Sale of Goods Carried by Sea

Sale of Goods Carried by Sea

Charles Debattista   LLD (Malta), MA (Oxon)
Senior Lecturer in the Faculty of Law
at the University of Southampton

Butterworths
London, Boston, Dublin, Edinburgh, Hato Rey,
Kuala Lumpur, Singapore, Sydney, Toronto, Wellington
1990

United Kingdom	Butterworth & Co (Publishers) Ltd, 88 Kingsway, LONDON WC2B 6AB and 4 Hill Street, EDINBURGH EH2 3JZ
Australia	Butterworths Pty Ltd, SYDNEY, MELBOURNE, BRISBANE, ADELAIDE, PERTH, CANBERRA and HOBART
Canada	Butterworths Canada Ltd, TORONTO and VANCOUVER
Ireland	Butterworth (Ireland) Ltd, DUBLIN
Malaysia	Malayan Law Journal Sdn Bhd, KUALA LUMPUR
New Zealand	Butterworths of New Zealand Ltd, WELLINGTON and AUCKLAND
Puerto Rico	Equity de Puerto Rico, Inc, HATO REY
Singapore	Malayan Law Journal Pte Ltd, SINGAPORE
USA	Butterworth Legal Publishers, AUSTIN, Texas; BOSTON, Massachusetts; CLEARWATER, Florida (D & S Publishers); ORFORD, New Hampshire (Equity Publishing); ST PAUL, Minnesota; and SEATTLE, Washington

© Charles Debattista 1990 except Appendix 2 © International Chamber of Commerce, Paris
Available from:
ICC UK
Centre Point
103 New Oxford Street
London WC1A 1QB

A CIP Catalogue record for this book is available from the British Library.

ISBN 0 406 11360 2

Typeset by Kerrypress Ltd, Luton, Bedfordshire.
Printed in Great Britain by Billing & Sons Ltd, Worcester

Preface

'Recently the Courts have been much exercised in attempting to say what a bill of lading is not. But what bills of lading really are is a question which, in spite of the great antiquity of such documents, has hitherto remained unanswered, and, one fears, remains, in the present state of affairs, unanswerable.'

Raymond E. Negus, 'The Negotiability of Bills of Lading' (1921) 37 LQR 442-461, at 461.

This book examines those legal principles of English law which govern the use of bills of lading in international trade. Traditionally dealt with in books covering the law of carriage of goods by sea, bills of lading are here examined in the context of the contract of sale of goods and of the contract setting up a letter of credit. Emphasis is consequently placed upon the tender of bills of lading by sellers to buyers and bankers. The book's starting point is, therefore, the bill's function as a document of title, that elusive characteristic to which Mr Negus despairingly referred in the Law Quarterly Review more than half a century ago.

The role of the bill of lading as a document of title sets cif and fob contracts apart from contracts of sale of goods in the domestic context in two senses. Firstly, it is this function which places the document at the centre of a triangle of contracts, the contract of sale, the contract of carriage and the letter of credit, each of which contracts will affect, and be affected by, the bill of lading. Secondly, it is this function which obliges and allows the seller to perform his duty of 'delivery' through the tender of documents and the shipment of goods. These two features distinguishing shipment sales from domestic sales provide the two themes which run through this book, namely, the domino-effect which one contract in the triangle has on the others: and the impact which dual performance — through tender of documents and shipment of goods — has upon accepted principles of the law of sale of goods.

The law is stated on the basis of materials available on 1 January 1990. My main priority throughout has been to state the current English legal principles as fully and as accurately as possible. I consequently decided not to anticipate the impact which regimes not yet in force under English law might have upon those principles. Thus, consideration of the 1980 United Nations Convention on Contracts for the International Sale of Goods, the 1980 United Nations Convention on International Multimodal Transport, and of the 1978 United Nations Convention on the Carriage of Goods by Sea, has been quite deliberately excluded. It seemed equally premature to forecast the impact rules yet in gestation might have upon this area of the law. Thus, the work of the Law Commission on Rights to Goods in Transit, (Working Paper No 112), is dealt with only by way of preliminary and general remark; the work of the Comite Maritime International on Seawaybills, only by passing reference; and the work of the same body on the Electronic Transfer of Rights to Goods in Transit, not at all. In each of these three cases, it appeared prudent to delay detailed treatment until after the organisations concerned had concluded their own deliberations. In the same vein, it should also be noted that a fuller version of the Court of Appeal's decision in *The Delfini* than that which appears in The Times is due to appear presently in the Lloyd's Law Reports. The complete report will afford readers the opportunity to assess the further nuances added by the Court of Appeal to the debate in *The San Nicholas*, nuances which it was not, regrettably, possible sensibly to incorporate into the text.

Finally, it is important to state that all references to Incoterms point towards Incoterms 1980. The International Chamber of Commerce has for some time been working on a revision of these rules and, as the book was going to print, this work came to fruition in the shape of Incoterms 1990. The revised rules come into force on 1 July 1990 and it has been possible, thanks to the courtesy of the ICC and to the endurance of the publishers, to incorporate the relevant parts of Incoterms 1990 in a separate appendix. It has also been possible to add Destination Tables to assist the reader in converting references to Incoterms 1980 to the appropriate rules in Incoterms 1990.

Apart from thanking my family for their patience throughout the writing of the book, I must acknowledge several debts of gratitude to a number of my colleagues, both in my own Faculty and elsewhere. My first debt is owed to the Law Faculty at Southampton; to the Faculty as such, for the readiness with which I was released from teaching duties for the term in which a large part of the text was written; and in particular to Emeritus Professor John Wilson, who read the whole manuscript in draft. Secondly, special thanks go to the Nordic Council, who very kindly invited me to take up a six-month Research Fellowship at the University of Oslo. Most of the book was written in Oslo, where I was given free access to the English law holdings of the Law Faculty's twin Institutes of Maritime Law and Private Law. Thirdly, I am indebted to a large number of students, and to practitioners attending courses of the Southampton Law Faculty's Institute of Maritime Law, for the many questions raised in discussion at seminars in Southampton and elsewhere: these questions have, I hope, given the book an edge which would not otherwise have been there. Fourthly, I am grateful to the various commercial organisations who have agreed to the reproduction of their contract forms into the appendices to the book. Lastly, but by no means least, I am very grateful to the publishers; their encouragement and assistance, given cheerfully and patiently throughout, made the production of the book a much more pleasurable task than it would otherwise have been.

Charles Debattista
Southampton
29 March 1990

Contents

Preface v
Table of statutes xiii
Table of cases xv

Chapter 1 Documentary sales on shipment terms: an introduction to contracts and duties in international sales 1

1. Documentary sales on shipment terms 3
2. Physical and documentary duties of sellers on shipment terms 5
   (a) Physical duties 5
       (i) Physical duties relating to the goods themselves 6
       (ii) Physical duties relating to the shipment of the goods 6
   (b) Documentary duties 9
3. The letter of credit described 10

PART I POSSESSION, PROPERTY, RISK AND TITLE TO SUE

Chapter 2 The bill of lading as a document of title 15

1. A framework of questions – and concepts 18
2. Documents of title, transferability, and negotiability 19
   (a) Transferability in general 20
   (b) Transferability of bills of lading 21
   (c) Negotiability 21
       (i) Better title 22
       (ii) The consideration point 24
3. The proprietary rights transferred 26
   (a) The right to delivery 27
   (b) Consequences of the transfer of the right to delivery 30
   (c) The Factors Acts and the Sale of Goods Act 33
   (d) The use of the bill of lading as a means of security 36
   (e) When the bill stops being a document of title 40

Chapter 3 Title to sue the carrier 43

1. How title to sue passes by contract 45
   (a) The statutory solution: section 1 of the Bills of Lading Act 1855 45

(i) Does the Act require a document of title at common law? 46
(ii) 'To whom the property in the goods shall pass' 47
(iii) Pledgees as consignees 48
(iv) 'Upon or by reason of such consignment or endorsement' 51
(b) The implied contract device 53
2. How title to sue arises in tort 56
(a) The tort plaintiff compared to the contract plaintiff 56
(b) Problems after *The Aliakmon* 60
(i) When the rule applies 61
(ii) The origins of the rule in the law of negligence 62
(iii) Is the general principle against recovery appropriate here? 63

Chapter 4 Transfer of property and risk 71

1. The concepts of property and risk: their nature and significance 72
(a) Property and possession 73
(b) Property and risk 75
2. Transfer of property and the Sale of Goods Act 1979 76
(a) Ascertainment and appropriation 77
(b) Unconditional appropriation 80
(c) Indicia of intention as to the passage of property 82
(i) Express clauses reserving property 82
(ii) Implied intention to reserve property 85
(d) Transfer of property and letters of credit 88
3. Transfer of risk 89
(a) Transfer of risk and the Sale of Goods Act 1979 91
(i) Section 20(2) 91
(ii) Section 20(3) 93
(iii) Section 32(2) 94
(iv) Section 32(3) 95
(v) Section 33 97
(a) The general rule in shipment sales 98
(i) Risk of loss or damage to the goods and breach of other duties 99
(ii) The rule in *Mash and Murrell* 99
(iii) Risk passes 'on or as from shipment' 100

PART II DOCUMENTARY DUTIES — A BILL ACCEPTABLE TO BUYERS AND BANKS

Chapter 5 Qualities of the bill of lading as a receipt 109

1. The bill's function as a receipt 111
2. Merchants' rights to demand a clear receipt from the carrier 115
(a) The seller: does he have a right to a firm receipt 116
(i) At common law? 116
(ii) Under the Carriage of Goods by Sea Act 1971? 117
(b) The buyer: does he have a right to a firm receipt 121
(i) At common law? 121
(ii) Under the Carriage of Goods by Sea Act 1971? 122

3. Requirements of the bill of lading as a receipt in sale contracts and in letters of credit   124
   (a) The bill must cover the contract goods and no others   126
      (i) Statements as to quantity   126
      (ii) Carrier's qualifications on the statement as to quantity   127
   (b) The bill must be 'clean'   130

Chapter 6   Qualities of the bill of lading as a contract   135

1. Terms of the carriage contract purchased by the buyer   137
      (i) The bill of lading as evidence of the contract of carriage between the seller and the carrier   138
      (ii) The bill of lading as the contract of carriage between the buyer and the carrier   138
2. The seller's duty relating to the carriage contract sold to the buyer   139
3. Carriage contract to provide continuous documentary cover to the destination port agreed in the sale contract   141
   (a) Bills giving carrier liberty to deviate   141
      (i) Where sale contract stipulates direct shipment   142
      (ii) Where sale contract does not stipulate for direct shipment   143
   (b) Deck stowage   148
      (i) Deck stowage unauthorised by the bill of lading   148
      (ii) Cargo stated to be carried on deck   150
      (iii) Bill of lading granting carrier liberty to stow on deck   151
   (c) Transhipment   152
      (i) Clauses in the bill stating that the goods will be transhipped   153
      (ii) Bills giving carrier liberty to tranship   154
         1. Where the bill gives 'through' cover   156
         2. Where the bill does not give 'through' cover   157
   (d) Bills with destination different to sale destination   159

Chapter 7   Bills of lading under charterparties   161

1. Business practice and the nature of the problems caused   162
2. Under which contractual terms is the buyer to sue the carrier?   164
   (a) Where the bill of lading is in the hands of the charterer   165
   (b) Where the bill of lading is in the hands of a third party   169
      (i) Incorporation in general   172
      (ii) Incorporation of arbitration clauses   174
3. Whom is the buyer to sue for short-delivery or damage to goods?   175
4. The bill of lading as a receipt where it is issued under a charterparty   179
   (a) Charterer selling cif   180
   (b) Charterer buying fob   182
5. Requirements of tender where a bill of lading is issued under a charterparty   182

Chapter 8 Seawaybills and combined transport documents 187

1. Seawaybills 188
    (a) Reasons for their use 188
    (b) The seawaybill as a document of title 189
        (i) Seawaybills and the right to delivery 190
        (ii) Seawaybills and the right of control 195
        (iii) Are seawaybills negotiable? 198
    (c) The seawaybill as a contract of carriage 199
        (i) The buyer's title to sue 200
        (ii) Seawaybills and the Carriage of Goods by Sea Act 1971 204
    (d) Seawaybills and letters of credit 207
2. Combined transport documents 211
    (a) Combined transport documents as documents of title 214
        (i) The traditional view: textbooks and the market 214
        (ii) The traditional view: an assessment 218
        (iii) The traditional view: overtaken by custom? 225
    (b) Combined transport documents and letters of credit 227

PART III REJECTION OF DOCUMENTS AND REJECTION
OF GOODS

Chapter 9 Rejection of documents and goods 229

1. Seller's physical and documentary duties as to the time of shipment:
    conditions of the contract 232
2. Documentary duties in general and repudiation 235
    (a) Arguments against applying the rule 237
    (b) Arguments in favour of applying the rule 239
    (c) The cases 240
    (d) Should the rule apply? 242
3. Buyer's remedy of rejection: practical constraints 244
    (a) Documents reach buyer before goods and buyer notices
         documentary defect 245
    (b) Documents reach buyer before goods and buyer does not notice
         documentary defect 245
    (c) Goods reach buyer before documents and buyer notices
         documentary defect 246
    (d) Goods reach buyer before documents and buyer does not notice
         documentary defect 247
4. Buyer's remedies of rejection: documents and goods 248
    (a) Independent rights of rejection 248
    (b) Damages for loss of the opportunity to reject documents 252
        (i) The type of loss which can be recovered 253
        (ii) Market losses 255
        (iii) Defect in the documents alone, causing no loss 257
    (c) Loss through estoppel of the right to repudiate 260
        (i) The doctrine of *Panchaud Freres* 260
        (ii) The effects of the doctrine 263

(a) Buyer estopped from rejecting goods on similar grounds 263
(b) Buyer estopped from recovering damages for loss of the opportunity to reject 264
(c) Buyer not estopped from rejecting goods on other grounds 266
(d) Summary of the effects of the doctrine 267
(iii) Is the buyer estopped through actions of the bank? 268

APPENDICES

Appendix 1 Statutes 273
(a) Sale of Goods Act 1979 273
(b) Carriage of Goods by Sea Act 1971 299
(c) Bills of Lading Act 1855 309

Appendix 2 ICC rules relevant to international trade 311

(a) Incoterms 1980 for CIF, C & F, FOB, FRC and CIP (ICC publication 350) 311
(b) Articles 25 and 26 of the Uniform Customs and Practice for Documentary Credits (ICC publication 400) 322
(c) Incoterms 1990 for CIF, FOB, CFR, FCA and CIP (ICC publication 460) with destination tables 324

Appendix 3 Commercial forms 345
(a) Form 100 of the Grain and Feed Trade Association 346
(b) ACL bill of lading 354
(c) An application for the opening of a letter of credit 358
(d) The General Council of British Shipping Waybill 360
(e) Genwaybill, the Baltic and International Maritime Council Non-Negotiable General Sea Waybill 364
(f) Combidoc, the Baltic and International Maritime Council Combined Transport Document 368

Index 373

Table of statutes

	PAGE
Bills of Exchange Act 1882	24, 26
s 27(2)	24
29(1)	23
30(1)	24
Bills of Lading Act 1855 .	19, 21, 22, 44,
	54, 194, 200, 214,
	215, 221, 222, 225, 226
s 1	9, 21, 24, 28, 37, 40, 41,
	45, 46, 47, 48, 50, 51, 52,
	53, 55, 56, 60, 61, 64, 65,
	74, 78, 79, 80, 105, 112,
	123, 124, 136, 137, 169,
	170, 190, 197, 198, 200,
	202, 203, 204, 208, 209,
	213, 216, 224
2	47, 54
3	112, 131
Bill of Sale Act 1878	35
s 4	36
Bills of Sale Act (1878) Amendment Act	
1882:	35
s 3	36
Carriage of Goods by Sea Act 1924 .	31,
	117, 223, 226
Carriage of Goods by Sea Act 1971	.19, 60,
	67, 113, 116, 117, 119,
	120, 121, 122, 131, 147,
	151, 156, 164, 170, 179,
	180, 181, 189, 194, 204,
	207, 210, 212, 213, 214
s 1	117
(2)	181, 205, 206
(3)	59
(4)	59, 206, 207, 214
(6)	205, 206
(7)	151
3	57
Schedule (Hague-Visby Rules)	
art I	59, 113, 117, 148, 165,
	171, 181, 200, 206, 207, 214
art II	206, 207
art III	165, 180, 181
r 1	57
2	57, 148
3	31, 118, 119, 120,
	122, 123, 124, 125, 180,
	181, 182, 206

	PAGE
Carriage of Goods by Sea Act 1971—*contd*	
art III—*contd*	
r 4	100, 113, 114, 115,
	118, 119, 120, 131,
	165, 179, 205, 206
5	115, 118, 120, 124
6	60
7	118, 205, 221, 233
8	145, 147, 165, 171
art IV	165
r 1	57, 60
2	60
4	145, 147
5	60, 171
art IV BIS	165
r 1	57, 58, 59, 60, 67, 112,
	204
2	59, 112
art V	117, 165, 172, 181, 182
art VI	22, 207
art VII	60
art VIII	165
art X	117, 214
Colonial Courts of Admiralty Act 1890:	221
Companies Act 1985	36, 84
s 396(1)	36, 85
399(1)	84
Companies Act 1989	36
s 95	84
396(1)	36
Factors Act 1889	21, 36, 38
s 1(4)	16, 27, 33, 34, 72, 73, 199
2	23, 34, 40, 49, 50, 72, 219
3	34, 38, 219
4	34, 219
8	23, 34, 72, 219
9	23, 34, 72, 219, 220
10	24
Law of Property Act 1925	
s 136(1)	20
Misrepresentation Act 1967	
s 2(1)	112
Sale of Goods Act 1893	
s 14(1), (2)	99
20(2)	92
(3)	102
25	34

PAGE

Sale of Goods Act 1893—*contd*

s 32(2)   140
38(2)   25

Sale of Goods Act 1979 . .   21, 26, 33, 35,
36, 38, 73, 199

s 2(5)   103
6,7   103
10   232
13, 14   6
16 . . . .   51, 61, 72, 76,
77, 79, 80, 83, 102, 103
17 . . . . 76, 78
(2)   85
18 . . . . 76, 82, 102
r 1 . . . . 76, 101, 102, 103
2   76
3   76
4   76
5 . . . .   72, 76, 77, 79,
80, 81, 82, 83,
84, 86, 102, 103
s 19 . . . .   72, 76, 78,
82, 84
(1)   82
(2) 85, 86
(3) 82, 85
20   75
(1) 90, 91, 100,
101, 102, 103
(2) 91, 92, 93
(3) 91, 93, 94

PAGE

Sale of Goods Act 1979—*contd*

s 24 . . . . 3, 34, 72, 73,
89, 198, 219
25 . . . . 23, 34, 72, 73,
84, 219, 220
(1)   220
26 . . . . 34, 219
27   3
29(1)   3
(4)   34
30(2)   240
(1) 94, 96, 194
(2) 91, 94, 95, 110, 136, 140
(3) 91, 95, 96, 97
33 . . . . .91, 97, 98, 99, 100
34, 35 . . . . 251, 266
Pt V (ss 38–48)   231
s 38–43   88
47 . . . . 34, 219
(2)   24
Pt VI (ss 49–54)   231
s 49   74
(1), (2)   74
51   152
(2)   257
53   152
(2)   257
61 . . . . 27, 33, 72, 101
(1) 76, 77, 78
Supreme Court Act 1981
s 20(2) 224

Table of cases

PAGE

A

Al Hofuf, The. See Scandinavian Trading Co A/B v Zodiac Petroleum SA and William
    Hudson Ltd, The Al Hofuf

Albazero, The, Albacruz (Owners) v Albazero (Owners) [1977] AC 774, [1976] 3 All ER
    129, [1976] 3 WLR 419, 120 Sol Jo 570, [1976] 2 Lloyd's Rep 467, 126 NLJ 953, HL .   52,
    86

Aliakmon, The. See Leigh and Sillivan Ltd v Aliakmon Shipping Co Ltd, The Aliakmon

Aluminium Industrie Vaassen BV v Romalpa Aluminium Ltd [1976] 2 All ER 552, [1976]
    1 WLR 676, 119 Sol Jo 318; affd [1976] 2 All ER 552, [1976] 1 WLR 676, 120 Sol Jo
    95, [1976] 1 Lloyd's Rep 443, CA 83

Anns v Merton London Borough Council [1978] AC 728, [1977] 2 All ER 492, [1977] 2
    WLR 1024, 141 JP 526, 121 Sol Jo 377, 75 LGR 555, 5 BLR 1, 243 Estates Gazette
    523, 591, HL 65

Antares, The. See Kenya Railways v Antares Co Pte Ltd, The Antares

Antares (No 2), The. See Kenya Railways v Antares Co Pte Ltd, The Antares (No 2)

Aramis, The [1987] 2 Lloyd's Rep 58; revsd [1989] 1 Lloyd's Rep 213, CA . . 48, 55, 62

Arcos Ltd v EA Ronaasen & Son [1933] AC 470, [1933] All ER Rep 646, 102 LJKB 346,
    149 LT 98, 49 TLR 231, 77 Sol Jo 99, 38 Com Cas 166, 45 Lloyd's Rep 33, HL . . 239

Ardennes, SS (Cargo Owners) v SS Ardennes (Owners) [1951] 1 KB 55, [1950] 2 All ER
    517, 66 (pt 2) TLR 312, 94 Sol Jo 458, 84 Ll L Rep 340 . . . . 138, 139

Astro Valiente Compania Naviera SA v Pakistan Ministry of Food and Agriculture (No 2),
    The Emmanuel Colocotronis (No 2) [1982] 1 All ER 823, [1982] 1 WLR 1096, 126 Sol
    Jo 343, [1982] 1 Lloyd's Rep 286 . . . . . . 172, 173, 175

A-G of Ceylon v Scindia Steam Navigation Co Ltd [1962] AC 60, [1961] 3 All ER 684,
    [1961] 3 WLR 936, 105 Sol Jo 865, [1961] 2 Lloyd's Rep 173, PC . . . 118

B

Bain (D H) v Field & Co Fruit Merchants Ltd (1920) 3 Ll L Rep 26; affd 5 Ll L Rep 16,
    CA 8

Bangladesh Chemical Industries Corpn v Henry Stephens Shipping Co Ltd and Tex-Dilan
    Shipping Co Ltd, The SLS Everest [1981] 2 Lloyd's Rep 389, [1981] Com LR 176,
    CA 170, 173

Banque de l'Indochine et de Suez SA v J H Rayner (Mincing Lane) Ltd [1983] QB 711,
    [1983] 1 All ER 468, [1982] 2 Lloyd's Rep 476; affd [1983] QB 711, [1983] 1 All ER
    1137, [1983] 2 WLR 841, 127 Sol Jo 361, [1983] 1 Lloyd's Rep 228, CA . . 48, 154

Barclays Bank Ltd v Customs and Excise Comrs [1963] 1 Lloyd's Rep 81 . . . 41

Baumwoll Manufactur von Carl Scheibler v Furness [1893] AC 8, 62 LJQB 201, 68 LT 1, 9
    TLR 71, 7 Asp MLC 263, 1 R 59, HL 177

Berg (V) & Son Ltd v Vanden Avenne-Izegem PVBA [1977] 1 Lloyd's Rep 499, CA . 262

Berger & Co Inc v Gill & Duffus SA [1984] AC 382, [1984] 2 WLR 95, 128 Sol Jo 47,
    [1984] LS Gaz R 429, sub nom Gill & Duffus SA v Berger & Co Inc [1984] 1 All ER
    438, [1984] 1 Lloyd's Rep 227, HL 251, 263

Bergerco USA v Vegoil Ltd [1984] 1 Lloyd's Rep 440 . . . . 143, 251, 269

Berkshire, The [1974] 1 Lloyd's Rep 185 179

PAGE

Biddell Bros v E Clemens Horst Co [1911] 1 KB 934, 80 LJKB 584, 104 LT 577, 27 TLR
331, 55 Sol Jo 383, 12 Asp MLC 1, CA; revsd sub nom Clemens Horst (E) Co v Biddell
Bros [1912] AC 18, [1911-13] All ER Rep 93, 81 LJKB 42, 105 LT 563, 28 TLR 42,
56 Sol Jo 50, 12 Asp MLC 80, 17 Com Cas 55, HL 4, 86, 244
Bond Worth Ltd, Re [1980] Ch 228, [1979] 3 All ER 919, [1979] 3 WLR 629, 123 Sol Jo
216   85
Boukadoura Maritime Corpn v Marocaine de l'Industrie et du Raffinage SA, The
Boukadoura [1989] 1 Lloyd's Rep 393   .   .   .   .   .   .   117, 131
Bowes v Shand (1877) 2 App Cas 455, [1874-80] All ER Rep 174, 46 LJQB 561, 36 LT
857, 25 WR 730, 3 Asp MLC 461, HL 92, 232
Brandt v Liverpool, Brazil and River Plate Steam Navigation Co Ltd [1924] 1 KB 575,
[1923] All ER Rep 656, 93 LJKB 646, 130 LT 392, 16 Asp MLC 262, 29 Com Cas 57,
CA 19, 44, 45, 54, 61, 64, 105, 112, 136, 200, 202,
210, 224
Bristol and West of England Bank v Midland Rly Co [1891] 2 QB 653, 61 LJQB 115, 65
LT 234, 40 WR 148, 7 TLR 627, 7 Asp MLC 69, CA   38
British Imex Industries Ltd v Midland Bank Ltd [1958] 1 QB 542, [1958] 1 All ER 264,
[1958] 2 WLR 103, 102 Sol Jo 69, [1957] 2 Lloyd's Rep 591   .   .   .   128
Brown, Jenkinson & Co Ltd v Percy Dalton (London) Ltd [1957] 2 QB 621, [1957] 2 All
ER 844, [1957] 3 WLR 403, 101 Sol Jo 610, [1957] 2 Lloyd's Rep 1, CA .   .   131
Browne v Hare (1858) 3 H & N 484; affd (1859) 4 H & N 822, 29 LJ Ex 6, 7 WR 619, sub
nom Hare v Browne 33 LTOS 334, 5 Jur NS 711, Ex Ch   86
Bunge Corpn v Tradax SA [1981] 2 All ER 513, [1980] 1 Lloyd's Rep 294, CA; affd
[1981] 2 All ER 513, [1981] 1 WLR 711, 125 Sol Jo 373, [1981] 2 Lloyd's Rep 1,
HL 230, 231, 237
Burdick v Sewell (1884) 13 QBD 159, CA; revsd sub nom Sewell v Burdick 10 App Cas 74,
54 LJQB 156, 52 LT 445, 33 WR 461, 1 TLR 128, 5 Asp MLC 376, HL . 25, 27, 28, 35, 37,
48, 50, 53, 54, 80, 137, 200
Burgos v Nascimento, McKeand, Claimant [1908] WN 237, 100 LT 71, 53 Sol Jo 60, 11
Asp MLC 181   25
Burstall & Co v Grimsdale & Sons (1906) 11 Com Cas 280 .   .   .   . 142, 145, 146, 150

C

Calcutta SS Co Ltd v Andrew Weir & Co [1910] 1 KB 759, 79 LJKB 401, 102 LT 428, 26
TLR 237, 11 Asp MLC 395, 15 Com Cas 172   168
Canada and Dominion Sugar Co Ltd v Canadian National (West Indies) Steamships Ltd
[1947] AC 46, [1947] LJR 385, 62 TLR 666, PC 114, 118
Candlewood Navigation Corpn Ltd v Mitsui OSK Lines Ltd, The Mineral Transporter, The
Ibaraki Maru [1986] AC 1, [1985] 2 All ER 935, [1985] 3 WLR 381, 129 Sol Jo 506,
[1985] 2 Lloyd's Rep 303, PC 66, 68
Carlberg v Wemyss Coal Co Ltd 1915 SC 616, 52 SLR 515   32
Cattle v Stockton Waterworks Co (1875) LR 10 QB 453, [1874-80] All ER Rep 220, 44
LJQB 139, 33 LT 475, 30 JP Jo 791   62
Cehave NV v Bremer Handelsgesellschaft mbH, The Hansa Nord [1976] QB 44, [1975] 3
All ER 739, [1975] 3 WLR 447, 119 Sol Jo 678, [1975] 2 Lloyd's Rep 445, CA .   . 236
Chellaram (P S) & Co Ltd v China Ocean Shipping Co [1989] 1 Lloyd's Rep 413   .   86
Ciudad de Pasto and Ciudad de Neiva, The. See Mitsui & Co Ltd v Flota Mercante
Grancolombiana, The Ciudad de Pasto and Ciudad de Neiva
Clemens Horst (E) Co v Biddell Bros. See Biddell Bros v E Clemens Horst Co
Colin and Shields v W Weddel & Co Ltd [1952] 2 All ER 337, [1952] 2 TLR 185, 96 Sol
Jo 547, [1952] 2 Lloyd's Rep 9, CA   136
Compagnie Commercial Sucres et Denrees v C Czarnikow Ltd, The Naxos [1989] 2 Lloyd's
Rep 462, CA   231
Compania Comerical y Naviera San Martin SA v China National Foreign Trade
Transportation Corpn, The Costanza M [1981] 2 Lloyd's Rep 147, CA   .   .   48
Compania Naviera Vasconzada v Churchill and Sim [1906] 1 KB 237, 75 LJKB 94, 94 LT
59, 54 WR 406, 22 TLR 85, 50 Sol Jo 76, 10 Asp MLC 177, 11 Com Cas 49   . 100, 114,
115, 130, 131, 132, 133

PAGE

Comptoir D'Achat et de Vente du Boerenbond Belge S/A v Luis de Ridder Ltda, The Julia
[1949] AC 293, [1949] 1 All ER 269, [1949] LJR 513, 65 TLR 126, 93 Sol Jo 101,
HL 87, 90, 98, 101
Congimex Companhia Geral de Comercio Importadora e Exportadora SARL v Tradax
Export SA [1983] 1 Lloyd's Rep 250, CA   5
Connolly Shaw Ltd v Nordenfjeldske SS Co (1934) 50 TLR 418, 78 Sol Jo 430, 49 Ll L Rep
183 .   .   .   .   145, 146, 147
Conoco (UK) Ltd v Limni Maritime Co Ltd, The Sirina [1988] 2 Lloyd's Rep 613 .   .   114
Costanza M, The. See Compania Comercial y Naviera San Martain SA v China National
Foreign Trade Transportation Corpn, The Costanza M
Covas v Bingham (1853) 2 E & B 836, 2 CLR 212, 23 LJQB 26, 18 JP 569, 18 Jur 596, sub
nom Bingham v Covas 22 LTOS 97, 2 WR 37   184
Coxe v Harden (1803) 4 East 211, 1 Smith KB 20   25
Cremer v General Carriers SA [1974] 1 All ER 1, [1974] 1 WLR 341, 117 Sol Jo 873, sub
nom Peter Cremer, Westfaelische Central Genossenschaft GmbH and Intergraan NV v
General Carriers SA, The Dona Mari [1973] 2 Lloyd's Rep 366 .   .   55, 62, 114, 132
Cunningham (J & J) Ltd v Robert A Munro & Co Ltd (1922) 28 Com Cas 42   .   .   92

D

D and F Estates Ltd v Church Comrs for England [1989] AC 177, [1988] 2 All ER 992,
[1988] 3 WLR 368, 132 Sol Jo 1092, 41 BLR 1, 15 Con LR 35, [1988] 2 EGLR 262,
[1988] NLJR 210, HL   63
Delfini, The. See Enichem Anic SpA v Ampelos Shipping Co Ltd, The Delfini
Diamond Alkali Export Corpn v Bourgeois [1921] 3 KB 443, [1921] All ER Rep 283, 91
LJKB 147, 126 LT 379, 15 Asp MLC 455, 26 Com Cas 310 .   .   214, 219, 220, 221, 222
Dona Mari, The. See Cremer v General Carriers SA
Donoghue (or McAlister) v Stevenson. See M'Alister (or Donoghue) v Stevenson
Dunelmia, The. See President of India v Metcalfe Shipping Co Ltd, The Dunelmia

E

Eastwood and Holt v Studer (1926) 31 Com Cas 251   87
El Amria and El Minia, The [1982] 2 Lloyd's Rep 28, 126 Sol Jo 411, [1982] Com LR 121,
CA 9, 139
Elafi, The. See Karlshamns Oljefabriker v Eastport Navigation Corpn, The Elafi
Elder Dempster Lines v Ishag, The Lycaon [1983] 2 Lloyd's Rep 548   .   .   32, 87, 196
Elli 2, The. See Ilyssia Cia Naviera SA v Bamaodah, The Elli 2
Emmanuel Colocotronis (No 2), The. See Astro Valiente Compania Naviera SA v Pakistan
Ministry of Food and Agriculture (No 2), The Emmanuel Colocotronis (No 2)
Empresa Exportadora de Azucar v Industria Azucarera Nacional SA, The Playa Larga and
The Marble Islands [1983] 2 Lloyd's Rep 171, CA   .   .   .   33, 159, 197, 251
Enichem Anic SpA v Ampelos Shipping Co Ltd, The Delfini [1988] 2 Lloyd's Rep 599; affd
(1989) Times, 11 August, CA   .   .   .   31, 41, 47, 51, 52, 105, 203, 213, 222
Epaphus, The. See Eurico SpA v Philipp Bros, The Epaphus
Eurico SpA v Philipp Bros, The Epaphus [1986] 2 Lloyd's Rep 387; on appeal [1987] 2
Lloyd's Rep 215, CA   160
Eurymedon, The. See New Zealand Shipping Co Ltd v A M Satterthwaite & Co Ltd

F

Federal Commerce and Navigation Co Ltd v Molena Alpha Inc, The Nanfri [1978] 1
Lloyd's Rep 581; revsd [1978] QB 927, [1978] 3 All ER 1066, [1978] 3 WLR 309, 122
Sol Jo 347, [1978] 2 Lloyd's Rep 132, CA; affd [1979] AC 757, [1979] 1 All ER 307,
[1978] 3 WLR 991, 122 Sol Jo 843, [1979] 1 Lloyd's Rep 201, HL .   .   .   173
Federspiel (Carlos) & Co SA v Charles Twigg & Co Ltd [1957] 1 Lloyd's Rep 240   .   81
Finlay (James) & Co Ltd v NV Kwik Hoo Tong Handel Maatschappij [1928] 2 KB 604, 97
LJKB 817, 139 LT 582, 44 TLR 643, 72 Sol Jo 468, 17 Asp MLC 566; affd [1929] 1
KB 400, [1928] All ER Rep 110, 98 LJKB 251, 140 LT 389, 45 TLR 149, 17 Asp
MLC 566, 34 Com Cas 143, CA   .   .   4, 234, 248, 249, 253, 254, 255, 256, 257, 258,
264, 265, 266

PAGE

Finska Cellulosaforeningen v Westfield Paper Co Ltd [1940] 4 All ER 473, 46 Com Cas 87,
68 Ll L Rep 75   .   .   .   .   95, 140, 146, 184
Fischel & Co v Spencer (1922) 12 Ll L Rep 36   156
Fletcher (W & R) (New Zealand) v Sigurd Haavik Aksjeselskap, The Vikfrost [1980] 1
Lloyd's Rep 560, CA   179
Frebold and Sturznickel (t/a Panda OHG) v Circle Products Ltd [1970] 1 Lloyd's Rep 499,
CA   218
Furst (Enrico) & Co v W E Fischer Ltd [1960] 2 Lloyd's Rep 340   154

G

Gabarron v Kreeft (1875) LR 10 Exch 274, 44 LJ Ex 238, 33 LT 365, 24 WR 146, 3 Asp
MLC 36   83
Gabbiano, The [1940] P 166, 109 LJP 74, 165 LT 5, 56 TLR 774, 84 Sol Jo 394, 45 Com
Cas 235, 19 Asp MLC 371   .   .   .   .   5, 98
Galatia, The. See Golodetz (M) & Co Inc v Czanikow-Rionda Co Inc, The Galatia
Garbis Maritime Corpn v Philippine National Oil Co, The Garbis [1982] 2 Lloyd's Rep
283   .   .   .   .   172, 173
Gardano and Giampari (or Giampieri) v Greek Petroleum George Mamidakis & Co [1961]
3 All ER 919, [1962] 1 WLR 40, 106 Sol Jo 76, [1961] 2 Lloyd's Rep 259   .   .   52
Gatoil International Inc v Tradax Petroleum Ltd, The Rio Sun [1985] 1 Lloyd's Rep 350   .   5,
92, 93, 95, 100
General Trading Co and Van Stolk's Commissiehandel, Re (1911) 16 Com Cas 95   .   233, 242,
247
Gill & Duffus SA v Berger & Co Inc. See Berger & Co Inc v Gill & Duffus SA
Ginzberg v Barrow Haematite Steel Co Ltd and Mckellar [1966] 1 Lloyd's Rep 343, 116
NLJ 752   87
Glyn, Mills Currie & Co v East and West India Dock Co (1882) 7 App Cas 591, [1881-5]
All ER Rep 674, 52 LJQB 146, 47 TLR 309, 31 WR 201, 4 Asp MLC 580, HL   .   29
Glynn v Margetson & Co [1893] AC 351, 62 LJQB 466, 69 LT 1, 9 TLR 437, 1 Asp MLC
366, 1 R 193, HL 145, 146, 223
Golodetz (M) & Co Inc v Czarnikow-Rionda Co Inc, The Galatia [1979] 2 All ER 726,
[1980] 1 WLR 495, [1979] 2 Lloyd's Rep 450; affd [1980] 1 All ER 501, [1980] 1
WLR 495, 124 Sol Jo 201, [1980] 1 Lloyd's Rep 453, CA   .   103, 125, 128, 129, 130, 140,
180, 188
Goodbody & Co and Balfour, Williamson & Co, Re (1899) 82 LT 484, 9 Asp MLC 69, 5
Com Cas 59, CA   186
Grant v Norway (1851) 10 CB 665, 20 LJCP 93, 16 LTOS 504, 15 Jur 296   .   112, 113, 122, 148
Groom (C) Ltd v Barber [1915] 1 KB 316, [1914-15] All ER Rep 194, 84 LJKB 318, 112
LT 301, 31 TLR 66, 59 Sol Jo 129, 12 Asp MLC 594, 20 Com Cas 71   .   .   .   104
Guaranty Trust Co of New York v Hannay & Co [1918] 2 KB 623, [1918-19] All ER Rep
151, 87 LJKB 1223, 119 LT 321, 34 TLR 427, CA   37

H

Hadley v Baxendale (1854) 9 Exch 341, [1843-60] All ER Rep 461, 23 LJ Ex 179, 23
LTOS 69, 18 Jur 358, 2 WR 302, 2 CLR 517   257
Hain SS Co Ltd v Tate and Lyle Ltd [1936] 2 All ER 597, 155 LT 177, 52 TLR 617, 80
Sol Jo 68, 19 Asp MLC 62, 41 Com Cas 350, 55 Ll L Rep 159, HL   .   .   139, 170
Hamilton & Co v Mackie & Sons (1889) 5 TLR 677, CA   175
Hanno (Heinrich) & Co BV v Fairlight Shipping Co Ltd, The Kostas K [1985] 1 Lloyd's
Rep 231   170
Hansa Nord, The. See Cehave NV v Bremer Handelsgesellschaft mbH, The Hansa Nord
Hansson v Hamel and Horley Ltd [1922] 2 AC 36, [1922] All ER Rep 237, 91 LJKB 433,
127 LT 74, 38 TLR 466, 66 Sol Jo 421, 15 Asp MLC 546, 27 Com Cas 321, 10 Ll L
Rep 199, 507, HL 141, 144, 153, 155, 156
Harland and Wolff Ltd v Burns and Laird Lines Ltd 1931 SC 722, 1931 SN 87, 1931 SLT
572, 40 Ll L Rep 286   207
Hayman & Son v M'Lintock 1907 SC 936, 9 F 936, 44 SLR 691, 15 SLT 63   .   .   .   41
Hedley Byrne & Co Ltd v Heller & Partners Ltd [1964] AC 465, [1963] 2 All ER 575,
[1963] 3 WLR 101, 107 Sol Jo 454, [1963] 1 Lloyd's Rep 485, HL .   .   .   62, 63

PAGE

Henderson & Co v Comptoir d'Escompte de Paris (1873) LR 5 PC 253, 42 LJPC 60, 29 LT
    192, 21 WR 873, 2 Asp MLC 98 . . . . . . 22, 193, 199
Henrik Sif, The. See Pacol Ltd v Trade Lines Ltd
Herroe and Askoe, The. See Rederiaktiebolaget Gustav Erikson v Ismail, The Herroe and
    Askoe
Heskell v Continental Express Ltd [1950] 1 All ER 1033, 94 Sol Jo 339, 83 Ll L Rep 438 . 29
Heyman v Darwins Ltd [1942] AC 356, [1942] 1 All ER 337, 111 LJKB 241, 166 LT 306,
    58 TLR 169, HL 230
Hickman Grain v Canadian Pacific Rly 36 Man R 322, 32 CRC 333, [1927] 1 WWR 317,
    [1927] 1 DLR 851; revsd [1928] SCR 170, 34 CRC 238, [1928] 1 DLR 1069 . . 197
Hilding, The (Part Cargoes Ex). See Kronprinsessan Margareta, The
Hilding, The (Part Cargoes Ex). See Parana, The
Hindley & Co Ltd v East Indian Produce Co Ltd [1973] 2 Lloyd's Rep 515 . . 5, 103
Hispanica de Petroleos SA v Vencedora Oceanica Navegacion SA, The Kapetan Markos
    NL (No 2) [1987] 2 Lloyd's Rep 321, CA 7, 50, 52
Holland Colombo Trading Society Ltd v Alawdeen [1954] 2 Lloyd's Rep 45 . 4, 158
Hong Kong Fir Shipping Co Ltd v Kawasaki Kisen Kaisha Ltd [1962] 2 QB 26, [1962] 1
    All ER 474, [1962] 2 WLR 474, 106 Sol Jo 35, [1961] 2 Lloyd's Rep 478, CA . 230
Houlder Bros & Co Ltd v Public Works Comr [1908] AC 276, 77 LJPC 58, 98 LT 684, 11
    Asp MLC 61, PC 95, 98
Howard v Shepherd (1850) 9 CB 297, 19 LJCP 249, 137 ER 907 45
Huilerie L'Abeille v Société des Huileries du Niger, The Kastellon [1978] 2 Lloyd's Rep
    203 256

I

Ibaraki Maru, The. See Candlewood Navigation Corpn Ltd v Mitsui OSK Lines Ltd, The
    Mineral Transporter, The Ibaraki Maru
Ilyssia Cia Naviera SA v Bamaodah, The Elli 2 [1985] 1 Lloyd's Rep 107, CA . 55, 61, 62,
    65, 201
Inglis v Robertson and Baxter [1898] AC 616, [1895-9] All ER Rep Ext 387, 67 LJPC 108,
    79 LT 224, 14 TLR 517, HL 38
Inglis v Stock. See Stock v Inglis
Intercontinental Export Co (Pty) Ltd v MV Dien Danielsen 1982 (3) SA 534 (N); revsd
    1983 (4) SA 275 (N) 167
Ireland v Livingston (1872) LR 5 HL 395, [1861-73] All ER Rep 585, 41 LJQB 201, 27 LT
    79, 1 Asp MLC 389 184
Irene's Success, The. See Schiffahrt und Kohlen GmbH v Chelsea Maritime Ltd, The Irene's
    Success
Ishag v Allied Bank International, Fuhs and Kotalimbora [1981] 1 Lloyd's Rep 92 . 219, 221,
    222, 223

J

Jalamohan, The. See Ngo Chew Hong Edible Oil Pte Ltd v Scindia Steam Navigation Co
    Ltd, The Jalamohan
Johnson v Agnew [1980] AC 367, [1979] 1 All ER 883, [1979] 2 WLR 487, 123 Sol Jo 217,
    39 P & CR 424, 251 Estates Gazette 1167, HL 230
Joyce v Swann (1864) 17 CBNS 84 86
Julia, The. See Comptoir D'Achat et de Vente du Boerenbond Belge S/A v Luis de Ridder
    Ltda, The Julia
Junior Books Ltd v Veitchi Co Ltd [1983] 1 AC 520, [1982] 3 All ER 201, [1982] 3 WLR
    477, 126 Sol Jo 538, 21 BLR 66, [1982] Com LR 221, [1982] LS Gaz R 1413, 1982
    SLT 492, HL 63
Jydsk Andels-Foderstofforretning v Grands Moulins de Paris (1931) 39 Ll L Rep 223 . 237,
    239, 240, 241

K

Kapetan Georgis, The. See Virgo Steamship Co SA v Skaarup Shipping Corpn, The
    Kapetan Georgis

PAGE

Kapetan Markos NL (No 2), The. See Hispanica de Petroleos SA v Vencedora Oceanica
  Navegacion SA, The Kapetan Markos NL (No 2)
Karberg (Arnhold) & Co v Blythe Green Jourdain & Co [1915] 2 KB 379; affd [1916] 1
  KB 495, [1914-15] All ER Rep Ext 1221, 85 LJKB 665, 114 LT 152, 32 TLR 186, 60
  Sol Jo 156, 13 Asp MLC 235, 21 Com Cas 174, CA 4, 5, 87, 98
Karlshamns Oljefabriker v Eastport Navigation Corpn, The Elafi [1982] 1 All ER 208,
  [1981] 2 Lloyd's Rep 679, [1981] Com LR 149 .   .   .   . 47, 51, 52, 65, 68, 77
Kastellon, The. See Huilerie L'Abeille v Société des Huileries du Niger, The Kastellon
Kaukomarkkinat O/Y v Elbe Transport-Union GmbH, The Kelo [1985] 2 Lloyd's Rep 85 .   55
Keighley, Maxted & Co and Bryan, Durant & Co (No 2), Re (1894) 70 LT 155, 7 Asp
  MLC 418, CA 125, 126
Kelo, The. See Kaukomarkkinat O/Y v Elbe Transport-Union GmbH, The Kelo
Kenya Railways v Antares Co Pte Ltd, The Antares [1987] 1 Lloyd's Rep 424, CA   . 139, 148
Kenya Railways v Antares Co Pte Ltd, The Antares (No 2) [1987] 1 Lloyd's Rep 424, CA . 139,
                                                                                      148
Kleinjan and Holst NV Rotterdam v Bremer Handelsgesellschaft mbH Hamburg [1972] 2
  Lloyd's Rep 11 .   .   .   . 82, 264, 265, 266, 269
Kostas K, The. See Hanno (Heinrich) & Co BV v Fairlight Shipping Co Ltd, The Kostas K
Kronprinsessan Margareta, The [1921] 1 AC 486, 90 LJP 145, 124 LT 609, 15 Asp MLC
  170, sub nom The Hilding (Part Cargoes Ex) 37 TLR 199, PC   .   .   . 87, 89
Kum v Wah Tat Bank Ltd [1971] 1 Lloyd's Rep 439, PC .   . 21, 190, 194, 195, 225, 226
Kwei Tek Chao (t/a Zung Fu Co) v British Traders and Shippers Ltd [1954] 2 QB 459,
  [1954] 1 All ER 779, [1954] 2 WLR 365, 98 Sol Jo 163, [1954] 1 Lloyd's Rep 16   . 94,
                             243, 248, 251, 255, 256, 257, 258, 259, 260, 264
Kwei Tek Chao (t/a Zung Fu Co) v British Traders and Shippers Ltd [1954] 2 QB 459,
  [1954] 3 All ER 165, [1954] 3 WLR 496, 98 Sol Jo 592, [1954] 2 Lloyd's Rep 114   . 94,
                             243, 248, 251, 255, 256, 257, 258, 259, 260, 264

L

Law and Bonar Ltd v British American Tobacco Co Ltd [1916] 2 KB 605, 85 LJKB 1714,
  115 LT 612, 13 Asp MLC 499, 21 Com Cas 350   .   .   .   .   . 96, 98
Leduc & Co v Ward (1888) 20 QBD 475, [1886-90] All ER Rep 266, 57 LJQB 379, 58 LT
  908, 36 WR 537, 4 TLR 313, 6 Asp MLC 290, CA 139, 166, 169
Leigh and Sillivan Ltd v Aliakmon Shipping Co Ltd, The Aliakmon [1983] 1 Lloyd's Rep
  203; revsd [1985] QB 350, [1985] 2 All ER 44, [1985] 2 WLR 289, 129 Sol Jo 69,
  [1985] 1 Lloyd's Rep 199, [1985] NLJ Rep 285, [1985] LS Gaz R 203, CA; affd
  [1986] AC 785, [1986] 2 All ER 145, [1986] 2 WLR 902, 130 Sol Jo 357, [1986] 2
  Lloyd's Rep 1, [1986] NLJ Rep 415, [1986] LS Gaz R 1810, HL   .   26, 41, 45, 46, 55, 56,
                             57, 58, 60, 61, 62, 65, 66, 67, 68, 75, 79, 80, 87,
                             113, 148, 178, 200, 201, 209, 213
Lexmead (Basingstoke) Ltd v Lewis [1982] AC 225, 268, [1981] 2 WLR 713, 125 Sol Jo
  310, [1981] RTR 346, [1981] 2 Lloyd's Rep 17, sub nom Lambert v Lewis [1981] 1
  All ER 1185, HL 69
Libau Wood Co v H Smith & Sons Ltd (1930) 37 Ll L Rep 296 .   .   . 125, 129, 130, 180
Lickbarrow v Mason (1787) 1 Smith's Leading Cases 703, 2 Term Rep 63, [1775-1802] All
  ER Rep 1, 6 East 20n; on appeal sub nom Mason v Lickbarrow (1790) 1 Hy Bl 357,
  sub nom Lickbarrow v Mason [1775-1802] All ER Rep 1, Ex Ch; revsd (1793) 4 Bro
  Parl Cas 57, [1775-1802] All ER Rep 1, 5 Term Rep 367, 6 East 22n, 2 Hy Bl 211,
  HL 213, 214, 218, 220
Lickbarrow v Mason (1794) 1 Smith's Leading Cases 703, 5 Term Rep 683   . 29, 213, 214, 218,
                                                                          220, 225
Lickbarrow v Mason (1794) 1 Smith's Leading Cases 703, 6 Term Rep 131   . 213, 214, 218
Lloyds Bank Ltd v Bank of America National Trust and Savings Association [1938] 2 KB
  147, [1938] 2 All ER 63, 107 LJKB 538, 158 LT 301, 54 TLR 599, 82 Sol Jo 312, 43
  Com Cas 209, CA   40
London Wine Co (Shippers) Ltd, Re [1986] PCC 121 77
Lycaon, The. See Elder Dempster Lines v Ishag, The Lycaon

M

M'Alister (or Donoghue) v Stevenson [1932] AC 562, 101 LJPC 119, 48 TLR 494, 37 Com Cas 350, 1932 SC (HL) 31, sub nom McAlister (or Donoghue) v Stevenson 147 LT 281, 76 Sol Jo 396, sub nom Donoghue (or McAlister) v Stevenson [1932] All ER Rep 1, 1932 SLT 317 . . . . 57, 62, 64, 68

McCarren & Co Ltd v Humber International Transport Ltd and Truckline Ferries (Poole) Ltd, The Vechscroon [1982] 1 Lloyd's Rep 301, [1982] Com LR 11 . . . 205

Mack (Hugh) & Co Ltd v Burns and Laird Lines Ltd (1944) 77 Ll L Rep 377 . 207, 223

McKelvie v Wallace Bros Ltd [1919] 2 IR 250, HL 52

Maheno, The [1977] 1 Lloyd's Rep 81 223

Manbre Saccharine Co v Corn Products Co [1919] 1 KB 198, [1918-19] All ER Rep 980, 120 LT 113, sub nom Mambre Saccharine Co v Corn Products Co 88 LJKB 402, 35 TLR 94, 24 Com Cas 89 104

Manchester Trust Ltd v Furness, Withy & Co Ltd [1895] 2 QB 539, 73 LT 110, 44 WR 178, 8 Asp MLC 57, 1 Com Cas 39, 14 R 739, sub nom Manchester Trust Ltd v Turner, Withy & Co Ltd 64 LJQB 766, 11 TLR 530, CA 177

Marble Islands, The. See Empresa Exportadora de Azucar v Industria Azucarera Nacional SA, The Playa Larga and The Marble Islands

Margarine Union GmbH v Cambay Prince SS Co Ltd [1969] 1 QB 219, [1967] 3 All ER 775, [1967] 3 WLR 1569, 111 Sol Jo 943, [1967] 2 Lloyd's Rep 315 . 61, 64, 66, 67

Margaronis Navigation Agency Ltd v Henry W Peabody & Co of London Ltd [1965] 2 QB 430, [1964] 3 All ER 333, [1964] 3 WLR 873, 108 Sol Jo 562, [1964] 2 Lloyd's Rep 153, CA 240

Marie Joseph, The. See Pease v Gloahec, The Marie Joseph

Marlborough Hill, The v Cowan & Sons [1921] 1 AC 444, 90 LJPC 87, 124 LT 645, 37 TLR 190, 15 Asp MLC 163, 5 Ll L Rep 362, 26 Com Cas 121, PC . 219, 221, 222, 224

Marshall, Knott and Barker Ltd v Arcos Ltd (1933) 44 Ll L Rep 384 . . . 186

Mash and Murrell Ltd v Joseph I Emanuel Ltd [1961] 1 All ER 485, [1961] 1 WLR 862, 105 Sol Jo 468, [1961] 1 Lloyd's Rep 46; revsd [1962] 1 All ER 77n, [1962] 1 WLR 16n, 105 Sol Jo 1007, [1961] 2 Lloyd's Rep 326, CA 99, 100

Mason v Lickbarrow. See Lickbarrow v Mason

Mayhew Foods Ltd v Overseas Containers Ltd [1984] 1 Lloyd's Rep 317 . . . 156

Merak, The (Owners of Cargo on Board) v The Merak (Owners), The Merak [1965] P 223, [1965] 1 All ER 230, [1965] 2 WLR 250, 108 Sol Jo 1012, [1964] 2 Lloyd's Rep 527, CA 175

Messers Ltd v Morrison's Export Co Ltd [1939] 1 All ER 92, 55 TLR 245, 83 Sol Jo 75, 62 Ll L Rep 217 . . . . 149, 150

Meyer (Montague L) Ltd v Travaru A/B H Cornelius of Gamleby (1930) 46 TLR 553, 74 Sol Jo 466, 37 Ll L Rep 204 149

Meyer (Arnold Otto), NV v Aune [1939] 3 All ER 168, 55 TLR 876, 83 Sol Jo 623, 64 Ll L Rep 121 158

Meyerstein v Barber (1866) LR 2 CP 38, 36 LJCP 48, 15 LT 355, 12 Jur NS 1020, 15 WR 173, 2 Mar LC 420; on appeal (1867) LR 2 CP 661, 36 LJCP 289, 16 LT 569, 15 WR 998; affd sub nom Barber v Meyerstein (1870) LR 4 HL 317, 39 LJCP 187, 22 LT 808, 18 WR 1041, 3 Mar LC 449 41

Mineral Transporter, The. See Candlewood Navigation Corpn Ltd v Mitsui OSK Lines Ltd, The Mineral Transporter, The Ibaraki Maru

Miramar Maritime Corpn v Holborn Oil Trading Ltd, The Miramar [1983] 2 Lloyd's Rep 319; on appeal [1984] 1 Lloyd's Rep 142, CA; affd [1984] AC 676, [1984] 2 All ER 326, [1984] 3 WLR 1, 128 Sol Jo 414, [1984] 2 Lloyd's Rep 129, HL . . 172, 175

Miramichi, The [1915] P 71, 84 LJP 105, 112 LT 349, 31 TLR 72, 59 Sol Jo 107, 13 Asp MLC 21, 1 P Cas 137 87

Mitchel v Ede (1840) 11 Ad & El 888 . . . . 32, 196

Mitsui & Co Ltd v Flota Mercante Grancolombiana SA, The Ciudad de Pasto and The Ciudad de Neiva [1989] 1 All ER 951, [1988] 1 WLR 1145, 132 Sol Jo 1182, [1988] 2 Lloyd's Rep 208, [1988] 34 LS Gaz R 54, CA 68, 86

Moralice (London) Ltd v E D and F Man [1954] 2 Lloyd's Rep 526 . . 239, 240, 244

Moss SS Co Ltd v Whinney [1912] AC 254, [1911-13] All ER Rep 344, 81 LJKB 674, 105 LT 305, 27 TLR 513, 55 Sol Jo 631, 12 Asp MLC 25, 16 Com Cas 247, HL . . 138

PAGE

N

Nai Matteini, The. See Navigazione Alta Italia SpA v Svenska Petroleum AB, The Nai Matteini

Nanfri, The. See Federal Commerce and Navigation Co Ltd v Molena Alpha Inc, The Nanfri

Napier (F E) v Dexters Ltd (1926) 26 Ll L Rep 62; on appeal 26 Ll L Rep 184, CA . 88

Naviera Mogor SA v Société Metallurgique de Normandie, The Nogar Marin [1988] 1 Lloyd's Rep 412, CA 131

Navigazione Alta Italia SpA v Svenska Petroleum AB, The Nai Matteini [1988] 1 Lloyd's Rep 452 . . . . 170, 173, 175

Naxos, The. See Compagnie Commercial Sucres et Denrees v C Czarnikow Ltd, The Naxos

Nea Tyhi, The [1982] 1 Lloyd's Rep 606, [1982] Com LR 9 . . . 64, 113, 148, 178

New Chinese Antimony Co Ltd v Ocean SS Co Ltd [1917] 2 KB 664, 86 LJKB 1417, 117 LT 297, 14 Asp MLC 131, 23 Com Cas 1, CA 114

New Zealand Shipping Co Ltd v A M Satterthwaite & Co Ltd [1975] AC 154, [1974] 1 All ER 1015, [1974] 2 WLR 865, 118 Sol Jo 387, sub nom The Eurymedon [1974] 1 Lloyd's Rep 534, PC 44

Newsom v Thornton (1805) 6 East 17, 2 Smith KB 207, [1803-13] All ER Rep 226 . . 218

Ngo Chew Hong Edible Oil Pte Ltd v Scindia Steam Navigation Co Ltd, The Jalamohan [1988] 1 Lloyd's Rep 443 179

Nippon Yusen Kaisha v Ramjiban Serowgee [1938] AC 429, [1938] 2 All ER 285, 107 LJPC 89, 159 LT 266, 54 TLR 546, 82 Sol Jo 292, 19 Asp MLC 154, 43 Com Cas 223, PC 87

Nogar Marin, The. See Naviera Mogor SA v Société Metallurgique de Normandie, The Nogar Marin

North Western Bank Ltd v Poynter, Son and Macdonalds [1895] AC 56, [1891-4] All ER Rep 754, 64 LJPC 27, 72 LT 93, 11 R 125, HL 39

Northern Steel and Hardware Co Ltd v John Batt & Co (London) Ltd (1917) 33 TLR 516, CA 97

O

Obestain Inc v National Mineral Development Corpn Ltd, The Sanix Ace [1987] 1 Lloyd's Rep 465 . . . . 66, 68

Official Assignee of Madras v Mercantile Bank of India Ltd [1935] AC 53, [1934] All ER Rep 237, 104 LJPC 1, 152 LT 170, 40 Com Cas 143, PC . . . 27, 34

Okehampton, The [1913] P 173, 83 LJP 5, 110 LT 130, 29 TLR 731, 12 Asp MLC 428, 18 Com Cas 320, CA 177, 178

Olley v Marlborough Court Ltd [1949] 1 KB 532, [1949] 1 All ER 127, [1949] LJR 360, 65 TLR 95, 93 Sol Jo 40, CA 139

Olympia Oil and Cake Co Ltd and Produce Brokers Co Ltd, Re [1915] 1 KB 233, 84 LJKB 281, sub nom Olympia Oil and Cake Co Ltd v Produce Brokers Co Ltd 111 LT 1107, 12 Asp MLC 570, 19 Com Cas 359 104

P

Pacific Molasses Co and United Trading Co Ltd v Entre Rios Compania Naviera SA, The San Nicholas [1976] 1 Lloyd's Rep 8, CA 51, 52, 80, 83, 173

Pacol Ltd v Trade Lines Ltd (1982) 126 Sol Jo 312, sub nom Pacol Ltd v Trade Lines Ltd and R/I Sif IV, The Henrik Sif [1982] 1 Lloyd's Rep 456, [1982] Com LR 92 . 176, 178, 179

Panchaud Frères SA v Etablissements General Grain Co [1970] 1 Lloyd's Rep 53, CA . 159, 242, 243, 245, 260, 262, 263, 264, 265, 266, 268, 269

Parana, The [1921] 1 AC 486, 90 LJP 145, 124 LT 609, 15 Asp MLC 170, sub nom The Hilding (Part Cargoes Ex) 37 TLR 199, PC 87, 89

Parchim, The [1918] AC 157, 87 LJP 18, 117 LT 738, 34 TLR 53, 14 Asp MLC 196, PC . 86, 101

PAGE

Pease v Gloahec, The Marie Joseph (1866) LR 1 PC 219, [1861-73] All ER Rep 353, Brown & Lush 449, 3 Moo PCCNS 556, 35 LJPC 66, 15 LT 6, 12 Jur NS 677, 15 WR 201, 2 Mar LC 394 24

Peter der Grosse, The (1875) 1 PD 414; affd (1876) 34 LT 749, 3 Asp MLC 195, CA . 132

Peyman v Lanjani [1985] Ch 457, [1984] 3 All ER 703, [1985] 2 WLR 154, 128 Sol Jo 853, 48 P & CR 398, CA 262

Photo Production Ltd v Securicor Transport Ltd [1980] AC 827, [1980] 1 All ER 556, [1980] 2 WLR 283, 124 Sol Jo 147, [1980] 1 Lloyd's Rep 545, 130 NLJ 188, HL . 32, 54, 139, 147, 230

Plaimar Ltd v Waters Trading Co Ltd (1945) 72 CLR 304, [1945] ALR 469 (Aust HC) . 158

Playa Larga, The. See Empresa Exportadora de Azucar v Industria Azucarera Nacional SA, The Playa Larga and The Marble Islands

Polenghi Bros v Dried Milk Co Ltd (1904) 92 LT 64, 53 WR 318, 21 TLR 118, 49 Sol Jo 120, 10 Com Cas 42 74

President of India v Metcalfe Shipping Co Ltd, The Dunelmia [1970] 1 QB 289, [1969] 3 All ER 1549, [1969] 3 WLR 1120, 113 Sol Jo 792, [1969] 2 Lloyd's Rep 476, CA . 136, 164, 166, 167, 168, 169, 180, 182

Proctor & Gamble Philippines Manufacturing Corpn v Kurt A Becher GmbH & Co KG [1988] 1 Lloyd's Rep 88; affd [1988] 2 Lloyd's Rep 21, CA . 232, 234, 235, 238, 244, 257, 258, 259

Produce Brokers Co Ltd v Olympia Oil and Cake Co Ltd [1916] 1 AC 314, [1914-15] All ER Rep 133, 85 LJKB 160, 114 LT 94, 32 TLR 115, 60 Sol Jo 74, 21 Com Cas 320, HL 104

Produce Brokers Co Ltd v Olympia Oil and Cake Co Ltd [1916] 2 KB 296, sub nom Olympia Oil and Cake Co v Produce Brokers Co 85 LJKB 1695, 114 LT 944, 13 Asp MLC 393; affd sub nom Produce Brokers Co Ltd v Olympia Oil and Cake Co Ltd [1917] 1 KB 320, [1916-17] All ER Rep 753, sub nom Olympia Oil and Cake Co v Produce Brokers Co 86 LJKB 421, 116 LT 1, 33 TLR 95, CA 104

Proodos C, The. See Syros Shipping Co SA v Elaghill Trading Co, The Proodos C

Pyrene Co Ltd v Scindia Steam Navigation Co Ltd [1954] 2 QB 402, [1954] 2 All ER 158, [1954] 2 WLR 1005, 98 Sol Jo 354, [1954] 1 Lloyd's Rep 321 . 6, 7, 8, 44, 95, 116, 138, 139, 166, 200, 201

R

Ranson Ltd v Manufacture d'Engrais (1922) 13 Ll L Rep 205 . . . . 95, 140

Rasnoimport V/O v Guthrie & Co Ltd [1966] 1 Lloyd's Rep 1 112

Rederiaktiebolaget Gustav Erikson v Ismail, The Herroe and Askoe [1986] 2 Lloyd's Rep 281 114

Reinhold & Co and Hansloh's Arbitration, Re (1896) 12 TLR 422 79

Restitution SS Co v Sir John Pirie & Co (1889) 61 LT 330, 5 TLR 641, 6 Asp MLC 428; affd 64 LT 491n, 6 TLR 50, 7 Asp MLC 11n, CA 128

Rio Sun, The. See Gatoil International Inc v Tradax Petroleum Ltd, The Rio Sun

Rodocanachi v Milburn (1886) 18 QBD 67, 56 LJQB 202, 56 LT 594, 35 WR 241, 3 TLR 115, 6 Asp MLC 100, CA 164, 165, 169, 181

Roseline, The [1985] AMC 552 . . . . 7, 170, 174

Royal Exchange Shipping Co v Dixon (1886) 12 App Cas 11, 56 LJQB 266, 56 LT 206, 35 WR 461, 3 TLR 172, 6 Asp MLC 92, HL 139, 148

S

SIAT di dal Ferro v Tradax Overseas SA [1978] 2 Lloyd's Rep 470; on appeal [1980] 1 Lloyd's Rep 53, CA 159, 171, 184, 185, 237, 238, 244, 245

SLS Everest, The. See Bangladesh Chemical Industries Corpn v Henry Stephens Shipping Co Ltd and Tex-Dilan Shipping Co Ltd, The SLS Everest

Samuel, Samuel & Co v West Hartlepool Steam Navigation Co (1906) 11 Com Cas 115 . 176, 177, 178

San Nicholas, The. See Pacific Molasses Co and United Trading Co Ltd v Entre Rios Compania Naviera SA, The San Nicholas

Sanders Bros v Maclean & Co (1883) 11 QBD 327, 52 LJQB 481, 49 LT 462, 31 WR 698, 5 Asp MLC 160, CA 27

PAGE

Sanix Ace, The. See Obestain Inc v National Mineral Development Corpn Ltd, The Sanix
   Ace
Saudi Crown, The [1986] 1 Lloyd's Rep 261 113
Scandinavian Trading Co A/B v Zodiac Petroleum SA and William Hudson Ltd, The Al
   Hofuf [1981] 1 Lloyd's Rep 81 7
Schiffahrt und Kohlen GmbH v Chelsea Maritime Ltd, The Irene's Success [1982] QB 481,
   [1982] 1 All ER 218, [1982] 2 WLR 422, 126 Sol Jo 101, [1981] 2 Lloyd's Rep 635,
   [1981] Com LR 219 . . . . 64, 67
Scruttons Ltd v Midland Silicones Ltd [1962] AC 446, [1962] 1 All ER 1, [1962] 2 WLR
   186, 106 Sol Jo 34, [1961] 2 Lloyd's Rep 365, HL 7
Sea Calm Shipping Co SA v Chantiers Navals de l'Esterel SA, The Uhenbels [1986] 2
   Lloyd's Rep 294 178
Seateam & Co K/S A/S v Iraq National Oil Co, The Sevonia Team [1983] 2 Lloyd's Rep
   640 . . . . 52, 173
Sevonia Team, The. See Seateam & Co K/S A/S v Iraq National Oil Co, The Sevonia Team
Sewell v Burdick. See Burdick v Sewell
Shackleford, The. See Surrey Shipping Co Ltd v Compagnie Continentale (France) SA, The
   Shackleford
Sheridan v New Quay Co (1858) 4 CBNS 618, 28 LJCP 58, 33 LTOS 238, 5 Jur NS 248,
   140 ER 1234 87
Shipton, Anderson & Co v John Weston & Co (1922) 10 Ll L Rep 762 . . 4, 98, 144, 146
Shipton, Anderson & Co v Weil Bros & Co [1912] 1 KB 574, 81 LJKB 910, 106 LT 372, 28
   TLR 269, 17 Com Cas 153 . . . . 239, 240, 241
Shipton Anderson & Co and Harrison Bros & Co, Re [1915] 3 KB 676, 113 LT 1009, sub
   nom Shipton Anderson & Co v Harrison Bros & Co 84 LJKB 2137, 31 TLR 598, 21
   Com Cas 138 87
Silver v Ocean SS Co Ltd [1930] 1 KB 416, [1929] All ER Rep 611, 99 LJKB 104, 142 LT
   244, 46 TLR 78, 73 Sol Jo 849, 18 Asp MLC 74, 35 Com Cas 140, 35 Ll L Rep 49,
   CA 114
Sirina, The. See Conoco (UK) Ltd v Limni Maritime Co Ltd, The Sirina
Skarp, The [1935] P 134, [1935] All ER Rep 560, 104 LJP 63, 154 LT 309, 51 TLR 541,
   41 Com Cas 1, 18 Asp MLC 576 133
Skips A/S Nordheim v Syrian Petroleum Co Ltd, The Varenna [1984] QB 599, [1983] 3 All
   ER 645, [1984] 2 WLR 156, 127 Sol Jo 840, [1983] 2 Lloyd's Rep 592, CA . 172, 173,
   174, 175
Smyth (Ross T) & Co Ltd v T D Bailey, Son & Co [1940] 3 All ER 60, 164 LT 102, 56
   TLR 825, 84 Sol Jo 572, 45 Com Cas 292, 67 Ll L Rep 147, HL . 5, 81, 82, 89, 104
Soproma SpA v Marine and Animal By-Products Corpn [1966] 1 Lloyd's Rep 367, 116 NLJ
   867 . . . . 158, 193
Spillers Ltd v J W Mitchell Ltd (1929) 33 Ll L Rep 89 144
State Trading Corpn of India Ltd v M Golodetz Ltd [1988] 2 Lloyd's Rep 182; revsd
   [1989] 2 Lloyd's Rep 277, CA 32, 54, 139, 143
Stein, Forbes & Co v County Tailoring Co (1916) 86 LJKB 448, 115 LT 215, 13 Asp MLC
   422 . . . . 74, 87
Sterns Ltd v Vickers Ltd [1923] 1 KB 78, [1922] All ER Rep 126, 92 LJKB 331, 128 LT
   402, CA 104
Stettin, The (1889) 14 PD 142, 58 LJP 81, 61 LT 200, 38 WR 96, 5 TLR 581, 6 Asp MLC
   395 32
Stindt v Roberts (1848) 5 Dow & L 460, 2 Saund & C 212, 17 LJQB 166, 6 LT 257, 12 Jur
   518 . . . . 45, 54
Stock v Inglis (1884) 12 QBD 564, 53 LJQB 356, 51 LT 449, 5 Asp MLC 294, CA; affd sub
   nom Inglis v Stock (1885) 10 App Cas 263, [1881-85] All ER Rep 668, 54 LJQB 582,
   52 LT 821, 33 WR 877, 5 Asp MLC 422, HL 90, 103
Suisse Atlantique Société d'Armement Maritime SA v Rotterdamsche Kolen Centrale NV
   [1967] 1 AC 361, [1966] 2 All ER 61, [1966] 2 WLR 944, 110 Sol Jo 367, [1966] 1
   Lloyd's Rep 529, HL 147
Surrey Shipping Co Ltd v Compagnie Continentale (France) SA, The Shackleford [1978] 1
   Lloyd's Rep 191; on appeal [1978] 2 Lloyd's Rep 154, CA 262
Sutro (L) & Co and Heilbut, Symons & Co, Re [1917] 2 KB 348, 86 LJKB 1226, 116 LT
   545, 33 TLR 359, 14 Asp MLC 34, 23 Com Cas 21, CA 223

PAGE

Svenska Traktor, Aktiebolaget v Maritime Agencies (Southampton) Ltd [1953] 2 QB 295,
[1953] 2 All ER 570, [1953] 3 WLR 426, 97 Sol Jo 525, [1953] 2 Lloyd's Rep 124 . 152
Syros Shipping Co SA v Elaghill Trading Co, The Proodos C [1981] 3 All ER 189, [1980]
2 Lloyd's Rep 390 262
Sze Hai Tong Bank Ltd v Rambler Cycle Co Ltd [1959] AC 576, [1959] 3 All ER 182,
[1959] 3 WLR 214, 103 Sol Jo 561, [1959] 2 Lloyd's Rep 114, PC 32

T

Tamvaco v Lucas (1859) 1 E & E 581, 592, sub nom Tanvaco v Lucas 28 LJQB 150, 301, 1
LT 161, 5 Jur NS 731, 1258, 7 WR 568, 120 ER 1027 126
Taylor & Sons Ltd v Bank of Athens (1922) 91 LJKB 776, 128 LT 795, 27 Com Cas 142 . 254,
256
Teheran-Europe Co Ltd v S T Belton (Tractors) Ltd [1968] 2 QB 545, [1968] 2 All ER
886, [1968] 3 WLR 205, 112 Sol Jo 501, [1968] 2 Lloyd's Rep 37, CA . . . 100
Thompson v Dominy (1845) 14 M & W 403, 14 LJ Ex 320, 5 LTOS 268, 153 ER 532 . 45,
54
Tillmanns & Co v SS Knutsford Ltd [1908] 1 KB 185; affd [1908] 2 KB 385, 77 LJKB
778, 24 TLR 454, 13 Com Cas 244, sub nom SS Knutsford Ltd v Tillmanns & Co 99
LT 399, CA; on appeal [1908] AC 406, [1908-10] All ER Rep 549, 77 LJKB 977, 99
LT 399, 24 TLR 786, 11 Asp MLC 105, 13 Com Cas 334, HL 178
Toepfer v Lenersan-Poortman NV [1980] 1 Lloyd's Rep 143, CA . . . 231
Toepfer v Peter Cremer (1975) 119 Sol Jo 506, [1975] 2 Lloyd's Rep 118, CA . . 262
Tokio Marine and Fire Insurance Co Ltd v Retla SS Co [1970] 2 Lloyd's Rep 91, US CA . 114
Tradax Internacional SA v Goldschmidt SA [1977] 2 Lloyd's Rep 604 . . 239, 241, 248, 263
Transcontainer Express Ltd v Custodian Security Ltd [1988] 1 Lloyd's Rep 128, [1988] 1
FTLR 54, CA 68
Tregelles v Sewell (1862) 7 H & N 574; affd (1863) 7 H & N 584 98
Triangle Steel and Supply Co v Korean United Lines Inc 63 BCLR 66 . . 66, 68
Tromp, The [1921] P 337, 90 LJP 379, 125 LT 637, 37 TLR 752, 15 Asp MLC 338 . 132, 133
Trucks and Spares Ltd v Maritime Agencies (Southampton) Ltd [1951] 2 All ER 982,
[1951] 2 TLR 1021, 95 Sol Jo 788, [1951] 2 Lloyd's Rep 345, CA . . . 31
Tsakiroglou & Co Ltd v Noblee Thorl GmbH [1962] AC 93, [1961] 2 All ER 179, [1961] 2
WLR 633, 105 Sol Jo 346, [1961] 1 Lloyd's Rep 329, HL . . . 95, 140, 223

U

Uhenbels, The. See Sea Calm Shipping Co SA v Chantiers Navals de l'Esterel SA, The
Uhenbels
United Baltic Corpn v Burgett and Newsam (1921) 8 Ll L Rep 190, CA . . . 226

V

Varenna, The. See Skips A/S Nordheim v Syrian Petroleum Co Ltd, The Varenna
Vargas Pena Apezteguia Y Cia SAIC v Peter Cremer GmbH [1987] 1 Lloyd's Rep 394 . 242,
257, 264, 265, 266, 267
Vechscroon, The. See McCarren & Co Ltd v Humber International Transport Ltd and
Truckline Ferries (Poole) Ltd, The Vechscroon
Venezuela, The [1980] 1 Lloyd's Rep 393 178
Vikfrost, The. See Fletcher (W & R) (New Zealand) v Sigurd Haavik Aksjeselskap, The
Vikfrost
Virgo Steamship Co SA v Skaarup Shipping Corpn, The Kapetan Georgis [1988] 1 Lloyd's
Rep 352 68
Vitol SA v Esso Australia Ltd, The Wise [1989] 1 Lloyd's Rep 96; on appeal [1989] 2
Lloyd's Rep 451, CA 3, 83, 98
Vladimir Ilich, The. See Waren Import Gesellschaft Krohn & Co v Alfred C Toepfer, The
Valdimir Ilich

W

Wait and James v Midland Bank (1926) 31 Com Cas 172 77

PAGE

Waren Import Gesellschaft Krohn & Co v Alfred C Toepfer, The Vladimir Ilich [1975] 1
    Lloyd's Rep 322   262
Waren Import Gesellschaft Krohn & Co v Internationale Graanhandel Thegra NV [1975] 1
    Lloyd's Rep 146   .   .   .   . 19, 34
Waring v Cox (1808) 1 Camp 369   25
Weis & Co v Produce Brokers' Co (1921) 7 Ll L Rep 211, CA 221, 226
White Sea Timber Trust Ltd v W W North Ltd [1932] All ER Rep 136, 148 LT 263, 49
    TLR 142, 77 Sol Jo 30, 44 Ll L Rep 390, 18 Asp MLC 367   149
Wiehe v Dennis Bros (1913) 29 TLR 250   .   .   .   .   .   . 76, 94, 102
Wilston SS Co Ltd v Andrew Weir & Co (1925) 31 Com Cas 111, 22 Ll L Rep 521   . 176, 178
Wimble Sons & Co v Rosenberg & Sons [1913] 3 KB 743, 82 LJKB 1251, 109 LT 294, 29
    TLR 752, 57 Sol Jo 784, 12 Asp MLC 373, 18 Com Cas 65, 302, CA   .   . 96, 97
Wise, The. See Vitol SA v Esso Australia Ltd, The Wise
Woodhouse AC Israel Cocoa Ltd SA v Nigerian Produce Marketing Co Ltd [1971] 2 QB
    23, [1971] 1 All ER 665, [1971] 2 WLR 272, 115 Sol Jo 56, [1971] 1 Lloyd's Rep 25,
    CA; affd [1972] AC 741, [1972] 2 All ER 271, [1972] 2 WLR 1090, 116 Sol Jo 392,
    [1972] 1 Lloyd's Rep 439, HL 114, 262

Y

Yelo v S M Machado & Co Ltd [1952] 1 Lloyd's Rep 183 212

Documentary sales on shipment terms: an introduction to contracts and duties in international sales

1. Documentary sales on shipment terms
2. Physical and documentary duties of sellers on shipment terms
   (a) Physical duties
      i. Physical duties relating to the goods themselves
      ii. Physical duties relating to the shipment of the goods
   (b) Documentary duties
3. The letter of credit described

Distance, and the risks incidental to it, are the factors which give rise to the contracts which are the subject of this book. Sales of goods which need to be carried by sea differ from straightforward domestic sales in a number of ways: they will normally be shipped at a port far from the legitimately watchful eye of the buyer; they traverse long distances, in the custody of the carrier, normally a company quite independent of either trader; moreover, the risks involved in such transit are greater than they would otherwise be; and, finally, the transaction is normally irreversible, in that the physical return of the goods to the seller is in practice unlikely to be a realistic option. To judge by these concerns, one would be forgiven for wondering, if only momentarily, why anyone would consider trading goods across the high seas. Clearly, though, people do, and, by all accounts, do so very profitably. One of the reasons why international trade has risen above the difficulties caused by distance is that the trading community, followed, at times reluctantly and at times even confusingly, by the law, has developed a number of contracts which cater for the peculiar needs of international commerce[1].

These contracts are known as c i f ('cost, insurance, freight'), c & f ('cost and freight') and f o b ('free on board')[2] contracts and they share

---

[1] For a description of the historical development of such contracts, see The Origin of F O B and C I F Terms and the Factors Influencing Their Choice, D.M. Sassoon, 1967 J B L 32; and Application of F O B and C I F Sales in Common Law Countries, D.M. Sassoon, in (1981) 1 European Transport Law, 50.

[2] While the terms c i f and c & f are inextricably linked with goods traded across the high seas, the term f o b can be and is used for domestic sales involving land transit: see Sassoon, *C I F & F O B Contracts*, 3rd edn, 1984 [hereinafter referred to as Sassoon], art 431.

1

a number of common characteristics. Firstly, although they are contracts of sale, they all stipulate for, or at any rate contemplate, the conclusion of contracts of carriage, insurance and, possibly, the opening of a letter of credit. Secondly, although the arrival of the goods at the agreed destination is something devoutly to be wished for by both seller and buyer, these contracts are concluded on shipment rather than arrival terms, with delivery at the loading port taking pride of place among the seller's physical obligations under the contract. This brings us to our third characteristic feature: the parties to a sale on shipment terms owe each other not only duties of a physical character, but also others, quite separate, of a documentary character.

Implicit in these features common to most c i f and f o b contracts are the two themes which run through the rest of this book. Firstly, problems which arise under one particular contract involved in the export of goods can frequently only be explained, and therefore solved, in terms of rules relating to another of those contracts. Thus, to take one example, a bill of lading may give, as the destination of the voyage, the phrase 'as per charterparty' and this could cause difficulties on a number of contractual planes[3]. It could cause a bank confirming a letter of credit to withhold payment under that letter of credit, because the relevant rules bar tender of such a bill. Even where no letter of credit is in place, the buyer may, especially if enticed by a falling market, be inclined to reject the bill when tendered under his c i f contract: the bill leaves him in doubt as to whether the bill of lading provides for discharge of the goods at the port agreed with the seller under the contract of sale; it leaves him in doubt as to whether he can sue the carrier if they are not discharged at that port; finally, it is likely to leave him in doubt as to the very identity of the carrier if the goods are damaged in transit. Thus, the same feature of the bill of lading, its reference to a charterparty, can be seen to have a domino-like effect upon the several contracts making up an export transaction.

Secondly, whereas a sale of goods in the domestic context imposes upon the seller one mode of performance, namely to deliver the goods, a sale of goods on shipment terms involves two types of performance, a physical and a documentary mode of performance. This duality of performance needs to be kept firmly in mind in examining certain aspects of the law on c i f and f o b contracts, particularly the areas of the passage of risk[4] and the remedies of rejection of goods and documents[5].

This book examines these two central themes, namely the domino-like effect of the contracts involved in an export transaction, and the duality of performance imposed on the exporter, in the context of c i f, c & f, and f o b contracts. These themes explain both the selection and

---

[3]   See Chapter 7, below, where the problems special to bills of lading under charterparties are discussed.
[4]   See Chapter 4, below.
[5]   See Chapter 9, below.

the organisation of the areas chosen for discussion[6]. Part I of the book
concentrates on the document which lies at the centre of the network
of contracts making up the export transaction, namely the bill of lading.
Here, we shall be looking at the bill as a document of commercial value:
its function as a document of title; the role it plays in giving the buyer
title to sue the carrier; and its relationship to the passage of property
and risk from seller to buyer. In Part II of the book, we shall be examining
the seller's duty validly to tender a bill of lading under a contract of
sale on shipment terms or under a letter of credit: what type of bill
of lading must a seller tender in performing either type of contract?
We shall look at the various contractual requirements from two aspects:
firstly, we shall examine the contractual requirements of the bill of lading
as a receipt, and secondly, we shall look at the contractual requirements
of the bill as a contract of carriage. We shall then look at the difficulties
arising under the contract of sale and under the letter of credit where
the seller tenders any of three special types of bill of lading: bills of
lading issued under charterparties, seawaybills and combined transport
bills of lading. In Part III of the book, we shall examine the effect which
the seller's dual mode of performance, physical and documentary, has
upon the buyer's right to terminate the sale contract on the grounds
of repudiatory breach.

Turning then to this chapter, we have three tasks: firstly, to examine
the precise sense in which the contracts here discussed are documentary
contracts on shipment terms; secondly, to set out in brief the physical
and documentary duties of traders selling or buying on shipment terms;
finally, to describe briefly the mechanism of a letter of credit.

1. DOCUMENTARY SALES ON SHIPMENT TERMS

When contracts concluded on c i f, c & f, or f o b terms are described
as documentary sales agreed on shipment terms, this says something
about the nature of the seller's obligations towards the buyer. The seller
of goods in a domestic context promises 'to deliver the goods . . . in
accordance with the terms of the contract of sale'[7] and delivery normally
happens at 'the seller's place of business, if he has one, and if not, his
residence.'[8] The seller of goods on shipment terms, on the other hand,
promises something quite different. The seller does not promise actual
delivery: he does not guarantee that the goods will reach the buyer in
any state or condition, within a given time[9] or indeed at all. He does,

---

6   For works covering a broader area, see Benjamin's *Sale of Goods*, 3rd edn, 1987,
    hereinafter referred to as Benjamin; Schmitthoff's *Export Trade, The Law and Practice
    of International Trade*, 8th edn , 1986, hereinafter referred to as Schmitthoff; and Sassoon.
7   See s 27 of the Sale of Goods Act 1979.
8   See s 29(1) of the Sale of Goods Act 1979.
9   This is so even where the contract is concluded on c i f or c & f 'arrived' terms: see
    The Wise [1989] 1 Lloyd's Rep 96 at 101, (remitted to the Commercial Court by the
    Court of Appeal on grounds irrelevant to the present point: see [1989] 2 Lloyd's Rep
    451) where Leggatt J interpreted a term that the goods were to arrive by a given date
    simply to mean that the vessel was *expected* to arrive within the given period.

however, promise, where he sells c i f or c & f, that he will ship goods, or procure goods shipped, for the agreed destination, which goods are covered by the documents stipulated for in the contract[10]; and where he sells f o b, he promises to deliver goods on board a nominated ship and to provide the buyer with any assistance required to obtain the documents necessary for discharge of the goods[11]. In this sense, these contracts are contracts promising shipment, rather than arrival, and they are contracts contemplating performance which is at once physical and documentary: thus, they can be said to be documentary sales on shipment terms.

From this basic principle flow a number of important consequences to which we shall return at greater length later, but which it would be helpful to state briefly and without qualification at this stage. Firstly, the seller does not take the risk of loss of or damage to the goods during transit. Secondly, that risk is generally passed on to the buyer at an early stage, namely, the point of shipment. Thirdly, the upshot of this is that the buyer's remedies for the loss of or damage to the goods during transit lie not against the seller but against the carrier or the insurer. Fourthly, those rights against third parties, carrier or insurer, are expressed and contained in certain shipping documents, e g the bill of lading and the policy of insurance, which, in certain circumstances, transfer rights of action against the carrier and the cargo insurer.

These propositions have given rise to a debate about whether c i f and c & f contracts and certain types of f o b contracts are sales of goods or sales of documents. Thus, for example, in *James Finlay & Co v NV Kwik Hoo Tong HM*, Scrutton LJ was persuaded that a c i f contract was a sale of documents by the fact 'that the goods may be lost before the documents are tendered and before the property has passed.'[12] A c i f sale is certainly a sale of documents in the sense that the buyer is bound to pay the price on tender of the documents stipulated for in the contract, even where such tender occurs before the arrival of the goods at the discharge port[13]. It is also a sale of documents in the sense that where a contract, calling itself a c i f contract, permits the seller to tender no documents at all and to claim payment simply on delivery of the goods, then such a contract will not be treated as a c i f contract[14]. However,

---

[10] See, for example, *James Finlay & Co v NV Kwik Hoo Tong Handel Maatschappij* [1919] 1 KB 400 at 407, 8; and *Shipton, Anderson & Co v John Weston & Co* (1922) 10 Ll L Rep 762 at 763.

[11] It is difficult to state the duties of the f o b seller in general terms, because, as we shall presently see, the f.o.b contract comes in a number of shapes and forms: see Benjamin, at para 1810.

[12] [1919] 1 KB 400, see particularly 407-8. This was a view to which the judge had earlier subscribed, as Scrutton J, in *Arnhold Karberg & Co v Blythe Green Jourdain & Co* [1915] 2 KB 379 at 388; affd by the Court of Appeal at [1916] 1 KB 495, but with disapproval of Scrutton J's dictum expressed at pp 511, 514.

[13] See *E Clemens Horst & Co v Biddell Bros* [1912] AC 18.

[14] *Holland Colombo Trading Society Ltd v Alawdeen* [1954] 2 Lloyd's Rep 45 at 50.

on the other hand, where the seller tenders documents which state goods to have been shipped which have not been shipped at all, the seller is clearly in breach of contract, and in this sense, the contract is in a very real way a sale of goods[15]. The contract contemplates performance in two modes: it would be accurate, therefore, to describe a contract on shipment terms as a sale of goods covered by documents[16].

2. PHYSICAL AND DOCUMENTARY DUTIES OF SELLERS ON SHIPMENT TERMS

It follows from what has been said that the duties imposed on sellers by contracts concluded on shipment terms can be conveniently classified as physical or documentary duties. These duties have been recited a number of times in the authorities[17]: as handy a compendium as any of the duties generally imposed in c i f and f o b contracts is provided by the relevant Incoterms, a voluntary set of rules first published in 1936 and since regularly revised[18] by the International Chamber of Commerce. The area covered by Incoterms is wider than the central themes underlying this book, which, it will be recalled, are the domino-like effect one contract in an export transaction may have upon another; and the problems caused by the dual mode in which the seller performs his obligations under sale contracts concluded on shipment terms. Rather than rehearse the duties in full here[19], it may be more helpful, therefore, simply to set out in brief the main duties imposed on the seller by such contracts, distinguishing between his physical and his documentary duties.

(a) Physical duties

The seller's physical duties can be looked at under two distinct aspects: those which relate to the goods themselves and those which relate more specifically to the shipment of the goods.

---

[15] See *Hindley & Co Ltd v East Indian Produce Co Ltd* [1973] 2 Lloyd's Rep 515. See also, for the view that a c i f contract is *not* a sale of documents, *Ross T Smyth & Co Ltd v TD Bailey, Son & Co* [1940] 3 All ER 60 at 70; and *The Gabbiano* [1940] P 166 at 174.

[16] Or as a 'sale of goods to be performed by the delivery of documents': see Bankes LJ in *Arnhold Karberg & Co v Blythe Green Jourdain & Co* [1916] 1 KB 495 at 511; or as a 'sale of documents representing goods': see Donaldson MR in *Congimex Companhia Geral de Comercio Importadora e Exportadora SARL v Tradax Export SA* [1983] 1 Lloyd's Rep 250. See, generally, Benjamin, para 1617.

[17] For c i f sales, see, for example, *The Rio Sun* [1985] 1 Lloyd's Rep 350 at 357, and other cases cited at Benjamin, para 1619. For f o b contracts, see Benjamin, para 1810.

[18] The current version is contained in Incoterms 1980, publication number 350 of the International Chamber of Commerce, obtainable from the UK Branch of the ICC at 103, New Oxford Street, London WC1A 1QB. The ICC also publish a useful Guide to Incoterms, publication no 354. The ICC are currently working on a new draft of Incoterms, which is planned to come into operation later in 1990.

[19] For the full list of obligations imposed by Incoterms c i f, c & f, and f o b, see Appendix 2.a.

i. Physical duties relating to the goods themselves

Disputes relating to the goods themselves commonly raise issues of specification: for example, did the protein content of the grain tally with the tolerance allowed in the contract of sale[20]? Although the jargon used in such clauses may be unfamiliar to those of us not concerned with the technical side of the trade, such clauses, and the obligations they impose, involve points of law which are essentially the same as those raised by the standard duties implied by the law into any straightforward domestic sale of goods: compliance with description[21], merchantability or fitness for a given purpose[22]. These duties, treated as they are in the major works covering the law of domestic sales[23], will not be dealt with here.

ii. Physical duties relating to the shipment of the goods

Disputes relating to the shipment of the goods, however, raise issues which bring the sale contract into close contact with the contract for the carriage of the goods by sea, issues which are of their nature quite unlikely to arise in the context of a domestic sale of goods. Thus, a contract of sale on shipment terms will contain terms stipulating who it is who must contract for the carriage of the goods. It will also contain terms imposing a time-table for a number of obligations having to do with the shipping arrangements: for example, the choice of a vessel, or the loading and the unloading of the goods. These duties will be dealt with at more appropriate junctures[24]; it is important, however, to make clear at the outset whose duty it is under the contract of sale to contract with the carrier for the carriage of the goods.

Where the contract is on cif or c&f terms, the situation is straightforward. The choice of that term by the parties indicates their intention to impose upon the seller the duty to conclude a contract of carriage with the carrier: this, in effect, is what is meant by the word 'freight' in the phrase 'cost, insurance, freight' or 'cost and freight'. The buyer becomes a party to the contract of carriage later, normally through the operation of section 1 of the Bills of Lading Act 1855[25]. Where the contract is on fob terms, though, the situation is rather more complex, because, in the words of Devlin J, '[t]he fob contract has become a flexible instrument.'[26] Three main types of fob contract have been

---

[20] See, for example, clause 5 of the standard cif contract for the shipment of feeding stuffs in bulk, issued by the Grain and Feed Trade Association, referred to hereinafter as GAFTA 100: see Appendix 3.a.

[21] See s 13 of the Sale of Goods Act 1979.

[22] See s 14 of the Sale of Goods Act 1979.

[23] See Benjamin, Part 4; Atiyah, *The Sale of Goods,* 7th edn, 1985, Chapters 11 and 12.

[24] See Chapter 4.2.(b) for the obligation to name a vessel within a given time; and Chapter 9. 1 & 2, for the terms as to time in the shipment of the goods.

[25] See Chapter 3, below.

[26] See *Pyrene Co Ltd v Scindia Navigation Co Ltd* [1954] 2 QB 402 at 424.

identified[27]: the straight form, the classic form, and the extended form. Each will be dealt with in turn.

The straight form is the simplest to describe[28], but the hardest to accommodate into traditional orthodox principles of the law of contract. Here, the arrangements for the carriage of the goods from the loading port are left to the buyer, the seller's duty being simply to load goods on a nominated vessel at a given port. The buyer is thus at once a party to the contract of sale and a party to the contract of carriage. The seller, on the other hand, while clearly a party to the contract of sale, would appear not to be a party to the contract of carriage, that contract being concluded between the carrier and the buyer. Such fastidiousness with the doctrine of privity of contract might, however, dismay the carrier, who might actually want to be bound by a contract of carriage with the seller so as to take advantage of exclusion clauses or limitation clauses contained in such a contract. This type of consideration clearly swayed Devlin J in *Pyrene Co Ltd v Scindia Navigation Co Ltd*[29]. In that case, a carrier was sued by a seller of goods sold on straight f o b terms and damaged during loading; the carrier pleaded in his defence a term limiting his liability under the contract of carriage concluded with the buyer; the seller, qua shipper, was held to be a party to this contract of carriage, the terms of which thus limited the carrier's liability towards the seller, originally outside the charmed circle of privity of contract. Devlin J was happy to brush aside any objections founded upon the doctrine of privity. In a dictum which comes close to capitulating to the civil law concept of a promise for the benefit of a third party, Devlin J said:[30]

> 'This is the sort of situation that is covered by the wider principle; the third party takes those benefits of the contract which appertain to his interest therein, but takes them, of course, subject to whatever qualifications with regard to them the contract imposes.'

This pragmatic, some would say too hastily dismissive[31], approach to the doctrine of privity is a characteristic feature of this area of the

---

[27] These three types of f o b contract are not exhaustive: see Benjamin, para 1801, and, for an example of an f o b contract which fitted none of the three main types precisely, see *The Roseline* [1985] AMC 552, a case discussed in another context at Chapter 7.2.(b).ii, below.

[28] It is also the one assumed to represent the intention of the parties in Incoterms: see the f o b terms, obligation B.1, in Appendix 2.a. The fact that it is the simplest to describe, and perhaps also the purest form of f o b contract has led to its sometimes being described, confusingly, as the 'classic' form: see *The Al Hofuf* [1981] 1 Lloyd's Rep 81 at 84; Schmitthoff, p 18; Benjamin, para 1802; and The Law of International Commercial Transactions (Lex Mercatoria), H. J. Berman and C. Kaufman, in 19 Harvard International Law Journal (1978) 221 at 233. The terminology is clearly unsettled: different adjectives again are used in Practising CIF and FOB Today, J. Lebuhn, in (1981) 1 European Transport Law 24, at 30-35, where the labels used were 'real' (straight), 'unreal' (classic), and 'extended'.

[29] [1954] 2 QB 402.

[30] Loc cit at 426.

[31] See *Scruttons Ltd v Midland Silicones Ltd* [1962] AC 446 at 471; and *The Kapetan Marcos NL (No 2)* [1987] 2 Lloyd's Rep 321 at 331, per Mustill LJ, as to which case, see further Chapter 3, fnn 35 and 47. Neither the House of Lords in *Scruttons*, nor the

law[32], and one to which we shall return from time to time in this book[33].

Although Devlin J was concerned in the *Pyrene* case only with the straight f o b form, he also described another two types of f o b contract, the classic and the extended forms. In the classic f o b sale, the buyer nominates the vessel and the seller concludes the contract of carriage for account of the buyer. This form is more likely to occur where the goods traded are shipped on a vessel 'willing to load any goods brought down to the berth or at least those of which she is notified,'[34] that is to say where the goods are carried on a vessel running a liner service on a regular route. Here, the contract of carriage will be recorded on a bill of lading, to which the seller is a party as agent, and to which the buyer is a party as principal.

The third type of f o b sale is the extended f o b contract, also known as the f o b contract with additional services. Here, the seller agrees to provide services for the buyer other than simply providing the goods for shipment at the agreed port. The additional services can include anything which the parties wish. Thus, they may agree that the seller will conclude the contract of carriage, or effect the policy of insurance, or both. Whatever the agreement, the charge for the additional service is payable by the buyer quite separately from the price for the goods[35], which are strictly the only object of the contract of sale. In this sense, the extended f o b contract is still different from the c i f contract, where the obligation to contract for the carriage of the goods is an integral part of the seller's duties under the sale contract, a duty for which he receives payment as a hidden part of the price of the goods[36]. In another sense, though, the two types of contract are similar: for here too, the seller becomes a party to the contract of carriage in his own right; and

---

Court of Appeal in *Marcos* found it necessary, however, to overrule Devlin J's judgment. Devlin J offerred another ratio for his decision, namely that the facts showed an intention to create a contract between the carrier and the shipper, a ratio about which the judge himself had reservations largely because it involved the rather artificial implication of a contract: see [1954] 2 QB 402 at 426, 7. However ambivalent Devlin J himself was about this alternative ratio, though, it does serve to allow his decision to survive the aspersions cast by the higher courts upon his 'wider principle.'

[32] And, indeed, of commercial law generally: see Twentieth Century Developments in Commercial Law, R.M. Goode, in (1983) 3 LS 283 at 288, 289.

[33] See, particularly, Chapter 3, on Title to Sue the Carrier.

[34] See *Pyrene Co Ltd v Scindia Navigation Co Ltd* [1954] 2 QB 402 at 424.

[35] These charges, namely the freight or the premium, may be payable by the buyer either directly to the carrier or the insurer, or indirectly, through the seller. In either case, the cost is for the buyer's account, such that the buyer takes the risk of any upward fluctuation in, say, the cost of the freight, between the time when the sale is concluded and the time when the freight is paid.

[36] But see *Bain v Field & Co Fruit Merchants Ltd* (1920) 3 Ll L Rep 26 at 29, (affd at 5 Ll L Rep 16), where Bailhache J suggested obiter that, where a sale contract was concluded on f o b extended terms, and the cargo was made up of 'comparatively small parcels', it was the duty of the seller to make the contract of carriage. The judge admitted, though, that this suggestion was out of step with the view generally held: see Sassoon, art 526.

the buyer becomes a party later, again normally through the operation of section 1 of the Bills of Lading Act 1855[37].

(b) Documentary duties

As we have seen, the documentary aspects of the seller's duties under sale contracts concluded on shipment terms are one of the two main factors distinguishing such contracts from domestic sales: sales concluded on shipment terms are consequently sometimes called 'documentary sales'. Where the contract is concluded on c i f, c & f, classic f o b, or extended f o b terms[38], the seller owes the buyer a duty to tender the commercial documents stipulated for in the contract, and at the centre of those documents lies the bill of lading[39].

The bill of lading is central to international trade because it provides traders with three crucial facilities. Firstly, on certain conditions being fulfilled, it gives the buyer a valuable bundle of rights against the carrier of the goods: the right to demand delivery of the goods on discharge; the right to sue on clear contractual terms for loss of or damage to the goods; and the right to rely on firm estoppels as to the state of the goods on shipment. Secondly, the bill of lading allows the buyer to speculate on the market while the goods are in transit by selling the bill on. Thirdly, the bill of lading allows both parties to raise finance on the strength of the document itself. All three of these facilities are crucial to the smooth running of trade on shipment terms. Thus, firstly, the buyer could hardly be expected to part with the price against a piece of paper which did not give him direct rights against the carrier. Secondly, international trade, particularly in commodities, is made at once less risky and more profitable by the use of a document which can be sold and bought while goods are still in transit. And finally, trade becomes more possible if banks can be persuaded to give credit on the strength of goods represented by a valuable document like a bill of lading.

Three consequences flow from the importance of the bill of lading to international trade. Firstly, given the significance of the document, it is not surprising that sale contracts on shipment terms will contain clear terms as to the type of bill of lading which the seller must tender to the buyer[40]. Secondly, it is equally unsurprising that documentary duties are probably to be regarded as contractual conditions, breach of

---

[37] See Chapter 3, below. Where the sale contract is of the extended f o b type, the only carriage contract to which the buyer can become a party is the contract contained in the bill of lading; he is not a party to any other contract of carriage agreed between the seller qua shipper and the carrier: see *The El Amria and El Minia* [1982] 2 Lloyd's Rep 28 particularly at 32.

[38] With the additional service of concluding the contract of carriage.

[39] Where the contract is concluded on straight f o b terms, the seller does not, of course, have a bill of lading to tender to the buyer; his duty is therefore to provide a mate's receipt which the buyer can then exchange with the carrier for a bill of lading: see Incoterms, f o b, B.7 and 9, at Appendix 2.a, below.

[40] See, for example, GAFTA 100, clause 14, in Appendix 3.a.

which gives the buyer a set of remedies separate and independent from his remedies for breach of the seller's physical duties relating to the goods[41]. Thirdly, so long as it is not wished to alter the fundamentals of sale contracts on shipment terms, any developments of, or even away from, the paper bill of lading will need somehow to give traders the same three facilities described above as crucial to international trade, namely rights against the carrier, the opportunity to speculate while the goods are in transit, and the ability to finance credit.

3. THE LETTER OF CREDIT DESCRIBED

Mention of the ability to raise credit on the strength of the bill of lading brings us to our last task in this chapter, namely to give a brief description of the way a letter of credit works[42]. One of the main worries in an international sale—much more so than in a domestic sale—relates to payment. The seller is anxious not to go to the expense of manufacture, packing and shipment before he receives firm assurances, readily ascertainable and enforceable, that payment will be made; the buyer, for his part, is keen not to pay before and unless he is certain that goods and documents which conform with the sale contract have left the seller and are on their way to him. The letter of credit reconciles these conflicting interests by concentrating entirely upon the negotiation of the shipping documents between the seller and the buyer. Stated in its simplest terms, the letter of credit allows documents and money to move in opposite directions, giving the seller a reliable paymaster within his own jurisdiction and giving the buyer a documentary screening mechanism at the point where payment is made to the seller.

The system works as follows: where the seller and buyer agree in the contract of sale on payment by letter of credit, the buyer will instruct a bank, typically within the buyer's jurisdiction, to open a credit in favour of the seller for the amount of the purchase price. The buyer's bank—the issuing bank—will correspond with a bank in the seller's jurisdiction, which bank will either advise the seller of the opening of the credit in his favour, or—much more valuable to the seller—confirm the credit opened by the issuing bank, that is to say, it will add its own undertaking to pay the purchase price. Payment is made on tender by the seller of shipping documents conforming to the instructions given by the buyer to the issuing bank in the application for the credit. These instructions form the basis upon which the banks will act in this matter, and it is essential that the buyer ensures that he instructs the bank to pay on tender of precisely those documents which the seller and buyer

---

[41] See Chapter 9. 2, below.

[42] For a detailed examination of the law relating to letters of credit, the reader is referred to *The Law of Bankers' Commercial Credits*, H.C. Gutteridge and M. Megrah, 7th edn, 1984, hereinafter referred to as Gutteridge and Megrah. The object of the description given in the text above is limited to giving the background necessary for an understanding of the issues discussed later in the book.

agreed upon in the contract of sale: for once the instructions are given, the banks will comply with them strictly, the letter of credit operating quite independently of the contract for the sale of goods underlying it. On shipping the goods, the seller tenders the full bundle of documents to the advising or confirming bank, which examines the bundle to make sure that the documents comply with the buyer's instructions. If they do, the seller is paid by the bank and the documents are passed up the line, as it were, to the buyer, who will either have already put the issuing bank in funds, or, if not, will pay that bank either then, against the documents, or later, under a trust receipt[43].

What do the banks receive in return for this service? Other than custom and commissions, the banks, as holders of the shipping documents, including the bill of lading, act safe in the knowledge that if, for some reason, payment of the sum of the credit is not made by the buyer, they can realise their security by claiming possession of the goods from the carrier. Thus, here too, we see the bill of lading, and the commercial functions it performs, at the centre of a mechanism which is essential to the smooth progress of international trade.

---

[43] See Chapter 2.3.(d), below.

PART I

Possession, property, risk and title to sue

CHAPTER 2

The bill of lading as a document of title

1. A framework of questions—and concepts

2. Documents of title, transferability and negotiability

   (a) Transferability in general

   (b) Transferability of bills of lading

   (c) Negotiability

      i. Better title

      ii. The consideration point

3. The proprietary rights transferred

   (a) The right to delivery

   (b) Consequences of the transfer of the right to delivery

   (c) The Factors Acts and the Sale of Goods Act

   (d) The use of the bill of lading as a means of security

   (e) When the bill stops being a document of title

The nature of the bill of lading as a document of title lies at the very centre of its use in international sales. It is this function of the document that sets international sales on shipment terms apart from domestic sales by allowing traders to effect delivery of the goods through the transfer of documents; it is also this function which draws a proprietary link between a particular trader and a particular parcel of goods while they are still in transit, thus giving him, as we shall see in the next chapter, a cause of action for loss or damage occurring to those goods while they are actually in the possession of the carrier. Finally, and perhaps most importantly, it is this function which facilitates the payment of the price through the banking system, for it is the bill of lading as a document of title which gives the banks their ultimate, though probably not their best, security in the letter of credit mechanism.

Given the importance of this function to the commercial utility of bills of lading, it is surprising that there appears to be little agreement about the precise definition of a document of title. Thus, the latest edition of Benjamin still finds it necessary to admit that '[T]here is no authoritative definition of "document of title to goods" at common law'[1]. One explanation for this lack of agreement on a crisp definition may be the very name which legal folklore has given the function: 'document of title'. The word 'title' must be one of the most chameleon-like in legal jargon, taking its significance from the context in which it is used rather than from any agreed sense as to its meaning. Thus, the word has been variously used to refer to ownership, possession, locus standi and risk. A look at the treatment in the literature of the phrase 'document of title' and of the concepts behind it will illustrate the point.

The discussion in Sassoon is the most obviously symptomatic of the plurality of meanings hiding behind the notion of a 'document of title'. He writes:[2]

> 'The bill of lading enables the buyer or his agent to obtain actual delivery of the goods on their arrival at the port of destination. But the bill of lading has greater significance than that. Possession of the bill of lading is equivalent to possession of the goods, and delivery of the bill of lading to the buyer or to a third party may (if so intended) be effective to pass the property in the goods to such person. The bill of lading is a document of title [as defined in s 1(4) of the Factors Act 1889] enabling the holder to obtain credit from banks before the arrival of the goods, for the transfer of a bill of lading can operate as a pledge of the goods themselves. In addition, it is by virtue of the bill of lading that the buyer or his assignee can obtain redress against the carrier for any breach of its terms and of the contract of carriage that it evidences. In other words the bill of lading creates a privity between its holder and the carrier as if the contract was made between them.'

It is clear from this extract that several concepts are at play: possession, both actual and constructive, property, title in the sense attributed by the Factors Acts, privity of contract and title to sue. On the other hand, to look at Scrutton on this matter, one might be forgiven for believing that this function of a bill of lading has to do exclusively with its capacity to transfer property, general or special:[3]

> '. . . the bill of lading serves also as:
>
> (2) A document of title, by the indorsement of which the property in the goods for which it is a receipt may be transferred, or the goods pledged or mortgaged as security for an advance.'

---

[1]   Benjamin, para 1433; see also Goode, *Proprietary Rights and Insolvency in Sales Transactions*, (hereafter, Goode, *Proprietary Rights*), 2nd edn, 1989, at p 59.

[2]   At para 131.

[3]   *Scrutton on Charterparties and Bills of Lading*, 19th edn, 1984, (hereinafter referred to as Scrutton), art 2. It is of interest to note that this is what the editors of Scrutton suggest also endows the bill of lading with the nature of a negotiable instrument: art 92.

This, in marked contrast to the view of the editor of Carver, who, in discussing the bill of lading as a document of title, concentrates on the right of the holder thereof to demand possession:[4]

> 'The right to have possession of the goods passes to the transferee of the bill of lading: that is the symbol of the goods, and a transfer of it is, symbolically, a transfer of the possession of the goods themselves.'

Finally, the editors of Benjamin, despite their initial hesitation, construct a definition which in effect comprises both notions of property and the right to demand possession of the goods:[5]

> '. . . a document relating to goods the transfer of which operates as a transfer of the constructive possession of the goods, and may operate as a transfer of the property in them.'

To seek unanimity, then, on a definition of a 'document of title' is likely to be unsuccessful and perhaps unnecessary now that English commercial lawyers seem to have survived without one for so long. On the other hand, though, there are a number of practical problems whose resolution depends in effect on whether a particular shipping document, be it a bill of lading, a waybill, a container transport document or a so-called 'through' bill of lading, is or is not a document of title. Thus, for example, the seller's performance of his documentary obligations depends in part on the tender of a 'negotiable'[6] bill of lading. Again, the buyer's rights against the carrier for damages in case the goods are lost or damaged may, as we shall see,[7] depend on whether or not he holds a document of title. And finally, the bank's readiness to open and pay under a letter of credit will depend in large part on the security interest it is offered by the traders involved through the tender of a document of title. Agreement, then, about which documents possess this magical quality there must be, even if it is difficult to analyse the precise constituents of that quality.

Given the obvious difficulties encountered by others in defining what a document of title is, it might be more instructive and easier to start, as it were, at the other end: to concentrate on the questions which are asked when an international sale of goods carried by sea goes wrong. We shall find that each of these questions evokes a separate legal concept: but our aim is, at any rate eventually, to formulate an integral definition of one concept, that of a document of title. That destination might be easier to reach if we could first agree on why we need to get there. This will be our first task in this chapter: to provide a framework within which to search for an understanding of the bill of lading as a document of title. Our second task will be to analyse two words commonly found in close proximity to the phrase 'document of title', i e 'transferable'

---

[4] Carver, *Carriage by Sea*, 13th edn, 1982, (hereinafter referred to as Carver) at s 1596.
[5] Benjamin, para 1433.
[6] Incoterms, CIF, A7; see Appendix 2.a.
[7] See Chapter 3, below.

and 'negotiable'; and this, because it is difficult to agree on a definition of that phrase without first unravelling the significance of either of those two words. Thirdly, and this is our eventual goal, we shall ask what it is precisely that we mean by 'title': what exactly does a bill of lading transfer?

1. A FRAMEWORK OF QUESTIONS—
AND CONCEPTS

Putting to one side, then, for a moment, questions of definition, there are in practice five questions which an adviser to a buyer of lost or damaged goods, currently in the hands of a carrier by sea, needs to ask. Each of these questions raises issues which need to be kept separate the one from the other.

1. Firstly, he may need to establish that his client actually has a right to demand possession of the goods from the carrier, such that delivery by the carrier to someone else would amount to a conversion for which the carrier would be liable.

2. Secondly, he may need to discover, for any one of a variety of purposes, whether the damaged goods were the property of his client. Both this question and the previous one deal with the proprietary rights of the buyer over the goods; however, the impact of their answers spills over into issues of tort and contract. Thus, for example, whether or not the document tendered by the seller to the buyer is one which transfers the right to possession and which can transfer property will determine whether the seller has discharged his obligations under the contract of sale, and therefore whether the buyer can reject the documents on tender. Again, the question as to whether the seller has performed his obligations will dictate whether the buyer's remedy lies against the seller under the sale contract, or against the carrier under the carriage contract or against the insurer under the insurance policy.

3. This last issue—which defendant is the buyer to sue—is dictated by the passage of risk from the seller to the buyer: if the risk of loss or damage has passed, then the seller is not an appropriate defendant, because he has performed his obligations by placing the goods on board and tendering the appropriate documents; if, on the other hand, the seller has not performed, then the risk of loss or damage in transit is still with him, which simply means that he is still a legitimate defendant for the buyer to sue.

4. If the buyer cannot sue the seller, then the next question which arises is : does the buyer have locus standi to sue the carrier? Again, the transfer or otherwise of a proprietary interest will have a direct bearing on this question. His locus standi will depend, in contract, partly on whether he has, at the time of the action, property in the goods, and in tort, on whether he had, at the time of the loss complained of, some proprietary interest in the goods.

5. Once title to sue is established, the next question will relate to regime: is the plaintiff's action in tort or in contract, and if the latter, is the contract governed by the Carriage of Goods by Sea Act 1971?

The first four of these questions—the transfer of possession, of property, of risk and locus standi—will be discussed in this Part of this book. An examination of the fifth question—regime applicable—more properly belongs in works dealing with the law relating to the carriage of goods by sea[8]. Our task now is to discover which of those four questions is the one the answer to which depends exclusively on whether a particular shipping document is a 'document of title': that inquiry will lead us to an understanding of that phrase and it requires an examination of the allied notions of negotiability and transferability.

2. DOCUMENTS OF TITLE, TRANSFERABILITY AND NEGOTIABILITY

As has already been indicated, a clear understanding of this area of the law is hampered by the absence of uniformly accepted definitions and by rough and ready assertions that bills of lading are, or should be, negotiable and transferable documents of title[9]. Apart from the difficulties to which we have already referred with the definition of the word 'title', what exactly is the difference between the concepts of 'negotiability' and 'transferability'[10]? And does a bill of lading possess either or both of those characteristics motu propriu, or only as a result of the Bills of Lading Act 1855? If the former, might there be other documents which may have come to possess, through their increased currency among commercial men and women, characteristics of 'negotiability' or 'transferability' even though they may not technically come within the terms of the Bills of Lading Act 1855?[11]

---

8 Scrutton, pp 412–419; Carver, ss 450A, 470–474 and 483–491.
9 Equally unhelpful are dicta suggesting the reverse in respect of other types of shipping document. See, for instance, *Waren Import Gesellschaft Krohn & Co v Internationale Graanhandel Thegra NV* [1975] 1 Lloyd's Rep 146 at 154, where Kerr L J speaks of delivery orders as 'non-transferable documents of title.'
10 Thus, when GAFTA 100 requires, at clause 14, (see Appendix 3.a), that the bill of lading or other shipping document tendered be 'in negotiable and transferable form', is it demanding the presence of two characteristics or one?
11 Thus, for example, if container transport documents have come to be considered as transferable, then transferees thereof would have the right to claim possession of the goods from the carrier; once that possessory right were exercised, the common law would imply a contract between the carrier and the transferee under the rule in *Brandt v Liverpool, Brazil & River Plate SN Co* [1924] 1 KB 175 and any privity of contract difficulties there might be with these documents would be solved without the assistance of the Bills of Lading Act 1855 (which on one analysis is inapplicable without express incorporation) and without the necessity of the tortuous type of privity-solving draftsmanship which commonly characterises such documents: see, for example, the definition of the word '[M]erchant' in COMBIDOC: see Appendix 3.f. These issues will, of course, be discussed at greater length in Chapter 8, in the context of waybills and combined transport documents respectively; the aim here is simply to lay the background, in terms of general principle, to these more specific debates.

(a) Transferability in general

It is impossible to answer these questions without tapping into a number of fundamental ideas in the law relating to personal property[12]. Our point of departure must be the reluctance of the common law to contemplate the transfer by A to B of things in action as opposed to that of things in possession:[13] a transfer of the latter, being tangible movables, could readily be identified and observed; a transfer of the former, being intangible, could not. Moreover, the ethereal nature of such a transfer, if allowed, might bring with it the danger of maintenance, that is to say the pursuit of remedies in the courts by those who lacked any legitimate interest in the original substance of the claim[14]. The courts of equity first[15], and then Parliament through the Law of Property Act 1925[16], did away with the common law's sensibilities on this matter; but the point of more direct relevance to us here is that even before developments in equity and under statute, the common law recognised the transfer by delivery, sometimes accompanied by endorsement, of certain types of things in action which were considered 'to be locked up in [a] document'[17]. These things in action were of two types, rights to goods and rights to the payment of money; there were consequently two species of document each symbolising each of those two types of right: documents of title to goods and documents of title to money, normally called 'instruments'. The transfer of either type of document from A to B passed the right 'locked up in' the document without the need of any formal assignment or of any notice to the debtor of the obligation: the document was in this sense freely transferable and it was this quality which earned it classification as a document of title. 'Transferability', then, makes a document of title; it describes, rather than qualifies, such a document. Consequently, to speak of a 'transferable document of title' is tautologous; and to speak of a 'non-transferable document of title' is an impossibility.

---

[12] For a lucid account of the impact of such principles across the general area of commercial law, see Goode, Chapter 2, to which account the text accompanying and surrounding this note is heavily indebted.

[13] A 'thing in action', as opposed to a 'thing in possession', is one which does not exist in the physical world and which is consequently not susceptible to physical possession. See *Keeton and Sheridan on Equity*, 1987, at p 225.

[14] See Treitel, *The Law of Contract*, 17th edn, 1987, (hereinafter referred to as Treitel), p 498, particularly the text accompanying notes 3-5.

[15] See Treitel, at pp 499-500, and the authorities cited therein.

[16] Section 136(1): 'Any absolute assignment by writing under the hand of the assignor ... of any ... legal thing in action, of which express notice in writing has been given to the ... person from whom the assignor would have been entitled to claim such ... thing in action, is effectual in law (subject to equities having priority over the right of the assignee) to pass and transfer from the date of such notice –
    (a) the legal right to such ... thing in action;
    (b) the legal and other remedies for the same;
    (c) the power to give a good discharge for the same without the concurrence of the assignor...'

[17] Goode, p 66.

(b) Transferability of bills of lading

Applying these principles of personal property law to bills of lading in particular, there are three points of which it would be useful to make at least a preliminary mention at this stage. Firstly, a bill of lading is said not automatically to be a document of title: apparently, it achieves the characteristic of transferability only if it is expressed to be transferable and by mercantile custom this is inferred from the designation of the consignee in the appropriate box on the front page[18] as 'Mr Buyer or Order' or simply as 'Order'[19]. Secondly, a bill of lading stated to be 'non-transferable'[20] may well be, for certain statutory purposes, a bill of lading[21] or even a 'document of title'[22]; it follows from what has been said in the previous paragraph, though, that such a bill cannot be a document of title at common law. Thirdly, to establish the proposition that transferability without assignment is the essence of a document's identity as a 'document of title' is not the same as stating what it is exactly that is transferred from A to B by delivery of the document. That is a separate question, to which reference has already been made at the start of this chapter[23] and to which we shall be returning at greater length presently[24].

(c) Negotiability

Before we do so, however, we need to return to our excursion among some fundamental principles of personal property law with a view to examining the characteristic of negotiability of documents of title. It will be clear from what has gone before in this chapter that, yet again, proper analysis is impossible without agreement as to terminology. There is no lack of support for the view that a bill of lading is negotiable in a less than complete sense[25] and two explanations are commonly given for this: the first refers to the strength of the title conferred on the holder

---

[18] See Appendix 3.b.

[19] See Benjamin, paras 1438 and 1446; Scrutton, art 92; and Bennett, *The History and Present Position of the Bill of Lading as a Document of Title to Goods*, (hereinafter referred to as Bennett, History), 1914, at p 17. The position as described in the text lies at the basis of the legal difficulties surrounding seawaybills and will therefore be addressed at greater length in Chapter 8.1.

[20] Although the market is more likely to use, somewhat confusingly as we shall presently see, the word 'non-negotiable': see, for example, the GCBS Waybill in Appendix 3.d.

[21] For the purposes of the Bills of Lading Act 1855, though, it is not totally clear whether the privity gap is closed by s 1 of that Act in the absence of a document of title as understood in the text: see below fn 117 and further at Chapter 3.1.(a).i.

[22] For the purposes of the Factors Act 1889 and the Sale of Goods Act 1979: see Chapter 2.3.(c), below.

[23] See Chapter 2.1, above.

[24] See Chapter 2.3.(a), below.

[25] See, for example, Benjamin, para 1449; Scrutton, art 92, note 1; Bennett, History, at pp 19-20; *Crossley Vaines on Personal Property*, Tyler and Palmer, 1973, (hereinafter referred to as CrossleyVaines), at p 213; and Raleigh-Butt, *The Law of Negotiable Instruments*, 1931, at pp 18 and 19; also, *Kum v Wah Tat Bank* [1971] 1 Lloyd's Rep 439 at 446.

of the document as against the true owner; the second to the doctrine of consideration. It is proposed to tackle each of these in turn.

First, though, another skirmish with definitions. As Professor Goode has indicated[26], confusion in this area is compounded by the unfortunate ambiguity evident throughout the literature, as to the precise meaning of the word 'negotiability' and as to the relationship of that concept to that of 'transferability[27]'. It would assist clarity in analysis to reserve the former term, 'negotiability', for that feature of documents of title to money whereby certain transferees obtained a better title than their predecessors; and to use the term 'transferability' in the sense used earlier on in this chapter, i e capable of transferring rights without formal assignment. Neither is it to be thought that the value of agreed definitions of these terms is purely aesthetic: when one or other of them appears in statutes without definition, then substantive issues like the applicability or otherwise of Hague-Visby limitation will turn on narrow questions of definition[28]. With definitions firmly established, even if not fully approved of, then, the issue before us is this: to what extent is it really meaningful to continue to suggest that a transferable bill of lading is not negotiable in the sense in which a bill of exchange is? The proposition that the bill of lading is not negotiable is commonly supported on two grounds, the first referring to better title, the second to consideration. Each will now be dealt with in turn.

i. Better title

We saw earlier[29] that documents of title could symbolise rights either to money or to goods and that both were readily transferable without assignment. The first—and, it should be said, main—sense in which they are said to differ is this: documents of title to money are 'negotiable' in the sense that they can pass to a bona fide transferee for value without

---

[26]   See Goode, p 67, fn 98 and also p 428, fn 9 for a similar point on 'negotiable instrument'. Ambiguity in the use of the word 'negotiability' has troubled commentators for some time: for an entertainingly exasperated account, see Negotiability and Estoppel, J. S. Ewart, (1900) 16 LQR 135, particularly 135–143 and 156.

[27]   See, for example, Carver, at para 1597, where the editor starts out by saying that '[t]he bill of lading is thus generally a negotiable instrument, carrying with it the right to demand and have possession of the goods described in it.' The editor footnotes a caveat, though, that what he means by 'negotiable' is 'no more than transferable— as transferring the right to possession', preferring to reserve the term 'negotiable' for the effect which the Bills of Lading Act 1855 has on the bill of lading, i e the transfer of contractual rights and liabilities. See also Schmitthoff, at p 511, fn 60. The ambivalence of definition is not restricted to the books: see *Henderson v Comptoir d'Escompte de Paris* (1873) LR 5 PC 253 at 259. See Chapter 8.1.(b).i, below.

[28]   See, for example, art VI of the Hague-Visby Rules, and its use of the phrase 'non-negotiable' to mean, pace Scrutton at art 92, note 2 and p 462, 'not transferable'. For a comprehensive survey of definitional problems in a number of relevant statutes, see Shipping Documentation for the Carriage of Goods and the Hamburg Rules, C.W. O'Hare, (1978) 52 ALJ 415 at 420–422.

[29]   At Chapter 2.2.(a), above.

notice a better title than that enjoyed by the transferor; documents of title to goods are not 'negotiable' in this sense. Thus, while the 'holder in due course' of a bill of exchange takes the entitlement to payment totally free of the defects in title and of the equities of all previous holders, the same cannot be said of the holder of a bill of lading, who, at common law, succeeds in a very real sense, to the title enjoyed by his predecessor. The bill of lading, it is said, only attains such a quality where it is transferred in the exceptional circumstances provided for in the Factors Act 1889, ss. 2, 8 and 9 and in the Sale of Goods Act 1979, ss 24 and 25[30].

The puzzling assumption behind this suggested contrast between the two documents is that a bill of exchange somehow need satisfy no requirements for it to be negotiable, whereas a bill of lading does: but this is patently wrong, as even a cursory reading of any of the discussions about the 'holder in due course' will show. Thus, Professor Goode writes:[31]

> 'Just as the bona fide purchaser of goods for value and without notice will in certain conditions obtain an overriding title, by way of exception to the nemo dat rule, so also will the holder of a bill [of exchange], *if fulfilling certain requirements*,[32] be a holder in due course and thus acquire title to the bill free from equities and defects in the title of his transferor.'

There follows in the text an examination of the requirements which s 29(1) of the Bills of Exchange Act 1882 demands if a bill of exchange is to confer on a holder the privileged status of a 'holder in due course' and on the bill he holds the special attribute of 'negotiability'. Surely, it follows that both bills of lading and bills of exchange are transferable and that both may, on the fulfilment of certain conditions, be negotiable in the sense described above. This is not, of course, to say that the two documents are equally potent in terms of the circumstances in which they can pass indefeasible title: thus, while a holder in due course may defeat the real creditor even if the holder received the bill of exchange from a thief[33], an endorsee of a bill of lading in a similar position cannot prevail over the real owner because that circumstance lies outside the cases envisaged by ss 24 and 25 of the Sale of Goods Act 1979. But this is simply to say that the two documents are negotiable in different, if sometimes overlapping, circumstances; not that one is negotiable while the other is not[34].

---

[30] As to which, see below at Chapter 2.3.(c). See, for an example of the explanation rehearsed in the text, Goode, p 428, fn 10 and p 551, fn 42.

[31] Goode, pp 445-449.

[32] Emphasis added.

[33] See Goode, p 445.

[34] For a spirited, if irreverent, explanation as to why documents of title to goods could not be called negotiable even if, in a very important sense, they were, see The Conflict of Law and Commerce, Lord Chorley, in (1932) 48 LQR 51, particularly at pp 55-59. It must be said, though, that the weight of opinion in the literature lies very heavily against the view expressed in the text: thus, see Symbolical Deliveries by Documents, F. Tudsbery, (1915) 31 LQR 84-92, and The Negotiability of Bills of Lading, R.E. Negus, (1921) 37 LQR 442-461. The majority view, however, is not without its own

ii. The consideration point

The second reason why bills of lading are said to be less than negotiable takes us to the doctrine of consideration and its peculiar application in the field of bills of exchange. The argument[35] runs thus. Certain provisions of the Bills of Exchange Act 1882 relax the normal requirements of the common law doctrine of consideration[36], the central thrust of those provisions being that in certain situations consideration can be assumed in the holder's favour without it having to be proved[37]. Those provisions— and the relaxation of the general requirement of consideration in English law—do not apply to bills of lading. Consequently, '[t]he transfer of a bill of lading does not pass property or title, ... unless value is given for the transfer'[38] and neither is it 'clear whether the gratuitous transfer of a bill of lading might operate by way of gift, if so intended.'[39] Finally, and here lies the sting, if an attempt at such a transfer were made, section 1 of the Bills of Lading Act 1855 would not work its magic and construct a contract between the voluntary transferee and the carrier.

The consequences described in the last two sentences are startling examples of the sorts of difficulties caused by the uncertainty surrounding the definition of the term 'negotiable'. Again, it might help here to concentrate on the substance of the issue—consideration—rather than on the concept of negotiability, which we reserved above as a useful way of describing the potency of the holder's title. Moreover, it is absolutely necessary to state precisely the 'consideration' question or questions which it is worth asking. Thus, it would be a waste of time to ask whether A is bound by his promise to give his cargo of oil, currently in transit, to B by tendering a bill of lading covering the cargo. Such a promise would fall foul of the doctrine of consideration whether the intended mode of performance was documentary (by tender of the bill of lading) or physical (by delivery of the oil). The questions which are worth asking, and which seem to attract a negative answer from the editors of Benjamin, arise after a bill of lading has been transferred to a voluntary endorsee; and they are:(a) does B have a possessory interest

---

difficulties. Thus, Mr Negus is driven simply to distinguish as 'peculiar' a Privy Council decision, *Pease v Gloahec, The Marie Joseph* (1866) LR 1 PC 219, which anticipated the better title rule contained in s 10 of the Factors Act 1889, now s 47(2) of the Sale of Goods Act 1979. Again, Bennett, History, nails his colours to the majority view at pp 20, 21; yet later he writes, at p 34, 'One of the essential characteristics of a negotiable instrument is that a "holder in due course" acquires a good title irrespective of that of his transferor and it has been the policy of the Factors' Acts to apply this principle in some measure to Bills of Lading.'

[35]   See Benjamin, paras 1449, 1453; and Bennett, History, at p 21.
[36]   Namely, ss 27(2) and 30(1) of that Act, which respectively read:
'27(2). Where value has at any time been given for a bill the holder is deemed to be a holder for value as regards the acceptor and all parties to the bill who became parties prior to such time.'
'30(1). Every party whose signature appears on a bill is prima facie deemed to have become a party thereto for value.'
[37]   See Goode, at pp 444–445.
[38]   Benjamin, para 1453.
[39]   Ibid at fn 68.

in the goods such that he can demand possession of the goods from the carrier; and (b) if the goods are handed over to B in a damaged condition, is the relationship between B and the carrier governed by the same contract which had been concluded by A and the carrier?

As we have seen, Benjamin answers both questions in the negative, largely on the basis of a cluster of early cases[40] in which the issue was whether the seller's agent at the port of destination to whom the bill of lading had been endorsed could, in his own name, claim possession of the goods in order to protect his principal's interests against the buyer's insolvency. Before the Sale of Goods Act 1893 expressly gave the agent such a right in s 38(2), he could only do so if he had obtained a proprietary interest—at the very least the right to claim possession—in the goods; in these cases, the courts held that he had not. Unfortunately, dicta in the judgments made mention of the fact that the agent was a voluntary endorsee and thus was laid the basis for the proposition that a voluntary transfer of a bill of lading does not in law grant the transferee the right, as against the carrier, to possession of the goods. It is clear now, though, that after the decision of the House of Lords in *Sewell v Burdick*[41], the answer to the question in these cases is provided by the requirement of intention; that is to say, the agent receives no proprietary interest on endorsement not because he is a volunteer but because there was no intention that he should receive such an interest[42]. Moreover, given s 38(2) of the Sale of Goods Act 1893, the question in these early cases quite simply no longer needs to be asked. For both these reasons, their value in connection with the two questions asked in the last paragraph is quite insignificant. Those questions, it will be recalled, were: (a) does a voluntary endorsee of a bill of lading acquire from the endorser the right to demand delivery of the goods from the carrier; (b) if the goods are delivered in a damaged state, is the endorsee's relationship with the carrier based on the same contract concluded between the endorser and the carrier?

It is submitted that there are now three reasons why positive answers are to be preferred to either of those questions. Firstly, as a matter of policy, it is difficult to see why, once A has endorsed the bill of lading to B, a voluntary transferee, B should not be able to exercise control over them while they are in the hands of the carrier: the exercise of such control would clearly accord with the expectations of the carrier who would doubtless be bemused by the suggestion that he was to check, before handing the goods over to B at the quayside, whether B had

---

[40] *Coxe v Harden* (1803) 4 East 211; *Waring v Cox* (1808) 1 Camp 369; *Burgos v Nascimento* (1908) 11 Asp MLC 181. The first two cases are digested in Bennett, History, at pp 21–24.

[41] (1884) 10 App Cas 74, discussed further at Chapter 2.3.(a), below. See, though, the Earl of Selborne LC at p 80, for what must be obiter support for the view that a voluntary transfer of a bill of lading is ineffective. It must be said that the dictum is echoed in none of the other speeches in the case.

[42] See *Burgos v Nascimento* (1908) 11 Asp MLC 181 at 183.

provided A with consideration for the bill. Moreover, the carrier's bemusement would turn to something beyond irritation at the suggestion that any action by B for loss, damage or short delivery would not be governed by the contract—and its limitations—which he, the carrier, had concluded with A[43]. Secondly, as a matter of logic, Benjamin's position is based on a definition of negotiability which elides that concept with transferability, a conflation of ideas to the risks of which we have already referred. The sections of the Bills of Exchange Act 1882 which lie at the basis of Benjamin's argument[44] and the two questions asked above about the effect of a voluntary transfer of a bill of lading go to the transferability of the documents rather than their negotiability. The issue throughout is whether transfer without proven consideration passes to the transferee rights against third parties, i e the drawee in a bill of exchange and the carrier in a bill of lading; it is not whether the holder has a stronger title as against the true creditor or owner. Thirdly, it is not at all clear, as a matter of law, that a voluntary transfer of goods by symbolic or constructive delivery is ineffective, for although the general rule is that, absent a deed or a declaration of trust, only physical delivery makes a gift effective, there are recognised exceptions to that rule, among which is the transfer of a bill of lading[45].

To conclude, then, a bill of lading is negotiable in the sense that where the requirements of the Sale of Goods Act 1979 are satisfied[46], the title of the holder of the bill prevails over that of the true owner. This characteristic it shares with bills of exchange, which are, less than surprisingly, governed by their own statute which establishes its own instances of negotiability. Bills of lading, it is further suggested, can effectively be the objects of gifts, such that their voluntary transfer passes to the endorsee those rights which normally travel with a document of title. Defining which rights do travel with a document of title was the third task set out at the start of this chapter and to that question we now return.

3. THE PROPRIETARY RIGHTS TRANSFERRED

We said earlier[47] that to describe a document as 'transferable' or as a 'document of title' was to say something important about the manner of its assignability; it did not, however, explain what it was precisely which was being assigned by transfer of the document. Once that is explained, we will, finally, have arrived at an understanding of what the common law means by the phrase 'document of title' and that will

---

[43]   If the accepted view were correct, and a voluntary transfer of a bill of lading were ineffective, there would, of course, be no action in tort because of *The Aliakmon* [1986] 2 Lloyd's Rep 1, as to which see below at Chapter 3.2.

[44]   See fn 36 above.

[45]   See Crossley Vaines, at pp 305-310, particularly p 308, fn (q) and text accompanying.

[46]   As to which, see below, at Chapter 2.3.(c).

[47]   At Chapter 2.2.(b), above.

be our first task in this section. Our second will be to work out the practical consequences of the transfer of a document of title at common law. The jigsaw would still, however, be incomplete if we were to leave out of account the list of documents described by the Sale of Goods Act 1979[48] as coming within the expression 'document of title': for it seems puzzling, at first sight, for the English common law to say, as it does[49], that only bills of lading are documents of title[50], and then to find a long list of other documents treated in a statute as if they too were documents of title. To find a way out of that apparent conundrum will be our third task. Our fourth will be to see how the function of the bill of lading as a document of title facilitates the financing of an international sale through the letter of credit system: our aim here will be to concentrate on the proprietary security which a bill of lading affords a bank paying under a letter of credit, rather than to give an exhaustive account of the rules relating to letters of credit. Finally, we shall be asking when it is that a bill of lading ceases being a document of title.

(a) The right to delivery

The use of colourful metaphorical language in answer to the question 'What does a bill of lading transfer to the endorsee?' has helped to conceal rather than to reveal the meaning of the phrase 'document of title'. The metaphor which most readily comes to mind, in that it is the one which is the most common in the literature, is that likening the bill of lading to a symbolic key to a floating warehouse. Nowhere are the dangers of attempting to encapsulate diverse legal concepts under one convenient label more clearly to be found than in the following extract from Lord Justice Bowen's judgment in the Court of Appeal's decision in *Sanders Bros v Maclean & Co* [51]:

---

[48] By incorporating, in s 61, the definition of 'document of title' contained in s 1(4) of the Factors Act 1889, which reads:
'The expression "document of title" shall include any bill of lading, dock warrant, warehouse-keeper's certificate, and warrant or order for the delivery of goods, and any other document used in the ordinary course of business as proof of the possession or control of goods, or authorising or purporting to authorise, either by endorsement or by delivery, the possessor of the document to transfer or receive goods thereby represented.'

[49] *Official Assignee of Madras v Mercantile Bank of India Ltd* [1935] AC 53 at 59. For a possible explanation as to why the bill of lading is accorded this special status, see Of Dock Warrants, WarehouseKeepers' Certificates, Etc, A.T. Carter, (1892) 8 LQR 301 at 302; and for a comment on this explanation, see Goode, *Proprietary Rights*, at p 61, fn 4.

[50] For the sake of completeness, and only peripherally to the central thrust of this chapter, mention should be made of a number of local Acts of Parliament whereby certain dock and warehouse warrants are assimilated to documents of title at common law: see Benjamin, para 1481.

[51] (1883) 11 QBD 327 at 341. To be fair to Lord Justice Bowen, though, it should be said that, barely a year later, he it was who, implicitly refining what he had said in *Sanders v Maclean*, dissented in the Court of Appeal in *Burdick v Sewell* (1884) 13 QBD 159 at 170-175, in a judgment which was then vindicated by the House of Lords at (1884) 10 App Cas 74.

'A cargo at sea while in the hands of the carrier is necessarily incapable of physical delivery. During [the] period of transit and voyage, the bill of lading by the law merchant is universally recognised as its symbol, and the indorsement and delivery of the bill of lading operates as a symbolical delivery of the cargo. Property in the goods passes by such indorsement and delivery of the bill of lading, whenever it is the intention of the parties that the property should pass, just as under similar circumstances the property would pass by an actual delivery of the goods. And for the purpose of passing such property in the goods and completing the title of the indorsee to full possession thereof, the bill of lading, until complete delivery of the cargo has been made on shore to some one rightfully claiming under it, remains in force as a symbol, and carries with it not only the full ownership of the goods, but also all rights created by the contract of carriage between the shipper and the shipowner. It is a key which in the hands of a rightful owner is intended to unlock the door of the warehouse, floating or fixed, in which the goods may chance to be.'

What precisely, to use Professor Goode's phrase[52], is 'locked up in' this symbol? Is it 'property', 'title', 'full possession', 'full ownership', or the 'rights created by the contract of carriage'? To put it another way, which of the five questions raised earlier on in this chapter[53] is answered exclusively by considering whether the document in the buyer's hands is a document of title at common law?

Since the decision of the House of Lords in *Sewell v Burdick*[54], it has been clear that the proprietary effect of the transfer of the bill of lading depends on the intention accompanying the transfer. In that case, the carrier sought to recover freight from an endorsee to whom the bill of lading had been transferred by way of security for a loan; the House of Lords, reversing the Court of Appeal's judgment, found against the carrier on the ground that the defendant endorsee was not a party to the contract of carriage; this was because s 1 of the Bills of Lading Act 1855 had not been triggered; and this in turn was because the endorsee had not acquired property in the goods, the intention of the parties having been simply to create a security interest in the endorsee. We shall return to the Bills of Lading Act aspect of the case in due course[55]; suffice it for the present to say that dicta in earlier cases, suggesting that property in the goods always and necessarily passes to the transferee on endorsement

---

[52]   See fn 17 above.
[53]   At Chapter 2.1, when we sought to set out a framework of questions which an adviser of an aggrieved buyer of goods carried by sea might ask—and of the concepts which he or she might need in order to answer those questions. The concepts were: possession, property, risk, locus standi and regime.
[54]   (1884) 10 App Cas 74.
[55]   At Chapter 3.1.(a).ii.

of the bill of lading[56], must now be treated as having been overtaken by the judgment in *Sewell's* case.

Simply to suggest, though, that the nature of the proprietary interest transferred by endorsement of a bill of lading depends on the intention of the parties surrounding the transfer is hardly satisfactory. There must be some starting point, some assumption as to the nature of the interest transferred, which parties can take to be an accurate reflection of the law's reaction to the transfer of a bill of lading from A to B. The common law starts from the assumption that the bill of lading contains the right to demand physical delivery of the goods at the port of destination and no more; thus Devlin J in *Heskell v Continental Express Ltd*[57] says:

'The reason why a bill of lading is a document of title is because it contains a statement by the master of a ship that he is in possession of cargo, and an undertaking to deliver it.'

For property to pass, there must be evidence of an intention so to pass and evidence as to which type of property it was the intention of the parties to pass. In the absence of such evidence, it is the right to demand delivery at the port of destination—sometimes known as constructive possession[58]—which will be deemed to have passed on transfer.

We have thus come to the stage where we can adopt a working definition of a 'document of title' at common law. *Transferability* of the *right to demand possession* of goods from a person currently *having physical possession* of them lies at the core of the common law notion of a 'document of title' and an accurate definition of that phrase should include those ingredients and those alone. Ambivalence about the meaning of words like 'title', 'transferability' and 'negotiability' has meant that a good number of definitions in the literature, some of which we looked at early on in this chapter[59], said either too much or too little. In a

---

[56] Such as those in *Glyn, Mills Currie & Co v East & West India Docks* (1882) 7 App Cas 591 at 596, 604, 618; and in *Lickbarrow v Mason* (1794) 5 Term Rep 683 at 686. Indeed, it has been argued elsewhere that the law has always been as stated in *Sewell v Burdick*: see Bennett, History, at pp 50–54. For an extremely interesting account of why *Lickbarrow v Mason* spawned the notion that the endorsement of the bill of lading always passed property in the goods, see Bills of Lading and Factors in Nineteenth Century English Overseas Trade, N. I. Miller, at 24 University of Chicago Law Review 257 (1957) particularly at 267–281, where the writer also traces the crab-like encroachments upon the *Lickbarrow* case made over the century or so which passed between the *Lickbarrow* litigation and *Sewell's* case. The central thrust of Mr Miller's article is that the judges confused the financing role of a factor with the trading role of a buyer; and that consequently they failed to distinguish between the trading function of the bill of lading as between merchants, and its financing function as between merchants and factors; that is to say, between its being an object of ownership and an object of security.

[57] [1950] 1 All ER 1033 at 1042B. See also, for a host of much earlier cases supporting the text in the proposition, Bennett, History, at pp 9–12.

[58] See Benjamin, paras 1433 and 1445; but see also Goode, at p 62, and Goode, *Proprietary Rights*, at p 13, for a salutary word of caution about the use of this expression, lest it be taken to imply that the carrier has a proprietary interest in the goods independent of that of the bailor, the holder of the bill.

[59] At pp 16–17.

seminal lecture on 'Concepts of Ownership, Possession and Sale'[60], however, Professor Goode puts forward a form of words which does neither:

> '[The document of title] must be issued or accepted by the bailee of goods, must thereby embody his undertaking to hold the goods for, and release them to, whoever presents the document and must be recognised by statute or mercantile usage as a document which enables control of the goods to pass by delivery of the document with any necessary indorsement.'

If the bailee is a carrier by sea, the same text can serve equally usefully to describe the function of a bill of lading as a document of title at common law.

(b) Consequences of the transfer of the right to delivery

It follows from that definition that it is only the first of the five questions our imaginary adviser asked towards the beginning of this chapter[61] that is answered exclusively by deciding whether the document in the buyer's hands is a document of title at common law: if the buyer holds such a document, he has a right to demand possession of the goods from the carrier. We need now to work through the practical consequences of the transfer to the buyer of that right, acquired through the transfer of the bill of lading. Those consequences can broadly be placed under three headings, though each is closely related to the other: the right to delivery is exclusive; the carrier must only deliver against presentation of the bill; and the location of the document tells the carrier who controls the delivery of the goods.

Firstly, no one other than the holder of the bill has a right as against the carrier to demand possession of the goods from the carrier. Although this sounds like impeccable common sense at first hearing, this consequence is not without its own problems. For one thing, the reverse side of the proposition, i e that the holder of a bill has a right as against the carrier to demand delivery, lies at the core of many of the problems surrounding maritime documentary fraud; for it is the credit reposed in the bill of lading as a document of title that makes bona fide players in an international trade transaction relinquish goods and/or large sums of money to fraudulent holders of such a document[62]. Again, the rule can sometimes work harshly against buyers who find that they cannot claim delivery of the goods from the carrier because, for reasons completely outside their own control, they have no bill of lading in their possession

---

[60] Published in Goode, Proprietary Rights, the quotation in the text appearing at p 9; see also p 61. In like vein, see The Multimodal Transport Document, J. Ramberg, in *International Carriage of Goods: some legal problems and possible solutions*, eds Schmitthoff and Goode, 1988, at p 6.

[61] At Chapter 2.1.

[62] For an exhaustive account of the practice of maritime fraud and of the means for its prevention and detection, see *International Maritime Fraud*, Eric Ellen and Donald Campbell, 1981; for a thorough account of the law as it relates in particular to the fraudulent use of bills of lading, see the proceedings of the 1983 Venice Colloquium on Bills of Lading published by the Comite Maritime International.

when the goods arrive at the port of destination. Thus, in *Trucks & Spares Ltd v Maritime Agencies (Southampton) Ltd*[63], a buyer of goods to whom, through no fault of his own, the bill of lading had not been endorsed, was denied an interim order by the Court of Appeal for delivery of the goods by the carrier. The carrier had, in fact, retained the bills of lading, with the shipper's agreement[64], as security against outstanding debts owed him by the shipper. This point was not lost on Hodson LJ, who dissented, not being as willing as his brethren presumably were to throw the buyer back on his remedies for non-performance of the sale contract against a seller who was clearly having difficulties meeting his financial commitments.

The second consequence of the transfer of the right to delivery on endorsement of the bill of lading is closely related to the first: delivery of the goods by the carrier without presentation of the bill of lading attracts severe sanctions against the carrier. The reason why the buyer may have no bill of lading on arrival of the vessel may be far more mundane than that in the *Trucks*[65] case: the shipping documents, including the bill of lading, may simply have been delayed in the post, either directly from the seller or, even more circuitously, through the banking system[66]. When faced with such delay, it may well be in the commercial interests of all parties concerned[67]—sellers, buyers, and carriers—to agree that the goods should be delivered, despite the absence of a bill of lading, the agreement taking the shape of an intricate framework of indemnities[68], the two central ribs of which are provided by an indemnity given by the seller to the buyer holding the latter harmless against the consequences of paying the price without tender of the bill[69]; and an indemnity given by the buyer to the carrier holding him harmless against the consequences of delivery of the goods without presentation of the bill. This latter indemnity is well sought, because as against the original shipper the carrier delivers in the absence of a bill very much

---

[63] [1951] 2 All ER 982.

[64] It should be recalled that a carrier need only issue a bill of lading if a demand for such issue is made by the shipper: Carriage of Goods by Sea Act 1971, Sch art III.3; the position was the same under the Carriage of Goods by Sea Act 1924, which was in force when the *Trucks* case was decided. The case provides a useful illustration of the difficulties in which buyers can find themselves because they, the parties ultimately interested in the issue of the bill of lading, have no right in law to demand its issue. We shall return to this point when discussing the function of the bill of lading as a receipt, in Chapter 5.

[65] See fn 63 above.

[66] For accounts of the various initiatives taken in the trade, particularly through the application of computer technology to the transmission of trade documents, see *Cargo Key Receipt and Transport Document Replacement*, Kurt Gronfors, 1982; and Goode, Proprietary Rights, at pp 78-83.

[67] The motive force against delay is, of course, the prospect of having a ship standing idly by waiting for the arrival of bits of paper; or rather, the prospect of having to pay demurrage for such enforced idleness.

[68] See Goode, Proprietary Rights, at pp 73-4; and for a practical example of such an intricate framework, see *The Delfini* [1988] 2 Lloyd's Rep 599; affd by the Court of Appeal (1989) Times, 11 August.

[69] See, for instance, GAFTA 100, clause 11 in Appendix 3.a.

at his peril: the shipper, who may well have had good cause not to dispatch the bill to the buyer too hastily[70], has a right of action in damages for wrongful delivery[71]. Moreover, in such an action, the carrier would be bereft of the protection of any limitation or exception to liability which the bill of lading might contain[72].

Finally, if the carrier receives instructions from the shipper suggesting that, although the bill of lading originally mentioned B1 as consignee, he is now to deliver to B2, must the carrier obey those instructions? As a matter simply of contract, and, indeed, of commercial reality, he is extremely likely to, because the shipper is the other party to the carrier's contract of carriage; the carrier's position in law, though, is not one exclusively determined by his contract of carriage with the shipper. What of the proprietary rights, if any, over the goods which B1 may claim on the grounds of his having been originally mentioned as consignee on the bill of lading? Might the carrier find himself liable in damages for conversion if he obeys the shipper's instructions and ignores B1's request for delivery of the goods? The answer is that it all depends on what has happened to the bill of lading. Before the shipper has transferred the bill of lading to B1, the carrier must, under his contract with the shipper, and can, there being no tort of conversion against B1, obey the shipper's instructions as to the change of consignee. The reason for this is that, even where the bill of lading is made out to a named consignee, here B1, or his order, the instruction originally written onto the bill is not irreversible[73]. Where, on the other hand, the bill of lading has been transferred to B1 before the shipper's change of instructions, the shipper's control over the possession of the goods moves away from him with the document[74] and the carrier should now take instructions only from B1. This, it must be remembered, states the position of the carrier firstly, in contract vis-a-vis the shipper; and secondly, in the tort of conversion vis-a-vis the original consignee. It does not tell us anything

---

[70] That is to say, in case of doubt as to the buyer's readiness or ability to pay the price.

[71] *The Stettin* (1889) 14 PD 142.

[72] *Sze Hai Tong Bank v Rambler Cycle Co Ltd* [1959] AC 576; perhaps this case needs to be re-examined after the decision of the House of Lords in *Photo Production v Securicor Transport* [1980] AC 827, as to which see Fundamental Breach and Deviation in the Carriage of Goods by Sea, C. Debattista, 1989 JBL 22; and *State Trading Corp of India Ltd v M Golodetz Ltd* [1989] 2 Lloyd's Rep 277. On another point altogether, given the traditionally draconian sanctions against delivery without presentation, the suggestion seems strange that the carrier may in some circumstances lose his right to demurrage if he unreasonably refuses the offer of an indemnity from the buyer in lieu of a bill of lading. Yet the editors of Scrutton, supported by an authority from Scotland, make just such a suggestion: see Scrutton, art 149 and *Carlberg v Wemyss Coal Co* 1915 SC 616. Carver's explanation for the inconsistency between a duty to deliver only against production of a bill of lading and the suggested duty reasonably to accept an indemnity is that the first refers to delivery, the second to discharge, an explanation which, with respect, fails to satisfy: see Carver, para 1593.

[73] See *Mitchel v Ede* (1840) 11 Ad & El 888 at 903; and *The Lycaon* [1983] 2 Lloyd's Rep 548, where the bill of lading had not been transferred and consequently the shipper was held to have been entitled to alter the carrier's instructions as to delivery. See Benjamin, para 1437.

[74] See Carver, s 1595.

about the status of a change of instructions by the shipper as to delivery to the original consignee under the sale contract between that consignee and the shipper. In other words, to say that the carrier is protected from an action for damages in conversion by the original consignee is not to preclude an action by that same consignee against the shipper who, qua seller, will doubtless have undertaken to ship goods covered by a bill of lading made out to the original consignee or to his order and to deliver[75] such a bill of lading to that consignee. The action by the original consignee against the seller lies both in contract and in tort: although the seller *has* shipped goods and tendered documents as promised, his purported alteration of the carrier's instructions puts him in breach of the implied condition of quiet possession of the goods[76]. Moreover, as the carrier's compliance with the seller's new instructions would result in a breach by the carrier of the contract of carriage between the carrier and the original consignee, those instructions would also likely constitute the tort of unlawful interference with contractual relations for which the seller would be liable to the buyer.[77]

(c) The Factors Acts and the Sale of Goods Act

The road towards a workable definition of a document of title at common law has been long and tortuous: it may consequently seem strange— and doubtless irritating to a newcomer to the subject—that confusion is further confounded by the intervention of statute law, which states quite categorically that there are many more documents of title than simply bills of lading[78]. Does this mean that different answers are given to the same question by two different sources of English law, the common law and statute; does it mean that the courts will have to decide which, in given circumstances, is to prevail; worse still, does it mean that we now have to unravel the definition of the phrase 'document of title' at which we have arrived?

Fortunately, the answer to all three questions is No. For it is not so much that the common law and the Sale of Goods Act 1979 are answering the same question differently, as much as that they are quite simply answering different questions; and this really takes us back to the list of questions and concepts with which this chapter started[79]. When the question being asked is 'Does the holder of this document have a right to demand of the person who currently holds the goods the physical delivery of those goods, such that a refusal would amount to a conversion of the goods by that person?', then the English lawyer will find the answer among the plethora of authorities which have gone to make up

---

[75] If the sale was contracted on CIF terms, see Incoterms CIF A7 in Appendix 2.a; or to render assistance in procuring a bill of lading, if the sale was contracted on FOB terms, see Incoterms FOB A9 in Appendix 2.a.

[76] See *Empresa Exportadora de Azucar v Industria Azucarera Nacional SA, The Playa Larga and The Marble Islands* [1983] 2 Lloyd's Rep 171 at 178-180.

[77] See *Salmond and Heuston on the Law of Torts*, 1987, 19th edn, pp 404-414.

[78] See s 1(4) of the Factors Act 1889, incorporated into the Sale of Goods Act 1979 by s 61 of that Act. Section 1(4) of the Factors Act 1889 is reproduced at fn 48, above.

[79] At Chapter 2.1.

the law as it has been stated in the preceding pages of this chapter, i e the answer to the question will depend on whether the document is a document of title at common law. When, on the other hand, the question being asked is 'Has the holder of this document acquired from his transferor a title to the goods which is better than that of previous holders, in the sense that he can ward off claims by previous holders?', then the English lawyer will have to look up a separate part of his law books for the answer, an answer which has been established in a number of statutory sections[80]. If the difference between these two questions is borne firmly in mind, it will come as no surprise to find that the list of documents which at common law gives a positive answer to the first question contains only one document; whereas the list which under statute law gives a positive answer to the second question contains many more[81]. Thus, the documents listed in section 1(4) of the Factors Act 1889 are negotiable without being transferable: where the relevant statutory requirements are satisfied[82], these documents transfer to their holders a better title than that enjoyed by previous holders. Their transfer does not, however, without the specific acknowledgement—or 'attornment'—to this effect by the carrier[83], give the holder the right to demand physical possession of the goods[84] from the carrier, who

---

[80] Sections 2-4, 8, 9 of the Factors Act 1889; and ss 24-26 and 47 of the Sale of Goods Act 1979.

[81] In Proprietary Rights, Professor Goode makes the point, at p 62, that the statutory list is wider, not simply longer, than the common law's list of one, in that s 1 (4) of the Factors Act 1889 includes an order to an actual possessor as well as an undertaking given by such a person. Because of s 29(4) of the Sale of Goods Act 1979, reproduced at fn 83 below, such an order does not, of course, transfer constructive possession of the goods, lacking as it does an acknowledgement by the carrier: it would, though, give the buyer a right to sue the seller for damages for failure to procure to the buyer a right of possession: see Goode, Proprietary Rights at pp 66-67.

[82] For a detailed analysis of the relevant sections of the Factors Act 1889 and the Sale of Goods Act 1979, see Benjamin, Chapter 7. The periodical literature is prolific, but Goode, Proprietary Rights, at pp 68-69, is of particular relevance to international sales, as is s 25 of the Sale of Goods Act 1893: The Reluctance to Create a Mercantile Agency, L.A. Rutherford and I.A. Todd, at (1979) 38 CLJ 346.

[83] See s 29(4) of the Sale of Goods Act 1979, which reads:
      'When the goods at the time of sale are in the possession of a third person, there is no delivery by seller to buyer unless and until the third person acknowledges to the buyer that he holds the goods on his behalf; but nothing in this section affects the operation of the issue or transfer of any document of title to goods.'
      The section provides us with a nice illustration of the difficulties caused by problems of definition. If by 'document of title', the statute here means 'as defined in s 1(4) of the Factors Act', then presumably no attornment is required for delivery orders to pass the right of control to the transferee, because the caveat would take those documents outwith the mischief of the requirement of attornment. To avoid that result, [flying as it would in the face of several authorities, among which *Waren Import Gesellschaft Krohn & Co v Internationale Graanhandel Thegra NV* [1975] 1 Lloyd's Rep 146 at 154], we need to interpret the phrase 'document of title' in a statutory provision in a common law sense, despite the fact that the selfsame statute itself defines that phrase: this is, in effect, what the editors of Benjamin do at paras 1479 and 577.

[84] Although attornment is not necessary for better title to pass in the circumstances allowed by the statute: see *Official Assignee of Madras v Mercantile Bank of India Ltd* [1935] AC 53 at 60 and Benjamin para 1480.

may[85] insist on checking with the shipper of the goods whether the holder of the document is the appropriate receiver of the goods. More succinctly, *these* documents of title do not, by virtue of their inclusion in the statutory list, transfer constructive possession of the goods[86].

It would, of course, have helped students of the subject, even if no one else, if different words were used to express the two quite different sets of ideas here at play. Thus, the question which the common law addresses is really a question of the transfer of the right to possession and consequently it would make sense to call the bill of lading a document of possession at common law[87]. The phrase 'document of title at common law' is too deeply ingrained in the literature for there to be any hope of changing our ways now. If we were so to change, though, it would make equally good sense to retain the phrase 'document of title' to signify those documents listed in the Sale of Goods Act 1979 as pieces of paper which pass to their holder a better title than that enjoyed by previous holders; this would be appropriate because the reason for the enactment, in the Factors Acts[88] and in the Sale of Goods Act 1979, of the relevant exceptions to the nemo dat rule, had to do exclusively with better title rather than with the right to possession. Merchants acting as financiers for traders frequently needed to raise funds on the basis of the security which they felt was provided by documents placed in their care which evidenced the possession by third parties of goods owned by those traders. Funds could only be raised on this basis if banks accepting such documents in security could be assured, not only that they would not thereby render themselves liable to unforeseen liabilities[89], but also that their security was beyond the reaches of the trader lying behind the merchant acting simply as a factor. The factor himself, of course, being fully aware of the title of the trader, held subject to that title: to grant the financier a security unaffected by that title would consequently violate the nemo dat rule, a rule which merchants viewed very much as a lawyer's rule in the worst sense of that phrase. The Factors Acts represented a victory for commercial practice over the strictures of the common law[90] and

---

[85] Indeed, probably *must*, as a matter of contract between himself and the shipper, at any rate where a bill of lading has been issued covering an amount larger than that quantified in, say, the delivery order; this, because of the presentation rule described above at Chapter 2.3.(b).

[86] See Benjamin, paras 1433 and 1474.

[87] In *Proprietary Rights*, Professor Goode suggests 'control document': see pp 59–60.

[88] Of which there were several: 1823, 1825, 1842, 1877 all four of which culminated in the one now in force, which dates from 1889.

[89] See the discussion of *Sewell v Burdick* (1884) 10 App Cas 74, and fn 56, both at Chapter 2.3.(a), above.

[90] By excluding documents of title from the definition of bills of sale, the Bills of Sale Acts 1878 and 1882 too played a part in facilitating the use of documents of title as a means of financing international trade. Bills of sale are instruments whereby a seller who retains possession of goods transfers the right to claim possession of the goods to a buyer: they may thus be used as a security for a loan by the 'buyer' to the 'seller'. The Bills of Sale Acts made compulsory the registration of such interests: registration would put third party purchasers of the goods from the 'seller' on notice of the 'buyer's' title to the goods, whose interest would therefore prevail over that of the third party. Likewise, however, it would act as a clog on the further use of the document as a

the history of the battle preceding that victory has been well documented elsewhere[91].

(d) **The use of the bill of lading as a means of security**

We have looked at the general contours of the mechanism whereby the banks come to play an important role in the financing of international sales through the letter of credit[92]. We saw there that the ultimate safeguard[93] against non-payment of the sum of the credit by the customer, i e the buyer, is the security afforded the bank by possession of the bill of lading, the document of title to the goods. Our task here is to examine the precise content of that security and how it is utilised by the banks in the letter of credit system.

Application forms for the opening of a letter of credit will normally contain a clause such as the following:

'I/we hereby authorise you to hold the documents called for by the terms of this credit and the merchandise to which they relate and the relative insurances as security for all liabilities incurred by you or your correspondents or agents in connection with this credit including expenses and charges of whatever nature incurred in relation to the said merchandise or the obtaining of possession or the disposal thereof (which expenses and charges I/we hereby

---

security instrument, if, for example, the buyer wished to obtain finance by pledging the documents to a financier, because registration would put all third parties dealing with the document on notice of other claims. The Bills of Sale Acts consequently excluded documents of title, as defined in the Factors Acts, from the requirement of registration: see s 4 of the Bills of Sale Act 1878 and s 3 of the 1882 Act. The upshot was that parties inclined to finance trade on the security of such documents could do so safely in the knowledge that their interest in the goods was free of other claims. Where the 'buyer', i e the creditor, is a company, it does not need to register its security interest under the Companies Act 1985. The new s 396(1)(b) makes registrable 'a charge on goods or any interest in goods, other than a charge under which the chargee is entitled to possession either of the goods or of a document of title to them.' The lending company holding a document of title in security would, on the hypothesis here envisaged, not need to register its interest under the Act and this for either of two reasons: either because the mere holding of a document of title does not constitute a charge (see *A Review of Security Interests in Property*, A. L. Diamond, para 23.9.18); or because, if it does, the lender would be a chargee entitled to possession of the goods or of the document of title to them, and therefore exempt from the duty to register.

91   See, *Chalmers Sale of Goods*, 1981, Mark, at pp 289-290; Of Dock Warrants, Warehouse-Keepers' Certificates, Etc, A. T. Carter, (1892) 8 LQR 301; Bennett, History, pp 25-42; The Conflict of Law and Commerce, Lord Chorley, (1932) 48 LQR 51, particularly at 65-71; The Pledge of Documents of Title in Ontario, Roderick J. Wood, 9 Canadian Business Law Journal 81 (1984), particularly at 81-87. For a detailed analysis of the relevant sections of the Factors Act 1889 and of the Sale of Goods Act 1979, see Benjamin Chapter 7.

92   At Chapter 1.3.

93   Although it is highly unlikely for the bank to rely solely on the security of the goods.

authorise you to incur and undertake to repay to you) and you may sell the said merchandise either before or after arrival at your discretion and without notice to me/us. I/we further agree to give you any additional security that you may from time to time require to cover my/our liabilities to you hereunder and in the event of your selling the merchandise to pay on demand the amount of any deficiency.'

What is the nature of the proprietary interest created by such a clause in favour of the issuing bank[94] through the possession of the shipping documents called for by the credit? There seem to be three possibilities: the bank may be a mortgagee, a pledgee or the holder of a lien. The case-law on the classification of the bank's interest appears to be quite inconclusive[95], although it might have been thought that the decision of the House of Lords in *Sewell v Burdick*[96] had definitively decided that the banker's interest was in the nature of a pledge. The case is not, however, authority for that proposition: their Lordships expressly eschewed any suggestion that the alleged liability on the part of the endorsee to pay freight to the carrier depended on whether the endorsee was a pledgee or a mortgagee[97]. Their Lordships preferred to rest their decision on the wider ground that the words 'the property' in section 1 of the Bills of Lading Act 1855[98] meant the full property, unencumbered by security interests of whatever kind.

It may be thought, of course, that the classification of the bank's security interest over the goods represented by a bill of lading is a matter worthy purely of academic pursuit. Indeed, the editors of Scrutton appear to be making just such a charge when they write[99]:

'... the difference between mortgages and pledges is immaterial from a commercial point of view, as it lies chiefly in the exact legal remedies for enforcing the security.'

It does seem strange, though, that such an important commercial device appears still to lack a firm legal classification. Indeed, despite the absence of binding authority, the major works on banking law have declared themselves strongly in favour of characterising the bank's interest as that

---

[94] It appears that a pledge is implied in favour of the intermediary bank: see Gutteridge and Megrah, at p 210. There appears to be no judicial authority for this proposition, the writers reading rather too much, it is submitted, into a dictum of Scrutton LJ in *Guaranty Trust Co of New York v Hannay* [1918] 2 KB 623 at 659.

[95] See the discussion in Carver, ss 1624, 5.

[96] (1884) 10 App Cas 74.

[97] Loc cit at pp 84, 95, 96, 98, 103. It should, however, be noted that Lord Blackburn tells us, at p 97, that all of their Lordships had, in argument, agreed with the suggestion that the endorsee's interest was in the nature of a pledge. For a different reading of this aspect of the case, see Bills of Lading and Factors in Nineteenth Century English Overseas Trade, N. I. Miller, 24 University of Chicago Law Review 256 (1957) at 280.

[98] See Appendix 1c.

[99] At art 101.

of a pledgee. Thus, in his book on modern banking law[100], Professor Ellinger explains that if the bank were a mortgagee, then it would own the goods subject to the mortgagor's right of redemption; if it were a pledgee, then it would have a right to claim possession of the goods together with the right of selling them[101]; and if it simply held a lien over the goods, then it would be entitled to hold on to the goods until payment of the sum of the credit by the buyer. Now it is quite clear from a reading of the standard form of clause reproduced above that the intention of the parties is to constitute a pledge, rather than either of the other two types of security.

The difficulty with describing the bank's interest as a pledge is that a pledge normally depends for its existence on the continued physical possession by the pledgee of the thing pledged[102] and this raises two questions in the context of bills of lading held by a bank in security, the first relating to the manner of the constitution of the pledge, the second to the manner of its possible loss.

Firstly, of course, the goods are not in the actual physical possession of the bank: they are in the hands of the carrier. The solution to this problem is simple and obvious: the bill of lading, as we have seen[103], is a document of title or possession at common law and consequently it provides the holder with the constructive possession of the goods[104]. What is not so clear is whether the existence of the pledge depends on the manner in which the front page of the bill of lading is completed: does it need to be made out to shipper's order[105], or to the order of the bank, and if the latter, which bank? Or is it possible to constitute the bank a pledgee by transferring to it a bill of lading made out, as it normally would be, to the buyer's order? There appears to be no authority in the case-law on this question, although the major work in the area takes the very firm view that for the pledge to exist, the bill of lading must be made out either to shipper's order, or to the order of the paying bank[106]. With respect, it is submitted that so long as the

---

[100] *Modern Banking Law*, 1987, see pp 568–573; see also Gutteridge and Megrah, at pp 211, 212.
[101] The right of resale subsists even in favour of a bank which has wrongfully accepted non-conforming documents rejected by the buyer: see Gutteridge and Megrah, at p 210.
[102] See Crossley Vaines, at p 459.
[103] At Chapter 2.3.(a), above.
[104] Such that delivery of the goods by the carrier to someone other than the bank, without presentation of the bill of lading, would amount to conversion: *Bristol and West of England Bank v Midland Rly Co* [1891] 2 QB 653. Delivery to the bank of documents which are documents of title only for the purposes of the Factors Act 1889 and the Sale of Goods Act 1979 would not, it is submitted, render the bank a pledgee of the goods, despite s 3 of the Factors Act 1889, which enacts that '[A] pledge of the documents of title to goods shall be deemed to be a pledge of the goods.' This is because that section only applies to pledges constituted by mercantile agents: see *Inglis v Robertson and Baxter* [1898] AC 616. See also Crossley Vaines, at pp 459–460.
[105] That is to say, by simply writing the word 'Order' in the box marked Consignee: see Appendix 3.b.
[106] See Gutteridge and Megrah, at p 212.

bill of lading is an order bill of lading[107], the pledge is effective whether or not the bill is made out to the order of the buyer; and this for three reasons. Firstly, the contrary view proceeds upon a misconceived view of what makes a bill of lading a document of title at common law. It is the fact that a bill of lading is an order bill which makes it a freely transferable commercial document passing the right to demand possession from holder to holder[108]; the named identity of the party who can, so to speak, 'give the order' by effecting the first transfer is quite irrelevant to the question of transferability, although it may tell us something, as we shall see[109], about the moment when property passes from seller to buyer. Secondly, if the bank's security depended on the manner in which the bill of lading is completed, it would be strange to find no stipulation on the matter either in applications for the opening of letters of credit or in the Uniform Customs and Practice for Documentary Credits. Thirdly, banks having themselves named as consignees on the face of bills of lading might, as we shall see[110], find themselves in the unwelcome position of assuming liabilities which they would not normally expect to shoulder. For all these reasons, it is suggested that an order bill of lading endorsed to a bank is effective to create a pledge of the goods it represents, whether it be made out to shipper's order, bank's order or buyer's order.

The second problem with the classification of the bank's interest as a pledge arises from a commercial practice which involves the surrender of the document of title by the bank before it is paid by the customer. This may seem a strange thing for the bank to do; however, if the buyer of the goods has been unable to put the issuing bank in funds for the sum of the credit, it may be that the only way he can obtain funds with which to satisfy the bank is by selling the goods, and the only way he can do that is by acquiring the documents. On the other hand, if surrender of the document of title to the buyer were to terminate the pledge, it would be difficult for an otherwise unsecured bank to agree to such a surrender. Unsurprisingly, the commercial community has found a way out of the impasse, and perhaps more remarkably, the law has reacted favourably. The device used is known as a 'trust receipt' or 'letter of trust' and its effect is to constitute the buyer a trustee for the benefit of the bank of the documents, goods and proceeds thereof[111]. Where the device is in place, the handing over of the documents of title does not extinguish the pledge[112]. Moreover, should the buyer become

---

[107] As opposed to a named or nominate or straight bill of lading, that is to say, a bill of lading which provides for consignment exclusively to one named person. We shall return to the difficulties involved in the use of such documents as a means of security when we discuss seawaybills in Chapter 8.1.(d).

[108] See Chapter 2.3.(b), above.

[109] In Chapter 4.

[110] In Chapter 3.1.(a).iii, below.

[111] See Gutteridge and Megrah, pp 215, 216.

[112] The authority cited for this welcome exception to the general rule is somewhat oblique: the case normally put forward is *North Western Bank Ltd v John Poynter, Son and Macdonalds* [1895] AC 56. The case was a Scottish appeal to the House of Lords and

insolvent before he has sold the goods, the bank can claim the goods as its own without competing with the general body of creditors; and should insolvency strike after the sale of the goods, the bank has a prior claim on the proceeds[113]. This is not to say that the use of the trust receipt is completely free of risk to the bank and the residual risk neatly illustrates the distinction between a document of possession at common law and a document of title for statutory purposes. For should the buyer, having sold or pledged the goods to a bona fide third party, fail to account for the proceeds to the bank, the third party's title prevails over that of the bank because the buyer is considered to be the bank's mercantile agent in the sale or pledge and the third party is consequently protected by section 2 of the Factors Act 1889[114].

(e) When the bill stops being a document of title

This chapter has, it is hoped, gone some way towards explaining how and why the bill of lading is such a valuable document in international sales. If the document possesses such significance in terms of the proprietary rights 'locked up'[115] in it, it may be as well to end the chapter by considering when the bill of lading stops being a document of title at common law.

Money may turn on the answer to this question either when commercial use is sought to be made of the bill, say by way of pledge, after the goods it represents have been discharged; or when the buyer wishes to sue the carrier under the bill of lading contract in circumstances where the goods have been delivered to him before presentation of the bill of lading. Thus in the first type of case, what proprietary interest does a bank possess which takes a bill of lading in security after the goods have been discharged at the port of destination? Does the handing over of the bill give the bank constructive possession of the goods such that, if the bank cannot recover the goods from the actual possessor, it can bring an action in conversion against the carrier? And in the second, does the buyer become a party to the contract of carriage through section 1 of the Bills of Lading Act 1855[116] where, against an indemnity, he has taken delivery of the goods without presenting a bill of lading; or

---

the argument before their Lordships centred on the question whether Scots law was the same as English law on the issue: English law was very much assumed, with no real discussion, to be that the pledgee could hand back the object of the pledge to the pledgor, in the circumstances which obtained, without extinguishing the pledge: see page 68 of the report. For a spirited argument that Scots law is not only different from, but better than, English law on this matter, see Pledge of Bills of Lading in Scots Law, A. Rodger, in 1971 Juridical Review 193-213, particularly 203 et seq.

[113] See *Modern Banking Law*, Ellinger, 1987, at pp 572, 3.

[114] See *Lloyds Bank Ltd v Bank of America National Trust and Savings Association* [1938] 2 KB 147; *Chalmers Sale of Goods*, Mark, 1981, at pp 295, 6; and Benjamin, para 1508. For a couple of ingenious devices whereby this risk is avoided, see *Modern Banking Law*, Ellinger, 1987, at p 573.

[115] See fn 17, above.

[116] For a detailed discussion, see Chapter 3, below.

is the document he presents after delivery a defunct document of title which no longer triggers the gap-filling effect of section 1 of that Act[117]?

The answer in broad terms is that the bill stops being a document of title at common law only when the goods are delivered to the person having a right to demand their delivery from the carrier: delivery, not discharge, is central to the continued functioning of the bill as a document of title[118]. Thus, where goods were discharged into a warehouse and held there to the order of the shipowner, delivery to the person entitled thereto, as opposed to mere physical discharge, had not taken place; consequently, the bill of lading was still a document of title capable of being pledged, notwithstanding the fact that it was transferred to the bank after discharge of the goods into the warehouse[119]. On the other hand, where delivery was made to the proper consignee without presentation of the bill of lading, the bill of lading stopped being a document of title capable of putting the buyer and the carrier in contractual privity through section 1 of the Bills of Lading Act 1855[120].

A moment's reflection on the raison d'etre of the bill of lading as a document of title will show that it must be right to say that the litmus test is delivery rather than discharge. If a document of title at common law is intended to facilitate the transfer between merchants of the possession of goods actually in the hands of a carrier, then it is only when the merchant holding that document realises his interest by taking possession of the goods that the document ceases to exercise that function: discharge from the vessel prior to that moment of delivery is simply part of the history and of no legal significance in this context[121].

---

[117] Implicit in this question is the assumption that for s 1 of the Bills of Lading Act 1855 to work, the bill of lading transferred must be a document of title; an interesting assumption, which was accepted as valid by Phillips J in *The Delfini* [1988] 2 Lloyd's Rep 599, (affd by the Court of Appeal, (1989) Times, 11 August), and one to which we shall return in Chapter 4.

[118] *Hayman & Son v M'Lintock* 1907 SC 936 at 951. See also Scrutton, at art 93 and Bennett, History, at pp 42–44 and 45–46.

[119] *Meyerstein v Barber* (1866) LR 2 CP 38; and *Barclays Bank v Customs and Excise Comrs* [1963] 1 Lloyd's Rep 81; see (1963) 26 MLR 442.

[120] *The Delfini* [1988] 2 Lloyd's Rep 599, (affd by the Court of Appeal, (1989) Times, 11 August) where an ingenious argument suggesting that the bill of lading only stopped being a document of title on, or at any rate only to the extent of, the full and complete performance of the contract of carriage was dismissed by Phillips J. The case illustrates yet again the risks involved in delivery without presentation, albeit supported by an indemnity. It now appears that contractual locus standi may be a price the buyer has to pay for delivery without presentation; on the other hand, it is unlikely to be paid too frequently because in most cases the carrier would not take the privity point against the buyer, lest the action were to degenerate into a tort action unprotected by contractual limitations. The privity point was pleaded by the carrier in *The Delfini* presumably because the ultimate receiver could not prove a proprietary interest in the oil at the time of the alleged loss and consequently any action in tort would have come to grief on the principle of *The Aliakmon* [1986] 2 Lloyd's Rep 1.

[121] Goode, *Proprietary Rights*, at pp 59, 60.

CHAPTER 3

Title to sue the carrier

1. How title to sue passes by contract

   (a) The statutory solution: section 1 of the Bills of Lading Act 1855

       i. Does the Act require a document of title at common law?

       ii. 'To whom the property in the goods shall pass'

       iii. Pledgees as consignees

       iv. 'Upon or by reason of such consignment or endorsement'

   (b) The implied contract device

2. How title to sue arises in tort

   (a) The tort plaintiff compared to the contract plaintiff

   (b) Problems after *The Aliakmon*

       i. When the rule applies

       ii. The origins of the rule in the law of negligence

       iii. Is the general principle against recovery appropriate here?

In the first chapter of this book, we saw how the dual mode of performance imposed on the seller by contracts concluded on shipment terms was directed towards creating a secure contractual framework for international trade. In the second chapter, we saw how the role of the bill of lading as a document of title at common law assured the buyer a proprietary interest in the goods while they were at sea, thus giving him the right to delivery of the goods at the port of discharge and, by way of corollary, the power to sell the goods in transit. However, the allocation of rights and duties in the sale contract and the transfer of the right to delivery by endorsement of the bill of lading would be worth little if the buyer was not assured a direct right of action, governed by a predictable and certain regime, against the person at least as likely as any other involved in international trade to be responsible for the loss of or damage caused to the goods in transit, i e the carrier. Indeed, if he is to be liable at all, the carrier too has good reason to wish for a clearly predictable relationship—a contractual relationship—with the buyer: the carrier's costs have been estimated on the basis of a network of exclusions and limitations of liabilities which he has largely determined in his contract with the shipper of the goods, a network which he, the carrier, would for obvious reasons wish to have transferred to the buyer of the goods.

That objective—the transfer of the contract between the carrier and the shipper to the buyer of the goods—would merit only the most cursory discussion were it not for the doctrine of privity in the English common law of contract. For we have seen[1] that the function of the bill of lading as a document of title transfers the right to delivery of the goods at the port of destination and little else; it forms no part of the nature of the bill as a document of title at common law to contravene one of the most fundamental doctrines of the common law, that is to say, that only parties to a contract can sue or be sued on it. To put it another way, while the transfer of the bill of lading has something to tell us about the right to demand delivery from the carrier[2], and may have something to tell us about the transfer of property[3], it has, of itself, nothing to tell us about the transfer of the contract of carriage as between the seller and the buyer of the goods.

Talk of the 'fundamental doctrine' of privity of contract in this area of the law is, however, somewhat misplaced. Commercial lawyers, particularly those concerned with areas of English commercial law which fall to be applied by our courts in cases with a foreign element, will be very familiar with the way in which the judges habitually pay the doctrine only a very transparent lip-service[4]. It will come as no surprise, therefore, that here too, solutions have been found, both statutory and judge-made[5], which allow the choice of English law as the law governing an international sale without the need for too much time being spent by litigants on the theoretical barricade of privity. This is not to say, though, that there is no room for argument in the matter of drawing a link of liability between the carrier and the buyer of goods; and our task in this chapter is to examine such room for argument as exists.

The discussion falls neatly into two parts: firstly, we shall be looking at two devices, the first manufactured by Parliament, the second fabricated by the courts, whereby the doctrine of privity is avoided as between the buyer of goods and the carrier: that is to say, we shall be looking at the workings of the Bills of Lading Act 1855 and at the rule in *Brandt*

---

1   At Chapter 2.3.(a).
2   The first of the questions asked by our hypothetical adviser at Chapter 2.1.
3   The second question asked, ibid; and see Chapter 4.
4   See, by way of illustration, *Pyrene Co Ltd v Scindia Navigation Co Ltd* [1954] 2 QB 402, discussed at Chapter 1.2.(a).ii, above. Examples abound: the application of exclusion clauses outside the confines of the contract where they originate: see *The Eurymedon* [1975] AC 154; the technical lack of consideration passing from the beneficiary under a letter of credit: see Gutteridge and Megrah, Chapter 4.
5   Where neither statutes nor the courts appear to help, businessmen take the problem, as it were, into their own hands, and show a remarkable degree of ingenuity in devising clauses which effectively draw circles around the doctrine: see, for example, the definition of '[M]erchant' in COMBIDOC and, generally, Chapter 8.

v Liverpool, Brazil & River Plate Steam Navigation Co Ltd [6]. Secondly, where for some reason or another, neither of those devices serves to put the buyer in contractual contact with the carrier, we shall be looking at the prospects of a tort action brought by a buyer alleging negligence on the part of the carrier in causing the loss of or damage to the goods. Here we shall be examining in particular the problems caused to buyers in this position by the decision of the House of Lords in *The Aliakmon*[7].

1. HOW TITLE TO SUE PASSES BY CONTRACT

(a) The statutory solution: section 1 of the Bills of Lading Act 1855

Before the passage of the Bills of Lading Act 1855, it was clear law that the doctrine of privity barred an action by the buyer of goods against the carrier whether for short delivery[8] or for complete non-delivery[9]. It appeared less clear, though, whether the doctrine bit quite as hard against a carrier who, on delivery of the goods, wished to recover demurrage from the buyer with whom the carrier was not in contractual privity[10]. Any possible suspicion that the application of the doctrine of privity in this area was anything other than even-handed was precluded by the enactment in 1855 of the Bills of Lading Act, the centrepiece of which was the first part of the preamble and section 1, which it would be useful to quote in full at this stage[11]:

> 'Whereas by the custom of merchants a bill of lading of goods being transferable by endorsement the property in the goods may thereby pass to the endorsee, but nevertheless all rights in respect of the contract contained in the bill of lading continue in the original shipper or owner, and it is expedient that such rights should pass with the property:...
>
> **1. Consignees, and endorsees of bills of lading empowered to sue.** Every consignee of goods named in a bill of lading, and every endorsee of a bill of lading, to whom the property in the goods shall pass upon or by reason of such consignment or endorsement, shall have transferred to and vested in him all rights of suit, and be subject to the same liabilities in respect of such goods as if the contract contained in the bill of lading had been made with himself.'

---

[6] [1924] 1 KB 575.

[7] [1986] 2 Lloyd's Rep 1.

[8] *Thompson v Dominy* (1845) 153 ER 532. After *Brandt v Liverpool* [1924] 1 KB 575, it is submitted that this case might well be decided differently; although it must be said that the former case was not cited, much less disapproved of in the latter.

[9] *Howard v Shepherd* (1850) 137 ER 907.

[10] *Stindt v Roberts* (1848) 17 LJQB 166.

[11] For the text of the Act in full, see Appendix 1.c. The Act received little attention in Parliament, Hansard recording merely that a fourth section of the Bills of Lading Bill, dealing with the arrest of vessels, was thrown out at the Committee stage: Hansard 1865, pp 68-70. For further discussion as to the legislative intention behind the Act, see Contracts with Consignees and Indorsees, P.N. Todd, 1984 LMCLQ 476 at 477.

The wording of the section raises a number of problems of interpretation most of which have been the object of comment in the literature for some time[12]. We shall here be concentrating on four questions. Firstly, when the Act says 'bill of lading', does it necessarily mean a bill of lading which is a document of title at common law? Secondly, and this is a question to which reference has already been made: when section 1 refers to the person 'to whom the property in the goods shall pass', does that include the situation where the bill is transferred solely for the purposes of security? Thirdly, does the section work where a pledgee of a bill of lading is named as consignee on the face of the bill? Finally, does property need to pass at the same time as the endorsement of the bill of lading for the section to be activated?

i. Does the Act require a document of title at common law?

For an Act which makes such a serious, if welcome, inroad into the doctrine of privity, the Bills of Lading Act 1855 is surprisingly silent on the precise nature of the shipping document to which it refers. Does the Act fill the privity gap between the carrier and the buyer when, in the presence of all other requirements, the buyer holds a document simply calling itself a bill of lading? Or does that document need also to be a document of title at common law? Thus, if a bill of lading made out simply to a named consignee is transferred to that consignee, does the consignee take the benefits and burdens of the shipper's contract with the carrier? What is the consignee's position as against the carrier if the bill of lading in his possession is expressed to be non-transferable? To put it another way, does a 'nominate' or 'straight' bill of lading come within the Bills of Lading Act[13]? There is now[14] some authority for the view that the Act does indeed require for its operation a bill of lading which is a document of title at common law and that consequently it is only triggered by 'order' bills of lading. It will be

---

[12] See On Some Defects in the Bills of Lading Act 1855, Carver, 6 LQR 289, where Lord Carver suggested, at p 292, that '[P]erhaps the time has arrived when fresh legislation on the subject may be attempted with advantage.' Almost a century later, the same plea for legislative clarification of the Act can still be heard: see Bulk Buyers and Economic Loss, P.N. Todd, at 1983 JBL 42 at 54; Contracts with Consignees and Indorsees, by the same writer at 1984 LMCLQ 476 at 486; The Bills of Lading Act 1855 Today, A.P. Bell, at 1985 JBL 124 at 132; The Significance of Tort in Claims in respect of Carriage by Sea, F.M.B. Reynolds, at 1986 LMCLQ 97 at 100-104, and 110; and Ownership and Obligation in Commercial Transactions, R.M. Goode, at (1987) 103 LQR 433 at 459.

[13] See Chapter 2.2.(b), particularly fn 21 and accompanying text. The question here raised in the text is predicated on the commonly held view that only an 'order' bill of lading is a document of title at common law. This assumption lies at the root of the difficulties surrounding the use of seawaybills and container transport documents: we shall consequently be tackling the validity of that assumption in Chapter 8.

[14] Heretofore, it has been assumed, or readily deduced, that the Act only applies to documents of title at common law: see The Bills of Lading Act 1855 Today, A.P. Bell, at 1985 JBL 124 at 128; and Bills of Lading and Third Parties, G.H. Treitel, at 1986 LMCLQ 294 at 297, and Benjamin, para 1456, where Professor Treitel draws such a conclusion from a short dictum by Lord Brandon in The Aliakmon [1986] 2 Lloyd's Rep 1.

recalled that in *The Delfini*[15], the central issue was whether the buyer was a party to the contract of carriage in circumstances where he had taken delivery of the goods without presenting the bill of lading. In deciding against the buyer, Phillips J held that section 1 of the Act could not work in the buyer's favour because at the time of endorsement the bill of lading was not a document of title. That reasoning entailed the proposition that the Act only applied to bills of lading which were documents of title: it must be said, though, that little argument appears, at any rate from the report, to have been addressed to this particular part of the reasoning[16]. Indeed, looked at as a matter of principle, it does seem strange that a bill of lading made out to a named consignee leaves the buyer and the carrier[17] in a worse position than they would have been in had there been other buyers interposed between the original shipper and the ultimate receiver: that hypothetical circumstance would appear to the two parties to be quite incidental to their legitimate expectations when they entered into their two original contracts, that of sale and that of carriage[18].

ii. 'To whom the property in the goods shall pass'

We saw earlier in this chapter how important it was for the commercial community to ensure that buyers of goods carried by sea were just as well protected against the risks of transit as were their sellers. It was, however, equally important to the trading fraternity that the inroad into privity effected by section 1 of the Bills of Lading Act 1855 be not taken too far: for if those who financed international sales by holding bills of lading in pledge were suddenly to find themselves at the receiving end of a contract of carriage, in the drafting of which they had played no part and in the performance of which they were not primarily

---

[15] *The Delfini* [1988] 2 Lloyd's Rep 599; affd by the Court of Appeal (1989) Times, 11 August.

[16] Counsel for the defendant carriers, arguing that there was no contract between the litigants, appears successfully to have founded himself on the opinion of Mustill J in *The Elafi* [1982] 1 All ER 208 at 217 that the act of endorsement must form 'an essential link in the chain of events by which title is transferred.' The dictum by Mustill J was addressed not to the main question under discussion in *The Delfini* but to the quite separate issue as to whether the property in the goods and the transfer of the bill of lading must both happen at the same time, i e the fourth question to be discussed in this part of the chapter. To draw the proposition in the text from Mustill J's dictum, addressed as it was to another issue and expressed in any case tentatively, is with respect to burden the dictum with more than it can reasonably bear.

[17] Because of the loss of the contractual limitations contained in the original bill of lading contract.

[18] The view expressed in the text receives some support from the consideration that where there is a string of other buyers interposed between the shipper and the ultimate receiver, they disappear, as it were, from the network of liability; and the contract of carriage, saving the carrier's rights against the shipper under s 2 of the Bills of Lading Act 1855, is between the carrier and the ultimate receiver: see Benjamin, para 1461. Thus, for the purposes of the contract of carriage, the law acts as if there were no string and makes only the ultimate receiver a party to the carrier's contract: it is difficult to see why the position should be different where the facts actually do fit the fiction, i e where there is no string but only a seller, a carrier and a buyer.

interested, the practice of advancing loans against the security of shipping documents might become too perilous to pursue, and the funds which that practice generated too difficult to find. Doubtless such commercial considerations preyed much on the minds of the judges[19] involved in the decision in *Sewell v Burdick*, to which reference has already been made[20]. In that case, the endorsee holding the bill of lading in security escaped liability for freight due under the contract of carriage because section 1 was held not to apply where the intention behind the transfer of the bill was simply the creation of a security interest in the transferee: 'property', it was decided, meant 'general'[21] or (even more cryptically) 'the'[22] property. Only a person to whom such property had passed[23] could take advantage of[24], or be sued through[25], section 1 of the Bills of Lading Act.

iii. Pledgees as consignees

Our next question is closely connected to our last: does section 1 of the Act work where the pledgee is mentioned as consignee on the face of the bill of lading, so as to make him a party to the contract of carriage: in other words, does the fact that the pledgee is a 'consignee' make him a section 1 bill of lading holder? Banks on occasion demand, in return for the opening of a letter of credit, that they be entered as consignees on the bill[26], presumably swayed by the impression that such a course of action puts them in a stronger position should they need to realise their security on the goods. The question here addressed is whether any possible improvement said to be brought about by such a practice is outweighed by any unexpected disadvantages which might affect the bank vis-a-vis the carrier.

It would help our inquiry if we were to isolate the risks which the banks run in the letter of credit system and against which the practice here described is said to protect them. Of course, where the bank has

---

[19] See particularly the dissenting judgment of Bowen LJ, in the Court of Appeal, at (1884) 13 QBD 159 at 175, a judgment subsequently vindicated in the House of Lords.

[20] (1884) 10 App Cas 74. See Chapter 2.3.(a) and (d) above.

[21] Per Lord Fitzgerald, at (1884) 10 App Cas 74 at 106.

[22] Per Bowen LJ in his dissenting judgment in the Court of Appeal at (1884) 13 QBD 159 at 175.

[23] Or who is estopped from denying that it had passed: see the *Costanza M* [1981] 2 Lloyd's Rep 147.

[24] Thus, the strictures put on the 1855 Act by the House of Lords in *Sewell v Burdick* might hinder, as much as assist, the holder of a bill of lading seeking to found a cause of action upon s 1 of that Act: see *The Aramis* [1989] 1 Lloyd's Rep 213 at 217, 218.

[25] Lord Carver disagreed with the decision of the House of Lords in *Sewell v Burdick*: see On Some Defects in the Bills of Lading Act 1855, at (1890) 6 LQR 289 at 292-294. His central objection appears to be that the carrier's recovery of shipping charges unpaid by the buyer is made to depend on the pledgee's decision as to whether the value of the goods in security is likely to be outweighed by the cost of freight and other charges.

[26] See, for example, the bill of lading in *Banque de l'Indochine et de Suez v JH Rayner (Mincing Lane) Ltd* [1983] 1 Lloyd's Rep 228 at 231.

been put in funds, then there is no risk of non-payment of the sum of the credit and no possible advantage in being named as consignee on the face of the bill. Where, on the other hand, the bank[27] is not put in funds by the buyer, then there are three types of risk against which it must protect itself. The first is incurred where the buyer becomes insolvent while the shipping documents are still with the bank. The second arises where the shipping documents are with the buyer in trust for the bank[28], but the buyer becomes insolvent before he has an opportunity to sell the goods and reimburse the bank. The third occurs again when the buyer holds the documents in trust for the bank, but instead of becoming insolvent, the buyer simply disappears without paying the bank after selling the documents to or pledging them with an innocent third party.

How, if at all, is the position of the bank improved in each of these three situations if it is named as consignee in the bill of lading? The third situation is the easiest to deal with. We have seen already[29] that the buyer in this case is deemed to be the bank's mercantile agent, capable of passing good title through the application of section 2 of the Factors Act 1889. The consequent risk to the bank is great and is incurred, it is submitted, whether or not the bank is named as consignee in the bill of lading.

The first two cases[30] are rather more difficult but lead, in effect, to much the same result as the first case just discussed: that is to say, that being named as consignee makes no difference to the bank's position, or at least, if it does, the change is actually for the worse. Whether or not the unpaid bank is named as consignee on the bill, the likelihood is that it will wish to realise its security by selling the goods on the open market and obtaining the best possible price, hopefully a price sufficient to cover the unpaid sum of the credit. The only real question is whether the bank can effect such a sale simply by selling the documents or whether it needs to take physical possession of the goods from the carrier and then make a physical sale or, at any rate, ship and sell under a new documentary sale, taking a bill in its own name. It is clear that the first of these options has enormous attractions for the bank, which can hardly be expected to relish the prospect of trading goods physically on its own account. Whether or not the bank can sell by simply transferring the documents depends on whether it can persuade a prospective buyer of two things: firstly, that the bill of lading gives the latter a right, as against the carrier, to delivery of the goods on discharge; secondly, that the bill of lading gives the new buyer a title which cannot

---

[27] And for the sake of simplicity, we shall take as our model, the issuing bank.
[28] For a description of the trust receipt, see Chapter 2.3.(d), above.
[29] At Chapter 2.3.(d); see fn 114 and accompanying text.
[30] The two cases can, at any rate for the purposes of the current discussion, be dealt with together, the only difference between the two being that, in the second, the documents are with the buyer at the time insolvency strikes and consequently the bank has to repossess them before it can realise its security over the goods.

be defeated by previous holders of the bill. The first of these requirements causes less of a problem than does the second, for so long as the bill of lading is a document of title at common law[31], then its transfer by the bank will pass the right to delivery of the goods from the carrier at the port of destination. The important point for the purposes of this discussion, though, is that this would be the position whether or not the bank is named as the consignee on the bill.

The second requirement, that is to say, the passing by the bank of an indefeasible title to the second buyer, causes difficulty, of course, because of the nemo dat rule: if the bank, which on our hypothesis is attempting to sell the goods by transferring the documents, only has a pledgee's title to the goods represented by the documents, then surely all it can pass is a pledgee's title: consequently, no one in the market will buy from a bank unless the bank's name appears as consignee. Contrast the happy position, the argument inexorably concludes, of the bank named as consignee on the bill: its title, stronger than a pledgee's, can easily be negotiated in the market place. The argument is flawed in three respects. Firstly, to assume that a pledgee cannot pass better title than he himself has is to ignore section 2 of the Factors Act 1889. Surely, if a buyer who sells documents in breach of trust with the bank is considered to be a mercantile agent for the bank he defrauds[32], then it must be at least as easy to consider the bank in the position here envisaged as the mercantile agent of the buyer. If the bank is a mercantile agent, then section 2 of the Factors Act 1889 allows the bank to pass a better title to a bona fide third party[33]. Secondly, to assume that the naming of the bank as a consignee alters the nature of the bank's title is to fly in the face of the House of Lords decision in *Sewell v Burdick*[34], which held that the nature of the title passed on endorsement depended on the intention accompanying that endorsement: it would be stretching the limits of construction unreasonably to pretend for a moment that parties to a letter of credit intend to pass to the bank anything more than a security interest in the goods[35]. Thirdly, if the point just made

---

[31]   That is to say an order bill; if the bank holds a 'straight' bill made out to the buyer, the endorsement of the bill by the bank to a second buyer would not, on the traditional analysis, transfer the right to delivery: see Chapter 2.2.(b): but see Chapter 8, below. On the orthodox view, the bank would find difficulty transferring the right to delivery by mere endorsement of the bill to a second buyer even if s 1 of the Bills of Lading Act were to apply, as argued above at Chapter 3.1.(a).(i), to bills of lading which were not documents of title at common law. That debate goes to the transfer of contractual rights and liabilities; this debate goes to the transfer of the right to delivery of the goods.

[32]   In circumstances, that is to say, where a buyer holding documents under a trust receipt sells them to an innocent third party whose title prevails over that of the defrauded bank: see fn 29 above and accompanying text.

[33]   The seller has, in our hypothesis, been paid and consequently is hardly likely to vaunt a better title against the bona fide third party.

[34]   (1884) 10 App Cas 74.

[35]   See Goode, at p 692, fn 194; and, for another illustration, arising in a totally different context, of the principle that being named as consignee on the face of a bill of lading is not conclusive of title: *The Kapetan Markos NL (No 2)* [1987] 2 Lloyd's Rep 321 at 330.

were wrong, and if the bank named as consignee did receive the 'general' property in the goods, then there would be a price to pay, for the bank, by dint of its own argument, would have manoeuvred itself into the position of a section 1 bill of lading holder, a status which brings with it contractual rights *and* duties. One of those duties may be to pay demurrage, a duty quite likely to be triggered in circumstances where the carrier has issued a bill naming as consignee a party not commonly equipped to organise the speedy reception of goods at the port of discharge, while the 'real' consignee, on our hypothesis the insolvent buyer, is in no position actually to present the bill of lading. Moreover, if banks were found, contrary to the views here expressed, to be section 1 bill of lading holders, they would likely be very vulnerable to attack by carriers where the latters' only alternative for the recovery of shipping charges lay in competition with the general body of creditors of insolvent buyers.

The position, then, would appear to be that where the buyer is insolvent, the unpaid bank can realise its security by simply selling the documents; that this is the case whether or not it appears as consignee on the face of the bill; and, finally, that if it does appear as consignee, the bank may well make itself liable under the contract of carriage.

iv. 'Upon or by reason of such consignment or endorsement'

It is clear from the wording of section 1 and from the discussion of the section so far that there are two conditions necessary for the application of the section: the buyer must hold[36] a bill of lading and he must have acquired the property in the goods. Our fourth question raises the issue of the precise relationship between those two requirements: must they happen contemporaneously, or does it suffice if the transfer of the bill and the passage of property both occur because of the same contract of sale? Must the link be temporal or causal? The practical point behind the question can be of some significance to buyers of goods, typically commodities, whose contracts stipulate a point at which property passes, a point totally divorced from the moment at which the bill is transferred to the buyer[37]. Again staying with commodities, where a cargo covered by a particular bill of lading is part of a bulk, property cannot pass, as we shall see, before the cargo to which the bill relates is separated[38]; the bill of lading may, however, be transferred to the buyer before the goods are separated, typically at the port of discharge. In either of these two cases, if section 1 requires a temporal link between its two conditions, then the buyer is not in contractual privity with the carrier; if the link required is purely causal, then he is.

---

[36] Although the section says 'endorsement', it has been held that this must mean physical transfer: see *The Delfini* [1988] 2 Lloyd's Rep 599 at 606, (affd by the Court of Appeal (1989) Times, 11 August).

[37] See, for example, the clause in *The San Nicholas* [1976] 1 Lloyd's Rep 8, whereby property in a cargo of molasses was to pass 'at the permanent hose connection of the vessel receiving the molasses at loading port.'

[38] Section 16 of the Sale of Goods Act 1979; see *The Elafi* [1982] 2 All ER 108 and generally Chapter 4.

Given the significance of the question, it is unfortunate that on almost every occasion when firm guidance might have been given by the courts, the judges found an alternative avenue towards their decision, making it unnecessary to find the law on this particular point. The uncertainty is exacerbated by the stark disagreement in which the major works find themselves: thus the editors of Scrutton favour a temporal link between endorsement and the passage of property[39], while the editor of Carver favours a causal link[40]. The judicial history of the debate is unhelpful. The decision of McNair J in *Gardano & Giampieri v Greek Petroleum Mamidakis & Co*[41] is clearly based[42] on the temporal view[43]; and Phillips J tended towards the same view in *The Delfini*[44]. On the other hand, Roskill LJ in *The San Nicholas*[45], Mustill J in *The Elafi*[46] and Lloyd J in *The Sevonia Team*[47] supported the causal interpretation. It has been

---

[39] See art 13.
[40] See para 98.
[41] [1961] 2 Lloyd's Rep 259, particularly at 265, 266.
[42] For another interpretation of the ratio of the case, see Contracts with Consignees and Indorsees, P.N. Todd, at 1984 LMCLQ 476 at 482, 483, where Mr Todd suggests that the finding that section 1 of the 1855 Act did not operate was not part of the ratio of McNair J's decision, 'which concerned the residual rights of the shipper even if property and risk had passed to the consignee'. It is, with respect, difficult to see how this consideration takes McNair J's observations on s 1 of the Act outside the ratio of the case: the question asked in the case stated was whether the endorsees of the bill were entitled, to the exclusion of the charterers, to claim against the owners for shortage and contamination; this question raised s 1 issues and *Albazero*-type issues ([1977] AC 774) and it is submitted that McNair J's answer to the case stated involved a decision on the law as to both issues.
[43] As is the decision of the Irish Court of Appeal in *McKelvie v Wallace Bros* [1919] 2 IR 250. The decision was upheld in the House of Lords without, however, argument being heard.
[44] [1988] 2 Lloyd's Rep 599 at 605–607, (affd by the Court of Appeal (1989) Times, 11 August). As we have seen, Phillips J was happy to base his decision against the cargo-interest on the basis that the bill of lading had ceased being a document of title by the time of endorsement.
[45] [1976] 1 Lloyd's Rep 8 at 13. The Lord Justice's view was expressed to be obiter because the point had come up for discussion in interlocutory proceedings. Lord Denning MR expressed no preference between the two interpretations of the Act; he was of the view, at p 11, that even on the temporal view, the property passed on endorsement of the bill of lading because the bill was made out to shipper's order. However, with respect, this is to ignore the express clause in the contract of sale stipulating that property was to pass at the permananent hose connection of the vessel at the discharge port. See also Benjamin para 1456 for the view that Denning MR was here guilty of confusing property with the right to delivery of the goods.
[46] [1982] 1 All ER 208 at 217. The judge's view was obiter (and expressed to be tentative) because the plaintiff buyer was found to have an action in tort, property having passed through appropriation 'by exhaustion': see Chapter 4.
[47] [1983] 2 Lloyd's Rep 640 at 643, 644; on this case, see generally, Contracts with Consignees and Indorsees, P.N. Todd, 1984 LMCLQ 476. The judge's view was obiter because Lloyd J preferred to rest his view that the contract had passed upon the other limb of the relevant part of the section. Property had to pass 'upon or by reason of' either endorsement or consignment; property here had passed on shipment, i e on consignment; and therefore s 1 worked. Where, on the other hand, property passes to the buyer before shipment on the defendant carrier's vessel, this limb of the section cannot operate to bring it into operation: see *The Kapetan Markos NL (No 2)* [1987] 2 Lloyd's Rep 321 at 329. In that case, neither could the section work through the application of its 'endorsement' limb, because the contract of sale was separate from the agreement which

said that the arguments based on textual interpretation are too finely balanced for resolution of the debate solely in those terms, the problem being that the Act draws too close a link between the transfer of contractual rights and the passage of property[48]. In terms of policy, it is submitted that the causal view is preferable to the temporal approach: it would be strange to exclude the application of the Act from areas of international trade where the parties take the trouble to establish in their sale contract the moment at which property passes simply because that point does not coincide with the purely accidental moment of physical transfer of the bill from seller to buyer; it would be even stranger to exclude the application of the Act from one of the most significant activities in international trade, that is to say the sale and carriage of commodities in bulk[49].

(b) The implied contract device

However widely the wording of section 1 of the 1855 Act is construed, there are cases which very clearly come outside its ambit. This would be the case, for example, if the buyer of the goods holds a shipping document other than a bill of lading; or if the holder of a bill of lading holds less than full property in the goods. We have already seen at the start of this chapter, however, that the argument on the ground will normally run very strongly against taking too strict a stand on privity, the cargo interest not wishing to argue his way out of a cause of action, the carrier preferring to run the risk of liability under a contract he knows than in a tort he does not. Thus, where goods had been delivered in a damaged condition or in a smaller quantity than that shipped, and in circumstances which lay outside the operation of the Act, it was generally in the interest of both parties to resolve their dispute as if they were indeed bound together by contract. This pretence caused no difficulty so long as both parties were happy to participate: the law's

---

led to the transfer of the bill of lading issued in respect of the goods on board the Kapetan Markos to the buyer: see Benjamin, para 1456, fn 91.

[48] See Benjamin para, 1456 and The Significance of Tort in Claims in respect of Carriage by Sea, F.M.B. Reynolds, (1986) LMCLQ 97 at 100 and 103.

[49] The Law Commission Working Paper on Rights to Goods in Bulk, No 112, suggests that a solution to this problem might be sought through one of three paths: firstly, by abolishing the requirement of ascertainment in the sale of commodities carried by sea; secondly, by disentangling altogether the buyer's locus standi under the contract of carriage from the passage of property under the contract of sale; and thirdly, by applying s 1 of the 1855 Act to the sale of a part of goods shipped in bulk through a fiction whereby property will be deemed to have passed, for the purposes of the section, despite the absence of ascertainment, if property would have passed upon or by reason of consignment, or indorsement of the bill of lading. The first of these suggestions will be reverted to in Chapter 4.2.(a) below. The second would give locus standi both to and against a mere holder of a bill of lading: to this extent, it would undo the good sense of the decision in *Sewell v Burdick* (1884) 10 App Cas 74, as to which see Chapter 3.1.(a).ii, above. The third suggestion, a fiction by-passing the requirement of ascertainment, leaves unanswered the question of interpretation discussed in the text above, namely whether the fiction would work where property and endorsement might have occurred at the same time or simply because of the same contract of sale.

sensitivity about the doctrine of privity, which it had taken the passage of the 1855 Act to avoid, could easily be ignored when cargo-interests and carriers simply agreed to settle a damage or shortage claim 'contractually', as it were, in spite of that doctrine. Indeed, as we have seen[50], the courts were on occasion quite well-disposed to going along with the illusion of a contract, at any rate where one was needed to give the carrier a cause of action[51].

Circumstances might arise, and in *Brandt v Liverpool Brazil and River Plate Steam Navigation Co Ltd*[52] they did, where the 'parties' did not both wish there to be a contract between them; and where, unless the alternative of a tort remedy existed, the court would need to find a contract if recovery was to be allowed. Thus, in *Brandt v Liverpool* itself, where a pledgee of the bill of lading who had taken delivery of goods sued the carrier in respect of damage caused to the goods in transit, it paid the carrier to take the technical point of privity: the exceptions contained in the bill of lading could not, on the law as it then stood, avail him as he had been guilty of deviation[53]. Moreover, the plaintiff could not recover in tort, presumably because the tort of which he complained had occurred before shipment, that is to say before he had acquired any possessory interest in the cargo. The Court of Appeal, affirming the judgment of Greer J found for the pledgee[54], a contract being inferred 'from the fact of taking delivery'[55]. Any qualms about the absence in fact of anything like an exchange of consideration between the parties were smartly dealt with by Scrutton LJ: the constituent ingredients of the contract here were, on the one hand, a promise by the pledgee 'to perform the terms of the bill of lading' and on the other, a promise by the shipowner 'to deliver the goods on the terms of the bill of lading.'[56]

The contract thus implied illustrates yet again[57] the readiness of common law judges to ignore the common law doctrine of privity of contract: and we have yet to learn how far they will be constrained, or indeed prepared, to go. The practical effect of the device is to grant a remedy where one would otherwise be barred, either by the difficulties of interpretation surrounding the Bills of Lading Act 1855 or by the

---

[50]   *Stindt v Roberts* (1848) 17 LJQB 166, referred to above at Chapter 3.1.(a), see fn 10.

[51]   Contrast the attitude of the court in *Thompson v Dominy* (1845) 153 ER 532; see fn 8, above. It is interesting in this context to note that when the 1855 Act recognised and preserved, in s 2, the implication of a contract of carriage from the receipt of goods, it only referred expressly to 'any liability of the consignee' rather than any rights: but see Benjamin, para 1457.

[52]   [1924] 1 KB 575.

[53]   Ibid at 597. It is arguable whether this is still the rule after *Photo Production Ltd v Securicor Transport Ltd* [1980] AC 827. See Fundamental Breach and Deviation in the Carriage of Goods by Sea, Debattista, 1989 JBL 22; and *State Trading Corpn of India Ltd v M Golodetz Ltd* [1989] 2 Lloyd's Rep 277.

[54]   Who, had the boot been on the other foot, would have been well protected from liability by *Sewell v Burdick* (1884) 10 App Cas 74: see Chapter 3.1.a.(ii) above.

[55]   Per Scrutton LJ at [1924] 1 KB 575 at 595.

[56]   Ibid.

[57]   See fn 4, above and accompanying text.

increasingly restrictive rules imposed on the recovery of damages in tort, to which rules we shall presently refer. In the absence of legislative amendment clarifying the workings of the 1855 Act and given the decision of the House of Lords in *The Aliakmon*[58], recourse to the device in *Brandt v Liverpool* is likely to grow to a point where contractual intention is constructed rather than construed; and where just decisions can only be reached at the expense of accepted principle. Thus in *The Elli 2*[59], the Court of Appeal allowed a claim for demurrage by a shipowner against a buyer of goods who had taken delivery without producing a bill of lading. In the context of the present discussion, the Court resolved two[60] issues. Firstly, a contract of carriage could be implied despite the fact that a bill of lading was not physically presented against delivery on every occasion: the giving of an undertaking on those occasions when a bill was not presented was quite sufficient[61]. Secondly, a contract could be implied even though freight was no longer due under the bill of lading: it was sufficient if 'other considerations, such as demurrage[62]' were outstanding. May LJ took care to distinguish the case before the court from cases where 'nothing remains to be done in performance of the relevant contract of carriage save physically to hand the goods over to the receiver'[63]. Indeed, it should be said that although the Court was clearly prepared to travel quite a distance away from the doctrine of consideration in implying a contract, May LJ was keen to put some restriction on the process. At page 115 of the report, he says:

'...no such contract should be implied on the facts of any given case unless it is necessary to do so: necessary, that is to say, in order to give business reality to a transaction and to create enforceable obligations between parties who are dealing with one another in circumstances in which one would expect that business reality and those enforceable obligations to exist.'

The difficulties involved in squaring business reality with orthodox doctrine were even more considerable in *The Aramis*[64], where no promise

---

[58] [1986] 2 Lloyd's Rep 1.

[59] [1985] 1 Lloyd's Rep 107.

[60] A third, which was dismissed summarily, and with respect, quite properly by May LJ at p 115 of the report, was whether 'some right of property should pass to the ultimate receiver of the goods by virtue of the endorsement of the bill of lading.' To have given a positive answer to this question would have been to introduce into the *Brandt v Liverpool* device the temporal view of s 1 of the 1855 Act discussed above at Chapter 3.1.(a).iv.

[61] Loc cit at 112 and 115. Thus, it is still not clear whether a *Brandt v Liverpool* contract can be implied when no document is presented against delivery. On the other hand, it is clear that a contract will be implied when the receiver presents a ship's delivery order attorned to by the carrier: see *Peter Cremer Westfaelische GmbH v General Carriers SA, The Dona Mari* [1973] 2 Lloyd's Rep 366.

[62] Loc cit at 115, per May LJ

[63] Loc cit at 116; see also *The Kelo* [1985] 2 Lloyd's Rep 85, where Staughton J was not prepared to infer a contract from the mere taking up of delivery in return for the presentation of freight pre-paid bills of lading.

[64] [1987] 2 Lloyd's Rep 58; revsd [1989] 1 Lloyd's Rep 213: see particularly p 225. See, generally, Powles, 1989 JBL 157, 160-165.

to deliver goods could be imputed to the carrier, there being no more goods to deliver. At first instance, Evans J nonetheless found that a contract could be implied from the fact that the carrier had delivered other goods, shipped in bulk with the plaintiff's goods, to other receivers under other bills of lading. In reversing Evans J, the Court of Appeal recognised the good sense and commercial convenience of the judge's decision but overturned it on the ground that it did unacceptable violence to traditional sensitivities about the doctrine of consideration[65]. The effect of the Court of Appeal's decision, it must be said, is to render the implied contract device the least useful when it is the most necessary, that is to say where the receiver receives no goods at all[66].

2. HOW TITLE TO SUE ARISES IN TORT

We have seen throughout the first part of this chapter that the natural habitat, as it were, of a relationship involving the carriage of goods by sea is contract. This coincides with the commercial expectations of the parties, who have organised their costs and insurance cover on the basis of freight charges and liabilities envisaged in the contract of carriage concluded between the carrier and the original shipper of the goods. Indeed, so natural is it for carriage to be regulated by contract that ways have been found around the doctrine of privity which put the ultimate receiver in direct contact, as it were, with the carrier. There are limits, however, to section 1 of the Bills of Lading Act 1855; there are even, it seems, limits to the workings of the *Brandt v Liverpool* device. Where these limits are exceeded, a plaintiff wishing to recover for loss of or damage to goods or for short-delivery will need to sue the carrier in the tort of negligence. Our first task in this part of the chapter will be to contrast the position of a tort plaintiff to that of a contract plaintiff in a claim for damage to goods or short-delivery. Our second will be to discuss the not inconsiderable difficulties put in the path of a tort plaintiff by the decision of the House of Lords in *The Aliakmon*[67].

(a) The tort plaintiff compared to the contract plaintiff

The preliminary point needs to be made that the issue in discussion here is not whether a receiver of goods should pursue his claim for damages

---

[65] See the note on the case by Mr P. De Val at 1987 LMCLQ 258.

[66] For a particularly telling note, see B. J. Davenport, in (1989) 105 LQR 174, where Mr Davenport writes, at p 178, '... the strength of English commercial law is that in the past the judges sought to give effect to good sense and underlying commercial convenience. If the judges of the past had adopted the attitude of the Court of Appeal in *The Aramis*, would we today have the letter of credit—or even the bill of exchange?' See also Bills of Lading and Implied Contracts, G. H. Treitel, in 1989 LMCLQ 162, where Professor Treitel argues that the Court of Appeal might have reached the same conclusion arrived at by Evans J, through an altogether more traditional route, namely the implication of contracts 'in law', to which the normally stringent requirements of the common law (e g business efficacy) do not apply.

[67] [1986] 2 Lloyd's Rep 1.

in respect of short-delivery or damage to goods in contract or in tort. The fact of the matter is that if there is a contract binding the parties together, the carrier will plead it, whether the plaintiff chooses to formulate his claim in contract or in tort. The question discussed here is rather: if there is no contract between the carrier and the plaintiff, can the latter sue the former in tort; and if the plaintiff is thus thrown on his tort action, is he in a worse or a better position than that in which he would have been had he been able to sue in contract?

Were it not for problems which we shall discuss presently[68], an action in negligence might well appear, to the plaintiff bereft of contractual locus standi, to be quite an attractive alternative. The goods were, after all, in the carrier's possession when the damage is alleged to have occurred and it should not be too difficult for the court to establish the existence of a duty owed to the plaintiff to take reasonable care of the goods: it should be quite easy, in other words, to characterise the plaintiff as a 'neighbour' of the carrier in Atkinian terms[69]. So far as concerns the burden of proof, it is true that the rules of negligence require the plaintiff to prove the defendant's fault, but this would, by and large, be the position were the plaintiff suing under a bill of lading contract governed by the Carriage of Goods by Sea Act 1971[70] and consequently he would be in no worse a position than that in which he would otherwise have been. The plaintiff's position in tort would be different, however, as far as concerns the effect of exclusion clauses and other limitations in the contract—and the difference would appear to act to his advantage. For a plaintiff not enjoying the benefits of a contract with the carrier is also unencumbered by its burdens: in the context of an action for shortage or damage to goods, what this means in practice is that the plaintiff is not restricted in his action in negligence by exclusions and limitations which would govern the contract of carriage if there was one.

This last advantage of a tort as against a contract action may have been eroded by art IV-bis 1 of the Hague-Visby Rules which reads[71]:

> 'The defences and limits of liability provided for in these Rules shall apply in any action against the carrier in respect of loss or damage to goods covered by a contract of carriage whether the action be founded in contract or in tort.'

---

[68] That is to say, difficulties with locus standi caused by the application of the rule against recovery of pure economic loss in negligence: *The Aliakmon* [1986] 2 Lloyd's Rep 1, see below, the immediately subsequent section of this chapter.

[69] That is to say, in terms of Lord Atkin's celebrated aphorism in his speech in *Donoghue v Stevenson* [1932] AC 562.

[70] See s 3 and Schedule, arts III.1 and 2, and IV.1. The qualification 'by and large' is required because, under the terms of the article last mentioned, the burden of proving the exercise of reasonable diligence in making the ship seaworthy is placed on the carrier. The advantage to the cargo-owner suing in contract is, however, illusory: he still needs to prove that the damage has resulted from unseaworthiness, a burden considerably weightier than that placed on the carrier.

[71] The article was one of the amendments to the original Hague Rules and was incorporated into the Carriage of Goods by Sea Act 1971.

On one view of this article, the contractual limitations on the carrier's liability of due diligence in the care of the goods would apply to an action in tort brought by a plaintiff even where that plaintiff was not in contractual privity with the carrier. On another, the article simply rehearses the position in English law as it is in any event, that is to say that a party to a contract can plead contractual exclusions when sued in tort by the other party. The judges have not as yet had an opportunity to indicate which interpretation is correct and the major works in the area are in stark disagreement[72]. The expression of opinion in the periodical literature is limited: Mr Anthony Diamond QC favours a third, middle-of-the-road view, marshalling formidable textual arguments against the wider view, which, he writes, would require 'a bold construction.[73]' Dr F.M.B. Reynolds, while admitting that the resolution of the question is 'doubtful and at present, it seems, merely a matter of assertion', appears to incline against the wider view, suggesting that it could be 'overtly adopted by legislation suitably framed.'[74] Others express a clear preference: for the wider view, Professor Basil Markesinis[75], Dr Malcolm Clarke[76], Professor William Tetley[77], and for the narrower, Professor G.H. Treitel[78].

It would be comforting to suggest that, with the House of Lords firmly set against recovery in negligence by a plaintiff who cannot prove a proprietary connection with the goods at the time of the alleged tort[79], the discussion about the true effect of art IV-bis 1 of the Hague-Visby Rules is redundant: if it is so difficult for the plaintiff to succeed in tort, we need not concern ourselves, the argument would run, with the availability of contractual exclusions to a carrier sued in tort. The argument would be wrong, and the comfort short-lived: for, as we shall see, *The Aliakmon* does not exclude claims in negligence by aggrieved receivers of goods in all circumstances. There may well be instances[80] where the claimant is not in contractual privity with the carrier, but

---

[72] Carver takes the first, wider view: s 563; Scrutton, the second, narrower view: p 458.

[73] See The Hague-Visby Rules, at 1978 LMCLQ 225 at 248–249. Mr Diamond suggests that a carrier who has entered into a contract of carriage with a shipper but is sued in tort by a third party, e g a bank, can take advantage of the Hague-Visby limitations; while a carrier who contracts, not with the shipper but with a transhipping carrier or with a time-charterer, and who is sued in either case by the owner of the goods cannot. It is not, with respect, immediately clear why, at any rate in terms of policy, a carrier should be allowed the indulgence of the Rules in the first case but not in the second.

[74] The Significance of Tort in Claims in respect of Carriage by Sea, at 1986 LMCLQ 97 at 108.

[75] In An Expanding Tort Law—The Price of a Rigid Contract Law, (1987) 103 LQR 354 at 389, 390.

[76] Note on *The Aliakmon*, at [1986] CLJ 382 at 383.

[77] Who May Claim or Sue for Cargo Loss or Damage, W. Tetley, 17 JMLC 407 at 421 (1986).

[78] In Bills of Lading and Third Parties, at 1986 LMCLQ 294 at 304, and Benjamin, para 1459.

[79] *The Aliakmon* [1986] 2 Lloyd's Rep 1, to be discussed presently at Chapter 3.2.(b).

[80] And Mr Diamond has given examples in the article, already mentioned above, at 1978 LMCLQ 225 at 248, 249.

can prove a proprietary connection with the goods at the time of the alleged tort, thus bringing himself outside the rule in *The Aliakmon*. Thus, for example, an owner of transhipped goods may need to sue the second carrier in tort if, say, the bill of lading issued by the first carrier excludes liability after discharge, or if the first carrier is insolvent; and can do so, despite *The Aliakmon*, if he can prove that the damage occurred while the goods were on the second carrier's vessel. Consequently, money may well turn on the meaning of art IV-bis 1 of the Hague-Visby Rules.

It is suggested that the wider interpretation, allowing the carrier the protection of contractual exclusions when sued in tort, is preferable. The simplest argument is provided by the wording of the article itself, which appears clear enough on a reading untrammelled by over-sensitive considerations of privity, which, as we have seen[81], receives somewhat cavalier treatment in this area in any event. The wider view is also closer to the general policy behind the Rules, which was to bring about a uniform regime of liability regulating the carriage of goods by sea: a policy, moreover, which is illustrated even more clearly in the immediately subsequent rule, art IV-bis 2[82], which extends the operation of contractual exclusions to tort actions brought against rather than by third parties. Again, section 1(3) of the Carriage of Goods by Sea Act 1971 gives the Rules the effect of law 'in relation to and in connection with the carriage of goods by sea', rather than to contracts for the carriage of goods by sea.

The textual arguments favouring the narrow view need to be addressed. Firstly, reference is made[83] to section 1(4) of the Carriage of Goods by Sea Act 1971 which says that

> '...nothing in this section shall be taken as applying anything in the Rules to any contract for the carriage of goods by sea, unless the contract expressly or by implication provides for the issue of a bill of lading or any similar document of title.'

Consequently, it is said, the Act and the Rules can only apply to an action in contract, not to one in tort. With respect, that is to draw too much from the section, which states simply that where it is sought to apply the Rules to a contract, then the issue of a bill of lading must be provided for. Secondly, it is argued[84], art IV-bis 1 talks of actions against 'the carrier', a term defined in art I(a) as one which 'includes the owner or the charterer who enters into a contract of carriage with a shipper'; this definition, when read into art IV-bis 1, must consequently exclude

---

81 See fnn 4 and 57 above and accompanying text.
82 'If such an action [whether founded in contract or in tort] is brought against a servant or agent of the carrier (such servant or agent not being an independent contractor), such servant or agent shall be entitled to avail himself of the defences and limits of liability which the carrier is entitled to invoke under these Rules.'
83 Scrutton, p 458.
84 See The Hague-Visby Rules, Anthony Diamond QC, 1978 LMCLQ 225 at 248, 249.

a carrier sued in tort. With respect, that conclusion would only follow from a definition which read: 'carrier means the owner or the charterer who enters into a contract of carriage with the plaintiff.' The definition in the Rules, on the other hand, is much easier to satisfy: the defendant in the example given above, that is to say the second carrier transhipping goods and sued in tort by an aggrieved cargo-owner, would clearly come within it. Thirdly, it is said[85] that art IV-bis 1 makes no mention of actions against the ship, as do various other articles[86], and that this must mean that art IV-bis 1 does not contemplate tort actions at all. But this, with respect, is to lose sight of the fact that those articles referring to actions against the ship tell us something about actions in rem rather than about the availability or otherwise of actions in tort. For all these reasons, it is suggested that where a tort action is brought against a carrier, the plaintiff is no better off, as regards exclusions and limitations[87], than he would have been had he had the benefit of a contract.

(b) Problems after *The Aliakmon*

If the buyer thrown upon his remedy in tort against the carrier is no worse off than he would have been in contract, then it might appear that he need not exercise himself about the precise limits of section 1 of the Bills of Lading Act 1855 and of the device in *Brandt v Liverpool*; for surely, a buyer left out in the cold by contract would be well protected by the tort of negligence. Unfortunately, though, the position is somewhat more complex, for since the decision of the House of Lords in *The Aliakmon*[88], it has become clear that a buyer restricted to a remedy in tort faces serious problems with establishing locus standi. Just as too close a connection between the transfer of title to sue in contract and the passage of property is at the root of the major issue of interpretation raised by section 1 of the 1855 Act[89], so too, a close link between title to sue in tort and the transfer of a proprietary interest in the goods has led to severe restrictions on tort actions against carriers. For after *The Aliakmon*, it is now settled that a plaintiff cannot sue in tort unless he can prove that, at the time of the alleged negligence causing the loss complained of, he had a proprietary interest in the goods, e g ownership or a right to delivery of the goods on discharge. Our tasks

---

[85]   Ibid.

[86]   For example, arts III.6, IV.1, 2, 5(a) and (h), VII.

[87]   If the view expressed in the text is correct, then where the Carriage of Goods by Sea Act 1971 applies, the time bar provided for in art III.6 would run as much against a plaintiff suing in contract as against one suing in tort. This would iron out any differences between the two actions both with regard to the period of limitation and with regard to the date of its commencement. On the other hand, if the view adopted in the text is wrong, or where, even if it is right, the Carriage of Goods by Sea Act 1971 does not apply, the tort plaintiff would be in a different position to that in which he would have been had he been suing in contract, both with regard to the length of the period of limitation and with regard to the date of its commencement: see generally, *Salmond and Heuston on the Law of Torts*, Heuston and Buckley, (hereinafter Salmond and Heuston), 1987, at pp 664–668.

[88]   [1986] 2 Lloyd's Rep 1.

[89]   See Chapter 3.1.(a).(iv) above, and particularly fn 39 and accompanying text.

here are three: firstly, to indicate when the rule applies; secondly, to examine the origins of the rule; and thirdly, to discuss whether the policy behind the rule is appropriate in this area of commercial activity.

i. When the rule applies

The first—and obvious—point to make is that the rule given the imprimatur of the House of Lords in *The Aliakmon*[90] does not bar negligence actions by cargo-claimants in all circumstances. The result of the case is that where the plaintiff cannot prove a possessory interest in the goods at the time of the alleged tort, he cannot sue in tort; thus, where the plaintiff can so prove, the tort of negligence is at his disposal. Thus, the buyer of goods who, in the example given in the preceding section, had his goods transhipped by a second carrier with whom he was not in contractual privity, and who could prove that the goods were damaged while they were on the second vessel, lies not only outside section 1 of the 1855 Act[91] and outside *Brandt v Liverpool*[92], but also outside the rule in *The Aliakmon*. Again, where the buyer of goods holding a bill of lading issued by the charterer of a vessel and constituting the contract between those parties[93], chooses to sue the shipowner, because, say, the charterer is insolvent, no amount of imaginative construction can create a contract between the buyer and the shipowner, who is nonetheless and *The Aliakmon* notwithstanding, liable in tort if the plaintiff can prove negligence causing loss to goods at a time when he owned them or was entitled to their delivery.

It is when he cannot prove this link of ownership or constructive possession at the time of the alleged negligence that the buyer cannot succeed in a tort action. That is most likely to happen when the lost or damaged goods in respect of which the plaintiff sues are part of a bulk shipped on board one vessel: again, the buyer of commodities is in trouble[94]. Where he has a bill of lading, the temporal interpretation of section 1 of the Bills of Lading Act 1855 can, if accepted, bar his path in contract[95]: if the property in the goods must pass at the same time as the bill of lading is transferred to the endorsee, then section 1 of the 1855 Act can pass no contract, once property in goods shipped in bulk can only pass on ascertainment, according to section 16 of the Sale of Goods Act 1979[96]. Again, where he has no bill of lading, his

---

90   [1986] 2 Lloyd's Rep 1.
91   Because he is not suing under a bill of lading issued to him by the second carrier.
92   In effect, for the same reason, that is to say, that he can present to the defendant carrier no document at all (cf *The Elli 2* [1985] 1 Lloyd's Rep 107) issued by the second carrier.
93   See Chapter 7.3, below.
94   The cases in which the problem has arisen have been described as 'freakish': see *Margarine Union GmbH v Cambay Prince SS Co Ltd* [1969] 1 QB 219 at 254. In Bulk Buyers and Economic Loss, at 1983 JBL 42, Mr P.N. Todd writes: 'it is difficult to see why this should be so, and if it is, then the freakish facts seem to have given rise to a disproportionate amount of litigation.'
95   See above Chapter 3.1.(a)(iv).
96   Section 16 of the Sale of Goods Act 1979 and s 1 of the Bills of Lading Act 1855 conspire to cause problems currently the subject of examination by the Law Commission: see Working Paper 112, Rights to Goods in Bulk, and Chapter 4.2.(a), below.

path in tort is barred for much the same reason: property cannot pass before ascertainment, which normally happens on discharge, by which time the negligent act will have occurred. It could be argued that where the goods are discharged, the court could infer a *Brandt v Liverpool* contract. While such a contract would be sustainable in principle where the carrier has actually undertaken delivery to the plaintiff by acknowledging a delivery order for the plaintiff's parcel of the goods shipped in bulk and there are at any rate some goods to deliver[97], the degree of fabrication required where neither feature is present would seem to be far too extreme[98]. Yet it is precisely that degree of fabrication to which parties (and judges sympathetic to the merits of individual cargo claims) may well be forced by the restrictions upon a tort action recently enshrined in *The Aliakmon*[99].

ii. The origins of the rule in the law of negligence

The proposition that a receiver of goods can only sue a carrier in negligence when he can prove that damage was caused through the carrier's fault to goods which were owned by the plaintiff receiver or to the delivery of which he was entitled at the time of the alleged act of negligence is an application of the general principle of the law of negligence against the recovery of pure economic loss. According to that general principle[100], the victim of a negligent act can only recover damages for foreseeable losses caused by that act where those losses consist of physical injury either to the plaintiff or to his property. Other losses are purely economic and they are not recoverable in the tort of negligence[101]. The principle is traditionally justified on two grounds. Firstly, recovery for loss which is purely financial would open the floodgates of liability to enormous numbers of claims between which it would be difficult, if not impossible, to make any rational distinction[102]. Secondly, purely economic losses are normally compensated through contract and should not be allowed to spill over into the tort of negligence[103], which, from its inception in *Donoghue v Stevenson*[104], was allowed to violate the common law doctrine of privity only because physical loss was seen to merit greater protection than that afforded by contract. The principle against recovery has had a long[105] and relatively

---

[97] *Peter Cremer Westfaelische GmbH v General Carriers SA, The Dona Mari* [1973] 2 Lloyd's Rep 366.

[98] An implied contract in the circumstances here envisaged would combine the two 'missing' features in *The Elli 2* [1985] 1 Lloyd's Rep 107 and in *The Aramis* [1987] 2 Lloyd's Rep 58, [reversed by the Court of Appeal, [1989] 1 Lloyd's Rep 213], that is to say, a bill of lading to present and a cargo to deliver.

[99] [1986] 2 Lloyd's Rep 1.

[100] See generally Salmond and Heuston, at pp 227–238.

[101] As opposed to the tort of negligent mis-statement generated by the decision in *Hedley Byrne & Co Ltd v Heller & Partners Ltd* [1964] AC 465.

[102] See Salmond and Heuston, at p 231.

[103] See Salmond and Heuston, at p 230.

[104] [1932] AC 562.

[105] Frequently said, (see, for example, *The Aliakmon* [1986] 2 Lloyd's Rep 1 at 4), to date back to *Cattle v Stockton Waterworks Co* (1875) LR 10 QB 453. It is strange, though, that the rule against the recovery of economic loss in the tort of negligence

untroubled history: it was threatened twice, falling once and then only in a type of case which could conveniently be cordoned off, safely distant from the general principles of negligence. This first threat was posed by the successful action brought by a victim of a negligent misstatement: the decision of the House of Lords in *Hedley Byrne & Co Ltd v Heller & Partners Ltd*[106] spawned the distinction between negligent statements and negligent acts, a distinction which allowed orthodoxy to prevail, at any rate over negligent acts. The second threat came in 1983 when, in *Junior Books Ltd v Veitchi Co*[107], a factory owner recovered damages for loss of profit caused by a defective floor installed by a sub-contractor with whom the plaintiff was not in contractual privity. This case could not be sent up a siding quite so conveniently as could *Hedley Byrne*; it has, nonetheless, been very firmly put in its place, largely by statements, both from the courts[108] and in the literature[109], that it was a case special on its facts, consequently leaving unchanged the traditional principle against recovery of pure economic loss.

iii. Is the general principle against recovery appropriate here?

A critique of the general principle just described, whether in terms of precedent or in terms of policy, would be beyond the scope of this book[110]. Suffice it here to describe the circumstances in which it has been applied to the detriment of receivers of goods carried by sea; and then to suggest four reasons why its application in this area of commercial activity is quite inappropriate.

The history of the application of the general principle against recovery of economic loss to the law of carriage of goods by sea is shared between

---

appears to predate the creation of that tort (in 1932) by almost 60 years: but see Negligence and Economic Loss, P.S. Atiyah, (1967) 83 LQR 248, where Professor Atiyah writes that 'since negligence was established it is doubtless right to regard [the case] as an authority for the purposes of the tort of negligence.'

[106] [1964] AC 465.

[107] [1983] 1 AC 520.

[108] *D & F Estates Ltd v Church Comrs for England* [1988] 3 WLR 368, where Lord Bridge said, at 381 G-H: 'The consensus of judicial opinion, with which I concur, seems to be that the decision of the majority [in *Junior Books*] is so far dependent upon the unique, albeit non-contractual, relationship between the pursuer and the defender in that case and the unique scope of the duty of care owed by the defender to the pursuer arising from that relationship that the decision cannot be regarded as laying down any principle of general application in the law of tort or delict.'

[109] See Salmond and Heuston, at p 230, where *Junior Books* is described as 'only a momentary interruption to the slow, pragmatic development of the law.'

[110] The literature is prolific: see the sources footnoted at p 81, fn 1, in Economic Loss in the Maritime Context, N.J.J. Gaskell, 1985 LMCLQ 81; and Economic Loss: Is the Pendulum Out of Control, P. Cane, (1989) 105 LQR 200; An Expanding Tort Law—The Price of a Rigid Contract Law, B. Markesinis, (1987) 103 LQR 354; Tort and Contract After *Junior Books*, J. Holyoak, (1983) 99 LQR 591; Physical Loss, Economic Loss and Products Liability, P.F. Cane, (1979) 95 LQR 117; Negligent Misstatements, Negligent Acts and Economic Loss, P.P. Craig, (1976) 92 LQR 213; The Fallacies of *Simpson v Thomson*, P.S. James, (1971) 34 MLR 149; and Negligence and Economic Loss, P.S. Atiyah, (1967) 83 LQR 248.

four judges, Lord Roskill, Lord Brandon, Lord Justice Mustill, and Lord Justice Lloyd. The story starts with an unsuccessful action in negligence by buyers of damaged cargo shipped in bulk, ascertained on discharge and covered by delivery orders which were not issued or acknowledged by the defendant shipowner: *Margarine Union GmbH v Cambay Prince SS Co Ltd*[111]. The arguments used on either side in that case were to form the nub of the debate over the next two decades and it would therefore be useful to rehearse them here. Roskill J (as he then was) was unimpressed by the two arguments for recovery put before him by counsel for the buyers, Mr Anthony Lloyd QC: firstly, that the receiver of the goods on discharge was a clearly foreseeable victim of the carrier's negligence and was therefore a 'neighbour' in Lord Atkin's terms[112] and that his status as such should not be affected by the type of shipping document he held[113]; secondly, and in the alternative, the plaintiff's locus standi in tort should not depend on the transfer of a proprietary interest from the seller to the buyer, but on the transfer of risk between those parties, such that if risk lay with the buyer, he should be entitled to sue the carrier for loss or damage for which the latter was responsible[114]. Counsel for the defendant shipowner, Mr Michael Mustill, was forthright in his use of orthodox principle to rebut both arguments: as for the first, it had long been the law that the tort of negligence could not be used to compensate a plaintiff for what had turned out to be a bad bargain with the seller; indeed, if tort were to allow such recovery there would be no need for section 1 of the Bills of Lading Act 1855 and the device in *Brandt v Liverpool*[115]. The defendant's riposte to the second argument was that the passage of risk was 'a concept of the law of sale of goods as between buyer and seller and had no relevance when one had to consider how far the duty of a tortfeasor extended.'[116] Mr Mustill's arguments prevailed on the day and Roskill J found for the defendant.

Fourteen years after Roskill J decided *The Margarine Union*, lawyers interested in this area of commercial law were regaled with the spectacle of another two first instance judgments, given within weeks of each other, in which Lloyd J and Mustill J (as they had by then become) were given the opportunity to decide whether the arguments they had canvassed as counsel in that case were right or wrong. In the event, they each decided they were right. In *The Irene's Success*[117], Lloyd J, on facts which

---

[111] [1969] 1 QB 219.

[112] *Donoghue v Stevenson* [1932] AC 562.

[113] [1969] 1 QB 219 at 232-234.

[114] Loc cit at 234-235.

[115] Loc cit at 225 and 235. This last twist in the argument was, with respect, neat but untidy: a tort action, if allowed, would be perfectly consistent with s 1 and *Brandt v Liverpool*, if Parliament and the courts wished to extend the exclusions and limitations which the carrier had negotiated with the seller to the former's relationship with the buyer.

[116] [1969] 1 QB 219 at 235. Again, this argument proves too much: the proprietary title which the shipowner contended was essential to the buyer's locus standi in tort was itself—like risk—a matter determined by the law of sale.

[117] [1982] 1 All ER 218. The judgment of Lloyd J was followed a few weeks later by Sheen J in *The Nea Tyhi* [1982] 1 Lloyd's Rep 606, at 611-613. The part of Sheen

were broadly similar to those in the earlier case[118], allowed recovery in tort, largely adopting arguments which must have sounded anything but novel to him. In *The Elafi*[119], Mustill J followed the decision of Roskill J in the *Margarine Union*, proceeding to find that the plaintiff had locus standi because property had passed, through a process of appropriation by exhaustion.

With 'two judges in favour of one view, and two in favour of another,'[120] it became clear that guidance from the higher courts was sorely needed. It was not long before *The Aliakmon*[121], a case with 'unusual'[122] facts, gave the House of Lords an opportunity to come down very firmly on the side of Roskill J. in the *Margarine Union* case, that is to say, against recovery. The facts of the case were 'rather special'[123], a feature which ought not to be disregarded in assessing the relevance of the decision to the type of problem which had theretofor raised the question of recovery of pure economic loss, viz. the carriage of cargo shipped in bulk. Buyers of a cargo of steel had found themselves in some financial embarrassment when they found it more difficult to sell the cargo than they had expected. They consequently came to an agreement with the sellers whereby the steel was to be held at the disposal of the sellers but at the risk of the buyers, while efforts were to be made by both parties to find a purchaser. The cargo was damaged in transit and the buyers sued the carriers, claiming locus standi both in contract and in tort. By the time the case reached the House of Lords, the only live issue was whether the plaintiffs could sue in negligence, the Court of Appeal having held that the plaintiffs could benefit neither from section 1 of the Bills of Lading Act 1855[124]

J's judgment which followed Lloyd J's was strictly obiter because he found that the cargo-owners had locus standi in contract. The judge favoured Lloyd J's views for two reasons: firstly, he found it difficult to reconcile Roskill J's judgment in the *Margarine Union* case with the speech of Lord Wilberforce in *Anns v Merton London Borough Council* [1978] AC 728 (but see what is said by Lord Brandon about Lord Wilberforce's speech at [1986] 2 Lloyd's Rep 1 at 7); secondly, Lloyd J's view 'circumvents a judicial exercise which, to my mind, is void of reality or merit', that is to say, the determination, with any degree of certainty, of the precise moment when a negligent act damaged goods while at sea.

[118] Except for the fact that here the reason the buyers could not sue in contract was that they had no bill of lading at the time of discharge: it is interesting to speculate whether the conclusion would be drawn quite so readily now, after the decision in *The Elli 2* [1985] 1 Lloyd's Rep 107: see Chapter 3.1.(b), above, particularly fn 59 and accompanying text.

[119] [1982] 1 All ER 208.

[120] Per Staughton J in *The Aliakmon* [1983] 1 Lloyd's Rep 203 at 207.

[121] [1986] 2 Lloyd's Rep 1.

[122] Loc cit at p 3.

[123] Loc cit at p 11.

[124] Because property had not passed upon or by reason of the endorsement of the bill of lading: see [1985] 1 Lloyd's Rep 199 at 204, 218, 219. Staughton J was reversed on this point: the judge had found that s 1 of the 1855 Act did in fact work to the plaintiff's benefit, property having passed on endorsement of the bill. The fact that property was re-vested in the sellers by the special agreement between the seller and the buyer did not have the effect of re-transferring the right to sue the carrier; by Staughton J's own admission, a 'somewhat technical ground': see [1983] 1 Lloyd's Rep 203 at 207. See generally on this point Bills of Lading and Third Parties, G.H. Treitel, 1986 LMCLQ 294 at 297.

nor from a *Brandt v Liverpool* contract[125]. It is clear from Lord Brandon's speech that their Lordships felt the merits to be very much against the plaintiffs. The plaintiffs' predicament was of their own making, for in accepting to take the risk without the property, they had made themselves vulnerable to loss without recovery[126]: had the buyers, in their special agreement with the sellers, extracted a promise that the sellers would sue the carriers for any damage caused to the cargo by the carriers, they would have avoided the problem which they now sought to solve by an unacceptable extension of tort principles[127]. Those principles were clear and essential to the certainty expected of commercial law and Lord Brandon could see no reason why any derogation should be made therefrom[128].

Quite apart from the debate about the justification, in terms of precedent and policy, for the general principle against recovery of damages in negligence for pure economic loss, there are, it is suggested, four grounds for taking cargo claimants out of the ambit of that principle. Firstly, in none of the five cases we have looked at in this section would recovery by the claimant have resulted in unpredictable liabilities being incurred by the carrier[129]: in each, there was and could only be one plaintiff, 'the last c i f buyer who might buy those goods while they were still afloat'[130]. It is, with respect, difficult to avoid gaining the impression that the mere incantation of the word 'floodgates' exercises at times an almost mesmerising compulsion against recovery[131].

Secondly, to link title to sue in negligence to the passage of risk makes much better sense than linking it to the transfer of a proprietary interest[132]. For surely, it is patently within the contemplation of a carrier that the party likely to suffer loss as a result of negligent acts on board ship is the receiver of the goods on discharge. Indeed, the law of sale responds to this commercial expectation through the rule, which we shall consider

---

[125] Because the buyers had acted as agents for the sellers in taking delivery of the goods from the carrier: see [1985] 1 Lloyd's Rep 199 at 204, 206 and 219. Staughton J had come to the same decision on this point, though for different reasons, i e that such a contract should not be implied simply from the fact of discharge and delivery: see [1983] 1 Lloyd's Rep 203 at 207.

[126] [1986] 2 Lloyd's Rep 1 at 4.

[127] Loc cit at 10. As to the position of the buyers had they not been able to extract such a promise from the sellers, see Ownership and Obligation in Commercial Transactions, R.M. Goode, at (1987) 103 LQR 433 at 453–459.

[128] Loc cit at 9.

[129] Contrast the 'collision' cases, of which *The Mineral Transporter* [1986] AC 1 is the most recent example, which are, it is suggested, readily distinguishable on this ground.

[130] Per Roskill J, reporting a part of Mr Lloyd QC's argument for the plaintiffs in *Margarine Union GmbH v Cambay Prince SS Co Ltd* [1969] 1 QB 219 at 234.

[131] See, for example, the treatment by Lord Brandon of the argument rehearsed in the text and advanced by counsel for the plaintiff in *The Aliakmon* [1986] 2 Lloyd's Rep 1 at 8, 9.

[132] See Sassoon at s 164, p 139; Who May Claim or Sue for Cargo Loss or Damage, W. Tetley, 17 JMLC 407 at 420; *Triangle Steel & Supply Co v Korean United Lines Inc* 63 BCLR 66. For a diametrically opposed view, see *The Sanix Ace* [1987] 1 Lloyd's Rep 465, particularly at 470.

in due course[133], that risk generally passes from seller to buyer 'on or as from shipment'[134]. To say that tort should follow contract in making the buyer's title to sue the carrier dependent on a proprietary interest is to argue that we should make the same mistake twice[135]. Again, to say that the passage of risk is a matter for the sale contract and of no relevance to the liability of the carrier in tort[136] is to ignore the sensitive inter-relationship between the contracts making up an international trade transaction. Moreover, as has already been said[137], the argument proves too much: for the transfer of a proprietary title is as much a function of the contract of sale as is the transfer of risk.

Thirdly, the argument that the carrier sued in tort by the receiver would lose the protection of those clauses which he had taken care to write into his contract with the shipper, and that therefore the claimant should, as a matter of policy, be denied recovery, is to assume that such a carrier would indeed lose the protection of such clauses. The plaintiff in *The Aliakmon* argued[138] that the opposite result could be achieved through a bailment on terms: the suggestion came to grief upon the important question as to who, on that analysis, would be the bailor, the seller or the buyer. It has been argued elsewhere in this chapter[139] that art IV-bis 1 of the Hague-Visby Rules would, where the Carriage of Goods by Sea Act 1971 applied[140], extend the protection of contractual exclusions to a carrier sued in tort. If the arguments there presented are correct, then the problem of policy here mentioned would disappear.

Finally, there is a sense in which the application of the general principle against recovery leads us, at any rate in this particular area of the law, back into a conundrum which was by all accounts solved over half a century ago. In the *Margarine Union* case[141], in *The Irene's Success*[142],

---

[133] In Chapter 4.

[134] See Benjamin, para 1694. In this context, it has been said, with justification, that although the facts in *The Aliakmon* were in many ways unusual, in one sense they were quite typical, for risk frequently passes before property in international sales: see Bills of Lading and Third Parties, G.H. Treitel, 1986 LMCLQ 294 at 298. Indeed, the same can be said of the bulk shipment cases, sometimes said to be 'freak' cases: see fn 94, above.

[135] See Chapter 3.2.(b), above, particularly text accompanying fn 89.

[136] As was argued by Mr Michael Mustill for the carrier in the *Margarine Union* case: see [1969] 1 QB 219 at 235.

[137] See above at fn 116.

[138] At [1986] 2 Lloyd's Rep 1 at 9, 10.

[139] At Chapter 3.2.(a).

[140] Where the Act does not apply, an argument has been advanced by Mr A.M. Tettenborn that the nature of bailment would lead to the same result: see Sellers, Buyers and Negligent Damage to Goods, at 1983 JBL 459 at 462. If the exclusion clauses in the seller's contract with the carrier are 'characterised as part of the law of property, rather than the law of contract', then on the nemo dat principle, the buyer would only take 'property' rights similar to those of the seller. With respect, the characterisation of exclusion clauses as creatures of property law requires a formidable act of faith.

[141] [1969] 1 QB 219.

[142] [1982] 1 All ER 218.

in *The Elafi*[143] and in *The Aliakmon*[144], each plaintiff would clearly have had locus standi to sue in contract had he had a bill of lading or a delivery order attorned to by the carrier covering the parcel of goods said to have been damaged by the carrier. The rule against recovery upheld by three of those cases requires the cargo-interest suing in negligence to have had a proprietary interest in the goods at the time of the alleged tort. That requirement would have been satisfied had the claimants had either a bill of lading or an attorned to delivery order. However, if any of the claimants had had one of those documents in their possession, they would have been able to sue in contract. This comes perilously close to concluding that the claimants could only succeed in tort if they could succeed in contract: and that proposition was the one which was laid to rest by *Donoghue v Stevenson*[145].

The judicial response to the decision of the House of Lords in *The Aliakmon* has been, with respect, deferential rather than enthusiastic[146]. Warmly followed in *The Sanix Ace*[147], it was acknowledged, it must be said, in a somewhat subdued manner, in *Transcontainer Express Ltd v Custodian Security Ltd*[148], a case in which the rule against recovery worked against, rather than in favour of, a carrier. It was again acknowledged without, it appears, any argument on the point, in *The Ciudad de Pasto*[149]. More importantly, however, *The Aliakmon* was distinguished by Hirst J in *The Kapetan Georgis*[150]: a charterer, sued by a shipowner whose vessel was damaged by an explosion, sought to recover from the shipper of dangerous goods in third party proceedings, claiming, inter alia, a cause of action in negligence. The shipper argued that such an action was unsustainable after *The Mineral Transporter*[151] and *The Aliakmon*[152] because the charterer's loss was purely economic.

---

[143] [1982] 1 All ER 208.
[144] [1986] 2 Lloyd's Rep 1.
[145] [1932] AC 562.
[146] The reaction in the literature has been varied. In ascending order of hostility to the decision, see the following: Bills of Lading and Third Parties, G.H. Treitel, 1986 LMCLQ 294, particularly at 301–304, where Professor Treitel is less impressed with the arguments based on certainty than with those relating to the exclusion clauses in the bill of lading; The Carrier and the non-owning Consignee—An Inconsequential Immunity, at 1987 JBL 12, where Mr A.M. Tettenborn, though broadly supportive of the decision, concludes that 'no shipping lawyer need get particularly excited about *The Aliakmon*'; Professor Schmitthoff, in Export Trade, at p 40, where he warns that the decision 'will not be welcomed by those engaged in international trade'; Note by Dr Malcolm Clarke in [1986] 45 CLJ 382; and, for the most uncompromising critique, see An Expanding Tort Law—The Price of a Rigid Contract Law, B. Markesinis, in (1987) 103 LQR 354 at 384–390, where Professor Markesinis suggests that the case is 'remarkable but for all the wrong reasons.'
[147] [1987] 1 Lloyd's Rep 465, and see fn 132, above.
[148] [1988] 1 Lloyd's Rep 128, see particularly 138.
[149] [1989] 1 All ER 951 at 953. As to this case, see further Chapter 4.2.(c).ii, below, fn 87.
[150] [1988] 1 Lloyd's Rep 352. The Court of Appeal decision in *The Aliakmon* [1985] 1 Lloyd's Rep 199, was also distinguished in *Triangle Steel and Supply Co v Korean United Lines Inc* 63 BCLR 66.
[151] [1986] AC 1.
[152] [1986] 2 Lloyd's Rep 1.

Hirst J found for the charterer, distinguishing *The Aliakmon* on the basis that the instant case was 'hallmarked by a physical damage claim somewhere up the chain[153].' This may well be a seam worth tapping: for, to continue in the same vein, the problem for cargo claimants who have been involved in this story, from the *Margarine Union* case to *The Aliakmon*, has been that they have suffered financially from a physical loss in respect of which no claim was brought against the carrier by someone else somewhere up the chain[154].

---

[153] [1988] 1 Lloyd's Rep 352 at 356. The judge based this distinction on an obiter dictum by Lord Diplock in *Lexmead (Basingstoke) Ltd v Lewis* [1981] 2 Lloyd's Rep 17.

[154] A point also made by Professor Basil Markesinis in An Expanding Tort Law—The Price of a Rigid Contract Law, (1987) 103 LQR 354 at 385.

CHAPTER 4

Transfer of property and risk

1. The concepts of property and risk: their nature and significance
   (a) Property and possession
   (b) Property and risk
2. Transfer of property and the Sale of Goods Act 1979
   (a) Ascertainment and appropriation
   (b) Unconditional appropriation
   (c) Indicia of intention as to the passage of property
       i. Express clauses reserving property
       ii. Implied intention to reserve property
   (d) Transfer of property and letters of credit
3. Transfer of risk
   (a) Transfer of risk and the Sale of Goods Act 1979
       i. Section 20(2)
       ii. Section 20(3)
       iii. Section 32(2)
       iv. Section 32(3)
       v. Section 33
   (b) The general rule in shipment sales
       i. Risk of loss or damage to the goods and breach of other duties
       ii. The rule in *Mash and Murrell*
       iii. Risk passes 'on or as from shipment'

In Chapter 2, we identified five issues which it would be helpful to keep separate in the law regulating contracts on shipment terms: the right to demand possession of the goods from the carrier; the property in the goods; the risk of loss or damage to the goods; the buyer's title to sue the carrier and the regime regulating cargo claims. In Chapter 2, the buyer's right to demand possession of the goods from the carrier was identified with the nature of the bill of lading as a document of title at common law. The buyer's title to sue the carrier in contract or in tort was discussed in Chapter 3.

Our aim here is to look at those aspects of the passage of property and risk from seller to buyer which cause special difficulty in the sale of goods on shipment terms[1]. We shall approach that aim in three steps: firstly, we need to distinguish between the notions of property and risk and establish why it is that lawyers need to decide when either passes from seller to buyer. Secondly, we shall look at sections 16, 18, rule 5, and 19 of the Sale of Goods Act 1979, namely the sections most likely, for reasons which will be explained, to be of significance in advising parties to a sale on shipment terms. Thirdly, we shall look at the transfer of risk as between seller and buyer, first under some special rules in the Sale of Goods Act 1979 and then under a number of principles developed by the common law.

1. THE CONCEPTS OF PROPERTY AND RISK: THEIR NATURE AND SIGNIFICANCE

To arrive at some understanding of the concepts of property and risk in the context of the international sale of goods, we need to recall some of the distinctions outlined earlier in Chapter 2. We saw there that to call a bill of lading a 'document of title at common law' is to refer to its ability to transfer from seller to buyer the right to claim possession of the goods from the carrier: it was suggested that it might, for these purposes, be more useful to call the bill of lading a 'document of possession'[2]. We saw also that this power to transfer the right to possession of the goods from seller to buyer without a formal assignment between them and without notification thereof to the carrier was what made the document 'transferable': this latter term was consequently redundant when attached to the phrase 'document of title at common law'[3]. Finally, we saw that, apart from being a document of title at common law, a bill of lading was also negotiable, in the sense that, where the conditions laid down by statute were satisfied[4], the transferee of a bill of lading might have a title stronger than that held by his transferor. Observed in this context, a bill of lading was also, in common with other documents[5], a document of title in a rather more accurate sense, that is to say, as a document symbolising ownership.

---

[1]   The remaining question of the five referred to in Chapter 2, namely regime, more properly belongs in works dealing exclusively with the law of carriage of goods by sea: see Chapter 2, fn 8, above.

[2]   See Chapter 2.3.(c), above.

[3]   See Chapter 2.2.(a), above.

[4]   That is to say, by ss 2, 8 and 9 of the Factors Act 1889 and by ss 24 and 25 of the Sale of Goods Act 1979.

[5]   See s 1(4) of the Factors Act 1889, incorporated into the Sale of Goods Act 1979 by s 61; s 1(4) of the Factors Act reads:

'The expression 'document of title' shall include any bill of lading, dock warrant,

(a) Property and possession

This distinction between a document of title at common law and a document of title for the purposes of the Sale of Goods Act 1979, i e the distinction between transferability and negotiability, reflects directly that between the right to possession and ownership. These two concepts, possession and ownership, and the difference between them, have attracted, not surprisingly, a welter of literature[6]: the distinction can perhaps most briefly be described, at any rate in this context, by referring to the different questions which either concept answers. To say that the holder of a bill of lading has a document 'of possession' is to say that he has a right, as against the carrier who currently holds the goods, to claim possession of them: non-delivery by the carrier, or delivery to a non-holder, would consequently make the carrier liable to the holder in conversion. To say, on the other hand, that the holder of a bill of lading[7] has a document 'of title' is to say that he can defend his claim to the goods, which he may possess either actually or constructively[8], against another person vaunting a claim against him. Thus, possession answers the question as to whether a seller or a buyer has the right to claim[9] the goods physically *from the carrier*; whereas ownership answers the question whether a particular[10] rival can bring a stronger claim to the goods *against the current pretender*, the holder of the goods or of the documents[11].

Possession, then, is about control of the goods, ownership about the relative ranking of claims and this is borne out by the contexts in which it is most frequently necessary to establish who owns a particular cargo. The most obvious cases are those envisaged by the Sale of Goods Act itself in sections 24 and 25, namely, where an innocent third party purchaser of the goods is allowed to prevail over a previous owner who has put a rogue in the position of misusing documents of title to the goods[12]. The second is where insolvency strikes either seller or buyer

---

warehouse-keeper's certificate, and warrant or order for the delivery of goods, and any other document used in the ordinary course of business as proof of the possession or control of goods, or authorising or purporting to authorise, either by endorsement or by delivery, the possessor of the document to transfer or receive goods thereby represented.'

[6] See, in particular, Goode, at 157–161; Goode, *Proprietary Rights*, pp 1–26; and The Concepts of 'Property', 'Title' and 'Owner' Used in the Sale of Goods Act 1893, Battersby and Preston, (1972) 35 MLR 268.

[7] Or of another type of document included in s 1(4) of the Factors Act 1889.

[8] Should they still be in the actual possession of the carrier.

[9] Or control, primarily through transfer: though see Chapter 8.1.(b) below for seawaybills.

[10] 'Particular' because of 'the elementary proposition of our law that title to tangible property, whether land or chattels, is relative. ... Given such a concept, the phrase 'owner of property' assumes significance only in relation to a particular issue with a particular person': see the seminal article by G. Battersby and A.D. Preston, The Concepts of 'Property', 'Title' and 'Owner' Used in the Sale of Goods Act 1893, (1972) 35 MLR 268 at 269; for a contrary view, see Absolute Title Financing, Iwan Davies, (1985) AngloAmerican Law Review 71, particularly at 72,73.

[11] Where the goods are still held physically by the carrier.

[12] See Chapter 2.3.(c), above.

and the creditors of the insolvent party wish to put the cargo within the estate of the insolvent, thus forcing the other party to the sale contract to compete with them in the insolvency for the goods which were the subject of the sale[13]. Finally, in time of war, the Crown will want to seize a cargo in Prize, by effectively jumping the queue of claims over a cargo, and this it can do by proving that the cargo was owned by an enemy alien[14].

There are, however, other reasons why a court might be called upon to decide where property in a cargo lay at a particular time, reasons altogether more germane to the law of international trade: the buyer's title to sue the carrier, whether in contract or in tort, may also depend upon the passage of property in the goods from the seller to the buyer; again, the seller's right to bring an action against the buyer for payment of the price may also depend upon whether or not property in the goods has passed to the buyer. Thus, to take title to sue first, we saw in Chapter 3 that for section 1 of the Bills of Lading Act 1855 to bridge the privity gap between the buyer and the carrier, not only does the plaintiff need to hold a bill of lading which is a document of title at common law entitling him to possession of the goods from the carrier[15]: the plaintiff also needs to show that property in the goods passed to him by the time of suit by dint of the same contract through which the bill of lading reached him[16]. Again, where the buyer has no contractual locus standi, he might have a tortious cause of action where he could prove that at the time of the tort alleged, he had a proprietary interest in the goods, which interest could be either the right to possession or property[17]. Finally, section 49 of the Sale of Goods Act 1979 makes the unpaid seller's action for the price against the buyer conditional upon property having passed to the buyer[18]. For any of the reasons here described, then, a court may

---

[13] See Goode, *Proprietary Rights*, 1985, at 2, 3 and 16. Thus, where the seller becomes insolvent, the buyer will argue that property had passed to him prior to the seller's insolvency, such that he would have a real right over the goods, thus excluding them from the claims of the seller's unsecured creditors. Likewise, where the buyer becomes insolvent, the seller will argue that property had not passed to the buyer before his insolvency, such that, if the goods have since reached the buyer, the seller could exercise a real right over them, thus excluding them from the claims of the buyer's unsecured creditors.

[14] See *The International Law of the Sea*, D. P. O'Connell, 1982, at 1113.

[15] See Chapter 3.1.(a).(i), above.

[16] See Chapter 3.1.(a).(ii) and (iv), above.

[17] See Chapter 3.1.(a).(ii), above.

[18] Section 49(1) reads: 'Where, under a contract of sale, the property in the goods has passed to the buyer, and he wrongfully neglects or refuses to pay for the goods according to the terms of the contract, the seller may maintain an action against him for the price of the goods.' Section 49(2) allows the seller to bring an action for the price, irrespective of whether property has passed to the buyer, where 'the price is payable on a day certain irrespective of delivery.' It is doubtful whether a stipulation that payment be made 'against documents' is one which comes within s 49(2) such that a seller could sue for the price, rather than for damages, if the buyer refuses to pay on tender: contrast *Polenghi Bros v Dried Milk Co Ltd* (1904) 10 Com Cas 42 to, for example, *Stein Forbes & Co v County Tailoring Co* (1916) 115 LT 215 and other cases cited and discussed in Benjamin at paras 1778, 1779.

need to decide who, at a particular time, had property in the goods in a sense quite distinct from the right to possession. Interestingly, though, we shall see that just as the nature of the document transferred from seller to buyer tells us something about the transfer of constructive possession, so it might tell us something about the passage of property.

(b) Property and risk

The same phrase as is used to signify the transfer of property, namely 'passage of property', is used to describe the transfer of risk from seller to buyer[19]. This may give the impression that risk, like property, is in a real sense a right which is sold by the seller to the buyer. This manner of thinking may cause difficulty when it is pointed out that in sale contracts concluded on shipment terms, the seller frequently 'passes' the risk to the buyer earlier than the property; and that, consequently, a seller on c i f terms might be entitled, on one view, to allocate goods to a contract which are damaged in transit before property therein has passed to the buyer[20]. We shall come to the separation in point of time between property and risk later in this chapter. Suffice it for the present to outline the following distinction between the two concepts.

Property is properly regarded as a right transferred from seller to buyer, confirming the buyer's claim over the goods in preference to those of other pretenders thereto. Risk, on the other hand, tells us something about the contractual, as opposed to the proprietary, relationship between the parties to the contract of sale: to say that risk has 'passed' from seller to buyer is one way of saying that the seller has discharged his physical duty under the contract of sale to deliver the goods to the buyer[21], such that the buyer's remedies, if any, for loss of or damage to the goods while in transit lie not against the seller, but against the third parties brought into privity with the buyer through the documents tendered by the seller, namely, the carrier or the insurer. If, on the other hand, risk has not 'passed' from seller to buyer, then this again is a short-hand way of saying that the seller has yet to deliver the goods to the buyer, that he is consequently still under a duty to deliver goods as described in the contract, and that he is therefore still liable to the buyer under the contract of sale for loss of or damage to the goods. The object of ascertaining where the risk of goods in transit lies is therefore to establish whether the seller is an appropriate defendant to a contractual claim brought by the buyer in respect of non-delivery, short-delivery or damage to cargo[22]: if the risk rests with the seller, then he is a proper defendant; if the risk has 'passed', then he is not.

---

[19] See, for example, the rubric to s 20 of the Sale of Goods Act 1979, which reads 'Risk prima facie passes with property.'

[20] See Chapter 4.3.(b).(iii), below.

[21] See, in similar vein, Risk in the Law of Sale, L. J. Sealy, [1972b] CLJ 225, particularly at 226, 227; and Atiyah, at 249.

[22] In Chapter 3.2.(b).(iii), we considered the suggestion that the passage of risk as between seller and buyer might also be useful as the trigger for an action in tort by the buyer against the carrier: *The Aliakmon* [1986] 2 Lloyd's Rep 1 does, of course, stand in the way of such a suggestion.

Having examined the distinction between the concepts of property and risk, and having outlined the significance of either notion in the context of sale contracts concluded on shipment terms, our next task is to look at the guidance given by the Sale of Goods Act 1979 as to when property passes to the buyer.

2. TRANSFER OF PROPERTY AND THE SALE OF GOODS ACT 1979

The Act starts from the proposition that property passes from seller to buyer when the parties intend it to pass; section 17 reads as follows:

'(1) Where there is a contract for the sale of specific or ascertained goods the property in them is transferred to the buyer at such time as the parties to the contract intend it to be transferred.

(2) For the purpose of ascertaining the intention of the parties regard shall be had to the terms of the contract, the conduct of the parties and the circumstances of the case.'

There follows in section 18 a list of five rules for ascertaining the intention of the parties: the first three of these rules regulate the passage of property in specific goods; the fourth refers to the sale of goods on sale or return terms. These first four rules can easily be discounted in the context of sale contracts concluded on shipment terms. Specific goods are defined in section 61(1) of the Act as

'goods identified and agreed on at the time a contract of sale is made'.

Thus, the first three of the rules given in section 18 of the Act relate to contracts the subject-matter of which would be, for example, 'this particular shipment of cars, identified by these chassis numbers.' Now while it is perfectly conceivable for such a contract to be concluded on c i f [23] or f o b terms, contracts concluded on such terms more commonly refer to goods of a particular type rather than to particular goods: thus, it is more likely that the parties will agree to sell and buy, for instance, 'cars of such and such a type.' To describe goods in this generic way would take them out of the Act's definition of specific goods, and consequently the sale outside section 18, rules 1 to 3. Rule 4 is unlikely to be relevant to international sales because, again, such contracts are unlikely to be on sale or return terms.

The sections of the Act which are relevant to sale contracts on shipment terms are section 16, section 18, rule 5, and section 19. Before we deal with these sections in detail, it would be helpful to outline the notions which are fundamental to their working, namely ascertainment and appropriation. Having outlined these notions, we shall then examine the workings of these several sections in the context of sale contracts on shipment terms and the ground will be covered in four steps: we

---

[23]   See, for example, *Wiehe v Dennis Bros* (1913) 29 TLR 250, discussed further at Chapter 4.3.(ii), below.

shall look first at the notion of unconditional appropriation; secondly, we shall examine the factors which evidence the intention of the parties as to the passage of property; finally, we shall look briefly at the passage of property where a letter of credit is in place.

(a) Ascertainment and appropriation

Section 16 lays down the rule that property in goods cannot pass to the buyer 'unless and until the goods are ascertained.' Goods are unascertained if they are packed or shipped together with other goods of the same type; thus, if fifty cars of a particular make are shipped on board a particular vessel and the shipper has agreed to sell twenty-five of them to the buyer, then the property in any of the cars cannot pass to the buyer before the shipment has been separated into two lots of twenty-five. However, such separation, though necessary, is not sufficient of itself to pass property in the cars: for property to pass, the cars must further be appropriated to the buyer. Ascertainment simply separates twenty-five cars away from another twenty-five cars; for property to pass, the seller must now allocate one of the two separated lots of cars to the buyer[24]. This process of allocation is called 'appropriation' by the Act in section 18, rule 5, in terms of which property in 'unascertained[25] or future goods by description[26]' passes to the buyer on

---

[24] A separate act of allocation to a particular contract of sale would not, however, be necessary to transfer the property where the seller has sold the other twenty-five cars shipped on the same vessel to the same buyer while the vessel was in transit. In this case, so long as all the cars of the contract type on the vessel are intended for the same buyer, the goods, originally unascertained, have been ascertained 'by exhaustion'. Here, ascertainment, accompanied by the intention to pass property, is sufficient so to pass, despite the absence of a separate act of allocation to the separate contracts under which the two batches of twenty-five cars are sold: see *The Elafi* [1982] 1 All ER 208; and *Wait & James v Midland Bank* (1926) 31 Com Cas 172. Ascertainment can only pass property through exhaustion in this way where it is clear that all the goods of the same type, on the same vessel, or in the same warehouse, are intended for the same buyer: see *Re London Wine Co (Shippers) Ltd* [1986] PCC 121 at 152–156.

[25] The text of s 18, r 5, causes some difficulty here for appropriation is said to be necessary to pass property in unascertained goods. If this is right, then s 16, which makes ascertainment necessary for the passage of property, is either contradicted or rendered otiose by s 18, r 5. For if appropriation passes property in unascertained goods, pace s 18, r 5, then it cannot be true, pace s 16, that property in such goods cannot pass without ascertainment; unless, that is, appropriation in s 18, r 5 is the same as ascertainment, in which case s 16 becomes redundant.

The truth, surely, is that the two notions are separate in law: ascertained goods too need to be appropriated, because goods separated from a larger bulk still need to be allocated to a particular buyer for property to pass; although, of course, in most cases, the two processes, separation and allocation would happen at the same time. If this is right, then the way out of the resulting conundrum is to read the word 'unascertained' in s 18, r 5, to mean 'originally unascertained, but now ascertained as required by s 16'. The difficult relationship between s 16 and s 18, r 5, was referred to by Mustill J in *The Elafi* [1982] 1 All ER 208 at 214, 215, where the judge concluded that 'it appears legitimate to place appropriation on the same broad basis as ascertainment', the result of which view, as has been indicated above, would be that s 16 would be rendered otiose.

[26] 'Future goods' are defined by s 61(1) as 'goods to be manufactured or acquired by the seller after the making of the contract of sale.'

an appropriation which is unconditional, that is to say, on an allocation which is undiluted by any evidence tending to show that the seller intended to reserve the property[27]. Thus, we return to the point at which we started, namely the intention of the parties, established in section 17 as the key criterion in the passage of property[28].

The rule that ascertainment is necessary, though not, as we have seen, sufficient for the passage of property in goods causes inconvenience in sales of commodities shipped in bulk and subsequently sold in smaller quantities while in transit[29]. The rule has consequently been subjected to recent and considerably critical scrutiny in a Law Commission Working Paper entitled 'Rights to Goods in Bulk'[30]. The application of the rule in international trade causes two problems. Firstly, if ascertainment is necessary for the passage of property from seller to buyer in part of a cargo shipped in bulk, then the part of the cargo sold to the buyer does not become subject to the claims of the buyer's general creditors, the goods being subject to the stronger and real claim of the seller[31]. Secondly, the buyer's locus standi in a cargo claim against the carrier, whether brought in contract or in tort, may also be prejudiced by the requirement of ascertainment. So far as concerns contractual locus standi, we saw in Chapter 3[32] that there were two interpretations of the link between property and locus standi under section 1 of the Bills of Lading Act 1855: was the section triggered into action only when passage of the property in the goods and the transfer of the bill of lading occurred at the same time; or was it sufficient for the two events simply to have happened because of the same contract of sale, albeit at different times? If the former interpretation were preferred[33], then the requirement of ascertainment would preclude the application of section 1 of the 1855 Act where part of a bulk is sold and the buyer would have no locus

---

[27] Goods which were, at the time the contract was concluded, unascertained and not unconditionally appropriated, but which have since been ascertained and unconditionally appropriated, do not become specific goods for the purposes of the Act; for goods to be specific, they must be 'identified and agreed on at the time a contract of sale is made', pace s 61(1).

[28] And elaborated upon in s 19, which, as we shall presently see, evinces an intention to reserve property from, inter alia, the manner of the seller's dealing with the shipping documents.

[29] This practice has been explained on the basis that cash-flow problems encourage purchasers to make frequent purchases of smaller quantities of commodities rather than to hold larger quantities in reserve: Law Commission Working Paper No 112, at p 2.

[30] Law Commission Working Paper No 112.

[31] Contrast the position of the buyers' creditors where the buyer had bought, prior to his insolvency, the entire contents of a tanker of oil rather than simply a part of it. Here, the cargo will, given unconditional appropriation, have passed into the estate of the buyer: the buyer's creditors would consequently have more assets from which to satisfy their debts, the seller, if yet unpaid, simply joining in the competition for payment.

[32] See Chapter 3.1.a.iv, above.

[33] Contrary to the view expressed at Chapter 3.1.(a).iv, above.

standi in contract[34]. Moreover, because of the rule in *The Aliakmon*[35], the buyer of part of a bulk would have no locus standi against the carrier in tort because he would have had no proprietary interest in the goods during transit, that is to say when the goods were damaged by the carrier's alleged act of negligence.

The Law Commission's Working Paper seeks to solve both[36] problems—proprietary rights on insolvency and locus standi against the carrier—by effectively doing away with the requirement of ascertainment where an undivided share in or a specified amount of an identified bulk is sold[37]. The effect of such a reform would be to protect the interests of the buyers's creditors on insolvency; and to establish the buyer's locus standi against the carrier.

The Working Paper is bedevilled throughout, though, by the nagging feeling that:

'section 16 expresses what in many cases is a sensible policy:

"...for how can we speak of someone as having bought goods if we cannot tell what it is that he has bought?"'[38]

Consequently, the reform suggested is limited in extraordinarily restrictive terms:

---

[34] It has been suggested that for this reason, 'there must be doubts as to whether a buyer under a c i f contract could be compelled to accept a bill of lading covering unascertained goods unless the contract specifically requires him to do so': see The Passing of Property in Part of a Bulk, A. Nicol, (1979) 42 MLR 129 at 141, where the proposition is based on the judgment in *Re Reinhold & Co and Hansloh's Arbitration* (1896) 12 TLR 422. (See also Benjamin, at para 1547.) If this proposition were correct in law, it would cause extreme inconvenience in practice: its effect would be to give the buyer carte blanche to repudiate the contract by rejecting the documents at any time before discharge of the goods for no other real reason than to take advantage of a decrease in the market value of the commodity. It is difficult, however, to see how the proposition can be supported by the decision in *Reinhold*, a judgment which seems, in any case, to have fallen by the judicial wayside. In his judgment, Mr Baron Pollock makes it clear that '...it was not necessary to discuss the general question whether a tender of a bill of lading for an undistinguished part of the cargo could be valid.' The reason the buyer's rejection of the shipping documents was upheld was that the certificates of inspection tendered did not expressly relate to the same parcel of goods to which the bills of lading referred.

[35] [1986] 2 Lloyd's Rep 1; see Chapter 3.2.b, above.

[36] The Working Paper recognises that, although an amendment to s 1 of the Bills of Lading Act 1855 would assist the buyer in establishing his locus standi against the carrier, such a reform would do nothing for the position of the buyer's creditors on insolvency. Nonetheless, the Working Paper does investigate the possibilities for reform of the 1855 Act: see above, Chapter 3, fn 49.

[37] The model adopted for such reform comes from section 2-105(4) of the Uniform Commercial Code of the United States of America: see Law Commission Working Paper No 112, paras 4.4-4.14.

[38] See Law Commission Working Paper 112, para 4.5, quoting from Goode, Proprietary Rights, 1st edn, 1985, at 14. Another difficulty with the suggested reform is that s 18, r 5, of the Sale of Goods Act, which passes property on unconditional appropriation, would be bereft of sense in the absence of ascertainment: see text accompanying fn 25, above. For a robust defence of s 16 of the Sale of Goods Act, see The Passing of Property in Part of a Bulk, Nicol, (1979) 42 MLR 129, particularly 132-135.

'Nevertheless, it is suggested that in principle any reform should be limited to goods which can be sufficiently identified so as to determine what it is that the buyer has bought. Realistically, this should probably be limited to specified parts of an identified bulk.'[39]

The impression is given that there is little heart behind a radical departure from section 16 of the Sale of Goods Act and perhaps this is because it is rightly felt that tinkering with section 16 of the Sale of Goods Act might disturb settled principle quite unnecessarily. It is not immediately clear why the law should be altered so as to favour the general creditors of an insolvent buyer over an unpaid seller by transferring the property in part of a bulk to the buyer before discharge. On the other hand, it is clear that the law falls harshly upon the buyer of part of a bulk by depriving him of locus standi against the carrier both in contract[40] and in tort[41]. If the real victim of the piece is the buyer deprived of locus standi, rather than his creditors bereft of one other asset in insolvency, then the solution lies not in the uprooting of section 16 of the Sale of Goods Act 1979, but in an appropriate amendment to section 1 of the Bills of Lading Act 1855. The buyer could be given locus standi against the carrier wherever it is intended that property[42] in the goods is to pass by reason of the same contract of sale under which the goods are consigned or the bill of lading transferred[43]. By shifting the emphasis from actual transfer of property to the intention to pass property, locus standi would pass to the buyer even though property, according to section 16 of the 1979 Act, could not.

(b) Unconditional appropriation

In the absence of a different intention, unconditional appropriation, coupled, where the goods sold are part of an undifferentiated bulk, with ascertainment, lies at the centre of the passage of property in sale contracts concluded on shipment terms. The notion is introduced into the Sale of Goods Act 1979 by section 18, rule 5, sub-section (1), which reads:

'18. Unless a different intention appears, the following are rules for ascertaining the intention of the parties as to the time at which the property in the goods is to pass to the buyer.

---

[39] Law Commission Working Paper, No 112, para 4.5; see also para 4.11 of the Working Paper.

[40] Because s 1 of the Bills of Lading Act 1855 cannot work if property can only pass on discharge of the part and if the section is only triggered when property and the bill of lading pass to the buyer at the same time: see Chapter 3.1.(a).iv, above.

[41] Because of the rule in *The Aliakmon* [1986] 2 Lloyd's Rep 1: see Chapter 3.2.b, above.

[42] By retaining the link between property and the transfer of contractual locus standi, pledgees of bills of lading would still lie outside the 1855 Act and the good sense of *Sewell v Burdick* (1884) 10 App Cas 74 will have been preserved: see Chapter 3, fn 49, above.

[43] The wording suggested in the text would decide the question of interpretation raised by the *San Nicholas* [1976] 1 Lloyd's Rep 8 in favour of the causal approach supported above at Chapter 3.1.(a).iv: s 1 would be triggered even though the bill of lading was transferred to the buyer at a time different to the time at which property could, according to s 16 of the 1979 Act, be transferred, i e ascertainment by discharge.

Rule 5.—(1) Where there is a contract for the sale of unascertained or future goods by description, and goods of that description and in a deliverable state are unconditionally appropriated to the contract, either by the seller with the assent of the buyer or by the buyer with the assent of the seller, the property in the goods then passes to the buyer; and the assent may be express or implied, and may be given either before or after the appropriation is made.'

We have earlier described unconditional appropriation as the act by which a seller allocates a particular parcel of goods to a particular contract, so that goods generically described as, say, 'cars of this type', are specifically attached to a contract of sale as 'these cars'. Consequently, in the context of sale contracts concluded on shipment terms, the act of appropriation will commonly be the 'last act to be performed by the seller' irreversibly[44] identifying the goods as those sold to the particular buyer[45]. The Act itself gives a very obvious illustration of one such 'last act', namely, the act of delivery to the carrier; section 18, rule 5, sub-section (2) reads:

'Where, in pursuance of the contract, the seller delivers the goods to the buyer or to a carrier or other bailee or custodier (whether named by the buyer or not) for the purpose of transmission to the buyer, and does not reserve the right of disposal, he is to be taken to have unconditionally appropriated the goods to the buyer.'

Were it not for the significance of the shipping documents in the transfer of property in goods carried by sea, a role to which we shall presently refer, the practical result of this sub-section would be that the property in such goods would typically pass upon the shipment of the goods. We shall see, however, that the shipping documents, or indeed the contract of sale itself, will commonly indicate an intention rebutting this prima facie presumption.

Appropriation in the sense here described needs to be distinguished from the c i f seller's obligation to declare the ship upon which he intends to load the goods, a declaration sometimes confusingly called a 'notice of appropriation'. Standard term c i f contracts commonly impose upon the seller the duty to notify the buyer of the vessel upon which the goods sold are to be shipped[46]. The commercial purpose of the duty is twofold. Where the buyer intends to receive the goods himself, receipt of the notice of appropriation enables him to make the necessary arrangements for receiving the goods at the port of discharge; where the buyer sells the goods while they are in transit, the notice enables him to describe the goods he sells as goods shipped on board the declared ship. The legal

---

[44] This is why s 18, r 5 of the Act insists on the assent of both parties to the appropriation: see Goode, *Proprietary Rights*, pp 19-20. Such assent is generally inferred from the terms of the contract or the practices of the trade: see *Ross T Smyth & Co Ltd v Bailey, Son & Co* [1940] 3 All ER 60; in a similar vein, see Atiyah, p 242.

[45] See *Carlos Federspiel & Co SA v Charles Twigg & Co Ltd* [1957] 1 Lloyd's Rep 240 at 255, per Parker J.

[46] See, for example, GAFTA 100, clause 10; a similar, though not identical, duty is imposed by Incoterms CIF 4.

effect of the notice of appropriation is that it defines the promise which the seller is bound to perform when he tenders the bill of lading to the buyer: consequently, a seller who had declared shipment on the *Mahout* was in repudiatory breach when he tendered a bill of lading stating goods to have been shipped on the *Mahsud*[47]. This notice of appropriation is a formal notification, defining the seller's contractual obligation as to the shipment of the goods[48]. 'Appropriation' in the sense in which that word is used by section 18, rule 5 of the Sale of Goods Act 1979, is a physical act identifying the goods and, if unconditional, causing the property in them to pass from seller to buyer. The two quite separate notions are easily confused by the untidy use of the word 'appropriation' to signify either concept. The phrase 'notice of appropriation' might usefully be substituted by 'declaration of shipment'[49], leaving the word 'appropriation' to be used in its proper context, namely in the passage of property from seller to buyer[50].

(c) Indicia of intention as to the passage of property

We have seen that, unless section 18 of the Sale of Goods Act 1979 is expressly excluded in the contract of sale, property in unascertained or future goods by description will pass on their being unconditionally appropriated to a particular contract[51]; we also saw that shipment of the goods indicated unconditional appropriation where the seller had not reserved the right of disposal[52]. Our task here is to examine the means through which the seller can reserve the right of disposal, such that appropriation be made conditional, such that in turn property would not pass on shipment of the goods. Section 19 of the Act provides us with the two main factors[53] which the Courts take into account in discerning the seller's intentions as to the passage of property: firstly, express clauses in the contract of sale itself; secondly, the manner in which the bill of lading is issued, and the way in which it is transferred to the buyer. Each of these two types of indicia will be dealt with in turn.

i. Express clauses reserving property

Section 19(1) reads as follows:

'Where there is a contract for the sale of specific goods or where goods are subsequently appropriated to the contract, the seller may,

---

[47] *Kleinjan & Holst NV Rotterdam v Bremer Handelsgesellschaft mbH Hamburg* [1972] 2 Lloyd's Rep 11.
[48] See *Smyth & Co v Bailey & Co* [1940] 3 All ER 60 at 66.
[49] The standard form of contract on shipment terms used by the Coffee Trade Federation Limited (1988 edition) employs the phrase 'Advice of Shipment' in clause 26.
[50] Professor Goode uses the word 'quasi-appropriation' to signify the seller's declaration of shipment: see Goode, *Proprietary Rights*, p 19. See also Benjamin, at paras 1623, 1687 and 1854.
[51] Sale of Goods Act 1979, s 18, r 5(1).
[52] Sale of Goods Act 1979, s 18, r 5(2).
[53] Section 19(3) deals with the effect which dishonour of the bill of exchange has on the passage of property.

by the terms of the contract or appropriation[54], reserve the right
of disposal of the goods until certain conditions are fulfilled; and
in such a case, notwithstanding the delivery of the goods to the
buyer, or to a carrier or other bailee or custodier for the purpose
of transmission to the buyer, the property in the goods does not
pass to the buyer until the conditions imposed by the seller are
fulfilled.'

The effect of the section is to enable the seller expressly to retain property
in the goods despite their ascertainment under section 16 and
appropriation under section 18, rule 5. Express clauses retaining title
commonly found in commodity contracts make property pass at a
particular physical juncture[55]; or at a particular time[56]; or at one of either[57].
Such clauses are commonly known as 'reservation of title' or 'Romalpa'
clauses, after a case of that name[58].

The object of a Romalpa clause is to protect the seller against the
consequences of non-payment by retaining property in the goods, thus
saving them from the claims of other creditors of the buyer where the
buyer becomes insolvent. The clause may, however, go further than simply
retain property in the goods sold against payment of the purchase price:
it may, for example, purport to give the seller title not only over the
goods themselves, but over the proceeds derived through their on-sale;

---

[54] It has been suggested that where the seller reserves title by the terms of the appropriation
rather than by the terms of the contract, he may be in breach of his contract with
the buyer: see The Post-Contractual Reservation of Title, J.R. Bradgate, 1988 JBL 477,
at 478, 480–481. The proposition appears to be based on the decision in *Gabarron
v Kreeft* (1875) LR 10 Exch 274: in that case, though, as is readily admitted in Mr
Bradgate's article, the goods were arguably not appropriated to the contract. The point
of the decision was, in any case, that an innocent third party purchaser of the bills
of lading from the seller prevailed over the original buyer: nothing turned on whether
or not the seller was in breach of his contract with the original buyer. As Mr Bradgate
illustrates, though, the estate of an insolvent buyer may well wish to recover damages
for such a breach where the market price of the goods has risen between the time
the contract was concluded and the time of the buyer's insolvency: see ibid at 484,
485.

[55] See, for example, *The San Nicholas* [1976] 1 Lloyd's Rep 8, where the contract of
sale stipulated that property would pass 'at the permanent hose connection of the vessel
receiving the molasses at loading port'; similar clauses are typical in contracts for the
sale of oil: see *The Wise* [1989] 2 Lloyd's Rep 451. See also the Plywood CIF Contract
Form 1957, Plycif (1957), adopted by the Timber Trade Federation, clause 10 of which
reads: 'Property in goods to be deemed for all purposes (except retention of vendors'
lien for unpaid purchase price) to have passed to Buyers when goods have been shipped.'

[56] See the f o b contract used by the North American Export Grain Association, Inc, which,
at clause 25, reads: 'Anything in this contract to the contrary notwithstanding, seller
shall retain title to the commodity until seller has been paid in full, it being understood
that risk of loss shall pass to buyer on delivery at discharge end of loading spout'.

[57] See the CIF Reselling Contract, adopted by the Timber Trade Federation of the United
Kingdom, Scanref 1964, clause 9 of which reads: 'Property in goods to be deemed for
all purposes, except retention of Vendor's lien for unpaid purchase price, to have passed
to Buyers when goods have been put on board the vessel, or if sold "afloat", at the
date of the contract.'

[58] *Aluminium Industrie Vaassen BV v Romalpa Aluminium Ltd* [1976] 1 WLR 676:
property was to pass when the buyer paid 'all that is owing to' the seller.

or it may purport to give the seller title over products which have been manufactured with the goods[59].

Where the buyer is a company, such clauses raise the question as to whether they constitute a charge on the company's property registrable under the Companies Act 1985[60]. Money turns on the point because, failing registration, a charge is void against 'an administrator or liquidator of the company, and any person who for value acquires an interest in or right over property subject to the charge'[61]: the seller would consequently have no right to claim possession of the goods in which title has been reserved from the on-buyer; neither would he have a secured right to their proceeds from the buyer. This assumes, however, that the clause creates a registrable charge over the company's property in favour of the seller: the buyer's other creditors would wish to argue that the clause does so create, so that their security is not prejudiced by the seller's alleged, but unregistered claim[62]. The position appears to be that where the clause seeks to reserve title over anything other than the goods sold themselves, or possibly over the proceeds of their onsale[63], then the charge

---

[59] For an exhaustive sampling of various retention of title clauses, see The Commercial Realities of Reservation of Title Clauses, Julie Spencer, 1989 JBL 220, particularly, 225–229.

[60] Where the buyer is not a company, the law does not as yet require the registration of the security interest constituted by a Romalpa clause, however wide the ambit of the clause. If the recommendations of Professor Diamond, in A Review of Security Interests in Property [HMSO, 1989, chapter 17] are adopted, though, all such clauses would need to be registered where the buyer is not a company: failing registration, the seller's interest is not protected against the claims of other creditors of the buyer. Even if this were to become the law, though, Professor Diamond would exclude from the requirement of registration Romalpa clause security interests where the seller has retained the right to dispose of the goods in a sale on shipment terms: see para 17.19. The case thus excluded arises in the following manner: a seller who protects his interest by a Romalpa clause in a contract concluded on shipment terms is also likely to make the bill of lading out to his order, thus reserving the right of disposal for the purposes of ss 18, r 5, and 19 of the Sale of Goods Act 1979. The object of reserving the right of disposal is to enable the seller to sell the goods to a third party while they are in transit in case the original buyer does not pay. That third party would only acquire good title against the original buyer if he, the third party, were unaware of the claims of the original buyer: see s 25 of the Sale of Goods Act 1979. Thus, if registration of the seller's security interest were required in such circumstances, this would in effect destroy the seller's right of disposal which he had intended to retain by making the bill of lading out to his own order under s 19 of the 1979 Act. That right is preserved by the exclusion of shipment sales from Professor Diamond's overall scheme of registration of security interests. For this benefit, there is, however, one price the seller must pay. If, against a falling market, the value of the goods on re-sale by the seller is less than the contract price agreed with the original, now insolvent, buyer, the seller's claim for damages from that buyer would be unsecured and would simply compete with the claims of other creditors.

[61] See the new s 399(1), which appears at s 95 of the Companies Act 1989.

[62] See *Cases and Materials in Company Law*, Sealy, 4th edn, 1989, Butterworths, p 391.

[63] See *Sale of Goods*, P.S. Atiyah, 1985, pp 358–364, particularly p 364.

is registrable under the Act: the wider the ambit of the clause, the more likely is it that the charge needs to be registered[64].

ii. Implied intention to reserve property

In the absence of clauses in the contract expressly defining the moment at which property passes, it will be left to the courts to ascertain the intention of the parties in this regard. Given the central role played by the bill of lading in sale contracts concluded on shipment terms, it is not surprising that the manner in which the bill of lading is issued and the way in which it is transferred to the buyer are significant factors in discerning that intention. The lead is given by section 19(2) of the Sale of Goods Act 1979 itself, which reads as follows:

> 'Where goods are shipped, and by the bill of lading the goods are deliverable to the order of the seller or his agent, the seller is prima facie to be taken to reserve the right of disposal.'

This presumption provides us with yet another illustration of the rule laid down earlier in the 1979 Act by section 17(2) that the intention of the parties is to be ascertained by looking to 'the terms of the contract, the conduct of the parties and the circumstances of the case.' Three main sets of circumstances need to be considered here[65]:

— where the bill of lading is made out to the order of the seller;
— where the bill of lading is made out to the order of the buyer;
— where the contract provides for payment in 'cash against documents'.

These three sets of circumstances provide pegs on which to hang such guidance as has been given by the courts in the decided cases rather than hard and fast rules as to the passage of property in each case. We shall find presently that it is difficult to predict with certainty what intention the courts will infer in any particular case. Talk of a general rule pointing in any one direction is consequently less appropriate than discovering which factors the courts are inclined to consider as relevant to the issue of passage of property.

---

[64] Thus where, for example, a clause reserved title in products a constituent part of which were the goods supplied by the seller, the charge created was held to be a floating charge under s 396(1)(f) of the 1985 Act, registrable under pain of nullity: see *Re Bond Worth* [1980] Ch 228 and other cases cited in *Company Law*, Farrar, Furey and Hannigan, 2nd edn, 1988, Butterworths, p 577; Pennington's *Company Law*, 1985, pp 524–525; and *Cases and Materials in Company Law*, Sealy, 4th edn, 1989, Butterworths, pp 391–3.

[65] For the sake of completeness, two other variants need to be mentioned: where payment is to be made by bill of exchange, and where payment is to be made by letter of credit. As for the first, s 19(3) of the 1979 Act lays down the rule that transfer of a bill of lading against a dishonoured bill of exchange does not pass property in the goods to the buyer. As for the second, namely where the sale contract provides for payment by letter of credit, this will be dealt with separately at Chapter 4.2.(d), below.

— Where the bill of lading is made out to the order of the seller

As we have already seen, where the bill of lading is taken out to the order of the seller or his agent, then section 19(2) raises a prima facie presumption that the seller intends to reserve the right of disposal[66]: where this presumption applies[67], the property in the goods does not pass on shipment[68], as it would otherwise do under section 18 rule 5(2), but on payment[69]. On the other hand, the fact that the bill of lading is taken out to the order of the seller does not necessarily preclude the passage of property on shipment. Thus, where the seller takes a bill of lading as agent of the buyer[70], or where the bill of lading is made available to the buyer[71], property may pass on shipment notwithstanding the fact that the bill has been taken out to the seller's order.

— Where the bill of lading is made out to the order of the buyer

Arguing a contrariu sensu from section 19(2) of the Sale of Goods Act 1979, it may seem that where a bill of lading is taken out to the order of the buyer, this would lend strength to the presumption laid down by section 18, rule 5(2) that property in the goods passes on shipment.

---

[66] The presumption appears to be strong enough to withstand rebuttal even where the seller parts company with the bill of lading: see *PS Chellaram & Co Ltd v China Ocean Shipping Co* [1989] 1 Lloyd's Rep 413 at 421, 422, per Carruthers J, New South Wales, Admiralty Division.

[67] Before the Court of Appeal's decision in *Mitsui & Co Ltd v Flota Mercante Grancolombiana SA, The Cuidad de Pasto, The Cuidad de Neiva*, there appeared to be some doubt as to whether the presumption in s 19(2) could apply to f o b sales. The doubt, raised by the editor of Carver at para 1621, was based on the argument that a seller f o b promised to deliver the goods free on board and that he therefore promised to pass property to the buyer on shipment. The argument confuses the seller's contractual duty to have goods shipped, *some part of which* are intended for the buyer with the separate issue as to when property *in particular goods* is to pass to the buyer: thus a seller f o b is quite entitled to ship goods on the nominated vessel without passing property in them at that moment. The majority opinion among the textbook writers was against the view put forward in Carver: see Benjamin, paras 1823, 1861; Sassoon, para 552; Goode, p 588. The point has now been settled in favour of the majority view by the Court of Appeal in *The Cuidad de Pasto* [1989] 1 All ER 951, see particularly 956 a–e, 959 g, 960 a.

[68] See, however, *Biddell Bros v E Clemens Horst Co* [1911] 1 KB 934 at 956, where Kennedy LJ suggests that property 'passes conditionally where the bill of lading for the goods, for the purpose of better securing payment of the price, is made out in favour of the vendor or his agent or representative.' With respect, the effect of s 19(2) is to stop property from passing rather than to pass property conditionally.

[69] At any rate, normally. The court may decide that the seller intends to reserve property in the goods until some condition other than payment is satisfied. Thus, in *The Albazero*, Brandon J held that the plaintiff sellers, a company closely associated with the buyers, intended to reserve title in a cargo of oil not until payment, but until the bill of lading was posted to the buyers: see [1977] AC 774 at 796–799 per Brandon J, at 809–811 per Roskill LJ, and 840, per Lord Diplock. Both Brandon J and the Court of Appeal were reversed by the House of Lords, but not on the question as to passage of property. See Carver, para 1611.

[70] See *Joyce v Swann* (1864) 17 CBNS 84 and other cases cited at Carver, para 1602 at fn 50.

[71] See *Browne v Hare* (1858) 3 H & N 484 and (1859) 4 H & N 822, discussed by Benjamin at para 1862; and *The Parchim* [1918] AC 157, see particularly at 171, 172.

There is, however, strong authority, both by way of decision[72] and by way of obiter dicta[73], against rushing headlong towards that presumption which, it seems, the courts are only too ready to rebut by evidence of a contrary intention. Thus, where the seller took a bill of lading out to the buyer's order, but retained possession of it until payment, it was held that property did not pass on shipment of the goods but on transfer of the bill of lading[74]. It is on the crest of this sort of authority that it is sometimes said that property usually passes on delivery of the documents to the buyer[75].

— Where the contract provides for payment in 'cash against documents'

Where the contract provides for payment in 'cash against documents', this is taken to be the clearest sign that the parties intend the property in the goods to pass on payment of the price[76]. The presumption raised by such a term is so strong that it survives the delivery of the goods to the buyer before the bill of lading reaches the discharge port: thus, where the seller took a bill of lading to his order under a contract stipulating for payment against documents, and where the seller then tendered a ship's delivery order to the buyer entitling the buyer to take possession of the goods from the carrier, it was held that the delivery of the goods to the buyer did not disturb the presumption that the property was to pass on payment of the price[77].

---

[72] See *The Kronprinsessan Margarita, The Parana* [1921] 1 AC 486.

[73] See, for example, *Arnhold Karberg & Co v Blythe Green Jourdain & Co* [1915] 2 KB 379 at 387, per Scrutton J; *The Julia* [1949] AC 293 at 309, per Lord Porter; and *The Lycaon* [1983] 2 Lloyd's Rep 548 at 554, per Lloyd J.

[74] See *The Kronprinsessan Margarita, The Parana* [1921] 1 AC 486 at 511–517, particularly at 515, where Lord Sumner said: 'Certainly no case was found, in which it was held that taking the bill of lading in the buyer's name, while withholding delivery of it until presentation and taking up of the documents, would not be, as an appropriation, ... conditional.' See also *Sheridan v New Quay Co* (1858) 140 ER 1234, where property was held to pass on transfer of the bill of lading in a case where payment was to be in cash against the bill of lading, and this despite the fact that the bill was taken for the buyer's order.

[75] See, for example, Carver, para 1610; Benjamin, para 1689 and The Passing of Property and the Risk under a CIF Contract, H. Goitein, (1947) 43 LQR 81 at 84. It is possible that, even where the bill of lading is made out to the buyer, and where the bill of lading and the goods have been passed to the buyer, a court might hold that the intention of the parties is that the seller reserves title to the goods until payment of the price: see *The Aliakmon* [1986] 2 Lloyd's Rep 1 at 4. The crucial circumstance leading to that decision was that the parties had agreed, by way of a new contract, that the buyers were to take delivery of the goods as agents of the sellers.

[76] See *The Miramichi* [1915] P 71 at 78, where the term agreed was 'by check against documents'; *Re Shipton Anderson & Co and Harrison Bros & Co* [1915] 3 KB 676 at 680; *Stein, Forbes & Co v County Tailoring* [1917] 86 LJKB 448; and *Eastwood and Holt v Studer* (1926) 31 Com Cas 251.

[77] *Ginzberg v Barrow Haematite Steel Co Ltd and Mckellar* [1966] 1 Lloyd's Rep 343. On the other hand, the presumption was disturbed where a contract which provided for payment in cash against a mate's receipt also expressly provided that the seller was to have a lien on the goods until payment of the price: see *Nippon Yusen Kaisha v Ramjiban Serowgee* [1938] AC 429, particularly at 444, where Lord Wright based the opinion of the Privy Council that property passed before payment on the view

(d) Transfer of property and letters of credit

So far we have asked the question as to when property passes from seller to buyer without being influenced by the existence or otherwise of a letter of credit lying astride the contract of sale. We have seen already that where a bill of lading is transferred to a bank under a letter of credit, the bank receives a pledgee's interest in the goods rather than full ownership: we saw also that this was the case whether the bill of lading was made out to the order of the seller, of the buyer, or of the bank[78]. Those propositions, both relating to the bank's interest in the goods under a letter of credit, are in no way affected by anything that has been said earlier in this chapter relating to the question of passage of property from seller to buyer. Our task here is to ask that same question, only now with the additional feature of payment through a letter of credit: where a letter of credit is in place, does this tell us anything about the intention of the parties to the contract of sale as to the transfer of property from seller to buyer? The question needs to be considered first from the point of view of commercial convenience, then on the basis of authority.

As far as concerns commercial convenience, it is difficult to believe that when traders choose the letter of credit as their method of payment they intend this preference to have an impact upon the passage of property in the goods as between themselves qua seller and buyer. They would, surely, see the passage of property as a matter solely for the contract of sale to dictate, either through express stipulation or through judicial implication. With the bank's financing role adequately secured by the pledge created by the letter of credit, the traders would surely be surprised to learn that their choice of this avowedly[79] separate banking contract might have an impact upon something as intimate to the contract of sale as the passage of property in the goods. They would, if asked, surely answer that payment through a letter of credit has no impact upon the passage of property in goods as between seller and buyer.

---

that as the seller could only have a lien over someone else's property, this must mean that property in the goods had passed on delivery free alongside, despite the term 'cash against documents'. It is difficult to accommodate this judgment into the Sale of Goods Act 1979 which, at ss 38–43 implies a lien in favour of the unpaid seller into all contracts of sale: as such a lien is automatically implied by statute, does this mean that a term providing for payment in 'cash against documents' does not reserve title to the seller? The opinion of the Privy Council appears to have been followed by no other English court, and the editors of Benjamin are forced to say of it 'only ... that the passing of property is a question of intention in each case': see paras 1487, 1499 and 1505, fn 19. See also *FE Napier v Dexters Ltd* (1926) 26 Ll L Rep 62 and 184, where property was held to have passed before payment of the price in a contract stipulating for payment in cash against mate's receipt: the passage of property was a question of fact decided by the arbitrator, whose judgment neither Roche J nor the Court of Appeal wished to disturb: see particularly (1926) Ll L Rep 184 at 189, per Scrutton LJ.

[78]   See Chapter 2.3.(d), above.

[79]   See art 3 of the Uniform Customs and Practice for Documentary Credits.

So far as concerns authority on the matter, there is no case deciding in terms that payment by letter of credit necessarily points towards or away from reservation of title in favour of the seller. Indeed, the most explicit dictum there is on this matter rather supports the view just expressed that payment by letter of credit has little impact upon the passage of property: '[t]he special circumstance of the existence of a confirmed banker's credit in this case is only indirectly relevant.'[80] On the other hand, though, it has been suggested that the use of letters of credit in international trade explains and justifies the readiness with which the courts will find that the seller has retained title under the contract of sale beyond the time of shipment. The argument runs as follows: if the seller were to pass property in the goods to the buyer on shipment, then all he would have to pledge to the bank is his lien while the goods are still in his possession and his right of stoppage in transit once the goods are on their way to the buyer; no bank would take this to be a realistic security and it should follow therefore that the seller is more likely than not to have reserved title where a letter of credit is in place[81]. The sting in the argument is, however, blunted by the observation that a bank holding a document of title is a pledgee of the goods covered whoever has the general property in the goods, whether the seller or the buyer: for even where the property has passed to the buyer, a pledge in favour of the bank has already been created by the buyer in the application for the opening of the letter of credit[82]. It is therefore submitted that payment by letter of credit is not one of the indicia relevant to the question of passage of property between the parties to the contract of sale.

3. TRANSFER OF RISK

We have already seen[83] that, although property and risk are both said to 'pass' from seller to buyer, the two notions are quite distinct the one from the other. To say that property has passed from seller to buyer is to make a statement about the buyer's claim over the goods in preference to those of other pretenders: that claim, indefeasible by third parties[84]

---

[80] See *The Kronprinsessan Margarita, The Parana* [1921] 1 AC 486 at 517. It will be recalled that the seller was here held to have reserved property in goods covered by a bill of lading made out to the order of the buyer. The editors of Benjamin suggest, at para 1491, fn 51, that property remained in the seller 'precisely because the bank had not undertaken a binding obligation towards him.' But this view of the case is difficult to square with the fact that the letter of credit was confirmed. The difficulty originates in the Privy Council's opinion itself, for Lord Sumner says, in the extract quoted in the text above, that the letter of credit was confirmed, yet then indicates that the seller was not a 'holder of an enforcible(sic) contract from a bank for payment.'

[81] See Benjamin at para 1484, where the argument is based on the authority of a dictum by Lord Wright in *Ross T Smyth & Co Ltd v TD Bailey, Son & Co* [1940] 3 All ER 60 at 68.

[82] See Chapter 2.3.(d), above.

[83] See Chapter 4.1.(b), above.

[84] Other than in cases covered by s 24 of the Sale of Goods Act 1979: see Chapter 2.3.(c), above.

has, in a very real sense, 'passed' from seller to buyer. On the other hand, to say that the risk in shipped goods has passed from seller to buyer is to make a statement solely about the contractual relationship between the parties: where the seller performs his duty to ship goods of the contract description, then risk has 'passed' only in the sense that the buyer must now look to the carrier under the contract of carriage, or to the cargo insurer under his insurance policy, for compensation if the goods are lost or damaged in transit. It is not so much that some right has 'passed' from the seller to the buyer, as that the seller is taken out of the buyer's possible range of defendants to a cargo claim.

This manner of looking at risk makes it easier to accept the passage of risk before property in sale contracts concluded on shipment terms: it starts to explain the proposition that a seller who still owns goods does not run the risk of their loss or damage in transit, a theme to which we shall turn at length in the concluding part of this chapter. This reverses the presumption established in section 20(1) of the Sale of Goods Act 1979, which reads as follows:

'(1) Unless otherwise agreed, the goods remain at the seller's risk until the property in them is transferred to the buyer, but when the property in them is transferred to the buyer the goods are at the buyer's risk whether delivery has been made or not.'

This section of the Act is, however, barely ever applicable to sale contracts concluded on shipment terms[85] and for this there are both commercial and legal reasons.

From the seller's point of view, selling on shipment terms involves two types of danger, a physical danger and a financial one: the first, the risk that the goods might be lost or damaged at sea before he is paid the price; the second, the risk that the buyer might fail to pay the price altogether. Either occurrence becomes less worrying to the seller if the seller stops being liable for the safe keeping of the goods when the goods are shipped on board the vessel and if title is reserved to the seller until payment. These commercial considerations are recognised by the law in the essential nature of a sale contract concluded on shipment terms. As we have seen[86], in such a contract, the seller performs his contractual obligation by shipping goods of the contract description on the contract vessel and by tendering the contractual documents to the buyer: he owes the buyer no duty to guarantee that the goods will actually reach the contractual destination. For these commercial and legal reasons, the general rule as to the passage of risk is, as we shall see, that the

---

[85]   See, for example, *Stock v Inglis* (1884) 12 QBD 564 at 573; affd *sub nom Inglis v Stock* (1885) 10 App Cas 263; and *The Julia* [1949] AC 293 at 309.

[86]   See Chapter 1, above.

risk in sale contracts on shipment terms passes from the seller to the buyer on or as from shipment of the goods[87].

Our task in this part of the chapter is twofold. Firstly, we shall be looking at a number of sections of the Sale of Goods Act 1979 which make express exception to that general rule. Secondly, we shall be looking at the workings of the general rule in detail and at how it can be justified even where the goods are lost or damaged either before they are sold or before they are appropriated to a particular contract.

(a) Transfer of risk and the Sale of Goods Act 1979

It has just been said that section 20(1) of the Sale of Goods Act 1979, whereby risk passes with property, is hardly ever likely to be relevant to contracts concluded on shipment terms. This does not mean, however, that the Act has nothing to tell us about the transfer of risk in international trade. The Act contains five sections which, in the context of domestic sales, provide exceptions to the rule in section 20(1) that risk passes with property: most of these sections put the risk of such loss effectively upon the party whose fault it was that the loss was caused. As the Act does not in terms limit the application of these sections to domestic sales, the question arises as to whether any of them might apply to sale contracts concluded on shipment terms. We shall see presently that that question raises difficult issues of interpretation: by and large, though, we shall see that little turns on the resolution of such issues, either because the relevant sections of the Act simply reflect the position as established by the common law[88]; or because the section very clearly does not apply to any[89] or to many[90] contracts concluded on shipment terms; or, finally, because the section clearly and sensibly applies to such contracts[91]. These sections will now be examined with a view to establishing whether or not they apply to, or at any rate reflect the position in, sale contracts concluded on shipment terms.

i. Section 20(2)

The first of these particular rules is contained in section 20 itself, sub-section (2) of which reads as follows:

> '(2) But where delivery has been delayed through the fault of either buyer or seller the goods are at the risk of the party at fault as regards any loss which might not have occurred but for such fault.'

---

[87] This general rule is sometimes expressly stated in the contract of sale. See, for example, the f o b contract used by the North American Export Grain Association Inc, clause 25 of which reads: 'Anything in this contract to the contrary notwithstanding, seller shall retain title to the commodity until seller has been paid in full, it being understood that risk of loss shall pass to buyer on delivery at discharge end of loading spout.'
[88] Thus, ss 20(2) and 32(2).
[89] Thus, s 33.
[90] Thus, s 32(3).
[91] Thus, s 20(3).

The application of this sub-section to contracts concluded on shipment terms has been the cause of some controversy[92]. To be sure, if a seller on c i f or f o b terms fails to ship the goods within the contract period, then he is in breach of contract[93] and the goods are clearly at his risk, in the sense that he is liable for any deterioration resulting from the delay. This would be the case quite independently of section 20(2) of the Act: for that consequence flows directly from the essential nature of such contracts as shipment rather than arrival contracts; and from the general rule referred to above that the risk of loss or damage in transit passes on shipment of the goods[94].

What is the position, however, where the seller ships the goods within the contract period but causes damage to the goods by delaying their discharge at the contractual destination, for example by giving the carrier new delivery instructions or by delaying the tender of the bill of lading? Who bears the risk of such post-shipment loss: the buyer, because of the general rule that risk passes on shipment; or the seller, because of section 20(2) of the Act? The answer to this question matters because it tells the buyer whom to sue for recovery of that loss: the carrier, if the risk lies on the buyer, the seller, if it does not.

The better view would appear to be that the risk of such loss lies on the seller, and that consequently the buyer can sue the seller for recovery of such loss: this, however, for reasons which go deeper than section 20(2). In the *The Rio Sun*[95], where the seller postponed discharge by delaying the tender of the bill of lading to the buyer, he was liable to the buyer for loss caused by the delay, despite the fact that this had the effect of putting the risk of post-shipment loss upon the seller. Bingham J based his decision on this point squarely upon the duty of the seller to tender a bill of lading: the seller's conduct in this regard 'was as clear a breach of contract by a c i f seller as one could well imagine ...'[96]. This therefore made it unnecessary for the judge to decide whether or not section 20(2) of the Act could apply to sale contracts on shipment

---

[92] See, for example, Benjamin, 2nd edn, para 1695, the text of which was altered in Benjamin, 3rd edn, para 1705, after the earlier text was discussed by Bingham J in *The Rio Sun* [1985] 1 Lloyd's Rep 350 at 362.

[93] See *Bowes v Shand* (1877) 2 App Cas 455 and Chapter 9.1, below.

[94] Where the contract is on f o b terms, if the seller's failure to ship within the contract period is attributable to a breach by the buyer of his contractual obligation to nominate a vessel, then the buyer is in breach and he cannot sue the seller for any ensuing loss. The goods are, in that sense, at the buyer's risk even though they have not yet been shipped. Again, though, it is probably true to say that this result flows from the essential nature of an f o b contract rather than from an application of s 20(2) of the Sale of Goods Act 1979: it is interesting that the main authority for the f o b buyer's obligation to nominate a vessel makes no mention of that sub-section: see *JJ & Cunningham Ltd v Robert A Munro & Co* (1922) 28 Com Cas 42, particularly at 46, where the proposition stated in this note is explicitly explained in terms of risk passing to the buyer before shipment, with no mention being made of s 20(2) of the Sale of Goods Act 1893.

[95] [1985] 1 Lloyd's Rep 350 at 361–362.

[96] Ibid at 362.

terms. The judge nevertheless went on to decide that it could: he could 'see no reason why the sub-section should not have the effect of putting upon [the seller] the risk of any loss which might not have occurred but for the delay which he caused.'[97] The difficulty with this alternative ratio is that it involves the assumption that a c i f or f o b seller effects some form of 'delivery' at the port of discharge, an assumption which sits ill with the nature of those contracts as shipment contracts. That assumption is, however, unnecessary, as a delay in discharge caused by the seller would very likely involve a breach of his duty to procure a contract of carriage on reasonable terms covered by a bill of lading made out for the contract destination[98]: consequently, on the facts here envisaged, the risk of post-shipment loss caused by delay attributable to the seller lies with the seller because he is in breach of his contractual obligations, rather than because section 20(2) imposes upon him duties which somehow arise after shipment of the goods[99].

ii. Section 20(3)

Bailment exists when goods are physically in the possession of someone who does not have property in them: the possessor, known as the bailee, owes the person who gave him possession, the bailor, a duty of care as to the custody of the goods while the bailment lasts[100]. Section 20(3) imposes this duty upon the bailee irrespective of the passage of risk under the contract of sale:

> 'Nothing in this section affects the duties or liabilities of either seller or buyer as a bailee or custodier of the goods of the other party.'

The sub-section has not attracted much litigation in the area of sale contracts concluded on shipment terms, doubtless because problems as to the care and custody of the goods in such contracts normally arise when the goods are in the physical possession not of the seller or buyer but of the carrier: lack of due diligence in the care of the cargo is therefore more commonly dealt with under the contract of carriage than under the contract of sale.

It is possible, however, to envisage situations where the seller is the bailee for the buyer and vice versa, and where, therefore, section 20(3) comes into play. Thus, where, for example, property in specific goods

---

97 Ibid.
98 See generally Chapter 6, below.
99 Likewise, if the buyer delays in exercising an option to nominate a discharge port and loss ensues from such delay, the buyer is in breach of an implied contractual duty to do so within a reasonable time: see *The Rio Sun* [1985] 1 Lloyd's Rep 350 at 358–359. This would put any loss caused by such delay at the buyer's risk, even if it actually occurred prior to shipment, either because the buyer was in breach of such duty or, pace Bingham J, because of s 20(2) of the Act: see ibid. Here again, though, it is submitted that recourse to the Act is difficult, because it involves the assumption that the seller 'delivers' at the port of discharge, and unnecessary, because the result would be the same once the buyer is in breach.
100 See, generally, Crossley-Vaines, Chapter 6.

sold on c i f terms passed before shipment, the seller was held to owe the buyer a bailee's duty of care while the thing sold was in the seller's possession: *Wiehe v Dennis Bros.*[101] This situation is, however, very atypical of contracts concluded on shipment terms, where property normally passes much later than, rather than before, shipment[102].

An altogether more likely set of circumstances triggering section 20(3) into action in this context arises where the buyer repudiates the contract by rejecting the goods against the seller for breach of a condition in the contract[103]. If property and risk had passed to the buyer before rejection, then it is clear that property[104], and probably risk[105], revert to the seller on the rejection of the goods. However, it is quite possible for the buyer who has so repudiated the contract against the seller to find himself still in physical possession of the goods: in the nature of things, the suggestion that the goods should be shipped again at the port of discharge because of a dispute between the buyer and the seller is hardly likely to commend itself to the carrier, at any rate where he has already been paid his freight. In this situation, the buyer in possession of the rejected goods is a bailee for the seller and, pace section 20(3), he owes the seller a duty of care in that capacity, despite the fact that property and risk have reverted to the seller.

iii. Section 32(2)

This section reads as follows:

> 'Unless otherwise authorised by the buyer, the seller must make such contract with the carrier on behalf of the buyer as may be reasonable having regard to the nature of the goods and the other circumstances of the case; and if the seller omits to do so, and the goods are lost or damaged in the course of transit, the buyer may decline to treat the delivery to the carrier as a delivery to himself or may hold the seller responsible in damages.'

The effect of the section is that where the seller fails in his duty to make a contract of carriage on reasonable terms, he is taken not to have performed his duty to deliver the goods[106]. Consequently, the goods remain at his risk, in the sense that he is liable to the buyer for any loss or

---

[101] (1913) 29 TLR 250.

[102] See Chapter 4. 2.(c), above.

[103] See, generally, Chapter 9, below.

[104] *Kwei Tek Chao (t/a Zung Fu Co) v British Traders and Shippers Ltd* [1954] 2 QB 459 at 473.

[105] See Risk in the Law of Sale, L. S. Sealy, in [1972B] CLJ 225 at 243.

[106] Taken, for this purpose, to be the handing over of the goods to the carrier; see s 32(1), which reads: 'Where, in pursuance of a contract of sale, the seller is authorised or required to send the goods to the buyer, delivery of the goods to a carrier (whether named by the buyer or not) for the purpose of transmission to the buyer is prima facie deemed to be a delivery of the goods to the buyer.' In contracts concluded on shipment terms, this section does not, of course, state the totality of the seller's duty to deliver, which includes, as well as the duty physically to ship the goods, the duty to tender documents covering the goods shipped: see Chapter 1, above.

deterioration resulting from this breach of his obligations under the contract of sale[107].

Though not restricted in terms to the sale of goods carried by sea, this section would appear, at any rate at first sight, to be particularly suited to contracts concluded on shipment terms, where sellers do typically contract for the carriage of the goods sold to the buyer's chosen port. The words 'make such contract [of carriage] with the carrier *on behalf of the buyer*', however, cause some difficulty. If interpreted strictly as meaning 'as agent for the buyer', these words would exclude from the application of the section contracts concluded on c i f , c & f , f o b with additional services or straight f o b terms[108]. In the first three of these types of contract, the seller concludes the contract of carriage in his own name and then transfers it to the buyer; in the last type of contract, the seller concludes no contract of carriage at all: in none of these types of contract does the seller contract with the carrier as agent for the buyer. Consequently, on this reading, section 32(2) would appear to be applicable only to f o b contracts of the classic variety, that is to say where the seller does contract with the carrier on the buyer's behalf. If this were the case, a c i f buyer of, say, animal carcasses requiring refrigeration would have no cause of action against the seller for loss caused by the fact that the contract of carriage concluded by the seller imposed no duty on the carrier to provide refrigerated storage on board ship.

Fortunately for buyers in this position, this rather technical point about the wording of section 32(2) seems never to have been pursued in litigation. Indeed, such dicta as we have appear to have assumed that the section applies to contracts on shipment terms across the board[109]. This, presumably, is because litigants have felt that, even if section 32(2) of the Act were inapplicable, the courts would simply arrive at the same result by implying a similar term of their own making and impose upon the seller an obligation to conclude a contract of carriage on reasonable terms[110]. Consequently, it is probably safe to say that section 32(2) of the Act applies to contracts on shipment terms[111], or that if it does not, this makes no difference in practice.

iv. Section 32(3)

This section reads as follows:

'Unless otherwise agreed, where goods are sent by the seller to the

---

[107] Rather, that is, than the carrier being liable for such loss under the contract of carriage.

[108] See *Pyrene Co Ltd v Scindia Navigation Co Ltd* [1954] 2 QB 402 at 424; and, generally, Chapter 1.2.(a).ii, above.

[109] *Houlder Bros & Co Ltd v Public Works Comr* [1908] AC 276 at 290; *Tsakiroglou & Co v Noblee Thorl GmbH* [1961] 2 All ER 179 at 183H, 191D and 194I; and *The Rio Sun* [1985] 1 Lloyd's Rep 350 at 359-360.

[110] See *Ranson v Manufacture d'Engrais* (1922) 13 Ll L Rep 205 and *Finska Cellulosaforeningen v Westfield Paper Company Ltd* (1941) 46 Com Cas 87, discussed further at Chapter 6, below, fn 24.

[111] Thus, see Atiyah, at 319.

buyer by a route involving sea transit, under circumstances in which it is usual to insure, the seller must give such notice to the buyer as may enable him to insure them during their sea transit; and if the seller fails to do so, the goods are at his risk during such transit.'

The effect of the section is to put upon the seller the risk of post-shipment loss where he has failed to give the buyer sufficient information to insure the goods while they are in transit. Although, again, the section appears to be particularly well suited to all contracts involving sea transit, on closer inspection it is clear that the section is inappropriate to most contracts concluded on shipment terms.

Thus, where the seller himself is under an obligation to effect insurance cover, the section is evidently inapplicable: the buyer needs no information from the seller in order to effect insurance, quite simply because he, the buyer, effects no insurance. Thus, the section is inapplicable to contracts concluded on c i f terms[112]; and to contracts concluded on f o b terms with the additional duty on the seller of effecting insurance.

Equally clearly, though for a slightly different reason, the section does not sit comfortably with sale contracts concluded on straight f o b terms. Here, the buyer concludes both the contract of carriage and the insurance contract: consequently, he is likely to have at his disposal all the information he requires to effect the insurance cover appropriate to the sea transit contracted for under the contract of carriage. It seems, however, that where in these circumstances the seller does have information which the buyer needs in order to effect appropriate cover, then section 32(3) imposes upon the seller the duty to pass such information to the buyer: thus, in *Wimble Sons & Co v Rosenberg & Sons* [113], the Court of Appeal held, by a majority, that the section could apply in such circumstances[114].

---

[112] *Law & Bonar Ltd v British American Tobacco Co* [1916] 2 KB 605. In this case, Rowlatt J held that a c i f seller was not liable under the section where the buyer found himself with no insurance cover for war risks: such cover was not 'usual' at the time the contract was made, and the section therefore imposed no duty on the seller to pass information to the buyer which would enable him to effect such cover. The judge was careful, however, to leave room for the application of the section 'to a contract c i f made at a time when insurances other than those to be provided by the seller—eg against war risks—are usual': see p 609. This dictum may have been uttered out of an excess of caution, for surely, in such circumstances, the seller would be caught by his common law duty to effect 'usual' insurance cover, rather than by any duty of notification under s 32(3) of the Act. It is just conceivable, though, that a contract concluded in such circumstances might expressly leave it to the buyer to effect such 'usual' war risk cover and in this, somewhat remote, possibility, s 32(3), or perhaps some implied term to the same effect, might impose upon the seller a duty of notification: see Benjamin, para 1701.

[113] [1913] 3 KB 743.

[114] The majority on this point was composed of Buckley and Vaughan Williams LJJ, both of whom rejected an ingenious, if technical, point which urged Vaughan Williams LJ to dissent on the law. The argument was that if, pace s 32(1), the f o b seller delivered the goods to the buyer by delivering them to the carrier, then the goods could not, for the purposes of s 32(3), be said to be *'sent* by the seller to the buyer by a route involving sea transit': see [1913] 3 KB 743 at 756-757, for the minority view, and 749-750 and 752 for the majority view.

In the result, though, it was held, again by a majority, that the seller was not in breach because the buyer did have all the facts necessary for effecting the appropriate insurance cover. Although the contract in the case was on straight f o b terms, it left the choice of vessel to the seller, who failed to give the name of the vessel to the buyer before the cargo was lost at sea: it was held by the majority[115] in the Court of Appeal that the buyer could have effected insurance cover without this item of information and that the seller was therefore not in breach. If the seller in *Wimble Sons & Co v Rosenberg & Sons*[116] was not in breach of section 32(3), the upshot of the case, it is suggested[117], is that the section will hardly ever be relevant to straight f o b contracts.

If the section is never, or hardly ever, applicable to contracts concluded on c i f terms, on f o b terms with the additional duty on the seller of effecting insurance, or on straight f o b terms, which contracts on shipment terms are left for section 32(3) to bite on? It would appear that there is no reason in principle for barring the application of the section to c & f contracts, to f o b contracts of the classic variety, and to f o b contracts with the additional duty imposed on the seller to effect the contract of carriage but not of insurance. These three types of contract impose the duty of concluding the contract of carriage on the seller and the duty to effect insurance cover on the buyer: in each of them, consequently, the seller is quite likely to have information about the carriage contract which the buyer will need to make arrangements for insurance cover[118]. The seller must pass such information to the buyer, failing which the goods are at the risk of the seller despite the fact that the goods may have been lost or damaged after shipment.

v. Section 33

This section reads as follows:

> 'Where the seller of goods agrees to deliver them at his own risk at a place other than that where they are when sold, the buyer must nevertheless (unless otherwise agreed) take any risk of deterioration in the goods necessarily incident to the course of transit.'

The section is clearly inapplicable to contracts concluded on shipment terms, where it is hardly likely that the seller will agree that the goods

---

[115] The majority here was composed differently: Hamilton LJ and Buckley LJ, with Vaughan Williams LJ dissenting.

[116] [1913] 3 KB 743, followed in *Northern Steel and Hardware Co Ltd v John Batt & Co (London) Ltd* (1917) 33 TLR 516.

[117] See, in a similar vein, Atiyah, at 314.

[118] There appears to be some doubt as to whether the section can apply at all where the transit involves carriage by some means other than 'sea transit', i e where the carriage is multi-modal: see Benjamin para 2006, where the editors come to the clearly desirable conclusion that the section can and should be judicially extended to cover this sort of case.

will travel at his risk[119]. Whether buying c i f or f o b , the buyer expects to run the risk of transit and this, not because of section 33 of the Sale of Goods Act, but quite simply because that is what he buys. The seller performs his obligations under the contract so long as, in c i f contracts, he ships goods, or procures goods shipped, for the agreed destination, which goods are covered by the shipping documents stipulated for in the contract[120]; and so long as, in f o b , he loads the goods on the nominated vessel at the port of loading, together with any additional obligations he may have assumed in the contract. If the seller has performed these duties, the buyer must look to the carrier for his remedy if the goods arrive at the discharge port the worse for wear. Consequently, the premise which triggers section 33 into operation is inapplicable here.

(b) The general rule in shipment sales

These remarks on section 33, referring as they do to the essential nature of c i f and f o b contracts as shipment rather than arrival contracts, bring us back to the general rule that the risk of loss or damage in transit passes to the buyer, generally separately from property, on or as from shipment. Our task now is to examine the workings of this rule in greater

---

[119] Thus, in *Law & Bonar Ltd v British American Tobacco Co Ltd*, Rowlatt J said that a clause stating that the goods were at seller's risk until actual delivery at the port of discharge was repugnant to a c i f contract: [1916] 2 KB 605 at 608. It is less clear whether a clause postponing payment, wholly or partly, to the discharge of the goods is equally repugnant. See *Houlder Bros & Co Ltd v Public Works Comr* [1908] AC 276 at 290; *The Julia* [1949] AC 293 at 312; and *The Gabbiano* [1940] P 166 at 174, 175 for the view that such clauses are difficult to accommodate in a c i f contract properly so called. The contrary view, that such clauses are quite consistent with c i f contracts, seems to have been assumed to be correct in a number of cases: see, for example, *Arnhold Karberg & Co v Blythe Green Jourdain & Co* [1915] 2 KB 379; affd [1916] 1 KB 495, and other cases cited at Benjamin, para 1615. It is difficult to reconcile the dicta on this point, other than by suggesting, as does Schmitthoff at 47, that the impact of such clauses on the nature of the contract depends on the intention of the parties; or, as does Benjamin at para 1615, that the effect of such clauses is simply to exempt the buyer from the obligation to pay the price, rather than to make the seller liable for breach for non-arrival, as he would be if risk were to remain with him. The better view seems to be that the courts are unlikely to interpret a clause in a c i f contract such as to impose upon the seller a guarantee of arrival: thus, in *Tregelles v Sewell* (1862) 7 H & N 574; affd (1863) 7 H & N 584, a clause 'delivered at Harburgh [the discharge port], cost, freight and insurance,' was construed as simply describing the destination of the goods rather than defining the point at which risk passed; and in *The Wise* [1989] 1 Lloyd's Rep 96, a clause 'Arrival: March 15-30 1986' was construed simply to mean that the vessel was expected to reach her destination by that date, rather than that the seller guaranteed such arrival. Moreover, Leggatt J was of the view that this would follow from the essential nature of a shipment contract even without an express clause passing risk at the loading port: see pp 100-101. [The case was remitted by the Court of Appeal to the Commercial Court on grounds irrelevant to the present point [1989] 2 Lloyd's Rep 451.] For comparative comments, see generally Out-Turn Clauses in CIF Contracts in the Oil Trade, J.J. Lightburn & G.M. Nienaber, 1987 LMCLQ 177, 183-185; Practising CIF and FOB Today, J. Lebuhn, (1981) 1 European Transport Law, 24 at 24-28; and The Law of International Commercial Transactions (Lex Mercatoria), H.J. Berman and C. Kaufman, in 19 Harvard International Law Journal, (1979) 221 at 235-237.

[120] *Shipton, Anderson & Co v John Weston & Co* (1922) 10 Ll L Rep 762 at 763.

detail than we have done so far. Before we do so, though, we must make two caveats to the rule that risk passes on or as from shipment.

i. Risk of loss or damage to the goods and breach of other duties

The first is that the fact that risk passes to the buyer on shipment does not mean that the seller is discharged from any liability towards the buyer under the contract of sale. While the passage of risk means that the seller has performed his duty to ship goods or procure shipped goods[121], or to load goods on board a vessel nominated by the buyer[122], it tells us nothing about whether the seller has performed his other duties under the contract. Thus, if, for example, the seller tenders a bill of lading made out for a destination other than that stipulated for in the contract of sale, he would be in breach of contract[123] regardless of the fact that he has performed his physical obligation to deliver goods of contract specification.

ii. The rule in Mash and Murrell[124]

The second caveat to the proposition that risk for loss or damage to goods in transit passes on or as from shipment is provided by the rule in *Mash and Murrell Ltd v Joseph I Emanuel Ltd*[125], a case in which the plaintiff buyers sued the sellers for damages in respect of a cargo of potatoes which reached the buyers in a rotten state. The upshot of the case can be stated thus: when we say that a seller on shipment terms must ship goods, procure shipped goods, or load goods on a nominated vessel in a 'merchantable' state[126], what we mean is that the goods must remain merchantable from the time of shipment until arrival at destination and for a reasonable time for disposal[127]. Thus, if the buyer

---

[121] In c i f and c & f contracts.

[122] In f o b contracts.

[123] Indeed, in repudiatory breach: see Chapter 6.3.(d), below.

[124] [1961] 1 All ER 485, per Diplock J; revsd on the facts at [1962] 1 All ER 77n, CA.

[125] Ibid.

[126] A duty imposed on every seller of goods by s 14(2) of the Sale of Goods Act 1893. The plaintiffs put their case in three different ways: a breach of the warranty imposed by s 14(1) of the 1893 Act that goods would be fit for the purpose for which the goods are required; a breach of the warranty of merchantability imposed by s 14(2) of the Act; and breach of a common law warranty in identical terms. Diplock J saw no great distinction between these three different avenues towards the same destination: see [1961] 1 All ER 485 at 489D.

[127] See [1961] 1 All ER 485 at 490 I. It has been argued that this warranty may be inconsistent with s 33 of the Sale of Goods Act 1979, which puts upon the buyer the risk of loss necessarily incident to the course of transit where the seller agrees to deliver them *at his own risk*: see Damage Resulting from Natural Decay under Insurance, Carriage and Sale of Goods Contracts, D. M. Sassoon, (1965) 28 MLR 180 at 189-191 and Deterioration of Goods in Transit, by the same author, at (1962) JBL 351. Professor Sassoon argues that if s 33 puts the risk of 'necessarily incident' loss upon the buyer where the seller delivers at his own risk, then a fortiori the same risk would rest on the buyer where he took the risk of any loss on or as from shipment. This result would jar, so Professor Sassoon argues, with the rule in *Mash & Murrell*; the inconsistency can be ironed out, the argument proceeds, by allocating the risk of extraordinary loss to the buyer under the usual rule in shipment sales (reflecting s 33), and that of 'necessarily

can prove that at the time of shipment, the goods were not, as it were, prospectively merchantable in that sense for a normal voyage, then the buyer has a right of action against the seller under the contract of sale[128]. In *Mash and Murrell*[129] itself, the Court of Appeal held that the voyage actually pursued by the carrier was not a normal voyage and that consequently the sellers were not in breach of the warranty of merchantability as drawn by Diplock J. Thus, the buyer's remedy, if any, lay against the carrier rather than against the seller[130].

iii. Risk passes 'on or as from shipment'

We return now to our main task in this part of the chapter, namely to examine the nature and effect of the rule that risk in sale contracts concluded on shipment terms passes on or as from the shipment of the goods. In the preliminary comments to this part of the chapter, we saw that the reversal of the assumption in section 20(1) that risk passes with property was justified by the very nature of the seller's obligations under a contract on shipment terms. If the seller's obligation is to ship goods covered by the stipulated documents, he is not in breach of contract simply because, without more[131], the goods have failed to arrive in the quantity or condition stated in the contract. This is what is meant by the proposition that risk in such contracts passes on or as from shipment, a proposition for which the authority is both clear and

---

incident' loss to the seller under the rule in *Mash & Murrell* (which provides an exception to s 33). With respect, the argument is based somewhat perilously on the supposition that s 33 of the Act has something to tell us about risk in shipment sales, a supposition which has been discussed in the text above at Chapter 4.3.(a).v. The rule in *Mash & Murrell* is much more clearly analysed simply as an exception to the general rule that risk in shipment sales passes on or as from shipment, quite independently of s 33 which, as has been argued above, has no application in this type of contract. The rule was adopted without critical comment by Bingham J in *The Rio Sun* [1985] 1 Lloyd's Rep 350 at 358, where a passing reference was made to the criticism of the case in Sassoon, pp 214-219, 2nd edn (see pp 247-253, 3rd edn). At 252, Sassoon makes mention of a dictum by Diplock LJ in *Teheran Europe Co v ST Belton Ltd* [1968] 2 QB 545 at 560, to the effect that he had stated the law in *Mash & Murrell* 'with incautious wideness'. With respect, the comparison is misplaced: the issue in *Mash & Murrell* was whether the implied term of merchantability applied to c i f contracts; that in *Teheran* was whether the implied term of fitness for purpose was wide enough to include the loss complained of by the plaintiff.

[128] Of course, if the buyer finds this difficult to prove, and if the master had signed a clean bill of lading stating the goods to have been shipped in apparent good order and condition, the buyer would have a claim against the carrier under the contract of carriage supported by the incontrovertible representation that the goods had been shipped in apparent good order and condition: see the Carriage of Goods by Sea Act 1971, Sch art III.4 and, where the Act does not apply, *Compania Naviera Vasconzada v Churchill and Sim* [1906] 1 KB 237.

[129] [1962] 1 All ER 77n.

[130] Of course, had the sellers actually contracted for a voyage which was not usual, that would have put them in breach of their quite separate obligation to conclude a contract of carriage on 'usual' terms: see Chapter 6.2, below.

[131] Although, as we have just seen, the seller may be liable for breaches of other duties under the contract: see Chapter 4.3.(b).i, above.

unimpeachable[132]. The practical effect of the transfer of risk is equally clear: as indicated earlier[133], once risk passes, the buyer's remedies, if any, for loss or damage to the goods in transit lie no longer against the seller but against the carrier or the cargo insurer.

The rule causes concern because it appears to allow the seller to pass property in goods which are, at that time, or even when the contract was concluded, lost or damaged. While the passage of risk on shipment but prior to the transfer of property appears perfectly unexceptionable, to pass risk 'as from shipment', prior to contract[134] or prior to appropriation to a particular contract, smacks of retroactivity and ought therefore to be avoided or carefully justified.

In this last part of the chapter, we shall be examining the rule that risk passes on or as from shipment, with a view to identifying the situations where its effect might be to allow the seller to pass property in lost or damaged goods. The essence of our question is whether a seller who passes property in goods which are lost or damaged is thereby putting himself in breach of contract. In answering that question, it is helpful to consider first how risk is allocated where the goods are lost or damaged *after* property has passed to the buyer; and then secondly, how risk is allocated where loss or damage occurs *before* property has passed. In either case, we also need to distinguish between a sale of specific goods, i e 'goods identified and agreed on at the time a contract of sale is made'[135] and a sale of goods which are unascertained at the time the contract is made. Although, as we have seen, sale contracts concluded on shipment terms more commonly relate to unascertained goods[136], the passage of risk in specific goods sold on shipment terms is being included here for the sake of completeness.

a. Where the loss or damage occurs *after* the property has passed

Where the goods are specific, property would normally pass when the contract is concluded[137], and risk would, on the basis of the normal presumption laid down in section 20(1) of the 1979 Act, pass with the

---

[132] *The Julia* [1949] AC 293 at 309, and other cases cited by Benjamin at para 1694, fn 77 for c i f contracts; and *The Parchim* [1918] AC 157 at 168-9, and other cases cited by Benjamin in para 1869, fn 4 for f o b contracts.

[133] See Chapter 4.1.(b) and 4.3, above.

[134] Thus, in c i f and c & f contracts, the seller can perform his contractual duty physically to deliver goods by procuring goods which are already at sea and bound for the agreed destination. If risk passes 'as from shipment', then the buyer bears the risk of loss or damage which precedes the contract under which he bought the goods. In f o b contracts, of course, there is no need for the 'or as from shipment' part of the rule, as the seller cannot sell goods already at sea on f o b terms: see Benjamin, para 1869.

[135] See s 61 of the Sale of Goods Act 1979.

[136] See Chapter 4.2, above.

[137] Under s 18, r 1, of the Sale of Goods Act 1979, which reads: 'Where there is an unconditional contract for the sale of specific goods in a deliverable state the property in the goods passes to the buyer when the contract is made, and it is immaterial whether the time of payment or the time of delivery, or both, be postponed.'

property: consequently, the buyer bears the risk of loss or damage occurring after the property has passed. This is true not only of ordinary domestic sales, but also of sale contracts concluded on shipment terms, and this even though property and risk may not pass together in such sales. Where it is clear from the contract that risk was intended to pass with property, notwithstanding the fact that the parties are contracting on c i f terms, then there is clearly no problem: the normal presumption in section 20(1) would apply and the risk of loss or damage lies with the buyer[138]. On the other hand, the contract or the surrounding circumstances may well make it clear that the passage of property is to be postponed, as well it might, given that the parties are free to depart from the presumption in section 18, rule 1[139]. Where the parties do depart, risk passes nonetheless on shipment, under the general rule applicable to contracts concluded on shipment terms. This, however, makes no difference in the situation here being examined, namely where the loss or damage occurs after the property has passed: no money turns on the proposition that risk passes before property, because the loss has on this hypothesis occurred after both property and risk have passed to the buyer.

Where the goods were unascertained when the contract was concluded, but are now ascertained and unconditionally appropriated to the buyer, and the loss or damage occurs after ascertainment and appropriation, then property has passed before the loss, under sections 16 and 18, rule 5 of the 1979 Act[140]. An example of this situation in the context of a contract concluded on shipment terms[141] is where the goods are damaged after discharge from an undifferentiated bulk into a clearly appropriated parcel of goods now belonging to the buyer. Risk here will have been with the buyer since shipment under the general rule that risk passes on or as from shipment. However, as the loss or damage has occurred after appropriation, the effect of the rule is not retrospective: the buyer is simply running the risk of loss or damage to the goods he owns.

b. Where the loss or damage occurs *before* the property has passed

Where the goods are specific, property will normally pass to the buyer under section 18, rule 1, as we have seen, when the contract is concluded.

---

[138] See *Wiehe v Dennis Bros* (1913) 29 TLR 250 at 252, where Scrutton J indicated obiter that this would be the position in such circumstances. The judge nonetheless found that the defendant seller was liable in damages to the plaintiff buyer because the seller had failed in his duty as bailee while the specific horse sold was in his custody. The case is basically an application of s 20(3) of the Sale of Goods Act 1893: see Chapter 4.3.(a).ii, above.

[139] The governing paragraph of s 18 starts with the words 'Unless a different intention appears...' The clearest example of such an intention to derogate from s 18, r 1, would be an express reservation of title clause in the contract itself. It is rather more doubtful whether the term 'cash against documents' would have this effect, since r 1 applies, in terms, whether or not the time of payment is postponed.

[140] Discussed earlier at Chapter 4.2.(a) and (b), above.

[141] Where the contract is not on shipment terms, the position is clear: property and risk will have passed together, through the combined operation of ss 18, r 5 and 20(1) of the Sale of Goods Act 1979.

Consequently, the situation envisaged here might arise where the loss or damage to the goods occurs before the contract is concluded. Whether or not the contract is negotiated on shipment terms, if the goods are *lost* before the contract is concluded, the contract is avoided: this, as a result of section 7 of the 1979 Act where the contract is on shipment terms[142], and as a result of section 6 of the same Act where it is not. Where, on the other hand, the goods had simply been *damaged* before the contract was concluded, then if the contract is on shipment terms[143], the risk of such damage would probably be borne by the buyer on the basis of the rule that the risk will have passed on or as from shipment. Property will have passed either at the time the contract is concluded, as envisaged in section 18, rule 1, or later[144]: whichever of the two it is, risk will have passed to the buyer, before property, as from shipment. Thus, the seller appears to be entitled to sell the buyer damaged goods, leaving the buyer to search for a remedy elsewhere in respect of such loss.

Where goods sold on shipment terms are unascertained or unappropriated when the goods are lost or damaged, property cannot have passed[145] at the time of loss or damage. The allocation of risk here depends on whether the loss or damage occurred before or after shipment. If goods which the seller had intended to send to the buyer are lost or damaged before shipment, then it would, of course, be a nonsense to suggest that any risk in any goods had passed to the buyer: in such a case, there are clearly no contract goods to speak of and the seller will simply have to find other goods of the contract type with which to satisfy his customer[146]. Risk is, after all, said to pass on or as from shipment and not a moment earlier[147]. However, where the loss or damage occurs after the shipment of contract goods in an undifferentiated bulk but before ascertainment or appropriation to a particular contract, the general rule would pass risk to the buyer as from the time of shipment: here again, consequently, the seller will have appropriated lost or damaged goods to the buyer, who would need to look elsewhere for his remedy, if any, for such loss or damage[148].

---

[142] Section 7 reads: 'Where there is an agreement to sell specific goods and subsequently the goods, without any fault on the part of the seller or buyer, perish before the risk passes to the buyer, the agreement is avoided.' An 'agreement to sell' is defined by s 2(5) as a contract of sale where the transfer of property in the goods is to 'take place at a future time or subject to some condition later to be fulfilled.' It would appear that a sale of specific goods on shipment terms would be an agreement to sell within this section, as property is very likely to pass at a future time or subject to a condition later to be fulfilled.

[143] If the contract is not on shipment terms, the result would be that the risk of such damage lies with the seller, on the basis that risk passes with property: s 20(1) of the 1979 Act.

[144] If s 18, rule 1 is derogated from by the contract: see fn 139, above.

[145] See ss 16 and 18, r 5 of the 1979 Act.

[146] See *Hindley & Co Ltd v East Indian Produce Co Ltd* [1973] 2 Lloyd's Rep 515.

[147] Although, of course, it is perfectly open to the parties to agree that risk in the goods passes to the buyer before shipment: see, for example, *The Galatia* [1979] 2 Lloyd's Rep 450.

[148] See *Inglis v Stock* (1885) 10 App Cas 263. Where the contract is not on shipment terms, both property and risk will normally be with the seller, property because of s 18, r 5, and risk because of s 20(1). Consequently, the seller is in breach of contract if the goods

The upshot is that the seller on shipment terms appears to be entitled to pass property in lost or damaged goods to the buyer in two sets of circumstances: firstly, where he sells specific goods which were damaged before the contract was concluded; secondly, where he sells or appropriates unascertained goods which were lost or damaged before the contract or before appropriation to it. It will have been noted that in either case, the law on the matter has here been stated somewhat cautiously: this, because the authorities on this particular application of the general rule are unclear[149], and because writers in the area are divided[150].

The view here adopted, namely that the seller can, in the circumstances envisaged, pass the property in lost or damaged goods to the buyer, can be supported by two arguments, the first of which is based on the essential nature of c i f and f o b contracts as shipment contracts; the second of which is based on practical convenience.

Firstly, it must be recalled that the retrospective passage of risk to the buyer does not mean that he is left without a remedy: it means simply that the seller has performed his duty of physical delivery and that the buyer must look elsewhere for a remedy if the goods do not arrive at the agreed destination, or if they arrive in a damaged state. This is the very reason why the parties have agreed on sale terms which envisage the purchase of carriage and insurance contracts[151].

---

are not delivered to the buyer in good condition. However, the position appears to be different where the sale is of an undifferentiated part of an identified bulk. Where the entire bulk has been destroyed, the seller might be able to plead frustration, performance being frustrated if the whole of the identified bulk has been lost. Where the entire bulk has been damaged, as opposed to lost, the buyer bears the risk of such loss: see *Sterns Ltd v Vickers Ltd* [1923] 1 KB 78. This latter case provides a rare instance, in the context of sale contracts which are not on shipment terms, of risk passing before property: see Atiyah, at 246-248 for a discussion of its exceptional nature in domestic sales.

[149] For the proposition stated in the text, see *C Groom Ltd v Barber* [1915] 1 KB 316 at 322-325; *Manbre Saccharine Co v Corn Products Co* [1919] 1 KB 198; and *Ross T Smyth & Co Ltd v TD Bailey & Son & Co* [1940] 3 All ER 60 at 70. Against that proposition, see *Olympia Oil & Cake Co Ltd and Produce Brokers Co Ltd* [1915] 1 KB 233, a decision of the Divisional Court. The contract in this case was not a c i f contract: see McArdie J in *Manbre Saccharine* [1919] 1 KB 198 at 201; moreover, the net result of the litigation in *Olympia* was that the seller *was* in the end held to have been entitled to appropriate goods which he knew to be lost, this on the basis of a custom to that effect: see the ensuing litigation at [1916] 1 AC 314, [1916] 2 KB 296, and [1917] 1 KB 320.

[150] In favour of the view stated in the text, see Sassoon, paras 252-253; and The Appropriation to a CIF Contract of Goods Lost or Damaged at Sea, J.D. Feltham, (1975) JBL 273. Against that view, see Goode, pp 595-7, and Benjamin, at paras 1678, 9, and 1697. For a third view, namely that a seller ought to be able to appropriate but not to contract for the sale of lost or damaged goods, see The Law of International Commercial Transactions (Lex Mercatoria), H.J. Berman and C. Kaufman, in 19 Harvard International Law Journal, (1978) 221 at 242.

[151] See *Manbre Saccharine Co v Corn Products Co* [1919] 1 KB 198 at 204; and The Appropriation to a CIF Contract of Goods Lost or Damaged at Sea, J.D. Feltham, (1975) JBL 273 at 275.

Secondly, the alternative view, namely that the seller in the circumstances envisaged is in breach of his contract of sale, would lead to a circuitous chain of litigation, likely to be extremely difficult of resolution. The effect of this alternative view would be that a seller would be liable to his buyer if he had passed property in goods which were, at that time, lost or damaged. Consider how this would work where loss or damage had occurred in a cargo of a commodity shipped in bulk and traded down a string. Each buyer would have a cause of action against his seller for breach of the seller's duty to deliver goods of contract specification; each seller would wish to rebut liability by proving that the goods were in perfect condition when he sold down the string. This proof might be difficult to muster in practice[152]; moreover, the ensuing, and expensive, litigation would be pursued between the parties least likely to have caused the loss or damage, namely the traders[153]. On the other hand, if the seller is not in breach and if consequently the buyer does bear, as is here suggested, the risk of loss or damage in the circumstances envisaged, the litigation ensuing from such loss or damage is altogether neater and more appropriately directed against the party most likely to have caused it, namely the carrier[154]. The result of the seller's discharge and the effect of the passage of risk as between seller and buyer would, on this hypothesis, be a cargo claim between the receiver and the carrier, a perfectly natural result in a sale contract concluded on shipment terms.

---

[152] The difficulty of proving where goods are lost is one of the arguments put by Mr J.D. Feltham in favour of the view adopted in the text: see The Appropriation to a CIF Contract of Goods Lost or Damaged at Sea, at (1975) JBL 273. The same issue is referred to in Benjamin: although the editors of Benjamin take the view that a seller *cannot* appropriate goods which are lost (see fn 150 above), they place the risk of deterioration, as opposed to loss, prior to appropriation upon the buyer, on the basis that risk passes on or as from shipment, because '[i]t will often be impossible to show whether the deterioration occurred before or after appropriation': see para 1680; but see Feltham, as above, at 277.

[153] At any rate until the original shipper sued the carrier under the contract of carriage. The curcuity of action which would ensue if the seller could *not* appropriate goods after loss or damage is anticipated by the editors of Benjamin at para 1679: it is explained away by the observation that each seller up the string can escape liability by inserting a clause in his contract to the effect that the buyer must accept the original appropriation made by the shipper.

[154] At any rate, if the buyer has either a bill of lading or a ship's delivery order for the same quantity: either document would give the buyer locus standi in contract, under s 1 of the Bills of Lading Act 1855 and under the rule in *Brandt v Liverpool* [1924] 1 KB 575: see, generally, Chapter 3, above. The buyer's locus standi in this situation is queried in Goode, at 596, and this is Professor Goode's main argument against the passage of risk in unappropriated goods: the buyer, it is argued, would have no remedy against the carrier, because s 1 of the 1855 Act would not apply. With respect, this assumes that for the Act to apply, property in the goods must have passed *at the same time as* the transfer of the bill of lading, but see *The Delfini* [see (1989) Times, 11 August] and above at Chapter 3.1.(a).iv.

PART II

Documentary duties—a bill acceptable to buyers and banks

CHAPTER 5

Qualities of the bill of lading as a receipt

1. The bill's function as a receipt

2. Merchants' rights to demand a clear receipt from the carrier

    (a) The seller: does he have a right to a firm receipt

        i. At common law?

        ii. Under the Carriage of Goods by Sea Act 1971?

    (b) The buyer: does he have a right to a firm receipt

        i. At common law?

        ii. Under the Carriage of Goods by Sea Act 1971?

3. Requirements of the bill of lading as a receipt in sale contracts and in letters of credit

    (a) The bill must cover the contract goods and no others

        i. Statements as to quantity

        ii. Carrier's qualifications on the statement as to quantity

    (b) The bill must be 'clean'

In Chapters 3 and 4, we concentrated on those aspects of the bill of lading which gave the buyer the right to demand possession of the goods from the carrier and the right to sue him for damages, whether in contract or in tort, if the goods were discharged in a quantity less than, or in a condition worse than, that in which they had been shipped. The bill's function as a document of possession and its role in establishing the buyer's title to sue are crucial to the commercial value of the document to the buyer: there is, however, more to the document than that. Once possession is acquired and title to sue established, the buyer aggrieved by short delivery or damage to goods has two further issues to resolve: he needs to prove first that the carrier has in fact delivered less goods, or worse, than were shipped; secondly, he needs to be clear about the contractual regime, if any, regulating his cause of action against the carrier. Both these issues form the substance of two further functions of bills of lading, as a receipt for goods and as evidence of the contract of carriage, typically discussed as such in carriage textbooks[1]. These two functions are also relevant, however, from the point of view of the contract of sale. The buyer is the party ultimately to benefit from the value of the bill as a receipt and as evidence of the contract of carriage: he it is who is likely to sue a negligent carrier under that contract on the basis of statements contained in that receipt. The seller, though, at any rate where the sale is on c i f or c & f terms, on classic f o b terms, or on f o b terms with additional services[2], is the party who, of the two parties to the sale contract[3], has the greater degree of control over the tenor and contents of the bill actually issued: however, he expects to be paid the price on tender of the shipping documents to the buyer or to the confirming bank and is therefore unlikely to be too particular about the precise contents of the bill of lading if this will delay the moment of issue of the bill and consequently the time of tender and payment. Thus, the situation is one where the party with the right to make demands of the carrier with regard to the contents of the bill of lading, the seller, has little incentive to do so; while the party with the incentive, the buyer, appears to have no right to make such demands at the point of issue of the bill, because he is not at that time privy to any contract with the carrier. In these circumstances, the buyer has a direct interest in how the seller exercises whatever control he has over the type of bill of lading issued by the carrier; hence, the sale contract will frequently contain terms describing the bill of lading which the seller must, in performance of his duties under the contract of sale, take from the carrier, in exercise of his rights under the contract of carriage. These terms in the sale contract give the seller the incentive to ensure, as far as the law and practice of carriage allow him to, that the bill issued to him by the carrier for transfer to the buyer be as favourable to the buyer as possible. Thus, for example, where Incoterms form part of a contract on c i f terms, the seller must tender a bill of lading which is clean; which covers the contract goods; and which is made out for the agreed port of destination[4]. The first two of the obligations just mentioned relate to the function of the bill of lading as a receipt and they will be discussed in this chapter; the last duty—to tender a bill

---

[1]   See, for example, Scrutton, arts 52 to 62 as to the receipt function and art 30 as to the role of the bill as evidence of the contract of carriage; likewise, Carver at paras 102-118 and 84-101.

[2]   Where the sale is on straight f o b terms, the seller will have nothing to do with the issue of the bill and will therefore be in no position to exercise any control over the form in which it is issued. See, generally, Chapter 1.2.(a).ii, above.

[3]   The bill is, of course, the carrier's document and, as we shall see, it is the carrier who has the ultimate degree of control over what it says about the goods and about the terms of the contract of carriage.

[4]   Standard form contracts too, like GAFTA form 100, may contain stipulations, in greater or less detail than Incoterms, relating to the bill of lading to be tendered by the seller to the buyer. Thus in clause 14, GAFTA 100 binds the seller to tender '[F]ull set(s) of on board Bill(s) of Lading and/or Ship's Delivery Order(s) in negotiable and transferable form.' Where the sale contract contains no express term about the bill of lading, s 32(2) of the Sale of Goods Act 1979 imposes upon the seller the duty to '. . . make such contract with the carrier on behalf of the buyer as may be reasonable having regard to the nature of the goods and other circumstances of the case . . .'

of lading made out for the destination in the sale contract—raises questions relating to the contractual role of the bill of lading and will be discussed in the next chapter.

Again, just as the receipt and contract functions of the bill of lading are of direct significance to the sale contract, so are they clearly linked to the letter of credit where the parties have chosen this mechanism as the method of payment. Thus, for example, the confirming bank will look to see whether a bill tendered by a seller is clean[5] or shipped[6]; or whether it allows for transhipment[7]. The first two qualities relate to issues raised, in terms of the law of carriage by sea, by the function of the bill as a receipt; the last, by the contractual role of the bill of lading. This chapter and the next will consequently include an examination of those areas of the law of letters of credit which have something to say about these functions of bills of lading.

Throughout the two chapters, we shall be looking at the receipt and contractual functions of bills of lading very much from the direction of the sale contract and from that of the letter of credit rather than from that of the contract of carriage: what rights does the buyer have as against the seller with regard to this or that aspect of the bill of lading tendered? And what must the confirming bank look for in a bill of lading tendered by the seller under a letter of credit? In order to understand why a buyer, or a bank, should expect tender of a particular type of bill of lading, however, it is clear that we need to draw upon explanations provided by the law of carriage of goods by sea. Thus, this chapter starts with an examination of what we mean exactly when we say, as carriage lawyers, that the bill of lading is a receipt: we shall be discussing here the binding effect on the carrier of statements about the goods acknowledged by him on the face of the bill. In the next section, we shall ask what rights the seller and the buyer have, as against the carrier, to demand issue of a clear receipt on shipment of the goods. Finally, we shall be asking what a c i f contract and a letter of credit require of a bill of lading tendered by the seller so far as concerns the receipt function of the bill.

1. THE BILL'S FUNCTION AS A RECEIPT

To say that the bill of lading is a receipt is to make a statement about its role in the evidential battle between the cargo-interest and the carrier in a short-delivery or damage claim. The essence of such a claim is that the carrier has not delivered what was shipped: two facts need, therefore, to be proved by the plaintiff, namely, what cargo was shipped and what

---

[5] See UCP art 34.
[6] See UCP art 27. This article will be dealt with in Chapter 9 in our discussion on combined transport documents. It is in the context of containerised transport that the distinction between 'shipped' and 'received' bills of lading is now of most relevance.
[7] See UCP art 29.

cargo was delivered. The plaintiff is likely to be the buyer[8], who will have acquired locus standi to sue the carrier in contract either through section 1 of the Bills of Lading Act 1855 or through the implication of a contract under the rule in *Brandt v Liverpool*[9]. As receiver of the goods, the buyer is well placed to prove what was delivered; in the nature of things, though, he will find it rather more difficult to prove what was shipped, loading having taken place in a foreign port in an operation over which he is unlikely to have exercised any supervision. Unassisted

---

[8]   Although, despite the sale and consequent transfer of locus standi to sue the carrier, the seller may, qua shipper, in certain circumstances retain his own standing to sue: see Benjamin, para 1460.

[9]   [1924] 1 KB 575 and see generally Chapter 4 above. The buyer may also have one or more of three separate causes of action based on the making of the statement itself rather than on breach of the obligation to deliver. With each, there are serious practical and doctrinal problems; but the main reason why both parties would sooner litigate in contract than elsewhere is simple: much better for the buyer a contractual action granting the protection of an estoppel against the carrier without further proof; much better for the carrier to defend an action in contract protected by exclusion clauses. Where, though, for some reason, s 1 of the Bills of Lading Act 1855 and *Brandt v Liverpool* cannot apply, three other possible avenues of redress exist: breach of warranty of authority, s 3 of the Bills of Lading Act 1855 and the torts of fraudulent or negligent misstatement. Each of these remedies is primarily directed against the actual signatory of the bill, who is quite likely in any case not to be good for the loss. But even if he is, there are other problems. Breach of warranty of authority was used by Mocatta J to allow recovery for short-delivery by an endorsee against the signatory of the bill: *Rasnoimport V/O v Guthrie & Co Ltd* [1966] 1 Lloyd's Rep 1. The judge came perilously close to using representational estoppel as a cause of action: see The Bill of Lading as a Receipt—missing oil in unknown quantities, C. Debattista, 1986 LMCLQ 468 at 472, 473; the reasoning has been called 'complex' and 'artificial' by Dr FMB Reynolds at (1967) 83 LQR 189, largely because the judge was constrained by the authority of *Grant v Norway* (1851) 20 LJCP 93, as to which see further down in this note. As for the buyer's position under s 3 of the Bills of Lading Act 1855, the section simply arms the plaintiff with an estoppel not with a cause of action: *that* has to be construed independently from an agreement or from the facts of the case: *Rasnoimport* (above) and Scrutton, art 59. Finally, actions for fraudulent or negligent misstatement require proof by the buyer of the defendant's fraud or negligence: s 2(1) of the Misrepresentation Act 1967, which would place the burden of disproving negligence on the defendant, would not be available because, ex hypothesi, the plaintiff here would not have 'entered into a contract' as required by the terms of that section. In neither action can the defendant, whether he be the carrier or the signatory, plead the limitations which would have availed him in a contractual action: this because, even if art IV-bis 1 of the Hague-Visby Rules is assumed normally to extend contractual exemptions to tort actions (see Chapter 3.2.(a) above), that article cannot apply to an action for misstatement, which is not an action 'in respect of loss of or damage to goods' within the terms of the article. For the same reason, a signatory sued for misstatement cannot plead his principal's exclusions because for art IV-bis 2 to extend those exclusions to him, the action must be 'such an action' as is described in art IV-bis 1. Should recovery against the carrier be sought, it is difficult to fix him with tortious liability for the signatory's misstatement, whether fraudulent or negligent, at any rate where the claim is for shortdelivery rather than damage to goods: and the reason, again, is the rule in *Grant v Norway* (1851) 20 LJCP 93 which states that a statement by an agent that goods have been shipped where they have not cannot be imputed to the shipowner. As to actions for negligent misstatements, see, generally, Scrutton, art 59 and The Hague-Visby Rules, Anthony Diamond QC, 1978 LMCLQ 225 at 255, 256; and, as to the rule in *Grant v Norway*, see *Bowstead on Agency*, edn F.M.B. Reynolds, 1985, London, pp 309, 310, fn 28; and The Significance of Tort in Claims in respect of Carriage by Sea, F.M.B. Reynolds, 1986 LMCLQ 97 at 108-110.

by some form of statement binding the carrier as to the quantity and condition of the goods on shipment, the buyer can see his claim for recovery quite easily defeated by his inability to prove precisely what goods were shipped. For his part, the carrier, on our hypothesis the party responsible for the loss, is unlikely to be particularly forthcoming with firm evidence of facts which would in effect establish his liability. The buyer is spared this evidential nightmare by the bill of lading, which carries on its face statements as to the quantity and apparent condition of the goods on shipment. These statements, made as they are by the carrier, raise against the latter a prima facie presumption that goods were shipped as stated.

A moment's reflection on the relative ease of access to the facts providing evidence of shipment will, however, show that this prima facie presumption in the cargo-interest's favour is something of a hollow victory: just as, without it, the buyer would find it difficult to prove what was shipped, so in spite of it, the carrier would find it relatively easy to lead evidence contradicting a statement which only binds him, as it were, provisionally or prima facie. Unless the statements on the bill really bind the carrier, they are practically worthless to the buyer in cases where they count, that is to say where the carrier is willing to undergo litigation which he is, presumably, confident of winning by providing evidence contradicting bill of lading statements. This much was recognised by the Carriage of Goods by Sea Act 1971 which introduced[10] an absolute ban on evidence contradicting statements on the bill as to the identity, quantity and apparent condition of the goods on shipment, where the bill has been transferred to a third party acting in good faith[11], e g the buyer.

It is tempting to conclude that, given the statutory ban on alternative evidence, buyers of goods covered by the Carriage of Goods by Sea Act 1971, are well protected by the Act against negligent or rapacious carriers; and that they need seek no further rights under the law of sale to extract

---

[10] In art III.4 of the Schedule to that Act, the relevant part of which reads: 'However, proof to the contrary shall not be admissible when the bill of lading has been transferred to a third party acting in good faith.' This article is commonly said to have done away with the rule in *Grant v Norway* (1851) 20 LJCP 93 in actions for short-delivery brought against the carrier by the buyer of the goods: see Scrutton, p 438. The editors of Benjamin, however, are not so easily persuaded: at para 1440, they argue that as the estoppel only works against a 'carrier', and as a 'carrier' is defined in art I(a) as a shipowner or charterer 'who enters into a contract of carriage with a shipper', a carrier who is not a party to such a contract (because no goods have been shipped) is not caught by art III.4. The argument is, with respect, difficult to rebut. However, the judicial distaste felt for *Grant v Norway*, illustrated by cases like *The Nea Tyhi* [1982] 1 Lloyd's Rep 606 (disapproved of, though on an unrelated point, by Lord Brandon in *The Aliakmon* [1986] 2 Lloyd's Rep 1] and *The Saudi Crown* [1986] 1 Lloyd's Rep 261, is such that the argument, for all its technical accuracy, is unlikely to find much sympathy in the courts.

[11] The good faith requirement would appear to be satisfied so long as the transferee did not have 'actual notice at the time of receiving the bill that the goods shipped did not correspond with the bill of lading statement': see The Hague-Visby Rules, Anthony Diamond QC, at 1978 LMCLQ, 225 at 253.

from their sellers bills of lading firmly binding the carrier to his statements thereon: once the law of carriage so heavily favours the receiver of goods, he has little need of further stipulation or regulation in his favour under the contract of sale or the letter of credit. Such a conclusion would be quite misleading and the reason for this lies deep in the entrails of the law regarding the force of statements binding those who make them. The legal device used to make statements binding by barring evidence contradicting them is the device of representational estoppel. That doctrine[12] cannot get off the ground unless there is a statement by the carrier in the first place; and even if the bill does contain a statement about the quantity and condition of the goods on shipment, the estoppel is effectively grounded if the statement is so hedged around with qualifications that it hardly amounts to a statement about shipment at all: the statement founding the estoppel needs to be clear and unequivocal[13]. We shall see further on in this chapter that, somewhat surprisingly, the carrier is under no automatic duty to issue a bill of lading at all, never mind one saying anything about the shipment of

---

[12] Whether operated in its judicial (see *Compania Naviera Vasconzada v Churchill & Sim* [1906] 1 KB 237) or its statutory (see the Carriage of Goods by Sea Act 1971, Sch, art III.4) manifestations. The two forms of the estoppel differ only slightly in that the first requires the buyer to prove that he acted to his prejudice upon the faith of the statement on which the estoppel is based; in the second, the buyer need not prove action in reliance. There is less to this distinction than meets the eye because the courts will take the buyer's burden of proof as discharged by the suggestion that the buyer accepted tender of the bill by the seller on the faith of the statements made therein by the carrier: *Silver v Ocean SS Co Ltd* [1930] 1 KB 416 at 428, 434 and 441: but see Scrutton, whose editors suggest, at 438, that 'the transferee is in a substantially stronger position under the Amended Rules [i e the Hague-Visby Rules], than he would be at common law'; in a similar sense, Carver at para 520. It seems that the carrier cannot defeat the estoppel by pleading that the receiver was bound, as buyer under the contract of sale, to accept the documents and that therefore the receiver cannot have accepted the bill on the faith of the carrier's representation: see *Peter Cremer, Westfaelische Central Genossenschaft GmbH and Intergraan NV v General Carriers SA, The Dona Mari* [1973] 2 Lloyd's Rep 366 at 372-375, particularly at 374: and see Carver, at para 116. As to the application of representational estoppel generally in this context, see Scrutton, art 56.

[13] See *Woodhouse AC Israel Cocoa Ltd SA v Nigerian Produce Marketing Co Ltd* [1972] AC 741; and other cases cited in *The Law Relating to Estoppel by Representation*, Spencer Bower and Turner, London, 1977, at 82. The upshot of this requirement in the context of statements on the face of bills of lading is that where the statement is equivocal, as it would be where it is qualified by a 'weight unknown' clause, the bill does not even provide prima facie evidence against the carrier, neither of the quantity shipped nor of the apparent condition. So far as concerns quantity, see *New Chinese Antimony Co Ltd v Ocean SS Co Ltd* [1917] 2 KB 664; there appears to be a growing hostility to such clauses at first instance, though: see *The Herroe and Askoe* [1986] 2 Lloyd's Rep 281, where it was also held that a separate signature by the master next to the statement of quantity had the effect of restoring the strength of that statement, thus by-passing the 'weight and quantity unknown' clause; and *The Sirina* [1988] 2 Lloyd's Rep 613, where Phillips J suggested that there must a limit to the effect of the Court of Appeal's judgment in the *New Chinese Antimony* case, (see particularly p 615 of the report). As for apparent condition, see *Canada and Dominion Sugar Co Ltd v Canadian National (West Indies) Steamships Ltd* [1947] AC 46; and *Tokio Marine and Fire Insurance Co Ltd v Retla SS Co* (USCt of Apps) [1970] 2 Lloyd's Rep 91. See, further, Scrutton at art 56, particularly fnn 29 and 30 and accompanying text;

the goods[14]; and, somewhat less surprisingly, that although carriers in fact do, as a matter of daily routine, issue bills of lading after shipment, the statements contained therein about the quantity and state of the goods on shipment are so qualified that, by the time the bill is transferred to a third party acting in good faith, namely the buyer, the evidence it provides is conclusive of very little indeed[15]. For these reasons, the buyer's position as a plaintiff-receiver in a cargo claim against the carrier is not so strong as might appear at first sight under the law of carriage and he may need to take precautions as a buyer under the sale contract and in the letter of credit in order to strengthen his position in a cargo claim against the carrier should such a claim eventually become necessary. The form which those precautions might take will be discussed in the third part of this chapter. Prior to that, though, and before we give up totally on the law of carriage, we need to examine precisely what rights each of the cargo-interests involved, i e the seller and the buyer, has as against the carrier with regard to the type of representations the carrier makes on the bill about the quantity and condition of the goods on shipment.

2. MERCHANTS' RIGHTS TO DEMAND A CLEAR RECEIPT FROM THE CARRIER

We have just seen that the value to the buyer of the bill of lading as a receipt is dependent on the existence and nature of the statement as to shipment on the face of the bill of lading: without a clear and unequivocal statement that goods in such and such a quantity and in apparent good order and condition have been shipped, the estoppel brought about either by the common law[16] or by statute[17] would be of no practical value because, despite the ban on alternative evidence, the statement 'binding' the carrier would state very little of any worth at all. This being the case, it is useful to ask whether the two cargo-interests involved at different stages of the carriage of goods by sea, the seller and the buyer, have any rights under the contract of carriage as to the terms in which the carrier's[18] statement as to shipment is drawn on the

---

and at art 60, particularly fnn 85 and 86 and accompanying text; Carver, at para 104; and, generally, for a historical and comparative survey of the legal strength of statements on bills of lading, see History and Development of the Bill of Lading, D.E. Murray, 37 Univ of Miami LR 689 (1983).

[14] See Chapter 5.2, below.

[15] See Chapter 5.3.(a) and (b), below.

[16] As in *Compania Naviera Vasconzada v Churchill and Sim* [1906] 1 KB 237.

[17] As by art III.4 of the Schedule to the Carriage of Goods by Sea Act 1971.

[18] The figures will typically originate with the seller, the shipper of the goods, who is, of course, in the best possible position to know what goods, in what quantity and condition, he has given to the carrier. It is clear, though, that once the carrier appends his signature to the statement on the bill the figures become, so far as concerns third parties like the buyer, the carrier's figures on the carrier's document. The carrier is protected against the consequences of inaccuracy in the figures given him by the shipper by an indemnity imposed by the Carriage of Goods by Sea Act 1971 in art III.5 of the Schedule to that Act. There appears to be no authority implying such an indemnity where the Act does not apply. See further on art III.5, Chapter 5.2.(a).ii, below.

face of the bill[19]. In each case, the question will be dealt with first under the common law, then under the Carriage of Goods by Sea Act 1971.

(a) The seller: does he have a right to a firm receipt

i. At common law?

It might have been thought that the shipper, as the initial cargo party to the contract of carriage[20], would have a common law right against the carrier to the issue of a bill of lading stating clearly and without reservation that goods have been shipped in a given quantity and in apparent good order and condition. There seems, however, to be no authority actually granting such a right to the seller qua shipper of the goods. It could doubtless be argued that authority is unnecessary, the right flowing inexorably from the definition of the bill of lading as a document of title. The definition of a document of title adopted in this book was taken, it will be recalled, from Professor Goode's work *Proprietary Rights and Insolvency in Sales Transactions*[21] and was in these terms:

> '[The document of title] must be issued or accepted by the bailee of *the goods*, must thereby embody his undertaking to hold *the goods* for, and release them to whoever presents the document and must be recognised by statute or mercantile usage as a document which enables control of *the goods* to pass by delivery of the document with any necessary indorsement.' (Emphasis added.)

The fact that the document of title, the bill of lading, must relate to *the goods* must mean, the argument would run, that the bill must contain a clear statement of which goods, in what quantity and apparent condition, are in the actual possession of the carrier: there would otherwise be no goods to which the right to delivery locked up in the document could attach. However welcome this argument might be to shippers claiming a right to unqualified statements on the bill as to the shipment of goods, the argument is flawed on two grounds. Firstly, it proceeds upon the assumption that a shipper of goods has a common law right to the issue of a document of title and the existence of this right is by no means obvious. The shipper may well need a document of title

---

[19] Excluded from the discussion at this point will be the case where one or other of the two cargo-interests also happens to be a charterer of the vessel on which the goods covered by the bill are carried. That type of case will be covered in Chapter 7 when we discuss the problems caused by bills of lading issued pursuant to charterparties.

[20] That is to say, in c i f and c & f sales, in f o b sales with additional services and in f o b sales of the classic type. In the third type of f o b sale, the so-called 'straight' variety, where the buyer takes the bill of lading directly from the carrier, the seller plays no part in the issue of the bill of lading, although he is nonetheless considered to be a party to the contract of carriage: see *Pyrene Co Ltd v Scindia Navigation Co Ltd* [1954] 2 QB 402 and, generally, fn 2 and Chapter 1.2.(a).ii, above.

[21] See above, Chapter 2.3.(a).

so as to perform his documentary obligations under the contract of sale, but it does not follow from that need that a right to such a document can be implied into a contract of carriage[22]. Secondly, even if the shipper did have a right, whether implied or expressed in the carriage contract, to the issue of a document of title by the carrier, it does not follow from the words in italics in the definition above that the shipper can insist on a clear and unequivocal statement as to the quantity and apparent condition in which the goods were shipped. The definition talks of an undertaking to hold the goods, without in any way stating how those goods must be described on the document. While a bill of lading saying absolutely nothing in the space reserved for the description of the goods would probably not be a document of title as defined[23], a bill saying '10 boxes each said to contain 5 personal computers', or one saying '100 tons of sugar' but 'weight unknown', or one saying simply 'particulars furnished by the shipper'[24] would clearly come well within the definition of a document of title. Thus it seems that, at any rate at common law, the carrier has an unrestricted right so to qualify statements on the bill as to make the document prima facie evidence of virtually nothing at all.

ii. Under the Carriage of Goods by Sea Act 1971?

The Hague-Visby Rules, incorporated into our law as a schedule to the Carriage of Goods by Sea Act 1971[25], alter the position in the shipper's favour, at any rate in theory, where the Act applies[26]. The Act deals largely with the contractual aspects of bills of lading, but it contains

---

[22] The fact that bills are invariably issued by carriers does not really take the point made in the text. The question here is whether a right to a particular type of receipt can ride upon a right to the issue of a document of title. If there is no right to the latter, then a right to the former cannot be established on this ground. Any other conclusion would found a legal right to a clear and unequivocal statement of shipment upon the practice that bills of lading are issued for goods on shipment: but see Carver, whose editor draws precisely this conclusion, in precisely this manner, at para 57, fn 30. Such authority as exists, decided albeit under the Hague Rules rather than at common law, tends very much against that conclusion: see fn 28, below.

[23] Because there would appear to be no goods to which the right to possession could attach.

[24] All three forms of words qualifying what would otherwise be firm statements on the face of bills of lading are treated as interchangeable: see The HagueVisby Rules, Anthony Diamond QC, 1978 LMCLQ 225 at 254. For a judicial expression of doubt, however, as to whether the qualification 'said to be' does have the same debilitating effect on a representation as to the quantity of goods shipped as a 'weight and quantity unknown' clause, see Evans J in *The Boukadoura* [1989] 1 Lloyd's Rep 393 at 399.

[25] And, before them, the Hague Rules, incorporated via the Carriage of Goods by Sea Act 1924, which on the point discussed here in the text, did not differ from the Hague-Visby Rules.

[26] The applicability or otherwise of the Carriage of Goods by Sea Act 1971 is a question containing its own particular brand of intriguing difficulty, which lies, however, strictly outside the confines of this book. The main sections of the Act attracting controversy in this context are s 1 of the Act and arts I, V and X of the Schedule to the Act. For discussions in the literature, see Scrutton, at 412-420; Carver, at ss 470-477, 484-497; and Diamond, The Hague-Visby Rules, 1978 LMCLQ 225 at 256-263.

also a small cluster of articles which relate to the receipt function of bills of lading[27]. Among that cluster, the articles of more direct relevance to us here are articles III.3 and III.5: these articles define the rights and liabilities of the shipper with regard to the type of receipt he can expect to receive from his carrier and it is those rights and liabilities which are under discussion here.

Article III.3 reads as follows:

> 'After receiving the goods into his charge the carrier or the master or the agent of the carrier shall, on demand of the shipper, issue to the shipper a bill of lading showing among other things—
> (a) The leading marks necessary for the identification of the goods as the same are furnished in writing by the shipper before the loading of such goods starts, provided such marks are stamped or otherwise shown clearly upon the goods if uncovered, or on the cases or coverings in which such goods are contained, in such a manner as should ordinarily remain legible until the end of the voyage.
> (b) Either the number of packages or pieces, or the quantity, or weight, as the case may be, as furnished in writing by the shipper.
> (c) The apparent order and condition of the goods.
> Provided that no carrier, master or agent of the carrier shall be bound to state or show in the bill of lading any marks, number, quantity, or weight which he has reasonable ground for suspecting not accurately to represent the goods actually received, or which he has no reasonable means of checking.'

Thus, where the Act applies, the shipper has the right to demand[28] of the carrier a bill of lading clearly stating the marks, quantity and

---

27   These are: art III.3, which lists a number of requirements on which the shipper may insist when the bill is issued; art III.4, which defines the evidential strength of the statements as to shipment carried on the bill; art III.5, which imposes liability on the shipper for inaccuracies in identifying marks and figures given to the carrier by the shipper; and art III.7, which gives the shipper the right to demand from the carrier a 'shipped' as opposed to a 'received for shipment' bill of lading. art III.4 has already been referred to in the first part of this chapter when we dealt with the evidential role of the bill of lading as a receipt; art III.7 will be dealt with when we discuss container transport documents in Chapter 8.

28   It is interesting to note that again, despite the intervention of statute, the carrier is not automatically placed under a duty to issue a bill of lading at all, much less one stating clearly the quantity and condition of the goods on shipment: see *Canada and Dominion Sugar Co Ltd v Canadian National (West Indies) Steamships Ltd* [1947] AC 46 at 57. A bold attempt was made by Mr N.D. Shaffer in 'Bills of Lading—Weight Unknown', at 1965 SLT 49 to argue that after the decision of the Privy Council in *A-G of Ceylon v Scindia Steam Navigation Co Ltd* [1962] AC 60, 'for all practical purposes the words "on demand of the shipper" at the commencement of the Rule may be disregarded,' such that, where the Rules apply, the carrier would be under an automatic duty to issue a bill complying with art III.3. That proposition, however welcome to cargo-interests, is simply too weighty to be borne by *Scindia*, in which the Privy Council held quite simply that a clause stating 'weight, contents and value when shipped unknown' did not qualify a statement on the bill as to the number

condition of the goods when the carrier takes charge of them. Given that carriers do invariably, very much for their own protection through bill of lading clauses, issue bills of lading to shippers of goods, the real content of the right created by this article is not so much the entitlement to demand a bill of lading: rather is it a right to ask for a bill with unqualified statements about the goods on delivery to the carrier. Thus, where, for example, the carrier wishes to qualify a statement that '100 tons of sugar' have been shipped by a clause saying that the 'weight, measure, marks, numbers, quality, contents and value [are] unknown'[29] the shipper can, if covered by the Carriage of Goods by Sea Act 1971, demand the deletion of the word 'weight' in that clause, such that the statement that 100 tons of sugar have been shipped stands without qualification[30].

Thus far, taking both article III.3 and article III.4 into account, the Act works very much in the shipper's favour, giving him as it does the right to demand a bill of lading with firm representations, binding on the carrier, as to the identity, quantity and state of the goods on delivery to the carrier. The Rules which the Act brings into force do not lose sight, however, of the fact that the figures and identifying marks which they impute to the carrier are, in truth, figures and marks which originate with the shipper. It was realised that there should consequently be some limit on the right of the shipper to insist upon the carrier's acknowledgement of marks or figures, at any rate when these are marks or figures which are solely within the shipper's ken. It was also recognised that the carrier ought to have a right of recourse against the shipper where the carrier found himself bound by article III.4 to figures and identifying marks which, albeit acknowledged by the carrier, originated with the shipper. The first objective—the setting of a limit on the shipper's right to insist on the carrier's adherence to the shipper's marks or figures—was reached through the proviso to article III.3 itself, which reserves to the carrier the right to say nothing at all about the identifying marks or quantity of the goods either where he has reasonable grounds for suspecting their accuracy, or simply where he has no reasonable means

---

of bags of rice shipped. Mr Shaffer himself advises caution in drawing the conclusion for which he argues from the decision of the Privy Council: see, further, The Bill of Lading as a Receipt—Missing Oil in Unknown Quantities, Debattista, 1986 LMCLQ 468 at 478, fn 37. See also, for a slightly different but closely related point, The Hague-Visby Rules, Anthony Diamond QC. 1978 LMCLQ 225 at 254, where Mr Diamond suggests that the issue of a bill should be deemed to be sufficient evidence of a demand, such that all qualifications not justified by the proviso to art III.3 would be ignored. 'At the present time, however,' Mr Diamond concludes, 'this step seems unlikely to be taken.' Twelve years on, we are no closer to the position advocated by Mr Diamond.

[29] A clause taken from the front page of the CONLINEBILL bill of lading and one which appears in more or less the same form in most bills of lading.

[30] By the same token, it might be argued that a carrier taking charge of a container stated on the bill as 'said to contain 100 word-processors' can be asked by the shipper to delete the words 'said to contain', at any rate where the intention behind those words is to qualify the representation as to the quantity of goods shipped.

of checking their accuracy[31]. The second aim—to grant the carrier recourse against the seller for the consequences of inaccurate marks and figures—was attained through the statutory imposition of an indemnity in the carrier's favour in article III.5 which reads as follows:

> 'The shipper shall be deemed to have guaranteed to the carrier the accuracy at the time of shipment of the marks, number, quantity and weight, as furnished by him, and the shipper shall indemnify the carrier against all loss, damages and expenses arising or resulting from inaccuracies in such particulars. The right of the carrier to such indemnity shall in no way limit his responsibility and liability under the contract of carriage to any person other than the shipper.'

Here the figures and identifying marks are, as it were, turned back on to the shipper with whom they originated. While the marks and figures are clearly the carrier's vis-a-vis third parties, like the buyer, in whose favour they constitute conclusive evidence under article III.4, they are, as between the carrier and the shipper, very much the shipper's marks and figures for which the shipper remains responsible towards the carrier.

To read articles III.3, III.4 and III.5 together, one might be forgiven a brief spell of admiration for the perfect lattice of provisions created by the Hague-Visby Rules safeguarding the interests of all three parties involved respectively in the drawing up, acknowledging and receiving of statements as to the goods on the bill of lading, i e the seller, the carrier and the buyer respectively. The shipper has simply to demand a clear acknowledgement from the carrier of statements entered on the bill by the shipper; those statements now constitute evidence of prima facie strength against the carrier in the shipper's favour, and of irrebuttable strength against the carrier in the buyer's favour; finally, the carrier retains throughout a right of recourse against the seller who shipped the goods for the consequences of inaccuracy in the marks or figures given him by the shipper. It starts to look as if the law of carriage by sea, at any rate where the Carriage of Goods by Sea Act 1971 applies, provides adequate security to the receiver of goods, such that he need not, qua buyer under the sale contract, or qua the party instructing the opening of a letter of credit, seek further protection through those contracts against the effects of a heavily qualified, and therefore evidentially worthless, receipt. Unfortunately for him, though, one part of the otherwise perfect

---

[31] A moment's reflection on this proviso will show that it contains a right which no carrier is likely to exercise and one to the exercise of which no shipper is likely to drive his carrier. A bill of lading with nothing on its face as to the quantity of the goods on delivery to the carrier is of little practical value to anyone: it would probably not be a document of title at common law, as we have seen above in the text accompanying fn 23. Carriers wishing to avoid making firm statements which they might later regret are far more likely to make heavily qualified statements about the goods than to make no statement at all. This must be why 'weight and quantity unknown' clauses, of the type seen at fn 29, above, are so common in bills of lading; it must also be why the proviso to article III.3 is the most neglected part of the Hague-Visby Rules, with no litigation and serious comment to its name: see Scrutton, pp 437, 8, and Carver, paras 518, 9.

framework of rules in the law of carriage is weak: it is the part which is likely to be of most interest to the buyer and the reason for its weakness is one to which reference has already been made in the general comments introducing this chapter. For all the rights which the Carriage of Goods by Sea Act 1971 grants the shipper as to the type of bill of lading he can demand from the carrier, the shipper is most unlikely so to quibble with the carrier as to risk delaying the issue of the bill of lading, and consequently the time when he can, qua seller or beneficiary under a letter of credit, obtain payment of the price. It is only by weaving into the texture of rules a number of stipulations in the buyer's favour under the sale contract and under the letter of credit that the seller can be persuaded to exercise the right given him by the Carriage of Goods by Sea Act 1971 to demand a clear receipt from the carrier. The incentive may, of course, not work: the seller may still fail to exercise the rights given him by the law of carriage. We ought consequently to ask, before we examine the buyer's rights under the contract of sale, whether, if the shipper fails to exercise his right to demand a bill with unqualified statements as to the goods on shipment, the buyer might not, under the law of carriage by sea, exercise a similar right himself.

(b) The buyer: does he have a right to a firm receipt

i. At common law?

The suggestion that a buyer not yet party to a contract of carriage[32] might have a right, under the law governing that contract, to dictate the terms in which receipt of the goods is acknowledged by the carrier is such an affront to the doctrine of privity that even greater care than usual should be taken in isolating those circumstances where the question is worth asking and why. The following illustration will serve both purposes: B buys 100 tons of sugar from S on c i f terms under a contract which incorporates Incoterms and which is otherwise completely silent as to the acceptability or otherwise of bills of lading containing 'weight and quantity unknown' clauses[33]. Payment is to be by letter of credit, the Uniform Customs and Practice for Documentary Credits to apply to the credit. S concludes the carriage contract with C, the carrier, and, for present purposes, we are to assume that the Carriage of Goods by Sea Act 1971 does not apply to that contract because we are here looking at the buyer's rights against the carrier at common law. B receives a telex from S declaring shipment on C's vessel and B learns that C's standard bill of lading acknowledges receipt of goods 'weight and quantity unknown'. The question we are asking is: does B have a common law righi as against C that the latter issue to S a bill of lading with a clear and unequivocal statement as to the quantity and condition of the goods on shipment, such that any subsequent shortage claim by B against C

---

[32] That is to say, before the bill of lading is transferred to him.
[33] Incoterms themselves allow the tender of bills containing such clauses: see fn 38, below.

will be governed[34] by the statement in the bill that 100 tons of sugar have been shipped?

The answer to that question is very clearly No and the reasons go deeper than the doctrine of privity. We have already seen that the seller, qua shipper of the goods under the contract of carriage, has no right to the issue of a bill of lading with unqualified statements as to the goods on shipment[35]. If the seller himself has no right to such a document, then a fortiori the buyer can have no such right. No amount of cajoling with the doctrine of privity can extend to the third party to the carriage contract, the buyer, a right which does not even exist in the second party to that contract, the shipper.

ii. Under the Carriage of Goods by Sea Act 1971?

Where the contract of carriage concluded between S and C is governed by the Carriage of Goods by Sea Act 1971, the answer cannot be so simple; for here, as we have seen[36], the seller does have a right, qua shipper of the goods, to demand a bill of lading with clear and unequivocal statements as to the goods at the time of delivery thereof to the carrier. There are three sets of arguments against and for extending that right to the buyer under the law of carriage[37].

The first set of arguments revolves around policy considerations. Against extending S's rights against the carrier to B, it could be argued that B has no one but himself to blame for the predicament in which he finds himself. For someone so keen to ensure that bills of lading tendered by the seller contained unqualified statements as to the quantity and condition of the goods on shipment, B was surprisingly complacent when negotiating his sale contract and when opening the letter of credit. Incoterms make it clear[38] that, in the absence of an express clause in the sale contract, the seller is entitled to tender a bill of lading with a 'weight and quantity unknown' clause and had B wished S to demand the deletion of that clause under article III.3 of the Schedule to the Carriage of Goods by Sea Act 1971, he should have inserted a clause in the contract of sale barring tender of a bill containing the offending qualification.

---

[34] Despite *Grant v Norway* (1851) 20 LJCP 93, which would not, it is submitted, apply to a short-delivery claim, as opposed to a claim for non-delivery: Scrutton, art 60, fn 72; but see, for a contrary view, Carver, para 102. For a discussion of these differing views, see The Bill of Lading as a Receipt—Missing Oil in Unknown Quantities, Debattista, 1986 LMCLQ 468, particularly at 470-473.

[35] See Chapter 5.2.(a).(i), above.

[36] Above at Chapter 5.2.(a).ii.

[37] The arguments will be tackled in that order, that is to say first those against, then those for extension, because, although finely balanced, the arguments against such an extension appear to have the edge over those for it.

[38] CIF A7, note (c), the relevant part of which reads: 'The following clauses do not convert a clean into an unclean bill of lading:...
  (c) clauses which disclaim on the part of the carrier knowledge of contents, weight, measurement, quality, or technical specification of the goods.'

B should moreover, as was his right under the UCP[39], have followed this through by barring tender of such a bill under the letter of credit. In the absence of such timely action, it is surely too late now for B to create novel carriage rights to help him out of his predicament. On the other hand, it is possible to argue that policy demands the creation by the courts of just such a right: for surely, the thrust of article III.3 is very much against the qualification of statements made by the carrier as to the quantity and condition of the goods on shipment. For reasons discussed above[40], the aim of the article was thwarted by granting the right it created to a party with little incentive to exercise it, namely the seller. Should not, therefore, the courts further the aim of this part of the Schedule to the Act by recognising a similar right in the buyer of the goods, the party ultimately interested in the strength of the representations on the face of the bill?

This brings us neatly to the second set of arguments, which revolve around the doctrine of privity. For even if the answer to the question at the end of the last paragraph were Yes, how could English courts 'recognise' such a right in the buyer, who is patently not privy to the contract of carriage at the time of its purported exercise? The Act does, after all, give the rights listed in article III.3 expressly to the shipper: to extend that right to the buyer, qua intended receiver of the goods, would, surely, require a totally unreasonable degree of judicial creativity. On the other hand, too much can too easily be made of privity arguments in this context: the buyer is, at the relevant time[41], about to enter into contractual relations with the carrier through the operation of section 1 of the Bills of Lading Act 1855[42] and it does seem pedantic to a fault to harp single-mindedly on a doctrine to which, as we have seen throughout this book, is honoured in the breach at least as much as in the observance in this area of commercial law. Neither does the fact that the Act grants the rights in article III.3 to the shipper take the point: it is in the nature of a new right extended by the courts from one which already exists that the existing right is narrower than the new one. In short, there is little real merit in the privity argument, which is perhaps why the editor of Carver, who alone in the literature considers the problem here discussed, fails to mention such considerations altogether.

The third set of arguments revolve, indeed, around Carver's discussion of the problem at para 521 of his work on carriage by sea. The editor of Carver is very much against extending to the buyer the seller's right to demand a bill of lading conforming to article III.3 of the Hague-

---

[39] See article 32 which reads, with added emphasis: 'Unless otherwise stipulated in the credit, banks will accept transport documents which bear a clause on the face thereof such as "shipper's load and count" or "said by shipper to contain" or words of similar effect.'

[40] At Chapter 5.2.(a).ii, above.

[41] That is to say, the time of issue of the bill of lading.

[42] Itself a privity-solver: see, generally, Chapter 3, above.

Visby Rules; and his reasons turn on the precise relationship between articles III.3 and III.5 of the Rules[43]. It will be recalled that article III.5 imposes upon the shipper an indemnity in the carrier's favour for the consequences of any inaccuracy in the marks and figures given the carrier by the shipper[44]. Carver describes this warranty as personal to the shipper, in that it is not one of the obligations transferred to the buyer on the operation of section 1 of the Bills of Lading Act 1855[45]; from the personal nature of the indemnity imposed by article III.5 on the shipper, Carver concludes that, once the shipper is the only party liable on the indemnity, then it is only the shipper who can insist on the requirements of article III.3 when the bill of lading is issued by the carrier. The reasoning appears attractive until one observes that it proceeds upon the ill-founded assumption that, if the receiver could demand a bill of lading complying with article III.3, this would automatically place upon his shoulders the burden of the indemnity imposed by article III.5. Surely, though, if a receiver were legitimately to demand a bill under article III.3 and were then to sue the carrier for short delivery, the result of inaccurate statements given by the shipper to the carrier would be the enforcement of the indemnity by the carrier against the shipper, not against the receiver. This is precisely why article III.5 then goes on to say that the carrier's right to the shipper's indemnity in no way limits his liabilities towards 'any person other than the shipper', for example the receiver. Carver's argument against extension is consequently based on too close a connection between articles III.3 and III.5 of the Hague-Visby Rules, a connection belied by the wording of the articles themselves.

It will be apparent that the textual arguments against and for extension are very finely balanced. It is nonetheless probably fair to predict that extending the seller's rights to the buyer would be likely to find little favour in an English court: the judges would be reluctant to grant contractual rights outside a carriage contract in order to avoid consequences which the buyer himself could easily have avoided through specific stipulation in the contract of sale and the letter of credit. It is therefore to stipulations in those contracts that we now turn.

3. REQUIREMENTS OF THE BILL OF LADING AS A RECEIPT IN SALE CONTRACTS AND IN LETTERS OF CREDIT

In the first part of this chapter, we saw why the function of the bill of lading as a receipt is so important to the buyer: the presumptions raised by statements in the bill against the carrier tip the evidential scales in the buyer's favour in an action for short-delivery or damage to goods.

---

[43] The argument is rehearsed and discussed in The Bill of Lading as a Receipt—Missing Oil in Unknown Quantities, Debattista, 1986 LMCLQ 468 at 479, from which most of the text accompanying this footnote is taken.

[44] See Chapter 5.2.(a).ii, above.

[45] Of this view also are the editors of Scrutton: see p 439.

We saw also, however, that the mechanism setting up these presumptions[46] is entrusted exclusively to the shipper of the goods, who in most cases will be the seller[47]; that, as shipper under the contract of carriage, the seller is quite unlikely to use this mechanism, partly because some of the statements originate in a very real sense with himself[48], and partly because the seller's right to prompt payment depends on prompt tender of the bill of lading, whose issue will be delayed by the seller's quibbling with the carrier about the details of statements as to the goods on shipment. It seems thus that the network of rules constructed by the law of carriage to ensure the issue of a bill of lading with firm and binding statements in the buyer's favour is of greater value in theory than in practice; and that if the buyer's interests are to be protected, this will have to be through terms, expressed or implied, in the sale contract and in the letter of credit. The object of these terms is to make payment of the price depend on the tender of a bill of lading making clear and unequivocal statements as to the identity, quantity and state of the goods on shipment: if payment of the price is made to depend on such tender, then the seller is given a reason, by the contract of sale and by the letter of credit, to exercise such rights as he has to a firm receipt under the law of carriage. The form and source of such terms are the subject of the third part of this chapter. We shall find that, at times, the courts are quite willing to imply such terms into the sale contract in the buyer's favour[49]; but that at others, they are not so ready to fill gaps into which the buyer has fallen by default[50]. Moreover, we shall also see how easy it is for one contract involved in the international trade transaction to be out of kilter with another[51]. For all these reasons, care needs to be taken by the buyer in the drafting both of his contract of sale and of his instructions to the bank issuing a letter of credit. We shall be discussing the requirements of the bill of lading as a receipt under these contracts in the following order: firstly, terms as to statements about the quantity of the goods; and secondly, those as to the 'cleanliness' of the bill.

---

[46] That is to say, demanding a bill of lading conforming to art III.3 of the Schedule to the Carriage of Goods by Sea Act 1971.

[47] Except where the sale is concluded on straight f o b terms, in which case the buyer is the 'shipper' of the goods and the seller will have no control over the type of bill of lading issued by the carrier: see, generally, fn 2 and Chapter 1.2.(a).ii, above.

[48] That is to say, the statements as to identifying marks and as to quantity.

[49] As, for example, in *Re Keighley, Maxted & Co and Bryan, Durant & Co (No 2)* (1894) 7 Asp MLC 418, where an undertaking to tender a bill of lading for the contract goods was readily implied.

[50] Thus, it is not at all clear whether the courts will imply a term imposing upon the seller a duty to provide a bill of lading which states without qualification the quantity in which the goods were shipped: contrast *The Galatia* [1979] 2 Lloyd's Rep 450; affd [1980] 1 Lloyd's Rep 453, with *Libau Wood Co v (H) Smith & Sons Ltd* (1930) 37 Ll L Rep 296.

[51] Contrast, for example, the seller's obligation under a c i f sale contract to tender a bill of lading stating the goods to have been shipped in the quantity stated in the sale contract, with his right under the Uniform Customs and Practice for Documentary Credits to tender a bill of lading stating the quantity to be within 5% more or less than that stated in the letter of credit: art 43(b), UCP.

(a) The bill must cover the contract goods and no others

The buyer has every reason to require of his seller a bill of lading making it immediately apparent on its face that it refers to the goods in the same quantity contracted for in the contract of sale. We saw in the first part of this chapter that the buyer's right against the carrier to the delivery of a particular cargo in a given quantity is very strongly affected by the statements made by the carrier on the bill; if those statements allow the carrier to discharge goods in a different quantity to that contracted for, the buyer is left with no remedy against the carrier[52]: the buyer would consequently need to seek redress elsewhere, that is to say, against the seller, quite possibly and inconveniently in a foreign jurisdiction. The requirement here mentioned raises issues as to the statement of quantity on the bill and as to the qualifications which the carrier might add to that statement.

i. Statements as to quantity

It has long been settled that the common law implies into c i f contracts a term that the seller shall tender to the buyer a bill of lading for the quantity of the goods stated in the sale contract[53]. Thus in *Re Keighley, Maxted & Co and Bryan, Durant & Co (No 2)*[54], a seller who had expressly reserved the right to ship more cargo than that sold, the excess to be held in trust for him, was held nonetheless to be under a duty to tender a bill of lading for the quantity bought by the buyer: any other result would have made it difficult for the buyer to sell the goods in transit and would thus have been wholly inconsistent with the very nature of a sale on shipment terms[55]. The sale contract in that case said nothing about the terms in which the quantity shipped was to be stated on the bill: where Incoterms are incorporated into the contract, though, the obligation to tender a bill of lading which 'must cover the contract goods' is expressed in clear terms, at any rate where the sale is on c i f terms[56].

The sale contract may, of course, itself not specify the quantity sold to any particular degree of precision. Thus contracts for the sale of commodities will frequently state the quantity sold as '[a stated quantity] 2% more or less'[57]. It is clear that the tolerance threshold allowed in the physical aspect of the performance of the contract ought also to

---

[52] Who will have performed his main obligation under the contract of carriage by discharging what the bill of lading says was shipped.

[53] The same term, it is submitted, will be implied in c & f contracts and in f o b contracts of the extended and classic varieties, that is to say, in those contracts where the seller is the party responsible for taking the bill of lading from the carrier: see, generally, fn 2 and Chapter 1.2.(a).ii, above.

[54] (1894) 7 Asp MLC 418. See also *Tamvaco v Lucas* (1859) 120 ER 1027, 1032, where the quantity shipped was actually within the limits set by the contract; yet a bill of lading indicating that those limits had been exceeded was held to be bad tender.

[55] Loc cit, particularly at 420, per Lopes J.

[56] See Incoterms, C I F A.7. There is, of course, no equivalent express term in Incoterms for f o b contracts, but see fn 53 above.

[57] See, for example, GAFTA 100, clause 2.

be reflected in the documentary aspect of performance, such that a seller may tender a bill stating shipment of a quantity within the allowed limits[58]. Even where the sale contract does not allow a tolerance threshold, problems relating to the precise quantity stated may arise with the tender of bills of lading under the letter of credit used to finance such a sale. Consider thus the following example: a sale contract gives, say, '500 tonnes of wheat' as the quantity sold; the letter of credit similarly envisages the tender of a bill of lading for 500 tonnes of wheat; yet the bill of lading actually tendered to the bank states that '495 tonnes of wheat' have been shipped. On these facts, and particularly against a falling market, the buyer may well expect the paying bank to reject the shipping documents on the ground that the bill of lading does not conform to the requirements of the letter of credit. The buyer will, however, be surprised to learn that the bank can, indeed must, accept the documents in the circumstances described above; for article 43(b) of the Uniform Customs and Practice for Documentary Credits allows, in the absence of specific provision in the letter of credit, tender by the seller of a bill of lading stating shipment of a quantity within 5% either way of that stipulated in the credit[59]. Consequently, the seller in our example is paid his price under the credit; the bank is not liable to the buyer for breach; and neither is the carrier, for he has performed his undertaking to deliver what was shipped. The buyer is not, of course, completely without a remedy: for the seller is clearly in breach of his undertakings to ship 500 tonnes of wheat and to tender a bill of lading for the same amount[60]. This avenue of redress is, however, hardly likely to commend itself to the buyer if it means obtaining judgment and execution against a foreign defendant, quite possibly in a foreign jurisdiction. Much better to have anticipated the problem through the simple device of stipulating in the letter of credit, as article 43(b) of the Uniform Customs allows the buyer to do, that the quantity of goods specified must not be exceeded or reduced.

ii. Carrier's qualifications on the statement as to quantity

From the buyer's point of view, it is not enough, of course, for the seller to tender a bill of lading stating that goods in the contract quantity

---

[58] There appears to be no authority for the proposition stated in the text; it does, however, seem to follow inexorably from the seller's obligation, express or implied, to tender a bill of lading 'for the contract goods': if 'the contract goods' are '500 tonnes of wheat 2% more or less', then a bill of lading stating shipment of '510 tonnes of wheat' would be a bill 'for the contract goods'.

[59] The relevant part of the article reads as follows: 'Unless a credit stipulates that the quantity of the goods specified must not be exceeded or reduced, a tolerance of 5% more or 5% less will be permissible...'

  The article goes on to say that '[t]his tolerance does not apply when the credit stipulates the quantity in terms of a stated number of packing units or individual items.' Thus, in a sale of 100 cars, or of 10 containers of word-processors, the problem referred to in the text could not arise.

[60] Unless, of course, the maxim de minimis non curat lex defeats the buyer's action for breach. This raises the interesting question as to whether the maxim de minimis has any role to play in the (a) physical; and (b) documentary performance of an international sale. The debate is larger than statements as to quantity and it will consequently be discussed in Chapter 9 treating Rejection of Documents and Goods.

have been shipped: for the reasons rehearsed earlier in this chapter[61], that statement is worth little as an evidential device in a short delivery claim if it is hedged round with qualifications like 'weight and quantity unknown' or 'shipper's load and tally' or 'said to weigh/contain'. We need now to ask, therefore, whether the seller[62] owes the buyer a duty under the contract of sale to tender a bill of lading with a clear and unequivocal statement as to the quantity of the goods on shipment. The question will be discussed firstly on the basis of the common law and then on the basis of Incoterms.

— The buyer's rights at common law

The position at common law is said[63] to be governed by the decision of Donaldson J in *The Galatia*[64], in which one of the issues was whether a seller c i f was entitled to tender to a buyer a bill of lading containing a 'weight and quantity unknown' clause. The judge held that he was thus entitled on the ground that, as the statement as to quantity on the bill acknowledged shipment of sugar 'said to weigh 200.8 tonnes', the 'weight and quantity unknown' clause in no way qualified that statement and indeed was perfectly consistent with it; consequently, the bill of lading was clean[65] and therefore its tender was valid.

---

61 See Chapter 5.1, above.

62 By which is meant the seller c i f , c & f or the seller on extended or classic f o b terms, that is to say, those shipment sales where the seller is the party responsible for taking out the bill of lading: see, generally, fn 2 and Chapter 1.2.(a).ii, above.

63 See Benjamin, para 1643; and Goode, pp 556, 7.

64 [1979] 2 Lloyd's Rep 450, particularly at 457, a judgment upheld in the Court of Appeal, whose judgment is reported at [1980] 1 Lloyd's Rep 453 but which adds nothing to Donaldson J's consideration of this point.

65 Donaldson J's decision on this point was expressed in terms of whether or not the bill of lading was internally consistent and, therefore, clean and, therefore valid. With respect, this analysis proceeds upon an interpretation of the word 'clean' somewhat wider than that which it generally bears, although it must be said at the outset that the word has been notoriously difficult for lawyers to define: see Benjamin, para 1643 and Carver, para 736, fn 58, and para 1617. There seem to be two views in contention: the narrow interpretation, calling a bill clean if it contains no qualification of the statement that the cargo has been shipped in apparent good order and condition; and the wider interpretation, calling a bill clean so long as it contains no inconsistencies concerning any of the representations made about the goods, including those about quantity. Clearly, if the wider sense is preferred, it should be easier for a judge to hold invalid the tender of a bill with a 'weight and quantity unknown' clause, though ironically Donaldson J, although adopting the wider view, held such tender to be valid. Be that as it may, such authority as exists very much favours the narrow interpretation of the word 'clean': see Salmon J in *British Imex Industries Ltd v Midland Bank* [1958] 1 QB 542 at 551, (whose view is, incidentally, adopted without contrary comment by Donaldson J in *The Galatia* itself at 455), and other cases cited by Carver, loc cit fn 59. Authority for the wider understanding is, to say the least, meagre: Donaldson J traces it to a judgment of Cave J in *Restitution SS Co v Sir John Pirie & Co* (1889) 6 Asp MLC 428, a case dealing with recovery of demurrage under a charterparty, where the judge refers, at 430, to a definition said to be given in Pollock and Bruce's *Law of Merchant Shipping*. This is curious because the relevant edition of that work, the fourth, published in 1881, defines a clean bill in the narrower of the two senses given above; at 341, the editors write: 'A bill of lading commonly states that the goods are

Donaldson J's judgment arguably leaves open the question as to whether tender is valid where a bill marked 'weight and quantity unknown' states the quantity on shipment without the 'said to weigh . . .' qualification: presumably, a buyer seeking to justify rejection on these facts could distinguish *The Galatia* on the basis that on such facts there would clearly be an inconsistency between the 'weight and quantity unknown' clause and the statement as to quantity. The buyer's argument in such a case could be supported by a judgment of Macnaghten J in *Libau Wood Co v H Smith & Sons Ltd*[66] in which the judge upheld a c i f buyer's rejection of a bill of lading which contained both an annotation stating that part of the cargo had been lost during loading and a 'weight and quantity unknown' clause. The sellers' argument that the latter type of clause was so common that it could not conceivably invalidate an otherwise valid tender[67], was given extremely short shrift by the judge. At page 300 of the report, Macnaghten J treats both clauses together as equally offensive to the nature of a c i f contract:

> '[I]f I followed [counsel for the sellers] aright every bill of lading is nothing more than an acknowledgement of the shipment of an unknown quantity of goods, the description of which may or may not be in accordance with the statement in the document. I think the argument of [counsel for the buyers] on that point is right. A bill of lading which the buyer is bound to accept must be a document acknowledging the shipment of a quantity of goods according with the quantity specified in the invoice and for which the seller demands payment. And if there is an invoice for a specified quantity and the bill of lading is for either an unknown quantity of goods or a quantity of goods substantially different from that in the invoice, the bill of lading would not be a proper bill of lading which the buyer would be compelled to accept.'

Thus, the position at common law, though not free from doubt, can be summarised as follows. Where the contract is silent as to the acceptability of bills of lading with 'weight and quantity unknown' clauses, the buyer (a) can reject a bill containing such a clause but also saying clearly that goods in a stated quantity have been shipped; (b) cannot reject a bill with such a clause, which bill only states that goods in a given quantity are said to have been shipped. The accuracy of

---

shipped in good order and condition, and are to be delivered in like good order and condition, and a bill of lading *in such a form* is commonly called a clean bill of lading.' (Emphasis added.) The editors go on to describe the evidential effects of 'weight and quantity unknown' clauses, at no stage suggesting that their use makes a bill unclean or invalid. Given the state of the authorities, to link statements as to quantity to the notion of cleanliness is, with respect, to risk confusion: contrast the approach of Macnaghten J in *Libau Wood Co v H Smith & Sons Ltd* (1930) 37 Ll L Rep 296 (to which reference will presently be made in the text) who deals with the matter on the basis of the much simpler and more appropriate question as to whether tender of bill of lading with qualifications as to quantity is 'proper'.

66   (1930) 37 Ll L Rep 296.

67   A circumstance which made Donaldson J 'not unhappy' to reach the (contrary) conclusion he did: see *The Galatia* [1979] 2 Lloyd's Rep 450 at 457.

proposition (a) depends on whether it is correct to distinguish, as suggested above, Donaldson J's judgment in *The Galatia*, (which albeit given in the Commercial Court, was later affirmed in the Court of Appeal), from Macnaghten J's judgment in *Libau Wood Co v H Smith & Sons Ltd*[68]. Given the uncertainty surrounding the position at common law, buyers keen to obtain from their sellers firm receipts issued by the carrier would be well advised to insert appropriate clauses in their contracts of sale, making it clear that bills of lading containing 'weight and quantity unknown' clauses are unacceptable.

— The buyer's rights under Incoterms

Buyers need to do exactly the same thing, but for exactly the opposite reason, where Incoterms are incorporated into the contract. Here, the position is quite clear: the tender of a bill of lading containing a 'weight and quantity' unknown clause is a valid tender[69]. The same rule is neatly reflected in the Uniform Customs and Practice for Documentary Credits, which also allow, in the absence of contrary instruction, tender by the seller of documents containing clauses such as 'shippers load and count' or 'said by shipper to contain' or words of similar effect[70]. Thus, where Incoterms are incorporated, or where a letter of credit is used for payment, a buyer anxious to obtain a bill of lading from the seller containing an unqualified statement as to the quantity of the goods on shipment must expressly include a clause to that effect in his contract of sale or in his instructions to the issuing bank.

(b) The bill must be 'clean'

As well as a statement relating to the quantity of goods shipped, the bill of lading contains one as to the apparent[71] order and condition in

---

[68] (1930) 37 Ll L Rep 296.
[69] See Incoterms, C I F A7, note (c), which reads as follows: 'The following clauses do not convert a clean into an unclean bill of lading: . . .c) clauses which disclaim on the part of the carrier knowledge of contents, weight, measurement, quality or technical specification of the goods.' The note to term A7 starts by defining a clean bill of lading to mean 'one which bears no superimposed clauses expressly declaring a defective condition of the goods or packaging', tending thus towards the narrower of the two interpretations described in fn 65, above, namely that the word 'clean' relates to the apparent order and condition of the goods and not to the quantity in which the goods are stated to have been shipped. Note (c), though, appears to elide the notions of quantity and cleanliness, as Donaldson J seems to do in *The Galatia* [1979] 2 Lloyd's Rep 450 at 457.
[70] See UCP art 32. The Banking Commission of the International Chamber of Commerce, the ICC agency charged with the occasional revision and constant monitoring of the operation of the UCP, has declared itself to be of the view that a 'weight and quantity unknown' clause is clearly a clause containing 'words of similar effect' for the purposes of this article, or rather, of its earlier counterpart as art 17 of the 1974 Revision. The Commission, however, found it impossible to come to a final view as to whether this article applied generally or only to containerised cargo: see, respectively, Decisions (1975-1979) of the ICC Banking Commission, 1980, Paris, at 39-40 and 35-37.
[71] The statement makes a representation about the external appearance of the goods rather than about their actual, internal condition: *Compania Naviera Vasconzada v Churchill and Sim* [1906] 1 KB 237.

which they are shipped. Where this statement is unqualified by reservations indicating a defect in the apparent condition or packaging of the goods, the bill of lading is said to be 'clean'[72]; where it is so qualified, it is said to be 'claused'. The reason for the buyer's strong preference for a clean bill of lading is abundantly clear from what has gone before[73]: the buyer's position in an action against the carrier for damage to goods will be radically affected by the statement made by the carrier as to the apparent condition in which the goods were shipped on board; whether the buyer is making use of the common law estoppel created in his favour by the judges[74], that established by the Carriage of Goods by Sea Act 1971[75], or that contained in section 3 of the Bills of Lading Act 1855[76], these estoppels are only as good as the representation on which they are based and consequently the buyer wants the best possible representation—a completely unqualified one. Moreover, and closely related to the reason just given, the buyer is unlikely to be able to sell the goods through another documentary sale while they are in transit if the document evidencing their shipment brazenly states that something was wrong with them on shipment. In these circumstances, it is not surprising to find that sale contracts very frequently stipulate in express terms that the seller must tender a clean bill of lading[77]; and it has been suggested that where there is no express term in the sale contract to that effect, one ought to be implied[78].

---

[72] As to the definition of the word 'clean', see the discussion at note 65 above.
[73] Chapter 5.1, above.
[74] See *Compania Naviera Vasconzada v Churchill and Sim* [1906] 1 KB 237.
[75] In art III.4 of the Schedule to the Act, reproduced at fn 10 above.
[76] Which sets up an estoppel against the signatory of the bill: see Appendix 1 and fn 9, above.
[77] Thus see GAFTA 100, clause 14; the Coffee Trade Federation F O B , C & F, C I F Contract, clause 36 D; and Rule 117(a)(i) of the Rules to Regulate Cane and Beet Raw Sugar Contracts C I F Free Out and C & F Free Out of the Sugar Association of London. Moreover, where Incoterms are incorporated, the seller is always under a duty to tender a clean bill: see Incoterms C I F A7. Where payment is through a letter of credit, this requirement is reflected in the UCP in art 34(b) which only allows tender by the seller of fouled or claused bills of lading when 'the credit expressly stipulates the clauses or notations which may be accepted.' This effectively means that claused bills can practically never be tendered under letters of credit: for in the nature of things a buyer is highly unlikely either to know of, or agree to, specific clauses as to apparent condition at the time of shipment.
[78] See Benjamin, at para 1643, text accompanying fn 37. So pervasive is the seller's obligation under the sale contract to tender a clean bill of lading that shippers frequently give, and honour, an indemnity holding the carrier harmless against the consequences of issuing a clean bill in circumstances where clausing would have been more appropriate: see Scrutton, art 59, fn 57. Such an indemnity must be expressed in the contract of carriage and cannot simply be implied against a shipper-charterer from the authority given him by the charterparty to present bills of lading to the master for signature: see *The Nogar Marin* [1988] 1 Lloyd's Rep 412; cf *The Boukadoura* [1989] 1 Lloyd's Rep 393. Where the purpose of the express indemnity is to encourage the carrier to make a fraudulent representation about the state in which the goods are shipped, the indemnity may be unenforceable: see *Brown Jenkinson & Co Ltd v Percy Dalton (London) Ltd* [1957] 2 QB 621, where Lord Evershed MR dissented and Pearce LJ only reluctantly joined Morris LJ in finding against enforceability.

The precise contours of the seller's duty are tolerably clear. Thus, a bill of lading stating that a cargo of, say, sugar in bags, has been shipped in apparent good order and condition can be rejected by the buyer if it goes on to say, for example, 'many bags torn and others damp'. Questions as to cleanliness may arise, however, where the bill says that the value, contents or condition are unknown: in such a case, can a buyer reject the bill of lading as against the seller on the ground that it is unclean? It is submitted that it is extremely unlikely that a court would allow rejection by the buyer on such grounds. The question has never arisen for decision in the quite the way it has been put above, that is to say in litigation brought by the seller against the buyer for wrongful rejection[79]. The reason for this, it is suggested, is that the law of carriage by sea safeguards the interests of buyers, qua receivers, to such a degree that rejection of the bill against the seller becomes quite unnecessary. The courts have always been extremely quick to protect buyers, and their estoppels, against carriers, by interpreting clauses seeking to qualify the statement that the goods were shipped in apparent good order and condition very strictly against the carrier. Thus, in *Compania Naviera Vasconzada v Churchill and Sim*[80], the carrier's statement that timber had been 'shipped in good order and condition' was held not to have been qualified by the words 'quality and measure unknown', the word 'condition' being interpreted as referring to 'external and apparent condition'[81], the word 'quality' to 'something which is usually not apparent, at all events to an unskilled person.'[82] The distinction was even used to the buyer's advantage in *The Tromp*[83], where the relevant clause read 'weight, quality, condition and measure unknown', and where it might therefore have been thought that the carrier had successfully qualified his representation that the goods had been shipped in good order and condition. In what is, with respect, a somewhat disingenuous part of his judgment[84], Duke J held that where the damage complained of was wetness in bagged potatoes, the statement 'shipped in good order' was left unqualified by the clause 'quality, condition unknown' because, while 'quality' and 'condition' might, on these facts, be taken to refer to the actual, internal state of the potatoes, the word 'order' must be taken to refer exclusively to their apparent

---

The reaction to the decision in the literature was equally ambivalent: for what is, with respect, a somewhat moralistic approach, see the note by REM in (1957) 73 LQR 438; for a rather more pragmatic view, see that by Mr F.J. Odgers in [1958] CLJ 20. It is, perhaps, unfortunate that this case did not reach the House of Lords, despite leave to appeal being given by the Court of Appeal.

[79] Although it did arise, in an oblique and hypothetical way, in *Peter Cremer, Westfaelische Central Genossenschaft GmbH and Intergraan NV v General Carriers SA, The Dona Mari* [1973] 2 Lloyd's Rep 366 at 375, where Kerr J indicates that a 'quality unknown' clause would not entitle buyers to reject a bill of lading because such words 'are ineffective to qualify a statement that the goods have been shipped in good order and condition.'

[80] [1906] 1 KB 237.

[81] Loc cit at 245.

[82] Ibid. In the same sense also, *The Peter der Grosse* [1876] 1 PD 414, where the relevant clause was 'weight, contents, and value unknown.'

[83] [1921] P 337.

[84] Loc cit at 348, 349.

state; and as to that, there was no qualification and the carrier was consequently bound by his representation that the potatoes had been shipped in apparent good order. A similar play on words was not available to Langton J in *The Skarp*[85], where the clauses were in effect identical to those in *The Tromp*[86], but where the cargo was timber, as in the *Compania Naviera* case[87]. The judge was clearly not inclined to allow the carrier to escape from the estoppel through the simple expedient of making a statement, 'shipped in good order and condition', which was then qualified out of existence by another, 'condition unknown':

> '[I]t is difficult to understand why the affirmation or acceptance of one untruth should be cleared by a deliberate statement of another untruth.'[88]

However compelling the reason for limiting the effect of the qualification, though, the judge had to achieve that result through reasoning which did no violence to the parties' contractual liberty: Langton J did so by construing the word 'condition' in the 'unknown' clause, though (remarkably) not in the 'shipped' clause, as referring to the actual quality of the cargo as timber: 'whether it was ripe or over-ripe or something of that sort'[89]; again, consequently, there was no qualification of the statement as to apparent condition, to which statement the carrier was therefore bound.

To such extremes of construction are the judges willing to go, in cargo claims against the carrier, so as to preserve the statement that goods have been shipped in good order and condition as a clear and unequivocal representation that they have, in law, been so shipped. This being the case, it seems that the buyer need seek no further protection against such clauses by stipulating in his sale contract that a bill of lading containing a 'condition unknown' clause cannot be tendered. Moreover, in the absence of such stipulation in the sale contract, rejection of such a bill would, it is submitted, be a repudiatory breach on the part of the buyer. The position is the same, only for even clearer reasons, where Incoterms are incorporated into the contract. The definition of a clean bill of lading, given in term C I F A7, as one which 'bears no superimposed clauses expressly declaring a defective condition of the goods or packaging' can, on no reasonable construction, exclude a bill saying simply that the quality or condition of the goods on shipment is 'unknown'. The same definition is adopted by the Uniform Customs and Practice for Documentary Credits in article 34(a)[90], with the result that, saving express contrary stipulation in the buyer's instructions to

---

[85] [1935] P 134.
[86] [1921] P 337. The clauses in *The Skarp* were: shipped 'in good order and condition' and 'condition, quality, description and measurement unknown.'
[87] [1906] 1 KB 237.
[88] [1935] P 134 at 144.
[89] Loc cit at 143.
[90] This article reads: 'A clean transport document is one which bears no superimposed clause or notation which expressly declares a defective condition of the goods and/ or the packaging.'

the issuing bank, tender of a bill containing a 'quality and condition unknown' clause is valid.

CHAPTER 6

Qualities of the bill of lading as a contract

1. Terms of the carriage contract purchased by the buyer

    i. The bill of lading as evidence of the contract of carriage between the seller and the carrier

    ii. The bill of lading as the contract of carriage between the buyer and the carrier

2. The seller's duty relating to the carriage contract sold to the buyer

3. Carriage contract to provide continuous documentary cover to the destination port agreed in the sale contract

  (a) Bills giving carrier liberty to deviate

    i. Where sale contract stipulates direct shipment

    ii. Where sale contract does not stipulate for direct shipment

  (b) Deck stowage

    i. Deck stowage unauthorised by the bill of lading

    ii. Cargo stated to be carried on deck

    iii. Bill of lading granting carrier liberty to stow on deck

  (c) Transhipment

    i. Clauses in the bill stating that the goods will be transhipped

    ii. Bills giving carrier liberty to tranship

      1. Where the bill gives 'through' cover

      2. Where the bill does not give 'through' cover

  (d) Bills with destination different to sale destination

In Chapter 5, we saw that while it is normally the seller who organises the issue of the bill of lading by the carrier at the port of loading[1],

---

[1] That is to say, where the sale is concluded on c i f , c & f , f o b with additional services, and f o b classic terms. Where the sale is on straight f o b terms, the seller will have little say over the form in which the bill of lading is issued by the carrier to the buyer: see Chapter 1.2.(a).ii above.

it is always the buyer who, qua receiver of the goods, eventually becomes the party most interested in the evidential function of that document as a receipt. The same is true of the contractual role of the bill of lading: through the operation of section 1 of the Bills of Lading Act 1855[2], it is the buyer who will look to the bill of lading both for his right to sue the carrier for short-delivery or damage to cargo and, at any rate where the buyer has not chartered the vessel carrying the goods[3], for the regime applicable to such an action[4]. Given the stake he has in the bill of lading as a contract of carriage, the buyer will wish the seller to obtain from the carrier the most favourable terms possible: at the very least, the buyer will expect the seller to procure a contract of carriage 'on usual terms'[5] or on terms which are 'reasonable having regard to the nature of the goods and other circumstances of the case'[6]. The central aim of this chapter is to investigate what is meant by 'usual' terms: to discover what sort of carriage contract a buyer is entitled to from his seller. Our first task will be to define precisely which terms of the seller's contract with the carrier pass to the buyer's contract with the carrier: we shall see that it is not every term agreed in the former contract which passes to the latter. Secondly, we shall examine the nature and source of the seller's obligation to the buyer to procure a contract of carriage on reasonable terms. Thirdly and finally, we shall focus on the central duty which that general obligation entails: namely, the duty to provide a carriage contract which gives the buyer continuous documentary cover against the carrier from the loading port to the destination agreed in the sale contract. In this last section of the chapter, we will be asking mainly whether the buyer, or the bank where a letter of credit is used, can legitimately reject a bill of lading which grants the carrier liberties to deviate, carry goods on deck, or tranship them on other vessels; we shall also see how discrepancies can arise between the destination agreed between the seller and the carrier in the contract of carriage and that agreed between the seller and the buyer in the contract of sale.

---

[2]   See Chapter 3.1.(a) above.

[3]   In which case, his contract with the carrier is contained in the charterparty: *President of India v Metcalfe Shipping Co Ltd, The Dunelmia* [1970] 1 QB 289. We shall be discussing this type of case in Chapter 7, when we deal with bills of lading issued under charterparties.

[4]   The same can be said, with one caveat, of buyers whose locus standi is based on the type of contract implied in *Brandt v Liverpool Brazil and River Plate Steam Navigation Co Ltd* [1924] 1 KB 575. The qualification relates to goods covered by delivery orders. Where a receiver of goods covered by a ship's delivery order attorned to by the carrier founds his contractual claim on the device in *Brandt v Liverpool*, the regime governing cargo claims is that provided for by the delivery order rather than by the bill of lading. Where the delivery order expressly incorporates bill of lading terms, the two would, of course, be the same. Where, on the other hand, the terms on the bill have not been incorporated into the delivery order, then the buyer (and, incidentally, the carrier) cannot take advantage of the terms of the bill of lading: see *Colin and Shields v W Weddel & Co Ltd* [1952] 2 Lloyd's Rep 9 at 17 and 19.

[5]   See Incoterms, C I F A2, A7; and C & F A2, A6.

[6]   See s 32(2), Sale of Goods Act 1979, which is discussed further at Chapter 6.2 below.

1. TERMS OF THE CARRIAGE CONTRACT PURCHASED BY THE BUYER

When we say that the seller owes the buyer a duty to procure and transfer a contract of carriage on usual or reasonable terms, to which contract of carriage are we referring: is it to the contract concluded, whether through written or oral terms, between the seller, qua shipper, and the carrier; or is it to a neater version of that contract, the version, perhaps, crystallised in the precise and easily accessible terms of the bill of lading[7]? The question is relevant to the issues discussed in this chapter because it is impossible to decide whether the seller has procured a proper contract of carriage for his buyer unless we first establish which contract of carriage the buyer is to scrutinise under the contract of sale. The short answer to the question is that the carriage contract which the buyer purchases from the seller is that contained in the bill of lading. Section 1 of the Bills of Lading Act 1855, it will be recalled[8], actually says so:

> 'Every consignee of goods named in a bill of lading, and every endorsee of a bill of lading, to whom the property in the goods shall pass upon or by reason of such consignment or endorsement, shall have transferred to and vested in him all rights of suit, and be subject to the same liabilities in respect of such goods as if the contract *contained in the bill of lading* had been made with himself.' (Emphasis added.)

The point seems at first sight to be too obvious for discussion; but a dictum by Lord Bramwell in the House of Lords decision in *Sewell v Burdick*[9] makes it necessary to go behind the bland words of the section in search of further explanation. In that case, Lord Bramwell said:

> 'There is, I think, another inaccuracy in the statute . . . It speaks of the contract contained in the bill of lading. To my mind there is no contract in it. It is a receipt for the goods, stating the terms on which they were delivered to and received by the ship, and therefore excellent evidence of those terms, but it is not a contract.'

It looks as if the Act is saying that the bill of lading, and only the bill of lading, contains all the terms of the contract of carriage; whereas Lord Bramwell seems to be suggesting that it does not. This apparent contradiction is resolved by distinguishing between the contractual role of the bill of lading as between the seller, qua shipper of the goods, and the carrier; and its contractual role as between the buyer, qua receiver of the goods, and the carrier.

---

[7] Excluded from discussion in this chapter is the question as to whether the buyer is bound by terms contained in a charterparty which is concluded between the seller and the carrier, and the terms of which are incorporated into the bill transferred to the buyer. This question will be dealt with in Chapter 7, when we shall be examining several problems arising from the issue of bills of lading under charterparties.

[8] From Chapter 3.1.(a).

[9] (1884) 10 App Cas 74 at 105.

i. The bill of lading as evidence of the contract of carriage between the seller and the carrier

As between the seller, as shipper, and the carrier, the bill of lading is excellent evidence of the terms of the contract of carriage: that contract may, however, contain other terms which were not recorded on the bill of lading but which are nonetheless binding as between these two parties. The reason for this, at first sight, somewhat surprising proposition[10] has to do with two basic propositions of general contract law, namely, that bilateral contracts are concluded on the exchange of mutual promises and that contracts generally need no written record for their validity. Thus, contracts of carriage, in common with most other contracts[11], may be made without any written record. Although this happens, of course, very rarely, the rule still means that, even where a bill of lading is issued, 'the issue of the bill of lading does not necessarily mark any stage in the development of the contract'[12]. The contract of carriage will, indeed, have typically been concluded some time before the issue of the bill of lading[13], which is normally issued after the goods are shipped. Consequently, if in the interim the shipper and the carrier agree to terms, whether orally or in writing, which they do not include on the bill of lading, the parties are nonetheless bound by such terms, which are no less part of their contract although not part of the bill of lading. Thus, in *The Ardennes*[14], an oral agreement made prior to the issue of the bill of lading, that a cargo of mandarin oranges would be shipped without deviation, was held to prevail over a term in the bill giving the carrier a liberty to deviate. Once a stipulation expressly disallowing deviation had been agreed between the parties, then nothing in the standard form of a bill of lading subsequently issued could alter that agreement[15].

ii. The bill of lading as the contract of carriage between the buyer and the carrier

As between the buyer, qua receiver of the goods, and the carrier, the bill of lading is the contract in the sense that it contains, and it alone contains, the contractual terms between those parties, thus excluding any terms agreed to between the shipper and the carrier outside the

---

[10] For surely, most shippers and carriers would expect the terms of their contract to be contained exclusively in the bill of lading.

[11] For the exceptions, see Treitel, pp 135–143.

[12] *Pyrene Co Ltd v Scindia Navigation Co Ltd* [1954] 2 QB 402 at 409, per Devlin J.

[13] The precise moment of conclusion of the contract of carriage will depend on the facts of each situation: the latest moment at which the contract may be said to exist is clearly the time of shipment of the goods; on the other hand, there is no reason to suppose that it might not have been concluded at a far earlier, and less formal, stage, for example when space was booked by telephone: see The Bill of Lading as the Contract of Carriage—Reassessment of *Leduc v Ward*, C. Debattista, [1982] 45 MLR 652 at 652, 653.

[14] [1951] 1 KB 55.

[15] See, for an illustration of the same rule in circumstances where the prior agreement was itself written rather than oral, *Moss SS Co Ltd v Whinney* [1912] AC 254.

parameters of the bill. The reason for the rule is quite clear: the buyer only has notice of those terms recorded on the bill and to bind him to any others would do violence to the fundamental principle of general contract law that express terms have contractual force only if they are notified to either party before or at the time of the conclusion of the contract[16]. Thus in *Leduc v Ward*[17], a carrier was sued by an endorsee for non-delivery in circumstances which the carrier pleaded came within an exclusion clause; the plaintiff alleged deviation by the carrier which, on the law as it then stood[18], would have deprived him of the protection of all exclusion clauses. The carrier argued that there was no deviation because the route taken on the voyage had been expressly and orally agreed to by the shipper in a stipulation not recorded on the bill. The Court of Appeal, however, held that that stipulation was not part of the contract between the endorsee and the carrier[19]; that as between those parties, the route taken was outside that allowed in the bill of lading; and that consequently, the carrier had deviated his way out of the exclusion clauses in the bill of lading[20]. By the same token, waiver of the carrier's deviation by the seller does not affect the buyer of the goods, who retains the right to repudiate the contract of carriage forfeited by the seller.[21]

2. THE SELLER'S DUTY RELATING TO THE CARRIAGE CONTRACT SOLD TO THE BUYER

If, then, the buyer's contract with the carrier is contained exclusively in the bill of lading, what duty does the seller owe the buyer with regard

---

[16] *Olley v Marlborough Court* [1949] 1 KB 532. The rule does not always work to the buyer's advantage. Thus, on the facts of *The Ardennes* [1951] 1 KB 55, had the action been brought by an endorsee of the bill of lading rather than by the shipper, the endorsee would doubtless have rather preferred to have inherited from the shipper the special term disallowing deviation than the bill of lading term which did not: see text accompanying fn 14.

[17] (1888) 20 QBD 475.

[18] See now *Photo Production v Securicor Transport Ltd* [1980] AC 827; *The Antares (Nos. 1 & 2)* [1987] 1 Lloyd's Rep 424; and *State Trading Corpn of India Ltd v M Golodetz Ltd* [1989] 2 Lloyd's Rep 277; see also Fundamental Breach of Charterparty, M. Clarke, 1978 LMCLQ 472; The Future of Deviation in the Law of Carriage of Goods, C.P. Mills, 1983 LMCLQ 587; and Fundamental Breach and Deviation in the Carriage of Goods by Sea, C. Debattista, 1988 JBL 22.

[19] On one reading, the ratio of the case is actually wider than the text suggests: it appears from parts of the judgments that the members of the court felt that the bill of lading contained all the terms of the contract of carriage, even as between the carrier and the shipper of the goods: see The Bill of Lading as the Contract of Carriage—A Reassessment of *Leduc v Ward*, C. Debattista, [1982] 45 MLR 652, particularly 660. If this is correct, then it is undesirable in the sense that it would make suspect the decision in *Pyrene Co Ltd v Scindia Navigation Ltd* [1954] 2 QB 402.

[20] For further illustrations of the same principle, see *Royal Exchange Shipping Co v Dixon* (1886) 12 App Cas 11, where a buyer was not affected by the seller's agreement with the carrier that goods could be stowed on deck; and *The El Amria and El Minia* [1982] 2 Lloyd's Rep 28, where a contract between the shipper and the carrier containing a jurisdiction clause different to that stipulated in the bill of lading was held not to avail the bill of lading holders.

[21] *Hain SS Co Ltd v Tate and Lyle Ltd* [1936] 2 All ER 597 at 602-603 and 608-609; see also Benjamin, para 1463.

to the type of carriage contract transferred to the buyer through tender of the bill of lading? The answer is sometimes expressly given in the sale contract itself, at any rate in very general terms. Thus, we have already seen that, where the contract is on c i f or c & f terms and Incoterms are incorporated into the contract, the seller 'must contract on usual terms . . . for the carriage of the goods to the agreed port of destination by the usual route'[22]. Where the contract is not on c i f or c & f terms[23], or where, even though it is, Incoterms are not incorporated, the courts have shown themselves to be extremely willing to imply such a term, whether of their own motion[24] or on the back of section 32(2) of the Sale of Goods Act 1979, which reads:

> 'Unless otherwise authorised by the buyer, the seller must make such contract with the carrier on behalf of the buyer as may be reasonable having regard to the nature of the goods and other circumstances of the case; and if the seller omits to do so, and the goods are lost or damaged in the course of transit, the buyer may decline to treat the delivery to the carrier as a delivery to himself or may hold the seller responsible in damages.'

The carriage contract must be concluded on 'reasonable'[25] terms, rather than on terms which will necessarily guarantee the buyer success in litigation against the carrier: so long as it provides the buyer with a cause of action against the carrier, the seller will have discharged this part of his responsibilities towards the buyer[26]. This principle permeates through our discussion, in the next part of this chapter, of the seller's duty to provide the buyer with a bill of lading giving him continuous documentary cover against the carrier.

---

[22] C I F A2, A7; similarly, C & F A2, A6. Another example of an express term establishing the seller's duty in this regard can be found in the Coffee Trade Federation's F O B, C & F and C I F Contract, at clause 13, the relevant part of which reads: 'It is an express condition of the contract that the sellers are under obligation: . . . B. to conclude with due diligence, on the customary terms, a contract for the carriage of the coffee by a usual route to the port of destination; . . .'

[23] That is to say, in this context, where the contract is on f o b extended or classic terms and where, consequently, the seller is responsible for organising the issue of the bill of lading.

[24] See *Ranson v Manufacture d'Engrais* (1922) 13 Ll L Rep 205, where Greer J allowed recovery in damages for breach of an implied term that goods would be carried on a steamship rather than a sailing ship, carriage on the former type of vessel having been found to be usual for the type of cargo sold. The report gives no indication that the sale contract stipulated for the tender of a bill of lading on usual terms; nor that s 32(2) of the Sale of Goods Act 1893 was used as the basis for the implication of the term by the judge. See also, in the same sense, *Finska Cellulosaforeningen v Westfield Paper Co Ltd* (1941) 46 Com Cas 87, particularly, on this point, at 91–93, where a war risk clause was held to be usual, the duty to tender a usual bill of lading being implied sub silentio.

[25] The time at which the particular term in the bill under scrutiny must be usual or reasonable is the time of shipment rather than the time of the sale contract: see, as to the reasonableness of the route taken, *Tsakiroglou & Co v Noblee Thorl GmbH* [1961] 2 All ER 179 at 185I–186B.

[26] See *The Galatia* [1979] 2 Lloyd's Rep 450 at 456, per Donaldson J; approved by the Court of Appeal at [1980] 1 Lloyd's Rep 453.

3. CARRIAGE CONTRACT TO PROVIDE CONTINUOUS DOCUMENTARY COVER TO THE DESTINATION PORT AGREED IN THE SALE CONTRACT

The contract of carriage contained in the bill of lading must give the buyer rights enforceable against the carrier in respect of the whole voyage, from the port of loading to the port of destination: and a bill of lading which fails to afford the buyer such continuous documentary cover against the carrier is not a contract of carriage on usual or reasonable terms and can consequently be rejected by the buyer. In *Hansson v Hamel and Horley*[27], Lord Sumner said:[28]

> 'When documents are to be taken up the buyer is entitled to documents which substantially confer protective rights throughout. He is not buying a litigation . . . These documents have to be handled by banks, they have to be taken up or rejected promptly and without any opportunity for prolonged inquiry, they have to be such as can be retendered to sub-purchasers, and it is essential that they should so conform to the accustomed shipping documents as to be reasonably and readily fit to pass current in commerce.'

Thus in that case, tender by the seller of a bill of lading covering only the second leg of a voyage during which goods were transhipped was held invalid by the House of Lords.

The requirement of continuous documentary cover will be discussed here in the context of three types of clause, all quite common in bills of lading, and each of which gives the carrier a liberty to act in a manner which might be thought to raise doubts as to whether the requirement is satisfied. Thus, where a bill of lading gives the carrier a liberty to deviate from the contract voyage, does the bill offend against the principle of continuous documentary cover, such that a buyer, inclined to reject against a falling market, might use that as a ground for rejection? Exactly the same question will be asked of bills of lading which give the carrier liberties to carry the goods on deck and to tranship. Deck stowage and transhipment also raise questions as to the validity of documentary tender where the bill of lading actually states that the goods will be stowed on deck or transhipped: consequently, the effect of such statements on tender will also be discussed. The cover must last to the port of destination, and to no other: our final task in this chapter will be to look at the rule that the bill of lading must be made out for the destination stipulated in the contract of sale.

(a) Bills giving carrier liberty to deviate

Can a buyer reject a bill of lading on the ground that it grants the

---

27   [1922] 2 AC 36.
28   Loc cit at p 46.

carrier a liberty to deviate[29]? Such liberties are frequently drawn in alarmingly wide terms; thus, for example, the relevant part of one bill of lading[30] reads as follows:

> '17. (1) The Carrier may at any time and without notice to the Merchant
>
> (a) use any means of Carriage whatsoever.
> (b) transfer the Goods from one conveyance to another, including but not limited to transhipping or carrying the same on another vessel than that named on the face hereof.
> . . . . .
> (d) proceed by any route in his discretion (whether or not the nearest or most direct or customary or advertised route), at any speed, and proceed to or stay at any place or port whatsoever, once or more often and in any order.
> . . . . .
>
> (2) The liberties set out in sub-clause (1) may be invoked by the Carrier for any purpose whatsoever, whether or not connected with the Carriage of the Goods, including loading or unloading other goods, bunkering, undergoing repairs, adjusting instruments, packing up or landing any persons, included but not limited to persons involved with the operation or maintenance of the vessel and assisting vessels in all situations. Anything done in accordance with sub-clause (1) or any delay arising therefrom shall be deemed to be within the contractual Carriage and shall not be a deviation.'

Given the remarkable latitude this clause appears to give the carrier, it may seem, at any rate at first sight, that a buyer might legitimately object to tender by the seller of a bill containing such a clause on the ground that it does not afford continuous documentary cover. For surely, whether or not the carrier actually deviates, a buyer accepting a bill with such a clause would, in the words of Lord Sumner[31], be 'buying a litigation'? Ought not the buyer, therefore, be allowed to reject the bill on that ground? It would be helpful to examine this question in two separate sets of circumstance: firstly, where the sale contract itself stipulates for direct shipment of the goods; secondly, where it does not.

i. *Where sale contract stipulates direct shipment*

Where the sale contract contains a term that shipment is to be direct[32],

---

[29] The issue discussed in the text relates to clauses giving the carrier a liberty to deviate, rather than to actual deviation by the carrier. It is clear that any remedy the buyer might have for actual deviation lies against the carrier rather than against the seller: see *Burstall & Co v Grimsdale & Sons* (1906) 11 Com Cas 280 at 291, an extract reproduced below in the text accompanying fn 53. See also Benjamin, paras 1464, 1638.

[30] Used by the Cunard Ellerman Line.

[31] See fn 28, above.

[32] A good number of standard term contracts of sale do quite the opposite, that is to say they expressly reserve to the seller the right to organise shipment direct or indirect: see, for example, GAFTA 100, clause 8: 'Shipment to be made . . . direct or indirect'; Contract No 3 (c i f for all Countries) of the Rubber Trade Association of London, page 2, the relevant part of which reads: 'To be shipped . . . direct, and/or indirect, with liberty to call . . . at other ports.' Judging by the cases which have come before the courts on this point, buyers stipulating for direct shipment have only done so by way of a special

then although there seems to be no authority precisely in point, it is suggested that the buyer can reject a bill of lading containing any form of clause giving the carrier a liberty to deviate. In *Bergerco USA v Vegoil*[33], a buyer was held entitled to reject goods on the grounds that they had not been shipped on a 'contractual ship'[34]: the parties had agreed that shipment would be direct to Bombay, whereas the vessel on which the cargo was loaded was actually scheduled to call at several intermediate ports. The case does not take quite the same question we are asking here, that is to say, whether a buyer can reject a bill of lading containing a liberty to deviate; and this for two reasons. Firstly, the central issue in the case was whether the buyers could reject goods, rather than whether they could reject documents[35]; secondly, the buyers' stated ground for rejection[36] was a scheduled departure from the 'direct' route agreed in the contract of sale, rather than a deviation by the carrier in purported exercise of a liberty to deviate in the bill of lading. There is, however, less to these objections than may appear at first sight. As for the first, Hobhouse J characterised the seller's breach as a failure to comply with an all-or-nothing stipulation to make a contractual shipment rather than a continuing promise on the part of the seller that the carrier would not deviate[37]: viewed in this light, the term broken by the sellers was simply the physical parallel of their obligation to tender a contractual bill of lading, and extrapolation from the former duty to the latter is consequently legitimate. As for the second, the supposed contrast between a scheduled departure and a liberty to deviate throws up a distinction without a difference: from the point of view of a sale contract stipulating for direct shipment, calls into port under a schedule and calls made in exercise of a liberty to deviate are quite the same thing. The decision by Hobhouse J in *Bergerco*[38] does, consequently, lend support to the proposition that a buyer can reject a bill of lading granting the carrier a liberty to deviate where the sale contract stipulates for direct shipment[39].

ii. *Where sale contract does not stipulate for direct shipment*

Where the contract of sale either says nothing about the route of transit

---

addition to the standard form used, sometimes as a quid pro quo for some indulgence allowed to the seller: thus, in *Bergerco USA v Vegoil Ltd* [1984] 1 Lloyd's Rep 440, the stipulation was extracted in return for an extension to the shipment period; again, in *State Trading Corpn of India Ltd v M Golodetz Ltd* [1988] 2 Lloyd's Rep 182, the direct shipment clause was specially incorporated into the standard form: see p 183; revsd [1989] 2 Lloyd's Rep 277.

33 [1984] 1 Lloyd's Rep 440.
34 Loc cit at 443.
35 The documents had, in fact, been accepted by the bank under a letter of credit: this circumstance was held not to estop the buyers from now rejecting the goods. As to this aspect of the case, see Chapter 9.4.(c).iii, below.
36 The fact that the market price for the commodity involved had fallen might also, of course, have had some part to play in the buyer's decision to reject: see [1984] 1 Lloyd's Rep 440 at 442.
37 See [1984] 1 Lloyd's Rep 440 at 443.
38 [1984] 1 Lloyd's Rep 440.
39 Cf Benjamin, para 1637, where the editors give the case as direct, rather than oblique, authority for the proposition stated here in the text.

or, as is quite commonly the case[40], expressly gives the seller the option of shipping 'direct or indirect', the position is not so clear. It is certain on authority that the buyer can reject a bill of lading granting the carrier a liberty to deviate where the extent of the liberty is uncertain because the clause itself is not printed on the bill[41]. This, however, hardly assists with the vast majority of bills of lading where the reverse is the case: that is to say where the liberty clause is clearly carried, in the terms such as those reproduced above[42], on the reverse side of the bill of lading. Can a buyer reject such a bill of lading in the absence of express stipulation for direct shipment in the sale contract? The editors of Benjamin, founding themselves on the judgment of Greer J in *Shipton, Anderson & Co v John Weston & Co* [43], suggest that the buyer can so reject where the clause is

> 'so wide that the ship might have called anywhere she liked and almost have gone round the world before she came to the port of discharge.'[44]

On the basis of that test, the clause reproduced above[45] would clearly vitiate tender of a bill of lading; and the editors of Benjamin would presumably justify rejection by the buyer because, in their words,

> 'the shipping documents "have to be taken up or rejected promptly" (*Hansson v Hamel and Horley Ltd* [1922] 2 AC 36 at 46) and this would not be possible if the buyer (or his bank) had to resolve such difficult questions of construction.'[46]

This view, it is submitted, gives cause for some concern: wide liberty clauses of the type exemplified above[47] are in very common use; the seller of the goods, qua shipper, has, at any rate in practice, little or no control over the terms in which they are drawn; and rejection, or its threat, by the buyer on this ground would put the seller in an impossible position against a falling market. This consideration of itself does not, of course, decide the case against the buyer's right to reject: it does at least, though, raise the question as to whether the right to reject is necessary to safeguard the buyer's interests. It is submitted that the law of carriage of goods by sea gives the buyer adequate protection against the unjustified use of liberty clauses by carriers; that, had the buyer wished for a greater degree of protection, namely, had he wished for a bill of lading ruling out any deviation, then he could have stipulated such a term expressly in the contract of sale; and that where he has not, it is clear that he is content with the protection granted him, qua receiver of the goods, by the law of carriage.

---

40   See the standard form clauses reproduced at fn 32 above.
41   *Spillers Ltd v J W Mitchell Ltd* (1929) 33 Ll L Rep 89.
42   See text accompanying fn 30 above.
43   (1922) 10 Ll L Rep 762.
44   Ibid at 763.
45   See text accompanying fn 30 above.
46   See Benjamin, para 1638.
47   See text accompanying fn 30 above.

That protection comes in three shapes: the rule in *Glynn v Margetson*[48]; by the residual doctrine of fundamental breach, as applied in *Connolly Shaw Ltd v Nordenfjeldske SS Co*[49]; and, where the Carriage of Goods by Sea Act 1971 applies, by the combined effect of articles III.8 and IV.4 of the Schedule to that Act. Through each of these devices, the law of carriage protects the receiver of goods against the unjustified use of liberty clauses: that protection makes it quite unnecessary further to allow the buyer a right of rejection which can so easily be abused against a falling market. We shall examine each form of protection in turn.

— The rule in *Glynn v Margetson*[50]

Under the rule in *Glynn v Margetson*, the courts will construe a clause giving the carrier a liberty to deviate down to the contractual voyage provided for in the contract of carriage, so as not to defeat the main object and purpose of that contract. Thus, in *Glynn v Margetson*[51] itself, a liberty clause in wide terms was held not to allow deviation to a port which was not on the route between the ports of loading and discharge. Consequently, where a buyer of a bill of lading containing a liberty clause is aggrieved by a deviation allegedly made in exercise of that liberty, his cause of action for damage or short delivery against the carrier is not defeated by the liberty clause if the actual use made of it by the carrier would defeat the commercial object of the contract of carriage. In these circumstances, it is difficult to see why the buyer needs also to have the right to reject the documents as against the seller. This point was made in a somewhat neglected part of Kennedy J's judgment in *Burstall & Co v Grimsdale and Sons*[52], a case in which rejection of a bill of lading by the buyer on the ground, inter alia, that it contained a liberty clause, was held unjustified. At the relevant part of the report, Kennedy J said[53]:

> 'Suppose, however, that the clause in the bill of lading would not, under the decision of the House of Lords in *Glynn v Margetson*[54], allow such a thing to be done as was done in this case, namely, calling at Bremen. Even then there is nothing for these buyers to complain of as against the shippers. The buyers have on this hypothesis got a contract which is, from the mercantile point of view, an ordinary contract, and they cannot say that there has been a power given to the carriers to deviate where a deviation might possibly injure or delay the delivery. The shippers' answer to any

---

[48] [1893] AC 351. The point made in the text about this case is taken in Benjamin, para 1638, but rejected for reasons which are, with respect, not entirely clear.
[49] (1934) 49 Ll L Rep 183.
[50] [1893] AC 351.
[51] Ibid.
[52] (1906) 11 Com Cas 280.
[53] Loc cit at 291.
[54] [1893] AC 351.

complaint by the buyers would be this, that the clause in the bill of lading which they, the shippers, have accepted under the through bill of lading is not a clause which enables the carriers to deviate. In other words, the shippers could say, "We have done nothing wrong in sending your goods by carriers whose contract does not entitle them as against you to deviate; therefore we have performed our duty in sending the goods, not only by a steamer destined to London, but also by a steamer that has no right to deviate." If there is a breach of that contract of carriage by deviating the buyers would have a right of action against the carriers, but it is clear that there could be no claim as against the shippers.'

The decision of Kennedy J in this case has not, it is submitted, received the exposure it deserves. The case has been explained away as one decided on its special facts, the liberty clause being usual and customary 'in the trade in question'[55]: with respect, though, it is difficult to see, at any rate from the report, that the case was either argued or decided with such constrictions in mind. The case was not even cited in *Shipton Anderson & Co v John Weston & Co*[56], which was, it will be recalled, the case upon which the editors of Benjamin base their view in favour of rejection. Stated at its very lowest, *Burstall & Co v Grimsdale and Sons*[57], conflicting as it does with the later decision in the *Shipton Anderson* case[58], leaves the question unsettled by authority; stated at its very highest, it decides the question against rejection, Kennedy J's judgment not having been cited in *Shipton Anderson*[59], in which the buyer was held, in any case, to have waived the right, which he allegedly had, to reject the bill of lading.

— A 'residual' doctrine of fundamental breach

The trigger operating the device in *Glynn v Margetson*[60] is the discrepancy between the voyage agreed in the contract of carriage and the apparently limitless extent of the liberty to deviate: the effect of the rule is, as it were, to read the latter down to the dimensions of the former. What, however, if the clause seeks to extend the limits of the former, the contract voyage, out to the dimensions of the latter, the deviation liberty clause? The clause reproduced above purports to do just that in its very last sentence, which reads: 'The exercise of any of the above liberties shall be deemed to be part of the contractual voyage.' A clause in broadly similar terms was the object of litigation in *Connolly Shaw Ltd v*

---

55   See Benjamin, para 1638.
56   (1922) 10 Ll L Rep 762. Neither, it seems, has the decision been considered in any other case; it was acknowledged, without observation, by Viscount Caldecote LCJ in *Finska Cellulosaforeningen v Westfield Paper Co Ltd* [1940] 4 All ER 473 at 478.
57   (1906) 11 Com Cas 280.
58   (1922) 10 Ll L Rep 762.
59   Ibid.
60   [1893] AC 351.

Nordenfjeldske SS Co[61], where Branson J decided that even such a clause could not be 'imported into the definition of the voyage' such as to 'lead to an entire frustration of a contract [of carriage]'[62]. Here again, consequently, the law of carriage offers the receiver of goods sufficient protection against unjustified use by the carrier of even the widest form of liberty clause: to grant the buyer the right to reject the documents against the seller would be to give him a quite gratuitous remedy.

— Carriage of Goods by Sea Act 1971

Finally, where the Carriage of Goods by Sea Act 1971 applies, article IV.4 of the Schedule to the Act allows only

> '[A]ny deviation in saving or attempting to save life or property at sea or any reasonable deviation . . .'

The exercise of a liberty clause outside the circumstances allowed by article IV.4 would, it is submitted, come to grief against article III.8, which renders null

> '[A]ny clause . . . relieving the carrier or the ship from liability for loss or damage to, or in connection with, goods arising from negligence, fault, or failure in the duties and obligations provided in this article or lessening such liability otherwise than as provided in these Rules . . .'

Again, through these articles of the Hague-Visby Rules, the law of carriage solves the buyer's problems if and when they arise: what need, then, of additional rights under the contract of sale? It must be recalled that the obligation of the seller is to procure for the buyer a contract of carriage giving the buyer continuous locus standi against the carrier, not one which gives the carrier no defences.

The use by a carrier of a clause giving him a liberty to deviate is hedged around both by judicial canons of construction and by substantive statutory rules: where the buyer has not thought to stipulate for direct carriage in the sale contract, it is suggested that he needs no further

---

[61] (1934) 49 Ll L Rep 183. The relevant part of the liberty to deviate clause read: 'and all such ports, places and sailings shall be deemed included within the intended voyage of the said goods.'

[62] Ibid at 191. Branson J's judgment sounds uncannily like an early version of the doctrine of fundamental breach, a doctrine assaulted by the House of Lords in *Suisse Atlantique Societe d'Armement Maritime SA v Rotterdamsche Kolen Centrale NV* [1967] 1 AC 361 and given decent burial in *Photo Productions v Securicor Transport Ltd* [1980] AC 827. Despite the uncomfortable affinity between that doctrine and this part of Branson J's judgment, it is clear that enough life is left in the doctrine to allow the judges to strike down clauses which, if applied, would deprive the agreement of 'the legal characteristics of a contract': see per Lord Diplock in the *Securicor* case [1980] AC 827 at 850E-F, and other cases cited in Fundamental Breach and Deviation in the Carriage of Goods by Sea, C. Debattista, 1989 JBL 22 at 34.

remedies under the contract of sale for deviation by the carrier, whether justified or not by the contract of carriage.

(b) Deck stowage

Our central question here is whether a seller can tender a bill of lading giving the carrier a liberty to carry the goods on deck. Deck carriage raises problems, however, in three different types of circumstance: where the bill of lading says nothing about carriage on deck, that is to say, where carriage on deck is unauthorised; where the bill says that the goods will actually be carried on deck; and where the bill gives the carrier a liberty to carry on deck. The law of sale, the law of carriage and the law relating to letters of credit each have something to say about each of these situations and the resulting overall position is therefore rather complex. It would be helpful consequently if we dealt with each case separately.

i. Deck stowage unauthorised by the bill of lading

Where the carrier stows goods on deck in the absence of any liberty so to do expressed on the bill of lading, the buyer can, if damage ensues, sue the carrier for breach of the latter's duty 'properly and carefully [to] stow' the goods[63]: the buyer's remedy[64] against the carrier[65] clearly emerges from the contract of carriage[66]. The question arises as to whether the carrier's breach under the contract of carriage also puts the seller in breach of the contract of sale, a breach in respect of which the buyer would have a separate remedy under the latter contract. The major

---

[63] Carriage of Goods by Sea Act 1971, Sch art III.2. Where the Act does not apply, a similar clause will be implied by the courts: *Royal Exchange Shipping Co v Dixon* (1886) 12 App Cas 11. The case involved four bills of lading, three of which specifically stipulated for under deck carriage, the fourth of which was silent as to the manner of stowage. The House of Lords held that the term would be implied into the fourth bill, and would have been implied into all four had all four been silent on the matter.

[64] It would appear from *Royal Exchange Shipping Co Ltd v Dixon* (1886) 12 App Cas 11 that the buyer's remedy under the contract of carriage would be free of any exclusions contained in that contract, unauthorised deck carriage being considered as a species of deviation: see Scrutton, art 86. The proposition that unauthorised deck carriage necessarily deprives the carrier of his contractual exclusions must now be suspect after *The Antares (Nos 1 & 2)* [1987] 1 Lloyd's Rep 424: see Fundamental Breach and Deviation in the Carriage of Goods by Sea, C. Debattista, 1989 JBL 22.

[65] In *The Nea Tyhi* [1982] 1 Lloyd's Rep 606, it was suggested in argument that the carrier, as opposed to the actual signatory, could escape liability on the basis that the signature of a bill of lading could not bind a carrier for goods carried on deck when such carriage was unauthorised by the bill, that is to say on the grounds of *Grant v Norway* (1851) 20 LJCP 93. The argument was greeted by Sheen J with something lying between irritation and contempt: see pp 610–611. *The Nea Tyhi* was disapproved of, but not on this point, in *The Aliakmon* [1986] 2 Lloyd's Rep 1.

[66] To which the Carriage of Goods by Sea Act 1971 can apply: art I(c) of the Schedule to the Act only excludes from its application 'cargo which by the contract of carriage is stated as being carried on deck and is so carried.' Unauthorised deck stowage is, by definition, not stated to be carried on deck.

textbooks agree that the seller would indeed be in breach of contract[67] and as authority for this view three first instance judgments are cited: *Montague L Meyer Ltd v Travaru A/B H Cornelius of Gamleby*[68]; *Messers Ltd v Morrison's Export Co*[69] and *White Sea Timber Trust Ltd v WW North Ltd*[70]. In each of these cases, the contract of sale expressly stipulated for carriage under deck[71]; the contract may, of course, fail to make such a stipulation and consequently it would be helpful to examine the question under both hypotheses.

Where the contract of sale contains an express term requiring shipment under deck, it is clear that authority supports the view traditionally adopted in the books[72]: that is to say, that the buyer has a separate remedy against the seller under the contract of sale for having failed to organise carriage under deck. It is suggested, however, that this view fits ill with the nature of c i f sales[73] as shipment, rather than arrival, contracts. The seller's duty in a shipment contract is performed by the shipment of goods under, and the tender of documents evidencing, a contract of carriage on usual terms: he does not promise that the goods will actually be carried, or that they will arrive, in the manner stipulated. Therefore, it is submitted, a seller under a shipment contract performs his duty, in this context, by tendering a bill of lading which neither states that the cargo will be carried on deck, nor that the carrier may so carry. On this analysis, tender of a bill of lading which is silent on the issue of deck stowage would be valid under the contract of sale, although the deck stowage itself would, of course, put the carrier in breach of his obligations under the contract of carriage. The traditional view— that the carrier's breach puts the seller in breach—in effect requires the seller to obtain a bill of lading expressly saying that the goods would not be carried on deck[74] and to guarantee to the buyer that the carrier would comply with that term. It is, however, difficult to see why the

---

67 See Benjamin, para 1537 and Sassoon para 58.
68 (1930) 37 Ll L Rep 204.
69 [1939] 1 All ER 92.
70 (1933) 44 Ll L Rep 390.
71 In *Messers Ltd v Morrison's Export Co Ltd* [1939] 1 All ER 92, the express term read 'to be loaded on deck one-third.' Branson J was happy to construe this to mean that the residue was to be stowed under deck.
72 Although *White Sea Timber Trust Ltd v WW North Ltd* (1933) 44 Ll L Rep 390 actually decided a different question, namely whether a shipment covered by four bills of lading was to be considered as one contract or as four contracts: held, one contract, and therefore deck carriage under one bill justified rejection of the cargo covered by all four. The case clearly proceeds, nonetheless, upon the basis that the sellers were in breach because of the carrier's unauthorised deck stowage.
73 And those f o b contracts where the seller is responsible for the procurement of the bill of lading.
74 The bill of lading tendered in *Montague L Meyer Ltd v Travaru A/BH Cornelius* (1930) 37 Ll L Rep 204 was, in fact, just such a bill of lading: see *White Sea Timber Trust Ltd v WW North Ltd* (1933) 44 Ll L Rep 390 at 391. Clearly, though, to no avail, as the seller was still held to be in breach, presumably because he was assumed to be under a duty to guarantee the carrier's compliance with the term on the bill of lading.

seller, who gives no guarantee that the carrier will not deviate[75], should guarantee that the carrier will carry the goods on deck.

Where the contract of sale contains no express term that the goods be carried under deck, again it is suggested by the editors of Benjamin that the seller, as well as the carrier, is responsible towards the buyer for unauthorised deck stowage:[76]

> 'Indeed the position seems to be that the buyer is entitled to reject goods carried on deck unless the contract of sale expressly permits such carriage. The "general proposition that the deck is not the place upon which to put cargo except by such special arrangement"[77] appears to apply as much to contracts of sale as to contracts of carriage.'

It is suggested, however, that the reasons given in the immediately preceding paragraph for denying the buyer a remedy against the seller and restricting him to his remedy against the carrier apply a fortiori here: for surely, had the buyer been so anxious to impose upon the seller a term guaranteeing performance of the carrier's duties under the carriage contract, he would have included an express term for on deck shipment in the sale contract. Moreover, the dictum by Branson J in *Messers Ltd v Morrison's Export Co Ltd* ,[78] cited in Benjamin, as authority for the general proposition that the buyer has a remedy against the seller for damage caused by deck stowage unless such stowage is expressly permitted in the sale contract, is, with respect, far too slim to support such a proposition. Branson J implied no new general term binding the seller to a promise that the carrier will carry on deck: the judge simply construed an express term that one third of the cargo would be carried on deck to mean that two-thirds would not.

For all these reasons, it is suggested that the buyer's remedy in respect of loss caused by deck stowage unauthorised by the bill of lading lies against the carrier rather than against the seller. It is further suggested that the position is unaffected by an express term in the contract of sale stipulating that the cargo will be carried under deck. It is important to note, though, that such authority as exists at present does not accord with the position as here described.

ii. Cargo stated to be carried on deck

Tender of a bill of lading actually stating that the cargo is carried on deck is valid, it is suggested, unless the sale contract excludes tender of such a bill; and unless stowage on deck is not usual for the particular type of cargo. There appears to be no authority for implying generally

---

[75] See *Burstall & Co v Grimsdale & Sons* (1906) 11 Com Cas 280, particularly at 291: see text accompanying fn 53 above; and Benjamin, paras. 1464 and 1638.
[76] Benjamin, para 1537.
[77] *Messers Ltd v Morrison's Export Co* [1939] 1 All ER 92 at 93.
[78] [1939] 1 All ER 92 at 93.

into sale contracts a term that goods be carried under deck. Neither, indeed, do Incoterms impose such a stipulation on the seller, who is thus free, at any rate under the contract of sale, to tender a bill stating that the cargo is carried on deck. Problems may arise, however, where a letter of credit is in place; for article 28(a) of the Uniform Customs and Practice for Documentary Credits prevents acceptance of such a document unless its tender is specifically authorised by the letter of credit:

'In the case of carriage by sea or by more than one mode of transport but including carriage by sea, banks will refuse a transport document stating that the goods are or will be loaded on deck, unless specifically authorised in the credit.'

Thus it appears that a seller can, as a seller, but cannot as a beneficiary of a letter of credit, tender a bill of lading stating goods to be carried on deck.

The resulting discrepancy between the two sets of rules is confusing both in practical terms and in terms of principle. In practice, the disparity between the rules is liable to cause delay or even litigation. Thus, where the market price of the goods sold is static or falling, a seller whose documents are rejected by the bank is likely only to request the buyer to alter his instructions to the bank and authorise acceptance of the documents by the bank. On the other hand, where the market price is rising, the seller may well be tempted to go further and purport to terminate the contract of sale on the basis of the buyer's wrongful rejection of documents. In terms of principle, the conflict between the position under the law of sale and that under the rules relating to letters of credit is equally untidy: it is not immediately clear why a bill of lading stating carriage on deck should be any more menacing to a buyer paying by letter of credit than to a buyer who is not. The position of the bank as the holder of the bill in security is affected by the statement that goods are carried on deck only in the sense that the Carriage of Goods by Sea Act 1971 would not apply[79] to any cargo claim it eventually brought against the carrier on realising its security: again, though, it is difficult to see why banks should be any happier with this where tender of such a bill is authorised by the letter of credit than when it is not. The practical upshot of the mismatch of rules in this area is that buyers instructing the opening of letters of credit should ensure that their instructions to the issuing bank make express mention of deck stowage, making it clear whether they wish the bank to accept or reject bills of lading stating goods to be carried on deck.

iii. Bill of lading granting carrier liberty to stow on deck

So far as concerns the contract of sale, the position of bills of lading granting the carrier a liberty to carry the goods on deck is very similar

[79] Unless the bill was one to which the Act applied by virtue of an express incorporation clause: see s 1(7) of the Act.

to that of bills of lading stating the goods actually to be carried on deck. There appears to be no generally implied term stipulating against such tender, and where Incoterms apply, no express term to that effect. Consequently, the seller can tender such a bill of lading unless either the sale contract expressly excludes such tender or deck stowage is unusual for the type of cargo involved. A buyer requiring tender of a bill without such a liberty should make specific provision to that effect both in the sale contract and, if this is the method chosen for payment, in the letter of credit. In the absence of such specific provision, the buyer's position is precarious under all three contracts to which he is a party, ie the letter of credit, the contract of carriage and the sale contract. So far as concerns the letter of credit, banks must accept a bill of lading granting the carrier a liberty to carry the goods on deck[80]. So far as concerns the contract of carriage, there is no rule preventing parties to a carriage contract from agreeing to give the carrier a liberty to stow the goods on deck: such a liberty must still, however, be exercised with due care for the cargo such that, should the carrier exercise the liberty unreasonably, the buyer would have a cause of action against the carrier[81]. So far as concerns the position of the buyer under the contract of sale, the buyer has no remedy against the seller, at any rate where stowage on deck is reasonable for the particular type of cargo concerned; where it is not, the seller is in breach and the buyer can recover any loss ensuing from the fact that the goods were carried on, rather than under, the deck[82].

(c) Transhipment

Transhipment occurs when the carrier with whom the shipper concludes the contract of carriage performs only part of the voyage on the vessel named in the contract, using other vessels, whether owned by the contractual carrier or by others, for the other parts of the voyage[83]. Transhipment is permissible under the law of carriage in three different

---

[80]   Art 28(b) of the UCP reads: 'Banks will not refuse a transport document which contains a provision that the goods may be carried on deck, provided it does not specifically state that they are or will be loaded on deck.'

[81]   *Svenska Traktor Aktiebolaget v Maritime Agencies (Southampton)* [1953] 2 QB 295.

[82]   The measure of damages is likely to be simply the difference between the value of the goods had they been stowed on deck and their value after transit on deck, that is to say, damages for breach of warranty under s 53 of the Sale of Goods Act 1979, rather than damages for non-delivery under s 51 of that Act. The reason is that although the breach primarily here complained of is a documentary breach—tender of a bill with a liberty to stow on deck in circumstances where such stowage is unreasonable— the buyer cannot recover for that breach because he has accepted the bill of lading giving the liberty. The buyer is consequently thrown upon recovery for the physical breach, ie shipment on deck in circumstances where such shipment was unreasonable for the cargo involved. See generally as to the difference between remedies for documentary and physical breaches, Chapter 9.

[83]   The term is at times also used to signify the use of modes of transport other than ships for the carriage of the goods over part of the voyage. Transhipment in this wider sense, and documents covering contracts involving transhipment in this sense, will be dealt with in the discussion on containerised transport in Chapter 8.

sets of circumstance: where it is necessary[84]; where the parties to the carriage contract agree that the goods will be transhipped; and where the parties to that contract agree that the goods may be transhipped. Our task in this part of this chapter, it will be recalled, is to examine the effect, on tender of documents under the contract of sale and under the letter of credit, of bill of lading clauses stating that transhipment will or may occur[85].

i. Clauses in the bill stating that the goods will be transhipped

It is clear that where the contract of sale and the letter of credit either expressly allow transhipment or are both silent on the matter, neither the buyer nor the bank can reject a bill of lading stating that the goods will be transhipped, provided it also expressly stipulates that responsibility for the entire voyage is covered by the same document. So far as concerns tender under a letter of credit, this much results explicitly from article 29(b) of the Uniform Customs and Practice for Documentary Credits, which reads:

> 'Unless transhipment is prohibited by the terms of the credit, banks will accept transport documents which indicate that the goods will be transhipped, provided the entire carriage is covered by one and the same transport document.'

There appears to be no authority establishing the same proposition for tender under the contract of sale, at any rate in the precise circumstances here envisaged, that is to say where the bill of lading states that goods will be transhipped. It is suggested, however, that this would follow inexorably from the term implied generally in shipment sales that documents tendered should afford the buyer continuous documentary cover[86]. The upshot is that tender of a bill of lading stating that the goods will be transhipped and containing a clause limiting the carrier's liability 'to the part of the transport performed by him on vessels under his management'[87] can, in the two cases here envisaged, be rejected by the buyer under the contract of sale, and must be rejected by the bank under the letter of credit.

The position is equally clear where the sale contract and the letter of credit expressly forbid transhipment. Whether or not the bill of lading covers the entire voyage, the document cannot validly be tendered by the seller in the teeth of express proscription in the contract of sale and in the letter of credit.

---

[84] In the sense that an excepted peril has made the voyage impossible to complete, or so clearly unreasonable to complete as to make it effectively impossible from a commercial point of view: see Scrutton, art 129.

[85] The first type of transhipment permissible by the law of carriage—necessary transhipment—lies outside our ambit, the right to tranship in such circumstances existing, as it does, quite independently of any clause in the bill of lading.

[86] *Hansson v Hamel and Horley Ltd* [1922] 2 AC 36.

[87] See Conlinebill liner bill of lading, clause 6, reproduced below at Chapter 6.3.(c).ii.

Throughout this part of the discussion, it has been assumed that the buyer's instructions to the banks under the letter of credit tally with what the sale contract says or does not say about transhipment. Where, through oversight, the two contracts do not tally, there is considerable room for, at worst, litigation and, at best, delay. Thus if the contract of sale expressly forbids transhipment, but the buyer omits to relay this information in his application for the opening of a letter of credit[88], the buyer can find himself in a position of some difficulty. The banks must honour the credit and pay the price to the seller: article 29(b) of the Uniform Customs and Practice for Documentary Credits says as much; consequently, the buyer has no cause for complaint against the banks on this score. He does, of course, have an action against the seller for breach of the transhipment provision in the sale contract. This remedy, though, if worth pursuing at all[89], is likely to be restricted to the loss resulting from the transhipment itself: the bill of lading accepted by the banks on the buyer's behalf will, on our hypothesis, have clearly stated that the goods would be transhipped, and consequently, the buyer will have lost any right to sue the seller for having been deprived of the opportunity to reject a bill of lading tendered in breach of the contract of sale[90].

The converse situation—where the sale contract expressly allows transhipment or is silent on the matter, but the letter of credit expressly forbids transhipment—is equally likely to cause problems for the buyer, though for different reasons. In this case, the bank must reject the bill of lading by virtue of the clear instruction given to that effect by the buyer. Against a rising market, the seller could, if so inclined, treat the opening of the credit forbidding transhipment as a repudiatory breach by the buyer of the sale contract, the type of credit to be opened by the buyer being a condition of the contract of sale[91]. Against a falling market, the seller would be unlikely to respond with such alacrity or force to the opening of the credit: the bill, however, would still be rejected by the bank, at any rate until the buyer had altered his instructions to the bank, or until the bank had been persuaded to pay the seller 'under reserve'[92].

ii. Bills giving carrier liberty to tranship

Given the perils which may chance upon a voyage by sea, the carrier will very frequently reserve to himself the right to tranship the goods

---

[88] Application forms for the opening of a letter of credit typically contain a box, headed 'Transhipment' for the insertion of such information: see Appendix 3.c.

[89] Against a foreign defendant, quite possibly in a foreign jurisdiction.

[90] Against a falling market, this remedy might be quite valuable: see generally Chapter 9.

[91] *Enrico Furst & Co v WE Fischer Ltd* [1960] 2 Lloyd's Rep 340 and other cases cited in Benjamin, at para 2192.

[92] That is to say, subject to the intermediary bank's right to claim repayment of the credit on objection to the bill being taken by the opening bank on similar grounds: *Banque de l'Indochine et de Suez SA v JH Rayner (Mincing Lane)* [1983] QB 711.

in certain events; thus, for example, clause 6 of the Conlinebill liner bill of lading reads:

'6. Substitution of Vessel, Transhipment and Forwarding.

Whether expressly arranged beforehand or otherwise, the Carrier shall be at liberty to carry the goods to their port of destination by the said or other vessel or vessels either belonging to the Carrier or others, or by other means of transport, proceeding either directly or indirectly to such port and to carry the goods or part of them beyond their port of destination, and to tranship, land and store the goods either on shore or afloat and reship and forward the same at Carrier's expense but at Merchant's risk. When the ultimate destination at which the Carrier may have engaged to deliver the goods is other than the vessel's port of discharge, the Carrier acts as Forwarding Agent only.

The responsibility of the Carrier shall be limited to the part of the transport performed by him on vessels under his management and no claim will be acknowledged by the Carrier for damage or loss arising during any other part of the transport even though the freight for the whole transport has been collected by him.'

Before we attempt to identify the bearing which such a clause has on tender of the bill of lading under the sale contract and under the letter of credit, it would be helpful first to establish how such a clause might be considered to raise problems with the requirement of continuous documentary cover. Clearly, the clause does not raise difficulties as obvious as those caused by the type of facts which occurred in *Hansson v Hamel & Horley*[93]. There, the seller tendered one bill of lading, covering only part of a journey carried out by two carriers with each of whom the seller had concluded a separate contract of carriage: it was thus clear that the bill of lading tendered failed to give any cover at all over one entire leg of the voyage[94]. Our hypothesis here, on the other hand, is one where the seller concludes one contract of carriage, with one carrier, covered by one bill of lading containing a liberty clause such as the one reproduced above. Again, here we have a clause which appears, at any rate on the surface, far less innocuous than one which states that the goods will be transhipped: the clause reproduced above simply reserves to the carrier the right to tranship, a right which might or might not in fact be exercised. For both these reasons, any objection by a buyer on tender of a bill containing such a clause might at first sight appear to be entirely unmeritorious: there is no obvious or immediate gap in documentary cover. This, however, is the very crux of the problem: though neither immediate nor obvious, the clause reveals the possibility of a gap in cover, which may or may not occur, but which might leave the buyer with no remedy against the carrier exercising the liberty. For the risk lies not so much in the liberty to tranship itself, but with the disclaimer

---

[93] [1922] 2 AC 36.
[94] Although the bill of lading tendered quite inappropriately called itself a 'through' bill of lading: see [1922] 2 AC 36 at 48.

of liability which commonly accompanies it; that is to say, in the second paragraph of the clause reproduced above, limiting the responsibility of the carrier to that part of the voyage performed on vessels under his management. Indeed, it would be helpful if our discussion of the effect of transhipment liberty clauses on tender of documents were to distinguish between bills which, while reserving to the carrier the liberty to tranship, expressly placed on one pair of shoulders responsibility for the whole voyage[95]; and bills which reserved the liberty to tranship to a carrier who accepted responsibility only for that part of the transit carried out by himself.

1. Where the bill gives 'through' cover

It is clear that where the sale contract and the letter of credit either expressly provide for, or are silent as to the tender of bills of lading with a liberty to tranship, the tender of such a bill giving 'through' documentary cover is valid. So far as concerns the contract of sale, Lord Sumner clearly hints as much in his speech in *Hansson v Hamel and Horley Ltd*[96] and it seems, in any case, quite clear as a matter of principle that this should be the case[97]. There might at one stage have been thought to exist a problem with that stage of the voyage during which the goods were on land, awaiting transhipment: for surely, here, the statutory regime normally applying to contracts of carriage by sea covered by a bill of lading, namely the Carriage of Goods by Sea Act 1971, could not apply, and consequently there would be a gap in continuous cover during that period. The point arose in the context of a cargo claim in *Mayhew Foods Ltd v Overseas Containers Ltd*[98], a case in which Bingham J decided that the Carriage of Goods by Sea Act 1971 applied to the whole transit, including the time during which the goods were awaiting transhipment

---

[95]   That is to say, where the bill of lading is truly a 'through' bill of lading: cf fn 94 above.

[96]   [1922] 2 AC 36 at 48.

[97]   See Benjamin, para 1632. *Fischel & Co v Spencer* (1922) 12 Ll L Rep 36 causes some difficulty for the proposition adopted in the text above and in Benjamin. This was a case where the sale was silent as to transhipment and where the bill of lading gave a liberty to tranship. No mention is made of any term in the bill disclaiming liability when the goods left the vessel named in the bill of lading; consequently it appears as though the bill gave continuous documentary cover. This notwithstanding, the Court, composed of Hewart LCJ, Bailhache and Salter JJ, decided that tender was invalid: the court felt bound by a finding of fact made by the arbitrator that a seller wishing to retain the right to tranship would customarily insert a stipulation to that effect in the sale contract. The terms in which the judgment was couched make it difficult to distinguish this case on the basis of special custom: it must be said, though, that the finding of fact by the arbitrator as to the general custom alleged by the buyer would not, of course, be binding in future cases. Given the obiter dictum by Lord Sumner in *Hansson v Hamel & Horley* [1922] 2 AC 36 at 48, uttered less than three months before the Court of Appeal's decision in *Fischel*, the latter decision must be treated with considerable caution. It is interesting to note that Bailhache J, who sat in *Fischel*, also gave the first instance judgment which was reversed first by the Court of Appeal and then by the House of Lords in *Hansson*. The case has received no attention in the courts, and only little attention in the literature: see Sassoon, art 94.

[98]   [1984] 1 Lloyd's Rep 317.

on land. There is now, consequently, clearly no problem with continuous documentary cover on this score[99].

So far as concerns the position of such bills tendered under letters of credit, the Uniform Customs and Practice for Documentary Credits say nothing expressly about the tender of such bills, that is to say 'through' bills, containing a liberty to tranship, in circumstances where the letter of credit either expressly allows tender of such a bill or where it is silent as to such tender. To be sure, the Uniform Customs do talk about bills giving the carrier a liberty to tranship, whether or not they afford full documentary cover and whether or not they are allowed by the credit. Thus, article 29(c)(i) reads:

> 'Even if transhipment is prohibited by the terms of the credit, banks will accept transport documents which:
>
> i. incorporate printed clauses stating that the carrier has the right to tranship . . .'

It follows from this article that where the bill gives through cover, and where transhipment is either expressly or tacitly allowed, a bill giving the carrier a liberty to tranship can, a fortiori, be tendered under a letter of credit.

The same article of the Uniform Customs can cause problems for a buyer who does not wish to be presented with a bill of lading giving the carrier a liberty to tranship. So far as concerns his rights under the contract of sale, he can, of course, stipulate against such tender expressly in that contract. If, however, the parties have agreed to payment by letter of credit, the buyer may still find that the bill of lading has been accepted: and nothing he says in his application for the opening of the letter of credit will prevent this, for the article makes it clear that an express prohibition of such tender in the letter of credit must be disregarded by the bank. The consequence for the buyer is that he can recover from the seller such losses as result directly from the physical act of transhipment, the seller having broken his obligation, expressed in the sale contract, to procure a carriage contract prohibiting transhipment. Given that a bill of lading clearly allowing transhipment has been accepted, the buyer will not, on the other hand, be able to recover damages for having been deprived of the opportunity of rejecting the documents[100].

2. Where the bill does not give 'through' cover

Where the bill of lading does not afford the holder continuous documentary cover, that is to say, where the carrier expressly disclaims responsibility for any part of the carriage not carried out by him, the law relating to letters of credit is completely out of joint with the law

---

[99] Indeed, it is doubtful whether there ever was: for continuous documentary cover requires that the contract of carriage sold to the buyer gives him a right of action against the carrier in respect of the entire transit; it does not, it is submitted, require that the responsibility of the carrier be uniform throughout that period.

[100] See generally Chapter 9.4.(c).iii, below.

relating to international sales. So far as concerns the contract of sale, it is clear that where the contract expressly prohibits tender of a bill with a liberty to tranship, then tender of such a bill constitutes a breach of contract[101]. Where the contract expressly allows tender of a bill containing a liberty to tranship, it is submitted that the clause allowing such tender should be construed to mean that the bill tendered must afford through cover: this would seem to follow from the general requirement of continuous documentary cover. Consequently, tender of a bill of lading not affording such cover would be invalid. It is suggested that the position is the same where the contract of sale is silent as to tender of bills of lading containing a liberty to tranship: the case-law on this last point, is however, conflicting. Some support for the suggestion made here can be gleaned from an obiter dictum in *Holland Colombo Trading Society Ltd v Alawdeen*[102]. On the other hand, McNair J in *Soproma SpA v Marine and Animal By-Products Corpn*[103] held that rejection of such a bill would be unjustified, at any rate where the transhipment had not yet occurred at the time of tender. McNair J put it thus:[104]

> 'As at present advised, I should not be disposed to hold that a bill of lading otherwise unobjectionable in form which did in fact cover the whole transit actually performed would be a bad tender merely because it contained a liberty not in fact exercised but which, if exercised, would not have given the buyers continuous cover for the portion of the voyage not performed by the vessel named in the bill of lading.'

With respect, this view misses the point of tender of documents in shipment sales: the criterion for validity of tender is not whether the documents afford continuous documentary cover on the facts which have happened and which are known to have happened; rather is it whether the documents offer, at the time of tender, the prospect of continuous cover whether or not the liberties contained therein are exercised[105].

Thus, it is suggested, in all three situations described above, tender of a bill giving less than complete cover would seem to be invalid under the contract of sale[106]. However, where the buyer pays through a letter of credit, tender would seem to be valid in all three cases. This, because

---

[101] It is suggested, moreover, that this would be the case whether or not the bill of lading gives continuous documentary cover.

[102] [1954] 2 Lloyd's Rep 45 at 53. The opinion there expressed was obiter because the sale in that case was not a shipment sale but one under which the seller undertook to ensure the arrival of the goods.

[103] [1966] 1 Lloyd's Rep 367.

[104] Loc cit at 388, 389.

[105] See Benjamin, para 1633. The position may be different where the only route available to the seller involves transhipment by but one shipping line whose standard bill excludes liability for loss after transhipment: see *Plaimar Ltd v Waters Trading Co Ltd* (1945) 72 CLR 304 at 316 (Aust HC).

[106] At any rate unless a contrary custom be proved in a particular trade: see *Arnold Otto Meyer NV v Aune* (1939) 64 Ll L Rep 121; but see *Soproma SpA v Marine and Animal By-Products Corpn* [1966] 1 Lloyd's Rep 367 at 389.

article 29(c)(i)[107] states clearly that the instruction as to tender in the letter of credit is irrelevant, and, by default, that the continuity of the cover it offers is equally irrelevant. The result is that whatever stipulations a buyer makes in his letter of credit, the banks will accept bills of lading giving the carrier a liberty to tranship and disclaiming liability for any parts of the voyage not carried out by him, the buyer being thrown, again, on his remedies, if any[108], against the seller. It is difficult to see what interest is served by this glaring contradiction between the rules on sale and those on letters of credit on this matter[109].

(d) Bills with destination different to sale destination

The destination in the bill of lading must be the same as that in the sale contract. Where Incoterms are incorporated into the contract, express stipulation is made to this effect[110]. Where Incoterms do not apply, it is clear that such an obligation will be implied: *SIAT di dal Ferro v Tradax Overseas SA*[111]. The central issue in that case was whether or not the buyers were entitled to reject a number of bills of lading[112] on the ground that they did not provide for carriage to the destination stipulated in the contract of sale. In one set of bills of lading, the discrepancy between the two was as obvious as it could be: the sale contract provided for carriage to Venice, whereas the bills of lading were made out for Ancona/Ravenna[113]. It was held that the buyer was entitled to reject: it availed the sellers nothing that they authorised the master, on arrival at Venice, to alter the destination on the bills to indicate 'Venice'

---

107 The article reads, in relevant part: 'Even if transhipment is prohibited by the terms of the credit, banks will accept transport documents which: i. incorporate printed clauses stating that the carrier has the right to tranship . . .'

108 The buyer may be caught by the doctrine in *Panchaud Freres SA v Etablissements General Grain Co* [1970] 1 Lloyd's Rep 53: see Chapter 9, text accompanying fn 189.

109 The banking rules become even more curious when one compares the position of ocean bills of lading giving a liberty to tranship and container transport documents giving the same liberty: the former, as we have seen, need not give continuous documentary cover; the latter do: see art 29(c)(ii), UCP and Chapter 8 below.

110 See, respectively, C I F A2 and A7; similarly, C & F A2 and A6. It is suggested that the same obligation would be implied in f o b sales where the seller had undertaken responsibility for procurement of the bill of lading.

111 [1980] 1 Lloyd's Rep 53. The sale contract in that case did not incorporate Incoterms; neither did it contain any express term stipulating that the destination in the bill of lading and the contract of sale should be the same. See also other authorities cited at Benjamin, para 1636; and *The Playa Larga* [1983] 2 Lloyd's Rep 171 at 184.

112 We learn from Megaw LJ that 'some 40 or 50 issues or sub-issues' were aired by the parties during the various stages of arbitration and litigation; thankfully, though, we learn also, early on in the judgment, that the 'real' issues were relatively few. To another two of the 'real' issues we shall return in due course: namely, the question as to whether a charterparty need be tendered when a bill of lading refers to such a contract, in Chapter 7.

113 See [1980] 1 Lloyd's Rep 53 at 60; the 'bills of lading in group 4'. In another two sets of bills of lading, the discrepancy arose because the bills simply gave as the port of discharge the phrase: 'As per charterparty'; see pp 59 and 60 of the report, for the bills of lading in groups 2 and 3. This aspect of the case will be dealt with in Chapter 7.

as the port of discharge[114]. The principle was clearly stated thus in Megaw LJ's judgment:[115]

> 'The buyer is not under any duty to speculate or to investigate, or to accept assurances outside the bill of lading. The bill of lading is the document to which he is entitled to look as being definitive of the contract of carriage binding on the shipowner, as being a contract entered into or in existence at the time of the shipment of the goods, so as to cover the whole of the carriage from the port of loading to the port of discharge provided for by the contract of sale . . . The buyer ought not to be put in the position of having, as it were, to buy the possibility of litigation in respect of the contracts of carriage and insurance, the risk and outcome of which may be unpredictable at the moment when the buyer has to make up his mind to accept or reject the documents.'

The seller's duty to procure a contract of carriage for the sale destination means not only that the destination named in the contract of carriage must be identical to that named in the contract of sale, but that the vessel engaged by the seller should be able to reach the sale destination. Thus, where a seller engaged a vessel which, because of its draught, could not reach the port agreed in the sale contract, he was in breach of that contract: it availed him nothing to plead that the choice of vessel had been agreed with the buyer in the contract of sale: *The Epaphus*[116].

---

[114] See loc cit at 62 for the very curious turn which events took.
[115] Loc cit at 63.
[116] [1986] 2 Lloyd's Rep 387 at 392, 393; affd by the Court of Appeal at [1987] 2 Lloyd's Rep 215.

CHAPTER 7

Bills of lading under charterparties

1. Business practice and the nature of the problems caused

2. Under which contractual terms is the buyer to sue the carrier?

   (a) Where the bill of lading is in the hands of the charterer

   (b) Where the bill of lading is in the hands of a third party

      i. Incorporation in general

      ii. Incorporation of arbitration clauses

3. Whom is the buyer to sue for short-delivery or damage to goods?

4. The bill of lading as a receipt where it is issued under a charterparty

   (a) Charterer selling c i f

   (b) Charterer buying f o b

5. Requirements of tender where a bill of lading is issued under a charterparty

Our discussion of the seller's documentary duties in shipment sales has so far concentrated on the tender by the seller to the buyer, or by the seller to a bank paying under a letter of credit, of a bill of lading performing by itself all three of the following functions, namely, acting as a document of title[1] and as a receipt[2], and providing evidence of the terms of the contract of carriage[3]. Our account of the seller's duties in this regard has not so far been cluttered by the practice, curious at first sight, of using bills of lading in tandem with another form of contract of carriage, a charterparty, within the confines of the same international sale. This practice raises a number of complex legal problems, each of which we shall examine in this chapter. Our first problem is this: if there are two shipping documents, which of the two provides the buyer, qua receiver of the goods, with a contract upon which he can sue the carrier for short-delivery or for damage to the goods? Secondly, if the

---

[1] See Chapter 2, above.
[2] See Chapter 5, above.
[3] See Chapter 6, above.

goods bought by the buyer have been carried on a vessel which is under charter, whom is the buyer to sue in a cargo claim, the shipowner, or the charterer? Thirdly, where a bill of lading is issued covering goods carried on a chartered ship, how strong a statement of the quantity and apparent condition of the goods on shipment can the merchants demand of the carrier in the bill of lading? And finally, can bills of lading referring to charterparties be tendered under the terms of shipment sales and under letters of credit? An understanding of these four problems, and an attempt at solving them, would, it is suggested, be greatly assisted by investigating the reasons why the practice arises in the first place; and that will be our first task in this chapter.

1. BUSINESS PRACTICE AND THE NATURE OF THE PROBLEMS CAUSED

The relationship between the various contracts involved in the sale, on shipment terms, of goods for export is complicated enough with one document, the bill of lading, recording the terms of the contract of carriage between the cargo-interest, whether seller or buyer[4], and the carrier. Further to confuse matters by adding to the transaction another document, whose function again is to record the contractual terms of carriage between the shipper and the carrier, seems to create complexity of the most gratuitous kind—unless, that is, a satisfactory explanation can be found for the practice.

The explanation lies in a fundamental distinction which needs to be drawn between the function of a charterparty and the functions of a bill of lading. A charterparty is a contract of carriage between a shipowner and a charterer for the use of a vessel for a given voyage or for a stipulated time. It is a contract of carriage—and only a contract of carriage. There is nothing in a charterparty which looks remotely like a representation by the shipowner that goods have been shipped on board the vessel in a given quantity and in apparent good order and condition. Neither does a charterparty of itself entitle anyone to claim possession of the goods on discharge: its possession represents no proprietary interest in the goods. The result is that a charterparty is not a receipt for goods and it is not a document of title at common law. A bill of lading, on the other hand, performs both of those functions in addition to its providing evidence of the terms of a contract of carriage.

Now whether or not a shipper of goods needs to charter a ship will depend on the nature of the goods he wishes to ship; and on the shipper's role in the market place. If the goods to be shipped under a sale contract are such, in nature and in quantity, that they can fill a whole vessel, then it is more likely than not that the shipper will think of chartering

---

[4]   See Chapter 3, above, for an account of the transfer of the contract of carriage contained in the bill of lading from seller to buyer.

a ship; for obvious reasons, this is commonly the case in the sale of commodities on shipment terms. If the shipper does not need all the space on a vessel for the performance of his obligations under the sale contract, he might still charter a vessel rather than simply book space on a ship running a liner service: he will do this if, apart from organising the carriage of his own goods, he wishes to participate in the freight market by carrying other shippers' goods for profit. Finally, the charterer of a vessel may not be a shipper of goods at all; he may simply be providing a freight service to shippers of goods by putting the vessel up as a 'general ship', in which case he is unlikely to be, at any rate initially, a party to a sale contract involving goods carried on the vessel he charters.

Where the shipper of goods, for any of the reasons described above, charters a vessel, his contract with the carrier will be recorded in the charterparty. Whatever his reason for chartering the vessel—whether it be to use the whole or part of the ship in performance of a contract of sale, or to provide a service to others by running a general ship— he will also need another document, a bill of lading, if his commercial interests and those of others are to be safeguarded; and this for two reasons. Firstly, although the charterer is entitled, as a bailor of the goods entrusted to the shipowner, to the return of the same goods in the same quantity and condition as shipped, the value of this right is much enhanced, for all the reasons we examined in Chapter 5 when looking at the receipt function of the bill of lading, if the shipowner is bound to a receipt stating the quantity and condition in which the goods were shipped. Secondly, it serves no one's interest for the commercial value of the goods to be locked in the vessel, as it were, for the duration of the transit. Where the goods are shipped in performance of a contract of sale, the seller-shipper needs a document of title to pass to the buyer-receiver the right to demand delivery on discharge; indeed, that buyer might wish to take advantage of market movements during the transit of the goods by selling to others down a string. For the same reason, shippers of goods loaded on a general ship under charter will want a bill of lading they can sell to their buyers, and the latter to their sub-buyers, who might include the charterer himself. In all of these situations, the charterer needs a document performing functions—as a receipt and as a document of title—which his contract with the shipowner, the charterparty, does not: in all of these cases, whether he is selling c i f or buying f o b, or not selling or buying at all, the charterer needs a bill of lading.

In the introduction to this chapter, we mentioned briefly the types of problems which arise when bills of lading and charterparties are used within the same transaction: which of the two documents contains the contract of carriage; who is the carrier, the shipowner or the charterer; and how strong a receipt can the charterer demand of the shipowner? For ease of reference, these issues can be called in turn: the identity of contractual terms; the identity of the carrier; and the cargo-interests' right to a firm receipt. Before we tackle each of these problems, it would be useful broadly to identify the situations in which each of them arises. In all of the cases described in the preceding paragraph, two things can happen to the bill of lading: the bill can be held (a) by the charterer, or (b) by a third party. The first issue—which document bears the contractual terms of carriage—arises in both situations (a) and (b); and this issue will be discussed here in the context of each of those two situations. The second problem—the identity of the carrier—arises only in situation (b), that is to say, where the bill of lading has reached the hands of a third party: in situation (a), where the bill of lading is in the hands of a charterer, it is clear that the shipowner, rather than the charterer, is the carrier. The third problem—the strength of the bill of lading as a receipt—arises in both situations (a) and (b): both the charterer and a bill of lading holder who is not a charterer are interested in the strength of the statements contained in the bill of lading as to the quantity and apparent condition of the goods on shipment. The receipt function of the bill of lading when in the hands of a merchant who has not chartered the vessel on which the goods are shipped—i e in situation (b)—has been discussed in Chapter 5: here, we shall be looking at the same function where the facts are complicated by the circumstance that the bill of lading holder also happens to be the charterer of the vessel on which the goods are shipped—i e in situation (a).

2. UNDER WHICH CONTRACTUAL TERMS IS THE BUYER TO SUE THE CARRIER?

Both the carrier and the buyer need to know which of the two documents, the charterparty or the bill of lading, governs the contractual relationship between them; and this, for two reasons. Firstly, there is always an advantage sought by one party in one document which the other party tries to thwart by pleading the other document as the contractual document, and the resolution of the dispute will therefore depend on which of the two documents governs. Thus, for example, the shipowner might be after the protection of an exclusion clause which exists in the bill of lading but not in the charterparty[5]; or the charterers might be attempting to escape from a time-bar which obstructs their action if the bill of lading applies, but not if the charterparty applies[6]. Secondly, both parties need to know whether or not the Carriage of Goods by Sea Act 1971 applies to any cargo claims which might arise between them. That Act does not apply to charterparties, unless it is expressly

---

[5]   As in *Rodocanachi v Milburn* (1886) 18 QBD 67.

[6]   As in *President of India v Metcalfe Shipping Co Ltd, The Dunelmia* [1970] 1 QB 289, where the charterparty contained an arbitration clause with no time-bar. Had the bill of lading prevailed, the charterers would have been defeated by the one year time-bar of the Hague Rules.

incorporated therein[7]; the Act does, however, apply motu propriu to a bill of lading issued under a charterparty where the bill governs the contractual regime[8] between the parties[9]. Thus, the parties need to know when the bill, rather than the charterparty, regulates the relationship between them; for upon this depend other important questions, such as the application of exclusion or limitation clauses or of time-bars.

For all these reasons, the parties need to know which document provides them with their contractual framework for the resolution of cargo claims and, as indicated above, analysis of the question is assisted by examining it in each of the two situations, (a) and (b), already referred to.

(a) Where the bill of lading is in the hands of the charterer

A charterer who is party to a sale contracted on shipment terms may come to hold a bill of lading in one of two ways. Firstly, the bill may be issued directly to him by the shipowner: this is likely to happen where the sale contract is concluded either on c i f terms and the seller takes a bill of lading for goods carried on the vessel which he has chartered; or on f o b terms and the buyer, who has chartered the vessel, takes a mate's receipt from the seller, which receipt he then exchanges for a bill of lading with the carrier[10]. It is clear on authority that any dispute between the charterer and the shipowner is regulated in these circumstances by the terms contained in the charterparty: *Rodocanachi v Milburn*[11], where it was held that a shipowner could not avail himself of an exclusion clause in a bill of lading in a cargo claim brought by the plaintiff charterer to whom the defendant had issued the bill. The bill of lading was clearly here a receipt for the goods shipped and a document of title: indeed after the charterparty had been concluded, the

---

[7] See the Carriage of Goods by Sea Act 1971, Sch, art V, the relevant part of which reads: 'The provisions of these Rules shall not be applicable to charter parties.' As indicated in the text above, the Rules may, of course, be incorporated expressly into the charterparty; they may also be incorporated in part: see, for example, Shellvoy 4, clause 28 (2), which reads: 'The provisions of Articles III (other than Rules 4 and 8) IV, IVbis and VIII of the ... Hague-Visby Rules are incorporated into this charter and shall be deemed to be inserted in extenso herein.'

[8] It will be argued below, at Chapter 7.4, that the Act may also be relevant to the receipt function of a bill of lading issued under a charterparty.

[9] See Carriage of Goods by Sea Act 1971, Sch, art I(b), the relevant part of which lays down that the Rules will apply to 'any bill of lading ... issued under or pursuant to a charter party from the moment at which such bill of lading...regulates the relations between a carrier and a holder of the same.'

[10] The shipowner would normally be expected to issue a mate's receipt, rather than a bill of lading, to the party who actually loads the goods, namely the seller, who would then pass the receipt to the buyer, who could in turn exchange it for the bill of lading with the shipowner. This is why Incoterms define the relevant documentary duties of the f o b seller as to '[p]rovide ... the customary clean document in proof of delivery of the goods alongside the named vessel' and to '[r]ender the buyer, at the latter's request, risk and expense, every assistance in obtaining a bill of lading.' (See Incoterms, F O B A7 and 9 respectively.)

[11] (1886) 18 QBD 67 and other cases cited in Benjamin, para 1444, fn 83; and in Carver, art 699, fn 2.

charterer sold the goods, presumably by transferring the bill of lading. The bill did not, however, provide evidence of the contractual terms between the parties. In the slightly later case of *Leduc v Ward*[12], Lord Esher put it in these words:

> '[W]here there is a charterparty, as between the shipowner and the charterer the bill of lading may be merely in the nature of a receipt for the goods, because all the other terms of the contract of carriage between them are contained in the charterparty; and the bill of lading is merely given as between them to enable the charterer to deal with the goods while in the course of transit.'

A charterer may also come to hold a bill of lading issued by the shipowner in a second, rather less direct, way: the bill of lading might have been issued by the shipowner to the shipper of the goods and the latter could then have transferred the bill to the charterer. This situation can arise in two types of case. In the first, which we shall call case (i) for ease of reference, the shipper sells goods to the charterer on f o b terms and the shipowner issues a bill of lading directly to the shipper, who then transfers it to the buyer-charterer[13]. In the second case, case (ii), the charterer runs the vessel as a general ship, loading goods belonging to other shippers; bills of lading are issued to each of these shippers; the charterer subsequently, and during transit, buys goods covered by one of the bills from one of the shippers.

Statements as to which document, the charterparty or the bill of lading, governs the contract of carriage between the buyer-charterer and the shipowner where the charterer has come by the bill indirectly have, it is suggested, been marred by a reluctance to distinguish between the situation in case (i) and that in case (ii). The turning point for the major textbooks in the field came in 1969, when the Court of Appeal delivered its judgment in *President of India v Metcalfe Shipping Co Ltd*[14]. Prior to the decision in that case, the editors both of Scrutton[15] and of Carver[16] took the view that where a charterer took a bill of lading only indirectly from a shipowner the bill of lading, rather than the charterparty, recorded

---

[12] (1888) 20 QBD 475 at 479. Lord Esher was a member of the court both in this case and in *Rodocanachi v Milburn*, see fn 5, above.

[13] This manner of proceeding would fit precisely none of the the three classes of f o b sales which Devlin J identified in *Pyrene Co v Scindia Navigation Co* [1954] 2 QB 402, as to which see Chapter 1, above. On these facts, the contract of carriage has clearly been concluded by the buyer: they consequently fit neither the classic nor the extended forms of f o b sales. The facts are closest to the straight form of f o b sale, subject to this caveat. In the straight form of f o b sale, one would expect the mate's receipt, rather than the bill of lading to be given to the shipper, who would then pass the receipt to the buyer, who would then exchange it for the bill of lading with the shipowner: see fn 10 above. The facts described in the text arose nonetheless in *President of India v Metcalfe Shipping Co Ltd, The Dunelmia* [1970] 1 QB 289 and it is, perhaps, unfortunate that this area of the law is dominated by a decision founded on somewhat special facts.

[14] [1970] 1 QB 289.

[15] 17th edn, p 46.

[16] 11th edn, p 340.

the terms of the contract of carriage between the charterer and the shipowner. In the current editions of those works, though, the editors take the opposite view, namely that the charterparty prevails over the bill of lading as the contractual document[17]. It will be suggested here that both views, the view that the bill of lading prevails over the charterparty and the reverse, are extreme, based as they are on the misconception that one document must, in some sense, be stronger than the other. Rather than compare the relative potency of either document, it is more helpful to distinguish between the way these two documents are issued and used in practice. This distinction is best illustrated by returning to the two cases (i) and (ii) described above.

Case (i), it will be recalled, envisaged a charterer buying goods f o b, the shipowner issuing a bill of lading to the seller-shipper, who then transfers the bill to the buyer. These were the facts in *President of India v Metcalfe Shipping Co Ltd*[18], where the shipowner unsuccessfully argued that a claim for damage to goods brought by the buyer-charterer was barred by a stipulation in the bill of lading: the charterparty was held by the Court of Appeal to contain the contract between the parties and that contract did not bar the charterer's action. In case (i), it is clear that the transfer of the bill of lading to the charterer is totally unconnected to the contract of carriage—the charterparty—previously concluded between the shipowner and the charterer. The transfer of the bill of lading is a direct result of the contract of sale between the seller and the buyer; none of the parties, seller, buyer and perhaps least of all the shipowner, intends the bill of lading to supplant the charterparty as the contract of carriage. The buyer in this case already has a contract of carriage, the charterparty; all he expects to obtain on transfer of the bill of lading is a receipt and a document of title and that, indeed, is all he got in the *President of India*[19] case. In case (i), so far as concerns the buyer's relationship with the shipowner, once a charterer, the buyer is always a charterer and nothing but a charterer.

Case (ii) is totally different. Here, the charterer starts life off as nothing but a charterer, running the vessel as a general ship for the benefit of other shippers and for his own profit. However, the charterer then buys a parcel of goods covered by a bill of lading from one of those shippers. The shipowner's contracts of carriage with the shippers and their buyers are, respectively, evidenced by and contained in[20] the bill of lading. Why

---

17 Carver, at para 701, writes unreservedly that the view stated in previous editions was wrong. The editors of Scrutton are somewhat more circumspect, suggesting that 'the bill of lading does not modify or vary the terms of the charterparty, at least where the charterparty provides that bills of lading are to be signed "without prejudice to this charterparty"': see art 32. It is, however, doubtful whether the ratio of the *President of India* case can be limited in this way: see *Intercontinental Export Co (Pty) Ltd v MV Dien Danielsen* 1982 (3) SA 534 (N); revsd on other grounds at 1983 (4) SA 275 (N).
18 [1970] 1 QB 289.
19 Ibid.
20 See, generally, Chapter 6.1, above.

should the fact that one of those buyers happens also to be the charterer make any difference? To be sure, the charterer already has a contract of carriage with the shipowner so far as concerns his use of the whole vessel; but he has also now bought another contract of carriage together with and covering a particular parcel of goods. The notion that the charterer in this case may have two contracts of carriage with the same shipowner appears strange only if the difference between the commercial purposes of the two contracts is ignored. The charterer negotiated the charterparty to regulate his use of the whole vessel as a commercial operation; the buyer of the particular bill of lading bought a particular parcel of goods which he legitimately expected would bring with it a particular regime of rights and duties: the fact that the charterer of the vessel and the buyer of the goods are both the same person does not alter the rather more important fact that he has made two contracts with the shipowner for two quite different purposes. It is not so much a question of whether the charterparty or the bill of lading applies as much as when the charterparty or the bill of lading applies. Thus, where the dispute between the parties relates, say, to the payment of hire, then clearly the charterparty applies; but where the dispute relates to short-delivery of or damage to the cargo bought by the charterer, then equally clearly the bill of lading applies. *Calcutta SS Co Ltd v Andrew Weir & Co*[21], an authority upon which the textbooks based their earlier view, was just such an illustration of case (ii): the court there held that the bill of lading applied to a dispute between the charterer and the shipowner relating to the condition in which the cargo pledged to the charterer was landed[22]. The case is therefore distinguishable from, and was indeed so distinguished in, the *President of India* case[23]. The suggestion in the current edition of Carver[24] that the *Calcutta SS Co* case[25] is no longer a reliable authority is consequently somewhat difficult to understand[26].

The crux of the matter, then, is this: did the bill of lading come to the charterer simply to perform functions—as a receipt and as a document of title—which a pre-existing contract of carriage—the charterparty— could not; or did the bill reach the charterer as a buyer of goods through a contract of sale completely independent of the original charterparty concluded between the buyer, qua charterer, and the shipowner? If the former is the case, the charterparty governs the entire contractual relationship between the shipowner and the charterer; if the latter, the charterparty or the bill of lading can provide contractual terms for the resolution of disputes between the parties, the choice of regime depending

---

21   [1910] 1 KB 759.
22   The consequence on the facts of the case was that the shipowners were exempted from liability for damage to the goods.
23   [1970] 1 QB 289 at 305, 308–309, 310.
24   At para 701, fn 10.
25   [1910] 1 KB 759.
26   As, indeed, is the suggestion in Sassoon that the *Calcutta SS Co* case [1910] 1 KB 759 might actually have been overruled by the *President of India* case [1970] 1 QB 289: see art 483.

on the subject matter of the particular dispute concerned. This statement of the law is altogether more sensitive to the real commercial expectations of all three parties involved than either of the rigid views adopted both before and after 1969 in the major works[27]. Moreover, the view here expressed heeds the warning expressed by Fenton Atkinson LJ in *President of India v Metcalfe Shipping Co Ltd, The Dunelmia*[28], namely that:

> '...the relations between shipowners, charterers and shippers respectively are to be determined as a question of fact upon the documents and circumstances of each particular case...'

(b) Where the bill of lading is in the hands of a third party

The buyer is most obviously a third party to a charterparty between the shipowner and the charterer where the sale is concluded on c i f terms and the seller charters the vessel on which the goods are carried, taking a bill of lading and transferring it to the buyer[29]. It follows inexorably from the doctrine of privity that the contractual relationship between the buyer and the carrier cannot be governed by the charterparty. It is equally clear, though, that the transfer of the bill of lading from the seller to the buyer cannot construct a contractual link between the shipowner and the buyer through the application of section 1 of the Bills of Lading Act 1855[30]. That section transfers contracts but it does not create them: if the bill of lading performs no contractual function on its issue[31], then its transfer can pass no contract where none exists. Thus, it seems to follow, again inexorably from the doctrine of privity, that the shipowner and the buyer have no contract of carriage binding them the one to the other. It will cause little surprise to point out that the courts have cavalierly brushed aside this inconvenient and technical application of the doctrine of privity[32]. Thus in *Leduc v Ward*[33], Lord

---

[27] It is, of course, in the nature of a sensitive statement of the law that there may well be cases which are difficult to place. Thus, the editors of Scrutton contemplate, at 329, just such a 'nice question': a shipper-charterer who sells his goods by transferring the bill of lading and then buys them again from the same buyer. These facts partake of case (i) in the sense that the bill of lading was originally issued to the charterer simply as a receipt and a document of title; but it also partakes of case (ii) in the sense that the bill eventually returns to the charterer as a result of a totally independent contract of sale, transferring goods, documents and contractual rights and liabilities relating to those goods. The editors of Scrutton suggest that a cargo dispute between the shipowner and the charterer would be governed by the bill of lading, rather than by the charterparty. With respect, it is submitted that this is correct, the hypothesis being considerably closer to case (ii) envisaged in the text above.
[28] [1970] 1 QB 289 at 310.
[29] The buyer may also find that he is not privy to a charterparty concluded by the shipowner when the sale is on f o b terms: see below, fn 35.
[30] See Chapter 3.1.(a), above.
[31] The contract of carriage between the shipowner and the seller-charterer is, as we have seen, contained in the charterparty: *Rodocanachi v Milburn* (1886) 18 QBD 67.
[32] The textbook writers have been slightly less cavalier with the doctrine than the courts: for a valiant attempt at a technical escape from a technical problem, see Scrutton, art 33, note.
[33] (1888) 20 QBD 475 at 479.

Esher said, without but a sidelong glance at the doctrine of privity,

> '...where the bill of lading is indorsed over, as between the shipowner and the indorsee the bill of lading must be considered to contain the contract, because the former has given it for the purpose of enabling the charterer to pass it on as the contract of carriage in respect of the goods.'

When *Hain SS Co v Tate and Lyle Ltd*[34] reached the House of Lords, Lord Atkin put paid to any notion that the shipowner and the receiver of goods could be thrust asunder by anything so technical as the doctrine of privity; at page 620 of the report, he says:

> 'The consignee has not assigned to him the obligations under the charterparty nor, in fact, any obligation of the charterer under the bill of lading, for ex hypothesi there are none. A new contract appears to spring up between the ship and the consignee on the terms of the bill of lading.'

The law on this point, then, is transparently clear, even though its congruence with the orthodox doctrine of privity is, if only in theory, problematic: the contract of carriage between a buyer not privy to a charterparty with the shipowner is contained in the bill of lading[35].

The simplicity of that statement of the law conceals, however, the complexity which has bedevilled much litigation in the area. While the terms of the contract of carriage are clear if they are all contained within the bill of lading itself, they are not so clear if the bill of lading purports to incorporate terms from another document, i e the charterparty. Where the bill of lading contains an incorporation clause referring to the charterparty, are all the terms of the charterparty transferred to the contract

---

[34] (1936) 52 TLR 617.

[35] The buyer may also be a third party to a charterparty concluded by the shipowner where the sale contract is on f o b terms. Thus, where the buyer sub-charters a vessel from a charterer, and receives, whether directly from the shipowner or indirectly through the seller who ships the goods, a bill of lading issued by the shipowner, the only document to which both the shipowner and the buyer are privy is the bill of lading, there being no charterparty to which they are both party. In these circumstances, it has been held repeatedly—and again, it should be said, with hardly any argument taken on the point—that the bill of lading creates a new contractual nexus between the shipowner and the sub-charterer: see *The SLS Everest* [1981] 2 Lloyd's Rep 389; *The Nai Matteini* [1988] 1 Lloyd's Rep 452; and *The Kostas K* [1985] 1 Lloyd's Rep 231, where the sub-charterer was not, however, the buyer of the cargo. The privity issue which arises in this type of case is much the same as that discussed in the text above, i e does the possession of the bill of lading of itself create a contract between its holder and the shipowner? Indeed, here, if the courts had felt it necessary to tackle one technical point with another, they might have reached their conclusion because rather than in spite of the Bills of Lading Act 1855: they might have argued that the buyer/sub-charterers, at any rate in the first two cases mentioned above, had indeed inherited bill of lading contracts through s 1 of the 1855 Act. The fact that even this amount of obvious justification was not resorted to is a measure of the courts' readiness simply to ignore technical points of privity in this context. (Cf *The Roseline* [1985] AMC 551 for the view that there is no contract in the first place between the shipper and the shipowner on these facts: sed quaere, see fn 49, below.)

between the buyer and the shipowner; and if not, then which terms are incorporated? These questions have attracted litigation in a good number of cases, some of which relate to the incorporation of charterparty clauses in general, and others to the incorporation of charterparty arbitration clauses in particular. The broad principles governing incorporation of either type of charterparty clause are the same; their application to arbitration clauses, however, require detailed and separate treatment.

Before we examine those general principles, it would be helpful to point out why it is important in practice to determine which charterparty clauses are transferred into the bill of lading by an incorporation clause in the latter document. It will be recalled[36] that there are two main reasons why the parties to a contract of carriage need to establish in general which document, the charterparty or the bill of lading, regulates their contractual relationship: firstly, to discover which terms can be availed of by either party to a cargo dispute; and secondly, to establish whether their contract of carriage is subject to the Carriage of Goods by Sea Act 1971. In the hypothesis being examined here, we have already seen that the bill of lading governs the contractual relationship between the carrier and the third party: the issue is not, therefore, which document governs, but which parts of the charterparty find their way into the governing document, ie the bill of lading. The practical significance of this issue can be explained nonetheless by the same two reasons given above. Thus, if, for example, the discharge port in a bill of lading is described simply 'As Per Charter Party', the carrier discharges his duty to deliver to the buyer by unloading the goods at the charterparty destination if the incorporation of the charterparty destination into the bill of lading is effective; and this, despite the fact that the buyer expected delivery at quite a different port under his contract of sale[37]. Consequently, the resolution of a dispute between the buyer and the carrier as to delivery will depend on whether incorporation has been effective. Again, we have seen that the Carriage of Goods by Sea Act 1971 applies to bills of lading issued under a charterparty from the moment at which it becomes a contract between the carrier and the holder of the bill, that is to say, from the moment the bill is transferred to the third party in the hypothesis here examined[38]. Where charterparty clauses are effectively incorporated into the bill of lading, they too become subject, like all the other clauses in the bill, to the 1971 Act, which in article III.8 of the Schedule to the Act renders 'null, void and of no effect' any term seeking to reduce the carrier's liability to a level beneath that provided for in the Act. Thus, any charterparty clause effectively incorporated into a bill of lading will be struck down by article III.8 if it comes to grief upon some other article of the HagueVisby Rules: a six-month time-bar in the charterparty would, for example, give way to the one-year time-bar in the Rules[39].

---

[36] See text accompanying fn 5, above.
[37] This is why, of course, the same facts, which occurred in *SIAT di dal Ferro v Tradax Overseas SA* [1980] 1 Lloyd's Rep 53, raise issues of tender between the seller and the buyer, which issues will be discussed below at Chapter 7.5.
[38] See the Carriage of Goods by Sea Act 1971, Sch, art I(b), reproduced at fn 9 above.
[39] See the Carriage of Goods by Sea Act 1971, art IV.5.

The Act thus has a direct impact on effectively incorporated charterparty clauses; and this, despite the fact that it does not generally apply to charterparties[40].

We said earlier that the broad principles regulating the incorporation of charterparty clauses into bills of lading were similar whether or not the clause sought to be incorporated was an arbitration clause; but that the incorporation of arbitration clauses required separate treatment, simply because of the way the case-law in this area had developed. We shall consequently deal with incorporation under two heads: incorporation in general and incorporation of arbitration clauses.

i. Incorporation in general

Whether or not a particular clause in a charterparty is effectively incorporated by a clause in a bill of lading seeking to do so depends on the answer to each of the following two questions: firstly, is the incorporation clause in the bill of lading apt to describe the clause in the charterparty sought to be incorporated? Secondly, would that clause, if incorporated, be consistent with other clauses in the bill of lading? If both questions can be answered affirmatively, then the clause is incorporated into the bill of lading and is part of the contract of carriage between the carrier and the holder of the bill; if either of the questions attracts a negative answer, then the clause is not incorporated. The two questions have been called the 'description' and the 'consistency' questions and they appear first to have been articulated in this form by Staughton J in *The Emmanuel Colocotronis (No 2)*[41]. Each raises its own problems, which will be examined in turn.

The first question—that relating to the issue of 'description'—raises three problems. Firstly, although it is clear that the starting point must be the incorporation clause actually carried on the bill of lading, is it legitimate also to look at any clause, in the charterparty itself, which clause identifies those charterparty clauses which are to be incorporated into the bill of lading? Thus, for example, in *The Garbis*[42], the bill of lading sought to incorporate 'all the terms whatsoever' of the charterparty; yet, the charterparty appeared to restrict the terms of that

---

[40] See Carriage of Goods by Sea Act 1971, Sch, art V, the relevant part of which is reproduced at fn 7, above.

[41] [1982] 1 Lloyd's Rep 286 at 289. The Court of Appeal declined to follow this case in *The Varenna* [1983] 2 Lloyd's Rep 592: the point of disagreement related to the particular answer given by Staughton J to his own second question—consistency— in the context of the attempted incorporation of an arbitration clause into a bill of lading, as to which see fn 56, below. The Court of Appeal cast no aspersions on Staughton J's general approach to issues of incorporation: indeed, the judge's two questions were again used by Donaldson MR in *The Miramar* [1984] 1 Lloyd's Rep 142 at 143, a judgment which met with the approval of the House of Lords at [1984] 2 Lloyd's Rep 129; the Court of Appeal was presided over by Donaldson MR both in *The Varenna* and in *The Miramar*.

[42] [1982] 2 Lloyd's Rep 283, particularly at 288.

incorporation by listing a number of clauses which were to be incorporated into any bill of lading issued thereunder. On these facts, were the wide terms of description contained in the bill of lading to be limited by the specific instructions as to incorporation given by the charterparty? Goff J decided that the bill of lading incorporation clause could not be so limited.[43] Secondly, what types of charterparty clause are aptly described, for the purposes of incorporation, by general terms of incorporation in the bill of lading: is it all types of charterparty clause, for example, the safe port warranty or a clause stipulating for the payment of bunkers, or is it a more limited type of clause? It is clear on authority[44]

'...that general words of incorporation in a bill of lading may be effective to incorporate terms of an identifiable charter-party which are relevant to the shipment, carriage and discharge of the cargo and the payment of freight...'

Thirdly, where the bill of lading covers goods carried on a vessel which is subject to more than one charterparty[45], which charterparty does the incorporation clause refer to? Again, it is clear on authority that, where no charterparty is specifically identified in the bill of lading, the clause must be taken to refer to the head-charter[46], at any rate unless the particular circumstances of the case indicate otherwise[47].

The second question—that relating to 'consistency'—raises the following problem: in deciding whether or not the clause sought to be incorporated is consistent with the other clauses contained in the bill of lading, to what degree is it permissible for the judges so to construe the particular charterparty clause as to iron out any inconsistency with the bill of lading? This issue has arisen largely, but not exclusively,

---

43 Cf *The Emmanuel Colocotronis (No 2)* [1982] 1 Lloyd's Rep 286 at 292, per Staughton J, who clearly thought it legitimate to examine also the incorporation clause contained in the charterparty. The Court of Appeal in *The Varenna*, though, preferred the view taken by Goff J: see [1983] 2 Lloyd's Rep 592 at 594 and 596.

44 *The Garbis* [1982] 2 Lloyd's Rep 283 at 287; see also other cases cited in Scrutton, at art 34, fn 35, and, generally, art 36; for a general review of the authorities, both on incorporation in general and on incorporation of arbitration clauses, see Incorporation of Charterparty Terms into a Bill of Lading, Donald A. Davies, 1966 JBL 326; Incorporation of Arbitration Clauses into Charterparty Bills of Lading, E. A. Marshall, 1982 JBL 478; and Incorporation of Charterparty Terms into Bill of Lading Contracts— a Case Rationalisation, W. J. Park, (1986) 16 VUWLR 177.

45 That is to say, where the vessel has been chartered and sub-chartered, possibly a number of times.

46 *The Sevonia Team* [1983] 2 Lloyd's Rep 640 at 644; *The San Nicholas* [1976] 1 Lloyd's Rep 8 at 11; and *The Nai Matteini* [1988] 1 Lloyd's Rep 452 at 459.

47 Thus, see, for example, *The SLS Everest* [1981] 2 Lloyd's Rep 389, where the Court of Appeal upheld Lloyd J's decision that the incorporation clause must be taken to refer to the sub-charter, a voyage-charter, rather than to the head-charter, a time-charter, on the ground that many of the clauses contained in a time-charterparty would be inapposite to a bill of lading covering the carriage of goods on a certain voyage; also in this sense, Kerr J in *The Nanfri* [1978] 1 Lloyd's Rep 581 at 591. With respect, this manner of reasoning blurs the distinction between the 'description' and the 'consistency' issues referred to in the text above; moreover, it destroys the certainty achieved by the simpler rule that the incorporation clause must be taken to refer to the head charter where another charterparty is not specifically identified in the clause.

in the context of cases relating to the incorporation of arbitration clauses from charterparties into bills of lading and it will consequently be discussed presently.

ii. Incorporation of arbitration clauses

It has already been said that litigation regarding the incorporation of charterparty clauses into bills of lading has revolved largely around whether arbitration clauses in charterparties have been effectively incorporated into bills of lading. The practical significance of this issue can hardly be overstated: for the reverse side of the question 'Does this arbitration clause apply?' is the question 'Can this claim currently before the court be stopped?'[48] Where the incorporation clause refers specifically to the arbitration clause contained in the charterparty, then the arbitration clause is incorporated into the bill of lading, at any rate unless it is inconsistent with an arbitration clause contained in the bill of lading itself[49]. Where, however, the incorporation clause in the bill is drawn in general terms, then the charterparty arbitration clause needs to negotiate the same two hurdles as any other charterparty clause if it is effectively to be incorporated into the bill of lading: description and consistency. Those two hurdles can be translated, for the purpose of the particular issue of arbitration clauses, as follows. Firstly, the incorporation clause must be drawn in terms wide enough to include an arbitration clause[50]; secondly, the charterparty arbitration clause must clearly be intended to apply both to disputes arising under the charterparty and to disputes arising under the bill of lading[51].

This last statement of the law conceals a number of issues which have been keenly litigated. Thus, for example, what general words of incorporation would aptly describe an arbitration clause? It is clear on

---

[48] See, for example, *The Varenna* [1983] 2 Lloyd's Rep 592, where the shipowner brought a claim for demurrage against the shippers and against the consignees, holders of the bill of lading containing an incorporation clause.

[49] An example of a charterparty arbitration clause which, though specifically referred to in the bill of lading incorporation clause, was inconsistent with the bill of lading itself, can be found in the Canadian decision in *The Roseline* [1985] AMC 551. There, the charterparty arbitration clause referred disputes to Paris, whereas the bill of lading referred disputes to the Federal Court of Canada; the incorporation clause specifically incorporated the charterparty arbitration clause. An action by the shipowners against the sellers, named as shippers in the bill of lading, for a declaration that the parties were bound by a contract referring disputes to French arbitration, failed on the ground that there was no contract between the shipowners and the sellers. It is difficult to see how a party named as shipper in the bill is *not* a party to the contract of carriage recorded in the bill: see Benjamin, para 1444, fn 87. The same result might have been achieved—the declaration refused—on a much narrower and, it is submitted, more correct ground, namely that the charterparty arbitration clause was not part of any contract between the seller and the shipowner: despite its specific mention in the incorporation clause, it failed the consistency hurdle because it was flatly contradicted by the relevant clause in the bill of lading.

[50] If it is not, then incorporation fails on the description issue.

[51] If it is not, then incorporation fails on the consistency issue.

authority that the word 'conditions'[52] in the incorporation clause does not adequately describe an arbitration clause, because an arbitration clause is not a term relating to the shipment, carriage and discharge of the cargo; consequently, the incorporation of the arbitration clause fails on the hurdle of 'description': *The Varenna*[53]. It is not quite so clear, however, whether the use of the word 'terms' in the incorporation clause is similarly inadequate to incorporate an arbitration clause[54]. Again, how clearly must the intention appear in the charterparty arbitration clause that the clause is to apply both to disputes arising under the charterparty and to those arising under the bill of lading? If the clause expressly says so in terms, then the clause would, if incorporated, fit the bill of lading perfectly and there would be no problem of 'consistency' between the clause and the bill of lading. Equally clearly, where the arbitration clause applies in terms to 'disputes under this charterparty', it does not fit neatly into the bill of lading and the courts will not manipulate the word 'charterparty' to mean 'bill of lading'[55]. On the other hand, where the arbitration clause applies to 'disputes under this contract', it is not certain on the current state of the authorities whether the courts will construe the words 'this contract' to include the bill of lading as well as the charterparty[56].

3. WHOM IS THE BUYER TO SUE FOR SHORT-DELIVERY OR DAMAGE TO GOODS?

In the second section of this chapter, we saw that where the bill of lading is held by a third party to a charterparty, for example by a buyer of goods on c i f terms where the goods are carried on a vessel chartered to the seller, the buyer's contract of carriage with the carrier is very clearly

---

52 A word described by Donaldson MR as 'a chameleon-like word which takes its meaning from its surroundings': see *The Varenna* [1983] 2 Lloyd's Rep 592 at 595.
53 Ibid. To this extent, *The Varenna* clearly overrules Staughton J's judgment in *The Emmanuel Colocotronis (No 2)* [1982] 1 Lloyd's Rep 286.
54 See *The Varenna* [1983] 2 Lloyd's Rep 592 at 597 and the authorities there cited. See also the Court of Appeal judgment in *The Miramar* [1984] 1 Lloyd's Rep 142, where, at 143, Donaldson MR suggests that the phrase 'all the terms whatsoever' was wide enough aptly to describe all the terms of the charterparty; it must be said, though, firstly, that the clause sought to be incorporated in *The Miramar* was not an arbitration clause; and secondly, that the clause was not in any case incorporated because it failed the consistency test.
55 *Hamilton v Mackie* (1889) 5 TLR 677. For a more recent indication of judicial attitudes, see the House of Lords judgment in *The Miramar* [1984] 2 Lloyd's Rep 129, a case which did not relate to an arbitration clause, but one which was clearly based on a somewhat restrictive attitude to 'verbal manipulation' of charterparty clauses, an attitude which, per Gatehouse J in *The Nai Matteini* [1988] 1 Lloyd's Rep 452, must be taken to apply equally restrictively to the incorporation of arbitration clauses. The phrase 'verbal manipulation' is ascribed by Gatehouse J in *The Nai Matteini* [1988] 1 Lloyd's Rep 452 at 456, to Russell LJ in *The Merak* [1964] 2 Lloyd's Rep 527 at 537.
56 Staughton J construed the phrase to encompass both disputes under the charterparty and those under the bill of lading: *The Emmanuel Colocotronis (No 2)* [1982] 1 Lloyd's Rep 286 at 289 and 292; however, this aspect of Staughton J's judgment was disapproved of by the Court of Appeal in *The Varenna* [1983] 2 Lloyd's Rep 592.

contained in the bill of lading[57] rather than in the charterparty[58]. Clearly, though, the buyer needs to pursue his cargo claim not only on the basis of the right contract but also against the right defendant. Indeed, in a sense, both issues—the identity of the buyer's contractual terms of carriage and the identity of the carrier—are part of the same question: what links this cargo claimant by way of contract to this defendant? The problem is caused by there being at least two possible contenders for the title of carrier, namely the shipowner and the charterer[59]. The buyer must get the right defendant within his sights, if only because time (and expense) wasted in pursuing the wrong party might extinguish any possible remedies he might have against the proper defendant[60]. Moreover, it is conceivable that a buyer on c i f terms may find that his seller, charterer of the vessel on which the goods were shipped, is also his carrier[61]; consequently, the buyer may need to pursue remedies both under the contract of carriage and, in the alternative under the contract of sale, against the same defendant and in the same case[62].

Despite—or, perhaps, because of—the importance of the question, it is easier to draw general guidance than specific prescription from the cases. Dicta are plentiful which warn that each case is to be taken on its own facts. For example, Walton J in *Samuel, Samuel & Co v West Hartlepool Steam Navigation Co*[63], says:

> 'Upon this point many cases were cited, and to some extent the authorities appear conflicting. But since the question is really a question of fact depending upon the documents and circumstances in each case, it may be that the apparent conflict arises mainly from the fact that the documents and circumstances are different in different cases.'[64]

This is not to say that the courts' decisions in this area are of little or no value; rather does it suggest that they are to be used with greater caution and judgment than is usual.

Subject to that caveat, it is possible to set out the two types of extreme case where the carrier's identity is virtually free of doubt; and Walton

---

[57] See text accompanying fn 35, above.
[58] Although, of course, as we have seen, certain parts of the charterparty may be incorporated into the bill of lading through an appropriate incorporation clause in the bill of lading.
[59] Although the party who is the carrier is hardly likely, if liable, to appreciate the accolade.
[60] As almost happened to the cargo-claimants in *The Henrik Sif* [1982] 1 Lloyd's Rep 456: see text accompanying fn 77, below.
[61] This would be the case, for example, where the seller has chartered a vessel on a demise-charterparty: see text accompanying fn 66, below.
[62] Thus, the plaintiff could, qua receiver, claim that the goods were not landed in the same condition as that in which they were shipped; and, failing that, the plaintiff could, qua buyer, claim that the goods were not shipped in such a state as to withstand the ordinary risks of transit: see Chapter 5, above.
[63] (1906) 11 Com Cas 115 at 125.
[64] In a similar vein, see Roche J in *Wilston SS Co Ltd v Andrew Weir & Co* (1925) 22 Ll L Rep 521, at 522.

J identified these cases in the extract which immediately follows the quotation given above:[65]

'There are certain more or less typical cases. For instance, there is the case ... where the charterparty amounts to what is called a demise of the vessel. In such a case it is reasonably clear that the contracts with the shippers under the bill of lading are between them and the charterers and not between them and the owners. Again, there is another class of cases in which the charterers by the charterparty do no more than undertake that a full cargo shall be shipped and guarantee payment of a certain freight. In such cases it is very often stipulated that upon shipment of a full cargo and upon the charterers paying or securing payment in the manner agreed upon of the excess (if any) of chartered freight over and above the bill of lading freight the charterer's liability under the charterparty is to cease. In such cases the contract of carriage under the bill of lading would ordinarily be between the owners and the shippers. ... And between the two types or classes which I have described there is a great variety of intermediate cases, ...'

Thus, where the vessel is chartered by demise charterparty[66], the carrier is likely to be the charterer[67]; and where the chartered vessel is put up by the charterer as a general ship, with the charterer fading out of the picture through the application of a cesser clause, the carrier is likely to be the shipowner. Most of the litigation has, unsurprisingly, related to neither of these extreme cases, but to Walton J's 'great variety of intermediate cases'.

In these intermediate cases, the buyer's starting point in his search for the proper defendant to a cargo claim, must be that the carrier is the shipowner. In *Manchester Trust v Furness*[68], Lindley LJ said:

'The plaintiffs, who are holders of the bills of lading, rely upon the general rule of law that prima facie at all events a bill of lading signed by the master is signed by the master as the servant or agent of the shipowner.'

This presumption is a weak one: it may be, but by no means always is, rebutted by factors pointing the finger of liability in a cargo claim away from the shipowner and towards the charterer. Thus, the fact that the charterer has put his signature to the bill of lading may well indicate to the cargo-interest that his contract of carriage is with the charterer rather than with the shipowner: *The Okehampton*[69]. On the other hand,

---

[65] *Samuel, Samuel & Co v West Hartlepool Steam Navigation Co* (1906) 11 Com Cas 115 at 125, 126.
[66] That is to say, where the charterer hires the ship itself, taking over control of the vessel from the owner, rather than simply contracting for its use, under the shipowner's direction, over a certain period or for a certain voyage: see, generally, Scrutton, arts 25, 26.
[67] *Baumwoll Manufactur von Carl Scheibler v Furness* [1893] AC 8.
[68] [1895] 2 QB 539 at 543.
[69] [1913] P 173. See also *Samuel, Samuel & Co v West Hartlepool Steam Navigation Co* (1906) 11 Com Cas 115.

in *The Nea Tyhi*[70], Sheen J found that the buyer's contract of carriage was with the shipowner, rather than with the charterer, despite the fact that the charterer's agent had signed the bill of lading; the decision in *The Okehampton*[71] was not cited and Sheen J seemed anxious to point out that if the buyer's claim lay against the shipowners rather than the charterers, their claim would be valueless because the shipowners had gone into liquidation[72]. On the other hand still, the charterer's signature on a bill of lading in the charterer's form persuaded Sheen J that the proper defendant to a cargo claim was the charterer in *The Venezuela*[73], despite the fact that the charterers signed 'as agents for the Master'.[74]

It is evidently difficult, as has already been indicated, to extrapolate from any of these cases[75] to a given set of facts. On the other hand, there are two instances, even within Walton J's 'great variety of intermediate cases'[76], where the identity of the carrier is clear. Firstly, the doctrine of estoppel might act to prevent the charterer of a vessel from denying that he is the carrier with whom the cargo-interest has contracted for the carriage of the goods. Thus, in *The Henrik Sif*[77], time-charterers through their agents had allowed the plaintiff cargo-interests to believe that they were the disponent owners of the vessel and that they were therefore the proper defendants to the plaintiffs' cargo claim; the plaintiffs consequently let their claim against the real shipowners be barred by the passage of time. Webster J held that the time-charterers were estopped from denying that they were the proper defendants in the plaintiffs' cargo claim, and this despite the fact that the bill of lading issued to the cargo-interests contained a demise clause.

This last circumstance—the demise clause in *The Henrik Sif*[78]—brings us to the second instance where the identity of the carrier is clear. A demise clause is a clause contained in a bill of lading indicating to the

---

[70]   [1982] 1 Lloyd's Rep 606, a case which was disapproved of by the House of Lords in *The Aliakmon* [1986] 2 Lloyd's Rep 1 at 11, but not on the point referred to in the text.

[71]   [1913] P 173.

[72]   See [1982] 1 Lloyd's Rep 606 at 609.

[73]   [1980] 1 Lloyd's Rep 393.

[74]   A similar signature by the charterers in *Tillmanns v SS Knutsford Ltd* [1908] A C 406; affd [1908] 1 KB 185, persuaded Channel J, and the House of Lords, that the carrier was the shipowner; the case was cited before Sheen J in *The Venezuela*: the judge's response was to cite Roche J's dictum in *Wilston SS Co Ltd v Andrew Weir & Co* (1925) 22 Ll L Rep 521 at 522 to the effect that each case had to be decided on its particular facts.

[75]   The cases cited in the previous paragraph are a selection from those in which the issue has arisen for decision: for other cases illustrating the difficulty of making firm predictions on given facts, see Scrutton, art 38.

[76]   See *Samuel, Samuel & Co v West Hartlepool Steam Navigation Co* (1906) 11 Com Cas 115 at 126.

[77]   [1982] 1 Lloyd's Rep 456. Webster J's judgment raises the crucial issue as to whether estoppel, or some sub-species of it, can be used to found, or simply to assist, a cause of action. At 1987 LMCLQ 260, F.M.B. Reynolds writes: 'On English views of estoppel at least, the decision goes to the verge of the law.' See also *The Uhenbels* [1986] 2 Lloyd's Rep 294.

[78]   [1982] 1 Lloyd's Rep 456.

holder that the carrier is the owner of the vessel; the clause in *The Henrik Sif*[79] read:

> 'If the ship is not owned by or chartered by demise to the company
> ... by whom this Bill of Lading is issued ... this Bill of Lading
> shall take effect only as a contract with the owner or demise charterer
> as the case may be as Principal made through the Agency of the
> said company ... who act as Agents only and shall be under no
> personal liability whatsoever in respect thereof.'

Subject to the caveat that the charterer may, in certain circumstances,
be estopped from relying on such a clause[80], the demise clause makes
it clear to the buyer of the goods that his carrier, the appropriate defendant
to a cargo claim, is the shipowner or demise charterer, and not the charterer
who issued the bill of lading[81].

4. THE BILL OF LADING AS A RECEIPT WHERE IT IS ISSUED UNDER A CHARTERPARTY

In the first part of this chapter, we asked why, at times, traders take
and carriers issue bills of lading covering goods carried on a vessel under
charter: one of the reasons was that, despite the existence of a charterparty
binding the shipowner and the charterer in contract, the charterer still
needed a receipt for goods loaded because this would provide him with
useful evidence as to the quantity and apparent condition of the goods
on shipment in any cargo claim he, or others eventually interested in
the goods, might wish to bring against the shipowner. Moreover, we
saw that this was the case whether the charterer was selling or buying
the goods shipped, and, indeed, even if the charterer had shipped the
goods independently of any contract of sale.

In Chapter 5, we saw that the strength of the evidence provided by
the bill of lading as to the quantity and apparent condition of the goods
on shipment depended crucially on the precise tenor of the relevant
statement on the bill: whether the strength of the presumptions raised
by the bill was prima facie or conclusive, those presumptions were only
as useful as the statement on which they were based[82]. Thus, for example,
a bill of lading stating that '100 tons of sugar' were shipped, 'weight
and quantity unknown', is, even in the hands of an endorsee protected
by the Carriage of Goods by Sea Act 1971[83], of little evidential value

---

[79] Ibid.
[80] As was the charterer in *The Henrik Sif* itself: [1982] 1 Lloyd's Rep 456.
[81] The clause has been well-received by the courts in this country; see *The Berkshire* [1974]
1 Lloyd's Rep 185 at 187-188; *The Vikfrost* [1980] 1 Lloyd's Rep 560; *The Henrik Sif* [1982]
1 Lloyd's Rep 456; and *The Jalamohan* [1988] 1 Lloyd's Rep 443. However, for a comparative,
and hostile, study of the clause, see Tetley, *Marine Cargo Claims*, 3rd edn, pp 248-259. A
similar cautionary note is struck in this country by F.M.B. Reynolds at 1987 LMCLQ 259
and 1988 LMCLQ 285. For a more benign attitude, see *Carriage of Goods by Sea*, J.F.
Wilson (hereinafter referred to as Wilson) Pitman, 1988, pp 220, 221; and Goode,
pp 605-607.
[82] See, generally, Chapter 5.1, above.
[83] In whose favour the Act endows the statement on the bill with the quality of conclusive
evidence: see the Carriage of Goods by Sea Act 1971, Sch, art III.4.

because it provides conclusive evidence of a very inconclusive statement[84]. Later in the same chapter, Chapter 5, we saw how the 1971 Act went some way[85] towards avoiding such a result by giving the shipper the right to demand a bill of lading which did, in fact, make a conclusive statement about the goods, upon which a conclusive estoppel could be founded against the carrier[86]: in our example, the shipper would be entitled to demand the deletion of the word 'weight' from the 'weight and quantity unknown' reservation on issue of the bill.

Our task in this part of this chapter is to examine whether a charterer is likewise entitled to demand from the shipowner, under the Carriage of Goods by Sea Act 1971, a bill of lading containing firm, unqualified representations on the bill of lading as to the marks, quantity and apparent condition of the goods on shipment. The question needs to be examined in two hypotheses: firstly, where the charterer sells goods on c i f terms; secondly, where the charterer buys goods on f o b terms and the bill of lading is issued to the shipper and then transferred to the buyer[87].

(a) **Charterer selling c i f**

Before examining whether a charterer shipping goods under a c i f sale is entitled to firm representations on the bill as to the quantity and condition of the goods on shipment, it would be helpful to consider why such a charterer should be at all interested in the strength of statements on the bill. The example with which the question was introduced will serve to illustrate the significance of the issue. Where the carrier's statement on the bill that 100 tons of sugar were shipped is qualified by a 'weight and quantity unknown' clause, the buyer might, against a falling market, be minded to reject the bill; and on one view of the authorities he may well be entitled to[88]. Normally, a seller could avoid this risk by exercising the right given him by the 1971 Act to ask the carrier to delete the offending clause on issue of the bill: should the seller be deprived of this right, and risk rejection by the buyer, simply because he happens to have chartered the vessel carrying the goods?

If the charterparty incorporates the Carriage of Goods by Sea Act 1971, or the Hague or Hague-Visby Rules[89], or article III of those

---

[84] See further on this point, Chapter 5, above at fn 13.

[85] The Act only went some way towards solving the problem, it will be recalled, because it gave the shipper alone the right to demand compliance with its terms as to the type of receipt the carrier was to issue; and the shipper was unlikely, unless goaded by his duties under the contract of sale, to delay issue of the bill by complaining about small-print qualifications to statements as to the goods on shipment.

[86] See the Carriage of Goods by Sea Act 1971, Sch, art III.3 and see, generally, Chapter 5.2, above.

[87] As happened in *President of India v Metcalfe Shipping Co Ltd, The Dunelmia* [1970] 1 QB 289.

[88] See the discussion of *The Galatia* [1979] 2 Lloyd's Rep 450 and of its relationship to *Libau Wood Co v H Smith & Sons* (1930) 37 Ll L Rep 296, at Chapter 5.3.(a).ii, above.

[89] The Visby amendments to the original Hague Rules did not alter art III.3.

Rules[90], or (arguably) article V of those Rules[91], then it seems clear that, in terms of article III of the Rules, the shipper, that is to say, in this case, the charterer, can demand a bill of lading containing unqualified statements as to the quantity of goods shipped.

The position is not quite so clear where the charterer has not thought to incorporate the Rules, wholly or partly, into the charterparty. The crux of the matter is whether the charterer can, qua shipper, use the relevant part of a statute, the Carriage of Goods by Sea Act 1971, in order to obtain the same type of strong receipt which he might have stipulated for by contract. The part of the statute which the charterer might wish to use is a segment of article V in the Schedule to the Act, which reads:

'. . . if bills of lading are issued in the case of a ship under a charter party they shall comply with the terms of these Rules.'

The point would be that, once the Act has the force of law[92], then article V imposes an obligation on the shipowner to issue bills of lading, on demand of the shipper, which comply with article III.3, that is to say, which give firm representations as to the quantity of the goods on shipment.

Views on the validity of this argument in the two main works in the area differ. The editors of Scrutton[93] find it difficult to extend the benefit of article III.3 of the Rules, through article V, to a shipper-charterer who has not incorporated the Rules, totally or partially, into his charterparty. In the hands of the charterer, the bill of lading is a mere receipt[94]; it is not a contract of carriage as defined by article I(b) of the Rules[95]; and article V cannot consequently apply in such a way as to trigger off article III.3 in the charterer's favour. The editor of Carver[96], on the other hand, takes the simpler view, based on the bland text of the legislation: section 1(2) of the Act gives the Rules the force of law; articles V and III form part of those Rules; article V clearly activates article III.3 'if bills of lading are issued in the case of a ship under a charter party'; and therefore a shipper-charterer can demand compliance

---

[90] The article which gives the shipper the right to demand firm representations on the bill of lading: see Appendix 1.b.
[91] The relevant part of art V reads: '. . . if bills of lading are issued in the case of a ship under a charter party they shall comply with the terms of these Rules.' See the text immediately following this footnote for further discussion of this article.
[92] See s 1(2) of the Act.
[93] At pp 417 and 460.
[94] *Rodocanachi v Milburn* (1886) 18 QBD 67 and see Chapter 7.2.(a), above.
[95] '"Contract of carriage" applies only to contracts of carriage covered by a bill of lading or any similar document of title, in so far as such document relates to the carriage of goods by sea, including any bill of lading or any similar document as aforesaid issued under or pursuant to a charter party from the moment at which such bill of lading or similar document of title regulates the relations between a carrier and a holder of the same.'
[96] At para 567.

with article III.3. It is suggested that the reasoning supporting the view adopted in Carver is compelling, both because it flows neatly from the wording of the Act; and because it is more consistent with the policy behind the relevant article of the Rules, namely article III.3, which was to enhance the commercial value of bills of lading by strengthening their function as receipts for goods shipped[97].

(b) Charterer buying f o b

Here the question, though in essence the same, is asked on the basis of a different set of facts: where the sale is concluded on f o b rather than c i f terms, and the bill of lading is issued by the shipowner to the seller who then transfers it to the buyer[98], can the buyer, qua charterer, contact the shipowner and demand the issue to the shipper of a bill of lading containing a firm, unqualified statement as to the quantity and apparent condition of the goods on shipment? It would seem to follow from what was said above that, here again, we have a bill of lading issued in the case of a ship under charter and that therefore the bill must comply with the terms of the Rules, i e article III.3. Rather surprisingly, the editor of Carver[99] suggests that article V only applies[100] 'where a bill of lading is issued to a charterer.' If this qualification is intended to exclude the application, by force of law, of article V, and thereby of article III.3, in the circumstances here contemplated, then it is suggested that such a restriction is not warranted by the wording itself of article V, which contemplates the situation where 'bills of lading are issued in the case of a ship under a charter party' and not simply one where bills of lading are issued to a charterer.

5. REQUIREMENTS OF TENDER WHERE A BILL OF LADING IS ISSUED UNDER A CHARTERPARTY

Thus far, we have concentrated on the difficulties caused by the issue of bills of lading under charterparties in the relationships between either trader, seller or buyer, and the carrier, whoever he may be. In a cargo claim brought by either trader against the carrier, issues may well arise

---

[97] The arguments are rehearsed at greater length in The Bill of Lading as a Receipt— Missing Oil in Unknown Quantities, C. Debattista, 1986 LMCLQ 468, particularly at pp 476–478; the central thrust of the position there taken is that a bill in the hands of a shipper-charterer must comply, as a matter of form, with art III.3; it is not to impose the whole structure of the Rules, as a contractual regime, on a bill of lading which, in the circumstances envisaged, is not a contract.

[98] As happened in *President of India v Metcalfe Shipping Co Ltd, The Dunelmia* [1970] 1 QB 289. Where the bill of lading is issued by the shipowner directly to the buyer-charterer, in exchange for the mate's receipt which the buyer has obtained from the seller, the buyer-charterer is, of course, in the legal sense, the shipper of the goods and he then has the same rights, if any, which a seller-charterer under a c i f contract has under art III.3 of the Rules.

[99] At para 567.

[100] Presumably, of course, other than where the 1971 Act or the Rules have not been incorporated, in whole or in part, into the charterparty.

regarding the identity both of the carrier and of the contractual terms under which the claim is brought; and again, whichever of the two parties sues the carrier, the evidential nature of the bill of lading as a receipt is, as we have seen, of crucial significance to the success of the claim.

Things start happening, however, well before a cargo claim is brought against the carrier. In Chapters 5 and 6, we looked at a number of qualities which a bill of lading must possess, relating first to its receipt and then to its contractual function, if it is to be acceptable to a buyer on shipment terms. Which of the two traders, seller or buyer, ends up bringing the cargo claim against the carrier in respect of goods carried on a vessel under charter depends upon whether the bill of lading and other documents are accepted or rejected by the buyer. If the buyer rejects, then the seller brings the claim against the carrier and faces some or all of the difficulties discussed in the earlier parts of this chapter; if the buyer accepts the documents, then the party facing those problems is the buyer. So what is the buyer to do: should he accept or reject bills of lading issued pursuant to a charterparty? This is the central point of this final part of the chapter: what are the requirements of tender, both under a sale on shipment terms[101] and under a letter of credit, where a bill of lading is issued under a charterparty?

Three issues are involved in the question and each will be dealt with in turn. Firstly, can the buyer, or the bank where a letter of credit is in place, reject a bill of lading simply on the basis that it seeks to incorporate terms from a charterparty? Secondly, if the buyer is not entitled to reject simply on that ground, can he demand sight of the charterparty in order to examine whether the contract of carriage tendered[102] conforms to the stipulations agreed in the contract of sale, for example so far as concerns the destination of the goods? Thirdly, whether or not the buyer does have sight of the charterparty, can the buyer reject documents where the contract of carriage tendered does not, as a result of an incorporated term, conform to the contract of sale?

Firstly, then, is the mere fact that a bill of lading refers to a charterparty of itself a legitimate ground for rejection of documents? So far as concerns the sale contract, there appears to be no authority for implying a term against tender by the seller of such a bill of lading. On the other hand, where the method of payment chosen is a letter of credit governed by the Uniform Customs and Practice for Documentary Credits, then unless

---

[101] In this context, this phrase includes c i f and c & f contracts; and f o b contracts where the seller fixes the charter and takes the bill either on behalf of the buyer (f o b classic form) or in his own name, then passing both to the buyer (f o b with additional services). In f o b contracts of the straight variety, the buyer will have negotiated the charterparty and will be fully aware of its contents; even if the bill of lading consequently comes to him via the seller, he has no cause for complaint about the bill having been issued subject to a charterparty.

[102] That is to say, the contract composed of the terms in the bill of lading itself and those effectively incorporated from the charterparty.

the letter of credit expressly allows for the tender of such a bill, the confirming bank will reject the documents.[103]

This discrepancy between the rules relating to the sale contract and those relating to letters of credit may cause problems for the unwary buyer. Where the contract of sale and the letter of credit are silent on the issue, the seller will expect to be entitled to tender a bill of lading subject to a charterparty, whereas the bank will expect that he is not so entitled. The letter of credit can always, of course, be varied by agreement between the buyer and the issuing bank: the cause of the resulting delay could, however, be very simply avoided if application forms for the opening of letters of credit contained, which they commonly do not, a specific query inquiring of the buyer whether such bills are acceptable.

Secondly, given that a buyer appears not to be entitled to reject the bill of lading on the mere ground that it seeks to incorporate charterparty terms, can he insist with the seller, on pain of rejection, that the charterparty[104], or a copy thereof, be tendered with the bill of lading, so as to ascertain whether the resulting contract of carriage complies with the contract of sale? The case-law on this point is unclear. On the one hand, Viscount Caldecote LCJ decided against the requirement of tender in *Finska Cellulosaforeningen v Westfield Paper Co Ltd*[105], where he held that buyers were not entitled to reject shipping documents on the ground that the charterparty was not tendered with the bill of lading[106]. On the other hand, there are a number of early cases which seem to indicate that it was quite common to tender the charterparty where there was one[107]. Moreover, more recently, there have been some hesitant expressions of unease with the notion that the buyer might be bound to accept from the seller a contract of carriage, sight unseen, which binds him to the carrier. Thus, in *SIAT di dal Ferro v Tradax Overseas SA*[108], both Donaldson J at first instance and Megaw LJ in the Court

---

[103] See UCP art 26(c)(i); the position is the same where the credit calls for a combined transport document: see art 25(c)(i).

[104] As for which charterparty where there is a string of sub-charters, see text accompanying fn 47, above.

[105] [1940] 4 All ER 473, see particularly pp 474-6.

[106] Caldecote LCJ's judgment was distinguished by Donaldson J in *SIAT di dal Ferro v Tradax Overseas SA* [1978] 2 Lloyd's Rep 470 at 492; affd [1980] 1 Lloyd's Rep 53 and discussed above at Chapter 6.3.(d), on the ground that in the *Finska* case there was a course of dealing between the parties to the sale contract which put the buyers on notice as to the terms of the charterparty incorporated into the bill of lading. To distinguish the *Finska* case on this ground is, with respect, to explain rather than to justify it: for a charterparty contains much more than the standard form on which it is built, and to impute knowledge of a particular fixture on the basis of a standard form does violence, surely, to the general principles of notice of contractual terms.

[107] See, for example, *Covas v Bingham* (1853) 2 E & B 836 and other cases cited in Benjamin, para 1645, fn 54. Moreover, the charterparty is listed as one of the documents to be tendered in *Ireland v Livingston* (1872) LR 5 HL 395 at 406: this was, however, only said by way of obiter.

[108] See particularly, [1980] 1 Lloyd's Rep 53 at 63, per Megaw LJ; and [1978] 2 Lloyd's Rep 470 at 492, per Donaldson J.

of Appeal lament, albeit somewhat obliquely, the absence of the charterparty on tender of a bill of lading giving the phrase 'As Per Charter Party' as the destination of the goods. In deciding that the buyers were entitled to reject the bills because the destination they incorporated into the bill of lading did not, in fact, tally with the destination in the sale contract[109], Donaldson J said that the bills of lading were also defective

> '... in that, in the absence of an accompanying copy of the charter-party, they did not show whether the other terms of the contract of carriage were consistent with the sale contract.'

Both Donaldson J and the Court of Appeal were loath, however, to base their decision on the simple ground that no charterparty was tendered: the Court of Appeal, through Megaw LJ, expressly eschewed giving any view on the matter[110]; and Donaldson J goes, if anything, slightly further in the opposite direction, that is to say that the seller is under no obligation, ordinarily at any rate, to tender the charterparty:[111]

> 'The mere fact that a bill of lading refers to a charter-party does not require the production of that charter, if its terms are not incorporated into the bill of lading contract or do not affect the buyers' rights.'

This last text is adopted as a correct statement of the law in the current edition of Benjamin[112]. It is, with respect, difficult to follow the logic here, both in principle and in practice. For how is the buyer to know what is incorporated, and whether what is incorporated affects his rights, if he is not entitled, in the first instance, to demand sight of the charterparty? Uncertainty on this issue vanishes where the sale contract is on c i f terms and governed by Incoterms: here, the buyer is entitled to demand sight of the charterparty, failing which he can legitimately reject the documents[113].

The answer to our third question solves, in a sense, the problems created by the general uncertainty surrounding our second. Whether or not the buyer is entitled to demand (or otherwise has) sight of the charterparty to which the bill of lading refers, is the buyer entitled to reject the documents if the resulting contract does not in fact comply with the stipulations of the contract of sale? It is clear from the *SIAT di dal Ferro*[114] case, that the buyer is entitled to reject in such circumstances and, conversely, that he is not entitled to reject where the contract of carriage composed through incorporation does so comply. In that case, it will be recalled[115], the buyers were held entitled to reject, inter alia,

---

[109] As to this aspect of the case, which formed the ratio on this point, see the third question below.
[110] See [1980] 2 Lloyd's Rep 53 at 63.
[111] [1978] 2 Lloyd's Rep 470 at 492.
[112] See para 1645.
[113] See Incoterms, C I F A7.
[114] [1978] 2 Lloyd's Rep 470; affd by the Court of Appeal at [1980] 1 Lloyd's Rep 53.
[115] See Chapter 6.3.(d), above.

a group of bills of lading showing the port of discharge 'As Per Charter Party', where the destination under the resulting contract of carriage[116], providing for discharge at '... one of (sic) two safe berths Venice and Ravenna ...', did not comply with the contract of sale, which provided for discharge in Venice[117]. This reasoning provides the buyer, however, with only half an answer; and the other half could work very much against him. For if the incorporated clause turned out, on subsequent examination, to be innocuous[118], the buyer would find himself liable towards the seller for wrongful rejection[119]. Blandly to advise, therefore, that the buyer is entitled to reject non-conforming documents which he has no right to see is effectively to give the buyer far too little and very much too late.

It appears, then, firstly, that a buyer cannot[120], but a bank can, reject a bill of lading simply on the basis that it seeks to incorporate charterparty terms. Secondly, at any rate where c i f Incoterms are not incorporated, the buyer is not entitled to demand sight of the charterparty to which the bill of lading refers. This second proposition might cause the buyer serious difficulty vis-a-vis the seller if the resulting contract of carriage complied with the sale contract. However, and thirdly, where the contract of carriage resulting from incorporation does not comply with the sale contract, the buyer is entitled to reject the documents, and this whether or not he has actually had sight of the charterparty on transfer of the bill.

---

[116] That is to say, after incorporation.

[117] See also *Marshall, Knott & Barker Ltd v Arcos Ltd* (1932) 44 Ll L Rep 384; cf *Re Goodbody & Co and Balfour, Williamson & Co* (1899) 5 Com Cas 59, where the sale contract contained a safe port warranty, thus ensuring that no discrepancy arose when a bill of lading was tendered which likewise provided for discharge at a safe port.

[118] If, for example, on the facts of the *SIAT di dal Ferro* case itself, the charterparty destination was simply 'Venice'.

[119] The actual buyer in the *SIAT di dal Ferro* case, even on the hypothesis here envisaged, would not have been so liable, because there were other grounds entitling him to repudiate the contract: see Chapter 6.3.(d), above.

[120] It need hardly be added that the parties to the sale contract are perfectly at liberty to stipulate in the contract of sale that tender of such a bill be excluded.

CHAPTER 8

Seawaybills and combined transport documents

1. Seawaybills

   (a) Reasons for their use

   (b) The seawaybill as a document of title

      i. Seawaybills and the right to delivery

      ii. Seawaybills and the right of control

      iii. Are seawaybills negotiable?

   (c) The seawaybill as a contract of carriage

      i. The buyer's title to sue

      ii. Seawaybills and the Carriage of Goods by Sea Act 1971

   (d) Seawaybills and letters of credit

2. Combined transport documents

   (a) Combined transport documents as documents of title

      i. The traditional view: textbooks and the market

         *The textbooks
         *The market

         — Specimen clauses

         — Incoterms f r c and c i p

      ii. The traditional view: an assessment

      iii. The traditional view: overtaken by custom?

   (b) Combined transport documents and letters of credit

Waybills and combined transport documents are relatively new shipping documents created by the market in response to technical advances made in the speed at which and the manner in which cargoes are transported across the seas. Both types of document appear on their face to be remarkably similar to traditional bills of lading[1]; both, however, put old certainties to the test and raise crucial issues about the buyer's right

---

[1]   See Appendices 3.b and 3.f.

to sue the carrier for damage to goods or short-delivery. If the buyer's locus standi against the carrier is in doubt, then so is the seller's right to tender such documents under a sale contracted on shipment terms[2]. It is primarily in the context of the seller's contractual duty to tender a bill of lading giving the buyer a cause of action against the carrier in a cargo claim that we shall be examining waybills and combined transport documents: is tender of either document valid under a sale contract on shipment terms[3]? We shall also be looking at the validity of tender of such documents under letters of credit.

1. SEAWAYBILLS

(a) Reasons for their use

Seawaybills are used when there is no intention to sell the goods while they are in transit and where there is consequently no intention to negotiate the documents. They are the sea-going counterparts of consignment notes, used in land transport, and airwaybills, used in air transport. Traders are frequently encouraged[4] to use seawaybills rather than bills of lading where they ship goods on their own account; where they sell goods to a company with which they are closely associated; or where they sell goods to a trusted customer buying exclusively for his own use. Traders are so encouraged for two reasons[5], both resulting directly from the assumption that waybills are not documents of title. Firstly, for the buyer to obtain delivery of the goods from the carrier, he need not present the actual document to the carrier before delivery: he need only prove that he is the person named as consignee on the face of the document. Consequently, postal delays cause none of the problems associated with delivery of goods without presentation of a bill of lading[6]. Secondly, given that seawaybills are not treated as

---

2   See Chapter 6.2, above, and *The Galatia* [1979] 2 Lloyd's Rep 450 at 456, per Donaldson J; approved by the Court of Appeal at [1980] 1 Lloyd's Rep 453.

3   Much the same question can be expressed in slightly different terms: would an international sale providing for the tender by the seller of a seawaybill be a sale contract concluded on shipment terms?

4   See, generally, Report on Maritime Fraud, United Nations Conference on Trade and Development, UNCTAD/ST/SHIP/8, Part II, hereinafter referred to as UNCTAD Report on Maritime Fraud.

5   For a comparison between the commercial practices in the use of seawaybills and in the use of bills of lading, see Goode, pp 566–569; Wilson, pp 158–160; and Tetley, *Main Cargo Claims*, 3rd edn, pp 997, 998. Seawaybills are more commonly used in liner rather than bulk trades: see Law Commission Working Paper No 112, Rights to Goods in Bulk, p 9, fn 28.

6   See Chapter 2.3.(b), above. The fact that the buyer does not need prompt tender of the seawaybill to facilitate delivery of the goods to him by the carrier does not mean that he does not need eventually to have physical possession of the document, which, though not considered to be a document of title, is nonetheless a receipt and a record of the contractual terms agreed. In case of damage to or loss of the goods, he may well wish to sue the carrier; if he has locus standi for such a claim (an issue which we shall be discussing later in this chapter), then the buyer will need the seawaybill in order to discover (a) the terms upon which the goods have been carried by the carrier; and (b) the statements on the seawaybill declaring the state in which the goods

documents of intrinsic commercial value, entitling their holders to possession of the goods on discharge, they are not as susceptible to fraudulent use as are traditional bills of lading[7].

Despite the practical advantages to be derived from the use of seawaybills, it is widely recognised that there are a number of legal problems as yet unresolved[8] and each of these will here be discussed in the context of the central question asked in the introduction to this chapter, namely, is tender of a seawaybill valid under a sale contract concluded on shipment terms? The issues are these: firstly, is a seawaybill a document of title? Secondly, does the buyer of goods covered by a seawaybill have contractual locus standi to sue the carrier in a cargo claim and, if so, is that contract governed by the Carriage of Goods by Sea Act 1971? Thirdly, can seawaybills be validly tendered under letters of credit? These questions revolve around those issues discussed when examining the bill of lading as a document of title at common law, and when investigating the role played by the bill in the transfer from seller to buyer of title to sue the carrier in a cargo claim, that is to say, those issues looked at previously in Chapters 2 and 3. The conclusions reached in those chapters form the background, consequently, to the problems here discussed in the context of seawaybills.

(b) The seawaybill as a document of title

It may seem strange to start an examination of the legal position of seawaybills as between the parties to a sale on shipment terms by asking whether the seawaybill is a document of title. For surely, to ask this question of a document which typically starts out by describing itself

---

were shipped or received for shipment by the carrier. Again, where the traders have agreed upon payment by a letter of credit, the document must, of course, be tendered within the period allowed in the credit.

[7] The use of seawaybills does not avoid every type of documentary fraud. The seller, with or without the collusion of the carrier, can, of course, still persuade the buyer to part company with his money on the faith of a seawaybill which represents goods to have been shipped when they have not. The buyer, however, cannot put the document to fraudulent use by selling on to a third party, the seawaybill being clearly marked 'non-negotiable' on its face. See UNCTAD Report on Maritime Fraud, para 30.

[8] The judges in England have had no opportunity, at any rate judicially, to pronounce upon any of the problems presently to be referred to in the text. So far as concerns the literature, seawaybills have attracted spirited, rather than plentiful, comment in the literature. Apart from the UNCTAD Report on Maritime Fraud, see The Bill of Lading—Do We Really Need It?, Lord Justice Lloyd, 1989 LMCLQ 47; Waybills—Conclusive Evidence with Respect to Details of the Cargo, C. Debattista, 1989 Il Diritto Marittimo; Wilson, pp 158-160; *Marine Cargo Claims*, W. Tetley, Chapter 45; *Cargo Key Receipt and Transport Document Replacement*, K. Gronfors, Scandinavian University Books, Gothenburg, 1982; Waybills and Short Form Documents: A Lawyer's View, Williams, 1979 LMCLQ 297; and *Conference Papers on Waybills and Short Form Documents*, Lloyd's of London Press, 1979. At the time of writing, the Comite Maritime International are working on a set of uniform rules relating to seawaybills.

as 'non-negotiable'[9] must be a futile exercise in speculation of the worst kind. There is reason, however, to consider afresh the commonly held view that a seawaybill is a not a document of title, for a number of radical consequences result from that view. Firstly, if seawaybills do not entitle the holder to delivery of the goods on discharge, then we need to discover how it is that the buyer acquires from the seller the right, as against the carrier, to demand such delivery. Secondly, if section 1 of the Bills of Lading Act 1855 can only be triggered by the transfer of a document of title at common law, then the buyer's locus standi in a cargo claim against the carrier is suspect, the contract of carriage with the carrier having been concluded by the seller of the goods, rather than by the buyer. Thirdly, if the source of the buyer's right to delivery of the goods and his locus standi are unclear, then it would seem that the tender of a seawaybill is not valid under a sale on shipment terms[10]. All three consequences described above would likely dismay traders who use seawaybills to simplify, rather than destroy, the elementary legal assumptions upon which their transaction is based. For surely, the object is to reduce questions of delivery and locus standi to a minimum uncluttered by string-sales and postal delays, rather than to question the fundamental assumptions underpinning the right to delivery and locus standi.

The question, then, whether a seawaybill is a document of title at common law needs squarely to be addressed and it entails three separate but closely related issues. Firstly, what role, if any, does the document itself play in passing from the seller to the buyer the right, as against the carrier, to demand delivery of the goods on discharge? Secondly, if the right to delivery does not depend on the possession of the seawaybill by the buyer, what is the effect of instructions given by the seller to the carrier to deliver to someone other than the buyer? Thirdly, is the seawaybill negotiable in the sense that its transfer passes to the transferee a title better than that possessed by the transferor? Each of these questions will be discussed in turn.

i. Seawaybills and the right to delivery

Firstly, is it transfer of the document which passes to the buyer the right to demand, as against the carrier, delivery of the goods at the port of discharge? It is clear from commercial practice and, occasionally from the document itself[11], that delivery does not depend on presentation;

---

[9]   See, for example, Genwaybill in Appendix 3.e. It is generally agreed that the phrase 'non-negotiable' in the forms means 'non-transferable', i e not a document of title at common law: see Goode, p 566; Benjamin, at para 1438; and *Kum v Wah Tat Bank Ltd* [1971] 1 Lloyd's Rep 439 at 446. For the distinction between the concepts of 'transferability/documents of title' and 'negotiability', see, generally, Chapter 2.2 above.

[10]   A conclusion reached by Sassoon at para 157; and by R. Williams, in Waybills and Short Form Documents: A Lawyer's View, 1979 LMCLQ 297 at 313.

[11]   See, for example, Chemtankwaybill 85, the relevant part of which reads: 'The cargo shipped under this Waybill will be delivered to the Party named as Consignee or its authorised agent, on production of proof of identity without any documentary formalities.'

consequently, it cannot be transfer of the document which entitles the buyer to delivery of the cargo and it is said to follow from this that the seawaybill is not a document of title at common law.

It will be recalled that the definition of the phrase 'document of title' adopted in this book was in the following terms[12]:

> '[The document of title] must be issued or accepted by the bailee of goods, must thereby embody his undertaking to hold the goods for, and release them to, whoever presents the document and must be recognised by statute or mercantile usage as a document which enables control of the goods to pass by delivery of the document with any necessary endorsement.'

It will also be recalled that documents of title to goods, together with documents of title to money, were particularly useful because their delivery transferred the relevant right without the need of a formal assignment or of notification to the debtor of the obligation, here the carrier[13]. The seawaybill is generally recognised not to be a document of title at common law in this sense[14], and this for three reasons, each of which will be examined in turn.

The first reason is closely linked to the main advantage to be derived from the use of seawaybills, namely the fact that there is no need to present the document to the carrier for the buyer to obtain delivery of the goods, which delivery depends rather on the buyer's proving that he is indeed the consignee. If presentation is not necessary for delivery, the argument runs[15], this must mean that no right to delivery is 'locked up in'[16] the document itself and this in turn leads to the conclusion that it is not a document of title. Though superficially attractive, the argument concentrates on the cosmetic features of a document of title rather than on its essence. The whole point of documents of title to goods is that rights to possession can be transferred without having formally to assign the obligation and without having to notify the debtor of the obligation. Those two essential ingredients of documents of title are indeed present in a seawaybill. It is clear that a carrier issuing a seawaybill undertakes to deliver the goods to the consignee[17]; it is equally

---

[12] The definition was Professor Goode's, cited at Chapter 2.3.(a) above and taken from a lecture on 'Concepts of Ownership, Possession and Sale', published in Goode, *Proprietary Rights*, p 9.

[13] See Chapter 2.2.(a), above.

[14] See Carriage of Goods by Sea, Wilson, 1988, London, p 159; and Benjamin, para 1446. Moreover, some seawaybills actually take the trouble to say so explicitly: see Chemtankwaybill 85, Conditions of Carriage 1, which states: 'This Waybill, which is not a document of title at common law, is subject to the terms and conditions, liberties and exceptions of the Voyage Charter Party dated as overleaf and to the provisions set out below.'

[15] See Benjamin, para 1446; and Liability of the Carrier in Multimodal Transport, Diamond, in *International Carriage of Goods: Some Legal Problems and Possible Solutions*, 35, at 52.

[16] See Goode, p 66 and Chapter 2, above, text accompanying fn 17.

[17] See, for example, Chemtankwaybill 85: 'The cargo shipped under this Waybill will be delivered to the Party named as Consignee or its authorised agent,...'

clear that none of the three persons involved in the transaction[18], namely the seller, the buyer and the carrier, would expect the carrier's obligation to deliver formally to be assigned to the buyer or notified to the carrier. Just as the use of a bill of lading is understood by merchants to pass the right to delivery from seller to buyer subject only to the informality of transfer and presentation, so the use of a seawaybill is understood by merchants to pass the same right subject only to the informality of proof of identity[19]. The difference between the two documents lies in the documentary procedures required when delivery of the goods is demanded of the carrier by the buyer: in bills of lading it is presentation, in seawaybills it is proof of identity. This difference is easily justified by the commercial context in which the two documents are used. A bill of lading is used when traders are trading, or at any rate wish to be in a position to trade, on the market, taking advantage of market movements by selling or buying down a string: nomination of the buyer as 'Mr Buyer or Order'[20] says as much. A seawaybill, on the other hand, is used, as we have seen, where there is intended to be but one buyer, the consignee[21]. Where a bill of lading is used, the possibility of there being a string of buyers makes it imperative that the best possible proof is presented by the party claiming delivery that he is, indeed, entitled to delivery: and what better proof than the very document itself issued by the carrier on shipment? On the other hand, in a 'closed' transaction, where only one buyer is in prospect, the party named as consignee, what need is there for presentation of the document if the buyer can establish his entitlement by proving his identity through some other means? To require presentation would either defer discharge or necessitate the chain of indemnities used where the transfer of bills of lading is delayed[22]. Either consequence is avoided by requiring simple proof of identity rather than presentation when the demand for delivery is made. Nonetheless, it is clear that neither assignment nor notification is necessary and, in this sense, the seawaybill is, not unlike a bill of lading, a document of title at common law.

The second argument supporting the commonly held view that the seawaybill is not a document of title at common law is that, even if the buyer is entitled to demand delivery of the goods from the carrier by proving that he is the person named as consignee on the seawaybill, the waybill is still not a document of title at common law because only the consignee has this right: he cannot endow other buyers, further down a string, with the same right. This argument is flawed on two grounds. Firstly, and like the first argument discussed above, it loses sight of the

---

[18] Whether these three persons are also contractual parties to the same contract is a separate matter, which will be discussed presently and independently from the issue here covered.

[19] See Chemtankwaybill 85, which goes on to say (see fn 17, above), 'on production of proof of identity without any documentary formalities.'

[20] Or simply as 'Order': see Chapter 2, fn 19, above.

[21] The document may also be used, of course, where there is no buyer, that is to say where the shipper ships the goods for his own account, a situation which is irrelevant to the issue here being examined.

[22] See Chapter 2.3.(a), above.

nub of the definition of a document of title. A document which contemplates the passage of the right to demand delivery of the goods from seller to buyer, without assignment of the carrier's obligation to deliver and without notification to the carrier, is a document of title at common law; and this is no less the case if the three parties using the document agree that it will have this effect only once. Secondly, the argument proves too much. It assumes that a seawaybill is either a document of title in exactly the same way as is a bill of lading, or not a document of title at all. For commercial needs to be satisfied, though, seawaybills do not need to be treated as if they were 'order' bills of lading, which they patently are not[23]; they need only to be recognised as documents of title at common law, which it is here suggested, they are. Commercial needs are, on the other hand, frustrated if the fundamental expectations of the buyer, namely, delivery of the goods under an enforceable contract of carriage, are denied.

The third reason why the seawaybill is considered not to be a document of title at common law is that, once a bill of lading is only a document of title if it is made out 'to order'[24], then a waybill, which of its nature is made out exclusively to a named consignee, cannot be a document of title. The assumption upon which this argument is based, however, is one supported by somewhat meagre authority. It is stated in the literature that a bill of lading not made out 'to order'[25] is not a document of title at common law[26]. The statement is invariably based on the opinion of the Judicial Committee of the Privy Council in an appeal from the Supreme Court of Hong Kong in the case of *Henderson & Co v Comptoir D'Escompte De Paris*[27]. The bill of lading in that case was, indeed, one not made out 'to order'; and Sir Robert Collier, in delivering the opinion of the Committee, did, indeed, conclude from that fact that 'this bill of lading was not a negotiable instrument.'[28] It is doubtful, however, whether the case provides any authority for the proposition that a straight bill of lading is not a document of title at common law. For the question before their Lordships was whether the bill of lading was 'negotiable' in the sense described earlier in this book[29], that is to say, in the sense of passing to the transferee a title better than the transferor's; the question here, on the other hand, is whether a seawaybill is a document of title at common law, that is to say, whether it allows the passage of the right to demand delivery without assignment or notification to the carrier.

---

[23] Where the parties need or want an 'order' bill of lading, then they will doubtless use one.

[24] Benjamin, paras 1438 and 1446; and see Chapter 2, fn 19, above.

[25] Variously called a 'straight', 'nominate' or 'straight consigned' bill of lading.

[26] See Benjamin, para 1446; Carver, para 1598; and Scrutton, art 92.

[27] (1873) LR 5 PC 253, followed on this point by McNair J in *Soproma SpA v Marine and Animal By-Products Corpn* [1966] 1 Lloyd's Rep 367 at 388. The bill of lading in *Soproma* was not made out 'to order': tender was consequently held to be invalid under a letter of credit which expressly provided for tender of a bill 'issued to order and blank endorsed'.

[28] (1873) LR 5 PC 253 at 260.

[29] See Chapter 2.2.(c), above.

The central issue in the case was whether a bank to whom the bill had been endorsed in security for a debt took free of the title of the original buyer. It was held that the bank's title was indeed indefeasible, the bank not being fixed with notice of prior equities by the mere fact that the bill of lading was made out to one named consignee. The result of the case was, therefore, that the bill of lading was negotiable in the sense that it passed an indefeasible title; the assumption[30] by Sir Robert Collier that the bill was not negotiable is consequently somewhat puzzling. There would appear to be two possible explanations for Sir Robert Collier's dictum. The first is that the judge was quite simply wrong: that the actual decision in the case (the bank took free of the buyer's equities) belies the dictum, uttered towards the beginning of the opinion, that a straight bill of lading is not negotiable. The second interpretation is that in assuming that the bill of lading was not negotiable, Sir Robert was referring to the commonly held view that a straight bill was not transferable, that is to say that it was not a document of title at common law[31]. This second interpretation of the judgment would, of course, still contradict the view here being expressed, namely that a seawaybill is a document of title in this sense. Sir Robert's assumption on the point was, however, based on no prior authority and, moreover, it was clearly not relevant to the point in issue before him. On either view of the much cited dictum, then, the authority of the case for the proposition that a straight bill of lading is not a document of title at common law is, to state it at its very lowest, suspect. So, consequently, is the view that once a straight bill of lading is not a document of title, neither is a seawaybill.

Thus all three arguments said to support the proposition that seawaybills are not documents of title at common law can be parried without too much difficulty. Firstly, the fact that presentation of the bill is not necessary for delivery means only that proof of the consignee's identity is easier where there can only be one consignee: it does not mean that the waybill is any the less a document which allows for transfer of the right to delivery without assignment or notification to the carrier. Secondly, the fact that a seawaybill contemplates the transfer of the right to delivery but once means only that it is a document of title with a limited life-span rather than that it is not a document of title. Thirdly,

---

[30]   For it was no more than an assumption: see (1873) LR 5 PC 253 at 260.

[31]   Where the question was whether a document was a document of title at common law, Lord Devlin fought shy of the suggestion that a non-negotiable bill of lading did not pass the right to demand delivery of the goods from the carrier. In *Kum v Wah Tat Bank Ltd* [1971] 1 Lloyd's Rep 439 at 445, 446, Lord Devlin is happier to suggest that the issue as to whether a non-negotiable bill is a document of title does not arise because s 32(1) of the Sale of Goods Act 1979 interprets shipment as delivery by the seller to the buyer, thus making the carrier the consignee's bailee. Section 32(1) of the Act does not, however, solve the problem outright: it may give the buyer the right to demand delivery of the goods from the carrier; the question as to whether a non-negotiable bill of lading is a document of title still needs to be answered, though, because upon that answer may depend the solution of other problems, e g whether the Bills of Lading Act 1855 and the Carriage of Goods by Sea Act 1971 apply to seawaybills, both issues to which reference will be made presently in the text.

to say that seawaybills, like straight bills of lading are not documents of title is to assume that such bills of lading are indeed not documents of title, a proposition for which the authority is rather poor. It consequently appears that the path is clear towards arguing that the right to delivery of goods shipped under a seawaybill can be transferred from seller to buyer without assignment and without notification to the carrier and that the document is, in this sense, a document of title at common law[32].

ii. Seawaybills and the right of control

Before we can confidently accept the compelling force of that proposition, however, we need to deal with a major concern, which surfaces time and again in the literature[33] about, seawaybills and the 'right of control'. It is widely felt that a seawaybill can never attain the same legal status within a simple two-party sale of goods as that enjoyed by a full-blooded 'order' bill of lading because, where goods are shipped under a seawaybill, the seller retains a power to defraud the buyer out of the goods by simply altering the delivery instructions originally given to the carrier, ordering the carrier to deliver to a third party. This power is said to weaken the trust which buyers and bankers can place in the seawaybill and much effort has consequently gone into devising mechanisms intended to improve the situation by restricting the seller's right of control over the goods while they are in transit[34].

The assumption which lies behind this type of concern about seawaybills is that the seller of goods shipped under a waybill exercises a stronger degree of control over the goods while in transit than does the seller of goods covered by a bill of lading; and that the position of buyers and banks buying or extending credit on the faith of goods shipped under a seawaybill is correspondingly weaker. The argument

---

[32] It will have been noticed that the proposition argued for in the text has not been supported by suggesting that the seawaybill has come to be treated as a document of title at common law by commercial custom. For a custom to pass muster, it must be certain, reasonable, and not repugnant: *Kum v Wah Tat Bank Ltd* [1971] 1 Lloyd's Rep 439 at 444. Lord Devlin said, obiter, in that case that a mate's receipt could not there be admitted as a document of title through commercial custom because it explicitly described itself as 'non-negotiable': the same obstacle would obstruct a similar custom relating to seawaybills. On the other hand, if a seawaybill were to be treated as a document of title for the reasons given in the text, the objection of 'repugnance' would not arise. To be sure, one would still need to explain away the word 'non-negotiable': but just as this has been interpreted to mean 'non-transferable', so it could be interpreted to mean 'transferable, but only once.'

[33] See the UNCTAD Report on Maritime Fraud, para 47; Wilson, pp 159 and 160; The Paperless Transfer of Transport Information and Legal Functions, K. Gronfors, in *International Carriage of Goods: Some Legal Problems and Possible Solutions*, ed C. Schmitthoff and Goode, pp 29–31; and Liability of the Carrier in Multimodal Transport, Diamond, ibid at 55–56.

[34] See, generally, Tetley, pp 988–990; and *Cargo Key Receipt and Transport Document Replacement*, K. Gronfors, Gothenburg, 1982.

runs as follows[35]. With an 'order' bill of lading, the document itself has 'locked up in'[36] itself the right to delivery of the goods at the port of discharge and it is, consequently, clear that the seller's right to instruct the carrier as to delivery passes to the buyer when the seller transfers the bill of lading to the buyer. With a seawaybill, on the other hand, once the buyer does not need physically to transfer the document to demand delivery of the goods from the carrier, this must mean that the transfer of the document from seller to buyer does not signify the passage of the right of control; it follows, therefore, that the seller's power to alter the carrier's delivery instructions survives the transfer of the document. The risks incurred, both by buyers and by bankers, in leaving the seller with such a degree of power far outweigh, the argument concludes, any possible advantages derived from the use of seawaybills.

Two points can be made about the argument outlined above. Firstly, the fact that the carrier can deliver the goods to the buyer without presentation of the seawaybill does not necessarily mean that the transfer of the document by the seller to the buyer is devoid of all legal significance: and we shall see presently that a number of legal consequences do ensue from such transfer. This observation leads us to the second point. So far as concerns the power of the seller to alter the carrier's delivery instructions, a seller is effectively in no stronger a position where he ships goods under a seawaybill than he is where he ships goods under an 'order' bill of lading: buyers and banks are, consequently, in no weaker a position.

This second point needs further elaboration, requiring as it does a comparison between the seller's power to alter the carrier's delivery instructions where a bill of lading is used and the same power where a seawaybill is used. When discussing this power in the context of bills of lading[37], we saw that where the seller altered his instructions to the carrier, the position of the seller and of the carrier respectively vis-à-vis the buyer differed according as to whether the bill had been transferred to the buyer before or after the seller gave new instructions to the carrier. Where the seller alters instructions before transfer of the bill, three consequences follow. Firstly, the carrier is bound by his contract with the seller qua shipper to obey the new instructions to deliver to a new consignee. Secondly, a carrier complying with such instructions is not liable towards the original consignee in conversion, the original consignee not being in possession of any document entitling him to receive possession of the goods from the carrier[38]. Thirdly, although the original

---

[35]   See The Paperless Transfer of Transport Information and Legal Functions, K. Gronfors, in *International Carriage of Goods: Some Legal Problems and Possible Solutions*, ed C. Schmitthoff and Goode, pp 29-31; and Liability of the Carrier in Multimodal Transport, Diamond, ibid at 55-6.

[36]   See Goode, p 66.

[37]   See Chapter 2.3.(b), above.

[38]   See *Mitchel v Ede* (1840) 11 Ad & El 888 at 903; *The Lycaon* [1983] 2 Lloyd's Rep 548; and Benjamin, para 1437.

consignee has no remedy against the carrier, he is, of course, entitled to sue the seller under the contract of sale for breach of the obligation to ship goods covered by shipping documents entitling him to delivery of the goods at the port of discharge. It would seem that the position is the same where the goods are shipped under a seawaybill rather than under an 'order' bill of lading. For here too, the carrier is bound by his contract with the shipper to deliver the goods to whoever is named by the shipper to be the consignee[39]. Again, the original consignee has no remedy in conversion against a carrier complying with the shipper's instructions: the 'original consignee' has stopped being a consignee and therefore lies completely outside the ambit of the document. Finally, it is true here too that, although the original consignee has no remedy against the carrier, he can sue the seller under the contract of sale.

Where a seller of goods covered by an 'order' bill of lading purports to give instructions to the carrier, after the transfer of the bill, to deliver to someone other than the consignee, the carrier complies with these instructions at his peril. Transfer of the bill to the buyer in circumstances which trigger section 1 of the Bills of Lading Act 1855 gives the buyer contractual locus standi to instruct the carrier as to delivery: compliance with instructions issued by the seller would put the carrier in breach of his contract with the buyer. Again, compliance with such instructions would make the carrier liable in conversion towards the buyer, who is entitled to possession of the goods by virtue of his holding a document of title at common law. Thirdly, the seller seeking to alter the carrier's instructions as to delivery would be liable towards the buyer, both in contract for breach of the contract of sale and in tort for interfering with the contract of carriage which by then will have come into being between the carrier and the buyer[40]. Is the position any different where the buyer holds a seawaybill instead of an 'order' bill of lading? If the seawaybill is a document of title at common law, allowing for the transfer of the right to delivery without assignment or notification, the consignee is entitled to delivery of the goods on discharge on proof of identity and compliance by the carrier with the seller's new instructions would make the carrier liable in conversion[41]. The question would then arise as to whether that action was subject to the terms contained in the seawaybill, that is to say, whether the carrier and the consignee were privy to the contract of carriage originally concluded by the carrier and the consignor. Who is likely to raise the question of privity? It is hardly likely to be the carrier, keen as he is sure to be to seek exemption or

---

[39] In a similar sense, see Benjamin, para 1438.

[40] On the hypothesis envisaged, although the seller will have discharged his obligations under the contract of sale to ship goods covered by a bill of lading made out to the order of the buyer, he is under a further implied obligation not to interfere with the working of the contract of carriage: see *The Playa Larga* [1983] 2 Lloyd's Rep 171, particularly at 180.

[41] See Tetley, p 985, fn 193, for a contrary view which Professor Tetley supports on *Hickman Grain v Canadian Pacific Rly* [1927] 1 DLR 851, a decision of the Manitoba Court of Appeal, which held that where a carrier by rail delivered goods to a buyer without presentation of a bill of lading made out 'to order', the carrier was liable to a third party purchaser for the market value of the goods covered by the bill.

limitation of liability in the contract recorded in the seawaybill. The buyer, on the other hand, might well plead the privity point[42], claiming recovery of damages at large, unlimited by the terms of the seawaybill. It is difficult, however, to see a Court taking too kindly to a privity point taken by a buyer quite happy to take the benefits of the seawaybill without its burdens. We shall see presently[43] that section 1 of the Bills of Lading Act 1855 arguably does apply to waybills; and that even if it does not, other devices are available to the courts should they wish to bridge the privity gap between the buyer of goods covered by a seawaybill and the carrier. Be that as it may, though, the question here being discussed is somewhat more limited and, moreover, it can be answered favourably to the buyer. Should a carrier, faced with new delivery instructions issued by a seller after transferring the seawaybill to the buyer, comply with such instructions? If compliance were to lead to an action in conversion by the buyer, the carrier is hardly likely to comply and the position of buyers and bankers holding such a document is consequently no worse than that of buyers and bankers holding an 'order' bill of lading. In these circumstances, to consider a seawaybill as a document of title at common law presents risks no greater to buyers or bankers paying money on the faith of such a document than to those paying money on the faith of an 'order' bill of lading.

iii. Are seawaybills negotiable?

Seawaybills declare themselves to be 'non-negotiable'[44], a description which, as we have seen[45], is generally taken to reflect the commonly held view that seawaybills are not documents of title at common law. Our last task in this part of this chapter is to ask whether these documents are negotiable in the sense described earlier in this book, that is to say, in the sense that the holder of a seawaybill might, in certain circumstances, have a better title than that of the true owner of the goods.[46]

Money turns on this question where a seller who has not yet passed the seawaybill to his buyer now sells elsewhere, altering the name of the consignee on the document and changing the carrier's delivery instructions accordingly. If the seawaybill is negotiable, the second buyer's title over the goods is indefeasible by the claims of the original consignee; if the seawaybill is not negotiable, then the general principle, nemo dat quod non habet, would prevent the seller from passing a title to the second consignee which was better than the first's. For the second buyer to be favoured in this way, he would need to bring the circumstances described above within the terms of section 24 of the Sale of Goods Act 1979; and for that section to be triggered into effect, we would need

---

[42]   Unless he too wished to apply a particular term in the seawaybill to his cargo claim against the carrier, e g an arbitration clause.

[43]   See Chapter 8.1.(c), below.

[44]   See, for example, Genwaybill, in Appendix 3.e, which calls itself a 'Non-negotiable General Sea Waybill'.

[45]   See fn 9, above.

[46]   See, generally, Chapter 2.2.(c) and Chapter 2.3.(c), above.

to bring seawaybills within the definition of 'document of title' in section 1(4) of the Factors Act 1889, which reads:

> 'The expression "document of title" shall include any bill of lading, dock warrant, warehouse-keeper's certificate, and warrant or order for the delivery of goods, and any other document used in the ordinary course of business as proof of the possession or control of goods, or authorising or purporting to authorise, either by endorsement or by delivery, the possessor of the document to transfer or receive goods thereby represented.'

Rather than 'defining' what a document of title is, this section simply lists a number of documents recognised by statute as passing to the holder, in given circumstances, a title better than the transferor's. Consequently, the seawaybill need only be aptly described by one of the phrases used in the section for it to be classed as a document of title for the purposes of the Sale of Goods Act 1979. The seawaybill is clearly not a 'dock warrant' or a 'warehouse-keeper's certificate'; neither is it a document 'authorising or purporting to authorise, either by endorsement or delivery, the possessor of the document to transfer or receive goods thereby represented': the fact that the buyer need not present the document at the port of discharge and the fact that he cannot pass on the right to delivery by transfer of the document take the seawaybill outside that part of the section. Similarly, the fact that presentation is not required prevents the seawaybill from being a 'document used in the ordinary course of business as proof of the possession ... of goods.' We have seen above[47], though, that the transfer of the document to the buyer does in effect mean that the power to alter the carrier's delivery instructions has passed to the buyer: consequently, the seawaybill can be considered to be a 'document used in the ordinary course of business as proof of the ... control of goods.' Likewise, a seawaybill constitutes an agreement between the shipper and the carrier that the carrier will deliver the goods to the consignee: the document can consequently be seen as a 'warrant or order for the delivery of goods'. Finally, and perhaps most controversially, the seawaybill may be considered to be a 'bill of lading'[48], a proposition to which we shall need to return in discussing the buyer's title to sue.

There are, then, three possible pegs on which to hang a seawaybill in section 1(4) of the Factors Act 1889. Any one of the three would serve to bring the seawaybill within the ambit of the section and would consequently make it a negotiable document for the purposes of the Sale of Goods Act 1979.

(c) The seawaybill as a contract of carriage

There can be little doubt but that a seawaybill plays the same contractual role as does an 'order' bill of lading, at any rate as between the carrier

---

[47] See Chapter 8.1.b.ii, above.
[48] On this hypothesis, a seawaybill would, like the straight bill of lading in *Henderson & Co v Comptoir D'Escompte De Paris* (1873) LR 5 PC 253, be negotiable.

and the shipper of the goods. While its issue 'does not necessarily mark any stage in the development of the contract'[49], the document does provide 'excellent evidence'[50] of the contract of carriage between the carrier and the shipper, evidence which can, however, be contradicted by proof of other terms to which the parties have agreed[51]. The function of an 'order' bill of lading as a record of the contract arrived at by the parties can just as easily be fulfilled by any other document; and there is no reason to suggest that a seawaybill performs this role in a manner better or worse than does a bill of lading.

The use of the seawaybill as a document witnessing the terms of a contract of carriage is not, however, free of problems. Here again, the seawaybill is commonly seen very much as a poor relation of the 'order' bill of lading, and this for two reasons. Firstly, it is frequently assumed that seawaybills are not covered by the Bills of Lading Act 1855 and that, consequently, the privity gap between the buyer and the carrier cannot be bridged through the magic of section 1 of that Act[52]. Secondly, it is stated, equally frequently, that the Hague-Visby Rules, applying as they do to contracts of carriage 'covered by a bill of lading or any similar document of title'[53], do not govern contracts of carriage recorded on a seawaybill, whether that contract is pleaded by or against a consignor or a consignee. Both issues take us directly back to the central question we set ourselves in the introductory remarks to this chapter, namely, whether seawaybills can validly be tendered under a sale contracted on shipment terms. For if the buyer's title to sue the carrier in a cargo claim is suspect; and if the regime under which that claim can be litigated is doubtful, then the validity of the tender of a seawaybill is equally open to doubt.

i. The buyer's title to sue

The receiver's title to sue a carrier in a cargo claim can be founded, of course, either in contract or in tort[54]. As a buyer, though, the receiver is entitled to expect from his seller a document which gives him, as against the carrier, an actionable contract of carriage on reasonable terms[55]. Given the restrictions to which an action in negligence has been subjected by the House of Lords in *The Aliakmon*[56], the buyer of goods shipped under a waybill may now be rather more concerned about his locus standi in contract than ever he was[57]. If the carrier is to be sued

---

[49] *Pyrene Co Ltd v Scindia Navigation Co Ltd* [1954] 2 QB 402 at 409, per Devlin J.
[50] *Sewell v Burdick* (1884) 10 App Cas 74 at 105.
[51] See Chapter 6.1.(i), above.
[52] See UNCTAD Report on Maritime Fraud, para 46.
[53] See art I(b) of the Rules.
[54] See, generally, Chapter 3, above, in particular Chapter 3.2.(a).
[55] See Chapter 6.2, above.
[56] [1986] 2 Lloyd's Rep 1; see Chapter 3.2.(b), above.
[57] The buyer's contractual locus standi is likely to depend exclusively on s 1 of the 1855 Act, it being difficult to apply the rule in *Brandt v Liverpool Brazil and River Plate Steam Navigation Co Ltd* [1924] 1 KB 575 to the delivery of goods shipped under

at all[58], he too is likely to prefer to defend an action in contract rather than one in tort, replete as the contract is likely to be with clauses limiting or excluding his liability. This community of interest, if not quite identity of purpose, has spawned a good number of clauses in seawaybills, devised to bridge the privity gap which is otherwise assumed to separate the buyer from the carrier. Thus, for example, the GCBS seawaybill reads, in relevant part, as follows:

> 'The Shipper accepts the said Standard Conditions on his own behalf and on behalf of the Consignee and the owner of the goods and warrants that he has authority to do so. The Consignee by presenting this Waybill and/or requesting delivery of the goods further undertakes all liabilities of the Shipper hereunder, such undertaking being additional and without prejudice to the Shippers own liability. The benefits of the contract, evidenced by this Waybill shall thereby be transferred to the Consignee or other persons presenting this Waybill.'

Given that such a clause, and others like it[59], serve both carrier and buyer well, its validity has, not surprisingly, yet to be examined by the courts[60]. It would doubtless be interesting to see a judicial reaction to such a clause, a study, if ever there was one, in defensive draftsmanship,

---

seawaybills. Although physical presentation of the bill of lading on discharge is not necessary for the implied contract device to work, (see *The Elli 2* [1985] 1 Lloyd's Rep 107, discussed at Chapter 3.1.(b), above), it is still not clear on authority whether the device will work where no undertaking is given to present the document on its arrival; and with seawaybills, of course, such an undertaking would not be expected. Secondly, there must be some consideration moving from the buyer, for example a promise to pay freight or demurrage: as Professor Tetley points out, (see Tetley, p 971), freight is normally pre-paid and demurrage is not normally due in trades where seawaybills are used. As far as English law is concerned, it would appear, therefore, that the buyer's locus standi in contract could only be based on s 1 of the Bills of Lading Act 1855; one other, though remote, possibility would be to use Devlin J's 'wider principle' enunciated in *Pyrene Co Ltd v Scindia Navigation Co Ltd* [1954] 2 QB 402 at 426: 'This is the sort of situation that is covered by the wider principle; the third party [here, the consignee] takes those benefits of the contract which appertain to his interest therein, but takes them, of course, subject to whatever qualifications with regard to them which the contract imposes.' In a similar sense, see Tetley, p 975; and see, generally, Liability of the Carrier in Multimodal Transport, Diamond, in *International Carriage of Goods: Some Legal Problems and Possible Solutions*, eds Schmitthoff and Goode, 35, at 54–55.

[58] It is conceivable that, *The Aliakmon* regardless, the buyer may well have locus standi against the carrier in tort, as, for example, where the contract of sale passes property to the buyer on shipment of the goods: *The Aliakmon* would here be assuaged, leaving the carrier open to an action in tort unprotected by contractual protection.

[59] The same purpose is intended, if through slightly different means, by the following clause, used in Nedlloyd's document, interestingly called a 'Non Negotiable Seawaybill Straight Bill of Lading':
'The Shipper accepts the said standard terms and conditions on his own behalf, on behalf of the Consignee and the Owner of the Goods, and authorises the Consignee to bring suit against the Carrier in his own name but as agent of the Shipper, and warrants that he has authority so to accept and authorise.'

[60] It would pay a carrier to challenge the validity of such a clause where the buyer's action in tort is barred by *The Aliakmon* [1986] 2 Lloyd's Rep 1, and where the carrier wishes to escape from liability towards the buyer altogether.

seeking to achieve its simple end however convoluted the means. For if the shipper contracts with the carrier not only on his own behalf, but also as agent of the buyer, does this not mean that the buyer is a party to the contract of carriage from its inception between the shipper and the carrier? If so, why does the buyer need 'further' to undertake the liabilities imposed by that contract, on presenting the document to or on demanding the goods from the carrier?[61] Again, why would the benefits enuring from the contract need to be 'transferred' to the buyer? Finally, and moreover, if the buyer is an initial party to the contract of carriage, does this mean that the document can only be tendered where the type of sale contract used reflects the agency device contemplated in the clause, that is to say, where the seller takes the bill of lading on behalf of the buyer, i e in a classic f o b contract?

The significant point behind these questions is not whether they challenge the validity of the clause[62], but whether the clause is actually necessary to achieve its objective, namely the bridging of the privity gap between the buyer and the carrier. The clause is based on the assumption that section 1 of the Bills of Lading Act 1855 does not apply to seawaybills: it is that assumption that needs now to be challenged.

Three arguments are commonly put forward in support of the proposition that seawaybills lie outside the ambit of the Bills of Lading Act 1855: each argument, together with a suggested answer, will be discussed in turn. Firstly, the Act is said only to apply to bills of lading which are documents of title at common law[63]; once the seawaybill is not a document of title in this sense, the Act cannot apply[64]. There are two answers to this argument. Firstly, it has been urged earlier that the 1855 Act works its magic on all bills of lading, not only upon those which are also commonly reputed to be documents of title at common

---

[61] Others have seen the second sentence of this clause as an attempt to apply to seawaybills the rule in *Brandt v Liverpool Brazil and River Plate Steam Navigation Co Ltd* [1924] 1 KB 575, and suggested that the clause might, on this view, be ineffective, largely on the grounds described at fn 57, above: see Waybills and Short Form Documents: a Lawyer's View, R. Williams, 1979 LMCLQ 297 at 311.

[62] It should be said, though, that there do seem to be limits to the courts' willingness to accept sham agency devices: see Lord Wilberforce in *The Eurymedon* [1975] AC 154 at 166-169. See also the cautionary note struck in this regard by R. Williams, in Waybills and Short Form Documents: A Lawyer's View, 1979 LMCLQ 297 at 311, 312.

[63] See The Bills of Lading Act 1855 Today, A.P. Bell, 1985 JBL 124 at 128; Bills of Lading and Third Parties, G.H. Treitel, 1986 LMCLQ 294 at 297; Waybills and Short Form Documents: a Lawyer's View, R. Williams, 1979 LMCLQ 297 at 308; and Benjamin, para 1456.

[64] See Tetley, p 968; and The Paperless Transfer of Transport Information and Legal Functions, by K. Gronfors, in *International Carriage of Goods: Some Legal Problems and Possible Solutions*, eds Schmitthoff and Goode, at pp 33-34. Cf section 32 of the United States Pomerene Act, which reads, in relevant part: 'If the bill is a straight bill such person [the transferee] also acquires the right to notify the carrier of the transfer to him of such bill and thereby to become the direct obligee of whatever obligations the carrier owed to the transferor of the bill immediately before the notification.'

law[65]. In arguing towards that proposition, however, it was conceded that the judgment of Phillips J in *The Delfini*[66] provided some authority for the contrary position: if, pace Phillips J, section 1 of the 1855 Act is only triggered into action by a document of title, then the second answer to the question here being discussed is that the seawaybill is a document of title at common law for the reasons given in an earlier part of this chapter[67].

The second argument said to take seawaybills outside the scope of the 1855 Act is that, whether or not it applies only to documents of title and whether or not the seawaybill is a document of title at common law, the Act applies in terms only to bills of lading; once a seawaybill is not a bill of lading, the Act cannot apply to seawaybills. The argument can just as easily be stood on its head: far and away from excluding certain types of bill of lading, the Act is clearly intended to apply to all types of bill of lading, whether 'order' or straight bills: had Parliament intended a more restrictive area of application, it would have made the restriction explicit. Thus, the Act must be taken to apply to a straight bill of lading and, if this is correct, there is no reason to suppose that it does not apply to a seawaybill, which is simply a straight bill of lading known by another name[68].

Finally, it could be argued that, whether or not the seawaybill is a document of title and whether or not the seawaybill is a bill of lading, the seawaybill comes to grief upon that part of section 1 which requires property in the goods to have passed 'upon or by reason of such consignment or endorsement'[69]. The argument would run thus: if the buyer need not present the seawaybill at the port of discharge before delivery of the goods, this must mean that property does not pass upon or by reason of its transfer to the buyer. The argument is misconceived in several senses. Firstly, the position as to delivery and presentation goes to the transfer of the right to delivery, whereas the requirement in section 1 here being discussed goes to another matter altogether, the transfer of property. Secondly, the property in goods shipped under a seawaybill may well pass on transfer of the document, which is likely to coincide with the moment at which the price is paid. Thirdly, even if the property in the goods does not pass at the same time as transfer of the seawaybill, this is not fatal to the application of the section, as long as the transfer of the document and the passage of the property are both causally connected to the same same contract of sale: as we have seen, this is arguably the case with bills of lading[70], and, if it is,

---

[65] See Chapter 3.1.(a).(i), above.
[66] [1988] 2 Lloyd's Rep 599; affd by the Court of Appeal (1989) Times, 11 August.
[67] See Chapter 8.1.(b).i, above.
[68] See Tetley, who, at pp977, 8, writes: 'The analogy of a waybill to a nominate bill of lading is fraught with difficulties. Yet it remains a possible legal basis for the waybill consignee's right to sue under the entire contract of carriage.'
[69] See, generally, Chapter 3.1.a.iv, above.
[70] Ibid.

there is no reason to suppose that the position is any different with seawaybills.

It seems possible to argue, consequently, that section 1 of the Bills of Lading Act 1855, couched as it is in terms wide enough to encompass seawaybills, does indeed transfer the contract of carriage from the seller to the buyer[71]. If this is correct, three results ensue. Firstly, clauses such as the one reproduced above from the GCBS seawaybill become redundant; secondly, amendment of the 1855 Act to accommodate seawaybills would be unnecessary[72]; and thirdly, there would be no reason to suspect the validity of the tender of seawaybills in sale contracts on shipment terms, at any rate on locus standi grounds.

ii. Seawaybills and the Carriage of Goods by Sea Act 1971

The buyer of goods on shipment terms is interested not only in having a secure contractual platform from which he can launch a cargo claim against the carrier; his concern is also to be party to a contract of carriage on reasonable[73]—and predictable—terms. The shipper too will want the terms of his contract with the carrier to be clear, at any rate as clear as they would have been had the contract been recorded in a bill of lading rather than a seawaybill. Certainty about the terms of the contract of carriage is, finally, also in the interests of the carrier, who needs to know the nature of his responsibility and the limits to his liability under the contract. All three parties, then, wish for a clear and predictable regime; and all three parties, and their insurers, will be familiar with and, at any rate where English law applies, expect the contract of carriage to be governed by, the Hague-Visby Rules.

Given this congruence of interest, it is not surprising to find that seawaybills will commonly incorporate the Hague-Visby Rules as the law governing the contract of carriage[74]. In view of this fact, it might at first sight appear superfluous to ask whether the Rules, or, in this country, the Carriage of Goods by Sea Act 1971, apply in the absence

---

[71] Professor Tetley argues that the buyer's right of suit can be implied from art IV bis 1 of the Hague Visby Rules, the article which applies to actions in tort the exclusions of liability which would protect the carrier in an action in contract: for Professor Tetley's argument, see Tetley, p 968; and for an earlier discussion of art IV bis 1, see Chapter 3.2.(a) above. Although the text above argues towards the same conclusion arrived at by Professor Tetley, namely that the buyer's contractual locus standi is secure, it is suggested that Professor Tetley imposes a heavier interpretation on art IV bis 1 than the article can reasonably bear. Firstly, it assumes that the Hague Visby Rules apply to seawaybills, (a matter to which we shall be referring presently); secondly, to say that the exceptions in the Rules apply to the buyer's tort action if he has one, is a far cry from saying that the Rules imply that the buyer has locus standi in contract.

[72] Contrast Diamond in Liability of the Carrier in Multimodal Transport, in *International Carriage of Goods: Some Legal Problems and Possible Solutions*, eds Schmitthoff and Goode, 35 at 55.

[73] See, generally, Chapter 6.2, above.

[74] See, for example, the incorporation clause in the GCBS Waybill, reproduced at Appendix 3.d

of such incorporation. There are, however, two reasons why we should persist with the inquiry.

Firstly, the effect of the Rules in a given case may well differ according as to whether they apply to the facts motu propriu or by virtue of contractual incorporation. Where the Rules apply by 'force of law'[75], their terms will prevail over any other provisions in the contract of carriage with which they conflict. Where, on the other hand, the Rules apply merely by virtue of contractual incorporation, their terms will not necessarily so prevail[76].

Secondly, incorporation of the Hague-Visby Rules into a seawaybill may, unless appropriate provision is made in the document itself, have a somewhat unexpected impact, at any rate where English law applies, on the value of the document as a receipt. Section 1(6)(b) of the Carriage of Goods by Sea Act 1971 applies the Rules with the force of law to:

'(b) any receipt which is a non-negotiable document marked as such if the contract contained in or evidenced by it is a contract for the carriage of goods by sea which expressly provides that the Rules are to govern the contract as if the receipt were a bill of lading...'

Thus far, it would appear that the Act responds to incorporation in a manner favourable to the cargo-interest, giving the Rules the force of law, thus allowing them to prevail over conflicting contractual terms[77], consequently solving the first difficulty to which reference has just been made. The sub-section then proceeds, however, to deprive the buyer of the goods of two major benefits he might have expected to derive through incorporation of the Rules; for the sub-section goes on to say:

'...but subject, where paragraph (b) applies, to any necessary modifications and in particular with the omission in Article III of the Rules of the second sentence of paragraph 4 and of paragraph 7.'

The effect of these words is twofold. Firstly, when the non-negotiable receipt is transferred to a buyer, the statements on its face do not provide him with conclusive evidence of what they say as against the carrier: this because the application of the second sentence of art III.4 of the Rules[78] is specifically ruled out. Secondly, by excluding the application of art III.7, the Act denies the shipper the right to demand the issue of a 'shipped' as opposed to a 'received' bill of lading: this right, though given by art III.7 to the shipper, normally works to the advantage of

---

[75] The words used in s 1(2) of the Carriage of Goods by Sea Act 1971.

[76] See Scrutton, pp 418, 419; and the UNCTAD Report on Maritime Fraud, para 45.

[77] For a case illustrating this effect, see *The Vechscroon* [1982] 1 Lloyd's Rep 301.

[78] Which reads: 'However, proof to the contrary shall not be admissible when the bill of lading has been transferred to a third party acting in good faith.' See Waybills and Short Form Documents: A Lawyer's View, R. Williams, 1979 LMCLQ 297 at 307, 308.

the buyer, who would much sooner receive a bill stating the precise date of shipment than one stating the date at which the carrier took the goods into his charge. If the shipper is deprived of the right to demand a 'shipped' bill of lading, the buyer has no hope of deriving the benefits of such a bill. Through section 1(6)(b) of the Act, then, incorporation of the Rules into a seawaybill has the rather curious effect of giving them the force of law in a somewhat attenuated way, giving the buyer a weaker document than he might have expected[79].

If, despite incorporation of the Rules, the buyer is in a worse position under the Rules than that in which he would have been had a bill of lading been issued, is it possible to argue that the Carriage of Goods by Sea Act 1971 applies motu propriu irrespective of incorporation? If the Act were to be thus applicable, the parties could gain entry into the Act through section 1(2), which states simply that the Rules shall have the force of law, rather than through section 1(6)(b), an altogether more contorted and debilitating means of access to the Rules[80].

The suggestion that the Act might apply to seawaybills has been discussed in, and rejected by, the bulk of the literature in the area[81]. The argument against the application of the 1971 Act is attractive in the simplicity of its logic. Section 1(4) of the Act reads:

> 'Subject to subsection (6) below, nothing in this section shall be taken as applying anything in the Rules to any contract for the carriage of goods by sea, unless the contract expressly or by implication provides for the issue of a bill of lading or any similar document of title.'

A seawaybill is not a document of title. Therefore, the Rules cannot apply to seawaybills other than through incorporation, in which case they apply by force of law in the attenuated version provided for in section 1(6)(b). Moreover, a reading of articles II and I(b) of the Rules

---

[79] In this regard, it is interesting to note the following clause in Nedlloyd's Non Negotiable Seawaybill Straight Bill of Lading: 'In either case [i e whether the Hague or Hague Visby Rules apply] the provisions of Article III Rule 4 of the Hague Visby Rules are deemed to be incorporated herein.'

[80] On this view, the Act would make the statements on the face of the bill as to the quantity and apparent condition of the goods on shipment conclusive in the hands of the buyer. The effect of the estoppel thus arising would still, of course, depend on the precise terms in which the statements were couched. Thus, if a statement that 100 crates of wine were qualified by the caveat that the weight and quantity of the goods shipped were unknown, then the effect of the statement would be nugatory. If the 1971 Act applied to seawaybills, whether through incorporation or otherwise, the shipper would have the right, under art III.3, to demand the deletion of the qualification; but, as we have seen, it might not be in the shipper's commercial interest to quibble with the carrier about the terms in which the goods have been described on shipment, at any rate, where the buyer has not thought to stipulate for the tender of a document making unqualified statements. See, generally, Chapter 5, above; Waybills: Conclusive Evidence with Respect to Details of the Cargo, C. Debattista, 1989, Il Diritto Marittimo, 127; and Tetley, pp 984, 5.

[81] Scrutton, p 416; Diamond, p 261; and see Waybills and Short Form Documents: A Lawyer's View, R. Williams, 1979 LMCLQ 297 at 299.

themselves make it clear that the Rules were never intended to apply to seawaybills. Article II applies the Rules to 'every contract of carriage of goods by sea'. The term 'contract of carriage' can only be applied, in terms of article I(b), 'to contracts of carriage covered by a bill of lading or any similar document of title'. Again, once a seawaybill is not a document of title, article II cannot apply the Rules to contracts of carriage recorded on a seawaybill.

Clearly, if, as has been argued above[82], a seawaybill is a document of title, then the basis upon which these arguments are constructed collapses[83] and it would follow that the Act would, quite simply, apply in precisely those circumstances in which it would apply to bills of lading where such a document is issued.

(d) Seawaybills and letters of credit

When examining the circumstances in which it might be preferable to use a seawaybill rather than a bill of lading[84], we saw that traders were encouraged to use the former document either where the goods were

---

[82] See Chapter 8.1.(b).(i), above.

[83] Others have sought different avenues through which seawaybills can enter into the Act. Thus, it has been suggested that art I(b) might 'be read in two ways, either to restrict the Hague Rules to bills of lading which are also documents of title, or to admit non-negotiable bills of lading in addition to documents of title': see Shipping Documentation for the Carriage of Goods and the Hamburg Rules, C.W. O'Hare, (1978) 52 ALJ 415 at 421. With respect, to accept the second alternative would be effectively to read out of existence the word 'similar' in art I(b): see Carver, para 495. A rather more complex avenue towards the application of the Rules to seawaybills revolves around art VI, which allows the parties to a contract of carriage recorded on a non-negotiable receipt to derogate from the Rules where the cargo shipped is not an 'ordinary commercial shipment[s] made in the ordinary course of trade'; it follows that where non-negotiable receipts are used in the ordinary course of trade, the parties are bound by the Act and they cannot derogate from the Rules: Carver hints at this argument in art 495, and Tetley develops it at pp 944–946 and 949–950. The difficulty with the argument is that it fails to get the document through the gatepost of s 1(4) of the Act, the section which applies the Act only to contracts expressly or impliedly providing for the issue of a bill of lading or any similar document of title. The gatepost is only successfully passed if a seawaybill is considered to be a document of title, as is suggested in the text above: a similar point was made by Andrews LCJ in the Court of Appeal of Northern Ireland in *Hugh Mack & Co Ltd v Burns and Laird Lines Ltd* (1944) 77 Ll L Rep 377 at 384; and by the Lord President Clyde in *Harland & Woolf Ltd v Burns and Laird Lines Ltd* 1931 SC 722 at 729 and 730; see also Scrutton, pp 461, 2. In jurisdictions untrammelled by s 1(4) of the Act, the same problem arises: art II of the Rules applies the Rules only to a 'contract of carriage by sea', a term defined by art I(b) as a contract covered by a 'bill of lading or similar document of title'. Professor Tetley avoids the difficulty by subjecting art II to art VI: art II does, indeed, start with the words 'Subject to the provisions of Article VI. . .'. Those words, however, are, surely, intended simply to underline what art VI says, namely that, where it applies, the parties may derogate from the Rules; they are not intended to apply the full rigour of the Rules to a 'contract of carriage' which lies outside the definition of that term given in art I(b): see Legal Problems at Common Law Associated with the Use of the Seawaybill, J.F. Wilson, 1989, Il Diritto Marittimo, 115.

[84] See Chapter 8.1.(a), above.

shipped for the shipper's own account or where there was no intention to sell the goods on beyond the first buyer. In the second type of case, the seller and the buyer might choose to organise payment of the price through a letter of credit and, where this happens, the question arises as to whether such a document is acceptable to banks.

There appears to be little doubt in the literature that seawaybills can legitimately be tendered under letters of credit[85]. Whether one considers a seawaybill to be a 'marine bill of lading'[86] or another 'transport document'[87], it is clear that a seawaybill satisfies the requirements for tender imposed respectively by article 26 or article 25[88]. Under one or other of those articles, a seawaybill can validly be tendered under a letter of credit, even if the letter of credit makes no express mention of the term 'seawaybill'.

This, however, does not tell the whole story about seawaybills and letters of credit: for although the validity of their tender appears to be beyond controversy, their value as security for the banks seems to be suspect. Thus, banks accepting seawaybills under letters of credit are variously advised to have themselves named as consignees[89] or as both shippers and consignees[90], so as to enhance the security value of these documents. It will be recalled that, earlier in this book[91], we asked whether it was advisable for banks to be named as consignees on bills of lading. We concluded that, where an unpaid bank held a bill of lading tendered to it under a letter of credit, it could realise its security through a documentary sale whether or not it was named as consignee on the bill; that if it were named as consignee, this might open it to liabilities under the contract of carriage through the operation of section 1 of the Bills of Lading Act 1855[92]; and that consequently, there was nothing to be gained, and possibly much to be lost, through the bank's being named as consignee on a bill of lading.

The issue we must now address is whether the same is the case with seawaybills and the short answer is that the position is different here and that there might well be circumstances where it is advisable for

---

[85] See Gutteridge & Megrah, p 127; and the UNCTAD Report on Maritime Fraud, para 48.

[86] It has been argued above that a seawaybill is simply a nominate bill of lading known by another name: see Chapter 8.1.(c).i, above.

[87] The term used in art 25 of the UCP.

[88] Art 26 lists the requirements for the tender of bills of lading, while art 25 lists those required of other transport documents. Both articles are reproduced at Appendix 2.b. The only relevant difference between the two is that, if the seawaybill is considered to be a species of 'marine bill of lading' rather than another 'transport document', it must contain a statement that the goods have been shipped on board, rather than one simply stating that the goods have been received for shipment: see art 26 (a) (ii) and (c) (iii) and art 27 (a).

[89] See Gutteridge & Megrah, p 211.

[90] See the UNCTAD Report on Maritime Fraud, para 49.

[91] See Chapter 3.1.(a).iii, above.

[92] If, that is, the courts were prepared to pay scant attention to the fact that the bill of lading is held by the bank only as a pledgee: see Chapter 3.1.(a).iii, above.

a bank to have itself named as consignee on the seawaybill. Two sets of circumstances need to be distinguished: firstly, where the bank has been put in funds, or has been otherwise secured, by the buyer when opening the letter of credit; secondly, where it has not, and where, consequently, the bank could only look to the goods shipped under the seawaybill as its security against the buyer's insolvency.

Where the bank has been paid, or otherwise secured, on the opening of the credit, the bank incurs no risk in accepting a seawaybill: as we have seen, it is entitled and bound so to accept under the Uniform Customs and Practice for Documentary Credits, and once it has been paid, the bank is already well protected against the buyer's insolvency. Consequently, no benefit enures to the bank by having itself named as consignee on the seawaybill in these circumstances. Indeed, the upshot would be confusion compounded by uncertainty as to the carrier's liability for damage to goods or short delivery. With the bank appearing on the seawaybill as consignee, the buyer may well find it impossible to gain access to the goods: despite the fact that the document is in the buyer's hands, the carrier is clearly bound to deliver to the party named as consignee, here the bank. This predicament is hardly likely to be one either intended or hoped for by any of the other parties involved in the transaction, the traders and the carrier, each of whom had chosen payment by letter of credit against tender of a seawaybill as a means of expediting rather than delaying payment and delivery. Neither can the bank resolve the impasse simply by endorsing the seawaybill to the buyer: even if the document is a document of title at common law[93], it is one which can transfer the right to delivery only once, and that one transfer has, on this hypothesis, already been effected—to the bank. For the buyer successfully to take delivery, the bank would need either to take delivery itself and pass the goods on to the buyer; or to ask the shipper to alter the carrier's delivery instructions[94], now naming the buyer as consignee. Moreover, if the bank, choosing the first of those alternatives, were itself to take delivery of the goods for transfer to the buyer, the carrier's liability for damage to goods or short delivery would be very uncertain. If a cargo claim were brought by the bank[95], it is doubtful whether section 1 of the Bills of Lading Act 1855 could be

---

[93] See Chapter 8.1.(b).i, above.
[94] Some seawaybills contemplate the possibility that the consignee himself might change the carrier's delivery instructions; see, for example, the seawaybill used by P&O Containers, which reads, in relevant part: 'Should the Consignee require delivery to a party and/or premises other than as shown above in the "Consignee" box, then written instructions must be given by the Consignee to the Carrier or his agent. Unless the Shipper expressly waives his right to control the Goods until delivery by means of a clause on the face hereof, such instructions from the Consignee will be subject to any instruction to the contrary by the Shipper.' Where the bank, named as consignee, holds a seawaybill containing such a clause, it can solve the impasse described in the text above by altering the carrier's delivery instructions itself.
[95] On the hypothesis envisaged in the text, the carrier would be liable neither in contract nor in tort to the buyer: s 1 of the 1855 Act could only work to the buyer's benefit if his name were substituted for that of the bank; and *The Aliakmon* [1986] 2 Lloyd's Rep 1 would obstruct a cause of action in tort.

triggered into operation, the document having been given to the bank by way of security[96]: consequently, if the carrier were liable towards the bank in tort, he would derive no contractual protection from the contract recorded in the seawaybill[97]. In conclusion, it would seem that confusion ensues and no purpose served by having the bank named as consignee on a seawaybill where the bank has taken the precaution of being put in funds or otherwise secured when opening the letter of credit.

On the other hand, where the bank has opened the letter of credit solely on the strength of the security provided by the seawaybill, the document provides little if any protection against the subsequent insolvency of the buyer[98] unless, that is, the bank is named as consignee on the document. It has been argued above[99] that the seawaybill is a document of title at common law, in the sense that the right to delivery of goods shipped under a seawaybill can pass from seller to buyer without a formal assignment and without notification to the carrier. This does not mean, however, that a seawaybill made out to the buyer provides as strong a means of security as does an 'order' bill of lading to a bank paying money under a letter of credit. While the goods shipped under a seawaybill can validly be pledged to the bank through the standard agreement commonly appearing in applications for the opening of letters of credit[100], the bank might find it far more difficult to enforce the pledge than it would have done had it held in security an 'order' bill of lading. If the buyer becomes insolvent, the bank will want to realise its security either by taking possession of the goods or by selling the goods on through a transfer of the seawaybill. The former alternative is not only cumbersome in fact, but also difficult in law, at any rate without the co-operation of the shipper of the goods: for if the buyer is named as consignee on

---

[96] See Chapter 3.1.(a).iii, above.

[97] It is unlikely that the carrier in *Brandt v Liverpool Brazil and River Plate Steam Navigation Co Ltd* [1924] 1 KB 575 would help construct a contract between the carrier and a bank named as consignee who took delivery of the goods against presentation of the seawaybill, this for the reasons given at fn 57 above. It should be added, though, that where English law applied, the carrier might, if the Carriage of Goods by Sea Act 1971 were to apply to seawaybills (see Chapter 8.1.(c).ii, above), be entitled to the protection given the carrier by that Act: see Chapter 3.2.(a), above.

[98] Where the buyer needs to sell the goods in order to earn the money required to pay the bank the sum of the credit, the bank need not, here, release the seawaybill under a trust receipt: the point of the trust receipt is that a buyer may need physical possession of the bill of lading either to obtain physical possession of the goods or to sell them on through a documentary sale: with a seawaybill, the buyer does not need the document to do the first; and cannot do the second, with or without the document. The bank may still, though, need to organise an alteration in the carrier's delivery instructions, making the buyer the consignee, so as to enable the buyer to make the money he needs to pay the bank. In these circumstances, the bank runs the same risk of a fraudulent disposition of the goods by the buyer, a risk explained more fully at Chapter 3.1.(a).iii, above.

[99] See Chapter 8.1.(b).i, above.

[100] Reproduced and discussed at Chapter 2.3.(d), above; in relevant part, that agreement read: 'I/we hereby authorise you to hold the documents . . . and the merchandise to which they relate as security . . . and you may sell the said merchandise either before or after arrival at your discretion and without notice to me/us.'

the seawaybill, the carrier can only deliver the goods to the bank if so instructed by the shipper. The second alternative, clearly the quickest and neatest from the bank's point of view, is impossible, particularly but not only, where the seawaybill is made out to the buyer. Where, on the other hand, the seawaybill names the bank as consignee, the first alternative, namely taking physical delivery of the goods from the carrier, is available in law[101]. The second, namely realising its security through a documentary sale, would still, however, be barred by the consideration that a seawaybill can only perform the function of a document of title at common law once[102].

The position of a bank paying out money against tender of a seawaybill under a letter of credit can, then, be summarised as follows. A bank opening a letter of credit under which a seawaybill is likely to be tendered should either ensure that it is put in funds, or otherwise secured, by the buyer for the sum of the credit when the letter is opened; or insist that it be named as shipper[103] and consignee, or at any rate as consignee, on the seawaybill: only thus could the bank ensure that, if the buyer became insolvent, it could realise its security over the goods by claiming their delivery from the carrier.

2. COMBINED TRANSPORT DOCUMENTS

Can a seller validly tender a combined transport document, to the buyer, directly under a contract of sale concluded on shipment terms; or indirectly to a bank, where a letter of credit is in place?[104] Much the same problems as bedevil the use of seawaybills in international trade afflict the use of combined transport documents, though, as we shall see, for a slightly different reason. The buyer expects to receive from his seller a document entitling him to demand delivery of the goods from the carrier; and

---

[101] The same difficulties discussed above, in the text accompanying fn 95, with regard to the cause of action under which a cargo claim might be pursued, would arise here: the carrier might well find himself liable, in a cargo claim brought by the bank qua consignee, on terms other than those agreed with the shipper of the goods.

[102] See *Legal Problems of Credit and Security*, R.M. Goode, 1988, 2nd edn, p 12.

[103] See the UNCTAD Report on Maritime Fraud, para 49. This device would avoid the bank having to seek the co-operation of the shipper in circumstances where the bank or the buyer could only gain access to the goods on a change of the carrier's delivery instructions.

[104] Bills of lading contemplating the shipment of goods in containers are known by a number of names. Thus, Atlantic Container Line Ltd call their document simply a Bill of Lading; COMBICONBILL calls itself a 'Combined Transport Bill of Lading'; P & O Containers call theirs a 'Bill of Lading for Combined Transport Shipment or Port to Port shipment'; and BIMCO'S COMBIDOC is called a 'Combined Transport Document.' In Scrutton, these documents are also called 'through' bills of lading, although the editors concede that this involves using that term loosely: see art 179; see also Schmitthoff, p 495; and Through Bills of Lading, Bateson, (1889) 20 LQR 424. The term 'through bill of lading' might more accurately be used to signify a bill of lading under which the carrier assumes responsibility for the goods from port to port, in unimodal transport, and from point to point, in multimodal transport: see Tetley, pp 926–927.

one which gives him the right to sue the carrier, under a reasonable and predictable regime, for short-delivery of or damage to the cargo. In our examination of seawaybills, we saw that the buyer's right to demand delivery of the goods and his locus standi in a cargo claim against the carrier pursued under the Carriage of Goods by Sea Act 1971 were both suspect because it was doubtful, on the traditional view, whether the document was a document of title at common law, it being described explicitly as a non-negotiable document. Here too, the crucial issue[105] is whether a combined transport document is a document of title at common law: the cause for doubt, though, is slightly different. Combined transport documents invariably confirm that goods have been received by the carrier rather than that they have actually been shipped on board[106]. It is commonly said that bills of lading are only documents of title if they confirm that goods have been shipped on board[107]. It is consequently

---

[105] For a thorough account of other problems raised by combined transport documents, see Benjamin, paras 1999-2011; Goode, pp 632, 633; and see also The Multimodal Transport Docuument, J. Ramberg, in *International Carriage of Goods: Some Legal Problems*, eds Schmitthoff and Goode, 1988, at p 1-18. The International Chamber of Commerce has sought to solve a number of the problems caused by multimodal transport in the law of carriage through the adoption of the Uniform Rules for a Combined Transport Document ICC Publication No 298; these rules 'do not, however,— and, indeed, they cannot—legislate for the commercial and financial standing of the CTD.' (See A Combined Transport Document, Lord Diplock, (1972) JBL 269 at 271, 272; The International Chamber of Commerce Rules for a Combined Transport Document, B. S. Wheble, 1976 LMCLQ 145; Benjamin, para 1998; Goode, pp 633-637; and Liability of the Carrier in Multimodal Transport, Diamond, in *International Carriage of Goods: Some Legal Problems*, eds Schmitthoff and Goode, 1988, at 35, particularly at 39-44.) From the point of view of tender under a sale on shipment terms, the next most significant problem after the question discussed in the text above is whether such documents provide the buyer with continuous documentary cover and whether they can therefore be tendered by the seller under a sale on shipment terms: see Chapter 6.3, above. There are two aspects to this problem: (a) whether the carrier has assumed responsibility for the entire transit, by whichever mode it is carried out; (b) whether the same regime applies to the entire transit. As for (a), if the document tendered by the seller does not place responsibility upon the carrier for the entire transit, then tender is affected by the same principles as are applicable to transhipment: see Chapter 6.3.(c).ii.2, above, Scrutton, art 181, and *Yelo v SM Machado & Co Ltd* [1952] 1 Lloyd's Rep 183 at 190-192. As for (b), the doubt arises in this way: the regime applicable to any particular cargo claim will normally depend on whether or not the stage of the carriage during which loss or damage occurred is known: see P & O Containers Bill of Lading for Combined Transport shipment or Port to Port shipment, cl 6. Consequently, the buyer's cover against the carrier may vary depending upon whether any international convention appropriate to a particular mode of transport applies to a particular loss known to have occurred while the goods were being carried by that mode: see Scrutton, art 180. This lack of uniform cover would not, it is suggested, vitiate tender of the document under a sale on shipment terms: the requirement, surely, is that the document provide continuous cover, not that it provide uniform cover; see Chapter 6, fn 99 above and, for a suggestion in like vein, Benjamin para 1993.

[106] All the documents listed above at fn 104 so confirm. This is hardly surprising in view of the type of cargo to which such documents relate: containers are frequently collected by carriers or their agents at inland container depots at a considerable distance from the point at which goods have traditionally been delivered to the carrier, namely, the ship's rail.

[107] See, for example, Benjamin, paras 1439, 1445 and 1448; Scrutton, art 181; Goode, p 553; and Tetley, p 929.

said to follow that combined transport documents cannot, for this reason, be considered to be documents of title[108].

Just as is the case with seawaybills[109], a number of questions are raised by the proposition that a combined transport document is not a document of title at common law. Firstly, and most obviously, if a combined transport document is not a document of title at common law, how does the endorsee derive the right, as against the carrier, to demand delivery of the goods at the port of discharge? Secondly, if transfer of a document of title is required to trigger section 1 of the Bills of Lading Act 1855 into operation[110], then does the endorsee of a combined transport document have contractual locus standi in a cargo claim against the carrier[111]; or can such a claim only be brought, if at all[112], in tort, leaving the carrier bereft of his contractual exclusions and limitations? Thirdly, does the combined transport document record, as the buyer would expect, a contract of carriage governed by the Carriage of Goods by Sea Act 1971? The first two of these questions, and probably the third[113], need to be answered affirmatively if we are to conclude that a seller of goods on shipment terms can legitimately tender a combined transport document to his buyer; and the answer to all three of these questions depends, in essence, on the crucial issue as to whether a combined transport document is a document of title at common law. Thus, transfer of the right to possession depends directly on whether the document transferred is a document of title at common law; again, the operation of section 1 of the Bills of Lading Act 1855 depends, on the view accepted by Phillips J in *The Delfini*[114], on the transfer of a document of title[115];

---

[108] See, for example, Benjamin, para 1994; and Some Legal Aspects of the Carriage of Goods by Container, S. Mankabady, [1974] 23 ICLQ 317, at 321, 322.

[109] See Chapter 8.1.(a), above.

[110] See *The Delfini* [1988] 2 Lloyd's Rep 599; affd by the Court of Appeal (1989) Times, 11 August.

[111] The 1855 Act is generally assumed not to apply to combined transport documents: see, for example, Carriage by 'Combined Transport'—Recent Developments, J. Goldring, (1978) ABLR 151 at 155.

[112] For the plaintiff to bring an action in tort, he would need to prove that he had a proprietary interest in the goods at the time of the loss: *The Aliakmon* [1986] 2 Lloyd's Rep 1. His proprietary interest would need to be founded on some circumstance other than the transfer to him of the combined transport document since, on the view traditionally held, the document is not a document of title.

[113] In circumstances where the seller's duty to tender a bill of lading evidencing a reasonable contract of carriage is satisfied by tendering a bill of lading governed by the Carriage of Goods by Sea Act 1971. See Chapter 6.2, above.

[114] [1988] 2 Lloyd's Rep 599; affd by the Court of Appeal (1989) Times, 11 August.

[115] Soon after the passage into law of the 1855 Act, it was suggested that even though a 'through' bill of lading was recognised by custom to be a document of title at common law, this did not bring the document within the Act, and this on the rather strange ground that the Act cannot have been intended to apply, in 1889, to documents which had not been in common use in 1855: see Through Bills of Lading, H. D. Bateson, (1889) 20 LQR 424 at 425; and On Some Defects in the Bills of Lading Act, Carver, (1890) 23 LQR 289 at 298. It is interesting that, so soon after 1855, writers were suggesting that 'through' bills of lading were documents of title, for as we shall presently see, this suggestion was rapidly buried under the weight of the reverse proposition on the basis of *Lickbarrow v Mason* 1 Smith's Leading Cases 703: the former view is the

and, finally, the applicability or otherwise of the Carriage of Goods by Sea Act 1971 depends on whether the combined transport document can be considered to be a 'bill of lading or similar document of title'[116].

Consequently, in this second part of this chapter we shall be examining the widely held view that a combined transport document is not a document of title at common law, a view taken both by the major textbooks in the area and by the market. It will be suggested that the justifications commonly put forward for that view, both in terms of principle and in terms of authority, are suspect. On the other hand, it will also be suggested that if the traditional view accurately reflects the state of the authorities, then it has been overtaken by a legally binding custom to the effect that a combined transport document is a document of title at common law. The existence of such a custom will be supported in part by referring to developments in the law relating to letters of credit: the position of combined transport documents under the Uniform Customs and Practice for Documentary Credits will form the subject of our last inquiry in this chapter.

(a) Combined transport documents as documents of title

i. The traditional view: textbooks and the market

*The textbooks

The attitude of the major textbook writers to the legal nature of combined transport documents can best be described as one of studied ambivalence. On the one hand, orthodoxy, said to be supported by the authority of *Lickbarrow v Mason*[117], must be followed and on this basis, combined transport documents are not documents of title at common law and cannot, consequently, be tendered under a sale contract concluded on shipment terms. On the other hand, the use of combined transport documents is so widespread and, to judge by the dearth of case-law in the area, so free of trouble, that it seems difficult and somewhat remote to suggest that there is something seriously wrong in law with these documents. Opinion in the textbooks ranges between cagey hostility, outright contradiction and guarded enthusiasm. Thus, Sassoon writes:[118]

---

one favoured in this chapter. Not so welcome, though, is the proposition that even though the 'through' bill of lading is, pace Bateson and Carver, a document of title, it lies outside the 1855 Act simply because the Act preceded the widespread use of 'through' bills. Surely, the question is not whether the Act preceded such bills, but whether the Act is so worded as to include them; and it will be suggested in this chapter that that test would appear to be amply satisfied.

116   See the Carriage of Goods by Sea Act 1971, s 1(4); Sch, art I(b), art X.
117   1 Smith's Leading Cases 703; see also *Diamond Alkali Export Corpn v Bourgeois* [1921] 3 KB 443.
118   Para 157; see also Application of FOB and CIF Sales in Common Law Countries, in (1981) 1 European Transport Law 50 at 56.

'The [combined transport] document (if no contrary marking or notation appears thereon) is considered negotiable (by usage) and the fact that it may be issued by someone other than the sea carrier does not appear to have given rise to any particular difficulties till now. Whether a c i f seller may tender such a document in performance of his contract (absent agreement thereon) is unsettled and unclear. However, the fact that the document usually does not establish privity with the shipowner could be construed as curtailing the rights of the c i f buyer and (it is thought) may be a valid ground for rejecting the same.'

The editors of Scrutton are less hostile, but less resolute with it; the text starts sympathetically:[119]

'. . . it is submitted that there would now be little difficulty in establishing that [combined transport bills of lading] are by custom treated as transferable documents of title and within the meaning of the expression "bill of lading" as used in the Bills of Lading Act 1855.'

Further on in the same article, though, the editors conclude:

'A combined transport bill of lading providing for carriage partly be sea and partly by some other means of transport is not a valid tender under a c i f contract, in the absence of agreement or usage to that effect; if the express terms of the contract provide for carriage by sea, evidence of such a usage will not be admitted.'

The editors of Benjamin are not so sanguine in their acceptance of the traditional view. After assuming that the proposition that combined transport documents are not documents of title at common law is correct on the authorities, they then make a guarded defence of such documents:[120]

'. . . it seems that in the present state of the authorities a shipper who wanted to be sure of getting a document of title would need to obtain a separate bill of lading for the part of the transit involving carriage by sea. The question whether combined carriage documents are documents of title is one which cannot yet be answered with certainty. The now common use of such documents, the increasing degree of their standardisation and their acceptability to banks under documentary credits may support the view that a custom, similar to that established in *Lickbarrow v Mason*, exists in relation to such documents, at least where they are issued by, or on behalf of, sea carriers; but for the present it awaits judicial recognition.'

*The market

The market, doubtless impatient at the scholarly hesitation in the textbooks, has not waited for judicial recognition of such a custom. Aware

---

[119] See art 181.
[120] At paras 1994 and 2000.

of the legal problems underlying combined transport documents, traders and carriers together have zealously searched for a pragmatic solution to those problems. The results of that search can be seen both in the documents themselves currently used by the trade and in two contract terms adopted by the International Chamber of Commerce in Incoterms 1980, namely f r c and c i p.[121] We shall look first at a number of specimen clauses and then at the contract terms f r c and c i p.

— Specimen clauses

As we have seen, the crucial question is whether the combined transport document transfers to the buyer the right to possession on discharge and the contract of carriage originally concluded by the seller and the carrier. The market's answer has been to attempt, through a number of clauses, to bridge the perceived privity gap by drafting the buyer into the document, as it were, with a view to endowing him with the right to demand possession of the goods on discharge and with a view to activating section 1 of the Bills of Lading Act 1855. The devices employed vary in complexity. Thus, most combined transport documents include the buyer in the definition of the word 'merchant', presumably on the basis that this would give the buyer a possessory interest in the goods and contractual locus standi against the carrier. Thus, the P & O Containers bill of lading reads, in relevant part, as follows:

> '"Merchant" includes the Shipper, Holder, Consignee, Receiver of the Goods, any Person owning or entitled to the possession of the Goods or of this Bill of Lading, any Person having a present or future interest in the Goods and anyone acting on behalf of any such person.'[122]

Moreover, the definition of the word 'holder' in the same document is couched in terms clearly assuming the operation of section 1 of the Bills of Lading Act 1855:

> '"Holder" means any Person for the time being in possession of this Bill of Lading to whom the property in the Goods has passed on or by reason of the consignment of the Goods or the endorsement of this Bill of Lading or otherwise.'

To this somewhat indirect approach might be contrasted the rather more brazen attitude adopted by the Negotiable FIATA Combined Transport Bill of Lading, which boldly proclaims itself to be a document of title; clause 3.1 of the document reads:

> 'By accepting this Bill of Lading the Merchant and his transferees agree with the Freight-Forwarder that, unless it is marked "non-

---

[121] Free carrier (named point) and freight, carriage and insurance paid to. These terms are respectively based on f o b and c i f terms, subject to the difference that they cater for carriage of the goods by container.

[122] For similar clauses, see Atlantic Container Line Ltd, cll 1 and 2; COMBICONBILL, cl 2; COMBIDOC, cl 2.

negotiable'', it shall constitute title to the goods and the holder, by endorsement of this Bill of Lading, shall be entitled to receive or to transfer the goods herein mentioned.'

The aim of these clauses is clearly to give combined transport documents the same legal effects as shipped on board bills of lading. The techniques adopted, though, are somewhat puzzling, for it is not entirely clear that parties can simply agree, by contract, that a particular document is a document of title where that characteristic is not given it by the general law. It will be recalled that a document of title was earlier defined as one which[123]:

'. . . must be issued or accepted by the bailee of goods, must thereby embody his undertaking to hold the goods for, and release them to, whoever presents the document and *must be recognised by statute or mercantile usage*[124] as a document which enables control of the goods to pass by delivery of the document with any necessary indorsement.'

The same point is made by the editors of Benjamin in the context of another type of document, the delivery order[125]:

'. . . if a document could become a document of title merely because of its terms, it is hard to see why a custom as to the transferability of bills of lading had to be proved in *Lickbarrow v Mason*; and the better view seems to be that a document can achieve this kind of transferability only by mercantile custom or by statute.'

If this is right, the clauses here examined do not achieve their objective of transferring to the buyer a possessory interest in the goods and contractual locus standi vis-à-vis the carrier.

— Incoterms f r c and c i p

The terms f r c and c i p were adopted by the International Chamber of Commerce in the 1980 version of Incoterms. These terms of sale are modelled respectively on the traditional f o b and c i f terms and adapted to the carriage of goods by container[126]. The point of difference relevant to us here between f o b and c i f on the one hand, and f r c and c i p on the other relates to their documentary requirements[127]. Whereas the traditional terms refer explicitly to the bill of lading[128], the new terms,

---

[123] See Chapter 2.3.(a), above.

[124] Emphasis added.

[125] See Benjamin, para 1474.

[126] See, generally, International Conventions Applicable to FOB and CIF Sales and to Multimodal Transport of Goods Sales, M.J. Shah, (1981) 1 European Transport Law, 67 at 79-81, 86-89. See Appendix 2.a.

[127] Another major difference, less relevant to us in this context, relates to the point at which risk passes from seller to buyer: the ship's rail in f o b and c i f terms is substituted by the point at which the goods are put into the charge of the carrier.

[128] See f o b A9, which imposes upon the seller the duty to '[r]ender the buyer, at the latter's request, every assistance in obtaining a bill of lading. . .'; and c i f A7, which imposes upon the seller the duty '[a]t his own expense [to] furnish to the buyer without delay a clean negotiable bill of lading . . . [which must be] "on board" or "shipped".'

with an eye to what are assumed to be 'new' documents used in the container trade, refer simply to 'any document'[129] or 'the usual transport document'[130]. These terms were clearly necessary to bring the language of the traditional c i f and f o b terms into line with containerised transport. They could not of themselves, though, and neither were they intended to, alter the orthodox assumption that combined transport documents were not documents of title at common law: without a reversal in that assumption, the new terms could not stand much chance of success in the market place[131]. Indeed, it is not surprising to find that goods packed in containers are still sold on c i f or f o b terms rather than on c i p or f r c terms, traders and carriers preferring to use traditional terms, however inaccurately, rather than newer terms, however appropriate[132].

The ambiguity apparent both in the textbooks and in the attitude of the markets to combined transport documents can only be resolved if two fundamental questions are asked: firstly, what authority is there for excluding combined transport documents from the general custom which holds bills of lading to be documents of title; secondly, if that authority is sound, has it been overtaken by a new custom to the effect that combined transport documents too are documents of title at common law? These two questions will now be considered in turn.

ii. The traditional view: an assessment

The view that combined transport documents are not documents of title at common law is based, as we have seen[133], on the proposition that bills of lading can only be documents of title if they state that goods have been shipped on board: it is not sufficient if they state simply that the goods have been received for shipment. That proposition is said to be supported by two main authorities, namely *Lickbarrow v Mason*[134]

---

[129] See f r c A13, which imposes upon the seller the duty to '[r]ender the buyer, at his request, risk and expense, every assistance in obtaining any document. . .'

[130] See c i p A7, which imposes upon the seller the duty '[a]t his own expense, [to] provide the buyer, if customary, with the usual transport document.'

[131] This, presumably, is why Schmitthoff suggests, at 54, that the c i p contract is only 'a genuine c i f contract if, according to the terms of the contract of sale, the seller is obliged to tender a genuine marine bill of lading or a delivery order on the ship and, on the transfer of these documents and the insurance document, the buyer or his transferee is placed into direct contractual relationship with the carrier and the insurer.' See also Liability of the Carrier in Multimodal Transport, Diamond, in *International Carriage of Goods: Some Legal Problems and Possible Solutions*, eds Schmitthoff and Goode, 35 at 57, fn 35.

[132] See, for example, *Frebold & Sturznickel v Circle Products* [1970] 1 Lloyd's Rep 499.

[133] See the introductory remarks to Chapter 8.2, above.

[134] A case which went through long and protracted litigation: (1787) 2 Term Rep 63; revsd *sub nom Mason v Lickbarrow* by the Exchequer Chamber at (1790) 1 Hy Bl 357; restored and venire de novo ordered by the House of Lords at (1793) 2 Hy Bl 211; second trial reported at (1794) 5 Term Rep 683; see also the note to *Newsom v Thornton* (1805) 6 East 17, 20n for the opinion of Buller J advising the House of Lords. All the judgments in the case are reproduced at 1 Smith's Leading Cases, 703 et seq.

and *Diamond Alkali Export Corpn v Bourgeois*[135]. That support is, however, weakened by two other decisions: the judgment of the Privy Council in *The 'Marlborough Hill' v Cowan & Sons*[136] and by the decision of Lloyd J in *Ishag v Allied Bank International, Fuhs and Kotalimbora*[137]. The status of the traditional proposition that bills of lading are only documents of title if they state the goods to have been shipped is consequently unclear, not only because these decisions stand on either side of it, but also because the authority for each of the four decisions is itself suspect. We shall look first at these four decisions in turn; we shall look then at the traditional view in terms of principle.

In *Lickbarrow v Mason*[138], the plaintiff was a transferee for value of bills of lading from a buyer of goods who had gone bankrupt before paying his seller. The unpaid seller, on learning of his buyer's bankruptcy, indorsed another part of the bill of lading to the defendants, requesting them to take possession of the goods from the carrier on his behalf: this the defendants did and sold the goods for the account of the unpaid seller. The plaintiffs successfully sued the defendants in trover for having converted the goods.

In assessing the relevance of the case to the issue here being discussed, namely whether a received for shipment bill of lading is a document of title at common law, it is important to recall the distinction, outlined earlier[139], between the notions of transferability and negotiability. Transferability was taken to mean that the transfer of a document passed, without assignment to the transferee or notification to the carrier, the right to demand possession of the goods from the carrier; this characteristic was what made a document a document of title at common law[140]. Negotiability, on the other hand, was taken to mean that the transfer of a document could, in certain circumstances[141], pass to the transferee a better title than that of the transferor.

Now the question in *Lickbarrow's* case was whether the plaintiffs derived title to the goods free of the title of the unpaid seller or of that of his transferees, the defendants. This question raised the issue of negotiability, not that of transferability. Did the plaintiff, a bona fide transferee of the document for value, obtain a better title to the goods than the transferor's, namely the defaulting buyer's? It was held that the plaintiff did indeed obtain such better title, which could not therefore be disturbed by the original seller or his transferee, the defendant. The

---

[135] [1921] 3 KB 443.
[136] [1921] 1 AC 444.
[137] [1981] 1 Lloyd's Rep 92.
[138] See fn 134, above.
[139] See Chapter 2.2, above.
[140] See Chapter 2.2.(a), above.
[141] That is to say, in the circumstances envisaged by ss 2-4, 8 and 9 of the Factors Act 1889 and by ss 24-26 and 47 of the Sale of Goods Act 1979.

case was thus an early foretaste of section 9 of the Factors Act 1889 and of section 25 of the Sale of Goods Act 1979[142]. The case was not, however, concerned with the issue of transferability: it did not raise the question as to whether transfer of the bill of lading passed to the plaintiff the right, as against the carrier, to demand delivery on discharge. It provides us with no authority, consequently, as to whether the bill of lading is a document of title at common law. Much less does it decide—and this is the proposition which lies at the root of our troubles with combined transport documents—that a bill of lading is only a document of title if it states that the goods have been shipped rather than that they have been received for shipment[143].

It was, nonetheless, for that proposition that McArdie J cited *Lickbarrow's* case more than a century later in *Diamond Alkali Export Corpn v Bourgeois*[144]. In this case, however, the issue here being discussed, namely whether a received for shipment bill of lading was a document of title such that it could be tendered under a c i f contract, did arise for decision. The plaintiff sellers sued the defendant buyers for wrongful rejection of documents: the buyers had rejected the documents partly[145] because the bill of lading tendered stated that the goods had been received for shipment rather than that they had been shipped on board. McArdie J held that the buyers were entitled to reject the documents on this ground: as c i f buyers, they were entitled to a transferable bill of lading and

---

[142] Subsection (1) of which reads as follows:
  '**Buyer in possession after sale.**—(1) Where a person having bought or agreed to buy goods obtains, with the consent of the seller, possession of the goods or documents of title to the goods, the delivery or transfer by that person, or by a mercantile agent acting for him, of the goods or documents of title, under any sale, pledge or other disposition thereof, to any person receiving the same in good faith and without notice of any lien or other right of the original seller in respect of the goods, has the same effect as if the person making the delivery or transfer were a mercantile agent in possession of the goods or documents of title with the consent of the owner.'
  The spirit of the section is clearly 'the broad general principle, that, wherever one of two innocent persons must suffer by the acts of a third, he who has enabled such third person to occasion the loss must sustain it', the same principle which, according to Ashurst J in *Lickbarrow's* case at (1787) 2 Term Rep 63 at 70 gave 'a strong and leading clue to the decision of the present case.'

[143] To be sure, the special verdict found by the jury was that 'by the custom of merchants, bills of lading, expressing goods or merchandizes *to have been shipped* by any person or persons to be delivered to order or assigns, have been, and are, at any time *after such goods have been shipped*, and before the voyage performed, for which they have been or are shipped, negotiable and transferable by the shipper or shippers of such goods to any other person or persons . . .': see (1794) 5 Term Rep 683 at 685, 686, (emphasis added). The bill of lading in the case was a 'shipped' bill of lading: but this was simply part of the story, nothing turning on the distinction between 'shipped' and 'received' bills of lading. The reference in the special verdict to transferability was, in any case and as is argued in the text above, outwith the ambit of the issue actually raised by the plaintiff's action.

[144] [1921] 3 KB 443 at 450, in a judgment described by Carver as 'unusually unsatisfactory': see Carver at para 1613, fn 93.

[145] The buyers had also pleaded, unsuccessfully, that they were entitled to reject on the ground of late shipment of the goods; and, successfully, that an inadequate insurance document had been tendered.

a received for shipment bill of lading was not transferable. The only judicial authority, however, which McArdie J could muster for this proposition was *Lickbarrow's* case: insofar, therefore, as *Lickbarrow's* case is suspect in this regard, so is McArdie J's judgment in the *Diamond Alkali* case.

In support of the proposition that only shipped bills of lading can be documents of title, we are left, therefore, with a first instance decision which made that proposition its ratio, basing itself on the authority of a previous judgment which actually provides no support for the proposition[146]. We now need to look at the two decisions going the other way, namely, *The Marlborough Hill*[147] and *Ishag v Allied Bank International, Fuhs and Kotalimbora*[148].

The question referred to the Privy Council in *The Marlborough Hill*[149] was whether the Supreme Court of New South Wales had jurisdiction under the Colonial Courts of Admiralty Act 1890 over a particular cargo claim brought by endorsees of bills of lading stating goods to have been received for shipment. The Act gave the court jurisdiction over claims brought by endorsees of 'any bill of lading'. The issue, therefore, was whether a received bill of lading was a bill of lading for the purposes of that Act and the Privy Council advised that it was. It has rightly been pointed out that the only question before the court was whether the document was a bill of lading for a specific statutory purpose[150]: the issue was neither whether a received for shipment bill of lading was a document of title at common law nor whether it was a bill of lading under the Bills of Lading Act 1855. On the other hand, it is clear from Lord Phillimore's opinion in the case that in their Lordships' view, the document before them was both a document of title and a bill of lading under the 1855 Act[151]. It is difficult, nonetheless, to suggest that

---

[146] This is truly an instance, though, where error communis facit ius: the proposition that only shipped bills of lading are documents of title at common law is so deeply ingrained that the Hague-Visby Rules (and the Hague Rules before them) treat received for shipment bills as somewhat manque. Thus, under art III.7, the shipper is entitled to demand the issue of a shipped bill of lading, or, failing that, a received for shipment bill annotated with the date of shipment. Again, where Incoterms c i f are incorporated into the contract of sale, it is clear that the seller must tender a shipped bill of lading: see Incoterms, c i f A7. See, for a general indication as to how the proposition in the text has insidiously entered the mythology of the area, Waybills and Short Form Documents: A Lawyer's View, R. Williams, [1979] LMCLQ 297 at 312, 313.

[147] [1921] 1 AC 444, particularly at 449.

[148] [1981] 1 Lloyd's Rep 92.

[149] [1921] 1 AC 444, see particularly 449.

[150] See McArdie J in *Diamond Alkali Export Corpn v Bourgeois* [1921] 3 KB 443 at 452; Benjamin, para 1448; and R. Negus, in The Evolution of Bills of Lading, (1921) 37 LQR 304 at 307, 308 and in The Negotiability of Bills of Lading, (1921) 37 LQR 442 at 446, 447.

[151] See [1921] 1 AC 444, particularly at 451, where Lord Phillimore expressly acknowledges, and later refutes, counsel's submission that a received for shipment bill of lading lies outwith the 1855 Act (see *Weis & Co v Produce Brokers Co* (1921) 7 Ll L Rep 211 at 212, where Bankes LJ clearly read Lord Phillimore's words in this sense; but see McCardie J in the *Diamond Alkali* case at [1921] 3 KB 443 at 452 for a different reading

the case provides us with binding authority[152] for either of these two propositions.

The decision of the Privy Council in that case was, however, assumed in *Ishag v Allied Bank International, Fuhs and Kotalimbora*[153] to have decided that a received for shipment bill of lading was a document of title. The central issue before Lloyd J was which of two claimants, both holders of bills of lading separately issued, was entitled to the possession of goods from the carrier and the crux was whether the plaintiff's bill of lading was a document of title at common law. That bill of lading stated the goods to be at the disposal of the carrier who, it was further stated in the bill, intended to ship them on a particular vessel. The goods were actually held at the disposal of the ship's agents in a warehouse belonging to a third party. Lloyd J decided that this document was a document of title despite the fact that the goods were not actually in the carrier's possession, or in that of his agents[154]:

> 'For myself, I can see no practical or commercial difference between goods being received by agents on behalf of the shipowners and held in their own warehouse and goods being held at the disposal of the agents in the warehouse of another. Nor is there any difference, as was suggested, between "for shipment" in a received for shipment bill and "intended to be shipped with" in the present document . . . In my judgment the legal effect of the bill of lading is precisely the same as in any other received for shipment bill of lading. I would hold that it is covered by the custom as found proved in *The Marlborough Hill*.'

With respect, and as has been pointed out elsewhere[155], it is difficult to see how the document in the *Ishag* case was a received for shipment bill of lading. Moreover, and as we have just seen, *The Marlborough Hill* cannot be taken to have decided that a received bill of lading is a document of title at common law. Finally, and as we shall presently be seeing, possession of the goods by the carrier lies at the very root of the definition of a document of title at common law, and this crucial ingredient was missing in the *Ishag* case. Authority for the proposition, consequently, that a received for shipment bill of lading is a document of title is as uncertain as that for the reverse rule. This proposition is

---

of Lord Phillimore's words); and at [1921] 1 AC 444 at 452, where Lord Phillimore concludes that '[i]f this document is a bill of lading, it is a negotiable instrument', by which he clearly meant that it was transferable. Since the decision of Phillips J in *The Delfini* [1988] 2 Lloyd's Rep 599, it is probably true to say that the 1855 Act requires a bill of lading which is also a document of title at common law for its operation: see Chapter 3.1.(a).i, above. Phillips J's judgment was affirmed by the Court of Appeal (1989) Times, 11 August.

152 An additional, if highly technical, complication is caused, of course, by the fact that this was a Privy Council opinion given in a case arising within an Australian jurisdiction: see McArdie J in the *Diamond Alkali* case [1921] 3 KB 443 at 452.

153 [1981] 1 Lloyd's Rep 92.

154 Ibid at 97.

155 See Benjamin, para 1448.

supported only by an obiter dictum in a Privy Council opinion and by a decision based upon that obiter in a judgment given at first instance[156].

Given the lack of firm guidance from the cases, we must consider whether combined transport documents stating that goods have been received for shipment ought, in principle, to be considered as documents of title at common law. The test must be whether or not a combined transport document comes within the definition of a 'document of title' adopted earlier[157] as a document which:

'. . . must be issued or accepted by the bailee of goods, must thereby embody his undertaking to hold the goods for, and release them to, whoever presents the document and must be recognised by statute or mercantile usage as a document which enables control of the goods to pass by delivery of the document with any necessary endorsement.'

Each of the various parts of this definition would appear to be satisfied by a combined transport document. Thus, the document is issued by the bailee of the goods[158], who undertakes to hold them for the holder of the document. Moreover, if, as has been argued above, authority is poor for excluding received for shipment bills from the general mercantile custom making bills of lading documents of title at common law, then there is no reason in law for omitting combined transport documents from that custom on that ground[159]. The fact that the document states the goods to have been received for shipment, rather than shipped, indicates simply that the bailment of the goods has started at an earlier point than it does with a shipped bill of lading: that, it is suggested,

---

[156] For the sake of completeness, it should be added that Lord Chief Justice Andrews gave a very sidelong glance at received for shipment bills of lading in *Hugh Mack & Co Ltd v Burns & Laird Lines Ltd* (1944) 77 Ll L Rep 377 at 383, where he suggested that such bills of lading were 'similar document[s] of title' for the purposes of the Carriage of Goods by Sea Act 1924.

[157] See Chapter 2.3.(a), above.

[158] The goods must be in the actual possession of the carrier throughout the transit if the document covering that transit is to be considered to be a document of title at common law. Thus where the goods were deposited, against a consignment note, with a freight forwarder who then delivered them to a carrier in return for a bill of lading, the consignment note was not a document of title, its issuer not being a bailee throughout the transit: *The Maheno* [1977] 1 Lloyd's Rep 81, 86-88 and Benjamin, art 1994; see, in this regard, the point made in the text above in connection with *Ishag v Allied Bank International, Fuhs and Kotalimbora* [1981] 1 Lloyd's Rep 92.

[159] The dissenting judgment of Scrutton LJ in *Re L Sutro & Co and Heilbut, Symons & Co* [1917] 2 KB 348, 359-364, particularly at 360-361, is interesting in this regard. Dissenting from the view that buyers should be entitled to repudiate a contract because part of the trip was effected by rail, Scrutton LJ says, at 360-361: '. . .many c f i contracts must involve some land transit. . . . How would the printed form [ie the bill of lading] about vessels and "ports" of discharge be applied to such written particulars? The answer has been given by the House of Lords in *Glynn v Margetson & Co* [1893] AC 351 [ie the terms would be construed to fit the particular contract].' The decision in *Sutro*, of course, went the other way: it was suggested by the House of Lords in *Tsakiroglou & Co Ltd v Noblee Thorl GmbH* [1962] AC 93 at 113, however, that the majority decision might not stand; see Benjamin, para 1994.

is a distinction in fact which makes no difference in law[160]. Moreover, it is a distinction which need hardly cause surprise: for it is in the nature of containerised transport that the carrier takes charge of the goods as bailee at an earlier point and that the ship's rail be moved, as it were, inland to container depots[161]. It follows, therefore, that the document covering such transport should, if it is to be accurate, state that goods have been received for shipment, rather than that they have actually been shipped. That statement takes nothing from the characteristic of a combined transport document as a document of title at common law.

If this is correct, then combined transport documents would do no violence to the orthodox understanding of the law relating to documents of title and several consequences would follow. Firstly, a buyer could not reject a combined transport document on the ground that it does not give him a right to demand possession of the goods from the carrier, stating as it does that the goods were received rather than shipped by the carrier. Secondly, the buyer—and the carrier—would have the benefit of a contract fabricated by section 1 of the Bills of Lading Act 1855. Thirdly, once the buyer and the carrier are safely brought into contractual privity by that Act, the gap-filling clauses examined earlier in this chapter[162] would be quite unnecessary. Fourthly, pledgees of such documents would clearly have a possessory interest in the goods represented by the documents: they could thus realise their security by claiming possession of the goods from the carrier and they could sue in tort in the case of damage or short-delivery[163]. Finally, the terms devised by the International Chamber of Commerce for use in containerised

---

[160] Others have argued that it is a distinction in fact which should make a difference in law. Thus, Mr R. E. Negus suggests, in The Evolution of Bills of Lading, (1921) 37 LQR 304 at 305, that a received for shipment bill of lading is not a document of title at common law because before the goods are shipped, they may well be in a shore warehouse which is not, like a ship, subject to arrest. This, however, is to lose sight of the fact that a seller or a buyer of goods covered by a received for shipment bill of lading can nonetheless bring an action in rem against the carrier, under the Supreme Court Act 1981, s 20(2)(g) or (h), and this whether or not the goods have actually been shipped. Again, Benjamin suggests, at para 1448, that if a received for shipment bill of lading were considered to be a document of title at common law, it would be easier for the seller to reclaim the goods from the carrier and deal physically with the goods in breach of his contract with the buyer. With respect, this reasoning is difficult to follow: a seller intent on defaulting on his initial sale contract could, qua bailor, so reclaim and re-sell whether or not the bill of lading stating the goods to have been received were considered a document of title; the only difference that would make would be that the seller might find it easier to deal with the goods for a second time through a documentary rather than a physical sale. Moreover, in either case, the buyer's position is clear: the seller is liable to the buyer under the original contract of sale; but the carrier is not liable to the initial buyer under the contract of carriage, to which that buyer is not privy, no bill of lading having been transferred to him.

[161] See, in a similar vein, *The Marlborough Hill v Cowan & Sons* [1921] 1 AC 444 at 451; and Goode, at p 556.

[162] See the text accompanying fn 122, above.

[163] Although the carrier could, and would, where the requirements of *Brandt v Liverpool Brazil and River Plate Steam Navigation Co Ltd* [1924] 1 KB 575 are satisfied, plead a new, implied, contract of carriage between himself and the buyer.

transport, namely, c i p and f r c, could safely be used as the combined transport equivalents of c i f and f o b terms.

On the other hand, if, for all the reasons traditionally put forward in the literature, a combined transport document is not a document of title at common law under the orthodox custom endowing bills of lading with that quality, then a new custom must be found which would extend that attribute to this 'new' type of document. Our next task is, therefore, to see whether such a new custom has indeed arisen.

iii. The traditional view: overtaken by custom?

There is no novelty about the proposition that, whether or not received for shipment bills of lading come within the custom recognised by *Lickbarrow v Mason*[164], such bills of lading are accepted by another commercial custom as documents of title at common law. Thus, late in the last century, Carver wrote[165]:

> 'Whether bills of lading of this kind do, or do not, come within the settled rule as to the effect of indorsing and delivering an ordinary bill of lading, it is the fact that for many years past through bills of lading have been treated by business men as documents of title, negotiable in the same manner as ordinary bills of lading. There can, I should think, be little doubt that custom has extended the rule of negotiability in this sense to these documents.'

---

[164] (1794) 5 Term Rep 683; see fn 134, above for a full account of the litigation.

[165] On Some Defects in the Bills of Lading Act 1855, (1890) 6 LQR 289 at 296; see also 299-300. It should be said that even though Carver accepted the transferability of such documents, he still saw difficulties with them on one of two grounds. Firstly, where the sea carrier was a party to the through bill of lading, Carver doubted whether the documents came within the Bills of Lading Act 1855, the use of these documents being more recent than the passage of that Act. Secondly, where the sea carrier was not directly a party to the through document, the 1855 Act could only work where both the through document, qua document of title, and the ocean bill of lading, the contract of sea carriage, were tendered to the buyer together. It is interesting that both these complaints are based on the proposition that a through bill of lading is a document of title at common law. As for the complaints themselves, the second has been overtaken by the practice, evidenced in the specimen documents referred to above, that the sea carrier is typically a party to the combined transport document; the first would, with respect, lead to the conclusion that the utility of a statute dies with its passage onto the statute book, a rather strange conclusion in the context of a statute dealing with commercial law. (See *Kum v Wah Tat Bank Ltd* [1971] 1 Lloyd's Rep 439 at 444, where Lord Devlin says: 'The function of the commercial law is to allow, so far as it can, commercial men to do business in the way in which they want to do it and not to require them to stick to forms that they may think to be outmoded. The common law is not bureaucratic.') For other early writings making the same point as Carver, see Through Bills of Lading, Bateson, (1889) 5 LQR 424 at 424 and 427; and The Conflict of Law and Commerce, Lord Chorley, (1932) 48 LQR 51 at 61-62.

We have seen already, however, that such a custom has yet to be judicially recognised[166], at any rate as one generally governing received for shipment bills of lading[167].

For such a custom to pass muster before our courts, it must satisfy the test laid down by the Privy Council in *Kum v Wah Tat Bank Ltd*[168]. That test was described by Lord Devlin in the following terms:[169]

> '. . . the question whether the alleged custom, if proved in fact . . ., is good in law, must be determined in accordance with the requirements of the English common law. These are that the custom should be certain, reasonable and not repugnant. It would be repugnant if it were inconsistent with any express term in any document it affects, whether that document be regarded as a contract or as a document of title.'

It should not be difficult to prove that, as a matter of fact, the trade treats combined transport documents in exactly the same way as if they were ordinary bills of lading. Carriers, traders and, as we shall presently see, banks deal with these documents in exactly the same way as they do with bills of lading: the whole thrust of the contractual clauses inserted in combined transport bills of lading is to bring about precisely that effect. If the custom be proved to exist in fact, our next task would be to establish that it is good in law. The effect of the custom, if admitted, would clearly be certain: the combined transport document would have the same legal effects as shipped bills of lading, that is to say, they would be covered by the Bills of Lading Act 1855 and by the Carriage of Goods by Sea Act 1971, and could not be rejected by a buyer on shipment terms, at any rate on the ground that the document stated the goods to have been received for shipment rather than shipped. For the reasons stated earlier[170], such a custom would seem to be perfectly reasonable in the context of modern means of transport. Finally, far and away from being repugnant to the express terms of the document, such a custom would effect precisely the consequence which a number of clauses, earlier

---

[166] See Benjamin, para 1994, quoted above, in the text accompanying fn 120.

[167] The cases of *Weis & Co v Produce Brokers' Co* (1921) 7 Ll L Rep 211 and in *United Baltic Corpn v Burgett & Newsam* (1921) 8 Ll L Rep 190 have been read as cases where received for shipment bills of lading were held to be good tender because of a custom to that effect in the particular trade: see Sassoon, paras 143-145; and Carver, para 1613, fn 93. As Sassoon freely concedes, though, the buyers in either case raised no objection to tender on the ground that the bills stated the goods to have been received rather than that they had been shipped on board. The sellers were successful before the Court of Appeal, not because the received for shipment bills they had tendered were documents of title, but because the bills they had tendered complied with a contractual stipulation that they were to ship the goods on a named vessel 'expected ready to load' on a given date and to tender a bill of lading dated 'accordingly', the latter word interpreted by the court to mean that the precise date of shipment need not be given on the bill.

[168] [1971] 1 Lloyd's Rep 439.

[169] Ibid at 444.

[170] See text accompanying fn 159, above.

examined[171], seek to bring about: indeed, the need for such clauses would, if the custom were to be admitted, disappear.

(b) Combined transport documents and letters of credit

Mention has just been made of the fact that banks negotiating shipping documents under letters of credit are quite happy to accept and pay against tender of combined transport documents. The current version of the Uniform Customs and Practice for Documentary Credits makes it clear[172] that such documents are acceptable: the section of the Uniform Customs dealing with the tender of transport documents starts, in article 25, by dealing with transport documents other than ocean bills of lading, which are dealt with separately in article 26[173]. Again, as with Incoterms c i p and f r c[174], the approach has been to assume that combined transport documents are somehow essentially different to ocean bills of lading, but then so to draft the rules as to make them as acceptable as ocean bills. The language is adapted, of course, to accommodate different practices: thus, 'loaded on board or shipped on a named vessel' in article 26(a)(ii) becomes 'dispatch or taking in charge of the goods, or loading on board, as the case may be' in article 25(a)(ii). In essence, though, article 25 is the mirror image for combined transport of the requirements imposed by article 26 for uni-modal transport and it is of interest that the only substantial difference between the two relates to the requirement of shipment: an ocean bill of lading must state that the goods have been shipped, whereas a combined transport document need only state that the goods have been received for shipment[175]. Thus, the feature of combined transport documents traditionally assumed to weaken their value as commercial documents—namely, the fact that they state goods to have been received for shipment rather than shipped—is first acknowledged, but then ignored. The upshot is that the combined transport document is acceptable so long as it is issued by or on behalf of a carrier[176] who is willing to take responsibility for the goods for the entire carriage[177].

What is the impact of the the acceptability of combined transport documents under the Uniform Customs and Practice upon the central question asked in this part of the chapter, namely whether these

---

[171] See text accompanying fn 122, above.
[172] For the position under the previous 1974 Revision of the UCP, see Combined Transport—a Banking View, B. Wheble, (1975) 10 ETL 648; and The Documentary Credit in Relation to Traditional and Multimodal Sales, B. Wheble, (1981) 16 ETL 100, at 105, 106.
[173] See Appendix 2.b.
[174] See text accompanying fn 131, above.
[175] See arts 25(a)(ii), 26(a)(ii), 25(b)(v), 26(c)(iii), 27(a), 47 (b)(i) and (iii) of the UCP.
[176] As opposed to a forwarding agent acting on behalf of the shipper: see arts 25(d), mirrored, for ocean bills, in 26(c)(iv). The FIATA Combined Transport Bill of Lading mentioned in art 25(d) is also acceptable where the letter of credit calls for an ocean bill of lading: see Opinions of the ICC Banking Commission 1984-1986, pp 39-41.
[177] See arts 25(a)(i) and 29(c)(ii); it seems as if the requirement of through cover does not apply to an ocean bill of lading giving the carrier a liberty to tranship: see Chapter 6, fn 109, above.

documents are documents of title at common law. The Uniform Customs do not and could not, of themselves, make a combined transport document a document of title[178]; and the value of such a document as security for money paid under a letter of credit depends not upon its acceptability under the Uniform Customs but upon its status at common law[179]. The acceptance of such documents by the banking community, though, clearly provides strong evidence that by custom, be it that recognised by *Lickbarrow's* case or a newer and wider one, combined transport documents are considered by the common law as documents of title.

---

[178] See, for a similar point made in the context of Incoterms c i p and f r c, fn 131, above.
[179] Thus, unless the combined transport document is recognised as a document of title at common law, the bank would have neither the right to claim possession of the goods from the carrier nor the right to sue him for damage to goods or short delivery: see Carriage by Combined Transport—Recent Developments, J. Goldring, (1978) **ABLR** 151.

PART III

Rejection of documents and rejection of goods

CHAPTER 9

Rejection of documents and goods

1. Seller's physical and documentary duties as to the time of shipment: conditions of the contract

2. Documentary duties in general and repudiation

   (a) Arguments against applying the rule

   (b) Arguments in favour of applying the rule

   (c) The cases

   (d) Should the rule apply?

3. Buyer's remedy of rejection: practical constraints

   (a) Documents reach buyer before goods and buyer notices documentary defect

   (b) Documents reach buyer before goods and buyer does not notice documentary defect

   (c) Goods reach buyer before documents and buyer notices documentary defect

   (d) Goods reach buyer before documents and buyer does not notice documentary defect

4. Buyer's remedies of rejection: documents and goods

   (a) Independent rights of rejection

   (b) Damages for loss of the opportunity to reject documents

      i. The type of loss which can be recovered

      ii. Market losses

      iii. Defect in the documents alone, causing no loss

   (c) Loss through estoppel of the right to repudiate

      i. The doctrine of *Panchaud Freres*

      ii. The effects of the doctrine

      a. Buyer estopped from rejecting goods on similar grounds

      b. Buyer estopped from recovering damages for loss of the opportunity to reject

     c. Buyer not estopped from rejecting goods on other grounds

     d. Summary of the effects of the doctrine

    iii. Is the buyer estopped through actions of the bank?

The effect in the general law of contract of repudiation of a contract on account of its breach is relatively clear: where one party to a contract is in breach of a condition, or of an innominate term the effects of the breach of which go to the root of the contract, the other party has the option of terminating the contract. The effect of such termination is that both parties are no longer bound by the primary, or performance, duties in the contract[1]; both parties remain bound, however, by secondary duties in the contract, namely duties imposed by terms regulating the remedies of the parties after breach[2]. The clarity of the present state of the law, at any rate in the general law of contract[3], is due in large part to the judgment of Diplock LJ in *Hong Kong Fir Shipping Co Ltd v Kawasaki Kisen Kaisha Ltd*[4] and to the speeches of Lords Wilberforce and Diplock in *Photo Production Ltd v Securicor Transport Ltd*[5]: these decisions helped throw light on what had previously been clouded by too rigid an adherence to the distinction between conditions and warranties[6], and by the confusion, inherent in the discredited doctrine of fundamental breach, between repudiation and rescission of a contract[7].

Given the relative ease with which the remedy of repudiation can be stated, it may seem strange that a particular manifestation of the remedy in the law of sales—rejection by the buyer—should merit an entire chapter to itself; just as strange, moreover, that it alone, of all the remedies

---

[1] Such as the duty to ship the goods, or the duty to pay the price.

[2] Such as an arbitration clause, or a liquidated damages clause: see *Heyman v Darwins* [1942] AC 356, particularly per Lord Macmillan at 373.

[3] There are doubts as to whether this general statement applies to the law of carriage of goods by sea: see Fundamental Breach and Deviation in the Carriage of Goods by Sea, C. Debattista, 1989 JBL 22.

[4] [1961] 2 Lloyd's Rep 478, 491-495.

[5] [1980] AC 827.

[6] Diplock LJ 's contribution to the law on repudiatory breach has not, for all its clarity, commanded unanimous support: see, for an entertaining critique of the *Hongkong* doctrine, Contract—The Buyer's Right to Reject Defective Goods, T. Weir, [1976] CLJ 33. There is no doubt, however, but that the *Hongkong* doctrine represents the law as accepted in the highest quarters: see *Bunge Corpn v Tradax SA* [1981] 2 Lloyd's Rep 1.

[7] Repudiation terminates, while rescission annuls, a contract. It is clear that no contractual term can 'survive' rescission, quite simply because rescission implies that no contract ever existed: consequently, there are no terms to survive. With repudiation, on the other hand, it is conceivable that terms devised by the parties to regulate the resolution of disputes might survive breaches giving rise to disputes. The conflation between these separate concepts—repudiation and rescission—formed the basis of the now discredited doctrine of fundamental breach, in virtue of which a party in serious breach of contract was deprived of the protection of contractual exclusion clauses: see *Photo Production v Securicor Transport* [1980] AC 827 per Lord Wilberforce at 844; and *Johnson v Agnew* [1980] AC 367 per Lord Wilberforce at 392, 393.

available to sellers and buyers whose contracts of sale are governed by English law[8], deserves attention here. It is suggested, however, that repudiation by the buyer of a contract on shipment terms is both complex and special enough to require detailed and exclusive treatment in a book having as one of its themes the dual mode of performance by the seller of his obligations under a sale on shipment terms; and this, for reasons both academic and practical or commercial.

As for the first type of consideration, we have seen throughout that a binary line runs down every international sale contract on shipment terms: the seller's duties towards the buyer come in two shapes, the physical and the documentary. It is not surprising, consequently, that that most radical of contractual remedies—repudiation—should need to be analysed in binary terms and herein lies the complexity: what exactly does 'repudiation' mean in the context of a contract which is performed in two modes, a physical mode and a documentary mode? This dual manner of performance—and the consequently dual aspect of rejection— sets repudiation in international shipment sales apart from repudiation in domestic sales. From a commercial point of view, at any rate judging by the cases which have come to light in the reports, repudiation of sale contracts involving the shipment of commodities represented by shipping documents is an important option in markets where a sudden drop in the price of the commodity can make a major difference to the value of the contract to the buyer: prompt action on the documents can help extricate the buyer from a contract which has turned out to be less advantageous than it once appeared to be. For all these reasons, we shall be concentrating here on the buyer's remedy of repudiation of contract for the seller's breach, reference being made to the major works in the area[9] for those other remedies which international sales share with their domestic counterparts.

Our central aim, then, is to examine the workings of the buyer's remedy of repudiation in international sale contracts on shipment terms. Our route starts with a consideration of the seller's duties to ship goods within the shipment period and to tender a bill of lading accurately stating shipment to have occurred within the shipment period. It is useful to start here because the authorities which have developed the law on rejection of documents and goods in shipment contracts all relate to the tender of bills of lading inaccurately stating the date of shipment[10].

---

[8]   See Parts V and VI of the Sale of Goods Act 1979, respectively for Rights of Unpaid Seller against the Goods and for Actions for Breach of the Contract.

[9]   See Benjamin, paras. 1751-1763, 1772-1785, 1892-1913; Sassoon, paras 302-334, 342-350; 691-714.

[10]   This is hardly a coincidence. Time is of the essence in the type of contract here discussed: see *Bunge Corpn v Tradax SA* [1981] 2 Lloyd's Rep 1, particularly at 12; and *Toepfer v LenersanPoortman NV* [1980] 1 Lloyd's Rep 143, particularly at 147-148; but see *The Naxos* [1989] 2 Lloyd's Rep 462, particularly at 474, 475, for the proposition that time is only of the essence in such contracts where the stipulated schedule is precise, Sir Michael Kerr dissenting at 471-473. It is not surprising that buyers wishing to repudiate will look for breach of a term relating to time as justification

Our second task will be to ask whether it is every documentary defect which is considered to be a condition, entitling the buyer to repudiate the contract, however minor the effects of the breach. Having established that the better view seems to be that all the seller's documentary duties are conditions, we shall then look at the practical constraints imposed upon the buyer's right of repudiation by the fact that the shipping documents and the goods rarely reach the buyer at the same time: essentially, how is the buyer to decide what to do if the other half, as it were, of the seller's performance has yet to arrive? Our fourth task will be to see how the law solves the buyer's conundrum by constructing two independent rights of rejection, namely a right to reject the documents and a right to reject the goods: here, we shall examine the sense in which these rights are independent; we shall see how the buyer can be compensated for being deprived of the opportunity to reject the documents; and finally, we shall see how, through the doctrine of estoppel, the buyer can lose his right to repudiate the contract.

1. SELLER'S PHYSICAL AND DOCUMENTARY DUTIES AS TO THE TIME OF SHIPMENT: CONDITIONS OF THE CONTRACT

The date of shipment goes to the very essence of c i f and f o b contracts as shipment rather than destination contracts[11]: given that the seller promises shipment, rather than arrival, of the goods, the least the buyer is entitled to expect is that the seller should perform his obligation as to shipment within the time allowed for in the contract. Thus, the time of shipment agreed in the sale contract is a condition of the contract, breach of which condition allows repudiation of the contract by the buyer: *Bowes v Shand*[12], where a buyer was held entitled to reject a cargo the bulk of which had been shipped in February in breach of a contract stipulating for shipment in March and/or April. The seller's duty physically to ship the cargo within the contract period is reflected in his documentary duty to tender a bill of lading accurately stating shipment within the same period[13]. As has already been indicated, the buyer's right of repudiation in shipment sales has been developed in cases dealing with the rejection of documents inaccurately stating the date of shipment.

---

for rejection. Although time stipulations are not generally considered to be conditions by the Sale of Goods Act 1979 (see s 10), the reverse is the case in the case of mercantile contracts: see Sassoon, para 59. Professor Treitel justifies this departure from the norm on two grounds, namely, 'that breach by delay is uniquely easy to establish'; and that '[D]elay is also of obvious commercial importance in dealing with commodities, which can fluctuate rapidly in value': see Treitel, pp 610,1. The second explanation serves rather better, with respect, than the first: for surely, the facility with which breach of a time stipulation can be established is not restricted to contracts involving commodities.

[11] See Chapter 1, above.
[12] (1877) 2 App Cas 455. See Benjamin, para 1532.
[13] *Procter & Gamble Philippines Manufacturing Corpn v Kurt A Becher GmbH & Co KG* [1988] 2 Lloyd's Rep 21 and earlier cases therein cited.

An understanding of the workings of repudiation in this area must therefore start with an explanation of the seller's duty[14] to tender a bill of lading accurately stating that the cargo has been shipped within the contract period.

Little time need be spent discussing whether or not the buyer has a right simply to a bill of lading stating a date of shipment: the fact of the matter is that bills of lading invariably do state a date of shipment, although it is, rather confusingly, described as the date of issue[15]; and, in any case, sale contracts very commonly contain an express term stipulating the seller's obligation to tender a dated bill of lading[16]. The question which is worth asking is whether the seller impliedly[17] promises the buyer that the date stated on the bill accurately represents the date of shipment. It is helpful to ask the question in three sets of circumstances: firstly, where the seller ships the goods within the contract period, but tenders a bill of lading inaccurately stating them to have been shipped out of time; secondly, the reverse case, that is to say, where the seller ships out of time, but tenders a bill of lading inaccurately stating shipment to have taken place within the contract period; thirdly, where, whether or not the seller has shipped within the contract period, he tenders a bill of lading giving a shipment date which, though within the shipment period, is nonetheless inaccurate. It will be seen that in all three cases, the seller is under an implied obligation to tender a bill of lading accurately stating shipment within the contract period.

In the first case, the seller has performed his duty physically to ship the goods within the contract period; but by tendering a bill of lading which inaccurately states shipment outside that period, the seller has failed to tender a document which correctly describes the goods being sold; consequently, he has failed to give the buyer a bill of lading which he could easily sell on the market. This much was held in the case *Re General Trading Co and Van Stolk's Commissiehandel*[18]. Any other result would have involved the assumption that performance of the seller's physical obligation to ship within the contract period is a discharge

---

[14] At any rate in those sale contracts where the seller is responsible for organising the issue of the bill of lading, that is to say, in c i f , c & f, f o b extended and f o b classic contracts.

[15] This is curious, given the importance attached to the date of shipment and given that the date of issue rarely, if ever, coincides with the date of shipment. Nonetheless it seems always to be assumed that the date given as the date of issue on the face of a bill (see Appendix 3.b) is the date on which the goods were actually shipped, saving, of course, the case where the bill starts off as a 'received for shipment' bill and eventually becomes a 'shipped' bill by express annotation of the date of actual shipment: see the Carriage of Goods by Sea Act 1971, Sch, art III.7.

[16] See, for example, Incoterms CIF A7: '[The bill of lading] must be dated within the period agreed for shipment.'

[17] The duty is sometimes made express: thus see clause 6 in GAFTA 100: 'Period of shipment . . . as per bill(s) of lading dated or to be dated . . .; the bills of lading to be dated when the goods are actually on board. Date of bill(s) shall be accepted as proof of date of shipment in the absence of evidence to the contrary.'

[18] (1911) 16 Com Cas 95, particularly at 101.

of his independent documentary duty to tender a bill of lading accurately describing the goods.

In the second case, the seller has failed to perform his duty physically to ship the goods within the contract period, but has managed to tender a bill of lading dissembling performance of that physical duty[19]. It is clear on authority that the tender of such a bill of lading constitutes a breach of 'a distinct and separate promise . . . to hand a bill of lading which would truly state that the [cargo was shipped within the contract period]'[20]. In this case, the seller is consequently in breach of both his physical duty to ship goods timeously and of his documentary duty to tender a bill of lading accurately describing the goods. We shall see later in this chapter[21] that the measure of damages compensating the buyer is different for each of these two breaches; suffice it for the present, though, simply to establish the separate existence of the duty to tender a bill of lading accurately stating shipment within the contract period.

In the third case, the seller tenders a bill of lading stating a shipment date which, while falling within the shipment period, does not accurately reflect the date when the goods were actually shipped: for example, the seller tenders a bill of lading stating shipment to have occurred on 25 October, whereas the goods were actually loaded on 26 October. If the contract stipulates September shipment, the seller is, of course, in breach both of his physical duty to ship the goods within the contract period and of his documentary duty to tender a bill of lading stating shipment within the same period. What is the position, however, where the contract stipulates for October shipment, that is to say, where the seller is not in breach of his physical duty to ship the goods timeously? Is he still in breach of his duty to tender a bill accurately stating shipment within the contract period? The situation was considered in the *James Finlay* case[22] by Greer LJ, who declined to give a firm answer to the question whether the seller was, in this case too, in breach of an obligation to tender an accurate bill of lading. It is now clear, though, that such a seller is in breach of his documentary duty: *Procter & Gamble Philippines Manufacturing Corpn v Kurt A Becher GmbH & Co KG*[23]. Again here,

---

[19]   To tender such a bill, the original shipper must have obtained the co-operation of the carrier, or at any rate of the party physically signing the bill on the carrier's behalf. Such co-operation might be obtained against an indemnity which the shipper offers the carrier or signatory in return for a bill which, stating shipment within the contract period, can easily be tendered to the buyer or to the bank under a letter of credit: see *James Finlay & Co Ltd v NV Kwik Hoo Tong Handel Maatschappij* [1929] 1 KB 400 at 408; and *Procter & Gamble Philippines Manufacturing Corpn v Kurt A Becher GmbH & Co KG* [1988] 2 Lloyd's Rep 21 at 22.

[20]   *James Finlay & Co Ltd v NV Kwik Hoo Tong Handel Maatschappij* [1929] 1 KB 400 at 413, per Greer LJ

[21]   See Chapter 9.4.(b), below.

[22]   [1929] 1 KB 400 at 412.

[23]   [1988] 2 Lloyd's Rep 21. The obligation in this case was made express in GAFTA 100, clause 6; it is clear from the judgments, though, that the duty to tender an accurate bill of lading—implied in the *James Finlay* case (above, fn 22)—would apply in this third type of case as well: see [1988] 2 Lloyd's Rep 21 at 27-29, 33.

the consequences of the seller's breach are a matter to which we shall be returning later in this chapter[24]; suffice it for the present to say simply that, after *Procter & Gamble*[25], a buyer establishing such a breach on the part of the seller is unlikely to recover much by way of damages in other than very exceptional circumstances.

In all three cases, then, namely where the seller is in breach of his documentary but not of his physical duty to ship timeously; where the seller attempts to conceal through the bill of lading a breach of his physical duty of timeous shipment; and where the seller is simply guilty of a documentary inaccuracy which falls within the shipment period; in all these cases, the seller is in breach of a duty, quite separate from his obligation physically to ship the goods within the contract period, to tender a bill of lading accurately stating shipment to have occurred within that period. The cases establishing and illustrating this documentary duty all arise from facts where the gap between the date of actual shipment and the date stated on the bill of lading was really very short indeed[26]. This observation leads us to our next question: does any breach of the seller's documentary duties, however minor, entitle the buyer to repudiate the contract?

2. DOCUMENTARY DUTIES IN GENERAL AND REPUDIATION

An inaccurate statement on the bill as to the date of shipment is, of course, only one type of defect on the grounds of which the buyer may feel entitled to repudiate the contract: it has been singled out for treatment in this chapter because most of our understanding of the remedy of repudiation in shipment sales emerges from cases relating to this particular type of documentary breach. In Chapters 5 and 6, however, we looked at a large number of qualities to which a buyer is entitled in his bill of lading, whether by express stipulation or through implication by the courts. Thus we saw, for example, that the seller must tender a clean bill of lading[27] and that the bill must provide the buyer with continuous documentary cover against the carrier in respect of the whole voyage from the loading port to the agreed destination[28]: failure by the seller to provide a bill satisfying either requirement very clearly puts him in breach of contract. The question here goes one step further: does any documentary breach, however minor in terms of its actual impact on the buyer, entitle the buyer to repudiate the contract? Or, to place the question within its general contractual setting, are documentary duties conditions or innominate terms?

---

[24] See Chapter 9.4.(b), below.
[25] [1988] 2 Lloyd's Rep 21.
[26] Thus, in none of the three cases mentioned in our discussion of the seller's documentary duty was the gap longer than ten days.
[27] See Chapter 5.3.(b), above.
[28] See Chapter 6.3, above.

The classification of contractual promises as conditions, warranties or innominate terms in the general law of contract is interesting both in terms of conceptual analysis and in terms of practical application[29]; its importance in this field of commercial activity is enhanced by the fact that an apparently slight drop in the international market value of a commodity shipped in large quantities can make withdrawal from a contract—or even its mere threat—extremely attractive to a buyer who now finds that he could have purchased the same cargo at a much cheaper price had he entered the market later rather than sooner. Consequently, from a buyer's point of view, the greater the number of conditions in his contract, the greater the chance of finding the seller in breach of one or other of them, and therefore the greater the opportunity of legitimating an otherwise wholly unmeritorious termination of the contract. Moreover, the opportunities for finding technical breaches of contract and for using them as pretexts for termination on purely commercial grounds would be greatly increased if every contractual requirement of every document contained in the bundle tendered by the seller were to enjoy the status of a condition. Is that status shared by every documentary duty imposed on the seller of goods on shipment terms?

The authorities in which the issue has been addressed are few and conflicting. The proposition, stated in *The Hansa Nord*[30], that

> 'the seller's obligation regarding documentation had long been made sacrosanct by the highest authority and that the express or implied provisions in a c i f contract in those respects were of the class . . . any breach of which justified rejection'

appears to have entered the law very much sub silentio: in *The Hansa Nord*[31] itself, no 'highest authority' appears actually to have been cited in support of the proposition. Moreover, the obligation allegedly broken by the seller in that case was his physical duty to ship goods 'in good condition' rather than his duty to tender documents indicating shipment in good condition: consequently, the case fails precisely to address the issue here discussed. Indeed, there seems to be a marked degree of judicial reluctance directly to challenge the proposition that documentary duties are conditions, even in cases where the courts have sought to restrict the buyer's right to repudiate the contract on the grounds of a documentary breach. Rather have the judges been content to raise the issue obliquely in slightly different terms: does the general maxim de minimis non curat lex apply to documentary duties in shipment sales?

There appears to be no case deciding in terms that the de minimis rule applies to none of the documentary duties in shipment sales; neither, however, does there appear to be any authority for the proposition that

---

[29] For what is, with respect, an illuminating and thorough account of the issue, see Treitel, pp 601–613.
[30] Per Roskill LJ at [1976] QB 44 at 70B.
[31] [1976] QB 44.

it applies to every such duty. The judges have been saved the difficulty of deciding the question largely because the cases before them have conveniently been easy of resolution through some other means[32]. Caution in this area is well justified, for the question touches two sensitive nerves running through the subject: the precise relationship between the physical and documentary modes of performance in shipment sales; and, in close proximity, the exact link between a shipment sale and a letter of credit. In the absence of clear authority, an attempt will here be made first to rehearse the arguments on either side and then to suggest which of the two views is preferable.

(a) Arguments against applying the rule

Three arguments have been put forward against applying the de minimis rule to documentary duties in shipment sales: certainty of application; consistency between the law of sale and that relating to letters of credit; and the balance of convenience between the parties. The first argument—based on considerations of certainty—is one very commonly put forward whenever the judges prefer the rigour of conditions to the haze of innominate terms: the all-or-nothing nature of conditions assists businessmen and their advisers in coming to decisions upon the accuracy and speed of which turn the disposition of large cargoes at sea and, possibly, enormous sums of money[33]. Those commercial decisions ought not to be delayed or complicated by criteria depending on a speculative assessment of likely loss. Thus, in *SIAT di dal Ferro v Tradax Overseas SA*, Megaw LJ asked:[34]

> '[O]ught the essential nature of the buyer's rights, when he is faced with defective documents, to vary according as to whether he is or is not in a string of buyers of the same goods; whether at the date of the tender of the defective documents he has or has not resold, whether on the same or different contractual terms; or whether thereafter he might desire to resell by passing on the documents, rather than taking delivery of the goods on his own account?'

---

[32] Thus, for example, in *SIAT di dal Ferro v Tradax Overseas SA* [1980] 1 Lloyd's Rep 53, the court found breaches so serious as not to require a decision as to whether other defects in the documents were saved by the de minimis rule. Again, in *Jydsk Andels-Foderstofforretning v Grands Moulins de Paris* (1931) 39 Ll L Rep 223, in applying the de minimis rule to a case where an amount slightly in excess of the contract quantity was tendered, MacKinnon J did not need to specify which of the two breaches, physical or documentary, he was applying it to, and this because the document—a weight certificate—arrived as the goods were being discharged: consequently, both goods and documents were rejected by the buyer at the same time.

[33] See, for example, Lord Roskill in *Bunge Corpn v Tradax SA* [1981] 2 Lloyd's Rep 1 at 12.

[34] [1980] 1 Lloyd's Rep 53 at 62. The issue discussed in the text did not arise for decision in *SIAT* because the Court found that there were defects in the bills of lading tendered which very clearly put the seller in repudiatory breach: the bills did not provide for carriage to the destination stipulated in the contract of sale, as to which see Chapter 6.3.(d), above. It was, therefore, unnecessary for the court to decide whether other documentary breaches alleged by the buyer were repudiatory or not.

The second argument too found a place in Megaw LJ's judgment in the same case. Counsel for the sellers suggested that whereas minor documentary breaches were clearly repudiatory in the sense that they entitled banks to reject documents tendered under letters of credit, the same was not the case as between seller and buyer where no letter of credit was in place. Megaw LJ suggests that even if there were authority for differentiating between tender in these two contracts,

> '. . the question would arise whether it is a desirable or defensible distinction; or whether it would lead to anomalies and uncertainties in an area of the law where such degree of certainty as can fairly be achieved is obviously commercially desirable.'[35]

The third argument is constructed by comparing the inconvenience caused to either party, on the one hand, by allowing rejection by the buyer on the slightest pretext; and, on the other, by allowing tender by the seller of documents in technical breach of the sale contract through the application of the de minimis rule. The rigour of a rule readily allowing rejection by the buyer is said to cause little harm to the seller, because

> '. . the law, in the absence of a contractual term to the contrary, allows a seller who has presented defective documents to re-present, tendering correct documents, so long as he does so before the last permissible date provided by the terms of the contract . . .'[36]

On the other hand, tender of documents which differ, however slightly, from those stipulated in the contract of sale, might put the buyer in an impossible situation in the market. In *Procter & Gamble Philippines Manufacturing Corpn v Kurt A Becher GmbH & Co KG*[37], a case dealing with tender of bills of lading mis-stating the date of shipment by only six to ten days, Kerr LJ put it thus:

> 'There is usually no difference whatever between goods loaded at the end of January instead of the beginning of February. The goods are the same. But this is not a trade in goods but in contracts for the shipment of goods. A January contract may be far more valuable than one for shipment in February. More important, on a plunging market the inability to present a bill of lading evidencing shipment within the contract period can have very serious financial consequences; the difference between the right to demand payment of the contract price on the one hand, and having to deal with "spot" goods of far lesser value, possibly involving considerable expenses in their disposal, on the other hand.'

---

[35] Ibid. For a contrary view, see Twentieth Century Developments in Commercial Law, R.M. Goode, (1983) 3 LS 283 at 285.

[36] *SIAT di dal Ferro v Tradax Overseas SA* [1980] 1 Lloyd's Rep 53 at 63.

[37] [1988] 2 Lloyd's Rep 21 at 22. This case cannot, of course, be taken to support the general proposition that any defect, however minor, in the documents tendered by the seller entitles the buyer to repudiate the contract. The case related to a mis-statement as to the date of shipment and did not purport to lay down a general rule covering other defects in the documents.

(b) Arguments in favour of applying the rule

On the other side of the debate, two arguments can be put forward in favour of the view that the de minimis rule should apply to any documentary breach by a seller under a shipment sale; and three authorities can be cited as lending it some degree of support. The arguments are based respectively on the avoidance of sharp practice and on the desirability of consistency between the physical and documentary duties imposed upon the seller; and the authorities are the first instance judgments of MacKinnon J in *Jydsk Andels-Foderstofforretning v Grands Moulins de Paris*[38]; of McNair J in *Moralice (London) Ltd v ED & F Man*[39]; and of Slynn J in *Tradax Internacional SA v Goldschmidt S.A.*[40]

The first argument has in effect already been referred to in this section of this chapter. If all documentary duties were categorised as conditions and if the rigour with which the law visits breach of such terms were not tempered at least by the de minimis rule, then the buyer's opportunity for extracting himself with more law than merit on his side would be large. Application of the de minimis rule would allow at any rate some room for the judge to bring a degree of discretion to bear against trumped up defects the real purpose of which is to harass the seller into a cheaper price.

The second argument is closely linked to the first. The judges already retain a small window of discretion through which to apply the de minimis rule where a seller is in breach of a condition imposing a duty as to the physical delivery of the goods. Thus, even in *Arcos Ltd v EA Ronaasen & Son*[41], a case where rejection of a cargo of timber was upheld by the House of Lords on the basis of breaches which were measured in fractions of an inch, Lord Atkin suggested that

> '[n]o doubt there may be microscopic deviations which businessmen and therefore lawyers will ignore.'[42]

If the de minimis rule, the argument runs, applies to those duties of the seller which relate to the goods, should it not also apply to those duties which relate to the documents?

---

[38] (1931) 39 Ll L Rep 223.
[39] [1954] 2 Lloyd's Rep 526.
[40] [1977] 2 Lloyd's Rep 604.
[41] [1933] AC 470. The readiness with which the House of Lords in this case treated a term that timber should be of a given dimension as a condition, and its breach by a marginal amount repudiatory, has been called suspect after more recent case-law: see *The Sale of Goods*, P. S. Atiyah, 7th edn, pp 98 and 52-57. The point of the case in the text above, though, remains intact, namely that even here, at the high water mark of the rigid application of the law on conditions, the House of Lords were prepared to countenance the application of the de minimis rule. Indeed, it applies a fortiori in the more relaxed atmosphere described by Professor Atiyah at pp 52-57 of his work.
[42] [1933] AC 470 at 479. The de minimis rule applies also to the seller's duty to tender the goods in the quantity agreed in the contract of sale: *Shipton, Anderson & Co v Weil Bros & Co* (1912) 17 Com Cas 153.

(c) The cases

All three authorities cited above as lending support to the proposition that the de minimis rule applies to all documentary duties in shipment sales fall well short of clearly establishing that proposition as a rule of law. In the first, *Jydsk Andels-Foderstofforretning v Grands Moulins de Paris*[43], a buyer was held by MacKinnon J not to have been entitled to repudiate a contract of sale which the seller had broken by shipping goods in excess of the amount stipulated for and by tendering a weight certificate for that excessive amount: the buyer could not repudiate because the excess in question came within the de minimis rule. There is no indication in the report of the case whether the judge treated the issue as one of rejection of goods or as one of rejection of documents. In truth, it was unnecessary for the judge to make such a distinction, for the facts were such that the offending document—a weight certificate—arrived (and was rejected) as the goods were being discharged (and rejected). Consequently, the case might just as well be authority for the proposition that the de minimis rule applies to the seller's physical duty to tender goods in the contract quantity[44] as of the other proposition—which is of more concern here—that it applies to his documentary duty as to quantity[45].

In the second case, *Moralice (London) Ltd v ED & F Man*[46], the plaintiff, a buyer/seller in the middle of a string, had been told by his seller, the defendant, that a bill of lading which was to be tendered under their contract of sale would show a slight discrepancy as to the amount of goods shipped. In view of that discrepancy, the plaintiff gave and honoured an indemnity to the bank paying under a letter of credit opened on the instructions of his buyer; the plaintiff had taken a similar indemnity from his seller, the defendant, and it was that second indemnity which the plaintiff now sought to enforce in this case. The defendant sought, unsuccessfully, to argue that the indemnity he had given the plaintiff was unenforceable for lack of consideration. Having decided that the indemnity was enforceable as a contract, McNair J then needed to establish that the indemnity fell to be enforced on its terms. For the second indemnity to apply, payment by the plaintiff under the first needed to be justified; the question, therefore, was: would the bank, apart from the indemnity given it by the plaintiff, have been entitled to reject the documents? McNair J decided[47] that the bank was entitled to reject and

---

[43] (1931) 39 Ll L Rep 223.

[44] See *Shipton, Anderson & Co v Weil Bros & Co* (1912) 17 Com Cas 153. Section 30(2) of the Sale of Goods Act, which expressly gives the buyer the right to reject either the excess or the whole quantity tendered, appears to be subject to the de minimis rule.

[45] The case was successfully cited before the Court of Appeal in *Margaronis Navigation Agency Ltd v Henry W Peabody & Co of London Ltd* [1965] 2 QB 430 as authority for the proposition that the de minimis rule could be invoked as much by a plaintiff as by a defendant: see pp 439F and 444B-C.

[46] [1954] 2 Lloyd's Rep 526.

[47] Loc cit at 532.

this because the de minimis rule did not apply in documentary credits. The judge added, by way of obiter, that the rule did apply as between the seller and the buyer 'if the contract was not complicated by the intervention of a letter of credit,'[48] giving as authority for that dictum the *Jydsk* case[49] cited above, a case which, as we have just seen, can just as easily be cited as authority for a quite separate proposition; and *Shipton, Anderson & Co v Weil Bros & Co Ltd*[50], a case which very clearly on its facts related to a breach by the seller of his physical duty to ship goods in the contract quantity rather than of his duty to tender documents in that quantity. The value of the case as authority for the proposition that the de minimis rule applies to all documentary duties imposed by shipment sales is consequently limited by two factors: firstly, McNair J's dictum in this regard was obiter, the position under the contract of sale being clearly incidental to the main issue, namely, was the bank entitled to reject; secondly, far from stating the proposition as one applying generally to documentary duties, McNair J took care to restrict its ambit to the seller's obligation regarding quantity.

In the third case, *Tradax Internacional SA v Goldschmidt SA*[51], the sale contract stipulated for shipment of barley containing no more than 4% foreign matter and for tender of shipping documents including a certificate of quality. When the goods arrived, the buyers learnt that the certificate of quality, which had not at that stage reached them, confirmed that the barley contained 4.10% foreign matter; the buyers rejected the documents on their subsequent arrival. After discharge of the goods at their destination, the buyers sold the goods for the sellers' account at price lower than the contract price: the sellers sued the buyers for the difference. Finding for the sellers, Slynn J held that the buyers were not entitled to reject the certificate of quality; or that if they were, they were estopped by their conduct from doing so. The buyers were, it seems, not entitled to reject the certificate of quality because it was a 'good' certificate, 'it [did] what it was intended to do' by showing 'that there was not a full compliance with the contractual term as to quality'[52]; moreover, the breach attested to by the certificate was within the de minimis rule and that it could 'not be treated as entitling a rejection either of a quality final certificate . . . or the goods.'[53] Slynn J went on to hold that even if the buyers were entitled to reject the certificate of quality because it did not conform to the contract, they had waived their right so to do because they had initially accepted the goods on arrival fully aware that the goods and the certificate of quality did not meet the contract specification as to foreign matter. It is the first part of the ratio which is directly relevant, for it is clear that of the three cases here examined, this is the one which comes closest to establishing that the de minimis rule applies to documentary duties. It is suggested

---

[48]   Ibid.
[49]   (1931) 39 Ll L Rep 223.
[50]   (1912) 17 Com Cas 153.
[51]   [1977] 2 Lloyd's Rep 604.
[52]   Loc cit at 612.
[53]   Loc cit at 613.

with respect, though, that the premise upon which the first part of the ratio is based is flawed by a misconception as to what constitutes a 'good' document. A 'good' document is not one which simply does what it is intended to do, but one which also does it in the manner stipulated in the contract. Thus, a bill of lading stating shipment out of time does what it is intended to do: it attests shipment on board on a given date; but it does not do it in the manner stipulated in the contract and, as we have seen[54], it can therefore be rejected. By parity of reasoning, the certificate of quality here was a certificate of quality, it was a bad certificate of quality and it could therefore be rejected[55]. If this is correct, then the authority of the first part of Slynn J's judgment must be suspect, although the result is, with respect, amply justified by the second part of the ratio, based on estoppel[56].

(d) Should the rule apply?

Given that the debate has not, as yet, been settled by authority, which of the two views is preferable? It is suggested that the de minimis rule ought not to be applied to the seller's documentary duties in shipment sales; and this, for the following reasons. It would be helpful to start with the mischief which the application of the de minimis rule is said to avoid, namely sharp practice by the buyer against a plunging market, and then to work our way backwards, as it were, from there. The buyer's reaction to tender of documents which fail to conform, in a minor way, to the contract of sale will depend, of course on whether or not that defect appears on the face of the documents; and on whether or not it is commercially desirable to repudiate the contract. It would also be helpful to isolate the different situations such considerations might give rise to.

The target of the de minimis rule in this area is the buyer who first accepts a bill of lading giving, say, '101 tonnes' as the quantity shipped, tendered under a contract providing for the shipment of 100 tonnes;

---

[54] *Re General Trading Co and Van Stolk's Commissiehandel* (1911) 16 Com Cas 95.

[55] It is possible that the argument rehearsed in the text was not open to Slynn J because the buyers appear to have accepted that the provision as to impurities was not part of the description of the goods: given that concession by the buyers, it would be difficult to argue that it could be rejected for the same reason that a bill of lading wrongly describing the date of shipment could be rejected. For this somewhat surprising concession, see [1977] 2 Lloyd's Rep 604 at 612; and see Benjamin, para 1727, for a view supportive of this part of Slynn J's judgment. It is interesting to contrast the concession made by the buyers in this case with that made by the sellers in *Vargas Pena Apezteguia Y Cia SAIC v Peter Cremer GmbH* [1987] 1 Lloyd's Rep 394 at 395 and 396: in *Vargas v Cremer*, it was common ground between the parties that a certificate of quality showing a fat content of 15.73% could be rejected by buyers who had stipulated for shipment of a cargo containing no more than 15% fat content. The concession went unremarked, both before the Commercial Court and before the arbitrators who had gone on to find that there was 'no difference whatsoever' between the market value of the commodity containing 15.73% and 15% fat content.

[56] As to which, see the discussion on *Panchaud Freres SA v Etablissements General Grain Co* [1970] 1 Lloyd's Rep 53, at Chapter 9.4.(c), below.

the market price having dropped, the buyer now, whether before or after arrival of the goods at the port of discharge, purports to repudiate the contract on the ground that the seller had tendered non-conforming documents. The de minimis rule would, it is said, prevent the buyer from so doing because, just as shipment of one extra tonne is a microscopic deviation[57], so is tender of a bill of lading stating such excess. The result would be the same, however, even if the de minimis rule were not applied to the seller's documentary duty in this case. For as we shall see[58], a buyer who accepts documents defective on their face is in certain circumstances estopped from later repudiating the contract: *Panchaud Freres SA v Etablissements General Grain Co*[59]. It seems, therefore, as if the de minimis rule is not necessary to prevent the sharpest form of practice which its proponents would employ it to avoid.

The rule in *Panchaud Freres*[60] does not, of course, apply in two slightly more complicated sets of circumstances. The buyer may, for example, decide promptly on tender of a bill of lading defective on its face to reject the document on the ground of a minor discrepancy: only de minimis would prevent such a buyer from terminating the contract for purely commercial reasons. Again, the defect in the document may not be as blatant as that given in the illustration above: it may not appear on the face of the document, as where, for example, the shipment is mis-stated by, say, one day, concealing a breach by the seller of his duty physically to ship within the contract period. We shall see later[61] that a buyer hoodwinked into accepting the documents in such circumstances can sue for damages for having been deprived of the opportunity of rejecting the documents: *Kwei Tek Chao v British Traders and Shippers Ltd*[62]. Again here, a judge inclined to throw out an action for recovery of such damages where it has been brought clearly for the purpose of capitalising on a drop in the market could not use *Panchaud Freres*[63] against the buyer: the judge would need de minimis. These two situations therefore raise the question of principle: should the buyer be entitled to reject, in the first case; and should he be entitled to recover damages for breach of the seller's documentary duty in the second, simply on the pretext of a minor defect in the documents?

To deprive the buyer of those remedies by applying the de minimis rule in these circumstances would be to ignore, it is suggested, an essential difference between the seller's physical duties and his documentary duties in shipment sales. The seller performs his physical duties in an imperfect world of commodities difficult to measure and of port operations difficult

---

[57] Lord Atkin's phrase in *Arcos Ltd v EA Ronaasen & Son*, see text accompanying fn 41, above.
[58] At Chapter 9.4.(c), below.
[59] [1970] 1 Lloyd's Rep 53.
[60] Ibid.
[61] At Chapter 9.4.(c), below.
[62] [1954] 2 QB 459.
[63] [1970] 1 Lloyd's Rep 53.

to control. It would be pedantry of the highest order to require perfect tender of the seller in respect of these duties. The same does not follow with regard to the seller's documentary duties. The point is not so much that shipping documents are completed and collected in a clinically careful environment: speed is and has to be very much of the essence, at the cost of precision and accuracy. The point, rather, is that accuracy is the only possible form of performance in the context of duties which are, by definition, a matter essentially of form. Both parties have, after all, chosen to trade on shipment terms, that is to say, on terms involving the tender of documents; both parties have contracted for the delivery not only of physical goods but also of pieces of paper, precisely described and therefore accurately to be tendered. As Kerr LJ put it in the *Procter & Gamble* case[64], 'this is not a trade in goods but in contracts for the shipment of goods': once the parties have elected to trade not only in goods, but also in contractual rights symbolised by documents, then the only form of tender can and must be perfect tender. Finally, it must, surely, be a nonsense to suggest that tender of documents under a letter of credit must be perfect, but not that under a contract of sale: these contracts operate together and the business community is ill-served by commercial law if such divergent answers were given to what is essentially the same question[65]. For all these reasons, it is suggested that the de minimis rule does not qualify the seller's duty to comply strictly with those conditions expressed or implied in a shipment sale relating to the tender of documents.

3. BUYER'S REMEDY OF REJECTION: PRACTICAL CONSTRAINTS

Throughout the first two parts of this chapter, reference has been made, albeit somewhat obliquely, to the buyer's dual rights of rejection which flow from the seller's dual modes of performance, namely physical and documentary. Having argued that documentary duties are in the nature of conditions, breach of which always entitles the buyer to repudiate the contract, we need now to examine what that option—repudiation— actually means in the context of a contract performed through two methods which rarely, if ever, coincide in time. Blandly to state that the buyer has the option, on the occurrence of a documentary breach by the seller, to repudiate the contract is to ignore the simple fact that a buyer might not, at the time the documents are tendered, wish to repudiate before he has had an opportunity to examine the goods when they arrive[66]. Again, where a sale contract is performed partly through

---

[64] [1988] 2 Lloyd's Rep 21 at 22.

[65] Contrast the views of McNair J in *Moralice (London) Ltd v ED & F Man* [1954] 2 Lloyd's Rep 526 at 532 to those of Megaw LJ in *SIAT di dal Ferro v Tradax Overseas SA* [1980] 1 Lloyd's Rep 53 at 62.

[66] The buyer appears to be in something of a cleft stick because it is clear that he cannot, on the other hand, wait and see the goods before he pays the price: *E Clemens Horst Co v Biddell Bros* [1912] AC 18.

the tender of documents, the remedy of repudiation must take account of the fact that the buyer may simply not know, at the time of tender, that the document is defective and that he can therefore repudiate: this because documents can easily conceal breaches of contract in a way that physical goods cannot. It is these practical constraints which set repudiation in shipment sales apart from the same remedy in domestic sales, where the mode of performance, and therefore the manner of terminating the contract for its breach, is unitary; it is these practical constraints which make a unitary concept of repudiation quite inappropriate for contracts in which performance is sophisticated through the use of documents. The object of this part of the chapter is to unravel those practical constraints and thus to lay out the background for the examination, which follows in the next part of the chapter, of the dual rights of rejection possessed by a buyer in shipment sales.

In unravelling those constraints, it would be helpful to distinguish between two main sets of circumstances: where the documents reach the buyer before the goods do; and where the goods reach the buyer before the documents do. Within each of those two situations, we need again to separate two types of case: where the buyer notices a defect in the documents; and where he does not. Each of these four hypotheses will be examined in turn.

(a) Documents reach buyer before goods and buyer notices documentary defect

It clearly follows from what was said in the second part of this chapter that the buyer here has an option to repudiate the contract for breach of condition. Thus where, for example, the destination given in the bill of lading tendered by the seller is not the same as that agreed in the contract of sale, the buyer can reject the documents without having to wait and see whether or not the goods are actually delivered at the port of discharge agreed in the sale contract[67]. The buyer is in no sense bound, of course, to repudiate: against a stable, or indeed, a rising market, the buyer may well decide that, whatever his legal rights, it would make commercial nonsense to reject the documents, particularly if the defect appears to be insignificant. There is, however, as we shall see, a price to pay for acquiescence at this stage; for should the buyer later wish to repudiate the contract, say when the goods arrive, he may find himself barred from doing so by the doctrine of estoppel[68].

(b) Documents reach buyer before goods and buyer does not notice documentary defect

In this situation, the buyer has accepted the documents and he is therefore very likely to have paid the seller, whether directly, or indirectly through

---

[67] *SIAT di dal Ferro v Tradax Overseas SA* [1980] 1 Lloyd's Rep 53.

[68] *Panchaud Freres SA v Etablissements General Grain Co* [1970] 1 Lloyd's Rep 53. See Chapter 9.4.(c), below.

a bank where a letter of credit is in place. The buyer's option to repudiate raises two separate problems here. Firstly, a buyer who has parted company with the price in return for documents which appeared good on their face is hardly likely to be inclined to part company with the goods on arrival, even if the goods are defective through the seller's breach to ship goods in conformity with the sale contract. Thus, for example, if a buyer has paid the contract price for a bundle of documents including an inspection certificate falsely stating, say, the moisture content of a commodity to be within the tolerance allowed in the contract, he may not be so keen simply to reject the cargo on arrival, despite the excessive moisture in the shipment and irrespective of price fluctuations in the market. The price has been paid to the seller: to return the goods to him may appear to the buyer rather like rewarding a fraud with interest. Much better, surely, to accept the goods, realise their actual value and recoup the loss by way of an action in damages: we shall see in the next part of this chapter that this is precisely one of the results which flows from there being two rights of rejection rather than one.

The second problem which the situation here discussed raises is rather less one of commercial judgment and rather more one of policy. The defect in the documents which the buyer failed to notice on tender may have had absolutely no effect on the physical condition of the goods themselves. This can be illustrated by the following example: a bill of lading is tendered, and paid for, wrongly stating the goods to have been shipped within the contract period; the goods were shipped one day outside the contract period; yet no physical loss is caused to the goods themselves; indeed, the goods are accepted by the buyer, who subsequently learns of the mis-dating of the bill of lading. In circumstances where the buyer has accepted tender of the documents and delivery of the goods, should he be able now to raise any complaint at all with the buyer? Does his acceptance of both modes of performance tendered by the seller not now estop him in some way from taking action? On the other hand, however, if the buyer were estopped, would this not lead to the result that a seller doubly in breach is in no way liable to the buyer? Again, we shall see presently that both results are avoided by the proposition that the two rights of rejection operate independently the one from the other and that the buyer's reaction to tender of the goods (in our example, acceptance) when he did not know of the defect in the documents (in our example, the statement of timely shipment where shipment was late) does not bar his right to compensation for market loss by having been deprived of the opportunity to repudiate the contract on tender of the documents.

(c) Goods reach buyer before documents and buyer notices documentary defect

In this case, the buyer notices on tender of documents the documentary defect putting the seller in breach: consequently, he is unlikely at this stage to pay, much less to have paid, the price. One might have thought, therefore, that rejection of the documents would be the obvious, and the only, answer. What, however, has happened to the goods in the meantime? In the hypothesis here examined, they reach the port of discharge before the documents reach the buyer. Where the buyer rejects the goods on arrival, for example because they were not shipped in accordance with the specifications agreed in the contract of sale, then the buyer clearly can and will reject the documents when they arrive. There is any number of reasons, however, why the buyer might have accepted the goods. Firstly, the goods may have been 'defective', in the sense that they did not tally with their description in the contract of sale, in a manner quite undiscoverable by the buyer at the time of discharge: this is likely to be the case where, for example, the goods have been shipped late. Secondly, the buyer may simply have decided to accept the goods, albeit defective through the seller's breach, for compelling commercial reasons: he may, for example, have an accommodating buyer further down the string; or he may himself find some other use to which he could put the defective goods, particularly if the market price for the commodity is rising. Thirdly, and most obviously, the buyer might have accepted the goods because they conformed to the stipulations agreed in the contract of sale: the documents might, nonetheless, be defective in a way clearly discoverable on arrival, as they would be, for example, if the bill of lading inaccurately states the goods to have been shipped outside the contract period[69]. Each of these three cases raises the same question: can the buyer reject the documents on arrival despite having first accepted the goods? We shall see presently that the answer depends in each case on the independent existence of the two rights of rejection and on the precise relationship between those two rights.

(d) Goods reach buyer before documents and buyer does not notice documentary defect

Again here, if the buyer has rejected the goods on arrival, then, of course, he can and will reject the documents on tender. However, the buyer may here too have accepted the goods for any of the three reasons given in the previous paragraph. The situation here envisaged differs from the previous one, though, in that here the buyer is hoodwinked into accepting the documents when they arrive because the defect in the documents is undiscoverable on their face, as it would be, for example, where the date of shipment is inaccurately stated to have occurred within the shipment period. The question which arises in this case is similar to the one raised in connection with situation (ii) discussed above and it is this: if the buyer has accepted the goods, for whatever reason, and has also accepted the documents, is he then estopped from claiming recovery of any loss suffered either by the fact that he has accepted the goods or by the fact that he has accepted the documents? The negative answer which the law gives to that question is a direct result of the

---

69 As happened in *Re General Trading Co and Van Stolk's Commissiehandel* (1911) 16 Com Cas 95.

separate existence of the right to reject the documents and the right to reject the goods.

4. BUYER'S REMEDIES OF REJECTION: DOCUMENTS AND GOODS

Taken together, the four situations described above raise three main questions, each of them a direct result of the simple fact that goods and documents rarely reach the buyer at the same time. Firstly, how does the buyer's reaction to one mode of delivery by the seller affect, if at all, his rights regarding the other mode of performance yet to be tendered by the seller? Secondly, where the seller successfully presents documents which are defective in a manner undiscoverable by the buyer (for example, where the bill of lading mis-states the date of shipment of the goods), to what extent is the buyer to recover compensation for having been deprived of the opportunity at least to consider rejecting the documents? Thirdly, where the buyer accepts documents containing defects which he noticed, or at any rate should have noticed, on tender, what effect, if any, does that acceptance have on the buyer's right later to repudiate the contract? Each of these three questions will be discussed in turn.

(a) Independent rights of rejection

In *James Finlay & Co Ltd v NV Kwik Hoo Tong Handel Maatschappij*[70] the Court of Appeal established the proposition that a seller of documents under a contract on shipment terms[71] owes the buyer not only an obligation to deliver goods tallying with the contract specification, but also a separate duty to tender documents conforming with the contract; and that, consequently, breach of either duty made the seller liable to the buyer. The point in issue in the case related to the quantification of damages for breach of the documentary duty to provide a bill of lading accurately stating the date of shipment: that central aspect of the case will be dealt with in the next part of this section when we discuss quantification of damages for loss of the opportunity to reject the documents. Suffice it here to say that *Finlay*[72] established the existence of separate rights of rejection of documents and goods.

It was left to Devlin J in *Kwei Tek Chao v British Traders and Shippers Ltd*[73] to work out the sense in which the two rights of rejection are not only separate but also independent: acceptance by the buyer of the

---

[70]   [1929] 1 KB 400.
[71]   That is to say, it is suggested, such sale contracts, whether c i f or f o b , which provide for tender of documents by the seller to the buyer: see, for example, *Tradax Internacional SA v Goldschmidt SA* [1977] 2 Lloyd's Rep 604 and other cases cited in Benjamin, para 1885; see also, Benjamin, para 1886.
[72]   [1929] 1 KB 400.
[73]   [1954] 2 QB 459.

performance tendered by the seller in one mode does not necessarily estop the buyer from rejecting the performance tendered by the seller in another mode. The independence of the two rights of rejection works, as it were, both ways: acceptance of the goods does not preclude rejection of the documents; and acceptance of the documents does not preclude rejection of the goods[74].

The crucial facts of the case were that the buyers, through banks paying under a letter of credit, accepted tender of documents, including a bill of lading wrongly stating shipment of the goods to have occurred within the period allowed in the contract of sale. The buyers subsequently accepted the goods on their arrival at the port of discharge. At the time the documents were negotiated through the banks, the buyers did not know that the goods had actually been shipped outside the contract period: indeed, the bill of lading gave them every reason to believe that shipment had been timely. At the time of arrival of the goods, though, it appeared that the buyers knew of the late shipment[75]: for reasons which will presently become clear, however, Devlin J was content to hold that knowledge of late shipment at this time was irrelevant to the 'broader grounds' on which his decision rested[76].

The buyers sued the sellers on two alternative causes of action, the relevant one[77] here being that for damages for breach of the sellers' contractual duty to tender a bill of lading accurately stating the date of shipment, that is to say, for breach of the separate documentary duty established in the *Finlay*[78] case. Counsel for the sellers argued against the application of the *Finlay*[79] case on the basis that here the buyers knew, at the time the goods were delivered, that the goods had not been shipped within the contract period, and that they therefore knew, at that time, that the bill of lading inaccurately stated the date of shipment. Devlin J held that, whether or not the buyers knew, at the time of delivery of the goods, that the goods had been shipped late, the fact of the matter was that they did not know, at the (earlier) time of tender of the documents, that the bill of lading was defective: it was for breach of the documentary duty that the buyers were seeking recovery and their right to recovery for that breach survived the buyers' later acceptance, possibly in full

---

[74] The case also raises the issue of quantification of damages where the buyer seeks compensation for having been deprived of the opportunity to reject the documents because the defect in the documents, eg mis-stating the date of shipment, is undiscoverable by the buyer at the time of tender. That aspect of the judgment will be examined in the next subsection of this chapter.

[75] There seems to have been some question as to this: contrast [1954] 2 QB 459, report of the facts at 463, and Devlin J's judgment at 473–4, 480 and 493; see Benjamin, para 1766, fn 19.

[76] [1954] 2 QB 459 at 480.

[77] The buyers' alternative cause of action was for repayment of the price as a claim for a consideration that had wholly failed; this claim was unsuccessful because Devlin J held that the mis-statement on the bill as to the date of shipment did not render the bill a nullity: see [1954] 2 QB 459 at 475, 476.

[78] [1929] 1 KB 400.

[79] Ibid.

possession of the facts, of the sellers' other mode of performance, namely acceptance of the goods. The crux of this part of the judgment is to be found in the following passage, which is cited in extenso because of its significance in the literature on the subject:[80]

> 'Here, ..., there is a right to reject documents and a right to reject goods, and the two things are quite distinct. A c i f contract puts a number of obligations upon the seller, some of which are in relation to the goods and some of which are in relation to the documents. So far as the goods are concerned, he must put on board at the port of shipment goods in conformity with the contract description, but he must also send forward documents, and those documents must comply with the contract. If he commits a breach the breaches may in one sense overlap, in that they flow from the same act. If there is a late shipment, as there was in this case, the date of the shipment being part of the description of the goods, the seller has not put on board goods which conform to the contract description, and therefore he has broken that obligation. He has also made it impossible to send forward a bill of lading which at once conforms with the contract and states accurately the date of shipment. Thus the same act can cause two breaches of two independent obligations.
>
> 'However that may be, they are distinct obligations, and the right to reject the documents arises when the documents are tendered, and the right to reject the goods arises when they are landed and when after examination they are found not to be in conformity with the contract. ...
>
> 'It follows, therefore, as a matter of principle, that the action of the plaintiff on the second breach cannot affect his right to damages on the first breach. They are distinct not merely in law, but also as a matter of business. Having a right to reject the documents separately from a right to reject the goods, it is obvious that as a matter of business very different considerations will govern the buyer's mind as he applies himself to one or other of those questions. When he has to make up his mind whether he accepts the documents, he has not parted with any money. If he parts with his money and then has to consider whether to reject the goods, wholly different considerations would operate. In the interval he may have had dealings with the goods; he may have pledged them to his bank, he may have agreed to resell the specific goods, and the position may have been entirely altered.'

For these reasons, both theoretical and practical in nature, Devlin J decided that the buyer's acceptance of the goods did not preclude him from rejecting documents, or rather, given that the defect in the documents was undiscoverable on tender, from recovering damages for having been deprived of the opportunity, at the time of tender of the documents, of rejecting those documents. Although the reverse proposition, namely

---

[80]   [1954] 2 QB 459 at 480–482.

that acceptance of the documents does not estop the buyer from later rejecting the goods did not arise for decision, the terms of Devlin J's judgment were clearly wide enough to support it[81]: this much was clearly acknowledged in *Bergerco USA v Vegoil Ltd*[82], where buyers who had accepted documents on tender were held entitled later to reject the goods on arrival.

The separate and independent existence of the two rights of rejection resolves the questions posed in situations (ii), (iii) and (iv) in the previous section of this chapter. Those questions, it will be recalled, were raised by the practical constraints which would fetter the buyer's right of repudiation if that right were unitary and if it had to be availed of on first tender by the seller, that is to say, if the option had to be exercised whenever the goods or the documents reached the buyer, whichever was the first.

Thus, in situation (ii), where the documents, arriving before the goods, contain a defect undiscoverable[83] by the buyer, the following three

---

[81] The progress of the argument before him was such that Devlin J felt constrained to discuss, (see [1954] 2 QB 459 at 484–489), by way of obiter, the workings of the reverse proposition on the hypothesis that, contrary to his view, there was but one right of repudiation in shipment sales. If that were the position, would any dealing with the documents constitute 'an act ... inconsistent with the ownership of the seller' within the terms of s 35 of the Sale of Goods Act 1979, the effect of which would be, in terms of that section, to preclude rejection of the goods? The question is of practical significance where a letter of credit is in place, as it was in the *Kwei Tek Chao* case itself: [1954] 2 QB 459; for under a letter of credit, it is common for the documents to be held by the banks in pledge: see Chapter 2.3.(d), above. Devlin J said that, on the given hypothesis, neither pledge nor, indeed, transfer of the bill of lading would be 'an act ... inconsistent with the ownership of the seller' within the terms of s 35; this, because where a bill of lading was transferred to a buyer, the most he could obtain by way of property (that is to say, subject to any express clause in the sale contract) was a conditional property, subject to the condition that the property would revert to the seller on rejection of the goods by the buyer: see *Kwei Tek Chao* [1954] 2 QB 459 at 487; *The Playa Larga* [1983] 2 Lloyd's Rep 171 at 187; and *Gill & Duffus SA v Berger Inc* [1984] 1 Lloyd's Rep 227 at 233. Consequently, the seller retained throughout a reversionary interest: and it was with that reversionary interest that the buyer could perform no act which was inconsistent. Thus, pledging the documents to a bank, or transferring them to a buyer further down a string, were both acts themselves subject to the condition of reversion to the seller, and could not, therefore, be inconsistent with the seller's reversionary interest. A contrariu sensu, the taking of physical possession of the goods by the buyer and the physical delivery of those goods to a sub-buyer would conflict with the seller's reversionary interest and would, consequently, bar the buyer from rejection by virtue of s 35 of the Sale of Goods Act 1979, so long as the buyer had had an opportunity to examine the goods as provided by s 34 of the Act.

[82] [1984] 1 Lloyd's Rep 440, particularly at 445, 446. See, for a discussion of other questions raised by this case, Chapter 6.3.(a).i, above.

[83] Where the defect, though hidden in the document, is actually 'discovered' by the buyer before acceptance, the buyer cannot reject the documents on this ground, for example, where the bill of lading mis-states shipment to have occurred within the shipment period: to allow him to reject the documents there and then in these circumstances would, in Lord Diplock's words in *Gill & Duffus SA v Berger Inc* [1984] 1 Lloyd's Rep 227 at 231, 'destroy the very roots of the system by which international trade ... is enabled to be financed.' The editors of Benjamin suggest at para 1675 that this is inconsistent with the independence of the two rights of rejection, presumably on the basis that if the buyer can prove the seller's breach of a documentary duty, he

propositions result from the separate and independent existence of the two rights of rejection. Firstly, acceptance of the documents does not preclude later rejection of the goods. We saw, however, that as the buyer is likely to have paid the price in return for the documents, he is quite unlikely to reject the goods: the second proposition, consequently, is that acceptance of the goods does not preclude an action by the buyer for damages for having been deprived of the opportunity to reject the documents on tender. Thirdly, compensation for loss of that opportunity can be claimed by the buyer even where the defect hidden in the document, for example, a statement inaccurately stating the goods to have been shipped within the contract period, had no physical effect on the goods.

In situation (iii), where the goods reach the buyer before the documents do, we saw that, even if the goods were in some way defective, the buyer might, for a number of different reasons, have chosen to accept the goods. Again here, acceptance of the goods by the buyer does not preclude later rejection by him of documents which he notices to be defective on tender.

In situation (iv), the defect in documents tendered after acceptance of the goods is undiscoverable by the buyer at the time of tender. Again, the separate and independent existence of the two rights of rejection means that the buyer's right vis-a-vis the documents is in no way prejudiced by his earlier acceptance of the goods: his right vis-a-vis the documents here, though, is clearly not so much a right to reject as much as one to recover compensation for loss of the opportunity to reject defective documents, that is to say, the same right to recovery which arose in situation (ii).

(b) Damages for loss of the opportunity to reject documents

Frequent mention has now been made of the buyer's right to recover compensation for the loss of the opportunity to reject documents which he has accepted where the defect is undiscoverable at the time of tender, for example where the bill of lading mis-states the time of shipment. We have seen that the right to such compensation is a direct result of the separate and independent existence of the two rights of rejection[84]:

---

should be able immediately to exercise the appropriate right of repudiation. Whether or not this follows as a matter of logic, it is suggested with respect that the policy considerations preferred by Lord Diplock are compelling; moreover, the buyer's interests are, as we shall presently see, adequately protected by his right to recover damages for the loss of the opportunity to reject the documents on tender: see Chapter 9.4.(b), below and Sale of Goods: Rules and Pseudo Rules, M. Arnheim, (1988) 132 Sol Jo 1130.

[84] It is sometimes suggested that the buyer might well have an alternative cause of action in tort, for fraudulent or negligent misrepresentation, where the seller himself has been responsible for the misstatement in the documents inducing acceptance by the buyer where rejection might have been more appropriate: see, for example, Goode, p 598. The absence of case-law illustrating the application of the two torts of misrepresentation in this field is not surprising: the documents commonly tendered by the seller to the buyer contain many representations made by third parties, but few, if any, by the seller himself. Even if a statement on a document originates with the seller, e g that relating to the quantity of goods shipped in a bill of lading, the statement is, at any rate on signature of the bill by the carrier, the carrier's statement, for which the seller cannot be held liable in the tort of misrepresentation.

our task now is to examine how such compensation is quantified. Three questions are here raised: firstly, what exactly is the loss for which the buyer is to be compensated and how does it differ from the loss caused by breach of the seller's physical duty to ship goods of the contract description? Secondly, do the damages recoverable by the buyer cover losses caused by fluctuations in the market price of the goods and, if so, fluctuations between which dates? Thirdly, can the buyer recover where the seller is only in breach of a documentary duty and where that breach causes no loss to the buyer?

i. The type of loss which can be recovered

Firstly, then, what exactly is the buyer's loss when he is deprived of the opportunity to reject the documents on tender? This is best arrived at by asking what the buyer might have done had he not been deprived of the opportunity to reject, that is to say, had the documents been genuine and shown on their face that the seller was in repudiatory breach of contract: for example, if the seller had tendered a bill of lading clearly stating that the goods had been shipped outside the contract period. Where the market price for the goods is falling[85], a genuine bill of lading would have avoided loss to the buyer which might arise in three different ways. Firstly, where the buyer had bought the goods for his own use, he might have rejected the documents and bought the same type of goods, or even the same goods, at the current, lower market rate. Wright J put it in these terms in *James Finlay & Co Ltd v NV Kwik Hoo Tong Handel Maatschappij*[86]:

> 'The buyer ... has the right to reject the tender of documents and refuse to pay ... if the shipment is not made in the contract month. The effect of misdating the bill of lading is to deprive him of that right by rendering its exercise impossible, if he relies, as in practice he generally must rely, and in law is entitled to rely, on the accuracy of the bill of lading date. He takes delivery of the goods and pays for them, because on the face of the bill of lading he is bound to do so under the contract, whereas if the bill of lading showed because it was a true document that the sellers could not enforce the contract, because the shipment was out of date, the buyer could and would refuse the tender and could obtain the same goods at their market price, which I assume to be lower than the contract price, that is, at a great saving to himself.'

Secondly, where the buyer had bought the goods in order to satisfy sub-buyers under contracts further down a string, the buyer might have made a windfall by rejecting the documents, buying the same type of goods, or even the same goods, at the lower market price, and selling them to his sub-buyers at the higher price agreed in the original contract with

---

[85] Where the market price rises, the buyer suffers no loss because he and his sub-buyers, if there are any, have bought the goods at a cheaper price.

[86] [1928] 2 KB 604 at 612; affd at [1929] 1 KB 400.

the sub-buyers[87]. Indeed,—and this is the third way the buyer might incur loss through having accepted incorrectly completed documents—the buyer might not only lose the opportunity of a windfall, but might also end up with rejected goods, bought expensively, which he can only sell at the cheaper market price: this would happen if sub-buyers learn of the late shipment and reject the goods against the buyer, their seller, on that ground.

It was this third type of situation which occurred in *James Finlay & Co Ltd v NV Kwik Hoo Tong Handel Maatschappij*[88]: buyers successfully sued sellers for damages after having accepted documents including a bill of lading incorrectly stating shipment to have occurred within the contract period. The issue throughout the litigation was one of quantum rather than liability: could the buyers recover the difference between the value of the goods when shipment should have taken place under the contract and their value when shipment did take place in breach of contract; or could they recover the difference between the contract price and the price of the goods realised at auction when the buyers, having learnt of the defect in the documents, mitigated their loss by selling at the cheaper market price? Both Wright J and the Court of Appeal[89] held that the proper measure of damages was the latter: the former reflected the loss caused by the seller's breach of his duty to ship goods within the contract period, rather than that caused by the seller's breach of his duty to tender a bill of lading accurately stating goods to have been shipped within the contract period. Indeed, where the seller's liability was based not on the seller's documentary breach, but on his physical breach, the courts had no option but to apply the former measure of damages, namely, the difference between the value of the goods on the contractual date of shipment and their value on the actual date of shipment. Thus, in *Taylor & Sons Ltd v Bank of Athens*[90], on facts broadly similar to the *Finlay* case[91], McCardie J awarded only nominal damages to the buyer because there was no difference in value between the value of the goods when they were shipped and their value when they should have been shipped. The cases are distinguishable[92] on the ground that in *Taylor*[93], which came to the judge by way of a case stated by an arbitrator, the loss for which the judge awarded damages was that caused by the seller's breach of his duty to ship within the contractual

---

[87]   The buyer would only be in a position to do this, of course, where he had not already bound himself to deliver goods on a particular ship by having tendered a notice of appropriation: see Chapter 4.2, above.

[88]   [1929] 1 KB 400.

[89]   [1928] 2 KB 604 and [1929] 1 KB 400 respectively.

[90]   (1922) 27 Com Cas 142.

[91]   [1929] 1 KB 400.

[92]   And were, indeed, so distinguished: see per Greer LJ at [1929] 1 KB 400 at 414, and per Sankey LJ at 416, 417. See also Benjamin, paras 1764, 1765, and Damages for Breach of a cif Contract, G.H. Treitel, 1988 LMCLQ 457 at 458, for the view that in *Taylor*, there *was* no documentary breach in respect of which loss could have been claimed or recovered.

[93]   (1922) 27 Com Cas 142.

period, and not that caused by the seller's breach of his documentary duty.

ii. Market losses

The second question raised by the quantification of the loss of the opportunity to reject documents is whether the buyer is allowed to recover losses which appear to be caused by market fluctuations; and if so, between which dates is the market fluctuation to be taken into account? The question arises because here again there is a difference between the way the courts have quantified the loss of the opportunity to reject the documents and the way they have quantified the loss caused by a breach of the seller's duty to ship goods of the contract description. It is clear from *Taylor*[94] that, at any rate so far as concerns breach of the duty physically to ship the goods within the contract period, the buyer is not entitled to recoup losses resulting from market fluctuations: to permit such recovery would be to allow the buyer to avoid the effects of what has turned out to be a bad bargain, and contracting parties are taken to have assumed the risk of their bargains turning sour on them. McCardie J put it this way[95]:

> 'It is vital to observe that the loss must result from the breach of warranty, as distinguished from a loss through having entered into the contract. It does not extend, I think, to a case where the loss results not from the breach of warranty but from an unfortunate or improvident bargain which the buyer may have made. Market falls are not generally due to a vendor's default. ... To impose the burden of such a loss on the seller would be to saddle him with something for which he is wholly free from blame.'

On the other hand, so far as concerns the loss caused to the buyer who has been deprived of the opportunity to reject documents containing a hidden defect, it is equally clear that the courts have had no such qualms about allowing recovery for what appear to be market losses. Thus, as we have seen, in the *Finlay* case[96], the buyer recovered the difference between the contract price and the price realised when the buyers sought to mitigate their loss by selling the goods at auction. This sum appeared to guard the buyer against a drop in market price between the time of contract and the time of the auction, which drop would otherwise have worked against him. Yet, no point as to market fluctuation was taken, either in argument or in the judgment. Again, in *Kwei Tek Chao v British Traders and Shippers Ltd*[97], the buyers recovered the difference between the contract price and the value of the goods when the buyers discovered that they could have rejected the documents had they known of the mis-statement as to the date of shipment. The buyers here, it will be recalled, had accepted the goods. They could not sensibly

---

[94] Ibid.
[95] Loc cit at 147.
[96] [1928] 2 KB 604; affd [1929] 1 KB 400.
[97] [1954] 2 QB 459.

sell the goods at auction because the market for the commodity had collapsed. The judge consequently awarded the difference between the market price and a very low salvage value for the goods, which on the figures in the case left the buyers with a substantial sum in damages. Again here, the buyers appear to have recovered a sum compensating them for having entered into a contract which subsequently turned out to be a bad bargain: yet not a voice was raised on this score, either in the argument or in the judgment[98].

How can the awards in *Finlay*[99] and in the *Kwei Tek Chao* case[100] be reconciled with the principle in *Taylor & Sons Ltd v Bank of Athens*[101] that a drop in the market is not a loss with which the buyer can saddle the seller? The question is raised in the main work on damages, *McGregor on Damages*, which suggests[102] that the buyer in each of the first two cases was 'claiming to be put into the position he would have been in not if the contract had been performed but if it had never been made.'[103] Recovery of such a claim was clearly out of kilter with the general principles of compensation in contract claims and the Court's view was, it is further suggested[104], 'based on compromise rather than on logic.' Such criticism of *Finlay*[105] and of *Kwei Tek Chao*[106] ignores, with respect, the crucial fact that a sale contract on shipment terms involves performance through two means, physical and documentary. Thus, the buyers in these cases were not claiming to be put in the position they would have been in had the contract not been made: they were not claiming protection from market movements. By recovering what might appear to be a market loss, they were rather claiming to be put in the position they would have been in had the documentary aspect of the contract been performed, that is to say, had the seller tendered an accurate bill of lading. Had the sellers performed, the buyers would indeed have been

---

[98]   The only judicial voice which seems to have been raised objecting to recovery based on *Finlay* principles is that of Donaldson J (as he then was) in *The Kastellon* [1978] 2 Lloyd's Rep 203, particularly at 204 and 207, where the judge characterises recovery on such grounds as based on a 'technicality' and on 'little merit.' The value of the case in terms of its authority on the question discussed in the text is limited: the question before Donaldson J was not whether *Finlay* should prima facie apply or how; but whether a force majeure clause in the contract protected the sellers from liability.

[99]   [1929] 1 KB 400.

[100] [1954] 2 QB 459.

[101] (1922) 27 Com Cas 142.

[102] *McGregor on Damages*, H. McGregor, 15th edn, London, 1988, para 831.

[103] A slightly different point is made by the editors of Benjamin, who are equally critical of the effect on the recovery of damages of *Finlay* and *Kwei Tek Chao*. At para 1769, they write: 'Such cases are, moreover, arguably inconsistent with the modern trend to restrict the right to reject where it is exercised simply for the purpose of escaping from a bad bargain: for to give a buyer damages for the loss of the right to reject puts him into the same financial position *as if he had indeed rejected*.' (Emphasis added.) It is suggested, with respect, that the arguments rehearsed in the text in answer to the criticisms of *Finlay* in *McGregor on Damages* also offer an answer to the criticism of the case in Benjamin.

[104] See fn 102.

[105] [1929] 1 KB 400.

[106] [1954] 2 QB 459.

able—and entitled—to purchase the goods at a lower market price. Viewed in that light, the 'market loss' was no more than the 'estimated loss directly and naturally resulting, in the ordinary course of events, from the breach' of which the rule in *Hadley v Baxendale*[107] and the Sale of Goods Act 1979[108] speak. The awards in *Finlay*[109] and *Kwei Tek Chao*[110] were thus the direct result of the breach of which the buyers complained, that is to say, the breach of the separate duty to tender genuine documents[111].

iii. Defect in the documents alone, causing no loss

The decisions in the *Finlay*[112] and *Kwei Tek Chao*[113] cases together indicate the high water mark of the separate existence of the right to reject the documents, for the loss of which right the law is prepared to award the buyer compensation through substantial damages. In both cases, the documentary breach which led to payment of the price, misstating the date of shipment—itself reflected a physical breach, shipping the goods outside the contract period. What, however, if the same documentary breach does not conceal a physical breach? What if the bill of lading inaccurately states the date of shipment in circumstances where both the stated date and the actual date fall within the contract period? Is the documentary duty to tender a genuine bill of lading so separate from the physical duty to ship within the contract period that the former gives the buyer a right of rejection, or, where the price is paid, a right to substantial damages, even where there is no breach of the physical duty to ship timeously? This, our third question relating to quantification, was anticipated by Greer LJ in *Finlay*[114] and was decided upon by the Court of Appeal in *Procter & Gamble Philippines Manufacturing Corpn v Kurt A Becher GmbH & Co KG*[115]. The question has also received attention in Benjamin, whose view against recovery[116] has now been vindicated by the decision in the *Procter & Gamble* case[117].

In the latter case, buyers had paid against documents inaccurately stating goods to have been shipped on 31 January; the goods were actually shipped on 6 and 10 February, both of which dates were within the contract period, which had been extended by agreement to 29 February.

---

[107] (1854) 9 Exch 341 at 354.
[108] At ss 51(2) and 53(2).
[109] [1929] 1 KB 400.
[110] [1954] 2 QB 459.
[111] See *Vargas Pena Apezteguia Y Cia SAIC v Peter Cremer GmbH* [1987] 1 Lloyd's Rep 394 at 399.
[112] [1929] 1 KB 400.
[113] [1954] 2 QB 459.
[114] [1929] 1 KB 400 at 412.
[115] [1988] 2 Lloyd's Rep 21.
[116] This is in line with Benjamin's generally restrictive attitude to recovery of damages on *Finlay* lines: see fn 103 above and Benjamin, para 1770; see also Damages for Breach of a c i f Contract, G. H. Treitel, 1988 LMCLQ 457, particularly at 459-462.
[117] [1988] 2 Lloyd's Rep 21.

The buyers claimed[118]substantial damages for breach of the seller's contractual duty[119] to tender a bill accurately stating the date of shipment; they sought quantification of their loss on the basis of *Finlay*[120]. The Court of Appeal found that, though the sellers were clearly in breach of their duty to tender a genuine bill of lading, the breach was not repudiatory because it did not conceal a breach of the physical duty to ship the goods within the contract period[121]. Once the documentary breach was not repudiatory, the buyers could only recover the loss caused by the mis-statement of the date of shipment on the bill, which was nil: consequently, the buyers received no damages at all.

The judgment is, with respect, clearly at odds with the separate existence of the seller's duty to tender genuine documents. If the breach complained of is documentary in nature, as it very clearly was both in *Finlay*[122] and in *Procter & Gamble*[123], then it is not immediately clear why the same documentary breach was any more serious in the first case than it was in the second, simply because in the first, the seller was also in breach of his physical duty to ship goods within the contract period. In terms of principle, either the two types of duty are separate, in which case, the losses caused by their breach are to be quantified separately; or they are not separate, in which case it is tenable to quantify out of existence the loss caused by a documentary breach because there has been no correspondent physical breach. Perhaps, it is of this case that it can be said, rather than of *Finlay*[124] or *Kwei Tek Chao*[125], that the reasoning is 'based on compromise rather than on logic;'[126] compromise, that is to say, between, on the one hand, a neat distinction between the two rights of rejection, and, on the other, a reluctance on the part of the judges to appear to be offering buyers an escape route from improvident bargains.

This tension between principle and policy can, it is suggested with respect, be felt in the terms of the judgment itself. Thus Kerr LJ is at pains to point out that the buyer in the position of *Procter & Gamble* might, in some circumstances, have a right to substantial damages:[127]

---

[118] The progress of proceedings from arbitration, where the buyers appear to have been the claimants, to litigation, where the sellers were the plaintiffs, was long and somewhat tortuous: see [1988] 2 Lloyd's Rep 21 at 27. The crucial point before the Commercial Court (see [1988] 1 Lloyd's Rep 88) and before the Court of Appeal was whether the buyers had a right to substantial damages for having been deprived of the opportunity to reject the documents.

[119] The duty was expressed in GAFTA 100, clause 6; but the Court of Appeal was clearly of the view that the duty would have been implied in the absence of the express term: see fn 23 above.

[120] [1929] 1 KB 400.

[121] See [1988] 2 Lloyd's Rep 21 at 28–30 and 32.

[122] [1929] 1 KB 400.

[123] [1988] 2 Lloyd's Rep 21.

[124] [1929] 1 KB 400.

[125] [1954] 2 QB 459.

[126] See *McGregor on Damages*, H. McGregor, 15th edn, London, 1988, para 831.

[127] [1988] 2 Lloyd's Rep 21 at 30; see also, per Nicholls LJ at 33.

'For instance, a falsely dated bill of lading becomes effectively unmerchantable ... once its true date is known. Its presentation by the seller was a breach of contract even if the goods were in fact shipped during the contractual shipment period, as in the present case. In such circumstances it may well be possible for the buyers to show that they suffered loss as the result of this breach. Thus, they may have found themselves "locked in" on a falling market by holding a non-transferable bill of lading, when they might otherwise have been able to sell the goods afloat, albeit at substantially less than their original contract price. Alternatively, they might be able to show that if the bill of lading had been correctly dated they could have used it to to fulfil a previously concluded sub-sale covered by a notice of appropriation with which they were now unable to comply.'

It is not altogether obvious why the buyers in either of the two examples envisaged by Kerr LJ should be entitled to substantial damages, while the buyers in *Procter & Gamble*[128] itself were not.

Although there appears not to have been any sub-sale to trouble the buyers in that case, it is clear that they were 'locked in' on a falling market such that they could not sell the goods afloat by transferring the documents: they had, instead, to await the arrival of the goods and sell them at 57% of the contract price[129]. Again, loss of a sub-sale, Kerr LJ's second example of recoverable loss, is another perfectly typical type of damage against which the buyer seeks protection when he insists on performance by the seller of his separate documentary duty to tender a genuine bill of lading[130]. With respect, neither of the examples given by Kerr LJ is in any sense exceptional: they are the stuff of which the independent right of rejection of documents, tendered in breach of independent documentary duties, is made.

It is, with respect, unfortunate that leave to appeal to the House of Lords was refused in *Procter & Gamble*[131]. On the present state of the authorities, it is difficult to state the law with any greater degree of certainty than this. Where the buyer is hoodwinked into paying against inaccurate documents, he can recover substantial damages for having been deprived of the opportunity to reject the documents in two sets of circumstances: either, firstly, where the inaccuracy in the documents conceals a breach by the seller of the physical duty to ship the goods as stipulated in the contract; or, secondly, where, although the documents do not conceal such a breach, the inaccuracy in the documents causes

---

[128] [1988] 2 Lloyd's Rep 21.
[129] See [1988] 2 Lloyd's Rep 21 at 24.
[130] Indeed, the buyers in *Kwei Tek Chao* had lost a sub-sale because of late shipment: see [1954] 2 QB 459 at 462, 463.
[131] [1988] 2 Lloyd's Rep 21 at 33.

the buyer an identifiable[132] commercial loss which he would not have suffered had the documents been accurate.

(c) Loss through estoppel of the right to repudiate

In our discussion[133] of the practical constraints upon the buyer's right to repudiate a contract on shipment terms, our first hypothesis was one where the documents reached the buyer before the goods did and where the buyer noticed a documentary defect on tender. We saw that the buyer could repudiate the contract by rejecting the documents, on the ground, say, that the bill of lading was not dated within the shipment period; but that, despite the serious nature of this breach, he was also entitled to accept the documents, as well he might where, for example, the market price for the commodity was rising. What, however, if the market price dropped again by the time the goods arrived at the port of discharge? Could the buyer now reject the goods, either on the ground that the bill of lading tendered did not conform to the contract or on the ground that the goods were shipped late? It would appear to follow from the separate and independent existence of the two rights to reject documents and goods that the buyer's acceptance of the documents in these circumstances would in no way fetter his right later to reject the goods on arrival. On the other hand, to permit repudiation in these circumstances would seem to allow the buyer brazenly to blow hot and cold on the same event, late shipment, albeit one giving rise to two breaches, one physical, the other documentary. To examine how the courts have resolved this dilemma is our central task in this third part of our discussion of the buyer's two rights of rejection.

i. The doctrine of Panchaud Freres

The case-law on the question is dominated by the Court of Appeal's decision in *Panchaud Freres SA v Etablissements General Grain Co*[134]. In that case, the documents were tendered and accepted before the arrival of the goods; this, despite the fact that it was clear that the goods might have been shipped outside the contract period: the bill of lading was dated within the contract period, while a certificate of quality tendered with the bill indicated that the goods had been inspected ashore after the contract period. The buyers rejected the goods on arrival, eventually on the grounds that the goods had been shipped late and that the bill of lading had been falsely dated[135]. The buyers' claim for recovery of

---

132 There is some indication in *Procter & Gamble* that the buyers had not taken the trouble sufficiently clearly to identify the precise nature of their loss, being content rather piously to mouthe the *Finlay* incantation: see [1988] 2 Lloyd's Rep 30 and 32.

133 At Chapter 9.3, above.

134 [1970] 1 Lloyd's Rep 53. The point was anticipated by Devlin J in *Kwei Tek Chao v British Traders and Shippers Ltd* [1954] 2 QB 459 at 481.

135 The buyers had originally rejected the goods on grounds which might have justified action against the carrier rather than rejection against the sellers, namely, that the goods did not correspond to their description on the bill of lading: see [1970] 1 Lloyd's Rep 53 at 56.

the price was thrown out by the Court of Appeal[136] in a decision which needed to side-step two principles the application of which might otherwise have given victory to the buyers.

The first was the well-established principle that 'our commercial law sets its face resolutely against any doctrine of constructive notice'[137] and it came to be relevant to the dispute between the parties in this way. The crucial issue was whether the buyers were, by accepting documents which clearly cast doubt on the date of shipment, later precluded from rejecting the goods for late shipment or for tender of a bill of lading falsely stating shipment to have been timely. The doctrine of waiver would clearly have defeated the buyers in this case, were it not for the somewhat unhelpful terms in which the facts were found at arbitration: whilst the buyers had learnt that the goods were shipped out of time after tender, 'they cannot be deemed to have been unaware' of that fact and of the false dating of the bill of lading at the time of tender[138]. To have held that the buyers had waived their right to repudiate the contract on these grounds would, on such a finding, have been perilously close to holding that they had forfeited their right by failing to act on knowledge which they should have had (constructive notice), rather than on knowledge which they did actually have (actual notice). Lord Denning MR avoided the difficulty through two easy steps: rather than calling for the application of the doctrine of waiver, this case called for the application of another doctrine; and that other doctrine was not so rigorous in its requirement of actual as opposed to constructive knowledge[139]. Lord Denning put it thus[140]:

> 'The present case is not a case of "waiver" strictly so called. It is a case of estoppel by conduct. ... Applied to the rejection of goods, the principle may be stated thus: If a man, who is entitled to reject goods on a certain ground, so conducts himself as to lead the other to believe that he is not relying on that ground, then he cannot afterwards set it up as a ground of rejection, when it would be unfair or unjust to allow him so to do.'

Though lip-service was paid to the view that rights should not be allocated by commercial law on the basis of constructive notice[141], it was clear

---

136 The proceedings were long and protracted, involving as they did a reference to arbitrators, an umpire, the relevant trade's Committee of Appeal, a case stated to Roskill J, and finally an appeal to the Court of Appeal. Indeed, so lengthy were the proceedings that there seems to have been some confusion as to who initiated them. It is clear from the report of the case at first instance that the claim was one for recovery of the price, brought by the buyers: see [1969] 2 Lloyd's Rep 109 at 111 and 118. It seems quite unlikely that the sellers should have claimed damages from the buyers, pace Denning MR [1970] 1 Lloyd's Rep 53 at 56, since the buyers had paid the purchase price on tender of documents.

137 See [1970] 1 Lloyd's Rep 53 at 57 per Denning MR and cases there cited.

138 [1970] 1 Lloyd's Rep 53 at 56.

139 For a similar view, see Benjamin, paras 1731 and 1735.

140 [1970] 1 Lloyd's Rep 53 at 57; see also at 59, where Winn LJ describes the principle as 'a requirement of fair conduct, ... negativing any liberty to blow hot and cold in commercial conduct.'

141 See [1970] 1 Lloyd's Rep at 57 and 60.

that the Court of Appeal was quite happy to estop the buyer from repudiating the contract where he knew or should have known at the time of tender of the facts now alleged to justify repudiation[142].

The second principle which seemed to support the buyers' entitlement to reject the goods was that which states that the buyer's right to reject the goods is separate and independent of his right to reject the documents, and that therefore acceptance of the documents could not restrict the buyer's right to reject the goods, whatever the buyer knew or should have known at the time of tender. In essence, the question before the court was whether that general principle, which clearly responded as we have seen to a number of commercial needs[143], was restricted by the doctrine, pace Denning MR, of estoppel by conduct, or by the requirement, pace Winn LJ, of fair conduct in commercial dealings. The court was clearly of the view that the two rights of rejection were not as independent as the buyers in this case would wish them to be. Winn LJ put it in this way:[144]

> '[I]n one sense of language of course, where there is a condition that a bill of lading in accordance with the contract terms, and a genuine correct bill of lading, should be tendered, breach of that obligation is a breach of a condition relating to the tender of such a document, whereas failure to deliver goods which were in fact shipped timeously within the contract period is a breach of a different condition: that is so in one sense of language—in another sense, much more realistic when one is talking of commercial matters, they are both really breaches of the same condition, that is to say of shipment within the contract period; since the requirement of the contract that a bill of lading be tendered is related to the obligation to ship timeously as a convenient form of producing

---

[142] It is this aspect of the judgments in the case that has raised eyebrows in some quarters: see, for example, Benjamin, para 900. The judicial history of *Panchaud* has nonetheless been relatively trouble-free. The case has been judicially considered or applied on several occasions: e g *Woodhouse AC Israel Cocoa Ltd SA v Nigerian Produce Marketing Co Ltd* [1971] 2 QB 23; *Toepfer v Peter Cremer* [1975] 2 Lloyd's Rep 118. The strongest judicial expression of doubt about the principle stated in the case has come from Donaldson J (as he then was) in *The Vladimir Ilich* [1975] 1 Lloyd's Rep 322, where, at 329, the judge said that 'even if *The African Knight* [i e *Panchaud Freres*] represents an unjustified extension of the law', it was not for him in that case to consider that point. Indeed, Donaldson J himself had no qualms about applying *Panchaud* barely three years later in *The Shackleford* [1978] 1 Lloyd's Rep 191. There have, to be complete, been occasions where the judges have been careful not to apply *Panchaud* beyond the parameters set out by the Court of Appeal in the case itself: see *V Berg & Son Ltd v Vanden Avenne-Izegem PVBA* [1977] 1 Lloyd's Rep 499 at 504, 505, per Lawton LJ; and *The Proodos C* [1980] 2 Lloyd's Rep 390 at 392, per Lloyd J; and yet at least one other occasion where the Court of Appeal decided that a party could not be taken to have elected whether or not to terminate a contract for breach unless he actually knew both of the facts giving rise to the option and of the right of election itself: *Peyman v Lanjani* [1985] Ch 457, where *Panchaud* was cited neither in the judgments nor in the arguments.

[143] See Chapter 9.4.(a), above.

[144] [1970] 1 Lloyd's Rep 53 at 60–61.

evidence, or of enabling the matter to be dealt with in chain transactions: one is ancillary to the other.'

To call documentary and physical duties, breaches and remedies ancillary to each other is, perhaps and with respect, to overstate the point[145]. Clearly, though, the Court of Appeal was not prepared so to distil documentary rights and remedies as to detach them completely from their physical raison d'etre, the sale of physical goods.

ii. The effects of the doctrine

a. Buyer estopped from rejecting goods on similar grounds

With waiver and the independence of the two rights of rejection safely out of harm's reach, then, the primary effect of *Panchaud Freres*[146] appears to be that where the buyer learns or ought to have learnt from the documents, on tender, that a defect in the documents entitles him to reject them, and yet he does not so reject, he is estopped from later raising that defect, or the breach by the seller of the physical duty reflected in that defect[147], as grounds for rejecting the goods on their arrival[148]. Two

---

[145] See Benjamin, para 1724. It is also, perhaps and with respect, this way of thinking that led the Court to characterise their decision as in some way derogating from the rule that a party who repudiates a contract for the wrong reason, or for none at all, is not precluded from later setting up a legitimate cause for repudiation existing at the time of the repudiation. If a buyer on shipment terms has but one right to repudiate, then *Panchaud* would indeed qualify that rule, and some justification would need to be found accommodating the qualification: see, for such justification, Benjamin, para 1739. It is suggested that the answer is to be found differently. The buyer has two rights to repudiate a contract on shipment terms; those two rights are in principle separate and independent; it is that principle which the decision in *Panchaud*, for good reasons of policy, qualifies rather than the rule allowing a change of ground justifying repudiation. The latter rule is in any case somewhat difficult of application in the context of shipment sales which are performed through two separate modes, physical and documentary; and others have gone so far as to suggest that the rule is, as a matter of general law, illusory: see Sale of Goods: Rules and Pseudo Rules, M. Arnheim, (1988) 132 Sol Jo 1130. The issue has arisen in cases where the buyer has sought to defend himself in an action by the seller for wrongful rejection of documents by pleading, after an initial rejection on documentary grounds, that the seller was in breach of a physical duty to ship goods conforming to the contract. In such circumstances, it was held by the House of Lords that the buyer could not now plead the seller's physical breach to avoid his own liability for wrongful rejection of documents, although he could plead the effects of that physical breach in reduction of the quantum of his own liability towards the seller: *Gill & Duffus SA v Berger Inc* [1984] 1 Lloyd's Rep 227. See, generally, Benjamin, paras 670, 675, 1740–1748; and Rights of Rejection in c i f Sales, G.H. Treitel, 1984 LMCLQ 565.

[146] [1970] 1 Lloyd's Rep 53.

[147] See, in particular, [1970] 1 Lloyd's Rep 53 at 58, per Denning MR.

[148] Clearly, the result would be the same where the goods reach the buyer before the documents do and the buyer accepts the goods in the knowledge, actual or constructive, that, say, goods had been shipped containing more impurities than allowed by the contract: *Panchaud* would estop the buyer from later rejecting the documents on that particular ground of non-contractual shipment or on the ground that a non-contractual certificate of quality had been tendered: *Tradax Internacional SA v Goldschmidt SA* [1977] 2 Lloyd's Rep 604, discussed further at Chapter 9.2.(c), above. See, in a similar sense, *The Sale of Goods*, Atiyah, 7th edn, p 399. *Panchaud* was not cited in *Tradax*

other propositions appear to follow from the judgments in *Panchaud Freres*[149] neither of which arose for decision in the case itself: each will be taken in turn.

b. Buyer estopped from recovering damages for loss of the opportunity to reject

Firstly, it would seem to follow by parity of reasoning from the Court of Appeal's decision that a buyer who accepts documents knowing them to be defective cannot recover damages from the seller for having been deprived of the opportunity to reject the documents: in such a case, the buyer is not deprived by the documents of the opportunity to do so, but by his own conduct in having accepted knowingly defective documents. The state of the authorities on this proposition is at once interesting and uncertain. In its favour is the judgment of Saville J in *Vargas Pena Apezteguia Y Cia SAIC v Peter Cremer GmbH*[150]; against, the judgment of Cooke J in *Kleinjan & Holst NV Rotterdam v Bremer Handelsgesellschaft mbH Hamburg*[151]. In both cases, buyers accepted documents when aware of defects therein[152], both buyers reserving their rights as they did so; in neither case was *Panchaud Freres*[153] cited. The crux of the debate is this: should the decisions in *Finlay*[154] and *Kwei Tek Chao*[155], compensating the buyer for loss of the opportunity to reject the documents, apply whether or not the buyer knows of a defect in the documents when he accepts and pays for them?

Cooke J in *Kleinjan & Holst v Bremer Handels*[156] thought they should so apply, because:[157]

> '... the decision in *Finlay's* case lays down a general rule as to the measure of damages in cases where the sellers have broken a condition of the contract by failing to tender proper documents and the buyers, not having rescinded, are entitled to recover damages for the breach. The reasons why the buyers have not rescinded are immaterial.'

Moreover, the buyers had expressly reserved their rights when accepting the documents, and this reservation must have included the buyers' right

---

v Goldschmidt, but it is suggested that the later case, decided by Slynn J, is clearly an application of the earlier Court of Appeal authority.

[149] [1970] 1 Lloyd's Rep 53.
[150] [1987] 1 Lloyd's Rep 394.
[151] [1972] 2 Lloyd's Rep 11.
[152] In *Kleinjan & Holst v Bremer Handels* [1972] 2 Lloyd's Rep 11, the documents did not represent the same goods as those described in the first, valid but inaccurate, notice of appropriation. In *Vargas v Cremer* [1987] 1 Lloyd's Rep 394, a certificate of quality indicated that the fat content in the commodity exceeded that allowed by the contract: as to this aspect of the case, see fn 55, above.
[153] [1970] 1 Lloyd's Rep 53.
[154] [1929] 1 KB 400.
[155] [1954] 2 QB 459.
[156] [1972] 2 Lloyd's Rep 11.
[157] Loc cit at 22.

to damages resulting from the sellers' breach of their documentary duties[158].

Saville J in *Vargas v Cremer*[159] decided that *Finlay*[160] was inapplicable where the buyer knew at the time of tender that the documents were defective. Rather than founding that conclusion on *Panchaud Freres*[161], though, the judge went back to first principles: recovery for breach of contract was limited to those losses caused by such breach; and the loss for which the buyers sought recovery in the case was not caused by the sellers' breach but by the buyers' own conduct. Saville J put it in these terms:[162]

> 'If the buyers know of the breach, however, then the position is different [to *Finlay*], for without more there is then no causal connection between the breach and the loss of the right to reject. The buyers know that they may reject if they wish to do so—the breach does not cause them to accept the documents. In such a case to award damages where the documents have been accepted on the basis of the difference between the contract and market prices at the date of the breach is to award damages that simply do not flow from the breach.'[163]

As for the buyers' reservation of their rights when accepting the defective documents, Saville J was, with respect, almost coldly dismissive:[164]

> '... they can only reserve what rights they have—if they choose to accept the documents with knowledge of the breach, then the rights they have are the rights attached to that case, and not those that would exist if they had taken a different course of action.'

It is submitted with respect that the reasons given by Saville J for his decision against the buyers in *Vargas v Cremer*[165] are compelling, both in terms of principle and authority. In terms of policy too, the decision is powerful: for to award the buyers damages on *Finlay* principles[166] would have the effect of allowing the buyers to blow hot and cold on a contract upon which the market had turned sour; then indeed could it be said of the rule in *Finlay*[167] that it puts a buyer 'into

---

[158] Loc cit at 21.
[159] [1987] 1 Lloyd's Rep 394.
[160] [1929] 1 KB 400.
[161] [1970] 1 Lloyd's Rep 53.
[162] [1987] 1 Lloyd's Rep 394 at 399.
[163] Such an award, which had in fact been made by GAFTA's Board of Appeal, would, Saville J pithily says later in his judgment (at [1987] 1 Lloyd's Rep 394 at 399) be 'neither fair nor compensation.'
[164] [1987] 1 Lloyd's Rep 394 at 399.
[165] [1987] 1 Lloyd's Rep 394.
[166] As happened in *Kleinjan & Holst v Bremer Handelsgesellschaft mbH Hamburg* [1972] 2 Lloyd's Rep 11. The decision of Cooke J in this case meets with the approval of Benjamin, at para 1767; indeed, it must be said that this was one of the reasons why Saville J readily gave the buyers leave to appeal from his decision to the Court of Appeal: see [1987] 1 Lloyd's Rep 394 at 400.
[167] [1929] 1 KB 400.

the position he would have been in not if the contract had been performed but if it had never been made.'[168] Saville J expressed these policy considerations quite frankly:[169]

> '... the conduct adopted by the buyers was not the result of the breach—that conduct was not caused or dictated by the fact that the documents showed an excess of fat but doubtless by the fall in the market which was quite unrelated to the breach in this case...'

Although Saville J gave the parties leave to appeal from his judgment to the Court of Appeal, the case appears to have gone no further and consequently the law in this area remains uncertain.

c. Buyer not estopped from rejecting goods on other grounds

Secondly, it seems to follow a contrariu sensu from the Court of Appeal's decision in *Panchaud Freres*[170] that the buyer is not estopped from later rejecting the goods on their arrival on some other ground. Thus if, on the facts of *Panchaud*[171] itself, the moisture content in the goods were outside the contractual allowance and the certificate of quality, apart from accurately stating the late date of shipment, falsely stated that moisture content in the goods was within the contractual allowance, then the buyer would, surely, not be estopped from rejecting the goods against the seller[172]: the estoppel must be limited to the ambit of those defects which first gave rise to it.

The quantification of damages in this case could cause even more difficulty than it did in the two cases discussed above, namely, *Kleinjan & Holst v Bremer Handelsgesellschaft mbH Hamburg*[173] and *Vargas v Cremer*[174]. Quantification would here raise the same question: could the buyer recover damages on *Finlay*[175] lines for having lost the opportunity to reject the documents? The question is, however, complicated here by this distinguishing feature: in the two cases previously discussed, the buyers rejected the goods because of the physical defect underlying the documentary defect despite knowledge of which they had accepted the

---

[168] *McGregor on Damages*, H. McGregor, 15th edn, London, 1988, para 831.

[169] [1987] 1 Lloyd's Rep 394 at 399.

[170] [1970] 1 Lloyd's Rep 53. See also Benjamin, para 1735.

[171] [1970] 1 Lloyd's Rep 53.

[172] In a similar sense, see Benjamin, para 1735. It is in this type of case that the buyer's right to examine the goods, enshrined in s 34 of the Sale of Goods Act 1979, retains any relevance to those shipment sales where the seller is under an obligation to tender documents and ship goods; for it is only through the survival of this right of examination beyond the acceptance of documents that the buyer can discover another legitimate cause for rejecting the goods: see Benjamin, para 1736. In other types of case, ss 34 and 35 (Acceptance) of the 1979 Act 'are not easy to apply to c i f contracts, in which there are separate rights to reject the goods and the documents:' Benjamin, paras 911 and 1735. Where the seller is under no duty to tender documents, e g in straight f o b contracts, then of course this difficulty does not arise: see Benjamin, paras 1886-1890.

[173] [1972] 2 Lloyd's Rep 11.

[174] [1987] 1 Lloyd's Rep 394.

[175] [1929] 1 KB 400.

documents on tender[176]; here, though, the buyers reject the goods on a totally different ground (moisture content), bearing no relationship to the documentary defect of which they were aware when accepting the documents (date of shipment stated to be late). It is submitted that this distinction makes no difference to the thrust of Saville J's reasoning in *Vargas v Cremer*[177]: in the example given, the buyer lost his opportunity to reject the documents through his own conduct (accepting the documents knowing the certificate to state late shipment) rather than through the seller's breach (shipping goods with excess moisture); the buyer has deprived himself of that opportunity once and for all and he cannot now revive it through an action for damages saving him from the effect of his own conduct; he can now only recover damages for such loss as results directly from the seller's breach, namely the effect of the excess moisture on the value of the goods[178].

d. Summary of the effects of the doctrine

If the views expressed above are correct, then the overall effect of the Court of Appeal's judgment in *Panchaud Freres* can be summarised in the following four propositions:

(a) Where the buyer learns or ought to have learnt from the documents, on tender, that a defect in the documents entitles him to reject them, and yet he does not so reject, he is estopped from later raising that documentary defect, or the physical breach it reflects, as grounds for rejecting the goods on their arrival[179].

(b) Where the buyer accepts goods when aware, or when he should have been aware, that they were shipped in a defective condition, such that he was entitled to reject them, he is estopped from later raising that physical defect, or the documentary defect reflecting it, as grounds for rejecting the documents on their arrival[180].

(c) The buyer considered in the first proposition stated above is also estopped from claiming damages for having lost the opportunity

---

[176] In *Kleinjan & Holst v Bremer Handels*, neither the goods nor the documents coincided with what the seller had promised to deliver in his notice of appropriation; in *Vargas v Cremer*, the fat content in the goods exceeded the contractual allowance, and the certificate of quality said so.

[177] [1987] 1 Lloyd's Rep 394.

[178] A similar problem is caused by a slightly different type of case raised by the editors of Benjamin at para 1731. Where a buyer accepts documents unaware of a defect therein and then, having learnt of the defect in the documents, accepts the goods on arrival, it is there suggested that the buyer is estopped from rejecting the documents (by which is presumably meant 'from recovering damages for loss of the opportunity to reject', i e *Finlay* damages) 'on account of that defect'. It is submitted with respect that this does not go quite far enough. By accepting the goods in the knowledge that he might have repudiated the contract on account of a defect in the documents, the buyer forfeits once and for all his right to compensation for the loss of the opportunity to reject the documents on any ground; and this for the reasons given in the text above.

[179] See text accompanying fn 146 above.

[180] See fn 148 above.

to reject the documents on tender[181], and this remains so whatever other documentary defects later come to light[182].

(d) Such a buyer is not, however, estopped from rejecting the goods on arrival on the grounds of a physical breach by the seller, other than that reflected in the documentary defect of which the buyer was aware on tender; neither is he estopped from claiming damages for such other breach[183].

iii. Is the buyer estopped through actions of the bank?

Throughout our examination of the implications of the Court of Appeal's decision in *Panchaud Freres*[184], we have assumed that the buyer has accepted documents defective on their face directly from the hands of the seller. The discussion would be incomplete without asking whether the buyer's position vis-a-vis the seller is different where a letter of credit is in place.

Where the banks accept documents which are clearly defective on their face, they are in breach of the most fundamental obligation under the contract setting up the letter of credit, namely the duty to pay the sum of the credit only against documents conforming to the instructions given by the buyer[185]; and the buyer can clearly look to his remedies under the letter of credit for breach of that obligation. The question which arises here, though, is whether acceptance by the banks of patently defective documents in any way estops the buyer from taking action which he might otherwise have taken under the contract of sale: does the doctrine enshrined in *Panchaud Freres*[186] bite against the buyer when the patently defective documents have been accepted, not directly by the buyer himself, but by the bank?

Money turns on the point in three different situations, which it would be useful to illustrate by adding two circumstances to the facts of *Panchaud*[187] itself; that is to say by assuming payment in the case by letter of credit; and by assuming that the banks had accepted the documents, which, it will be recalled, clearly showed an inconsistency as to the date of shipment.

---

[181] See text accompanying fn 163 above.

[182] See text accompanying fn 173 above.

[183] See text accompanying fn 170 above.

[184] [1970] 1 Lloyd's Rep 53.

[185] See art 2 of the UCP, which defines a documentary credit as an 'arrangement ... whereby a bank ..., acting at the request and on the instructions of a customer ... is to make payment ... against stipulated documents, provided that the terms and conditions of the credit are complied with.' See also art 15, which reads in relevant part: 'Documents which appear on their face to be inconsistent with one another will be considered as not appearing on their face to be in accordance with the terms and conditions of the credit.'

[186] [1970] 1 Lloyd's Rep 53.

[187] Ibid.

Our first situation arises where the buyer accepts and pays for the documents from the bank[188]: can he then purport to reject the documents and/or the goods as against the seller on the documentary defect apparent on the face of the documents (misdating) or the physical breach it reveals (late shipment)? Proposition (a) stated above as the direct result of the *Panchaud Freres*[189] case would clearly prevent the buyer from so doing: the buyer cannot, it is submitted, blow hot and cold on the patently defective[190] documents, accepting them as against the bank, but purporting to reject them as against the seller[191]. Secondly, if the buyer accepts and pays for the documents from the bank, can he then reject the goods on arrival on some ground other than that which was apparent on the face of the document, for example on the ground that the goods were not of contract specification? It follows from proposition (d) stated above that the buyer can so reject, acceptance of the documents first by the banks, then by himself from the banks, making no difference to his right to reject goods on new grounds. Thirdly, if the buyer who accepts and pays for the documents from the bank, then discovers another documentary defect which was not apparent on the face of the documents, can he sue the seller for having been deprived of the opportunity to reject the documents? If, as is suggested in proposition (c) above, the judgment of Saville J in *Vargas v Cremer*[192] is to be preferred to that of Cooke J. in *Kleinjan & Holst v Bremer Handelsgesellschaft mbH Hamburg*[193], then it would follow that the buyer cannot so recover; and this, not so much because the banks' acceptance of the documents binds the buyer, but because his own acceptance of the documents has severed the causal link between the newly-discovered breach by the seller and the loss suffered by the buyer.

---

[188] As well he might, if he has already put the bank in funds for the sum of the letter of credit. Where the buyer rejects the documents against the bank, he is then likely to reject the goods because he is in no position to claim possession of them from the carrier, having no bill of lading in hand: the bank is left out of pocket, to the tune of the sum of the credit paid to the seller; and the prospects for recovery by the bank from the seller, in the circumstances envisaged, are poor: see Reflections on Letters of Credit—III, Professor Roy Goode, 1983 JBL 443.

[189] [1970] 1 Lloyd's Rep 53.

[190] If the banks accept conforming documents, the buyer is not, of course, estopped from later rejecting the goods; this is a direct result of the separate and independent existence of the rights to reject documents and goods: see *Bergerco USA v Vegoil* [1984] 1 Lloyd's Rep 440 at 445,6.

[191] It is clear that this result follows whether or not the banks instructed under a letter of credit are, for the purposes of the contract of sale, agents for the buyer. This is a difficult question, upon which there is more opinion in the textbooks than there are decisions in the cases, possibly because, as the text above attempts to show, most 'agency'-type questions can actually be solved through easier means. Such opinion as has been expressed, though, suggests that the banks do not act as agents for buyers when accepting or rejecting documents: see Goode, pp 661 and 668; *Documentary Letters of Credit*, E.P. Ellinger, 1970, University of Singapore Press, pp 66–67 and 151; Benjamin, para 2215.

[192] [1987] 1 Lloyd's Rep 394.

[193] [1972] 2 Lloyd's Rep 11.

Thus in all three cases envisaged above, the doctrine in *Panchaud*[194] bites, if at all, against the buyer personally; its application is in no sense affected by the parties' use of a letter of credit as the method of payment under their contract of sale.

---

[194] [1970] 1 Lloyd's Rep 53.

Appendices

Statutes

a. Sale of Goods Act 1979
b. Carriage of Goods by Sea Act 1971
c. Bills of Lading Act 1855

A. SALE OF GOODS ACT 1979

An Act to consolidate the law relating to the sale of goods [6 December 1979]

PART I
CONTRACTS TO WHICH ACT APPLIES

1.(1) This Act applies to contracts of sale of goods made on or after (but not to those made before) 1 January 1894.

(2) In relation to contracts made on certain dates, this Act applies subject to the modification of certain of its sections as mentioned in Schedule 1 below.

(3) Any such modification is indicated in the section concerned by a reference to Schedule 1 below.

(4) Accordingly, where a section does not contain such a reference, this Act applies in relation to the contract concerned without such modification of the section.

PART II
FORMATION OF THE CONTRACT

Contract of sale

2.(1) A contract of sale of goods is a contract by which the seller transfers or agrees to transfer the property in goods to the buyer for a money consideration, called the price.

(2) There may be a contract of sale between one part owner and another.

(3) A contract of sale may be absolute or conditional.

(4) Where under a contract of sale the property in the goods is transferred from the seller to the buyer the contract is called a sale.

(5) Where under a contract of sale the transfer of the property in the goods is to take place at a future time or subject to some condition later to be fulfilled the contract is called an agreement to sell.

(6) An agreement to sell becomes a sale when the time elapses or the conditions are fulfilled subject to which the property in the goods is to be transferred.

3.(1) Capacity to buy and sell is regulated by the general law concerning capacity to contract and to transfer and acquire property.

(2) Where necessaries are sold and delivered to a minor or to a person who by reason of mental incapacity or drunkenness is incompetent to contract, he must pay a reasonable price for them.

(3) In subsection (2) above 'necessaries' means goods suitable to the condition in life of the minor or other person concerned and to his actual requirements at the time of the sale and delivery.

Formalities of contract

4.(1) Subject to this and any other Act, a contract of sale may be made in writing (either with or without seal), or by word of mouth, or partly in writing and partly by word of mouth, or may be implied from the conduct of the parties.

(2) Nothing in this section affects the law relating to corporations.

Subject matter of contract

5.(1) The goods which form the subject of a contract of sale may be either existing goods, owned or possessed by the seller, or goods to be manufactured or acquired by him after the making of the contract of sale, in this Act called future goods.

(2) There may be a contract for the sale of goods the acquisition of which by the seller depends on a contingency which may or may not happen.

(3) Where by a contract of sale the seller purports to effect a present sale of future goods, the contract operates as an agreement to sell the goods.

6. Where there is a contract for the sale of specific goods, and the goods without the knowledge of the seller have perished at the time when the contract is made, the contract is void.

7. Where there is an agreement to sell specific goods and subsequently the goods, without any fault on the part of the seller or buyer, perish before the risk passes to the buyer, the agreement is avoided.

The price

8.(1) The price in a contract of sale may be fixed by the contract, or may be left to be fixed in a manner agreed by the contract, or may be determined by the course of dealing between the parties.

(2) Where the price is not determined as mentioned in subsection (1) above the buyer must pay a reasonable price.

(3) What is a reasonable price is a question of fact dependent on the circumstances of each particular case.

9.(1) Where there is an agreement to sell goods on the terms that the price is to be fixed by the valuation of a third party, and he cannot or does not make the valuation, the agreement is avoided; but if the goods or any part of them have been delivered to and appropriated by the buyer he must pay a reasonable price for them.

(2) Where the third party is prevented from making the valuation by the fault of the seller or buyer, the party not at fault may maintain an action for damages against the party at fault.

Conditions and warranties

10.(1) Unless a different intention appears from the terms of the contract, stipulations as to time of payment are not of the essence of a contract of sale.

(2) Whether any other stipulation as to time is or is not of the essence of the contract depends on the terms of the contract.

(3) In a contract of sale 'month' prima facie means calendar month.

11.(1) Subsections (2) to (4) and (7) below do not apply to Scotland and subsection (5) below applies only to Scotland.

(2) Where a contract of sale is subject to a condition to be fulfilled by the seller, the buyer may waive the condition, or may elect to treat the breach of the condition as a breach of warranty and not as a ground for treating the contract as repudiated.

(3) Whether a stipulation in a contract of sale is a condition, the breach of which may give rise to a right to treat the contract as repudiated, or a warranty, the breach of which may give rise to a claim for damages but not to a right to reject the goods and treat the contract as repudiated, depends in each case on the construction of the contract; and a stipulation may be a condition, though called a warranty in the contract.

(4) Where a contract of sale is not severable and the buyer has accepted the goods or part of them, the breach of a condition to be fulfilled by the seller can only be treated as a breach of warranty, and not as a ground for rejecting the goods and treating the contract as repudiated, unless there is an express or implied term of the contract to that effect.

(5) In Scotland, failure by the seller to perform any material part of a contract of sale is a breach of contract, which entitles the buyer either within a reasonable time after delivery to reject the goods and treat the contract as repudiated, or to retain the goods and treat the failure to perform such material part as a breach which may give rise to a claim for compensation or damages.

(6) Nothing in this section affects a condition or warranty whose fulfilment is excused by law by reason of impossibility or otherwise.

(7) Paragraph 2 of Schedule 1 below applies in relation to a contract made before 22 April 1967 or (in the application of this Act to Northern Ireland) 28 July 1967.

12.(1) In a contract of sale, other than one to which subsection (3) below applies, there is an implied condition on the part of the seller that in the case of a sale he has a right to sell the goods, and in the case of an agreement to sell he will have such a right at the time when the property is to pass.

(2) In a contract of sale, other than one to which subsection (3) below applies, there is also an implied warranty that—

(a) the goods are free, and will remain free until the time when the property is to pass, from any charge or encumbrance not disclosed or known to the buyer before the contract is made, and

(b) the buyer will enjoy quiet possession of the goods except so far as it may be disturbed by the owner or other person entitled to the benefit of any charge or encumbrance so disclosed or known.

(3) This subsection applies to a contract of sale in the case of which there appears from the contract or is to be inferred from its circumstances an intention that the seller should transfer only such title as he or a third person may have.

(4) In a contract to which subsection (3) above applies there is an implied warranty that all charges or encumbrances known to the seller and not known to the buyer have been disclosed to the buyer before the contract is made.

(5) In a contract to which subsection (3) above applies there is also an implied warranty that none of the following will disturb the buyer's quiet possession of the goods, namely—

(a) the seller;

(b) in a case where the parties to the contract intend that the seller should transfer only such title as a third person may have, that person;

(c) anyone claiming through or under the seller or that third person otherwise than under a charge or encumbrance disclosed or known to the buyer before the contract is made.

(6) Paragraph 3 of Schedule 1 below applies in relation to a contract made before 18 May 1973.

13.(1) Where there is a contract for the sale of goods by description, there is an implied condition that the goods will correspond with the description.

(2) If the sale is by sample as well as by description it is not sufficient that the bulk of the goods corresponds with the sample if the goods do not also correspond with the description.

(3) A sale of goods is not prevented from being a sale by description by reason only that, being exposed for sale or hire, they are selected by the buyer.

(4) Paragraph 4 of Schedule 1 below applies in relation to a contract made before 18 May 1973.

14.(1) Except as provided by this section and section 15 below and subject to any other enactment, there is no implied condition or warranty about the quality or fitness for any particular purpose of goods supplied under a contract of sale.

(2) Where the seller sells goods in the course of a business, there is an implied condition that the goods supplied under the contract are of merchantable quality, except that there is no such condition—

(a) as regards defects specifically drawn to the buyer's attention before the contract is made; or

(b) if the buyer examines the goods before the contract is made, as regards defects which that examination ought to reveal.

(3) Where the seller sells goods in the course of a business and the buyer, expressly or by implication, makes known—

(a) to the seller, or

(b) where the purchase price or part of it is payable by instalments and the goods were previously sold by a credit-broker to the seller, to that credit-broker,

any particular purpose for which the goods are being bought, there is an implied condition that the goods supplied under the contract are reasonably fit for that purpose, whether or not that is a purpose for which such goods are commonly supplied, except where the circumstances show that the buyer does not rely, or that it is unreasonable for him to rely, on the skill or judgment of the seller or credit-broker.

(4) An implied condition or warranty about quality or fitness for a particular purpose may be annexed to a contract of sale by usage.

(5) The preceding provisions of this section apply to a sale by a person who in the course of a business is acting as agent for another as they apply to a sale by a principal in the course of a business, except where that other is not selling in the course of a business and either the buyer knows that fact or reasonable steps are taken to bring it to the notice of the buyer before the contract is made.

(6) Goods of any kind are of merchantable quality within the meaning of subsection (2) above if they are as fit for the purpose or purposes for which goods of that kind are commonly bought as it is reasonable to expect having regard to any description applied to them, the price (if relevant) and all the other relevant circumstances.

(7) Paragraph 5 of Schedule 1 below applies in relation to a contract made on or after 18 May 1973 and before the appointed day, and paragraph 6 in relation to one made before 18 May 1973.

(8) In subsection (7) above and paragraph 5 of Schedule 1 below references to the appointed day are to the day appointed for the purposes of those provisions by an order of the Secretary of State made by statutory instrument.

Sale by sample

15.(1) A contract of sale is a contract for sale by sample where there is an express or implied term to that effect in the contract.

(2) In the case of a contract for sale by sample there is an implied condition—

(a) that the bulk will correspond with the sample in quality;

(b) that the buyer will have a reasonable opportunity of comparing the bulk with the sample;

(c) that the goods will be free from any defect, rendering them unmerchantable, which would not be apparent on reasonable examination of the sample.

(3) In subsection (2) (c) above 'unmerchantable' is to be construed in accordance with section 14 (6) above.

(4) Paragraph 7 of Schedule 1 below applies in relation to a contract made before 18 May 1973.

PART III
EFFECTS OF THE CONTRACT

Transfer of property as between seller and buyer

16. Where there is a contract for the sale of unascertained goods no property in the goods is transferred to the buyer unless and until the goods are ascertained.

17.(1) Where there is a contract for the sale of specific or ascertained goods the property in them is transferred to the buyer at such time as the parties to the contract intend it to be transferred.

(2) For the purpose of ascertaining the intention of the parties regard shall be had to the terms of the contract, the conduct of the parties and the circumstances of the case.

18. Unless a different intention appears, the following are rules for ascertaining the intention of the parties as to the time at which the property in the goods is to pass to the buyer.

Rule 1.—Where there is an unconditional contract for the sale of specific goods in a deliverable state the property in the goods passes to the buyer when the contract is made, and it is immaterial whether the time of payment or the time of delivery, or both, be postponed.

Rule 2.—Where there is a contract for the sale of specific goods and the seller is bound to do something to the goods for the purpose of putting them into a deliverable state, the property does not pass until the thing is done and the buyer has notice that it has been done.

Rule 3.—Where there is a contract for the sale of specific goods in a deliverable state but the seller is bound to weigh, measure, test, or do some other act or thing with reference to the goods for the purpose of ascertaining the price, the property does not pass until the act or thing is done and the buyer has notice that it has been done.

Rule 4.—When the goods are delivered to the buyer on approval or on sale or return or other similar terms the property in the goods passes to the buyer:—

(a) when he signifies his approval or acceptance to the seller or does any other act adopting the transaction;

(b) if he does not signify his approval or acceptance to the seller but retains the goods without giving notice of rejection, then, if a time has been fixed for the return of the goods, on the expiration of that time, and, if no time has been fixed, on the expiration of a reasonable time.

Rule 5.—(1) Where there is a contract for the sale of unascertained or future goods by description, and goods of that description and in a deliverable state are unconditionally appropriated to the contract, either by the seller with the assent of the buyer or by the buyer with the assent of the seller, the property in the goods then passes to the buyer; and the assent may be express or implied, and may be given either before or after the appropriation is made.

(2) Where, in pursuance of the contract, the seller delivers the goods to the buyer or to a carrier or other bailee or custodier (whether named by the buyer or not) for the purpose of transmission to the buyer, and does not reserve the right of disposal, he is to be taken to have unconditionally appropriated the goods to the contract.

19.(1) Where there is a contract for the sale of specific goods or where goods are subsequently appropriated to the contract, the seller may, by the terms of the contract or appropriation, reserve the right of disposal of the goods until certain conditions are fulfilled; and in such a case, notwithstanding the delivery of the goods to the buyer, or to a carrier or other bailee or custodier for the purpose of transmission to the buyer, the property in the goods does not pass to the buyer until the conditions imposed by the seller are fulfilled.

(2) Where goods are shipped, and by the bill of lading the goods are deliverable to the order of the seller or his agent, the seller is prima facie to be taken to reserve the right of disposal.

(3) Where the seller of goods draws on the buyer for the price, and transmits the bill of exchange and bill of lading to the buyer together to secure acceptance or payment of the bill of exchange, the buyer is bound to return the bill of lading if he does not honour the bill of exchange, and if he wrongfully retains the bill of lading the property in the goods does not pass to him.

20.(1) Unless otherwise agreed, the goods remain at the seller's risk until the property in them is transferred to the buyer, but when the property in them is transferred to the buyer the goods are at the buyer's risk whether delivery has been made or not.

(2) But where delivery has been delayed through the fault of either buyer or seller the goods are at the risk of the party at fault as regards any loss which might not have occurred but for such fault.

(3) Nothing in this section affects the duties or liabilities of either seller or buyer as a bailee or custodier of the goods of the other party.

Transfer of title

21.(1) Subject to this Act, where goods are sold by a person who is not their owner, and who does not sell them under the authority or with the consent of the owner, the buyer acquires no better title to the goods than the seller had, unless the owner of the goods is by his conduct precluded from denying the seller's authority to sell.

(2) Nothing in this Act affects—

(a) the provisions of the Factors Acts or any enactment enabling the apparent owner of goods to dispose of them as if he were their true owner;

(b) the validity of any contract of sale under any special common law or statutory power of sale or under the order of a court of competent jurisdiction.

22.(1) Where goods are sold in market overt, according to the usage of the market, the buyer acquires a good title to the goods, provided he buys them in good faith and without notice of any defect or want of title on the part of the seller.

(2) This section does not apply to Scotland.

(3) Paragraph 8 of Schedule 1 below applies in relation to a contract under which goods were sold before 1 January 1968 or (in the application of this Act to Northern Ireland) 29 August 1967.

23. When the seller of goods has a voidable title to them, but his title has not been avoided at the time of the sale, the buyer acquires a good title to the goods, provided he buys them in good faith and without notice of the seller's defect of title.

24. Where a person having sold goods continues or is in possession of the goods, or of the documents of title to the goods, the delivery or transfer by that person, or by a mercantile agent acting for him, of the goods or documents of title under any sale, pledge, or other disposition thereof, to any person receiving the same in good faith and without notice of the previous sale, has the same effect as if the person making the delivery or transfer were expressly authorised by the owner of the goods to make the same.

25.(1) Where a person having bought or agreed to buy goods obtains, with the consent of the seller, possession of the goods or the documents of title, under any sale, pledge, or other disposition thereof, to any person receiving the same in good faith and without notice of any lien or other right of the original seller in respect of the goods, has the same effect as if the person making the delivery or transfer were a mercantile agent in possession of the goods or documents of title with the consent of the owner.

(2) For the purposes of subsection (1) above—

(a) the buyer under a conditional sale agreement is to be taken not to be a person who has bought or agreed to buy goods, and

(b) 'conditional sale agreement' means an agreement for the sale of goods which is a consumer credit agreement within the meaning of the Consumer Credit Act 1974 under which the purchase price or part of it is payable by instalments, and the property in the goods is to remain in the seller (notwithstanding that the buyer is to be in possession of the goods) until such conditions as to the payment of instalments or otherwise as may be specified in the agreement are fulfilled.

(3) Paragraph 9 of Schedule 1 below applies in relation to a contract under which a person buys or agrees to buy goods and which is made before the appointed day.

(4) In subsection (3) above and paragraph 9 of Schedule 1 below references to the appointed day are to the day appointed for the purpose of those provisions by an order of the Secretary of State made by statutory instrument.

26. In Sections 24 and 25 above 'mercantile agent' means a mercantile agent having in the customary course of his business as such agent authority either—

(a) to sell goods, or
(b) to consign goods for the purpose of sale, or
(c) to buy goods, or
(d) to raise money on the security of goods.

PART IV
PERFORMANCE OF THE CONTRACT

27. It is the duty of the seller to deliver the goods, and of the buyer to accept and pay for them, in accordance with the terms of the contract of sale.

28. Unless otherwise agreed, delivery of the goods and payment of the price are concurrent conditions, that is to say, the seller must be ready and willing to give possession of the goods to the buyer in exchange for the price and the buyer must be ready and willing to pay the price in exchange for possession of the goods.

29.(1) Whether it is for the buyer to take possession of the goods or for the seller to send them to the buyer is a question depending in each case on the contract, express or implied, between the parties.

(2) Apart from any such contract, express or implied, the place of delivery is the seller's business if he has one, and if not, his residence; except that, if the contract is for the sale of specific goods, which to the knowledge of the parties when the contract is made are in some other place, then that place is the place of delivery.

(3) Where under the contract of sale the seller is bound to send the goods to the buyer, but no time for sending them is fixed, the seller is bound to send them within a reasonable time.

(4) Where the goods at the time of sale are in the possession of a third person, there is no delivery by seller to buyer unless and until

the third person acknowledges to the buyer that he holds the goods on his behalf; but nothing in this section affects the operation of the issue or transfer of any document of title to goods.

(5) Demand or tender of delivery may be treated as ineffectual unless made at a reasonable hour; and what is a reasonable hour is a question of fact.

(6) Unless otherwise agreed, the expenses of and incidental to putting the goods into a deliverable state must be borne by the seller.

30.(1) Where the seller delivers to the buyer a quantity of goods less than he contracted to sell, the buyer may reject them, but if the buyer accepts the goods so delivered he must pay for them at the contract rate.

(2) Where the seller delivers to the buyer a quantity of goods larger than he contracted to sell, the buyer may accept the goods included in the contract and reject the rest or he may reject the whole.

(3) Where the seller delivers to the buyer a quantity of goods larger than he contracted to sell and the buyer accepts the whole of the goods so delivered he must pay for them at the contract rate.

(4) Where the seller delivers to the buyer the goods he contracted to sell mixed with goods of a different description not included in the contract, the buyer may accept the goods which are in accordance with the contract and reject the rest, or he may reject the whole.

(5) This section is subject to any usage of trade, special agreement, or course of dealing between the parties.

31.(1) Unless otherwise agreed, the buyer of goods is not bound to accept delivery of them by instalments.

(2) Where there is a contract for the sale of goods to be delivered by stated instalments which are to be separately paid for, and the seller makes defective deliveries in respect of one or more instalments, or the buyer neglects or refuses to take delivery of or pay for one or more instalments, it is a question in each case depending on the terms of the contract and the circumstances of the case whether the breach of contract is a repudiation of the whole contract or whether it is a severable breach giving rise to a claim for compensation but not to a right to treat the whole contract as repudiated.

32.(1) Where in pursuance of a contract of sale, the seller is authorised or required to send the goods to the buyer, delivery of the goods to a carrier (whether named by the buyer or not) for the purpose of transmission to the buyer is prima facie deemed to be a delivery of the goods to the buyer.

(2) Unless otherwise authorised by the buyer, the seller must make such contract with the carrier on behalf of the buyer as may be reasonable having regard to the nature of the goods and the other circumstances of the case; and if the seller omits to do so, and the goods are lost or damaged in course of transit, the buyer may decline to treat the delivery

to the carrier as a delivery to himself or may hold the seller responsible in damages.

(3) Unless otherwise agreed, where goods are sent by the seller to the buyer by a route involving sea transit, under circumstances in which it is usual to insure, the seller must give such notice to the buyer as may enable him to insure them during their sea transit; and if the seller fails to do so, the goods are at his risk during such sea transit.

33. Where the seller of goods agrees to deliver them at his own risk at a place other than that where they are when sold, the buyer must nevertheless (unless otherwise agreed) take any risk of deterioration in the goods necessarily incident to the course of transit.

34.(1) Where the goods are delivered to the buyer, and he has not previously examined them, he is not deemed to have accepted them until he has had a reasonable opportunity of examining them for the purpose of ascertaining whether they are in conformity with the contract.

(2) Unless otherwise agreed, when the seller tenders delivery of goods to the buyer he is bound on request to afford the buyer a reasonable opportunity of examining the goods for the purpose of ascertaining whether they are in conformity with the contract.

35.(1) The buyer is deemed to have accepted the goods when he intimates to the seller that he has accepted them, or (except where section 34 above otherwise provides) when the goods have been delivered to him and he does any act in relation to them which is inconsistent with the ownership of the seller, or when after the lapse of a reasonable time he retains the goods without intimating to the seller that he has rejected them.

(2) Paragraph 10 of Schedule 1 below applies in relation to a contract made before 22 April 1967 or (in the application of this Act to Northern Ireland) 28 July 1967.

36. Unless otherwise agreed, where goods are delivered to the buyer, and he refuses to accept them, having the right to do so, he is not bound to return them to the seller, but it is sufficient if he intimates to the seller that he refuses to accept them.

37.(1) When the seller is ready and willing to deliver the goods, and requests the buyer to take delivery, and the buyer does not within a reasonable time after such request take delivery of the goods, he is liable to the seller for any loss occasioned by his neglect or refusal to take delivery, and also for a reasonable charge for the care and custody of the goods.

(2) Nothing in this section affects the rights of the seller where the neglect or refusal of the buyer to take delivery amounts to a repudiation of the contract.

PART V
RIGHTS OF UNPAID SELLER AGAINST THE GOODS

Preliminary

38.(1) The seller of goods is an unpaid seller within the meaning of this Act—

(a) when the whole of the price has not been paid or tendered;

(b) when a bill of exchange or other negotiable instrument has been received as conditional payment, and the condition on which it was received has not been fulfilled by reason of the dishonour of the instrument or otherwise.

(2) In this Part of this Act 'seller' includes any person who is in the position of a seller, as, for instance, an agent of the seller to whom the bill of lading has been indorsed or a consignor or agent who has himself paid (or is directly responsible for) the price.

39.(1) Subject to this and any other Act, notwithstanding that the property in the goods may have passed to the buyer, the unpaid seller of goods, as such, has by implication of law—

(a) a lien on the goods or right to retain them for the price while he is in possession of them;

(b) in case of the insolvency of the buyer, a right of stopping the goods in transit after he has parted with the possession of them;

(c) a right of re-sale as limited by this Act.

(2) Where the property in goods has not passed to the buyer, the unpaid seller has (in addition to his other remedies) a right of withholding delivery similar to and co-extensive with his rights of lien or retention and stoppage in transit where the property has passed to the buyer.

40. In Scotland a seller of goods may attach them while in his own hands or possession by arrestment or poinding; and such arrestment or poinding shall have the same operation and effect in a competition or otherwise as an arrestment or poinding by a third party.

Unpaid seller's lien

41.(1) Subject to this Act, the unpaid seller of goods who is in possession of them is entitled to retain possession of them until payment or tender of the price in the following cases:—

(a) where the goods have been sold without any stipulation as to credit;

(b) where the goods have been sold on credit but the term of credit has expired;

(c) where the buyer becomes insolvent.

(2) The seller may exercise his lien or right of retention notwithstanding that he is in possession of the goods as agent or bailee or custodier for the buyer.

42. Where an unpaid seller has made part delivery of the goods, he may

exercise his lien or right of retention on the remainder, unless such part delivery has been made under such circumstances as to show an agreement to waive the lien or right of retention.

43.(1) The unpaid seller of goods loses his lien or right of retention in respect of them—

    (a) when he delivers the goods to a carrier or other bailee or custodier for the purpose of transmission to the buyer without reserving the right of disposal of the goods;

    (b) when the buyer or his agent lawfully obtains possession of the goods;

    (c) by waiver of the lien or right of retention.

(2) An unpaid seller of goods who has a lien or right of retention in respect of them does not lose his lien or right of retention by reason only that he has obtained judgement or decree for the price of the goods.

Stoppage in transit

44. Subject to this Act, when the buyer of goods becomes insolvent the unpaid seller who has parted with the possession of the goods has the right of stopping them in transit, that is to say, he may resume possession of the goods as long as they are in course of transit, and may retain them until payment or tender of the price.

45.(1) Goods are deemed to be in course of transit from the time when they are delivered to a carrier or other bailee or custodier for the purpose of transmission to the buyer, until the buyer or his agent in that behalf takes delivery of them from the carrier or other bailee or custodier.

(2) If the buyer or his agent in that behalf obtains delivery of the goods before their arrival at the appointed destination, the transit is at an end.

(3) If, after the arrival of the goods at the appointed destination, the carrier or other bailee or custodier acknowledges to the buyer or his agent that he holds the goods on his behalf and continues in possession of them as bailee or custodier for the buyer or his agent, the transit is at an end, and it is immaterial that a further destination for the goods may have been indicated by the buyer.

(4) If the goods are rejected by the buyer, and the carrier or other bailee or custodier continues in possession of them, the transit is not deemed to be at an end, even if the seller has refused to receive them back.

(5) When goods are delivered to a ship chartered by the buyer it is a question depending on the circumstances of the particular case whether they are in the possession of the master as a carrier or as agent to the buyer.

(6) Where the carrier or other bailee or custodier wrongfully refuses to deliver the goods to the buyer or his agent in that behalf, the transit is deemed to be at an end.

(7) Where part delivery of the goods has been made to the buyer or his agent in that behalf, the remainder of the goods may be stopped in transit, unless such part delivery has been made under such circumstances as

to show an agreement to give up possession of the whole of the goods.

46.(1) The unpaid seller may exercise his right of stoppage in transit either by taking actual possession of the goods or by giving notice of his claim to the carrier or other bailee or custodier in whose possession the goods are.

(2) The notice may be given either to the person in actual possession of the goods or to his principal.

(3) If given to the principal, the notice is ineffective unless given at such time and under such circumstances that the principal, by the exercise of reasonable diligence, may communicate it to his servant or agent in time to prevent a delivery to the buyer.

(4) When notice of stoppage in transit is given by the seller to the carrier or other bailee or custodier in possession of the goods, he must re-deliver the goods to, or according to the directions of, the seller; and the expenses of the re-delivery must be borne by the seller.

Re-sale etc by buyer

47.(1) Subject to this Act, the unpaid seller's right of lien or retention or stoppage in transit is not affected by any sale or other disposition of the goods which the buyer may have made, unless the seller has assented to it.

(2) Where a document of title to goods has been lawfully transferred to any person as buyer or owner of the goods, and that person transfers the document to a person who takes it in good faith and for valuable consideration, then—

    (a) if the last-mentioned transfer was by way of sale the unpaid seller's right of lien or retention or stoppage in transit is defeated; and

    (b) if the last-mentioned transfer was made by way of pledge or other disposition for value, the unpaid seller's right of lien or retention or stoppage in transit can only be exercised subject to the rights of the transferee.

Rescission: and re-sale by seller

48.(1) Subject to this section, a contract of sale is not rescinded by the mere exercise by an unpaid seller of his right of lien or retention or stoppage in transit.

(2) Where an unpaid seller who has exercised his right of lien or retention or stoppage in transit re-sells the goods, the buyer acquires a good title to them as against the original buyer.

(3) Where the goods are of a perishable nature, or where the unpaid seller gives notice to the buyer of his intention to re-sell, and the buyer does not within a reasonable time pay or tender the price, the unpaid seller may re-sell the goods and recover from the original buyer damages for any loss occasioned by his breach of contract.

(4) Where the seller expressly reserves the right of re-sale in case the buyer should make default, and on the buyer making default re-sells the goods, the original contract of sale is rescinded but without prejudice to any claim the seller may have for damages.

PART VI
ACTIONS FOR BREACH OF THE CONTRACT
Seller's remedies

49.(1) Where, under a contract of sale, the property in the goods has passed to the buyer and he wrongfully neglects or refuses to pay for the goods according to the terms of the contract, the seller may maintain an action against him for the price of the goods.

(2) Where, under a contract of sale, the price is payable on a day certain irrespective of delivery and the buyer wrongfully neglects or refuses to pay such price, the seller may maintain an action for the price, although the property in the goods has not passed and the goods have not been appropriated to the contract.

(3) Nothing in this section prejudices the right of the seller in Scotland to recover interest on the price from the date of tender of the goods, or from the date on which the price was payable, as the case may be.

50.(1) Where the buyer wrongfully neglects or refuses to accept and pay for the goods, the seller may maintain an action against him for damages for non-acceptance.

(2) The measure of damages is the estimated loss directly and naturally resulting, in the ordinary course of events, from the buyer's breach of contract.

(3) Where there is an available market for the goods in question the measure of damages is prima facie to be ascertained by the difference between the contract price and the market or current price at the time or times when the goods ought to have been accepted or (if no time was fixed for acceptance) at the time of the refusal to accept.

Buyer's remedies

51.(1) Where the seller wrongfully neglects or refuses to deliver the goods to the buyer, the buyer may maintain an action against the seller for damages for non-delivery.

(2) The measure of damages is the estimated loss directly and naturally resulting, in the ordinary course of events, from the seller's breach of contract.

(3) Where there is an available market for the goods in question the measure of damages is prima facie to be ascertained by the difference between the contract price and the market or current price of the goods at the time or times when they ought to have been delivered or (if no time was fixed) at the time of the refusal to deliver.

52.(1) In any action for breach of contract to deliver specific or ascertained goods the court may, if it thinks fit, on the plaintiff's application, by its judgment or decree direct that the contract shall be performed specifically, without giving the defendant the option of retaining the goods on payment of damages.

(2) The plaintiff's application may be made at any time before judgment or decree.

(3) The judgement or decree may be unconditional, or on such terms and conditions as to damages, payment of the price and otherwise as seem just to the court.

53.(1) Where there is a breach of warranty by the seller, or where the buyer elects (or is compelled) to treat any breach of a condition on the part of the seller as a breach of warranty, the buyer is not by reason only of such breach of warranty entitled to reject the goods; but he may—

    (a) set up against the seller the breach of warranty in diminution or extinction of the price, or

    (b) maintain an action against the seller for damages for the breach of warranty.

(2) The measure of damages for breach of warranty is the estimated loss directly and naturally resulting, in the ordinary course of events, from the breach of warranty.

(3) In the case of breach of warranty of quality such loss is prima facie the difference between the value of the goods at the time of delivery to the buyer and the value they would have had if they had fulfilled the warranty.

(4) The fact that the buyer has set up the breach of warranty in diminution or extinction of the price does not prevent him from maintaining an action for the same breach of warranty if he has suffered further damage.

(5) Nothing in this section prejudices or affects the buyer's right of rejection in Scotland as declared by this Act.

Interest, etc

54. Nothing in this Act affects the right of the buyer or the seller to recover interest or special damages in any case where by law interest or special damages may be recovered or to recover money paid where the consideration for the payment of it has failed.

PART VII
SUPPLEMENTARY

55.(1) Where a right, duty or liability would arise under a contract of sale of goods by implication of law, it may (subject to the Unfair Contract Terms Act 1977) be negatived or varied by express agreement, or by the course of dealing between the parties, or by such usage as binds both parties to the contract.

(2) An express condition or warranty does not negative a condition or warranty implied by this Act unless inconsistent with it.

(3) Paragraph 11 of Schedule 1 below applies in relation to a contract made on or after 18 May 1973 and before 1 February 1978, and paragraph 12 in relation to one made before 18 May 1973.

56. Paragraph 13 of Schedule 1 below applies in relation to a contract made on or after 18 May 1973 and before 1 February 1978, so as to make provision about conflict of laws in relation to such a contract.

57.(1) Where goods are put up for sale by auction in lots, each lot is prima facie deemed to be the subject of a separate contract of sale.

(2) A sale by auction is complete when the auctioneer announces its completion by the fall of the hammer, or in other customary manner; and until the announcement is made any bidder may retract his bid.

(3) A sale by auction may not be notified to be subject to a reserve or upset price, and a right to bid may also be reserved expressly by or on behalf of the seller.

(4) Where a sale by auction is not notified to be subject to a right to bid by or on behalf of the seller, it is not lawful for the seller to bid himself or to employ any person to bid at the sale, or for the auctioneer knowingly to take any bid from the seller or any such person.

(5) A sale contravening subsection (4) above may be treated as fraudulent by the buyer.

(6) Where, in respect of a sale by auction, a right to bid is expressly reserved (but not otherwise) the seller or any one person on his behalf may bid at the auction.

58. In Scotland where a buyer has elected to accept goods which he might have rejected, and to treat a breach of contract as only giving rise to a claim for damages, he may, in an action by the seller for the price, be required, in the discretion of the court before which the action depends, to consign or pay into court the price of the goods, or part of the price, or to give other reasonable security for its due payment.

59. Where a reference is made in this Act to a reasonable time the question what is a reasonable time is a question of fact.

60. Where a right, duty or liability is declared by this Act, it may (unless otherwise provided by this Act) be enforced by action.

61.(1) In this Act, unless the context or subject matter otherwise requires,—

'action' includes counterclaim and set-off, and in Scotland condescendence and claim and compensation;

'business' includes a profession and the activities of any government department (including a Northern Ireland department) or local or public authority;

'buyer' means a person who buys or agrees to buy goods;

'contract of sale' includes an agreement to sell as well as a sale:

'credit-broker' means a person acting in the course of a business of credit brokerage carried on by him, that is a business of effecting introductions of individuals desiring to obtain credit—

(a) to persons carrying on any business so far as it relates to the provision of credit, or

(b) to other persons engaged in credit brokerage;

'defendant' includes in Scotland defender, respondent and claimant in multiple poinding;

'delivery' means voluntary transfer of possession from one person to another;

'documents of title to goods' has the same meaning as it has in the Factors Acts;

'Factors Act' means the Factors Act 1889, the Factors (Scotland) Act 1890, and any enactment amending or substituted for the same;

'fault' means wrongful act or default;

'future goods' means goods to be manufactured or acquired by the seller after the making of the contract of sale;

'goods' includes all personal chattels other than things in action and money, and in Scotland all corporeal moveables except money; and in particular 'goods' includes emblements, industrial growing crops, and things attached to or forming part of the land which are agreed to be severed before sale or under the contract of sale;

'plaintiff' includes pursuer, complainer, claimant in a multiple-poinding and defendant or defender counter-claiming;

'property' means the general property in goods, and not merely a special property;

'quality', in relation to goods, includes their state or condition;

'sale' includes a bargain and sale as well as a sale and delivery;

'seller' means a person who sells or agrees to sell goods;

'specific goods' means goods identified and agreed on at the time a contract of sale is made;

'warranty' (as regards England and Wales and Northern Ireland) means an agreement with reference to goods which are the subject of a contract of sale, but collateral to the main purpose of such contract, the breach of which gives rise to a claim for damages, but not to a right to reject the goods and treat the contract as repudiated.

(2) As regards Scotland a breach of warranty shall be deemed to be a failure to perform a material part of the contract.

(3) A thing is deemed to be done in good faith within the meaning of this Act when it is in fact done honestly, whether it is done negligently or not.

(4) A person is deemed to be insolvent within the meaning of this Act if he has either ceased to pay his debts in the ordinary course of business or he cannot pay his debts as they become due, whether he has committed an act of bankruptcy or not, and whether he has become a notom bankrupt or not.

(5) Goods are in a deliverable state within the meaning of this Act when they are in such a state that the buyer would under the contract be bound to take delivery of them.

(6) As regards the definition of 'business' in subsection (1) above, paragraph 14 of Schedule 1 below applies in relation to a contract made on or after 18 May 1973 and before 1 February 1978, and paragraph 15 in relation to one made before 18 May 1973.

62.(1) The rules in bankruptcy relating to contracts of sale apply to those contracts, notwithstanding anything in this Act.

(2) The rules of the common law, including the law merchant, except in so far as they are inconsistent with the provisions of this Act, and in particular the rules relating to the law of principal and agent and the effect of fraud, misrepresentation, duress or coercion, mistake, or other invalidating cause, apply to contracts for the sale of goods.

(3) Nothing in this Act or the Sale of Goods Act 1893 affects the enactments relating to bills of sale, or any enactment relating to the sale of goods which is not expressly repealed or amended by this Act or that.

(4) The provisions of this Act about contracts of sale do not apply to a transaction in the form of a contract of sale which is intended to operate by way of mortgage, pledge, charge, or other security.

(5) Nothing in this Act prejudices or affects the landlord's right of hypothec or sequestration for rent in Scotland.

63.(1) Without prejudice to section 17 of the Interpretation Act 1978 (repeal and re-enactment), the enactments mentioned in Schedule 2 below have effect subject to the amendments there specified (being amendments consequential on this Act).

(2) The enactments mentioned in Schedule 3 below are repealed to the extent specified in column 3, but subject to the savings in Schedule 4 below.

(3) The savings in Schedule 4 below have effect.

64.(1) This Act may be cited as the Sale of Goods Act 1979.

(2) This Act comes into force on 1 January 1980.

SCHEDULE 1

1.—(1) This Schedule modifies this Act as it applies to contracts of sale of goods made on certain dates.

(2) In this Schedule references to sections are to those of this Act and references to contracts are to contracts of sale of goods.

(3) Nothing in this Schedule affects a contract made before 1 January 1894.

2. In relation to a contract made before 22 April 1967 or (in the application of this Act to Northern Ireland) 28 July 1967, in section 11(4) after 'or part of them', insert 'or where the contract is for specific goods, the property in which has passed to the buyer,'.

3. In relation to a contract made before 18 May 1973 substitute the following for section 12:—

In a contract of sale, unless the circumstances of the contract are such as to show a different intention, there is—

    (a) an implied condition on the part of the seller that in the case of a sale he has a right to sell the goods, and in the case of an agreement to sell he will have such a right at the time when the property is to pass;

    (b) an implied warranty that the buyer will have and enjoy quiet possession of the goods;

    (c) an implied warranty that the goods will be free from any charge or encumbrance in favour of any third party, not declared or known to the buyer before or at the time when the contract is made.

4. In relation to a contract made before 18 May 1973, omit section 13(3).

5. In relation to a contract made on or after 18 May 1973 and before the appointed day, substitute the following for section 14:—

(1) Except as provided by this section and section 15 below and subject to any other enactment, there is no implied condition or warranty about the quality or fitness for any particular purpose of goods supplied under a contract of sale.

(2) Where the seller sells goods in the course of a business, there is an implied condition that the goods supplied under the contract are of merchantable quality, except that there is no such condition—

    (a) as regards defects, specifically drawn to the buyer's attention before the contract is made; or

    (b) if the buyer examines the goods before the contract is made, as regards defects which that examination ought to reveal.

(3) Where the seller sells goods in the course of a business and the buyer, expressly or by implication, makes known to the seller any particular purpose for which the goods are being bought, there is an implied condition that the goods supplied under the contract are reasonably fit for that purpose, whether or not that is a purpose for which such goods are commonly supplied, except where the circumstances show that the buyer does not rely, or that it is unreasonable for him to rely, on the seller's skill or judgment.

(4) An implied condition or warranty about quality or fitness for a particular purpose may be annexed to a contract of sale by usage.

(5) The preceding provisions of this section apply to a sale by a person who in the course of a business is acting as agent for another as they apply to a sale by a principal in the course of a business, except where that other is not selling in the course of a business and either the buyer knows that fact or reasonable steps are taken to bring it to the notice of the buyer before the contract is made.

(6) Goods of any kind are of merchantable quality within the meaning of subsection (2) above if they are as fit for the purpose or purposes for which goods of that kind are commonly bought as it is reasonable to expect having regard to any description applied to them, the price (if relevant) and all the other relevant circumstances.

(7) In the application of subsection (3) above to an agreement for the sale of goods under which the purchase price or part of it is payable by instalments any reference to the seller includes a reference to the person by whom any antecedent negotiations are conducted; and section 58(3) and (5) of the Hire-Purchase Act 1965, section 54(3) and (5) of the Hire-Purchase (Scotland) Act 1965 and section 65(3) and (5) of the Hire-Purchase Act (Northern Ireland) 1966 (meaning of antecedent negotiations and related expressions) apply in relation to this subsection as in relation to each of those Acts, but as if a reference to any such agreements were included in the references in subsection (3) of each of those sections to the agreements there mentioned.

6. In relation to a contract made before 18 May 1973 substitute the following for section 14:—

(1) Subject to this and any other Act, there is no implied condition or warranty about the quality or fitness for any particular purpose of goods supplied under a contract of sale.

(2) Where the buyer, expressly or by implication, makes known to the seller the particular purpose for which the goods are required, so as to show that the buyer relies on the seller's skill or judgment, and the goods are of a description which it is in the course of the seller's business to supply (whether he is the manufacturer or not), there is an implied condition that the goods will be reasonably fit for such purpose, except that in the case of a contract for the sale of a specified article under its patent or other trade name there is no implied condition as to its fitness for any particular purpose.

(3) Where goods are bought by description from a seller who deals in goods of that description (whether he is the manufacturer or not), there is an implied condition that the goods will be of merchantable quality; but if the buyer has examined the goods, there is no implied condition as regards defects which such examination ought to have revealed.

(4) An implied condition or warranty about quality or fitness for a particular purpose may be annexed by the usage of trade.

(5) An express condition or warranty does not negative a condition or warranty implied by this Act unless inconsistent with it.

7. In relation to a contract made before 18 May 1973, omit section 15(3).

8. In relation to a contract under which goods were sold before 1 January 1968 or (in the application of this Act to Northern Ireland) 29 August 1967, add the following paragraph at the end of section 22(1):—

'Nothing in this subsection affects the law relating to the sale of horses.'

9. In relation to a contract under which a person buys or agrees to buy goods and which is made before the appointed day, omit section 25(2).

10. In relation to a contract made before 22 April 1967 or (in the application of this Act to Northern Ireland) 28 July 1967, in section 35(1) omit '(except where section 34 above otherwise provides)'.

11. In relation to a contract made on or after 18 May 1973 and before 1 February 1978 substitute the following for section 55:—

(1) Where a right, duty or liability would arise under a contract of sale of goods by implication of law, it may be negatived or varied by express agreement, or by the course of dealing between the parties, or by such usage as binds both parties to the contract, but the preceding provision has effect subject to the following provisions of this section.

(2) An express condition or warranty does not negative a condition or warranty implied by this Act unless inconsistent with it.

(3) In the case of a contract of sale of goods, any term of that or any other contract exempting from all or any of the provisions of section 12 above is void.

(4) In the case of a contract of sale of goods, any term of that or any other contract exempting from all or any of the provisions of section 13, 14 or 15 above is void in the case of a consumer sale and is, in any other case, not enforceable to the extent that it is shown that it would not be fair or reasonable to allow reliance on the term.

(5) In determining for the purpose of subsection (4) above whether or not reliance on any such term would be fair or reasonable regard shall be had to all the circumstances of the case and in particular to the following matters—

    (a) the strength of the bargaining positions of the seller and buyer relative to each other, taking into account, among other things, the availability of suitable alternative products and sources of supply;
    (b) whether the buyer received an inducement to agree to the term or in accepting it had an opportunity of buying the goods or suitable alternatives without it from any source of supply;
    (c) whether the buyer knew or ought reasonably to have known of the existence and extent of the term (having regard, among other things, to any custom of the trade and any previous course of dealing between the parties);
    (d) where the term exempts from all or any of the provisions of section 13, 14 or 15 above if some condition is not complied with, whether it was reasonable at the time of the contract to expect that compliance with that condition would be practicable;
    (e) whether the goods were manufactured, processed, or adapted to the special order of the buyer.

(6) Subsection (5) above does not prevent the court from holding, in accordance with any rule of law, that a term which purports to exclude or restrict any of the provisions of section 13, 14 or 15 above is not a term of the contract.

(7) In this section 'consumer sale' means a sale of goods (other than a sale by auction or by competitive tender) by a seller in the course of a business where the goods—

(a) are of a type ordinarily bought for private use or consumption; and

(b) are sold to a person who does not buy or hold himself out as buying them in the course of a business.

(8) The onus of proving that a sale falls to be treated for the purposes of this section as not being a consumer sale lies on the party so contending.

(9) Any reference in this section to a term exempting from all or any of the provisions of any section of this Act is a reference to a term which purports to exclude or restrict, or has the effect of excluding or restricting, the operation of all or any of the provisions of that section, or any liability of the seller for breach of a condition or warranty implied by any provision of that section.

(10) It is hereby declared that any reference in this section to a term of a contract includes a reference to a term which although not contained in a contract is incorporated in the contract by another term of the contract.

(11) Nothing in this section prevents the parties to a contract for the international sale of goods from negativing or varying any right, duty or liability which would otherwise arise by implication of law under sections 12 to 15 above.

(12) In subsection (11) above 'contract for the international sale of goods' means a contract of sale of goods made by parties whose places of business (or, if they have none, habitual residences) are in the territories of different States (the Channel Islands and the Isle of Man being treated for this purpose as different States from the United Kingdom) and in the case of which one of the following conditions is satisfied:—

(a) the contract involves the sale of goods which are at the time of the conclusion of the contract in the course of carriage or will be carried from the territory of one State to the territory of another; or

(b) the acts constituting the offer and acceptance have been effected in the territories of different States; or

(c) delivery of the goods is to be made in the territory of a State other than that within whose territory the acts constituting the offer and the acceptance have been effected.

12. In relation to a contract made before 18 May 1973 substitute the following for section 55:—

Where a right, duty or liability would arise under a contract of sale by implication of law, it may be negatived or varied by express agreement, or by the course of dealing between the parties, or by such usage as binds both parties to the contract.

13.—(1) In relation to a contract on or after 18 May 1973 and before 1 February 1978 substitute for section 56 the section set out in sub-paragraph (3) below.

(2) In relation to a contract made otherwise than as mentioned in sub-paragraph (1) above ignore section 56 and this paragraph.

(3) The section mentioned in sub-paragraph (1) above is as follows:—

(1) Where the proper law of a contract for the sale of goods would, apart from a term that it should be the law of some other country or a term to the like effect, be the law of any part of the United Kingdom, or where any such contract contains a term which purports to substitute, or has the effect of substituting, provisions of the law of some other country for all or any of the provisions of sections 12 to 15 and 55 above, those sections shall, notwithstanding that term but subject to subsection (2) below, apply to the contract.

(2) Nothing in subsection (1) above prevents the parties to a contract for the international sale of goods from negativing or varying any right, duty or liability which would otherwise arise by implication of law under sections 12 to 15 above.

(3) In subsection (2) above 'contract for the international sale of goods' means a contract of sale of goods made by parties whose places of business (or, if they have none, habitual residences) are in the territories of different States (the Channel Islands and the Isle of Man being treated for this purpose as different States from the United Kingdom) and in the case of which one of the following conditions is satisfied:—

  (a) the contract involves the sale of goods which are at the time of the conclusion of the contract in the course of carriage or will be carried from the territory of one State to the territory of another; or
  (b) the acts constituting the offer and acceptance have been effected in the territories of different States; or
  (c) delivery of the goods is to be made in the territory of a State other than that within whose territory the acts constituting the offer and the acceptance have been effected.

14. In relation to a contract made on or after 18 May 1973 and before 1 February 1978, in the definition of 'business' in section 61(1) for 'or local or public authority' substitute 'local authority or statutory undertaker'.

15. In relation to a contract made before 18 May 1973 omit the definition of 'business' in section 61(1).

(Sch 2: para 1 repealed by the SL(R) Act 1981; para 2 amends the Law Reform (Frustrated Contracts) Act 1943, s 2(5)(c); para 3 amends the Frustrated Contracts Act (Northern Ireland) 1947, s 2(5)(c); para 54 amends the Hire-Purchase Act 1964, s 27(5); paras 5–7 amend the Hire-Purchase Act 1965, ss 230, 54, 58 (repealed); paras 8–10 amend the Hire-Purchase (Scotland) Act 1965, ss 20, 50, 54 (repealed); paras 11–14 amend the Hire-Purchase Act (Northern Ireland) 1966, ss 20, 54, 62, 65 (repealed); para 15 substitutes the Uniform Laws on International Sales Act 1967, s 1(4) ante; para 16 amends the Supply of Goods (Implied Terms) Act 1973, s 14(1); para 17 substitutes words in s 15(1) of that Act which have subsequently been repealed; para 18 amends the Consumer Credit Act 1974, s 189(1); paras 19, 20 amend the Unfair Contract Terms Act 1977, ss 6, 14; paras 21, 22 amend ss 20, 25 of that Act, which apply to Scotland only.)

SCHEDULE 3

Repeals

Chapter	Short Title	Extent of Repeal
56 & 57 Vict c 71	Sale of Goods Act 1893	The whole Act except section 26.
1967 c 7	Misrepresentation Act 1967	Section 4. In section 6(3) the words ',except section 4(2),'.
1967 c 14 (NI)	Misrepresentation Act (Northern Ireland) 1967	Section 4.
1973 c 13	Supply of Goods (Implied Terms) Act 1973	Sections 1 to 7 Section 18(2).
1974 c 39	Consumer Credit Act 1974	In Schedule 4, paragraphs 3 and 4
1977 c 50	Unfair Contract Terms Act 1977	In Schedule 3, the entries relating to the Sale of Goods Act 1893.

SCHEDULE 4

1. In this Schedule references to the 1893 Act are to the Sale of Goods Act 1893.

2. An order under section 14(8) or 25(4) above may make provision that it is to have effect only as provided by the order (being provision corresponding to that which could, apart from this Act, have been made by an order under section 192(4) of the Consumer Credit Act 1974 bringing into operation an amendment or repeal making a change corresponding to that made by the order under section 14(8) or 25(4) above).

3. Where an offence was committed in relation to goods before 1 January 1969 or (in the application of this Act to Northern Ireland) 1 August 1969, the effect of a conviction in respect of the offence is not affected by the repeal by this Act of section 24 of the 1893 Act.

4. The repeal by this Act of provisions of the 1893 Act does not extend to the following provisions of that Act in so far as they are needed to give effect to or interpret section 26 of that Act, namely, the definitions of 'goods' and 'property' in section 62(1), section 62(2) and section 63 (which was repealed subject to savings by the Statute Law Revision Act 1908).

5. The repeal by this Act of section 60 of and the Schedule to the 1893 Act (which effected repeals and which were themselves repealed subject to savings by the Statute Law Revision Act 1908) does not affect those savings, and accordingly does not affect things done or acquired before 1 January 1894.

6. In so far as the 1893 Act applied (immediately before the operation of the repeals made by this Act) to contracts made before 1 January 1894 (when the 1893 Act came into operation), the 1893 Act shall continue so to apply notwithstanding this Act.

B. CARRIAGE OF GOODS BY SEA ACT 1971

An Act to amend the law with respect to the carriage of goods by sea.
[8 April 1971]

BE IT ENACTED by the Queen's most Excellent Majesty, by and with the advice and consent of the Lords Spiritual and Temporal, and Commons, in this present Parliament assembled, and by the authority of the same, as follows:

1.—(1) In this Act, 'the Rules' means the International Convention for the unification of certain rules of law relating to bills of lading signed at Brussels on 25 August 1924, as amended by the Protocol signed at Brussels on 23 February 1968 [and by the protocol signed at Brussels on 21 December 1979.][1]

(2) The provisions of the Rules, as set out in the Schedule to this Act, shall have the force of law.

(3) Without prejudice to subsection (2) above, the said provisions shall have effect (and have the force of law) in relation to and in connection with the carriage of goods by sea in ships where the port of shipment is a port in the United Kingdom, whether or not the carriage is between ports in two different States within the meaning of Article X of the Rules.

(4) Subject to subsection (6) below, nothing in this section shall be taken as applying anything in the Rules to any contract for the carriage of goods by sea, unless the contract expressly or by implication provides for the issue of a bill of lading or any similar document of title.

[(5) – Repealed by the Merchant Shipping Act 1981, Sch.]

(6) Without prejudice to Article X(c) of the Rules, the Rules shall have the force of law in relation to –
- (a) any bill of lading if the contract contained in or evidenced by it expressly provides that the Rules shall govern the contract, and
- (b) any receipt which is a non-negotiable document marked as such if the contract contained in or evidenced by it is a contract for the carriage of goods by sea which expressly provides that the Rules are to govern the contract as if the receipt were a bill of lading,

but subject, where paragraph (b) applies, to any necessary modifications and in particular with the omission in Article III of the Rules of the second sentence of paragraph 4 and paragraph 7.

---

[1] Added by the Merchant Shipping Act 1981, s 2(1).

(7) If and so far as the contract contained in or evidenced by a bill of lading or receipt within paragraph (a) or (b) of subsection (6) above applies to deck cargo or live animals, the Rules as given the force of law by that subsection shall have effect as if Article 1(c) did not exclude deck cargo and live animals.

In this subsection 'deck cargo' means cargo which by the contract of carriage is stated as being carried on deck and is so carried.

2.—(1) If Her Majesty by Order in Council certifies to the following effect, that is to say, that for the purposes of the Rules
  (a) a State specified in the Order is a contracting State, or is a contracting State in respect of any place or territory so specified, or
  (b) any place or territory specified in the Order forms part of a State so specified (whether a contracting State or not),
the Order shall, except so far as it has been superseded by a subsequent Order, be conclusive evidence of the matters so certified.

(2) An Order in Council under this section may be varied or revoked by a subsequent Order in Council.

3. There shall not be implied in any contract for the carriage of goods by sea to which the Rules apply by virtue of this Act any absolute undertaking by the carrier of the goods to provide a seaworthy ship.

4.—(1) Her Majesty may by Order in Council direct that this Act shall extend, subject to such exceptions, adaptations and modifications as may be specified in the Order, to all or any of the following territories, that is:
  (a) any colony (not being a colony for whose external relations a country other than the United Kingdom is responsible),
  (b) any country outside Her Majesty's dominions in which Her Majesty has jurisdiction in right of Her Majesty's Government of the United Kingdom.

(2) An Order in Council under this section may contain such transitional and other consequential and incidental provisions as appear to Her Majesty to be expedient, including provisions amending or repealing any legislation about the carriage of goods by sea forming part of the law of any of the territories mentioned in paragraphs (a) and (b) above.

(3) An Order in Council under this section may be varied or revoked by a subsequent Order in Council.

5.—(1) Her Majesty may by Order in Council provide that section 1(3) of this Act shall have effect as if the reference therein to the United Kingdom included a reference to all or any of the following territories, that is —
  (a) the Isle of Man;

(b) any of the Channel Islands specified in the Order;

(c) any colony specified in the Order (not being a colony for whose external relations a country other than the United Kingdom is responsible);

(d) any associated state (as defined by section 1(3) of the West Indies Act 1967) specified in the Order;

(e) any country specified in the Order, being a country outside Her Majesty's dominions in which Her Majesty has jurisdiction in right of Her Majesty's Government of the United Kingdom.

(2) An Order in Council under this section may be varied or revoked by a subsequent Order in Council.

6.—(1) This Act may be cited as the Carriage of Goods by Sea Act 1971.

(2) It is hereby declared that this Act extends to Northern Ireland.

(3) The following enactments shall be repealed, that is—

(a) the Carriage of Goods by Sea Act 1924,

(b) section 12(4)(a) of the Nuclear Installations Act 1965,

and without prejudice to section 38(1) of the Interpretation Act 1889, the reference to the said Act of 1924 in section 1(1)(i)(ii) of the Hovercraft Act 1968 shall include a reference to this Act.

(4) It is hereby declared that for the purposes of Article VIII of the Rules section 502 of the Merchant Shipping Act 1894 (which, as amended by the Merchant Shipping (Liability of Shipowners and Others) Act 1958, entirely exempts shipowners and others in certain circumstances from liability for loss of, or damage to, goods) is a provision relating to limitations of liability.

(5) This Act shall come into force on such day as Her Majesty may by Order in Council appoint, and, for the purposes of the transition from the law in force immediately before the day appointed under this subsection to the provisions of this Act, the Order appointing the day may provide that those provisions shall have effect subject to such transitional provisions as may be contained in the Order.

SCHEDULE

The Hague Rules as amended by the Brussels Protocol 1968.

Article I

In these Rules the following words are employed, with the meaning set out below:

(a) 'Carrier' includes the owner or the charterer who enters into a contract of carriage with a shipper.

(b) 'Contract of carriage' applies only to contracts of carriage covered by a bill of lading or any similar document of title, in so far as such document relates to the carriage of goods by sea, including any bill of lading or any similar document as aforesaid issued under or pursuant to a charter party from the moment at which such bill of lading or similar document of title regulates the relations between a carrier and a holder of the same.

(c) 'Goods' includes goods, wares, merchandise, and articles of every kind whatsoever except live animals and cargo which by the contract of carriage is stated as being carried on deck and is so carried.

(d) 'Ship' means any vessel used for the carriage of goods by sea.

(e) 'Carriage of goods' covers the period from the time when the goods are loaded on to the time they are discharged from the ship.

Article II

Subject to the provisions of Article VI, under every contract of carriage of goods by sea the carrier, in relation to the loading, handling, stowage, carriage, custody, care and discharge of such goods, shall be subject to the responsibilities and liabilities, and entitled to the rights and immunities hereinafter set forth.

Article III

1. The carrier shall be bound before and at the beginning of the voyage to exercise due diligence to —
    (a) Make the ship seaworthy.
    (b) Properly man, equip and supply the ship.
    (c) Make the holds, refrigerating and cool chambers, and all other parts of the ship in which goods are carried, fit and safe for their reception, carriage and preservation.

2. Subject to the provisions of Article IV, the carrier shall properly and carefully load, handle, stow, carry, keep, care for, and discharge the goods carried.

3. After receiving the goods into his charge the carrier or the master or agent of the carrier shall, on demand of the shipper, issue to the shipper a bill of lading showing among other things —
    (a) The leading marks necessary for identification of the goods as the same are furnished in writing by the shipper before the loading of such goods starts, provided such marks are stamped or otherwise shown clearly upon the goods if uncovered, or on the cases or coverings in which such goods are contained, in such a manner as should ordinarily remain legible until the end of the voyage.
    (b) Either the number of packages or pieces, or the quantity, or weight, as the case may be, as furnished in writing by the shipper.
    (c) The apparent order and condition of the goods.
Provided that no carrier, master or agent of the carrier shall be bound

to state or show in the bill of lading any marks, number, quantity, or weight which he has reasonable ground for suspecting not accurately to represent the goods actually received, or which he has had no reasonable means of checking.

4. Such a bill of lading shall be prima facie evidence of the receipt by the carrier of the goods as therein described in accordance with paragraph 3(a), (b) and (c). However, proof to the contrary shall not be admissible when the bill of lading has been transferred to a third party acting in good faith.

5. The shipper shall be deemed to have guaranteed to the carrier the accuracy at the time of shipment of the marks, number, quantity and weight, as furnished by him, and the shipper shall indemnify the carrier against all loss, damages and expenses arising or resulting from inaccuracies in such particulars. The right of the carrier to such indemnity shall in no way limit his responsibility and liability under the contract of carriage to any person other than the shipper.

6. Unless notice of loss or damage and the general nature of such loss or damage be given in writing to the carrier or his agent at the port of discharge before or at the time of the removal of the goods into the custody of the person entitled to delivery thereof under the contract of carriage, or, if the loss or damage be not apparent, within three days, such removal shall be prima facie evidence of the delivery by the carrier of the goods as described in the bill of lading.

The notice in writing need not be given if the state of the goods has, at the time of their receipt, been the subject of joint survey or inspection.

Subject to paragraph 6*bis* the carrier and the ship shall in any event be discharged from all liability whatsoever in respect of the goods, unless suit is brought within one year of their delivery or of the date when they should have been delivered. This period may, however, be extended if the parties so agree after the cause of action has arisen.

In the case of any actual or apprehended loss or damage the carrier and the receiver shall give all reasonable facilities to each other for inspecting and tallying the goods.

6*bis*. An action for indemnity against a third person may be brought even after the expiration of the year provided for in the preceding paragraph if brought within the time allowed by the law of the Court seized of the case. However, the time allowed shall be not less than three months, commencing from the day when the person bringing such action for indemnity has settled the claim or has been served with process in the action against himself.

7. After the goods are loaded the bill of lading to be issued by the carrier, master, or agent of the carrier, to the shipper shall, if the shipper so

demands, be a 'shipped' bill of lading, provided that if the shipper shall have previously taken up any document of title to such goods, he shall surrender the same as against the issue of the 'shipped' bill of lading, but at the option of the carrier such document of title may be noted at the port of shipment by the carrier, master, or agent with the name or names of the ship or ships upon which the goods have been shipped and the date or dates of shipment, and when so noted, if it shows the particulars mentioned in paragraph 3 of Article III, shall for the purpose of this article be deemed to constitute a 'shipped' bill of lading.

8. Any clause, covenant, or agreement in a contract of carriage relieving the carrier or the ship from liability for loss or damage to, or in connection with, goods arising from negligence, fault or failure in the duties and obligations provided in this article or lessening such liability otherwise than as provided in these Rules, shall be null and void and of no effect. A benefit of insurance in favour of the carrier or similar clause shall be deemed to be a clause relieving the carrier from liability.

Article IV

1. Neither the carrier nor the ship shall be liable for loss or damage arising or resulting from unseaworthiness unless caused by want of due diligence on the part of the carrier to make the ship seaworthy, and to secure that the ship is properly manned, equipped and supplied, and to make the holds, refrigerating and cool chambers and all other parts of the ship in which goods are carried fit and safe for their reception, carriage and preservation in accordance with the provisions of paragraph 1 of Article III. Whenever loss or damage has resulted from unseaworthiness the burden of proving the exercise of due diligence shall be on the carrier or other person claiming exemption under this article.

2. Neither the carrier nor the ship shall be be responsible for loss or damage arising or resulting from —
   (a) Act, neglect, or default of the master, mariner, pilot, or the servants of the carrier in the navigation or in the management of the ship.
   (b) Fire, unless caused by the actual fault or privity of the carrier.
   (c) Perils, dangers and accidents of the sea or other navigable waters.
   (d) Act of God.
   (e) Act of war.
   (f) Act of public enemies.
   (g) Arrest or restraint of princes, rulers or people, or seizure under legal process.
   (h) Quarantine restrictions.
   (i) Act or omission of the shipper or owner of the goods, his agent or representative.
   (j) Strikes or lockouts or stoppage or restraint of labour from whatever cause, whether partial or general.
   (k) Riots and civil commotions.
   (l) Saving or attempting to save life or property at sea.

(m) Wastage in bulk or weight or any other loss or damage arising from inherent defect, quality or vice of the goods.

(n) Insufficiency of packing.

(o) Insufficiency or inadequacy of marks.

(p) Latent defects not discoverable by due diligence.

(q) Any other cause arising without the actual fault or privity of the carrier, or without the fault or neglect of the agents or servants of the carrier, but the burden of proof shall be on the person claiming the benefit of this exception to show that neither the actual fault or privity of the carrier nor the fault or neglect of the agents or servants of the carrier contributed to the loss or damage.

3. The shipper shall not be responsible for loss or damage sustained by the carrier or the ship arising or resulting from any cause without the act, fault or neglect of the shipper, his agents or his servants.

4. Any deviation in saving or attempting to save life or property at sea or any reasonable deviation shall not be deemed to be an infringement or breach of these Rules or of the contract of carriage, and the carrier shall not be liable for any loss or damage resulting therefrom.

5(a) Unless the nature and value of such goods have been declared by the shipper before shipment and inserted in the bill of lading, neither the carrier nor the ship shall in any event be or become liable for any loss or damage to or in connection with the goods in an amount exceeding [666.67 units of account][2] per package or unit or [2 units of account per kilogramme][3] of gross weight of the goods lost or damaged, whichever is the higher.

(b) The total amount recoverable shall be calculated by reference to the value of such goods at the place and time at which the goods are discharged from the ship in accordance with the contract or should have been so discharged.

The value of the goods shall be fixed according to the commodity exchange price, or, if there be no such price, according to the current market price, or, if there be no commodity exchange price or current market price, by reference to the normal value of goods of the same kind and quality.

(c) Where a container, pallet or similar article of transport is used to consolidate goods, the number of packages or units enumerated in the bill of lading as packed in such article of transport shall be deemed the number of packages or units for the purpose of this paragraph as far as these packages or units are concerned. Except as aforesaid such article of transport shall be considered the package or unit.

(d) The unit of account mentioned in this Article is the special drawing right as defined by the International Monetary Fund. The amounts

---

[2]   Words replaced by the Merchant Shipping Act 1981, s 2(3)(a).
[3]   Words replaced by the Merchant Shipping Act 1981, s 2(3)(b).

mentioned in sub-paragraph (a) of this paragraph shall be converted into national currency on the basis of the value of that currency on a date to be determined by the law of the Court seized of the case.[4]

(e) Neither the carrier nor the ship shall be entitled to the benefit of the limitation of liability provided for in this paragraph if it is proved that the damage resulted from an act or omission of the carrier done with intent to cause damage, or recklessly and with knowledge that damage would probably result.

(f) The declaration mentioned in sub-paragraph (a) of this paragraph, if embodied in the bill of lading, shall be prima facie evidence, but shall not be binding or conclusive on the carrier.

(g) By agreement between the carrier, master or agent of the carrier and the shipper other maximum amounts than those mentioned in sub-paragraph (a) of this paragraph may be fixed, provided that no maximum amount so fixed shall be less than the appropriate maximum mentioned in that sub-paragraph.

(h) Neither the carrier nor the ship shall be responsible in any event for loss or damage to, or in connection with, goods if the nature or value thereof has been knowingly mis-stated by the shipper in the bill of lading.

6. Goods of an inflammable, explosive or dangerous nature to the shipment whereof the carrier, master or agent of the carrier has not consented with knowledge of their nature and character, may at any time before discharge be landed at any place, or destroyed or rendered innocuous by the carrier without compensation and the shipper of such goods shall be liable for all damages and expenses directly or indirectly arising out of or resulting from such shipment. If any such goods shipped with such knowledge and consent shall become a danger to the ship or cargo, they may in like manner be landed at any place, or destroyed or rendered innocuous by the carrier without liability on the part of the carrier except to general average, if any.

Article IV *bis*

1. The defences and limits of liability provided for in these Rules shall apply in any action against the carrier in respect of loss or damage to goods covered by a contract of carriage whether the action be founded in contract or in tort.

2. If such an action is brought against a servant or agent of the carrier (such servant or agent not being an independent contractor), such servant or agent shall be entitled to avail himself of the defences and limits of liability which the carrier is entitled to invoke under these Rules.

3. The aggregate of the amounts recoverable from the carrier, and such

---

[4]   Words replaced by the Merchant Shipping Act 1981, s 2(4).

servants and agents, shall in no case exceed the limit provided for in these Rules.

4. Nevertheless, a servant or agent of the carrier shall not be entitled to avail himself of the provisions of this article, if it is proved that the damage resulted from an act or omission of the servant or agent done with intent to cause damage or recklessly and with knowledge that damage would probably result.

Article V

A carrier shall be at liberty to surrender in whole or in part all or any of his rights and immunities or to increase any of his responsibilities and obligations under these Rules, provided such surrender or increase shall be embodied in the bill of lading issued to the shipper. The provisions of these Rules shall not be applicable to charter parties, but if bills of lading are issued in the case of a ship under a charter party they shall comply with the terms of these Rules. Nothing in these Rules shall be held to prevent the insertion in a bill of lading of any lawful provision regarding general average.

Article VI

Notwithstanding the provisions of the preceding articles, a carrier, master or agent of the carrier and a shipper shall in regard to any particular goods be at liberty to enter into any agreement in any terms as to the responsibility and liability of the carrier for such goods, and as to the rights and immunities of the carrier in respect of such goods, or his obligation as to seaworthiness, so far as this stipulation is not contrary to public policy, or the care or diligence of his servants or agents in regard to the loading, handling, stowage, carriage, custody, care and discharge of the goods carried by sea, provided that in this case no bill of lading has been or shall be issued and that the terms agreed shall be embodied in a receipt which shall be a non-negotiable document and shall be marked as such.

Any agreement so entered into shall have full legal effect.

Provided that this article shall not apply to ordinary commercial shipments made in the ordinary course of trade, but only to other shipments where the character or condition of the property to be carried or the circumstances, terms and conditions under which the carriage is to be performed are such as reasonably to justify a special agreement.

Article VII

Nothing herein contained shall prevent a carrier or a shipper from entering into any agreement, stipulation, condition, reservation or exemption as to the responsibility and liability of the carrier or the ship for the loss or damage to, or in connection with, the custody and care and handling of goods prior to the loading on, and subsequent to the discharge from, the ship on which the goods are carried by sea.

Article VIII

The provisions of these Rules shall not affect the rights and obligations of the carrier under any statute for the time being in force relating to the limitation of the liability of owners of sea-going vessels.

Article IX

These Rules shall not affect the provisions of any International Convention or national law governing liability for nuclear damage.

Article X

The provisions of these Rules shall apply to every bill of lading relating to the carriage of goods between ports in two different States if:
- (a) the bill of lading is issued in a contracting State,
  or
- (b) the carriage is from a port in a contracting State,
  or
- (c) the contract contained in or evidenced by the bill of lading provides that these Rules or legislation of any State giving effect to them are to govern the contract,

whatever may be the nationality of the ship, the carrier, the shipper, the consignee, or any other interested person.

[*The last two paragraphs of this article are not reproduced. They require contracting States to apply the Rules to bills of lading mentioned in the article and authorize them to apply the Rules to other bills of lading.*]

[*Articles 11 to 16 of the International Convention for the unification of certain rules of law relating to bills of lading signed at Brussels on 25 August 1924 are not reproduced. They deal with the coming into force of the Convention, procedure for ratification, accession and denunciation, and the right to call for a fresh conference to consider amendments to the Rules contained in the Convention.*]

C. BILLS OF LADING ACT 1855

An Act to amend the Law relating to Bills of Lading

[14 August 1855]

Whereas, by the custom of merchants, a bill of lading of goods being transferable by endorsement, the property in the goods may thereby pass to the endorsee, but nevertheless all rights in respect of the contract contained in the bill of lading continue in the original shipper or owner; and it is expedient that such rights should pass with the property: And whereas it frequently happens that the goods in respect of which bills of lading purport to be signed have not been laden on board, and it is proper that such bills of lading in the hands of a bona fide holder for value should not be questioned by the master or other person signing the same on the ground of the goods not having been laden as aforesaid.

1. Every consignee of goods named in a bill of lading, and every endorsee of a bill of lading, to whom the property in the goods therein mentioned shall pass upon or by reason of such consignment or endorsement, shall have transferred to and vested in him all rights of suit, and be subject to the same liabilities in respect of such goods as if the contract contained in the bill of lading had been made with himself.

2. Nothing herein contained shall prejudice or affect any right of stoppage in transitu, or any right to claim freight against the original shipper or owner, or any liability of the consignee or endorsee by reason or in consequence of his being such consignee or endorsee, or of his receipt of the goods by reason or in consequence of such consignment or endorsement.

3. Every bill of lading in the hands of a consignee or endorsee for valuable consideration, representing goods to have been shipped on board a vessel, shall be conclusive evidence of such shipment as against the master or other person signing the same, notwithstanding that such goods or some part thereof may not have been so shipped, unless such holder of the bill of lading shall have had actual notice at the time of receiving the same that the goods had not been in fact laden on board; Provided, that the master or other person so signing may exonerate himself in respect of such misrepresentation by showing that it was caused without any default on his part, and wholly by the fraud of the shipper, or of the holder, or some person under whom the holder claims.

ICC rules relevant to international trade

a. Incoterms 1980 for CIF, C & F, FOB, FRC and CIP (ICC publication 350)
b. Articles 25 and 26 of the Uniform Customs and Practice for Documentary Credits (ICC publication 400)
c. Incoterms 1990 for CIF, FOB, CFR, FCA and CIP (ICC publication 460)

A. INCOTERMS 1980 FOR CIF, C & F, FOB, FRC AND CIP (ICC PUBLICATION 350)

CIF

CIF means 'Cost, Insurance and Freight'. This term is the same as C & F but with the addition that the seller has to procure marine insurance against the risk of loss or of damage to the goods during the carriage. The seller contracts with the insurer and pays the insurance premium. The buyer should note that under the present term, unlike the term 'Freight/Carriage and Insurance paid to', the seller is only required to cover insurance on minimum conditions (so-called FPA conditions).

A. The seller must:

1. Supply the goods in conformity with the contract of sale, together with such evidence of conformity as may be required by the contract.

2. Contract on usual terms at his own expense for the carriage of the goods to the agreed port of destination by the usual route, in a seagoing vessel (not being a sailing vessel) of the type normally used for the transport of goods of the contract description, and pay freight charges and any charges for unloading at the port of discharge which may be levied by regular shipping lines at the time and port of shipment.

3. At his own risk and expense obtain any export licence or other governmental authorization necessary for the export of the goods.

4. Load the goods at his own expense on board the vessel at the port of shipment and at the date or within the period fixed or, if neither date nor time has been stipulated, within a reasonable time, and notify the buyer, without delay, that the goods have been loaded on board the vessel.

5.   Procure, at his own cost and in a transferable form, a policy of marine insurance against the risks of carriage involved in the contract. The insurance shall be contracted with underwriters or insurance companies of good repute on FPA terms, and shall cover the CIF price plus ten per cent. The insurance shall be provided in the currency of the contract, if procurable[1].

Unless otherwise agreed, the risk of carriage shall not include special risks that are covered in specific trades or against which the buyer may wish individual protection. Among the special risks that should be considered and agreed upon between the seller and buyer are theft, pilferage, leakage, breakage, chipping sweat, contact with other cargoes and other peculiar to any particular trade.

When required by the buyer, the seller shall provide at the buyer's expense, war risk insurance in the currency of the contract, if procurable.

6.   Subject to the provisions of article B.4 below, bear all risks of the goods until such time as they shall have effectively passed the ship's rail at the port of shipment.

7.   At his own expense furnish to the buyer without delay a clear negotiable bill of lading for the agreed port of destination, as well as the invoice of the goods shipped and the insurance policy or, should the insurance policy not be available at the time the documents are tendered, a certificate of insurance issued under the authority of the underwriters and conveying to the bearer the same rights as if he were in possession of the policy and reproducing the essential provisions thereof. The bill of lading must cover the contract goods, be dated within the period agreed for shipment, and provide by endorsement or otherwise for delivery to the order of the buyer or buyer's agreed representative. Such bill of lading must be a full set of 'on board' or 'shipped' bills of lading, or a 'received for shipment' bill of lading duly endorsed by the shipping company, to the effect that the goods are on board, such endorsement to be dated within the period agreed for shipment. If the bill of lading contains a reference to the charter-party, the seller must also provide a copy of this latter document.

Note: A clean bill of lading is one which bears no superimposed clauses expressly declaring a defective condition of the goods or packaging.

The following clauses do not convert a clean into an unclean bill of lading:

a) clauses which do not expressly state that the goods or packaging are unsatisfactory, e g 'second-hand cases', 'used drums', etc: **b)** clauses which emphasize the carrier's non-liability for risks arising through the nature of the goods or the packaging: **c)** clauses which disclaim on the part of the carrier knowledge of contents, weight, measurement, quality, or technical specification of the goods.

---

[1]   CIF A.5 provides for the minimum terms (FPA) and period of insurance (warehouse to warehouse). Whenever the buyer wishes more than the minimum liability to be included in the contract, then he should take care to specify that the basis of the contract is to be 'Incoterms' with whatever addition he requires.

8. Provide at his own expense the customary packing of the goods, unless it is the custom of the trade to ship the goods unpacked.

9. Pay the costs of any checking operations (such as checking quality, measuring, weighing, counting) which shall be necessary for the purpose of loading the goods.

10. Pay any dues and taxes incurred in respect of the goods up to the time of their loading, including any taxes, fees or charges levied because of exportation, as well as the costs of any formalities which he shall have to fulfil in order to load the goods on board.

11. Provide the buyer, at the latter's request and expense (see B.5), with the certificate of origin and the consular invoice.

12. Render the buyer, at the latter's request, risk and expense, every assistance in obtaining any documents, other than those mentioned in the previous article, issued in the country of shipment and/or of origin and which the buyer may require for the importation of the goods into the country of destination (and, where necessary for their passage in transit through another country).

B. The buyer must:

1. Accept the documents when tendered by the seller, if they are in conformity with the contract of sale, and pay the price as provided in the contract.

2. Receive the goods at the agreed port of destination and bear, with the exception of the freight and marine insurance, all costs and charges incurred in respect of the goods in the course of their transit by sea until their arrival at the port of destination, as well as unloading costs, including lighterage and wharfage charges, unless such costs and charges shall have been included in the freight or collected by the steamship company at the time freight was paid.

   If war insurance is provided, it shall be at the expense of the buyer (see A.5).

   Note: If the goods are sold 'CIF landed', unloading costs, including lighterage and wharfage charges, are borne by the seller.

3. Bear all risks of the goods from the time when they shall have effectively passed the ship's rail at the port of shipment.

4. In case he may have reserved to himself a period within which to have the goods shipped and/or the right to choose the port of destination, and he fails to give instructions in time, bear the additional costs thereby incurred and all risks of the goods from the date of the expiration of the period fixed for shipment, provided always that the goods shall have been duly appropriated to the contract, that is to say, clearly set aside or otherwise identified as the contract goods.

5. Pay the costs and charges incurred in obtaining the certificate of origin and consular documents.

6. Pay all costs and charges incurred in obtaining the documents mentioned in article A.12 above.

7. Pay all customs duties as well as any other duties and taxes payable at the time of or by reason of the importation.

8. Procure and provide at his own risk and expense any import licence or permit or the like which he may require for the importation of the goods at destination.

C & F

C & F means 'Cost and Freight'. The seller must pay the costs and freight necessary to bring the goods to the named destination but the risk of loss of or damage to the goods, as well as of any cost increases, is transferred from the seller to the buyer when the goods pass the ship's rail in the port of shipment.

A. The seller must:

1. Supply the goods in conformity with the contract of sale, together with such evidence of conformity as may be required by the contract.

2. Contract on usual terms at his own expense for the carriage of the goods to the agreed port of destination by the usual route, in a seagoing vessel (not being a sailing vessel) of the type normally used for transport of goods of the contract description, and pay freight charges and any charges for unloading at the port of discharge which may be levied by regular shipping lines at the time and port of shipment.

3. At his own risk and expense obtain any export licence or other governmental authorization necessary for the export of the goods.

4. Load the goods at his own expense on board the vessel at the port of shipment and at the date or within the period fixed or, if neither date nor time has been stipulated, within a reasonable time, and notify the buyer, without delay, that the goods have been loaded on board the vessel.

5. Subject to the provisions of article B.4 below, bear all risks of the goods until such time as they shall have effectively passed the ship's rail at the port of shipment.

6. At his own expense furnish to the buyer without delay a clean negotiable bill of lading for the agreed port of destination, as well as the invoice of the goods shipped. The bill of lading must cover the contract goods, be dated within the period agreed for shipment, and provide by endorsement or otherwise for delivery to the order of the buyer or buyer's agreed representative. Such bill of lading must be a full set of 'on board' or 'shipped' bills of lading, or a 'received for shipment' bill of lading duly endorsed by the shipping company to the effect that the goods are on board, such endorsement to be dated within the period

agreed for shipment. If the bill of lading contains a reference to the charter-party, the seller must also provide a copy of this latter document.

Note: A clean bill of lading is one which bears no superimposed clauses expressly declaring a defective condition of the goods or packaging.

The following clauses do not convert a clean into an unclean bill of lading:
a) clauses which do not expressly state that the goods or packaging are unsatisfactory, e g 'second-hand cases', 'used drum', etc.; **b)** clauses which emphasize the carrier's non-liability for risks arising through the nature of the goods or the packaging; **c)** clauses which disclaim on the part of the carrier knowledge of contents, weight, measurement, quality, or technical specification of the goods.

7. Provide at his own expense the customary packaging of the goods, unless it is the custom of the trade to ship the goods unpacked.

8. Pay the costs of any checking operations (such as checking quality, measuring, weighing, counting) which shall be necessary for the purpose of loading the goods.

9. Pay any dues and taxes incurred in respect of the goods, up to the time of their loading, including any taxes, fees or charges levied because of exportation, as well as the cost of any formalities which he shall have to fulfil in order to load the goods on board.

10. Provide the buyer, at the latter's request and expense (see B.5), with the certificate of origin and the consular invoice.

11. Render the buyer, at the latter's request, risk and expense, every assistance in obtaining any documents, other than those mentioned in the previous article, issued in the country of shipment and/or of origin and which the buyer may require for the importation of the goods into the country of destination (and, where necessary, for their passage in transit through another country).

B. The buyer must:

1. Accept the documents when tendered by the seller, if they are in conformity with the contract of sale, and pay the price as provided in the contract.

2. Receive the goods at the agreed port of destination and bear, with the exception of the freight, all costs and charges, incurred in respect of the goods in the course of their transit by sea until their arrival at the port of destination, as well as unloading costs, including lighterage and wharfage charges, unless such costs and charges shall have been included in the freight or collected by the steamship company at the time freight was paid.

Note: If the goods are sold 'C & F landed', unloading costs, including lighterage and wharfage charges, are borne by the seller.

3. Bear all risks of the goods from the time when they shall have effectively passed the ship's rail at the port of shipment.

4.   In case he may have reserved to himself a period within which to have the goods shipped and/or the right to choose the port of destination, and he fails to give instructions in time, bear the additional costs thereby incurred and all risks of the goods from the date of the expiration of the period fixed for shipment, provided always that the goods shall have been duly appropriated to the contract, that is to say, clearly set aside or otherwise identified as the contract goods.

5.   Pay the costs and charges incurred in obtaining the certificate of origin and consular documents.

6.   Pay all the costs and charges incurred in obtaining the documents mentioned in article A.11 above.

7.   Pay all the customs duties as well as any other duties and taxes payable at the time of or by reason of the importation.

8.   Procure and provide at his own risk and expense any import licence or permit or the like which he may require for the importation of the goods at destination.

FOB

FOB means 'Free on Board'. The goods are placed on board a ship by the seller at a port of shipment named in the sales contract. The risk of loss of or damage to the goods is transferred from the seller to the buyer when the goods pass the ship's rail.

A. The seller must:

1.   Supply the goods in conformity with the contract of sale, together with such evidence of conformity as may be required by the contract.

2.   Deliver the goods on board the vessel named by the buyer, at the named port of shipment, in the manner customary at the port, at the date or within the period stipulated, and notify the buyer, without delay, that the goods have been delivered on board.

3.   At his own risk and expense obtain any export licence or other governmental authorization necessary for the export of the goods.

4.   Subject to the provisions of articles B.3 and B.4 below, bear all costs and risks of the goods until such time as they shall have effectively passed the ship's rail at the named port of shipment, including any taxes, fees or charges levied because of exportation, as well as the costs of any formalities which he shall have to fulfil in order to load the goods on board.

5.   Provide at his own expense the customary packing of the goods, unless it is the custom of the trade to ship the goods unpacked.

6.   Pay the costs of any checking operations (such as checking quality, measuring, weighing, counting) which shall be necessary for the purpose of delivering the goods.

7. Provide at his own expense the customary clean document in proof of delivery of the goods on board the named vessel.

8. Provide the buyer, at the latter's request and expense (see B.6) with the certificate of origin.

9. Render the buyer, at the latter's request, risk and expense, every assistance in obtaining a bill of lading and any documents, other than that mentioned in the previous article, issued in the country of shipment and/or of origin and which the buyer may require for the importation of the goods into the country of destination (and, where necessary, for their passage in transit through another country).

B. The buyer must:

1. At his own expense, charter a vessel or reserve the necessary space on board a vessel and give the seller due notice of the name, loading berth of and delivery dates to the vessel.

2. Bear all costs and risks of the goods from the time when they shall have effectively passed the ship's rail at the named port of shipment, and pay the price as provided in the contract.

3. Bear any additional costs incurred because the vessel named by him shall have failed to arrive on the stipulated date or by the end of the period specified, or shall be unable to take the goods or shall close for cargo earlier than the stipulated date or the end of the period specified and all the risks of the goods from the date of expiration of the period stipulated, provided, however, that the goods shall have been duly appropriated to the contract that is to say, clearly set aside or otherwise identified as the contract goods.

4. Should he fail to name the vessel in time or, if he shall have reserved to himself a period within which to take delivery of the goods and/or the right to choose the port of shipment, should he fail to give detailed instructions in time, bear any additional costs incurred because of such failure, and all the risks of the goods from the date of expiration of the period stipulated for delivery, provided, however, that the goods shall have been duly appropriated to the contract, that is to say, clearly set aside or otherwise identified as the contract goods.

5. Pay any costs and charges for obtaining a bill of lading if incurred under article A.9 above.

6. Pay all costs and charges incurred in obtaining the documents mentioned in articles A.8 and A.9 above, including the costs of certificates of origin and consular documents.

FRC

This term has been designed to meet the requirements of modern transport, particularly such 'multimodal' transport as container or 'roll on-roll off' traffic by trailers and ferries.

It is based on the same main principle as FOB except that the seller fulfils his obligations when he delivers the goods into the custody of the carrier at the named point. If no precise point can be mentioned at the time of the contract of sale, the parties should refer to the place or range where the carrier should take the goods into his charge. The risk of loss of or damage to the goods is transferred from seller to buyer at that time and not at the ship's rail.

'Carrier' means any person by whom or in whose name a contract of carriage by road, rail, air, sea or a combination of modes has been made. When the seller has to furnish a bill of lading, waybill or carrier's receipt, he duly fulfils this obligation by presenting such a document issued by a person so defined.

A. The seller must:

1.   Supply the goods in conformity with the contract of sale, together with such evidence of conformity as may be required by the contract.

2.   Deliver the goods into the charge of the carrier named by the buyer on the date or within the period agreed for delivery at the named point in the manner expressly agreed or customary at such point. If no specific point has been named, and if there are several points available, the seller may select the point at the place of delivery which best suits his purposes.

3.   At his own risk and expense obtain any export licence or other official authorization necessary for the export of the goods.

4.   Subject to the provisions of article B.5 below, pay any taxes, fees and charges levied in respect of the goods because of exportation.

5.   Subject to the provisions of article B.5 below, bear all costs payable in respect of the goods until such time as they will have been delivered in accordance with the provisions of article A.2 above.

6.   Subject to the provisions of article B.5 below, bear all risks of the goods until such time as they have been delivered in accordance with the provisions of article A.2 above.

7.   Provide at his own expense the customary packing of the goods, unless it is the custom of the trade to dispatch the goods unpacked.

8.   Pay the cost of any checking operations (such as checking quality, measuring, weighing, counting) which shall be necessary for the purpose of delivering the goods.

9.   Give the buyer without delay notice by telecommunication channels of the delivery of the goods.

10.   In the circumstances referred to in article B.5 below, give the buyer prompt notice by telecommunication channels of the occurrence of said circumstances.

11.   At his own expense, provide the buyer, if customary, with the usual document or other evidence of the delivery of the goods in accordance with the provisions of article A.2 above.

12. Provide the buyer with the commercial invoice in proper form so as to facilitate compliance with applicable regulations and, at the buyer's request and expense, with the certificate of origin.

13. Render the buyer, at his request, risk and expense, every assistance in obtaining any document other than those mentioned in article A.12 above issued in the country of departure and/or of origin and which the buyer may require for the importation of the goods into the country of destination (and, where necessary, for their passage in transit through another country).

B. *The buyer must:*

1. At his own expense contract for the carriage of the goods from the named point and give the seller due notice of the name of the carrier and of the time for delivering the goods to him.

2. Bear all costs payable in respect of the goods from the time when they have been delivered in accordance with the provisions of article A.2 above, except as provided in article A.4 above.

3. Pay the price as provided in the contract.

4. Bear all risks of the goods from the time when they have been delivered in accordance with the provisions of article A.2 above.

5. Bear any additional costs incurred because the buyer fails to name the carrier, or the carrier named by him fails to take the goods into his charge, at the time agreed, and bear all risks of the goods from the date of expiry of the period stipulated for delivery, provided, however, that the goods will have been duly appropriated to the contract, that is to say, clearly set aside or otherwise identified as the contract goods.

6. Bear all costs, fees and charges incurred in obtaining the documents mentioned in article A.13 above, including the cost of consular documents, as well as the cost of certificates of origin.

CIP

This term is the same as 'Freight/Carriage paid to. . .' but with the addition that the seller has to procure transport insurance against the risk of loss of or damage to the goods during the carriage. The seller contracts with the insurer and pays the insurance premium.

A. *The seller must:*

1. Supply the goods in conformity with the contract of sale, together with such evidence of conformity as may be required by the contract.

2. Contract at his own expense for the carriage of the goods by a usual route and in a customary manner to the agreed point at the place of destination. If the point is not agreed or is not determined by custom,

the seller may select the point at the place of destination which best suits his purpose.

3. Subject to the provisions of article B.3 below, bear all risks of the goods until they shall have been delivered into the custody of the first carrier, at the time as provided in the contract.

4. Give the buyer without delay notice by telecommunication channels that the goods have been delivered into the custody of the first carrier.

5. Provide at his own expense the customary packing of the goods, unless it is the custom of the trade to dispatch the goods unpacked.

6. Pay the costs of any checking operations (such as checking quality, measuring, weighing, counting) which shall be necessary for the purpose of loading the goods or of delivering them into the custody of the first carrier.

7. At his own expense, provide the buyer, if customary, with the usual transport document.

8. At his own risk and expense obtain any export licence or other governmental authorization necessary for the export of the goods, and pay any dues and taxes incurred in respect of the goods in the country of dispatch, including any export duties, as well as the costs of any formalities he shall have to fulfil in order to load the goods.

9. Provide the buyer with the commercial invoice in proper form so as to facilitate compliance with applicable regulations and, at the buyer's request and expense, with the certificate of origin.

10. Render the buyer, at the latter's request, risk and expense, every assistance in obtaining any documents, other than those mentioned in the previous article, issued in the country of loading and/or of origin and which the buyer may require for the importation of the goods into the country of destination (and, where necessary, for their passage in transit through another country).

11. Procure, at his own cost, transport insurance as agreed in the contract and upon such terms that the buyer, or any other person having an insurable interest in the goods, shall be entitled to claim directly from the insurer, and provide the buyer with the insurance policy or other evidence of insurance cover. The insurance shall be contracted with parties of good repute and, failing express argreement, on such terms as are in the seller's view appropriate having regard to the custom of the trade, the nature of the goods and other circumstances affecting the risk. In this latter case, the seller shall inform the buyer of the extent of the insurance cover so as to enable him to take out any additional insurance that he may consider necessary before the risks of the goods are borne by him in accordance with article B.2.

The insurance shall cover the price provided in the contract plus ten per cent and shall be provided in the currency of the contract, if procurable.

When required by the buyer, the seller shall provide, at the buyer's expense, war risk insurance in the currency of the contract, if procurable[2].

B. The buyer must:

1. Receive the goods at the agreed point at the place of destination and pay the price as provided in the contract, and bear, with the exception of the freight and the cost of transport insurance, all costs and charges incurred in respect of the goods in the course of their transit until their arrival at the point of destination, as well as unloading costs, unless such costs and charges shall have been included in the freight or collected by the carrier at the time freight was paid.

2. Bear all risks of the goods from the time when they shall have been delivered into the custody of the first carrier in accordance with article A.3.

3. Where he shall have reserved to himself a period within which to have the goods forwarded to him and/or the right to choose the point of destination, and should he fail to give instructions in time, bear the additional costs thereby incurred and all risks of the goods from the date or expiry of the period fixed, provided always that the goods shall have been duly appropriated to the contract that is to say, clearly set aside or otherwise identified as the contract goods.

4. Bear all costs, fees and charges incurred in obtaining the documents mentioned in article A.10 above, including the cost of consular documents as well as the cost of certificates of origin.

5. Pay all customs duties as well as any other duties and taxes payable at the time of or by reason of the importation.

---

[2] It should be observed that the insurance provision under A.11 of the present term differs from that under A.5 of the CIF term.

B. ARTICLES 25 AND 26 OF THE UNIFORM CUSTOMS AND PRACTICE FOR DOCUMENTARY CREDITS (ICC PUBLICATION 400)

Article 25

Unless a credit calling for a transport document stipulates as such document a marine bill of lading (ocean bill of lading or a bill of lading covering carriage by sea), or a post receipt or certificate of posting:

a. banks will, unless otherwise stipulated in the credit, accept a transport document which:
    i   appears on its face to have been issued by a named carrier, or his agent, and
    ii   indicates dispatch or taking in charge of the goods, or loading on board, as the case may be, and
    iii consists of the full set of originals issued to the consignor if issued in more than one original, and
    iv   meets all other stipulations of the credit.

b. Subject to the above, and unless otherwise stipulated in the credit banks will not reject a transport document which:
    i   bears a title such as 'Combined transport bill of lading', 'Combined transport document', 'Combined transport bill of lading or port-to-port bill of lading', or a title or a combination of titles of similar intent and effect, and/or
    ii   indicates some or all of the conditions of carriage by reference to a source or document other than the transport document itself (short form/blank back transport document), and/or
    iii indicates a place of taking in charge different from the port of loading and/or a place of final destination different from the port of discharge, and/or
    iv   relates to cargoes such as those in containers or on pallets, and the like, and/or
    v   contains the indication 'intended', or similar qualification, in relation to the vessel or other means of transport, and/or the port of loading and/or the port of discharge.

c. Unless otherwise stipulated in the credit in the case of carriage by sea or by more than one mode of transport but including carriage by sea, banks will reject a transport document which:
    i   indicates that it is subject to a charter party, and/or
    ii   indicates that the carrying vessel is propelled by sail only.

d. Unless otherwise stipulated in the credit, banks will reject a transport document issued by a freight forwarder unless it is the FIATA Combined Transport Bill of Lading approved by the International Chamber of Commerce or otherwise indicates that it is issued by a freight forwarder acting as a carrier or agent of a named carrier.

Article 26

If a credit calling for a transport document stipulates as such document a marine bill of lading:

a. banks will, unless otherwise stipulated in the credit, accept a document which:

    i   appears on its face to have been issued by a named carrier, or his agent, and

    ii indicates that the goods have been loaded on board or shipped on a named vessel, and

    iii consists of the full set of originals issued to the consignor if issued in more than one original, and

    iv meets all other stipulations of the credit.

b. Subject to the above, and unless otherwise stipulated in the credit, banks will not reject a document which:

    i   bears a title such as 'Combined transport bill of lading', 'Combined transport document', 'Combined transport bill of lading or port-to-port bill of lading', or a title or a combination of titles of similar intent and effect, and/or

    ii indicates some or all of the conditions of carriage by reference to a source or document other than the transport document itself (short form/blank back transport document), and/or

    iii indicates a place of taking in charge different from the port of loading, and/or a place of final destination different from the port of discharge, and/or

    iv relates to cargoes such as those in containers or on pallets, and the like.

c. Unless otherwise stipulated in the credit, banks will reject a document which:

    i   indicates that it is subject to a charter party, and/or

    ii indicates that the carrying vessel is propelled by sail only, and/or

    iii contains the indication 'intended', or similar qualification in relation to

- the vessel and/or the port of loading — unless such document bears an on board notation in accordance with article 27(b) and also indicates the actual port of loading, and/or

- the port of discharge — unless the place of final destination indicated on the document is other than the port of discharge, and/or

    iv is issued by a freight forwarder, unless it indicates that it is issued by such freight forwarder acting as a carrier, or as the agent of a named carrier.

C. INCOTERMS 1990 FOR CIF, FOB, CFR, FCA AND CIP (ICC PUBLICATION 460)

In force from 1 July 1990.

Cost, insurance and freight . . . (named port of destination) CIF

'Cost, Insurance and Freight' means that the seller has the same obligations as under CFR but with the addition that he has to procure marine insurance against the buyer's risk of loss of or damage to the goods during the carriage. The seller contracts for insurance and pays the insurance premium.

The buyer should note that under the CIF term the seller is only required to obtain insurance on minimum coverage.

The CIF term requires the seller to clear the goods for export.

This term can only be used for sea and inland waterway transport. When the ship's rail serves no practical purposes such as in the case of roll-on/roll-off or container traffic, the CIP term is more appropriate to use.

A. The seller must

A.1. Provision of goods in conformity with the contract

Provide the goods and the commercial invoice, or its equivalent electronic message, in conformity with the contract of sale and any other evidence of conformity which may be required by the contract.

A.2. Licences, authorisations and formalities

Obtain at his own risk and expense any export licence or other official authorisation and carry out all customs formalities necessary for the exportation of the goods.

A.3. Contract of carriage and insurance

(a) Contract of carriage

Contract on usual terms at his own expense for the carriage of the goods to the named port of destination by the usual route in a seagoing vessel (or inland waterway vessel as appropriate) of the type normally used for the transport of goods of the contract description.

(b) Contract of insurance

Obtain at his own expense cargo insurance as agreed in the contract, that the buyer, or any other person having an insurable interest in the goods, shall be entitled to claim directly from the insurer and provide the buyer with the insurance policy or other evidence of insurance cover.

The insurance shall be contracted with underwriters or an insurance company of good repute and, failing express agreement to the contrary, be in accordance with minimum cover of the Institute Cargo Clauses (Institute of London Underwriters) or any similar set of clauses. The duration of insurance cover shall be in accordance with B.5 and B.4. When required by the buyer, the seller shall provide at the buyer's expense war, strikes, riots and civil commotion risk insurances if procurable. The minimum insurance shall cover the price provided in the contract plus ten per cent (ie 110%) and shall be provided in the currency of the contract.

A.4. Delivery

Deliver the goods on board the vessel at the port of shipment on the date or within the period stipulated.

A.5. Transfer of risks

Subject to the provisions of B.5, bear all risks of loss of or damage to the goods until such time as they have passed the ship's rail at the port of shipment.

A.6. Division of costs

Subject to the provisions of B.6

- pay all costs relating to the goods until they have been delivered in accordance with A.4, as well as the freight and all other costs resulting from A.3, including costs of loading the goods on board and any charges for unloading at the port of discharge which may be levied by regular shipping lines when contracting for carriage;
- pay the costs of customs formalities necessary for exportation as well as all duties, taxes and other official charges payable upon exportation.

A.7. Notice to the buyer

Give the buyer sufficient notice that the goods have been delivered on board the vessel as well as any other notice required in order to allow the buyer to take measures which are normally necessary to enable him to take the goods.

A.8. Proof of delivery, transport document or equivalent electronic message

Unless otherwise agreed, at his own expense provide the buyer without delay with the usual transport document for the agreed port of destination.

This document (for example, a negotiable bill of lading, a non-negotiable sea waybill or an inland waterway document) must cover the contract goods, be dated within the period agreed for shipment, enable the buyer to claim the goods from the carrier at destination and, unless otherwise agreed, enable the buyer to sell the goods in transit by the transfer of the document to a subsequent buyer (the negotiable bill of lading) or by notification to the carrier.

When such a transport document is issued in several originals, a full set of originals must be presented to the buyer. If the transport document contains a reference to a charter party, the seller must also provide a copy of this latter document.

Where the seller and the buyer have agreed to communicate electronically, the document referred to in the preceding paragraphs may be replaced by an equivalent electronic data interchange (EDI) message.

2A.9. Checking—packaging—marking

Pay the costs of those checking operations (such as checking quality, measuring, weighing, counting) which are necessary for the purpose of delivering the goods in accordance with A.4.

Provide at his own expense packaging (unless it is usual for the particular trade to ship the goods of the contract description unpacked) which is required for the transport of the goods arranged by him. Packaging is to be marked appropriately.

A.10. Other obligations

Render the buyer at the latter's request, risk and expense, every assistance in obtaining any documents or equivalent electronic messages (other than those mentioned in A.8) issued or transmitted in the country of shipment and/or of origin which the buyer may require for the importation of the goods and, where necessary, for their transit through another country.

Provide the buyer, upon request, with the necessary information for procuring insurance.

B. The buyer must

B.1. Payment of the price

Pay the price as provided in the contract of sale.

B.2. Licences, authorisations and formalities

Obtain at his own risk and expense any import licence or other official authorisation and carry out all customs formalities for the importation of the goods and, where necessary, for their transit through another country.

B.3. Contract of carriage

No obligation.

B.4. Taking delivery

Accept delivery of the goods when they have been delivered in accordance with A.4 and receive them from the carrier at the named port of destination.

B.5. Transfer of risks

Bear all risks of loss of or damage to the goods from the time they have passed the ship's rail at the port of shipment.

Should he fail to give notice in accordance with B.7, bear all risks of loss of or damage to the goods from the agreed date or the expiry date of the period fixed for shipment, provided, however, that the goods have been duly appropriated to the contract, that is to say, clearly set aside or otherwise identified as the contract goods.

B.6. Division of costs

Subject to the provisions of A.3, pay all costs relating to the goods from the time they have been delivered in accordance with A.4 and, unless such costs and charges have been levied by regular shipping lines when contracting for carriage, pay all costs and charges relating to the goods whilst in transit until their arrival at the port of destination, as well as unloading costs including lighterage and wharfage charges.

Should he fail to give notice in accordance with B.7, pay the additional costs thereby incurred for the goods from the agreed date or the expiry date of the period fixed for shipment, provided, however, that the goods have been duly appropriated to the contract, that is to say, clearly set aside or otherwise identified as the contract goods.

Pay all duties, taxes and other official charges as well as the costs of carrying out customs formalities payable upon importation of the goods and, where necessary, for their transit through another country.

B.7. Notice to the seller

Whenever he is entitled to determine the time for shipping the goods and/or the port of destination, give the seller sufficient notice thereof.

B.8. Proof of delivery, transport document or equivalent electronic message

Accept the transport document in accordance with A.8 if it is in conformity with the contract.

B.9. Inspection of goods

Pay, unless otherwise agreed, the costs of pre-shipment inspection except when mandated by the authorities of the country of exportation.

B.10. Other obligations

Pay all costs and charges incurred in obtaining the documents or equivalent electronic messages mentioned in A.10, and reimburse those incurred by the seller in rendering his assistance in accordance therewith.

Provide the seller, upon request, with the necessary information for procuring insurance.

Free on board . . . (named port of shipment) FOB

'Free on Board' means that the seller fulfils his obligation to deliver when the goods have passed over the ship's rail at the named port of shipment. This means that the buyer has to bear all costs and risks of loss of or damage to the goods from that point.

The FOB term requires the seller to clear the goods for export.

This term can only be used for sea or inland waterway transport. When the ship's rail serves no practical purpose, such as in the case of roll-on/roll-off or container traffic, the FCA term is more appropriate to use.

A. The seller must

A.1. Provision of goods in conformity with the contract

Provide the goods and the commercial invoice, or its equivalent electronic message, in conformity with the contract of sale and any other evidence of conformity which may be required by the contract.

A.2. Licences, authorisations and formalities

Obtain at his own risk and expense any export licence or other official authorisation and carry out all customs formalities necessary for the exportation of the goods.

A.3. Contract of carriage and insurance

(a) Contract of carriage

No obligation.

(b) Contract of insurance

No obligation.

A.4. Delivery

Deliver the goods on board the vessel named by the buyer at the named port of shipment on the date or within the period stipulated and in the manner customary at the port.

A.5. Transfer of risks

Subject to the provisions of B.5, bear all risks of loss of or damage to the goods until such time as they have passed the ship's rail at the named port of shipment.

A.6. Division of costs

Subject to the provisions of B.6

- pay all costs relating to the goods until such time as they have passed the ship's rail at the named port of shipment;
- pay the costs of customs formalities necessary for exportation as well as all duties, taxes and other official charges payable upon exportation.

A.7. Notice to the buyer

Give the buyer sufficient notice that the goods have been delivered on board.

A.8. Proof of delivery, transport document or equivalent electronic message

Provide the buyer at the seller's expense with the usual document in proof of delivery in accordance with A.4.

Unless the document referred to in the preceding paragraph is the transport document, render the buyer, at the latter's request, risk and expense, every assistance in obtaining a transport document for the contract of carriage (for example, a negotiable bill of lading, a non-negotiable sea waybill, an inland waterway document, or a multimodal transport document).

Where the seller and the buyer have agreed to communicate electronically, the document referred to in the preceding paragraph may be replaced by an equivalent electronic data interchange (EDI) message.

A.9. Checking—packaging—marking

Pay the costs of those checking operations (such as checking quality, measuring, weighing, counting) which are necessary for the purpose of delivering the goods in accordance with A.4.

Provide at his own expense packaging (unless it is usual for the particular trade to ship the goods of the contract description unpacked) which is required for the transport of the goods, to the extent that the circumstances relating to the transport (eg modalities, destination) are made known to the seller before the contract of sale is concluded. Packaging is to be marked appropriately.

A.10. Other obligations

Render the buyer at the latter's request, risk and expense, every assistance in obtaining any documents or equivalent electronic messages (other than those mentioned in A.8) issued or transmitted in the country of shipment and/or of origin which the buyer may require for the importation of the goods and, where necessary, for their transit through another country.

Provide the buyer, upon request, with the necessary information for procuring insurance.

B. The buyer must

B.1. Payment of the price

Pay the price as provided in the contract of sale.

B.2. Licences, authorisations and formalities

Obtain at his own risk and expense any import licence or other official authorisation and carry out all customs formalities for the importation of the goods and, where necessary, for their transit through another country.

B.3. Contract of carriage

Contract at his own expense for the carriage of the goods from the named port of shipment.

B.4. Taking delivery

Take delivery of the goods in accordance with A.4.

B.5. Transfer of risks

Bear all risks of loss of or damage to the goods from the time they have passed the ship's rail at the named port of shipment.

Should he fail to give notice in accordance with B.7, or should the vessel named by him fail to arrive on time, or be unable to take the goods, or close for cargo earlier than the stipulated time, bear all risks of loss of or damage to the goods from the agreed date or the expiry date of the period stipulated for delivery, provided, however, that the goods have been duly appropriated to the contract, that is to say, clearly set aside or otherwise identified as the contract goods.

B.6. Division of costs

Pay all costs relating to the goods from the time they have passed the ship's rail at the named port of shipment.

Pay any additional costs incurred, either because the vessel named by him has failed to arrive on time, or is unable to take the goods, or will close for cargo earlier than the stipulated date, or because the buyer has failed to give appropriate notice in accordance with B.7, provided, however, that the goods have been duly appropriated to the contract, that is to say, clearly set aside or otherwise identified as the contract goods.

Pay all duties, taxes and other official charges as well as the costs of carrying out customs formalities payable upon importation of the goods and, where necessary, for their transit through another country.

B.7. Notice to the seller

Give the seller sufficient notice of the vessel name, loading point and required delivery time.

B.8. Proof of delivery, transport document or equivalent electronic message

Accept the proof of delivery in accordance with A.8.

B.9. Inspection of goods

Pay, unless otherwise agreed, the costs of pre-shipment inspection except when mandated by the authorities of the country of export.

B.10. Other obligations

Pay all costs and charges incurred in obtaining the documents or equivalent electronic messages mentioned in A.10 and reimburse those incurred by the seller in rendering his assistance in accordance therewith.

Cost and Freight . . . (named port of destination) CFR

'Cost and Freight' means that the seller must pay the costs and freight necessary to bring the goods to the named port of destination but the risk of loss of or damage to the goods, as well as any additional costs due to events occurring after the time the goods have been delivered on board the vessel is transferred from the seller to the buyer when the goods pass the ship's rail in the port of shipment.

The CFR term requires the seller to clear the goods for export.

This term can only be used for sea and inland waterway transport. When the ship's rail serves no practical purpose, such as in the case of roll-on/roll-off or container traffic, the CPT term is more appropriate to use.

A. The seller must

A.1. Provision of goods in conformity with the contract

Provide the goods and the commercial invoice, or its equivalent electronic message, in conformity with the contract of sale and any other evidence of conformity which may be required by the contract.

A.2. Licences, authorisations and formalities

Obtain at his own risk and expense any export licence or other official authorisation and carry out all customs formalities necessary for the exportation of the goods.

A.3. Contract of carriage and insurance

(a) Contract of carriage

Contract on usual terms at his own expense for the carriage of the goods to the named port of destination by the usual route in a seagoing vessel (or inland waterway vessel as appropriate) of the type normally used for the transport of goods of the contract description.

(b) Contract of insurance

No obligation.

A.4. Delivery

Deliver the goods on board the vessel at the port of shipment on the date or within the period stipulated.

A.5. Transfer of risks

Subject to the provisions of B.5, bear all risks of loss of or damage to the goods until such time as they have passed the ship's rail at the port of shipment.

A.6. Division of costs

Subject to the provisions of B.6

- pay all costs relating to the goods until they have been delivered in accordance with A.4 as well as the freight and all other costs resulting from A.3(a), including costs of loading the goods on board and any charges for unloading at the port of discharge which may be levied by regular shipping lines when contracting for carriage;
- pay the costs of customs formalities necessary for exportation as well as all duties, taxes and other official charges payable upon exportation.

A.7. Notice to the buyer

Give the buyer sufficient notice that the goods have been delivered on board the vessel as well as any other notice required in order to allow the buyer to take measures which are normally necessary to enable him to take the goods.

A.8. Proof of delivery, transport document or equivalent electronic message

Unless otherwise agreed, at his own expense provide the buyer without delay with the usual transport document for the agreed port of destination.
  This document (for example, a negotiable bill of lading, a non-negotiable sea waybill or an inland waterway document) must cover the contract goods, be dated within the period agreed for shipment, enable the buyer to claim the goods from the carrier at destination and, unless

otherwise agreed, enable the buyer to sell the goods in transit by the transfer of the document to a subsequent buyer (the negotiable bill of lading) or by notification to the carrier.

When such a transport document is issued in several originals, a full set of originals must be presented to the buyer. If the transport document contains a reference to a charter party, the seller must also provide a copy of this latter document.

Where the seller and the buyer have agreed to communicate electronically, the document referred to in the preceding paragraphs may be replaced by an equivalent electronic data interchange (EDI) message.

A.9. Checking—packaging—marking

Pay the costs of those checking operations (such as checking quality, measuring, weighing, counting) which are necessary for the purpose of delivering the goods in accordance with A.4.

Provide at his own expense packaging (unless it is usual for the particular trade to ship the goods of the contract description unpacked) which is required for the transport of the goods arranged by him. Packaging is to be marked appropriately.

A.10. Other obligations

Render the buyer at the latter's request, risk and expense, every assistance in obtaining any documents or equivalent electronic messages (other than those mentioned in A.8) issued or transmitted in the country of shipment and/or of origin which the buyer may require for the importation of the goods and, where necessary, for their transit through another country.

Provide the buyer, upon request, with the necessary information for procuring insurance.

B. *The buyer must*

B.1. Payment of the price

Pay the price as provided in the contract of sale.

B.2. Licences, authorisations and formalities

Obtain at his own risk and expense any import licence or other official authorisation and carry out all customs formalities for the importation of the goods and, where necessary, for their transit through another country.

B.3. Contract of carriage

No obligation.

B.4. Taking delivery

Accept delivery of the goods when they have been delivered in accordance with A.4 and receive them from the carrier at the named port of destination.

B.5. Transfer of risks

Bear all risks of loss of or damage to the goods from the time they have passed the ship's rail at the port of shipment.

Should he fail to give notice in accordance with B.7, bear all risks of loss of or damage to the goods from the agreed date or the expiry date of the period fixed for shipment, provided, however, that the goods have been duly appropriated to the contract, that is to say, clearly set aside or otherwise identified as the contract goods.

B.6. Division of costs

Subject to the provisions of A.3(a), pay all costs relating to the goods from the time they have been delivered in accordance with A.4. and, unless such costs and charges have been levied by regular shipping lines when contracting for carriage, pay all costs and charges relating to the goods whilst in transit until their arrival at the port of destination, as well as unloading costs including lighterage and wharfage charges.

Should he fail to give notice in accordance with B.7, pay the additional costs thereby incurred for the goods from the agreed date or the expiry date of the period fixed for shipment, provided, however, that the goods have been duly appropriated to the contract, that is to say, clearly set aside or otherwise identified as the contract goods.

Pay all duties, taxes and other official charges as well as the costs of carrying out customs formalities payable upon importation of the goods and, where necessary, for their transit through another country.

B.7. Notice to the seller

Whenever he is entitled to determine the time for shipping the goods and/or the port of destination, give the seller sufficient notice thereof.

B.8. Proof of delivery, transport document or equivalent electronic message

Accept the transport document in accordance with A.8 if it is in conformity with the contract.

B.9. Inspection of goods

Pay, unless otherwise agreed, the costs of pre-shipment inspection except when mandated by the authorities of the country of exportation.

B.10. Other obligations

Pay all costs and charges incurred in obtaining the documents or equivalent electronic messages mentioned in A.10 and reimburse those incurred by the seller in rendering his assistance in accordance therewith.

Free Carrier . . . (named place) FCA

'Free Carrier' means that the seller fulfils his obligation to deliver when he has handed over the goods, cleared for export, into the charge of the carrier named by the buyer at the named place or point. If no precise point is indicated by the buyer, the seller may choose within the place or range stipulated where the carrier shall take the goods into his charge. When, according to commercial practice, the seller's assistance is required in making the contract with the carrier (such as in rail or air transport) the seller may act at the buyer's risk and expense.

This term may be used for any mode of transport, including multimodal transport.

'Carrier' means any person who, in a contract of carriage, undertakes to perform or to procure the performance of carriage by rail, road, sea, air, inland waterway or by a combination of such modes. If the buyer instructs the seller to deliver the cargo to a person, eg a freight forwarder who is not a 'carrier', the seller is deemed to have fulfilled his obligation to deliver the goods when they are in the custody of that person.

'Transport terminal' means a railway terminal, a freight station, a container terminal or yard, a multi-purpose cargo terminal or any similar receiving point.

'Container' includes any equipment used to unitise cargo, eg all types of containers and/or flats, whether ISO accepted or not, trailers, swap bodies, ro-ro equipment, igloos, and applies to all modes of transport.

A. The seller must

A.1. Provision of goods in conformity with the contract

Provide the goods and the commercial invoice, or its equivalent electronic message, in conformity with the contract of sale and any other evidence of conformity which may be required by the contract.

A.2. Licences, authorisations and formalities

Obtain at his own risk and expense any export licence or other official authorisation and carry out all customs formalities necessary for the exportation of the goods.

A.3. Contract of carriage and insurance

(a) Contract of carriage

No obligation. However, if requested by the buyer or if it is commercial practice and the buyer does not give an instruction to the contrary in due time, the seller may contract for carriage on usual terms at the buyer's risk and expense. The seller may decline to make the contract and, if he does, shall promptly notify the buyer accordingly.

(b) Contract of insurance

No obligation.

A.4. Delivery

Deliver the goods into the custody of the carrier or another person (eg a freight forwarder) named by the buyer, or chosen by the seller in accordance with A.3(a), at the named place or point (eg transport terminal or other receiving point) on the date or within the period agreed for delivery and in the manner agreed or customary at such point. If no specific point has been agreed, and if there are several points available, the seller may select the point at the place of delivery which best suits his purpose. Failing precise instructions from the buyer, the seller may deliver the goods to the carrier in such a manner as the transport mode of that carrier and the quantity and/or nature of the goods may require.

Delivery to the carrier is completed:

(i) In the case of rail transport when the goods constitute a wagon load (or a container load carried by rail) the seller has to load the wagon or container in the appropriate manner. Delivery is completed when the loaded wagon or container is taken over by the railway or by another person acting on its behalf.

When the goods do not constitute a wagon or container load, delivery is completed when the seller has handed over the goods at the railway receiving point or loaded them into a vehicle provided by the railway.

(ii) In the case of road transport when loading takes place at the seller's premises, delivery is completed when the goods have been loaded on the vehicle provided by the buyer.

When the goods are delivered to the carrier's premises, delivery is completed when they have been handed over to the road carrier or to another person acting on his behalf.

(iii) In the case of transport by inland waterway when loading takes place at the seller's premises, delivery is completed when the goods have been loaded on the carrying vessel provided by the buyer.

When the goods are delivered to the carrier's premises, delivery is completed when they have been handed over to the inland waterway carrier or to another person acting on his behalf.

(iv) In the case of sea transport when the goods constitute a full container load (FCL), delivery is completed when the loaded container is taken over by the sea carrier. When the container has been carried to an operator of a transport terminal acting on behalf of the carrier, the goods shall be deemed to have been taken over when the container has entered into the premises of that terminal.

When the goods are less than a container load (LCL), or are not to be containerised, the seller has to carry them to the transport terminal. Delivery is completed when the goods have been handed over to the sea carrier or to another person acting on his behalf.

(v) In the case of air transport, delivery is completed when the goods have been handed over to the air carrier or to another person acting on his behalf.

(vi) In the case of unnamed transport, delivery is completed when the goods have been handed over to the carrier or to another person acting on his behalf.

(vii) In the case of multimodal transport, delivery is completed when the goods have been handed over as specified in (i)-(vi), as the case may be.

A.5. Transfer of risks

Subject to the provisions of B.5, bear all risks of loss of or damage to the goods until such time as they have been delivered in accordance with A.4.

A.6. Division of costs

Subject to the provisions of B.6

- pay all costs relating to the goods until such time as they have been delivered to the carrier in accordance with A.4;
- pay the costs of customs formalities as well as all duties, taxes, and other official charges payable upon exportation.

A.7. Notice to the buyer

Give the buyer sufficient notice that the goods have been delivered into the custody of the carrier. Should the carrier fail to take the goods into his charge at the time agreed, the seller must notify the buyer accordingly.

A.8. Proof of delivery, transport document or equivalent electronic message

Provide the buyer at the seller's expense, if customary, with the usual document in proof of delivery of the goods in accordance with A.4.

Unless the document referred to in the preceding paragraph is the transport document, render the buyer at the latter's request, risk and expense, every assistance in obtaining a transport document for the contract of carriage (for example, a negotiable bill of lading, a non-negotiable sea waybill, an inland waterway document, an air waybill, a railway consignment note, a road consignment note, or a multimodal transport document).

When the seller and the buyer have agreed to communicate electronically, the document referred to in the preceding paragraph may be replaced by an equivalent electronic data interchange (EDI) message.

A.9. Checking—packaging—marking

Pay the costs of those checking operations (such as checking quality, measuring, weighing, counting) which are necessary for the purpose of delivering the goods to the carrier.

Provide at his own expense packaging (unless it is usual for the particular trade to send the goods of the contract description unpacked) which is required for the transport of the goods, to the extent that the circumstances relating to the transport (eg modalities, destination) are made known to the seller before the contract of sale is concluded. Packaging is to be marked appropriately.

A.10. Other obligations

Render the buyer at the latter's request, risk and expense, every assistance in obtaining any documents or equivalent electronic messages (other than those mentioned in A.8) issued or transmitted in the country of delivery and/or of origin which the buyer may require for the importation of the goods and, where necessary, for their transit through another country.

Provide the buyer, upon request, with the necessary information for procuring insurance.

B. *The buyer must*

B.1. Payment of the price

Pay the price as provided in the contract of sale.

B.2. Licences, authorisations and formalities

Obtain at his own risk and expense any import licence or other official authorisation and carry out all customs formalities for the importation of the goods and, where necessary, for their transit through another country.

B.3. Contract of carriage

Contract at his own expense for the carriage of the goods from the named place, except as provided for in A.3(a).

B.4. Taking delivery

Take delivery of the goods in accordance with A.4.

B.5. Transfer of risks

Bear all risks of loss of or damage to the goods from the time they have been delivered in accordance with A.4.

Should he fail to give notice in accordance with B.7, or should the carrier named by him fail to take the goods into his charge, bear all risks of loss of or damage to the goods from the agreed date or the expiry date of any period stipulated for delivery, provided, however, that the goods have been duly appropriated to the contract, that is to say, clearly set aside or otherwise identified as the contract goods.

B.6. Division of costs

Pay all costs relating to the goods from the time when they have been delivered in accordance with A.4.

Pay any additional costs incurred, either because he fails to name the carrier, or the carrier named by him fails to take the goods into his charge at the agreed time, or because he has failed to give appropriate notice in accordance with B.7, provided, however, that the goods have been duly appropriated to the contract, that is to say, clearly set aside or otherwise identified as the contract goods.

Pay all duties, taxes and other official charges as well as the costs of carrying out customs formalities payable upon importation of the goods and, where necessary, for their transit through another country.

B.7. Notice to the seller

Give the seller sufficient notice of the name of the carrier and, where necessary, specify the mode of transport, as well as the date or period for delivering the goods to him and, as the case may be, of the point within the place where the goods should be delivered to the carrier.

B.8. Proof of delivery, transport document or equivalent electronic message

Accept the proof of delivery in accordance with A.8.

B.9. Inspection of goods

Pay, unless otherwise agreed, the costs of pre-shipment inspection except when mandated by the authorities of the country of exportation.

B.10. Other obligations

Pay all costs and charges incurred in obtaining the documents or equivalent electronic messages mentioned in A.10 and reimburse those incurred by the seller in rendering his assistance in accordance therewith and in contracting for carriage in accordance with A.3(a).

Give the seller appropriate instructions whenever the seller's assistance in contracting for carriage is required in accordance with A.3(a).

Carriage and insurance paid to . . . (named place of destination) CIP

'Carriage and insurance paid to . . .' means that the seller has the same obligations as under CPT but with the addition that the seller has to procure cargo insurance against the buyer's risk of loss of or damage to the goods during the carriage. The seller contracts for insurance and pays the insurance premium.

The buyer should note that under the CIP term the seller is only required to obtain insurance on minimum coverage.

The CIP term requires the seller to clear the goods for export.

This term may be used for any mode of transport including multimodal transport.

A. The seller must

A.1. Provision of goods in conformity with the contract

Provide the goods and the commercial invoice, or its equivalent electronic message, in conformity with the contract of sale and any other evidence of conformity which may be required by the contract.

A.2. Licences, authorisations and formalities

Obtain at his own risk and expense any export licence or other official authorisation and carry out all customs formalities necessary for the exportation of the goods.

A.3. Contract of carriage and insurance

(a) Contract of carriage

Contract on usual terms at his own expense for the carriage of the goods to the agreed point at the named place of destination by a usual route and in a customary manner. If a point is not agreed or is not determined by practice, the seller may select the point at the named place of destination which best suits his purpose.

(b) Contract of insurance

Obtain at his own expense cargo insurance as agreed in the contract, that the buyer, or any other person having an insurable interest in the goods, shall be entitled to claim directly from the insurer and provide the buyer with the insurance policy or other evidence of insurance cover.

The insurance shall be contracted with underwriters or an insurance company of good repute and, failing express agreement to the contrary, be in accordance with minimum cover of the Institute Cargo Clauses (Institute of London Underwriters) or any similar set of clauses. The duration of insurance cover shall be in accordance with B.5 and B.4. When required by the buyer, the seller shall provide at the buyer's expense war, strikes, riots and civil commotion risk insurances if procurable. The minimum insurance shall cover the price provided in the contract plus ten per cent (ie 110%) and shall be provided in the currency of the contract.

A.4. Delivery

Deliver the goods into the custody of the carrier or, if there are subsequent carriers, to the first carrier, for transportation to the named place of destination on the date or within the period stipulated.

A.5. Transfer of risks

Subject to the provisions of B.5, bear all risks of loss of or damage to the goods until such time as they have been delivered in accordance with A.4.

A.6. Division of costs

Subject to the provisions of B.6

- pay all costs relating to the goods until they have been delivered in accordance with A.4 as well as the freight and all other costs resulting from A.3 including costs of loading the goods and any charges for unloading at the place of destination which may be included in the freight or incurred by the seller when contracting for carriage;

- pay the costs of customs formalities necessary for exportation as well as all duties, taxes or other official charges payable upon exportation.

A.7. Notice to the buyer

Give the buyer sufficient notice that the goods have been delivered in accordance with A.4 as well as any other notice required in order to allow the buyer to take measures which are normally necessary to enable him to take the goods.

A.8. Proof of delivery, transport document or equivalent electronic message

Provide the buyer at the seller's expense, if customary, with the usual transport document (for example, a negotiable bill of lading, a non-negotiable sea waybill, an inland waterway document, an air waybill, a railway consignment note, a road consignment note or a multimodal transport document).

Where the seller and the buyer have agreed to communicate electronically, the document referred to in the preceding paragraph may be replaced by an equivalent electronic data interchange (EDI) message.

A.9. Checking—packaging—marking

Pay the costs of those checking operations (such as checking quality, measuring, weighing, counting) which are necessary for the purpose of delivering the goods in accordance with A.4.

Provide at his own expense packaging (unless it is usual for the particular trade to send the goods of the contract description unpacked) which is required for the transport of the goods arranged by him. Packaging is to be marked appropriately.

A.10. Other obligations

Render the buyer at the latter's request, risk and expense, every assistance in obtaining any documents or equivalent electronic messages (other than those mentioned in A.8) issued or transmitted in the country of dispatch and/or of origin, which the buyer may require for the importation of the goods and where necessary, for their transit through another country.

B. The buyer must

B.1. Payment of the price

Pay the price as provided in the contract of sale.

B.2. Licences, authorisations and formalities

Obtain at his own risk and expense any import licence or other official authorisation and carry out all customs formalities for the importation of the goods and, where necessary, for their transit through another country.

B.3. Contract of carriage

No obligation.

B.4. Taking delivery

Accept delivery of the goods when they have been delivered in accordance with A.4 and receive them from the carrier at the named place of destination.

B.5. Transfer of risks

Bear all risks of loss of or damage to the goods for the time they have been delivered in accordance with A.4.

Should he fail to give notice in accordance with B.7, bear all risks of the goods from the agreed date or the expiry date of the period fixed for delivery provided, however, that the goods have been duly appropriated to the contract, that is to say, clearly set aside or otherwise identified as the contract goods.

B.6. Division of costs

Subject to the provisions of A.3, pay all costs relating to the goods from the time they have been delivered in accordance with A.4 and, unless such costs and charges have been included in the freight or incurred by the seller when contracting for carriage in accordance with A.3(a), pay all costs and charges relating to the goods whilst in transit until their arrival at the agreed place of destination, as well as unloading costs.

Should he fail to give notice in accordance with B.7, pay the additional costs thereby incurred for the goods from the agreed date or the expiry date of the period fixed for dispatch provided, however, that the goods have been duly appropriated to the contract, that is to say, clearly set aside or otherwise identified as the contract goods.

Pay all duties, taxes and other official charges as well as the costs of carrying out customs formalities payable upon importation of the goods and, where necessary, for their transit through another country.

B.7. Notice to the seller

Whenever he is entitled to determine the time for dispatching the goods and/or the destination, give the seller sufficient notice thereof.

B.8. Proof of delivery, transport document or equivalent electronic message

Accept the transport document in accordance with A.8 if it is in conformity with the contract.

B.9. Inspection of goods

Pay, unless otherwise agreed, the costs of pre-shipment inspection except when mandated by the authorities of the country of exportation.

B.10. Other obligations

Pay all costs and charges incurred in obtaining the documents or equivalent electronic messages mentioned in A.10 and reimburse those incurred by the seller in rendering his assistance in accordance therewith.

Provide the seller, upon request, with the necessary information for procuring insurance.

Destination tables for Incoterms 1990

CIF 1980	CIF 1990	FOB 1980	FOB 1990	C&F 1980	CFR 1990
A1	A1	A1	A1	A1	A1
A2	A3(a) & A6	A2	A4 & A7	A2	A3(a) & A6
A3	A2	A3	A2	A3	A2
A4	A4 & A7	A4	A5 & A6	A4	A4 & A7
A5	A3(b)	A5	A9	A5	A5
A6	A5	A6	A9	A6	A8
A7	A8	A7	A8	A7	A9
A8	A9	A8	A10	A8	A9
A9	A9	A9	A10	A9	A6
A10	A6	–	A3	A10	A10
A11	A10			A11	A10
A12	A10				
B1	B1 & B8	B1	B3 & B7	B1	B8
B2	B4 & B6	B2	B5 & B6	B2	B4 & B6
B3	B5	B3	B6	B3	B5
B4	B6 & B7	B4	B5	B4	B5, B6 & B7
B5	B6	B5	B10	B5	B6
B6	–	B6	B10	B6	B10
B7	B6	–	B1	B7	B6
B8	B2	–	B2	B8	B2
–	B3	–	B4	–	B1
–	B9	–	B8	–	B3
		–	B9	–	B9

FRC 1980	FCA 1990	CIP 1980	CIP 1990
A1	A1	A1	A1
A2	A4	A2	A3(a) & A6
A3	A2	A3	A5
A4	A6	A4	A7
A5	A6	A5	A9
A6	A5	A6	A9
A7	A9	A7	A8
A8	A9	A8	A2
A9	A7	A9	A1 & A10
A10	–	A10	A10
A11	A8	A11	A3(b)
A12	A1	–	A4
A13	A10		
–	A3		
B1	B3 & B7	B1	B1 & B6
B2	B6	B2	B5
B3	B1	B3	B5 & B6
B4	B5	B4	B10
B5	B6	B5	B6
B6	B10	–	B2
–	B2	–	B3
–	B4	–	B4
–	B8	–	B7
–	B9	–	B8
		–	B9

Commercial forms

a. Form 100 of the Grain and Feed Trade Association
b. ACL bill of lading
c. An application for the opening of a letter of credit
d. The General Council of British Shipping Waybill
e. Genwaybill, the Baltic and International Maritime Council Non-negotiable General Sea Waybill
f. Combidoc, the Baltic and International Maritime Council Combined Transport Document

Effective 1st April 1987

Printed in England and issued by

THE GRAIN AND FEED TRADE ASSOCIATION

BALTIC EXCHANGE CHAMBERS, 28 ST. MARY AXE, LONDON, EC3A 8EP

CONTRACT FOR SHIPMENT OF FEEDING STUFFS IN BULK
C.I.F. TERMS

TALE QUALE

LONDON .... 19........

No. 100
Copyright

SELLERS ....

INTERVENING AS BROKERS ....

BUYERS ....

have this day entered into a contract on the following terms and conditions. Wherever the word "cakes" is used, this is agreed to mean goods of the contractual description.

1. GOODS

Broken cakes and/or meal in a proportion, having regard to the characteristics of the goods and methods of handling, to be taken and paid for as cakes. Goods in bulk but Buyers agree to accept up to 15% in stowage bags, such bags to be taken and paid for as cakes and any cutting to be paid for by Buyers. Sellers have the option of shipping the whole or part of the quantity in excess of 15% in bags, in which case the excess over 15% shall be delivered in bulk and Sellers shall be responsible for cutting the excess bags which shall remain their property.

2. QUANTITY

2% more or less. Sellers have the option of shipping a further 3% more or less than the contract quantity. The excess above 2% or the deficiency below 2% shall be settled on the quantity thereof at shipment at market value on the last day of discharge of the vessel at the port of destination; the value to be fixed by arbitration, unless mutually agreed. Should Sellers exercise the option to ship up to 5% more, the excess over 2% shall be paid for provisionally at contract price. The difference between the contract price and the market price calculated in accordance with the provisions of this clause, shall be adjusted in the final invoice.

3. PRICE—At ....

per 1000 kilos
per 1016 kilos or 2240 lbs., } gross weight, cost, insurance and freight to ....

4. BROKERAGE

on the mean contract quantity, goods lost or not lost, contract fulfilled or not fulfilled, unless such non-fulfilment is due to the successful application of the Prohibition Clause or the Force Majeure Clause. Brokerage shall be due on the day shipping documents are exchanged or if the goods are not appropriated then the Brokerage shall be due on the 30th consecutive day after the last day for appropriation or advice of shipment. .... % of the contract price to be paid by Sellers

5. QUALITY

★Delete as ★At time of loading to be fair average of the season's shipments.
applicable ★At time and place of shipment to be about as per sealed sample marked .... in the possession of ....

Warranted to contain not less than .... % of oil and protein combined and not more than 2½% of sand and/or silica. Should the whole or any portion not turn out equal to warranty, the goods must be taken at an allowance to be agreed or settled by arbitration as provided for below, except that for any deficiency of oil and protein there shall be allowances to Buyers at the following rates viz: 1% of the contract price for each of the 1st 3 units of deficiency under the warranted percentage; 2% of the contract price for the 4th and 5th units and 3% of the contract price for each unit in excess of 5 and proportionately for any fraction thereof. When the combined content of oil and protein is warranted within a margin (as for example 40/42%) no allowance shall be made if the analysis results below the minimum warranted the allowance for deficiency shall be computed from the mean of the warranted content. For any excess of sand and/or silica there shall be an allowance of 1% of the contract price for each unit of excess and proportionately for any fraction thereof. Should the goods contain over 5% of sand and/or silica the Buyers shall be entitled to reject the goods, in which case the contract shall be null and void for such quantity rejected.

The goods are warranted free from castor seed and/or castor seed husk, but should the analysis show a percentage of castor seed husk not exceeding .005% the Buyers shall not be entitled to reject the goods, but shall accept them with the following allowances: ¼% of contract price if not exceeding .001%, 1% of contract price if not exceeding .002% and 1½% of contract price if not exceeding .005%.

Should the first analysis show the goods free from castor seed and/or castor seed husk such analysis shall be final but in the event of the first analysis showing castor seed husk to be present a second sample may be analysed at the request of either party and the mean of the two analyses shall be taken as final. Should the parcel contain castor seed husk in excess of .005% Buyers shall be entitled to reject the parcel, in which case the contract shall be null and void for such quantity rejected. Nevertheless, should Buyers elect to retain the parcel they shall be entitled to a further allowance for any excess over .005% of castor seed husk, to be settled by agreement or arbitration. For the purpose of sampling and analysis each parcel shall stand as a separate shipment. The right of rejection provided by this clause shall be limited to the parcel or parcels found to be defective.

6. PERIOD OF SHIPMENT—As per Bill(s) of Lading dated or to be dated _____ the Bill(s) of Lading to be dated when the goods are actually on board. Date of the Bill(s) of Lading shall be accepted as proof of date of shipment in the absence of evidence to the contrary. In any month containing an odd number of days, the middle day shall be accepted as being in both halves of the month.

7. SALES BY NAMED VESSELS—For all sales by named vessels, the following shall apply:—
(a) Position of vessel is mutually agreed between Buyers and Sellers:
(b) The word 'now' to be inserted before the word 'classed' in the Shipment and Classification Clause:
(c) Appropriation clause cancelled if sold 'shipped'.

8. SHIPMENT AND CLASSIFICATION—Shipment to be made in good condition, direct or indirect, with or without transhipment from _____ by first class steamer(s) and/or power engined ship(s) classed not lower than 100 A1 or British Corporation B.S. or top classification in American, French, Italian, Norwegian, West German or other equal ranking Registers.

9. EXTENSION OF SHIPMENT—The contract period for shipment, if such be 31 days or less, shall, if desired by the Shipper, be extended by an additional period of not more than 8 days, provided that the Shipper gives notice claiming extension by telegram or telex sent not later than the next business day following the last day of the originally stipulated period. The notice need not state the number of additional days claimed, and such notice shall be passed on by Sellers to their Buyers respectively in due course after receipt. Sellers shall make an allowance to Buyers, to be deducted in the invoice from the contract price, based on the number of days by which the originally stipulated period is exceeded, as follows: for 1, 2, 3, or 4 additional days, ½% of the gross c.i.f. price; for 5 or 6 additional days, 1% of the gross c.i.f. price; for 7 or 8 additional days 1½% of the gross c.i.f. price. If, however, after having given notice to the Buyers as above, the Sellers fail to make shipment within such 8 days, then the contract shall be deemed to have called for shipment during the originally stipulated period plus 8 days, at contract price less 1½% and any settlement for default shall be calculated on that basis. If any allowance becomes due under this clause, the contract price shall be deemed to be the original contract price less the allowance and any other contractual differences shall be settled on the basis of such reduced price.

10. APPROPRIATION—
(a) Notice of Appropriation stating the vessel's name and the approximate weight shipped shall, within (i) 10 consecutive days if shipped from the U.S. Gulf and/or U.S. and/or Canadian Atlantic/Lake Ports, (ii) 14 consecutive days if shipped from any other port, from the date of the Bill(s) of Lading be despatched in accordance with sub-clause (e) by or on behalf of the Shipper direct to the first Buyers or to the Selling Agent or Brokers named in the contract. The Non-Business Days Clause shall not apply.
(b) Notice of Appropriation stating the vessel's name and the approximate weight shipped, shall, within the period stated in sub-clause (a) be despatched in accordance with sub-clause (e) by or on behalf of subsequent Sellers to their Buyers or to the Selling Agent or Brokers named in the contract, but if Notice of Appropriation is received by subsequent Sellers on or after the period stated in sub-clause (a) from the date of the Bill of Lading, their Notice of Appropriation shall be deemed to be in time if despatched:—
(1) On the same calendar day, if received not later than 1600 hours on any business day.
(2) Not later than the next business day, if received after 1600 hours or on a Non-Business Day.
(c) A Selling Agent or Brokers receiving a Notice of Appropriation shall despatch like Notice of Appropriation in accordance with the provisions of this clause. Where the Shipper or subsequent Sellers despatch the Notice of Appropriation to the Selling Agent, such Selling Agent may despatch Notice of Appropriation either direct to the Buyers or to the Brokers.
(d) The Shipper's Notice of Appropriation and every subsequent Sellers' Notice of Appropriation shall state the date or the presumed date of the Bill of Lading which shall be for information only and shall not be binding, but in fixing the period laid down by this clause for despatching Notices of Appropriation the actual date of the Bill of Lading shall prevail.
(e) Notices of Appropriation shall be despatched by telegram, telex or other method of rapid written communication, or by letter if delivered by hand on day of writing. Every such Notice of Appropriation shall be open to correction of any errors occurring in transmission, provided that the sender is not responsible for such errors, and for any previous error in transmission which has been repeated in good faith.
(f) Should the vessel arrive before receipt of the appropriation and any extra expenses be incurred thereby, such expenses shall be borne by Sellers.
(g) When a valid Notice of Appropriation has been received by Buyers it shall not be withdrawn except with their consent.
(h) A Notice of Appropriation despatched to the Brokers named in the contract shall be considered an appropriation despatched to the Buyers.
(i) An appropriation shall not be deemed invalid if the date of the Bill of Lading is within the contract period and if on that date the vessel named is at the port of loading and carrying goods of the contractual description and quantity.
(j) In the event of less than 95 tons being tendered by any one vessel, Buyers shall be entitled to refund of any proved extra expenses for sampling, analysis and lighterage incurred thereby at port of discharge.
(k) In the event of more than one shipment being made, each shipment shall be considered a separate contract, but the margin of the mean quantity sold shall not be affected thereby.

11. PAYMENT—Payment .... % of invoice amount by cash in ....

    ★Delete as applicable   ★(a) in exchange for and on presentation of shipping documents

    ★(b) in exchange for shipping documents on or before arrival of the vessel at destination, at Buyers' option;

    Sellers, however, have the option of calling upon Buyers to take up and pay for the documents on or after .... consecutive days from the date of the Bill(s) of Lading.

    In the event of the shipping documents not being available when called for by the Buyers on or arrival of the vessel at destination, Sellers may provide other documents or an indemnity entitling Buyers to obtain delivery of the goods and payment shall be made by Buyers in exchange for same, but such payment shall not prejudice Buyers' rights under the contract when shipping documents are eventually available. Should Sellers fail to present shipping documents or other documents or an indemnity entitling Buyers to take delivery, Buyers shall take delivery under an indemnity provided by themselves and shall pay for the documents when presented. Any reasonable extra expenses, including the costs of such indemnity or extra landing charges incurred by reason of the failure of Sellers to provide such documents, shall be borne by Sellers and allowed for in the final invoice but such payment shall not prejudice Buyers' rights under the contract when shipping documents are eventually available. Costs of collection shall be for the account of Sellers, but if Buyers demand presentation only through a bank of their choice, in that event any additional collection costs shall be for the account of Buyers.

    Any balance to be settled on rendering final invoice.
    Final invoices may be prepared by either party and shall be settled without delay, and if not so settled a dispute shall be deemed to have arisen which may be referred to arbitration as herein provided.

12. INTEREST—If there has been unreasonable delay in any payment interest appropriate to the currency involved shall be charged. If such charge is not mutually agreed, a dispute shall be deemed to exist which shall be settled by arbitration.
    Otherwise, interest shall be payable only where specifically provided in the terms of the contract or by an award of arbitration.

13. RYE TERMS—In the event of goods shipped in tankers or in oil compartments of oil/ore carriers arriving at destination damaged or out of condition, Buyers must accept delivery but shall be entitled to an allowance for deterioration calculated on a percentage based on contract price to be fixed by arbitration unless mutually agreed.
    Samples shall be taken and sealed at port of discharge jointly by Sellers and Buyers or their representatives. In the event of Buyers receiving an allowance from Sellers under this clause, Sellers and Buyers shall give each other all reasonable assistance in the prosecution of claims for recovery from shipowners and/or other parties. Any sum recovered under this clause shall be for the benefit of Sellers, and any proved reasonable extra expenses incurred by Buyers in connection with the claim are to be deducted. Buyers shall furnish Sellers on settlement of Rye Terms Allowance with the usual documents required by average adjusters for preparation of average statement and return to Sellers the Policy(ies) and/or certificate(s) received from them and in addition documents for claiming against the ship or any other party, failing which Buyers shall pay such contribution to average as Sellers may be unable to recover in consequence.

14. SHIPPING DOCUMENTS—Shipping documents shall consist of:—
    1. Invoice. 2. Full set(s) of on board Bill(s) of Lading and/or Ship's Delivery Order(s) and/or other Delivery Order(s) in negotiable and transferable form. Such other Delivery Order(s) if required by Buyers, to be certified by the Ship Owners, their Agents or a recognised Bank. 3. Policy(ies) and/or Insurance Certificate(s) and/or Letter(s) of Insurance in the currency of the contract. The Letter(s) of Insurance to be certified by a recognised Bank if required by Buyers. 4. Other documents as called for under the contract. Should documents be presented with an incomplete set of Bill(s) of Lading or should other Shipping Documents be missing, payment shall be made provided that delivery of such missing documents be guaranteed, such guarantee to be signed, if required by Buyers, by a recognised Bank. Acceptance of this guarantee shall not prejudice Buyers' rights under this contract. No clerical error in the documents shall entitle Buyers to rejection or to delay payment provided that Sellers furnish at the request of Buyers a guarantee to be counter-signed by a recognised Bank, if required by Buyers. Sellers shall be responsible for any loss or expense incurred by Buyers on account of such error. Buyers agree to accept documents containing the Chamber of Shipping War Deviation Clause and/or other recognised official War Risk Clause.

15. DUTIES, TAXES, LEVIES, ETC.—All export duties, taxes, levies, etc., present or future, in country of origin shall be for Sellers' account. All import duties, taxes, levies etc., present or future, in country of destination, shall be for Buyers' account.

16. DISCHARGE—Discharge shall be as fast as the vessel can deliver in accordance with the custom of the port but in the event of shipment being made under liner Bill(s) of Lading, discharge shall be as fast as the vessel can deliver in accordance with the terms of the Bill(s) of Lading. The cost of discharge from hold to ship's rail shall be for Sellers' account, from ship's rail overboard for Buyers' account. If documents are tendered which do not provide for discharging as above, or contain contrary stipulations, Sellers shall be responsible to Buyers for extra expenses incurred thereby. Discharge by grab(s) shall be permitted unless specifically excluded at the time of contract. If shipment is effected by Lash Barge, then the last day of discharge shall be the day of discharging the last Lash Barge at the Port of Destination.

17. WEIGHING—Final settlement shall be made on the basis of gross delivered weights and the goods shall be weighed at time and place of discharge at port of destination herein named at Buyers' expense. Sellers have the right to superintend. If discharge is carried out by grab, the method of weighing is to be mutually agreed between Buyers and Sellers and/or their respective agents. In case of damage the discharged weight shall be determined on the basis of an analysis made of samples of the damaged and undamaged part of the goods. Additional weight due to damage not to be paid for, unless Rye Terms apply.

18. DEFICIENCY—Any deficiency on Bill of Lading weight to be paid for by Sellers and any excess over Bill of Lading weight to be paid for by Buyers at contract price, unless the Pro Rata Clause applies.

19. SAMPLING AND ANALYSIS—
    (a) Samples of each parcel shall be drawn in accordance with the Rules for the Sampling of Feedingstuffs and Cereal By-Products of the Grain and Feed Trade Association Number 121 (such rules forming part of this contract and of which both parties hereto shall be deemed to be cognisant), on or before removal from the ship or quay, sealed in not less than 6 portions (numbered 1 to 6) jointly by Sellers and Buyers or their representatives. If one of the parties refuses to draw and/or seal samples or is not represented, the other party shall, under advice to the defaulting party, call in a competent organisation at the port, for the appointment of an

independent superintendent to act on behalf of the defaulting party. Extra expenses incurred in this connection shall be borne by the defaulting party. For Soyabean Meal and/or Pellets, Corn Gluten Feed and Citrus Pulp Pellets the sample(s) for the first analysis shall be drawn in accordance with the Sampling Rules No. 121 in moisture proof containers and the analysis result for moisture from this sample will be reported on the Certificate of Analysis and used as the calculating factor for a second and third analysis test.

(b) Each analysis shall show the number of the sample analysed.

(c) If required by Buyers, any one of the sealed samples except No. 1 shall, within 14 consecutive days of sealing be despatched to

★Laboratorium van Het Comite van Graanhandelaren B.V., Elbeweg 141, 3198 LC Europoort-Rotterdam

★Salamon & Seaber, 178 Old Street, London EC1V 9BP, or to

Laboratorium van Het Comite van Graanhandelaren B.V., Elbeweg 141, 3198 LC Europoort-Rotterdam, for analysis. In the event that this option is not decided at the time of the Contract, the choice of Analyst shall be that of the instructing party. Within 14 consecutive days of receipt of the Certificate of Analysis of this sample Buyers shall send a true copy thereof to Sellers stating whether they accept this analysis or whether they require a second analysis.

(d) Sellers have the right, within 14 consecutive days of receipt by them of the true copy of the Certificate of Analysis, to give notice to Buyers that they require a second analysis. If a second analysis is required another of the sealed samples shall be despatched without delay to Dr. Bernard Dyer & Partners (1948) Ltd., 20 Eastcheap, London, EC3M 1EL, for analysis. The mean of the two analyses shall be accepted as final if the variation does not exceed ½%.

(e) If the variation stated in paragraph (d) above does exceed ½% then at the request of either party, made within 14 consecutive days of receipt (by them) of the true copy of the certificate of the second analysis, and on notice being given to the other party a third sealed sample shall be despatched without delay to Dr. Aug. Voelcker & Sons, 380 Bollo Lane, Acton, London, W3 8QU, for analysis and the mean of the two analyses nearest to each other shall be accepted as final and binding on both parties.

(f) The party requiring any of the respective analyses shall be responsible for the despatch of the relative sample(s) and shall give directly, or through an agent or representative acting on their behalf, to the analyst concerned instructions specifying what analyses are to be carried out, both to be done within the time limit stated hereinbefore, and shall send to the other party a true copy of the relative Certificate of Analysis within 14 consecutive days of receiving it from the analyst.

(g) Should the buyers or any representatives acting on their behalf, fail to both despatch samples and instruct the analyst within 14 consecutive days of their sealing as above provided, or fail to forward the certificate in the said 14 days, then any claim for rejection or for an allowance in respect of any matters dealt with herein shall be deemed to be waived and absolutely barred.

(h) Should either party require further analyses but fail to make application therefore and to send samples within the time limit as above, or fail to forward the certificate, then the analysis or the mean of the two analyses then existing shall be deemed to be final.

(i) In case of resales the Notices Clause shall apply.

(j) The cost(s) of the analysis(es) for each separate warranty shall be borne by Buyers in cases where no allowance is payable but by Sellers if Buyers are entitled to an allowance.

(k) Methods of Analysis to be as prescribed by The Grain and Feed Trade Association, being the GAFTA Regulations, Form 130, for the time being in force. Analysts shall state what methods they have used on the Certificate of Analysis.

(l) Any one of the sealed samples shall be retained for Arbitration purposes if required.

★Delete as applicable

(m) ANALYSIS FOR CASTOR SEED AND/OR CASTOR SEED HUSK

(1) For goods sold to/discharged at ports in Belgium, France, Holland, West Germany, Norway, Sweden and Denmark, the first analysis for Castor seed and/or Castor seed husk shall be made by:—

For goods discharged at Belgian Ports—   Arbitrage-en Verzoeningskamer Voor Granen en Zaden v.z.w.o., Borzestraat 29. Antwerp, Belgium.

" " " " Dutch Ports—   Laboratorium van Het Comite van Graanhandelaren B.V., Elbeweg 141, 3198 LC Europoort-Rotterdam.

" " " " French Ports—   Laboratoire Municipal de Bordeaux, Rue du Professeur Vezes, 33300 Bordeaux, France.

" " " " West German Ports—   Institut für Angewandte Botanik, 2000 Hamburg 36, Marseiller Strasse 7.

" " " " Norwegian, Swedish or Danish Ports—   Steins Laboratorium APS, Holsbjergvej 42, 2620 Albertslund, Denmark.

on sealed sample No. 1 which shall, within 10 consecutive days of sealing, be despatched to the appropriate analyst. If a second analysis for Castor seed and/or Castor seed husk is required such analysis shall be made by Messrs. Salamon & Seaber on the sample already in their possession for test for oil and protein, but if a sample is not in their possession, on one sent to them without delay after receipt of the analysis certificate in respect of the first analysis for Castor seed and/or Castor seed husk.

(2) For goods discharged at other ports the first analysis for Castor seed and/or Castor seed husk shall be made by Messrs. Salamon & Seaber on Sealed sample No. 1 which shall, within 10 consecutive days of sealing, be despatched to the analyst and which shall also be used for other analyses if required. If a second analysis for Castor seed and/or Castor seed husk is required, such analysis shall be made by Dr. Bernard Dyer & Partners (1948) Ltd. If a sealed sample is not in the possession of Dr. Bernard Dyer's laboratory when a second analysis is required one of the other sealed samples, which shall also be used for other analyses if required, shall be sent to Dr. Bernard Dyer's laboratory without delay after receipt of the analysis certificate in respect of the first analysis for Castor seed and/or Castor seed husk.

(3) When the contractual quantity is represented by more than one sample, the analyst shall mix the samples together in proportion to the weight represented by each sample.

(n) ANALYSIS FOR SAND AND/OR SILICA

(1) For goods discharged at ports in Belgium, France, Holland, West Germany, Norway, Sweden and Denmark, the first analysis for sand and/or silica shall be made by the same laboratories as provided for the determination of Castor seed and/or Castor seed husk. Sealed sample No. 1, shall, within 10 consecutive days of sealing be despatched to the appropriate analyst. If a second analysis for sand and/or silica is required such analysis shall be despatched to the appropriate analyst.

in their possession for test for oil and protein but, if a sample is not already in their possession, on one sent to them without delay after receipt of the Analysis Certificate in respect of the first analysis for sand and/or silica. If a third analysis for sand and/or silica is required, such analysis shall be made by Dr. Bernard Dyer & Partners (1948) Ltd. If a sealed sample is not in the possession of Dr. Bernard Dyer's laboratory when a third analysis is required one of the other sealed samples, which shall also be used for other analyses if required, shall be sent to Dr. Bernard Dyer's laboratory without delay after receipt of the Analysis Certificate in respect of the second analysis for sand and/or silica.

(2) For goods discharged at other ports the first analysis for sand and/or silica shall be made by Messrs. Salamon & Seaber on Sealed sample No. 1 which shall, within 10 consecutive days of sealing, be despatched to the analyst and which shall also be used for other analyses if required. If a second analysis for sand and/or silica is required one of the other sealed samples, which shall also be used for other analyses if required, shall be sent to Dr. Bernard Dyer's laboratory without delay after receipt of the Analysis Certificate in respect of the first analysis for sand and/or silica. If a third analysis for sand and/or silica is required such analysis shall be made by Dr. Aug. Voelcker & Sons. If a sealed sample is not in the possession of Dr. Aug. Voelcker & Sons' laboratory when a third analysis is required one of the other sealed samples, which shall also be used for other analyses if required, shall be sent to Dr. Aug. Voelcker & Sons' laboratory without delay after receipt of the Analysis Certificate in respect of the second analysis for sand and/or silica.

(3) When the contractual quantity is represented by more than one sample, the analyst shall mix the samples together in proportion to the weight represented by each sample.

20. (o) SAMPLING AND ANALYSIS OF SOYABEAN MEAL AND GLUTENFEED IN BULK DISCHARGED AT ROTTERDAM AND AMSTERDAM—
For sampling and analysis of Soyabean Meal and Glutenfeed, in bulk, discharged at Rotterdam and Amsterdam, Laboratorium van Het Comite van Graanhandelaren, Rotterdam, will be responsible for the quartering down of samples required for all tests. The resulting sample(s) will be forwarded by them to the Analysts in accordance with the Sampling and Analysis Clause.

(p) Unless a specific request is made to and acknowledged by the Association, samples will be disposed of 6 months after being received by the Association.

21. LATENT DEFECT—The goods are not warranted free from defect, rendering same unmerchantable which would not be apparent on reasonable examination, any statute or rule of law to the contrary notwithstanding.

INSURANCE—Sellers shall provide insurance on terms not less favourable than those set out hereunder, and as set out in detail in The Grain and Feed Trade Association Form 72 viz:—

(a) Risks Covered:—
Cargo Clauses (W.A.), with average payable, with 3% franchise or better terms—Section 2 of Form 72
War Clauses (Cargo)   —Section 4 of Form 72
Strikes, Riots and Civil Commotions Clauses (Cargo)   —Section 5 of Form 72

(b) Insurers—The insurance to be effected with first class Underwriters and/or Companies who are domiciled or carrying on business in the United Kingdom or who, for the purpose of any legal proceedings, accept a British domicile and provide an address for service of process in London, but for whose solvency Sellers shall not be responsible.

(c) Insurable Value—Insured amount to be for not less than 2% over the invoice amount, including freight when freight is payable on shipment or due in any event, ship and/or cargo lost or not lost, and including the amount of any War Risk premium payable by Buyers.

(d) Freight Contingency—When freight is payable on arrival or on right and true delivery of the goods and the insurance does not include the freight, Sellers shall effect insurance upon similar terms, such insurance to attach only as such freight becomes payable, for the amount of the freight plus 2%, until the termination of the risk as provided in the above mentioned clauses, and shall undertake that their policies are so worded that in the case of particular or general average claim the Buyers shall be put in the same position as if the C.I.F. value plus 2% were insured from the time of shipment.

(e) Certificates/Policies—Sellers shall give all policies and/or certificates and/or letters of insurance provided for in this contract, (duly stamped if applicable), for original and increased value (if any) for the value stipulated in (c) above. In the event of a certificate of insurance being supplied, it is agreed that such certificate shall be exchanged by Sellers for a policy if and when required, and such certificate shall state on its face that it is so exchangeable. If required by Buyers, Letter(s) of Insurance shall be guaranteed by a recognised Bank, or by any other guarantor who is acceptable to Buyers.

(f) Total Loss—In the event of total or constructive total loss, or where the amount of the insurance becomes payable in full, the insured amount in excess of 2% over the invoice amount shall be for Sellers' account and the party in possession of the policy(ies) shall collect the amount of insurance and shall thereupon settle with the other party on that basis.

(g) Currency of Claims—Claims to be paid in the currency of the contract.

(h) War and Strike Risks/Premiums—Any premium in excess of ½% to be for account of Buyers. The rate of such insurance not to exceed the rate ruling in London at time of shipment or date of vessel's sailing, whichever may be adopted by Underwriters. Such excess premium shall be claimed from Buyers, wherever possible, with the Provisional Invoice, but in no case later than the date of vessel's arrival, or not later than 7 consecutive days after the rate has been agreed with Underwriters, whichever may be the later, otherwise such claim shall be void unless, in the opinion of arbitrators, the delay is justifiable. Sellers' obligation to provide War Risk Insurance shall be limited to the terms and conditions in force and generally obtainable in London at time of shipment.

(i) Where Sellers are responsible for allowances or other payments to Buyers under Rye Terms or other contractual terms, (and which risks are also covered by the insurance provided by Sellers), the Buyers, on receipt of settlement, shall immediately return to Sellers the insurance documents originally received from them and shall, if required, subrogate to Sellers all right of claim against the Insurers in respect of such matters.

22. PROHIBITION—In case of prohibition of export, blockade or hostilities or in case of any executive or legislative act done by or on behalf of the government of the country of origin or of the territory where the port or ports of shipment named herein is/are situate, restricting export, whether partially or otherwise, any such restriction shall be deemed by both parties to apply to this contract and to the extent of such total or partial restriction to prevent fulfilment whether by shipment or by any other means whatsoever and to that extent this contract or any unfulfilled portion thereof shall be cancelled. Sellers shall advise Buyers without delay with the reasons therefor and, if required, Sellers must produce proof to justify the cancellation.

23. FORCE MAJEURE, STRIKES ETC.—Sellers shall not be responsible for delay in shipment of the goods or any part thereof occasioned by any Act of God, strike, lockout, riot or civil commotion, combination of workmen, breakdown of machinery, fire or any cause comprehended in the term "force majeure". If delay in shipment is likely to occur for any of the above reasons, the Shipper shall give notice to the Buyers by telegram or telex or by similar advice within 7 consecutive days of the occurrence, or not less than 21 consecutive days before the commencement of the contract period, whichever is later. The notice shall state the reason(s) for the delay. If after giving such notice an extension to the shipping period is required, then the Shipper shall give further notice not later than 2 business days after the last day of the contract period of shipment stating the port or ports of loading from which the goods were intended to be shipped, and shipments effected after the contract period shall be limited to the port or ports so nominated. If shipment be delayed for more than one calendar month, Buyers shall have the option of cancelling the delayed portion of the contract, such option to be exercised by Buyers giving notice to be received by Sellers not later than the first business day after the additional calendar month. If Buyers do not exercise this option, such delayed portion shall be automatically extended for a further period of one month. If Shipment under this clause be prevented during the further one month's extension, the contract shall be considered void. Buyers shall have no claim against Sellers for delay or non-shipment under this clause provided that Sellers shall have supplied to Buyers, if required, satisfactory evidence justifying the delay or non-fulfilment.

24. NOTICES—Any Notices received after 1600 hours on a business day shall be deemed to have been received on the business day following. A Notice to the Brokers or Agent shall be deemed a Notice under this Contract. All Notices given under this Contract shall be given by letter, if delivered by hand on the day of writing, or by telegram or by telex or by other method of rapid written communication. In case of resales all Notices shall be passed on without delay by Buyers to their respective Sellers or vice versa.

25. NON-BUSINESS DAYS—Saturdays, Sundays and the officially recognised and/or legal holidays of the respective countries and any days which The Grain and Feed Trade Association may declare as Non-Business Days for specific purposes, shall be Non-Business Days. Should the time limit for doing any act or giving any notice expire on a Non-Business Day, the time so limited shall be extended until the first Business Day thereafter. The period of shipment shall not be affected by this clause.

26. PRO RATA—

(a) Should any of the above mentioned quantity form part of a larger quantity of the same or a different period of shipment of bags of the same mark, or of a similar quality, whether in bags or bulk or whether destined to more than one port, no separation or distinction shall be necessary.

(b) All loose collected, damaged goods and sweepings shall be shared by and apportioned pro-rata in kind between the various receivers thereof at the port of discharge named in the contract, buying under contracts containing this clause. In the event of this not being practicable, or any of them receiving more or less than his pro-rata share or apportionment, he shall settle with the other(s) on a pro-rata basis in cash at the market price and each receiver shall bear his proportion of the depreciation in market value. The pro-rata statement shall be established by the Sellers or their representatives in conjunction with the receivers or their representatives.

(c) The above pro-rata apportionment between receivers shall have no bearing on the establishment of final invoices with Sellers and for the purpose of these final invoices, the total quantity of loose collected, damaged goods and sweepings shall be regarded as delivered to those receivers who did not receive their full invoiced quantity.

(d) In the case of excess or deficiency, the difference between the invoiced and the total delivered quantity shall be settled at the market price by final invoices to be rendered by receivers, who have received more or less than that paid for, to their immediate Sellers without taking into consideration the above pro-rata apportionment between receivers.

(e) If an excess quantity is delivered to one or more receiver and a deficient quantity is delivered to one or more receiver, the excess and deficiency shall be settled between them at the market price. Final invoices shall be established with immediate Sellers for any balance resulting from this settlement.

(f) All Shippers, Sellers and Buyers of any part of such larger quantity as aforesaid under contracts containing this clause shall be deemed to have entered into mutual agreements with one another to the above effect, and to agree to submit to arbitration all questions and claims containing them or any of them in regard to the execution of this clause. All Sellers shall be responsible for the settlement by the respective Buyers in accordance with this clause within a reasonable time.

(g) The market price wherever mentioned in this clause shall be the market price on the last day of discharge of the vessel in the port of destination, such price to be fixed by arbitration unless mutually agreed.

(h) In the event of this clause being brought into operation, any allowances payable in respect of condition, or quality, or under any of the other guarantees contained in this contract, shall be based upon the actual weight received by the Buyers and not on the pro-rata weight.

(i) In the event of any conflict in terms the method of apportionment applicable to the port of discharge published by The Grain and Feed Trade Association shall, where applicable, take precedence over sub-clauses (b) to (h) above.

(j) In the event that Clause (a) applies or that the goods subsequently become co-mingled, and that the goods were shipped by more than one shipper and destined for one or more ports of discharge, then after the adjustment between receivers under the terms of this clause, the shippers shall settle pro-rata between themselves in proportion to their bill of lading quantities.

Such settlements shall be made in cash and in the event of two or more discharging ports being involved, then the settlement price shall be the average of the market prices on the last day of discharge in the respective ports.

27. DEFAULT—In default of fulfilment of contract by either party, the following provisions shall apply:—

(a) The party other than the defaulter shall, at their discretion have the right, after giving notice by letter, telegram or telex to the defaulter, to sell or purchase, as the case may be, against the defaulter, and such sale or purchase shall establish the default price.

(b) If either party be dissatisfied with such default price or if the right at (a) above is not exercised and damages cannot be mutually agreed, then the assessment of damages shall be settled by arbitration.

(c) The damages payable shall be based on the difference between the contract price and either the default price established under (a) above or upon the actual or estimated value of the goods, on the date of default, established under (b) above.

(d) In no case shall damages include loss of profit on any sub-contracts made by the party defaulting against or others unless the Arbitrator(s) or Board of Appeal, having regard to special circumstances, shall in his/their sole and absolute discretion think fit.

(e) Damages, if any, shall be computed on the quantity appropriated if any but, if no such quantity has been appropriated then on the mean contract quantity, and any option available to either party shall be deemed to have been exercised accordingly in favour of the mean contract quantity.

(f) Default may be declared by Sellers at any time after expiry of the contract period, and the default date shall then be the first business day after the date of Sellers' advice to their Buyers.

If default has not already been declared then (notwithstanding the provisions stated in the appropriation clause) if notice of appropriation is not passed by the 10th consecutive day after the last day for appropriation laid down in the contract, where the appropriation clause provides for 7 or more days for despatch of the appropriation, or if notice of appropriation is not passed by the 4th business day after the last day for appropriation laid down in the contract where the appropriation clause provides for less than 7 days for despatch of the appropriation, the Sellers shall be deemed to be in default, and the default date shall then be the first business day thereafter.

28. CIRCLE—Where Sellers repurchase from their Buyer or from any subsequent Buyer the same goods or part thereof, a circle shall be considered to exist as regards the particular goods so repurchased, and the provisions of the Default Clause shall not apply. (For the purpose of this Clause the same goods shall mean goods of the same description, from the same country of origin, of the same quality, and, where applicable, of the same analysis warranty, for shipment to the same port(s) of destination during the same period of shipment). Subject to the terms of the Prohibition Clause in the contract, if goods are not appropriated, or, having been appropriated documents are not presented, invoices based on the mean contract quantity shall be settled between each Buyer and his Seller in the circle by payment by Buyers to their Sellers of the excess of the Sellers' invoice amount over the lowest invoice amount in the circle. Payment shall be due not later than 15 consecutive days after the last day for appropriation, or, should the circle not be ascertained before the expiry of this time, then payment shall be due not later than 15 consecutive days after the circle is ascertained. All Sellers and Buyers shall give every assistance to ascertain the circle and when a circle shall have been ascertained in accordance with this Clause same shall be binding on all parties to the circle. As between Buyers and Sellers in the circle, the non-presentation of documents by Sellers to their Buyers shall not be considered a breach of contract. Should any party in the circle prior to the due date of payment commit any act comprehended in the Insolvency Clause of his contract, the circle shall be considered broken, and the Insolvency Clause shall apply.

29. INSOLVENCY—If before the fulfilment of this contract, either party shall suspend payments, commit an act of bankruptcy, notify any of his creditors that he is unable to meet debts or that he has suspended or that he is about to suspend payment of his debts, convene, call or hold a meeting of creditors, convene, call or hold a meeting to go into liquidation (other than for reconstruction or amalgamation) or shall apply for an official moratorium, have a petition presented for winding up, or shall have a Receiver appointed (any of which acts being hereinafter called an 'Act of Insolvency'), then the party committing such Act of Insolvency shall forthwith transmit by telex or telegram or by other method of rapid written communication a notice of the occurrence of such Act of Insolvency to the other party to the contract and, upon proof (by either the other party to the contract or the Receiver or person representing the party committing the Act of Insolvency) that such notice was thus given within two business days of the occurrence of the Act of Insolvency, the contract shall be closed out at the market price ruling on the business day following the giving of the Notice.

If such Notice be not given as aforesaid, then the other party, on learning of the occurrence of the Act of Insolvency, shall have the option of declaring the contract closed out at either the market price on the first business day after the date when such party first learnt of the occurrence of the Act of Insolvency or at the market price ruling on the first business day after the date when the Act of Insolvency occurred.

In all cases the other party to the contract shall have the option of ascertaining the settlement price on the closing out of the contract by re-purchase or re-sale, and the difference between the contract price and the repurchase or re-sale price shall be the amount payable or receivable under this contract.

30. DOMICILE—Buyers and Sellers agree that, for the purpose of proceedings either legal or by arbitration, this contract shall be deemed to have been made in England, and to be performed there, any correspondence in reference to the offer, the acceptance, the place of payment, or otherwise, notwithstanding, and the Courts of England or arbitrators appointed in England, as the case may be, shall, except for the purpose of enforcing any award made in pursuance of the arbitration clause hereof, have exclusive jurisdiction over all disputes which may arise under this contract. Such disputes shall be settled according to the law of England, whatever the domicile, residence or place of business of the parties to this contract may be or become. Any party to this contract residing or carrying on business elsewhere than in England or Wales, shall for the purpose of proceedings at law or in arbitration be considered as ordinarily resident or carrying on business at the offices of The Grain and Feed Trade Association, and if in Scotland, he shall be held to have prorogated jurisdiction against himself to the English Courts; or if in Northern Ireland to have submitted to the jurisdiction, and to be bound by the decision of the English Courts. The service of proceedings upon any such party by leaving the same at the office of The Grain and Feed Trade Association, together with the posting of a copy of such proceedings to his address abroad, or in Scotland or in Northern Ireland, shall be deemed good service, any rule of law or equity to the contrary notwithstanding. Where goods forming the subject of this contract are not for consumption in Great Britain or Northern Ireland nothing in the foregoing shall make the sale subject to the provisions of the Agriculture Act for the time being in force. Nevertheless parties to the contract accept the method of analysis prescribed in the Regulations made under the said Act.

31. ARBITRATION—

(a) Any dispute arising out of or under this contract shall be settled by arbitration in accordance with the Arbitration Rules, No. 125, of The Grain and Feed Trade Association, in the edition current at the date of this contract, such Rules forming part of this contract and of which both parties hereto shall be deemed to be cognisant.

(b) Neither party hereto, nor any persons claiming under either of them shall bring any action or other legal proceedings against the other of them in respect of any such dispute until such dispute shall first have been heard and determined by the arbitrator(s) or a Board of Appeal, as the case may be, in accordance with the Arbitration Rules and it is expressly agreed and declared that the obtaining of an award from the arbitrator(s) or a Board of Appeal, as the case may be, shall be a condition precedent to the right of either party hereto or of any persons claiming under either of them to bring any action or other legal proceedings against the other of them in respect of any such dispute.

32. INTERNATIONAL CONVENTIONS—

The following shall not apply to this contract:—
(a) the Uniform Law on Sales and the Uniform Law on Formation to which effect is given by the Uniform Laws on International Sales Act 1967;
(b) the United Nations Convention on Contracts for the International Sale of Goods of 1980; and
(c) the United Nations Convention on Prescription (Limitation) in the International Sale of Goods of 1974 and the amending Protocol of 1980.

BILL OF LADING

COPY

B/L NO.

SHIPPER'S NAME AND ADDRESS

S.S. CONTRACT NO.

SHIPPER'S REFERENCE NO.

FORWARDER REF.

PARTICULARS DECLARED BY SHIPPER

CONSIGNED TO:

FORWARDER

ACL

NOTIFY PARTY

PRE-CARRIAGE BY*

PLACE OF RECEIPT*

OCEAN VESSEL

PORT OF LOADING

PORT OF DISCHARGE

PLACE OF DELIVERY*

TYPE OF MOVE

ON-CARRIAGE BY*

MARKS AND NOS.
CONTAINER/SEAL NO.

PARTICULARS DECLARED BY SHIPPER
QUANTITY AND DESCRIPTION OF GOODS

GROSS WEIGHT
IN KILOS

MEASUREMENTS
IN CUBIC METERS

* Applicable only when document used as Through Bill of Lading

FREIGHT CHARGES
PAYABLE AT

BY

SHIPPERS DECLARED VALUE $ _____

SUBJECT TO EXTRA FREIGHT AS PER TARIFF AND CLAUSE 6 OF THIS B. L.

CARRIER'S RECEIPT — Received in apparent external good order and condition except as otherwise noted herein, the containers whose numbers are listed above said to contain the goods or in the case of breakbulk cargo the number of pieces or packages listed above, to be transported to such place as agreed, authorized or permitted herein and there to be delivered to the authorized receiver. The shipment to be transported by the ocean vessel, feeder vessel or other means of transportation (rail, truck or air), subject to the terms and conditions noted on this page and overleaf and also when applicable subject to the Carrier's published tariffs on file with the Federal Maritime Commission, Washington, D.C. USA or with the Canadian Transport Commission, Ottawa, Ont. Canada, such tariffs also being available from any port agent listed on the reverse side hereof. In accepting this Bill of Lading the Merchant agrees to be bound by its terms and conditions. ACL shall have the right to ship goods in containers and to stow all types of containers on deck or underdeck. In witness of the contract herein the Carrier has signed (3) original Bill(s) of Lading, one of which being accomplished the other(s) to be void.

FOR **ACL**

ACL CANADA INC.

BY _____

PLACE AND DATE OF ISSUE

12M 4/87

ATLANTIC CONTAINER LINE B.V.

CANADA

Toronto
20 Dundas St. West
Toronto, Ont. M5G 2C2
Phone: (416) 591-5700
Fax: (416) 977-8516

UNITED STATES

For General Cargo
To All Destinations
ACL USA INC.
80 Pine Street
New York, N.Y. 10005
Phone: (212) 908-2000

For Automobile Traffic
To All Destinations
Motorships, Inc.
482 Hudson Terrace
Englewood Cliffs, N.J. 07632
Phone: (201) 871-0700

EUROPE

Antwerp, Belgium
Incotrans
Cassiersstraat 15/19
B-2000 Antwerp, Belgium
Phone Code 32/31-315890

Bremen, West Germany
Incotrans GMBH Linienagentur
Gruenemweg 26
Postfach 104567
2800 Bremen 1
Bremen, West Germany
Phone Code 49/421-320383

Gothenburg, Sweden
ACL AB
P.O. Box 8888
S-402 72 Gothenburg,
Sweden
Phone Code 46/31-616900

Le Havre, France
ACL Division
Compagnie General Maritime
Quai de l'Europe
76600 Le Havre
Bremen, West Germany
Phone Code 33/35-268100

ENDORSEMENTS

ACL CANADA INC.

Montreal
740 rue Notre-Dame
Montréal, Quebec H3C 3X6
Phone: (514) 871-3333
Fax: (514) 871-3251

Baltimore
ACL USA INC.
5 Light Street
Baltimore, Md. 21202
Phone: (301) 659-7800

Portsmouth
ACL USA INC.
P.O. Box 609
Portsmouth Va. 23705
Phone: (804) 398-9400

Liverpool, England
Cunard-Brocklebank Ltd.
Atlantic Container Line Div.
Cunard House, Cotton Exchange Bldg.
Old Hall Street, Liverpool L3 9BN
Phone Code 44/51-2273000

London, England
ACL Division
Cunard Brocklebank, Ltd.
Kingsworthy Bldg. - Chobham Farm
Leyton Road, Stratford,
London, E15 1DG
Phone Code 44/1-5550211

Philadelphia
ACL USA INC.
Public Ledger Building, Suite 1235
Philadelphia, Pa. 19106
Phone: (215) 922-7931/35

Rotterdam, Holland
Incotrans Holland BV
Seattleweg 17
P.O. Box 7320
3000 HH Rotterdam
Phone: (010) 428-5555

Southampton, England
ACL Division
Cunard Brocklebank, Ltd.
South Western House
Canute Road
Southampton SO9 1ZA
Phone. Code 44/703-29933

Halifax
1770 Market Street, Suite 505
Halifax, N.S. B3J 3M3
Phone: (902) 425-3711
Fax: (902) 425-3711

Boston
Sprague Steamship Co.
50 Congress Street
Boston, Mass. 02109
Phone: (617) 227-6713

TERMS AND CONDITIONS

1. DEFINITIONS.
In this Bill of Lading ACL means Atlantic Container Line BV, a limited liability company located in Rotterdam Trade Register No. 156582, and the word 'Carrier' includes ACL, the vessel, owners and any of their employees, agents, contractors or sub-contractors. The words 'Carriage by Water' and 'Vessel' shall include any substitute vessel, feeder, ship, barge or watercraft. The word 'Merchant' includes the shipper, the consignee, the holder of the Bill of Lading and the owner of the goods. The words 'on board' mean on board any mode of transportation used or procured by the carrier, including rail, road and air transport.

2. CONTRACTING PARTIES
The contract evidenced by this Bill of Lading is between the Merchant and ACL/the vessel. It is agreed that only ACL and the vessel *in rem* shall be liable as carriers under this contract. Claims may be sent to any ACL office or port agent listed above.

3. RESPONSIBILITY.
I. ACL shall be responsible for the goods from the time when the goods are received by ACL at the port of loading to the time when they are delivered or dispatched by ACL.

unit in excess of the package or shipping unit limitation amount as laid down by the Hague Rules 1924, as amended by the Hague Visby Rules 1968, or any legislation making these rules or part of these rules compulsorily applicable in this Bill of Lading.

Such limitation amount according to the Hague Rules 1924, is, in the United States in accordance with the U.S. Carriage of Goods by Sea Act (US/500) and in Canada, in accordance with the Water Carriage of Goods Act (Can/500).

If no other limitation amount is applicable as either set forth above or statutorily, the compensation shall not, however, exceed the equivalent of 10,000 poincare francs per package or unit or 30 poincare francs per kilogram of gross weight of the goods, whichever is higher.

The words 'shipping unit' as used in the US Carriage of Goods by Sea Act shall mean each physical unit or piece of cargo not shipped in a package, including articles or things of any description whatsoever, except goods shipped in bulk and, irrespective of weight or measurement, units employed in calculating freight charges.

If ACL has consented to payment of freight and charges in other currencies than U.S. or Canadian dollars and such other currencies are devalued before payment, then the conversion of U.S. or Canadian currencies shall be effected at the highest bank selling rate on the date of payment.

c) All dues, taxes and charges or other expenses in connection with the goods shall be paid by the Merchant.

d) The Merchant shall reimburse ACL in proportion to the amount of freight for any increase of war risk insurance premium and war risk increase of the wages of the Master, officers and crew and for any increase of the cost for bunkers and for deviation or delay caused by war or warlike operations or by government directions in such connection.

e) The Merchant warrants the correctness of the declaration of contents, insurance, weight, measurement or value of the goods but ACL reserves the right to have the contents inspected in order to ascertain the weight, measurement or value for the purpose of verifying the freight basis. If on such inspection it is found that the declaration is not correct it is agreed that a sum equal either to five times the difference between at the port of discharge, and also during any previous or subsequent periods of carriage by water under this Bill of Lading, and such custody carriage shall be subject at all such times to the Hague Rules contained in the International Convention for the Unification of Certain Rules Relating to Bills of Lading dated 25th August, 1924, as amended by the Protocol signed at Brussels on the 23rd February, 1968 (Hague Visby Rules), or to any legislation making such Rules, whether amended by the above Brussels Protocol or not, compulsorily applicable to this Bill of Lading, including the Carriage of Goods by Sea Act of the United States, approved April 16th, 1936, which Rules and Act shall be deemed to be incorporated herein. The provisions of said Act or Rules (except as otherwise specifically provided herein) shall govern before the shipment is loaded on and after it is discharged from the vessel while the shipment is in the custody and possession of the carrier. It is agreed that such Act or Rules shall also apply to containers carried on deck and that the carrier has the right to ship goods in container stowed on deck or under deck.

II. When either the place of receipt or place of delivery set forth herein is an inland point in Canada , the USA or Europe, the responsibility of ACL with respect to the transportation to and from the sea terminal ports will be as follows

a) Within countries in Europe, to transport the goods in accordance with any mandatory national law or, in the absence thereof, subject to the inland carrier's own contracts and tariffs.

b) Between countries in Europe, to transport the goods

(1) if by road, in accordance with the Convention on the Contract for the International Carriage of Goods by Road, dated 19th May, 1956 (CMR).

(2) if by rail, in accordance with the International Agreement on Railway Transports, dated 25th February, 1961 (CIM).

(3) if by air, in accordance with the Convention for the Unification on certain Rules relating to International Carriage by Air, signed Warsaw 12th October, 1929, as amended by the Hague Protocol, dated 28th September, 1955.

c) Between points in the USA or Canada, to procure transportation by carriers (one or more) authorized by competent authority to engage in transportation between such points, and such transportation shall be subject to the inland carriers' contracts of carriage and tariffs. ACL guarantees the fulfilment of such inland carriers' obligations under their contracts and tariffs.

III. As to services incident to through transportation, ACL undertakes to procure such services as necessary. All such services will be subject to the usual contracts of persons providing the services. ACL guarantees the fulfilment of the obligations of such persons under the pertinent contracts.

IV. When the goods have been damaged or lost during through transportation and it cannot be established in whose custody the goods were when the damage or loss occurred, the damage or loss shall be deemed to have occurred during the carriage by water and the Hague Rules as defined above shall apply.

4. DELAY
ACL does not accept responsibility for any direct or indirect loss or damage sustained by the Merchant through delay, unless ACL is liable for consequences of delay under any laws, statutes, agreements or conventions of a mandatory nature.

5. DEFENCES AND LIMITS FOR SERVANTS, ETC.
If an action for loss or damage to goods is brought against any insurer, servant agent, independent contractor or sub-contractor, including but not restricted to stevedores, carpenters, or watchmen, such person shall be entitled to avail himself of the defences and limits of liability which the carrier is entitled to invoke under this contract. For the purpose of this clause, all such persons are entitled to this contract made on their behalf by the carrier. The aggregate of the amounts recoverable from the carrier or from the above mentioned persons shall in no case exceed the limits provided in this Bill of Lading.

6. PACKAGE/SHIPPING UNIT LIMITATION AND DECLARED VALUE.
The carrier shall not, unless a declared value has been noted in accordance with the below ad valorem section of this clause be or become liable for any loss or damage to or in connection with the transportation of goods in an amount per package or shipping

AD VALOREM: DECLARED VALUE OF PACKAGE OR UNIT.
The carrier's liability, if any, per package or shipping unit in accordance with the above package limitation section of this clause may be increased to a higher value per package or shipping unit by a declaration in writing to such an effect by the shipper upon delivery to the carrier, such higher value being inserted on the reverse page of this Bill of Lading and extra freight paid. In such case, if the actual value of the goods per package or per shipping unit shall exceed such declared value, the value shall nevertheless be deemed to be the declared value and the carrier's liability, if any, shall not exceed the declared value and any partial loss or damage shall be adjusted pro rata on the basis of such declared value.

7. TIME BAR
All liability whatsoever of the carrier shall cease unless suit is brought within 12 months after delivery of the goods or the date when the goods should have been delivered.

8. PACKING AND MERCHANT-OWNED EQUIPMENT.
The Merchant shall be liable for any loss, damage or injury caused by faulty packing of goods within containers and trailers and on flats when such packing has been performed by the Merchant or on behalf of the Merchant.

ACL does not accept responsibility for the functioning of reefer containers or trailers, not owned nor leased by ACL.

9. ROUTE
The goods may be carried by any route whatsoever, whether or not the most direct or advertised or customary route, via any ports or places in any order whatsoever and for whatsoever purpose visited, together with other goods of every kind, dangerous or otherwise whether stowed on or under deck. Vessels may sail with or without pilots, undergo repairs, adjust equipment, drydock and tow vessels in all situations.

10. SUBSTITUTION OF VESSEL AND TRANSHIPMENT.
ACL has the right, but not the obligation, to carry the goods by any substitute vessel, or by any other means of transport whether by water, land or air, and may discharge the goods at any place for transhipment, tranship, land or store the goods either onshore or afloat and reship or forward the same.

11. BOTH TO BLAME COLLISION CLAUSE.
If the vessel comes into collision with another vessel as a result of the negligence of the other vessel and any act, neglect or default of the Master, Mariner, Pilot or the Servants of the Carrier in the navigation or in the management of the vessel, the Merchant will indemnify the Carrier against all loss or liability to the other or non-carrying vessel or her Owner in so far as such loss or liability represents loss of or damage to any claim whatsoever of the Owner of the said goods paid or repayable by the other non-carrying vessel or her Owner to the Owner of said cargo and set off, or recouped or recovered by the other or non-carrying vessel or her Owner as part of his claim against the carrying vessel or carrier. The foregoing provisions shall also apply where the Owner, Operator or those in charge of any vessel or vessels or objects other than, or in addition to, the colliding vessels or objects are at fault in respect of a collision or contact.

12. DELIVERY OF GOODS
If the goods are not taken by the Merchant within a reasonable time of ACL calling upon him to take delivery, ACL shall be at liberty to put the goods in safe custody on behalf of the Merchant at the Merchant's risk and expense.

13. FREIGHT AND CHARGES.

a) Freight to be paid in cash without discount and, whether pre-payable or payable at destination, to be considered as earned on receipt of the goods and not to be returned, goods lost or not lost.

b) Freight and all other amounts mentioned in this B/L are, at the option of ACL, to be paid in the currency named in this B/L or of the country of the port of loading or port of discharge, at the highest selling rate of exchange for banker's sight draft current on the date of the freight agreement or on the date of this B/L, or for prepayable freight of the day of loading, or for freight payable at destination on the day when the vessel is entered at the Customs House or on the date of withdrawal of the delivery order.

the correct freight and the freight charged or to double the correct freight less the freight charged, whichever sum is the smaller, shall be payable as liquidated damages to ACL notwithstanding any other sum having been stated on the B/L as freight payable. The Merchant shall hold the carrier harmless from any fines or damages resulting from any misdeclaration of description or of weight or measurement of the goods.

14. LIEN
ACL shall have a lien on the goods or part of the goods (including any Merchant owned containers or equipment) for any amount due to ACL under this Bill of Lading (and for costs of recovering same) and shall be entitled to sell or otherwise dispose of such goods to recover any such amounts and may enforce such lien in any reasonable manner.

15. GENERAL AVERAGE.
General Average to be adjusted at any port or place at the carrier's option, and to be settled according to the York-Antwerp Rules, 1974, this covering all goods, whether carried on or under deck. The amended Jason Clause to be considered as incorporated herein. Such security including a cash deposit as the carrier may deem sufficient to cover the estimated contribution by the goods and any salvage and special charges thereon, shall, if required, be submitted to the carrier prior to delivery of the goods.

16. HINDRANCES ETC. AFFECTING PERFORMANCE.

(1) The carrier shall use reasonable endeavours to complete the transport and to deliver the goods at the place designated for delivery.

(2) If at any time the performance of the contract as evidenced by this Bill of Lading is or will be affected by any hindrance, risk, delay, difficulty or disadvantage of whatsoever kind, and if by virtue of sub-clause (1) the carrier has no duty to complete the performance of the contract, the carrier (whether or not the transport is commenced) may elect to

(a) treat the performance of this contract as terminated and place the goods at the Merchant's disposal at any place which the carrier shall deem safe and convenient; or

(b) deliver the goods at the place designated for delivery.

In any event the carrier shall be entitled to full freight for goods received for transportation and additional compensation for extra costs resulting from the circumstances referred to above.

17. JURISDICTION
Disputes arising under this Bill of Lading shall be determined at the option of the Merchant, either by the Commercial Court in London in accordance with English law or by the U.S. District Court for the Southern District of New York in accordance with the laws of the United States. For traffic to or from Canada, jurisdiction will be limited to the Commercial Court in London only.

18. SEPARABILITY.
The terms of this Bill of Lading shall be separable, and if any provision hereof, or any part of any provision be held to be invalid or unenforceable, such holding shall not affect the validity or enforceability of any other provision or part thereof in this Bill of Lading.

GOODS OF DANGEROUS OR DAMAGING NATURE AND RADIOACTIVE MATERIAL MUST NOT BE TENDERED FOR SHIPMENT UNLESS WRITTEN NOTICE OF THEIR NATURE AND THE NAME AND ADDRESS OF THE SENDER AND THE RECEIVER HAVE BEEN PREVIOUSLY GIVEN TO ACL, SUB-CARRIERS, MASTER OR AGENT OF THE VESSEL AND THE NATURE IS DISTINCTLY MARKED ON THE OUTSIDE OF THE PACKAGE OR PACKAGES AS REQUIRED BY APPLICABLE STATUTES OR REGULATIONS AND IN ADDITION ON EACH CONTAINER, FLAT, TRAILER, ETC. A SPECIAL STOWAGE ORDER GIVING CONSENT TO SHIPMENT MUST ALSO BE OBTAINED FROM ACL. THE MERCHANT WILL BE LIABLE FOR ALL CONSEQUENTIAL DAMAGE AND EXPENSE IF ALL THE FOREGOING PROVISIONS ARE NOT COMPLIED WITH.

PLEASE COMPLETE THIS BY TYPEWRITER OR IN BLOCK CAPITALS USING BALL POINT PEN | FOR BANK USE ONLY

DOCUMENTARY CREDIT APPLICATION ❖ BARCLAYS	

To
BARCLAYS BANK PLC _____ Branch   Date

Customer/Applicant: Address: Customer's Reference	Name and Address of beneficiary

Please open an *IRREVOCABLE* Letter of Credit *(see note 1)*

☐ Mail Only   ☐ Mail with brief details Teletransmitted   ☐ Full details Teletransmitted with no mail confirmation

Advising Bank:
(Bank use only)

Amount (see note 1)   ☐ Up to
(in words and figures)
(specify currency)   ☐ About

Available by drafts on Barclays Bank PLC or its correspondents at *(see note 1)*

☐ sight   ☐ _____days sight   ☐ _____days after _____

for_____per cent of the _____invoice value, accompanied by the following documents:
(see note 2)

Invoice *(see note 3)*
Full set of clean on board blank endorsed BILLS OF LADING *(see note 4)* marked notify:

INSURANCE policy or certificate *(in duplicate)* endorsed in blank for the invoice value of the goods plus_____
per cent, covering:
(see note 5)

Any other Documents:

Brief description of goods:
(see note 6)

Shipment from: to At latest by:	Partnerships ☐ Allowed ☐ Prohibited	Transhipments ☐ Allowed ☐ Prohibited *See note 1*

Documents to be presented within_____days of shipment but in any event within the validity of the credit.

Credit to expire on   in the beneficiary's country.

Additional Information *(see note 7)*

375 (4/85)/CRE 201

IF APPLICABLE PLEASE INDICATE

☐   Forward Contract No...........   —   Maturity   .. Rate   ... .

☐   CFC Account No.

TERMS AND CONDITIONS

In consideration of your issuing this Letter of Credit

a)   We authorise you to debit our account with all your commissions/charges and expenses together with those of your correspondents where applicable as and when they become due and with drawings either: (i) on presentation if drafts are drawn at sight or where no drafts are involved, or, (ii) at maturity in respect of accepted drafts in which case we hereby undertake to provide you with funds not later than 3 days before maturity, unless you have been previously provided with funds for this purpose.

b)   Where drafts are drawn in a currency other than Sterling, your demand for reimbursement from us will be calculated, unless previously agreed to the contrary, at your selling rate of exchange for the currency concerned, for the day you effect payment, or receive advice from your branch or correspondent that payment has been made. Interest where applicable is payable by us from the date of payment by your branch/correspondent until reimbursement currency is available to you, and any exchange risks are for our account.

c)   Where the beneficiary is not required to provide an insurance document, we undertake to arrange such insurance and deliver the relative policies/certificates to you on request. If the insurance is not arranged to your satisfaction you are authorised to arrange such insurance at our expense.

d)   The relative shipping documents, as and when received by you, are to be delivered to us provided all costs, expenses and interest have been paid. If we fail to pay, you are authorised to sell the goods, and we undertake to pay on demand the amount of any deficiency on such sale.

e)   It is agreed that this credit is subject to Uniform Customs and Practice for Documentary Credits (1983 Revision) I.C.C. Publication No. 400.

Clause (f) below should only be completed when full or part cash cover is being provided

f)   To provide you with security you are authorised immediately to

(i) debit our account with _____ (say _____

_____)

(ii) buy the sum of _____ (say _____

_____)

on our behalf and debit our account with the Sterling equivalent.

Such sums to be held by you until all claims regarding this Letter of Credit have been satisfied.

For and on behalf of _____
                        (Insert Company Name)

Capacity of Signatory(ies) _____

NOTES

ALL DELETIONS AND ALTERATIONS TO BE INITIALLED

1)   Indicate instruction to be followed by placing a tick or cross in appropriate box. One item only is to be completed in each section.

2)   Insert Term of Contract, C.I.F., F.O.B., etc.

3)   Indicate if required in duplicate, triplicate etc.

4)   If Bill of Lading not required delete and insert other transport document (e.g. Air Waybill, Forwarding Agents Receipts etc.) indicating name and address of consignee.

5)   If the insurance is being arranged by the beneficiary, complete this clause and state risks to be covered, Marine/Air/War etc. If insurance is being arranged by applicant, see note (c) above.

6)   Goods description may include reference to proforma invoices or contracts but such documents should not be attached.

7)   Include any additional information such as whether beneficiary has agreed to pay bank charges outside the U.K. and beneficiary's bankers (if known).

FOR BANK USE ONLY	AUTHORISING BRANCH TO INDICATE BELOW
BRANCH AUTHORISATION	BY PLACING TICK IN BOX IF FULLY CASH COVERED ☐
	ISB USE ONLY
	SIGNATURES VERIFIED

TO INTERNATIONAL SERVICES BRANCH

NON-NEGOTIABLE
SEA WAYBILL

Shipper

UK Customs
Assigned No.   SWB No.

Shipper's Reference

F/Agent's Reference

Consignee

Name of Carrier

Notify Party and Address (leave blank if stated above)

The contract evidenced by this Waybill is subject to the exceptions, limitations, conditions and liberties (including those relating to pre-carriage and on-carriage) set out in the Carrier's Standard Conditions of Carriage applicable to the voyage covered by this Waybill and operative on its date of issue: if the carriage is one where had a Bill of Lading been issued the provisions of the Hague Rules contained in the International Convention for unification of certain rules relating to Bills of Lading dated Brussels 25th August, 1924, as amended by the Protocol signed at Brussels on the 23rd February, 1968 (the Hague Visby Rules) would have been compulsorily applicable under Article X, the said Standard Conditions contain or shall be deemed to contain a Clause giving effect to the Hague Visby Rules. Otherwise the said Standard Conditions contain or shall be deemed to contain a Clause giving effect to the provisions of the Hague Rules. In neither case shall the proviso to the first sentence of Article V of the Hague Rules or the Hague Visby Rules apply. The Carrier hereby agrees (i) that to the extent of any inconsistency the said clause shall prevail over the said Standard Conditions in respect of any period to which the Hague Rules or the Hague Visby Rules by their terms apply, and (ii) that for the purpose of the terms of this Contract of Carriage this Waybill falls within the definition of Article 1(b) of the Hague Rules and the Hague Visby Rules.
The Shipper accepts the said Standard Conditions on his own behalf and on behalf of the Consignee and the owner of the goods and warrants that he has authority to do so. The Consignee by presenting this Waybill and/or requesting delivery of the goods further undertakes all liabilities of the Shipper hereunder such undertaking being additional and without prejudice to the Shipper's own liability. The benefits of the contract evidenced by this Waybill shall thereby be transferred to the Consignee or other persons presenting this Waybill.
Notwithstanding anything contained in the said Standard Conditions, the term Carrier in this Waybill shall mean the Carrier named on the front thereof.
A copy of the Carrier's said Standard Conditions applicable hereto may be inspected or will be supplied on request at the office of the Carrier or the Carrier's Principal Agents.

Pre-Carriage by*   Place of Receipt by Pre-Carrier*

Vessel   Port of Loading

Port of Discharge   Place of Delivery by On-Carrier*

Marks and Nos;   Container No.   Number and kind of packages; Description of Goods   Gross Weight   Measurement

*Applicable only when document used as a Through Bill of Lading

© GCBS 1979

AVAILABLE FROM

THE CARLTON BERRY CO. LTD.
PRINTERS TO LLOYD'S OF LONDON

PHONE: 01-623 7100 Extn. 3166

Particulars declared by Shipper

RECEIVED FOR CARRIAGE as above in apparent good order and condition, unless otherwise stated hereon, the goods described in the above particulars.

Freight Details; Charges etc.

Ocean Freight Payable at

Place and Date of Issue

Signature for Carrier; Carrier's Principal Place of Business

GCBS
SWB
1979

711

Printed by The Carlton Berry Co. Ltd.
Authorised and licensed by the
General Council of British Shipping.

The Sea Waybill is offered on outward liner services from the UK as follows:-

ANDREW WEIR - on behalf of Bank Line

Continent Pacific Islands Service "SHIPPED ONLY"

ATLANTIC CARGO SERVICES A.B. (LINER SHIPPING AGENCIES LTD)

Florida, U.S. Gulf ports and Mexico

BEN LINE

Joint Service

UKWAL (Elder Dempster Lines Ltd - The Guinea Gulf Line
Ltd - The Nigerian National Shipping Line Ltd
- Compagnie Maritime Zairoise - Palme Line Ltd
- Black Star Line Ltd - Hoegh Lines)

West Africa (CONFIRMATION AWAITED FROM COMPAGNIE MARITIME
ZAIROISE AND HOEGH LINES)

BOOKER LINE

Barbados and Trinidad

CANADIAN PACIFIC STEAMSHIP LIMITED

Tilbury to Montreal

CAYZER IRVINE SHIPPING - on behalf of Clan Line &
Union Castle

Red Sea, India, Sri Lanka, Bangladesh, East Africa,
Mauritius

NIGERIAN NATIONAL SHIPPING LINE LIMITED

Joint Service

UKWAL (Elder Dempster Lines Ltd - The Guinea Gulf
Line Ltd - The Nigerian National Shipping Line
Ltd - Compagnie Maritime Zairoise - Palm
Line Ltd - Black Star Line Ltd - Hoegh Lines)

West Africa (CONFIRMATION AWAITED FROM COMPAGNIE
MARITIME ZAIROISE AND HOEGH LINES)

NORTH SEA FERRIES

Hull to Rotterdam and Zeebrugge)
) "RECEIVED FOR SHIPMENT"
Ipswich to Rotterdam   )

OCEAN AGENCIES LIMITED - on behalf of Elder Dempster
Lines Ltd and The Guinea Gulf Line Ltd

Joint Service

UKWAL (Elder Dempster Lines Ltd - The Guinea Gulf
Line Ltd - The Nigerian National Shipping Line
Ltd - Compagnie Maritime Zairoise - Palm
Line Ltd - Black Star Line Ltd - Hoegh Lines)

West Africa (CONFIRMATION AWAITED FROM COMPAGNIE
MARITIME ZAIROISE AND HOEGH LINES)

P & O

Services to be confirmed

CUNARD-BROCKLEBANK LIMITED

Red Sea, Seychelles, India, Bangladesh, Sri Lanka

ELLERMAN CITY LINERS

Company Services

South Africa, Mozambique, India, Pakistan, Bangladesh
Mediterranean and Iberian Peninsula

Joint Services

Ellerman - P & O	Persian Gulf
Ellerman - Clan - Harrison	East Africa
Ellerman - Strath	Mediterranean
Ellerman - Prince	Mediterranean
Prince - Ellerman	Mediterranean
Ellerman - Prince - Zim	Israel
Ellerman - MacAndrews Joint	London to Lisbon & Gibraltar
Container Service	

THOS & JAS HARRISON LIMITED

Venezuela, Colombia, U.S. Gulf,   ) "RECEIVED FOR
Mexico, Belize, Red Sea, East Africa   ) SHIPMENT"

LAMPORT AND HOLT LINE

Services to be confirmed

(to next column)

UNITED BALTIC CORPORATION LIMITED

Joint Services

Ellerman - MacAndrews Joint Container Services

Lisbon and Gibraltar

COMPANIES LICENSED TO PRINT THE SEA WAYBILL

Cayzer Irvine Shipping Ltd 1 Seething Lane London, EC3N 4EE	A C Shaw (Export Sales) Ltd 127 Cheapside London, EC2V 6DH
Mawdsley Reed Ltd 25 Dickson Street Liverpool, L3 7HB	Systemforms Ltd Gainsborough House 10a Gainsborough Road Woodford Green Essex, IG8 8EE
Ozalid (UK) Ltd Cowdray Avenue Colchester Essex	Transcar Ltd 43-44 New Bond Street London, SW1
Rank Xerox (UK) Ltd Bridge House Oxford Road Uxbridge Middlesex	P C Richardson & CO Ltd 6 Whittington Avenue London, EC3V 1JY
Rockliff Brothers Ltd 2 Rumford Street Liverpool, L2 8SZ	The Carlton Berry Co Ltd 35 Crutched Friars London EC3

APRIL 1980

5/0565

CODE NAME: "GENWAYBILL"

Shipper

**NON-NEGOTIABLE
GENERAL SEA WAYBILL
FOR USE IN SHORT-SEA
DRY CARGO TRADE**

GSWB No.

Reference No.

Consignee (not to order)

Notify address

Vessel

Port of loading

Port of discharge

Description of cargo	Marks and Nos.	Number and kind of packages	Gross weight	Measurement

Particulars declared by the Shipper

(of which
being responsible for loss or damage howsoever arising)
on deck at Shipper's risk; the Carrier not

SHIPPED on board the cargo specified above, according to Shipper's declaration in apparent good order and condition – unless otherwise stated herein – weight, measure, marks, numbers, quality, contents and value unknown, for delivery at the port of discharge or so near thereto as the Vessel may safely get, always afloat.

The cargo shipped under this Waybill will be delivered to the Party named as Consignee or its authorised agent, on production of proof of identity without any documentary formalities. The Carrier to exercise due care ensuring that delivery is made to the proper party. However, in case of incorrect delivery, no responsibility will be accepted unless due to fault or neglect on the part of the Carrier.

FOR CONDITIONS OF CARRIAGE SEE OVERLEAF.

Issued pursuant to Voyage Charter Party indicated hereunder

Charter Party (Code name, place and date of issue)

Freight payable in accordance therewith.

Freight payable at

Place and date of issue

Signature

Printed and sold by
Fr. G. Knudtzons Bogtrykkeri A/S, 55 Toldbodgade, DK-1253 Copenhagen K.
by authority of The Baltic and International Maritime Council (BIMCO),
Copenhagen, Copyright.

THE BALTIC AND INTERNATIONAL MARITIME COUNCIL (BIMCO)

NON-NEGOTIABLE

GENERAL SEA WAYBILL

FOR USE IN SHORT-SEA DRY CARGO TRADE

CODE NAME: "GENWAYBILL"

Conditions of Carriage.

(1) All the terms, conditions, liberties, clauses and exceptions of the Voyage Charter Party, as dated overleaf, shall be deemed to be incorporated in this Waybill and shall govern the transportation of the cargo described on the front page of this Waybill. In addition, the provisions set out below shall apply to this Waybill.

(2) Paramount Clause
(a) This Waybill is a non-negotiable document. It is not a bill of lading and no bill of lading will be issued. However, it is agreed that the Hague Rules contained in the International Convention for the Unification of certain rules relating to Bills of Lading, dated Brussels the 25th August 1924 as enacted in the country of shipment shall apply to this Waybill. When no such enactment is in force in the country of shipment, the corresponding legislation of the country of destination shall apply, but in respect of shipments to which no such enactments are compulsorily applicable, the terms of the said Convention shall apply in exactly the same way.

(b) *Trades where Hague-Visby Rules apply.*
In trades where the International Brussels Convention 1924 as amended by the Protocol signed at Brussels on February 23rd 1968 – the Hague-Visby Rules – apply compulsorily, the provisions of the respective legislation shall also apply to this Waybill.

(c) The Carrier shall in no case be responsible for loss of or damage to cargo howsoever arising prior to loading into and after discharge from the Vessel or while the goods are in the charge of another Carrier nor in respect of deck cargo.

(d) It is agreed that whenever the Brussels Convention and the Brussels Protocol or statutes incorporating same use the words "Bill of Lading" they shall be read and interpreted as meaning "Waybill".

(3) General Average

General Average shall be adjusted, stated and settled according to York-Antwerp Rules 1974 or any modification thereof at the place (if any) agreed in the Voyage Charter Party, as dated overleaf, otherwise in London.

Cargo's contribution to General Average shall be paid to the Carrier even when such average is the result of a fault, neglect or error of the Master, Pilot or Crew. The Charterers, Shippers and Consignees expressly renounce the Netherlands Commercial Code, Art. 700, and the Belgium Commercial Code, Part II, Art. 148.

If the adjustment of General Average or the liability for any collision in which the Vessel is involved while performing the carriage under the terms of the Voyage Charter Party, as dated overleaf, which govern the transportation of the cargo described on the front page of this Waybill, falls to be determined in accordance with the law and practice of the United States of America, the following clauses shall apply:

New Jason Clause

In the event of accident, danger, damage or disaster before or after the commencement of the voyage, resulting from any cause whatsoever, whether due to negligence or not, for which, or for the consequence of which, the Carrier is not responsible, by Statute, contract or otherwise, the cargo, shippers, consignees or owners of the cargo shall contribute with the Carrier in general average to the payment of any sacrifices, losses or expenses of a general average nature that may be made or incurred and shall pay salvage and special charges incurred in respect of the cargo.

If a salving vessel is owned or operated by the Carrier, salvage shall be paid for as fully as if the said salving vessel or vessels belonged to strangers. Such deposit as the Carrier, or his agent, may deem sufficient to cover the estimated contribution of the cargo and any salvage and special charges thereon shall, if required, be made by the cargo, shippers, consignees or owners of the cargo to the Carrier before delivery.

Both-to-Blame Collision Clause

If the Vessel comes into collision with another vessel as a result of the negligence of the other vessel and any act, neglect or default of the Master, Mariner, Pilot or the Servants of the Carrier in the navigation or in the management of the Vessel, the owners of the cargo carried hereunder will indemnify the Carrier against all loss or liability to the other or non-carrying vessel or her owners in so far as such loss or liability represents loss of, or damage to, or any claim whatsoever of the owners of the said cargo, paid or payable by the other or non-carrying vessel or her owners to the owners of the said cargo and set-off, recouped or recovered by the other or non-carrying vessel or her owners as part of their claim against the carrying vessel or the Carrier.

The foregoing provisions shall also apply where the owners, operators or those in charge of any vessel or vessels or objects other than, or in addition to, the colliding vessels or objects are at fault in respect of a collision or contact.

For particulars of cargo, freight, destination, etc., see overleaf.

Code Name: "COMBIDOC"

Consignor

Consigned to order of

Notify address

CT Doc. No.

Reference No.

Negotiable

COMBINED TRANSPORT DOCUMENT

Issued by The Baltic and International Maritime Conference (BIMCO) and the International Shipowners' Association (INSA), subject to International Chamber of Commerce Uniform Rules for a Combined Transport Document (ICC Publication No. 298).

July 1st, 1977

Place of receipt

Port of loading

Place of delivery

Quantity and description of goods

Ocean vessel

Port of discharge

Marks and Nos.

Name of sub-contractors for carriage by inland waterways *

Date of sub-contract for carriage by inland waterways *

Gross weight, kg. Measurement, m³

Particulars above declared by Consignor

Freight and charges

RECEIVED the goods in apparent good order and condition and, as far as ascertained by reasonable means of checking, as specified above unless otherwise stated.

The CTO, in accordance with and to the extent of the provisions contained in this CT Document, and with liberty to sub-contract, undertakes to perform and/or in his own name to procure performance of the combined transport and the delivery of the goods, including all services which are necessary to such transport from the place and time of taking the goods in charge to the place and time of delivery and accepts responsibility for such transport and such services.

One of the CT Documents must be surrendered duly endorsed in exchange for the goods or delivery order.

IN WITNESS whereof CT Document(s) has/have been signed in the number indicated below, one of which being accomplished the other(s) to be void.

Freight payable at	Place and date of issue
Number of original CT Documents	Signed for the Combined Transport Operator (CTO)

As agent(s) to the CTO

Note:

The Merchant's attention is called to the fact that according to Clauses 10 to 12 of this CT Document, the liability of the CTO is, in most cases, limited in respect of loss of or damage to the goods and delay. The liability of the CTO in respect of loss or damage occurring during carriage by inland waterways shall be covered by the provisions of his contract with the sub-contractors mentioned above (*) and dated as likewise indicated (*).

p.t.o.

COMBINED TRANSPORT DOCUMENT

CODE NAME: "C O M B I D O C"

Issued July 1st. 1977

I. GENERAL PROVISIONS

1. Applicability. Notwithstanding the heading "Combined Transport Document", the provisions set out and referred to in this CT Document shall also apply if the transport as described on the face of the Document contrary to the original intentions of the parties is performed by one mode of transport only.

2. Definitions. "CTO" means the party on whose behalf this CT Document has been signed. "Merchant" includes the Shipper, the Receiver, the Consignor, the Consignee, the Holder of this CT Document and the Owner of the Goods. "Delivery" means delivering the goods to or placing the goods at the disposal of the party entitled to receive them.
"Goods" means the cargo accepted from the Consignor and includes any container, transportable tank, not supplied by or on behalf of the CTO. "Franc" means a unit consisting of 65.5 milligrammes of gold of millesimal fineness 900.

3. CTO's Tariff. The terms of the CTO's applicable Tariff at the date of shipment are incorporated herein. Copies of the relevant provisions of the applicable Tariff are available from the CTO upon request. In the case of inconsistency between this CT Document and the applicable Tariff, this CT Document shall prevail.

4. Time Bar. The CTO shall be discharged of all liability under this CT Document unless suit is brought within nine months after,
i) the delivery of the goods, or
ii) the date when the goods should have been delivered, or
iii) the date when in accordance with Clause 14, failure to deliver the goods would, in the absence of evidence to the contrary, give to the party entitled to receive them the right to treat the goods as lost.

5. Law and Jurisdiction. Disputes arising under this CT Document shall be determined at the option of the Claimant by the courts and subject to Clause 11 of this CT Document in accordance with the law at
(a) the place where the goods were taken in charge by the CTO or the place designated for delivery, or
(b) the place where the CTO has his principal place of business, or

in which case such higher value shall be the limit amount greater than the actual loss to the person entitled to make the claim.
(4) The CTO shall not, in any case, be liable for an amount greater than the actual loss to the person entitled to make the claim
(5) The CTO shall not be liable to pay compensation if the loss or damage was caused by
(a) an act or omission of the Merchant, or person other than the CTO acting on behalf of the Merchant or or from whom the CTO took the goods in charge,
(b) insufficient or defective condition of the packing or marks
(c) handling, loading, stowage or unloading of the goods by the Merchant or any person acting on his behalf,
(d) inherent vice of the goods,
(e) strike, lockout, stoppage or restraint of labour, the consequences of which the CTO could not avoid by the exercise of reasonable diligence.
(f) any cause or event which the CTO could not avoid and the consequences of which he could not prevent by the exercise of reasonable diligence.
(g) a nuclear incident if the operator of a nuclear installation or a person acting for him is liable for this damage under an applicable international Convention or national law governing liability in respect of nuclear energy.
(6) The burden of proving that the loss or damage was due to one or more of the causes or events mentioned in sub-clause (5) shall rest upon the CTO.
When the CTO establishes that, in the circumstances of the case, the loss or damage could be attributed to one or more of the causes or events specified in (b) to (g) of sub-clause (5), it shall be presumed that it was so caused. The claimant shall, however, be entitled to prove that the loss or damage was not, in fact, caused wholly or partly by one or more of these causes or events.

11. When the Stage of Transport Where the Loss or Damage Occurred is Known.
(1) The liability of the CTO in respect of such loss or damage shall be determined:
(a) by the provisions contained in any international Convention or national law, which provisions:
i) cannot be departed from by private contract, to the detriment of the claimant, and
ii) would have applied if the claimant had made a separate and direct contract with the CTO in respect of the particular stage of transport where the loss or damage occurred and received as evidence thereof any particular document which must be issued in order to make such international Convention or national law applicable, or
(b) in respect of any carriage by sea, by the Hague Rules contained in the International Convention for the Unification of Certain Rules relating to Bills of Lading, dated 25th August, 1924, even if these Rules do not apply to the carriage by sea by virtue of sub-paragraph (a) of this Clause 10. Furthermore the Hague Rules shall apply to all goods, whether carried on deck or under deck, or
(c) by the provisions of Clause 10 in cases where the provisions of sub-paragraphs (a) and (b) of this Clause do not apply.

the CTO of the goods as therein described in respect of the particulars which he had reasonable means of checking. Proof to the contrary shall not be admissible when this CT Document is issued in negotiable form and has been transferred to a third party acting in good faith.

17. Consignor's Responsibility. The Consignor shall be deemed to have guaranteed to the CTO the accuracy at the time the goods were taken in charge by the CTO of the description of the goods, marks, numbers, measurements, quantity and weight, as furnished by him, and the Consignor shall indemnify the CTO against all loss, damage and expenses arising or resulting from inaccuracies in or inadequacy of such particulars. The right of the CTO to such indemnity shall in no way limit his responsibility and liability under this CT Document to any person other than the Consignor.

18. Dangerous Goods.
(1) if any goods shipped comply with rules which are mandatory according to the national law or by reason of international Convention, relating to the carriage of goods of a dangerous nature, and shall in every respect be in the condition for carriage required. If such goods are delivered to the CTO without the exact nature of the danger before or in writing of the exact nature of the goods being taken in charge by the CTO and indicate to him, if need be the precautions to be taken.
(2) If the Consignor fails to provide such information and the CTO is unaware of the dangerous nature of the goods and the necessary precautions to be taken and if, at any time, they are deemed to be a hazard to life or property, they may at any place be unloaded, destroyed or rendered harmless, as circumstances may require, without compensation, and the Consignor shall be liable for all loss, damage, delay or expenses arising out of their being taken in charge, or their carriage, or of any service incidental thereto.
The burden of proving the CTO knew the exact nature of the danger constituted by the carriage of the said goods shall rest upon the person entitled to the goods.
(3) if any goods become a danger to the ship or cargo, they may in like manner be landed at any place or destroyed or rendered innocuous by the CTO without liability on the part of the CTO except to General Average, if any.

19. Consignor-packed Containers, etc.
(1) If a container has not been filled, packed or stowed by the CTO, the CTO shall not be liable for any loss of or damage to its contents and the Merchant shall cover any loss or expense incurred by the CTO, if such loss, damage or expense has been caused by
(a) negligent filling, packing or stowing of the container;
(b) the contents being unsuitable for carriage in container; or
(c) the unsuitability or defective condition of the container unless the container has been supplied by the CTO and the unsuitability or defective condition would not have been apparent upon reasonable inspection at or prior to the time when the container was filled, packed or stowed.

II. PERFORMANCE OF THE CONTRACT

6. Methods and Routes of Transportation.
(1) The CTO is entitled to perform the transport in any reasonable manner and by any reasonable means, methods and routes.
(2) In accordance herewith, for instance, in the event of carriage by sea, vessels may sail with or without pilots, undergo repairs, adjust equipment, drydock and tow vessels in all situations.

7. Optional Stowage.
(1) Goods may be stowed by the CTO by means of containers, trailers, transportable tanks, flats, pallets, or similar articles of transport used to consolidate goods.
(2) Containers, trailers and transportable tanks, whether stowed by the CTO or received by him in a stowed condition from the Merchant, may be carried on or under deck without notice to the Merchant.

8. Hindrances, etc. Affecting Performance.
(1) The CTO shall use reasonable endeavours to complete the transport and to deliver the goods at the place designated for delivery.
(2) If at any time the performance of the contract as evidenced by this CT Document is or will be affected by any hindrance, risk, delay, difficulty or disadvantage of whatsoever kind, and if by virtue of sub-clause (1) the CTO has no duty to complete the performance of the contract, the CTO (whether or not the transport is commenced) may elect to
(a) treat the performance of this contract as terminated and place the goods at the Merchant's disposal at any place which the CTO shall deem safe and convenient, or
(b) deliver the goods at the place designated for delivery
In any event the CTO shall be entitled to full freight for goods received for transportation and additional compensation for extra costs resulting from the circumstances referred to above.

III. CTO's LIABILITY

9. (1) The CTO assumes liability and undertakes to pay compensation for loss of or damage to the goods occurring within the time of taking them into his charge and the time of delivery, to the extent set out in this CT Document.
(2) The CTO accepts responsibility for the acts and omissions of his agents or servants, when such agents or servants are acting within the scope of their employment as if such acts and omissions were his own; further, he accepts responsibility for the acts and omissions of any other persons whose services he uses for the performance of the contract evidenced by this CT Document.

10. When the Stage of Transport Where the Loss or Damage Occurred is Not Known.
(1) Compensation as per Clause 9 (1) shall be calculated by reference to the value of such goods at the place and time they are or in accordance with the contract of combined transport they should have been delivered to the Consignee.
(2) The value of the goods shall be determined according to the current commodity exchange price or, if there is no such price, according to the current market price or, if there is no commodity exchange price or current market price, by reference to the normal value of goods of the same kind and quality.
(3) Compensation shall not exceed 30 francs per kilo of gross weight of the goods lost or damaged unless, with the consent of the CTO, the Consignor has declared a higher value for the goods and such higher value has been stated in this CT Document.

(2) Without prejudice to the provisions of Clause 15, when, under the provisions of sub-clause (1), the liability of the CTO shall be determined by the provisions of any international Convention or national law, this liability shall be determined as though the CTO were the carrier referred to in any such Convention or national law. However, the CTO shall not be exonerated from liability where the loss or damage is caused or contributed to by the acts or omissions of the CTO in his capacity as such, or his servants or agents when acting in such capacity and not in the performance of the carriage.

12. Delay. The CTO is liable to pay compensation for delay only when the stage of transport where a delay occurred is known, and to the extent that there is liability according to the provisions in Clause 11, sub-clause (1), paragraph (a). However, the amount of such compensation shall not exceed the amount of the freight for that stage of transport, provided that this limitation is not contrary to the applicable international Convention or national law.

13. Notice of Loss. Except with Clause 14 of this CT Document the CTO shall be deemed prima facie to have delivered the goods as described in this CT Document unless notice of loss of, or damage to, the goods, indicating the general nature of such loss or damage, shall have been given in writing to the CTO or to his representative at the place of delivery before or at the time of removal of the goods into the custody of the person entitled to delivery thereof under this CT Document, or, if the loss or damage is not apparent, within seven consecutive days thereafter.

14. Delivery/Non-Delivery of Goods.
(1) If the goods are not taken delivery of by the Merchant within a reasonable time after the CTO has called upon him to take delivery, the CTO shall be at liberty to put the goods in safe custody on behalf of the Merchant at the Merchant's risk and expense.
(2) Failure to deliver delivery within 90 days after the date when it would be reasonable to allow diligent completion of the combined transport operation shall, in the absence of evidence to the contrary, give to the party entitled to receive delivery the right to treat the goods as lost.

15. Defences and Limits for the CTO, Servants, etc.
(1) The defences and limits of liability provided for in this CT Document shall apply in any action against the CTO for loss of, damage or delay to the goods, whether the action be founded in contract or in tort.
(2) If an action for loss or damage to the goods is brought against a servant, agent or independent contractor, such person shall be entitled to avail himself of the defences and limits of liability which the CTO is entitled to invoke under this CT Document.
(3) The aggregate of the amounts recoverable from the CTO and his servants, agents or independent contractors shall in no case exceed the limits provided for in this CT Document.
(4) The CTO shall not be entitled to the benefit of the limitation of liability provided for in Clause 10 if it is proved that the loss or damage resulted from an act or omission of the CTO done with intent to cause damage or recklessly and with knowledge that damage would probably result.

IV. DESCRIPTION OF GOODS

16. CTO's Responsibility. This CT Document shall be prima facie evidence of the taking in charge by

(2) The provisions of sub-clause (1) of this Clause also apply with respect to trailers, transportable tanks, flats and pallets which have not been filled, packed or stowed by the CTO.
(3) The CTO does not accept liability for the functioning of reefer equipment or trailers supplied by the Merchant.

V. FREIGHT AND LIEN

20. Freight.
(1) Freight shall be deemed earned on receipt of the goods by the CTO and shall be paid in any event.
(2) The Merchant's attention is drawn to the stipulations concerning currency in which the freight and charges are to be paid, rate of exchange, devaluation and other contingencies relative to freight and charges in the relevant tariff conditions. If no such stipulation as to devaluation exists or is applicable the following clause to apply:
If the currency in which freight and charges are quoted is devalued or revalued between the date of the freight agreement and the date when the freight and charges are paid, then all freight and charges shall be automatically and immediately changed in proportion to the extent of the devaluation or revaluation of the said currency. When the CTO has consented to payment in other currency than the above mentioned currency, then all freight and charges shall be paid on the day preceding payment – be paid at the highest selling rate of exchange for banker's sight draft current on the day when such freight and charges are paid. If the banks are closed on the day when the freight is paid the rate to be used will be the one in force on the last day the banks were open.
(3) For the purpose of verifying the freight basis, the CTO reserves the right to have the contents of containers, trailers and similar articles of transport inspected in order to ascertain the weight, measurement, value, or nature of the goods. If on such inspection it is found that the declaration is not correct, it is agreed that a sum equal either to five times the difference between the correct freight and the freight charged or to double the correct freight less the freight charged, whichever sum is the smaller, shall be payable as liquidated damages to the CTO notwithstanding any other sum having been stated on this CT Document as the freight payable.
(4) All dues, taxes and charges levied on the goods and other expenses in connection therewith shall be paid by the Merchant.

21. Lien. The CTO shall have a lien on the goods for any amount due under this contract and for the costs of recovering the same, and may enforce such lien in any reasonable manner.

VI. MISCELLANEOUS PROVISIONS

22. General Average.
(1) General Average to be adjusted at any port or place at the CTO's option, and to be settled according to the York-Antwerp Rules 1974, this covering all goods, whether carried on or under deck. The New Jason Clause as approved by BIMCO to be considered as incorporated herein.
(2) Such security including a cash deposit as the CTO may deem sufficient to cover the estimated contribution of the goods and any salvage and special charges thereon shall, if required, be submitted to the CTO prior to delivery of the goods.

23. Both-to-Blame Collision Clause. The Both-to-Blame Collision Clause as adopted by BIMCO to be considered incorporated herein.

Index

Agent
mercantile, bank as, 50
voluntary endorsee, as, 25
Airwaybill
use of, 188
Arbitration clause
incorporation from charterparty to bill
of lading, 174, 175

Bailment
bailee-
carrier as, 30
duties and liabilities of, 93, 94
meaning, 93
Bank
bill of lading incorporating charterparty
terms, rejection of, 183–186
consignee, as, 48–51
estoppel of buyer's right of action, 268–
270
letters of credit. *See* LETTER OF CREDIT
mercantile agent, as, 50
pledgee's title, passing, 50
sale of documents by, 49
seawaybill, acceptance of, 208–211
section 1 bill of lading holder, as, 51
security interest over goods-
classification of, 37
pledge, as, 37–40
realisation of, 48–51
surrender, time of, 39
Bill of exchange
bill of lading, and, 22, 23
consideration, doctrine of, 24
holder in due course, entitlement of, 23
negotiability, instances of, 26
Bill of lading
bill of exchange, and, 22, 23
bundle of rights, 9
buyer, control of over, 110
charterer, in hands of, 165–169
charterparty, under. *See* CHARTERPARTY,
BILL OF LADING UNDER
'claused', 131
'clean', 130–134
consignee, bank named as, 48, 49
contract, as. *See* CARRIAGE CONTRACT
date of shipment, stating, 233–235

Bill of lading-*continued*
delivery-
consignee, alteration of, 32, 33
constructive possession, 29
document of title, bill ceasing to be
on, 40, 41
exclusive right to, 30, 31
right to, 27–29
symbol of, as, 25
transfer of right, consequences of, 30–
33
without presentation of bill, 31, 32
destination as per charterparty, 2
document of commercial value, as, 3
document of possession, as, 35, 72, 73
document of title, as-
bank, time of surrender by, 39
bill ceasing to be, time of, 40, 41
common law, at, 29, 30, 35, 72
definition, 15–19
framework for understanding, 17–19
ownership, symbolising, 72
received for shipment bill as, 220–222
shipment of goods, confirming, 212
transfer by bank, effect of, 49, 50
evidence of contract, as-
buyer, interest of, 110, 136
function as, 44
generally, 109–111
nature of, 15
possession, right to demand, 16, 17
statutory intervention, 33–36
transfer of property, for, 16, 17. *See
also* transferability, *below*
working definition of, 29
facilities provided by, 9, 10
finance raised by, 9
functions of, 162
gift, object of, 26
goods, relating to, 116
holder, rights of, 20
importance in international trade, 9, 10
intention as to passing of property-
buyer, made out to order of, 86, 87
cash against document, payment in,
97
seller, made out to order of, 86
role as to, 85

Bill of lading-*continued*
negotiability-
better title, giving, 22, 23
consideration, doctrine of, 24-26
generally, 21, 22, 72, 219
less than complete sense, in, 21
transferability, and, 19, 22, 73
negotiable, tender of, 17
non-transferable, stated to be, 21
pledge, creating, 37-40
receipt, as. *See* RECEIPT, BILL OF LADING
AS
sale of, 9
security-
interest of bank, classification of, 37-
40
means of, as, 36-40
seller, control of over, 110, 135
transfer of-
intention accompanying, 28
proprietary effect of, 28
transferability-
assignment, without, 22
characteristic, achieving, 21
expressly stated, 21
generally, 20, 72, 219
negotiability, and, 19, 22, 73
voluntary endorsee, rights of, 24-26

C & f contracts
characteristics, 2
goods, shipment of, 6
meaning, 1
sales of goods or documents, debate on,
4, 5
seller, promise of, 3, 4
Cargo
claim-
right defendant, against, 176-179
right to sue. *See* TITLE TO SUE
tender, requirements of, 182-186
clean bill, requirement of, 130-134
shipped and delivered, evidence of, 111,
112
Carriage contract
bill of lading-
contract itself, as, 138, 139
destination different to sale
destination, 159, 160
evidence, as, 137
role of, 136
buyer, expectation of, 136
charterparty as, 162, 163
seawaybill as. *See* SEAWAYBILL
seller, duty of, 139, 140
terms-
buyer, purchased by, 137-139
implied, 140
reasonable, 140
relevant questions, 137

Carriage contract-*continued*
terms-*continued*
usual, 136
whole voyage, rights enforceable for-
carrier given liberty to deviate, 142-
148. *See also* CARRIER
deck stowage-
carrier having liberty of, 151, 152
problems with, 148
statement of in bill, 150, 151
unauthorised, 148-150
destination different to sale
destination, 159, 160
requirement, 141
transhipment-
carrier having liberty of, 154-159
clauses stating, 153, 154
meaning, 152
permissible, 152, 153
Carrier
bailee as, 30
bill of lading, no duty to issue, 114
contractual relationship with buyer,
advantage of, 43, 44
deck stowage, liberty of, 151, 152
delivery by-
bill of lading, without presentation
of, 30, 31
consignee, alteration of, 32, 33
deviation, liberty to-
Carriage of Goods by Sea Act
provisions, 147
direct shipment-
sale contract not stipulating, 143,
144
sale contract stipulating, 142, 143
fundamental breach, residual doctrine
of, 146
Glynn v Margetson, rule in, 145, 146
wide terms, in, 142, 144
identity of, 176-179
right to demand possession from, 30, 31
shipper, right of recourse against, 119
title to sue. *See* TITLE TO SUE
transhipment, liberty of-
letter of credit, validity of tender, 158,
159
no through cover given, 157, 158
objection to, 155
reservation of, 154, 155
through cover, bill giving, 156, 157
Charge
reservation of title clause as, 84
Charterer
bill of lading in hands of, 165-169
Charterparty, bill of lading under
buyer having sight of, 184-186
carrier and buyer, contractual terms
binding-
charterer, bill in hands of, 165-169

Charterparty, bill of lading under-
continued
carrier and buyer, contractual terms
binding-*continued*
doctrine of privity, effect of, 170
document governing, 164, 165
incorporation into bill, 170-175
third party, bill in hands of, 169-175
charterparty, function of, 162, 163
contracts involved, relationship between,
162-164
incorporation of terms-
arbitration clause, of, 174, 175
consistency, 173
description, issue of, 172, 173
generally, 170, 171
importance of determining, 171
rejection of bill, 183-186
problems with, 161-164
receipt, bill as. *See* RECEIPT, BILL OF
LADING AS
short-delivery or damage, person sued
for-
carrier, identity of, 176-179
demise charterparty, 177
generally, 175, 176
shipowner, 177, 178
tender, requirements of, 182-186
C i f contracts
characteristics, 2
goods, shipment of, 6
meaning, 1
quantity of goods, implied term as to,
126
sales of goods or documents, debate on,
4, 5
seller, promise of, 3, 4
Combined transport documents
document of title, as—
custom, recognised by, 225-227
definition, coming within, 223
goods received, confirming, 212
Incoterms, 218, 218
market, view of, 215-218
received for shipment bills, 220-223
rejection by buyer, 224
shipment of goods, not confirming,
212, 213
specimen clauses, 216, 217
textbooks, view of, 214, 215
trade, treatment by, 226
traditional view, 218-225
transferability, issue of, 219, 220
endorsee, locus standi of, 213
generally, 187, 188
letters of credit, and, 227, 228
valid tender of, 211
Contract
bill of lading as. *See* CARRIAGE
CONTRACT

Contract-*continued*
de minimis rule—
application of, 236, 242-244
arguments against applying 237, 238
arguments for applying, 239
case law, 240-242
privity, doctrine of—
avoidance of, 44, 45
charterparty, terms governing third
party in, 170
fundamental, 44
implied contract device, 53-56
negligence, violation by action for, 62
seawaybill clauses avoiding, 201, 202
repudiation-
binary analysis, 231
effect of, 230
estoppel, loss of right through. *See*
ESTOPPEL
international shipment sales, in, 231
rejection by buyer, 230, 231. *See also*
REJECTION OF DOCUMENTS AND
GOODS
technical breaches, 236
terms, classification of, 236
title to sue passing by. *See* TITLE TO
SUE
tort plaintiff and contract plaintiff
compared 56-60

Document of title
bill of lading as. *See* BILL OF LADING
combined transport documents as. *See*
COMBINED TRANSPORT DOCUMENTS
definition of—
common law, at, 29, 30, 116
statutory intervention, 36-40
delivery—
right to, 27-30
transfer of right, consequences of, 30-
33
documents being, 16-18
Factors Act, documents within, 36-40
negotiability, 21, 22
Sale of Goods Act, documents within,
27, 36-40
seawaybill as. *See* SEAWAYBILL
transferability, 20
Documentary sales on shipment terms
bill of lading. *See* BILL OF LADING
conditions of contract, 236
consequences, 4
de minimis rule-
application of, 236, 242-244
arguments against applying, 237, 238
arguments for applying, 239
case law, 240-242
description as, 3, 4

Documentary sales on shipment terms-*continued*
goods-
    duties as to, 5, 6
    shipment of, 6-9
letter of credit. *See* LETTER OF CREDIT
risk. *See* RISK, TRANSFER OF
seawaybills, use of, 189
seller-
    documentary duties of, 9, 10, 17, 232-235
    physical duties of, 5-9, 232-235
    promise of, 3, 4

Estoppel
representational, doctrine of, 114, 131
right to repudiate, loss of-
    actions of bank, through, 268-270
    damages, recovery of, 264-266
    effect of doctrine, 263-269
    Panchaud Frerès, doctrine of, 260-263
    rejection of goods-
        on other grounds, 266, 267
        on similar grounds, 263
    summary of doctrine, 267

F o b contracts
additional services, 8
characteristics, 2
classic form, 8
extended form, 8
meaning, 1
sales of goods or documents, debate on, 4, 5
seller, promise of, 3, 4
straight form, 7

Insurance
seller, information given to buyer by, 95-97

Letter of credit
application for opening, 36
bank-
    proprietary interest of, 37
    readiness to pay, 17
    risks run by, 48, 49
    service of, 11
bill referring to charterparty, acceptance of, 183, 184
combined transport documents, and, 227, 228
receipt, requirements of bill of sale as. *See* BILL OF LADING AS
seawaybill tendered under, 207-211
system, 10, 11
transfer of property, and, 88, 89
transhipment, tender in case of, 158, 159
use of, 10, 11
Locus standi. *See* TITLE TO SUE

Negligence
economic loss-
    action for, 62
    general principle against recovery for, 63-69
negligent mis-statement, action for, 63
title to sue arising in. *See* TITLE TO SUE
Negotiability
better title, giving, 22, 23
bill of lading, of. *See* BILL OF LADING
consideration, doctrine of, 24-26
meaning, 22, 24

Ownership
possession, and right to, 73
ranking of claims, concerning, 73

Pledge
consignee, pledge as 48-51
security interest of bank as, 37-40
Possession, right to
control of goods, concerning, 73
ownership, and, 73
property, and, 73-75
Property
locus standi, and, 51-53, 78-80
passage of-
    bill of lading, role of. *See* BILL OF LADING
    intention as to, 82
    letter of credit, and 88, 89
    meaning, 75
    possession, and, 73-75
    reservation clauses-
        express, 82-85
        implied, 85-87
right transferred from buyer to seller, as, 75, 76
risk, and, 75, 76
Romalpa clause, 82-85
title to sue, and. *See* TITLE TO SUE
transfer, Sale of Goods Act provisions-
    appropriation-
        meaning, 77, 82
        notice of, 81, 82
        unconditional, 80-82
    ascertainment of goods, 77-80
    intention of parties, ascertaining, 76, 80, 81
    relevant sections, 76
where lying, decision on, 74, 75

Receipt, bill of lading as
buyer, right of-
    Carriage of Goods by Sea Act, under, 122-124
    common law, at, 121, 122
    Hague-Visby Rules, and, 123, 124
    policy considerations, 122, 123
    privity, doctrine of, 121-123

Receipt, bill of lading as-*continued*
  charterparty, issued under-
    charterer buying f o b, where, 182
    charterer selling c i f, where, 180-182
    generally, 179, 180
    Hague-Visby Rules, incorporation of,
      180-182
  evidence contradicting, ban on, 113
  function of, 111-115
  generally, 109-111
  Hague-Visby Rules, and, 118-121
  marks, quantity and condition of goods,
    showing, 118-121
  merchants' right to demand, 115
  qualification of, 115
  representational estoppel, doctrine of,
    114, 131
  sale contracts and letters of credit, in-
    'claused' bill, 131
    clean, bill to be, 130-134
    contract goods only, covering, 126-130
    generally, 124, 125
    quantity, statements as to, 126-130
  seller, right of-
    Carriage of Goods by Sea Act, under,
      117-121
    common law, at, 116, 117
    Hague-Visby Rules, under, 117-121
Rejection of documents and goods
  buyer, remedy of-
    acceptance of goods and rejection of
      documents, 250-252
    independent rights, 248-252
    loss of opportunity to reject. *See*
      opportunity to reject documents,
      loss of, *below*
    restraints on. *See* remedy, restraints
      on, *below*
  date of shipment as condition, 232-235
  de minimis rule-
    application of, 236, 242-244
    arguments against applying, 237, 238
    arguments for applying, 239
    case law, 240-242
  documentary defects, 232, 235
  documents alone, defect in, 257-260
  opportunity to reject documents, loss of-
    compensation for, 252, 253
    market losses, 255-257
    no loss caused, where, 257-260
    type of loss recoverable, 253-255
  remedy, restraints on-
    defective documents reaching buyer
      before goods, 245, 246
    documentary defect noticed, 245-247
    documentary defect not noticed, 245-
      248
    generally, 244, 245
    goods reaching buyer before
      documents, 246-248

Rejection of documents and goods-
  continued
  repudiation of contract-
    estoppel, loss of right through. *See*
      ESTOPPEL
    rejection by buyer, 230, 231
  seller-
    duties of, 231
    inaccurate bill of lading, tendering,
      233-235
    shipment of goods within contract
      period, 233
Reservation of title clause
  charge, as, 84
  letter of credit, payment by, 89
  use of, 83
Risk, transfer of
  contract of sale, under, 99, 105
  contractual relationship, concerned
    with, 75
  general rule-
    caveats, 99, 100
    statement of, 90, 91, 98
  loss or damage, occurrence of-
    after passing of property, 101, 102
    before passing of property, 102-105
  Mash & Murrell, rule in, 99, 100
  on or as from shipment-
    meaning, 100, 101
    unappropriated goods, 103
    unascertained goods, 102, 103
  practical effect, 101
  property and risk compared, 75, 76, 89
  retrospective, 104
  Sale of Goods Act, and-
    bailment, effect of, 93, 94
    contract of carriage on reasonable
      terms, 94, 95
    delay, effect of, 91-93
    deterioration of goods, 97, 98
    insurance of goods, 95-97
    provisions on, 91
    rejection of goods, 94
  transfer of property compared, 89, 90
Romalpa clause
  charge, as, 84
  object of, 83

Sale of goods contracts
  carriage, contract of. *See* CARRIAGE
    CONTRACT
  performance, duality of, 2
  shipment, promising, 3, 4
  types of, 1
Seawaybill
  contract of carriage, as-
    Bills of Lading Act, application of,
      202-204
    buyer's title to sue, and, 200-204

Seawaybill-*continued*
  contract of carriage, as-*continued*
    Carriage of Goods by Sea Act, and,
      204-207
    generally, 199, 200
    Hague-Visby Rules, incorporation of,
      204-207
    privity gap, clauses bridging, 201, 202
  document of title, as—
    common law, at, 192-195
    control, right of, 195-198
    definition, 191
    delivery instructions, alteration of,
      195, 196
    delivery, right to, 190-195
    generally, 189, 190
    non-negotiable, being, 190, 198, 199
  letters of credit, tendered under, 207-211
  sale contract concluded on shipment
    terms, validity under, 189
  security, acceptance as, 208-211
  use—
    advantages of, 191
    reasons for, 188, 189
Security
  bill of lading, of, 36-40
  letter of credit. *See* LETTER OF CREDIT
Shipment
  evidence of, 113

Title
  document of. *See* DOCUMENT OF TITLE
  meaning, 16
  sue, to. *See* TITLE TO SUE
Title to sue
  Bills of Lading Act, effect of—
    conditions for application, 51-53
    document of title, whether requiring,
      46, 47
    pledgee as consignee, 48-51
    property in goods, passing of, 47, 48,
      51-53, 74

Title to sue-*continued*
  Bills of Lading Act, effect of-*continued*
    section 1, wording of, 45, 46
  combined transport document, rights of
    endorsee, 213
  implied contract, passing by, 53-56
  property, and, 51-53, 78-80
  shipping document other than bill of
    lading, buyer holding, 53
  tort, arising in—
    Aliakmon, problems after, 60-69
    alternative to contract action, as, 56,
      57
    buyer seeking remedy, establishment
      by, 60, 68, 74
    Carriage of Goods by Sea Act, effect
      of, 59, 60
    fault, proof of, 57
    Hague-Visby Rules, effect of, 57-60,
      67
    locus standi, establishment of, 60, 68,
      74
    passage of risk, linked to, 66, 67
    proprietary interest in goods, proof
      of—
      application of rule, 60-62
      general principle against recovery,
        and, 63-69
      tort plaintiff and contract plaintiff
        compared, 56-60
  waybill, goods shipped under, 200-204
Tort
  title to sue arising in. *See* TITLE TO SUE
Transferability
  bill of lading, of. *See* BILL OF LADING
  concept of, 19, 20

Waybill
  generally, 187
  seawaybill. *See* SEAWAYBILL
  delivery, by, 20